Law from the Tigris to the Tiber:
The Writings of Raymond Westbrook

Volume 1: The Shared Tradition

Raymond Westbrook
October 1, 1946 – July 23, 2009

Law from the Tigris to the Tiber:
The Writings of Raymond Westbrook

Volume 1
The Shared Tradition

RAYMOND WESTBROOK

Edited by
BRUCE WELLS and RACHEL MAGDALENE

EISENBRAUNS
Winona Lake, Indiana
2009

Library of Congress Cataloging-in-Publication Data

Westbrook, Raymond.
  Law from the Tigris to the Tiber : the writings of Raymond Westbrook. /
    Raymond Westbrook ; edited by Bruce Wells and Rachel Magdalene.
      v.   cm.
  Includes bibliographical references and index.
  Contents: v. 1. The Shared tradition — v. 2. Cuneiform and biblical
sources.
  ISBN 978-1-57506-177-1 (set (2 vols.); hardback : alk. paper) — ISBN
  978-1-57506-175-7 (volume 1; hardback : alk. paper) — ISBN 978-1-57506-
  176-4 (volume 2; hardback : alk. paper)
    1. Law—Middle East—History. 2. Law, Ancient. 3. Jewish law.
  4. Roman law. 5. Law, Greek. I. Wells, Bruce. II. Magdalene,
  F. Rachel. III. Title.
    KL147.W477   2009
    340.5′394—dc22

                                                      2009040568

Contents

Preface

On July 23, 2009, as the preparations for this collection were nearing completion, Raymond Westbrook, the W. W. Spence Professor of Semitic Languages in the Department of Near Eastern Studies at Johns Hopkins University, passed away. We had been contemplating the production of these volumes for some time and began work on them in earnest about one year ago, spurred in part by the progression of his illness. Although we had hoped to deliver the completed collection as a surprise, his rapid decline did not permit us to do that. Instead, we made Professor Westbrook aware of the project several weeks before his passing. We are, however, deeply saddened that he was not able to see it in its final form. He was an important role model and mentor for us over the years, and we offer these volumes as a modest tribute to his scholarly achievements, his impact on the field, and his particular contributions to our academic development.

Raymond Westbrook earned his B.A. in Law from Oxford University in 1968, studying with David Daube, H. L. A. Hart, and other prominent legal scholars. He then took his Ll.M. at Hebrew University of Jerusalem, where he worked with Reuven Yaron. Westbrook was called to the Bar of England and Wales in 1976 and practiced law for a brief time. His Ph.D. in Assyriology was completed in 1982 at Yale University under J. J. Finkelstein and C. Wilcke. He arrived at Johns Hopkins in 1987, after he had taught in the Faculty of Law at Hebrew University of Jerusalem.

Westbrook published three books, edited or co-edited five additional volumes, and produced over 90 articles. His books include *Studies in Biblical and Cuneiform Law* (Gabalda, 1988); *Old Babylonian Marriage Law* (Berger, 1988); and *Property and the Family in Biblical Law* (Sheffield Academic Press, 1991). Among his edited volumes are *Amarna Diplomacy: The Beginnings of International Relations* (with R. Cohen; Johns Hopkins University Press, 2000); *Security for Debt in Ancient Near Eastern Law* (with R. Jasnow; Brill, 2001); *A History of Ancient Near Eastern Law* (Brill, 2003); *Women and Property in Ancient Near Eastern and Mediterranean Societies* (with D. Lyons; Center for Hellenic Studies,

2005); and *Isaiah's Vision of Peace in Biblical and Modern International Relations: Swords into Plowshares* (with R. Cohen; Palgrave Macmillan, 2008). A complete list of his publications (at least through 2008) can be found in the bibliography in volume 2.

Deciding the contents of these volumes took some time. In the end, we felt it best to focus on the 25 years of his work that followed directly after the completion of his dissertation in 1982 and to publish what we believe were his most significant works from that period, whether or not previously reprinted. Thus, exceedingly short articles, reviews, dictionary entries, and articles in handbooks and the like are generally excluded. Due to its import, we have included one article published in 1977 and thereby have the exception that proves the rule.

The volumes' structure emerged relatively quickly. Westbrook published across a broad scope. Nonetheless, we felt that these articles could be readily divided into five major areas: 1) his theoretical work on the shared legal tradition of the so-called law codes of the ancient Near East and classical world; 2) his study of particular substantive bodies of law across this large region; 3) the application of his theory and method to Greek and Roman law; 4) his general work on cuneiform legal sources; and 5) his general work on biblical law. These categories were then divided into two volumes named respectively *The Shared Tradition* and *Cuneiform and Biblical Sources*. Such division is not rigid, however, as Westbrook used sources from the ancient Near East, Greece, and Rome as appropriate, whatever topic was before him.

We wish to thank Jim Eisenbraun, publisher of Eisenbrauns, for his ready enthusiasm for the project since its inception. He was always at hand to answer our questions, to guide us, and to lend support. Our colleague, Cornelia Wunsch, willingly assisted with a host of difficult tasks that arose throughout the course of our work; the volumes are greatly improved thanks to her generous labors on our behalf. Finally, because this project was produced for the most part in the Wells' home, we would also both like to thank Marcy Wells, Bruce's wife, for her many gifts of hospitality, which made this project possible.

Bruce Wells
F. Rachel Magdalene
Munich, August 22, 2009

About the Editors

Bruce Wells received his Ph.D. in Near Eastern Studies in 2003 from The John Hopkins University. He is Assistant Professor of Hebrew Bible in the Department of Theology at Saint Joseph's University in Philadelphia. He is currently on a one-year leave at the Ludwig-Maximilians-Universität in Munich as a Research Fellow with the Alexander von Humboldt Foundation. Wells is the author of *The Law of Testimony in the Pentateuchal Codes* (Harrassowitz, 2004) and co-author with Raymond Westbrook of *Everyday Law in Biblical Israel: An Introduction* (Westminster John Knox, 2009).

F. Rachel Magdalene holds a J.D. from the University of Colorado School of Law and a Ph.D. in Biblical Interpretation (Hebrew Bible) from the University of Denver and Iliff School of Theology Joint Ph.D. Program. She also did supplemental doctoral studies in Assyriology, Hebrew Bible, and ancient comparative law at The Johns Hopkins University. She practiced tax and securities law for twelve years before pursuing her Ph.D. She is currently Visiting Research Scholar at the Universität Leipzig and Guest of the Faculty at Humboldt-Universität zu Berlin. She has taught biblical studies, religious studies, and law at both the undergraduate and graduate levels. Magdalene is the author of *On the Scales of Righteousness: Neo-Babylonian Trial Law and the Book of Job* (Brown Judaic Studies, 2007); co-author with James P. Kutner of *Study Guide to Due Diligence: Process, Participants and Liability* (College for Financial Planning Press, 1988); and an editor on G. K. Scott, et al., eds., *Due Diligence: Process, Participants and Liability* (Longman Financial Services, 1988).

Introduction
The Idea of a Shared Tradition

Bruce Wells*

It was November of 2004 at the annual meeting of the Society of Biblical Literature in San Antonio, Texas. Victor Avigdor Hurowitz had just finished presenting a paper on the prologue to the Code of Hammurabi. There was plenty of time for discussion, and several people raised their hands. After answering one or two questioners, Hurowitz looked to his left, gestured toward the back of the room, and said something on the order of, "And here we have Hammurabi himself to give us his opinion." We all glanced in that direction, and up stood Raymond Westbrook. The question that Professor Westbrook asked has long since faded from our memories, but the epithet bestowed on him that day will not soon be forgotten.

Raymond Westbrook was recognized by many as the world's leading authority on the legal systems of the ancient Near East. He was foremost an Assyriologist, having devoted much of his work to the analysis of cuneiform legal texts from Mesopotamia and Anatolia, as well as so-called peripheral sites such as Emar, Alalakh, and Amarna. He was also a biblical scholar, championing a reading of biblical legal texts substantially informed by a knowledge of cuneiform law. Finally, he was a Classicist, with articles to his name that included detailed studies of early Greek and Roman law. In addition to all of this, his office was filled with books on the contemporary law and legal history of Britain, the United States, Israel, China, and India, to name just a few. He could just as easily speak to

---

* With contributions from F. Rachel Magdalene.

questions of modern legal philosophy or the Magna Carta as he could to the Code of Hammurabi. He was a comparative law scholar par excellence.

Many of his publications were devoted to promulgating his own particular theory on the nature of ancient Near Eastern law and on how historians ought to approach the surviving records that give us insight into these early legal systems. Furthermore, he demonstrated the usefulness of his approach in numerous studies where his careful legal analysis of ancient texts produced creative and, for many, compelling solutions to age-old problems. Given Westbrook's varied constituencies, however, his publications appeared in a wide variety of venues, from the usual Assyriological suspects to law reviews to Festschrifts for biblical scholars to historical journals. This diversity of venues seems to have had the effect of diluting the force of his overall argument. It is difficult at times for readers, even specialists in these disciplines, to see all the components of his theory and to appreciate the full weight of the evidence. We believed a venue was needed where the different pieces of his work could be brought together to form a fuller and more concentrated version of his argument. Hence, the volume before you.

A Common Legal Tradition

We have entitled this volume *The Shared Tradition*. The title represents the essence of the theory that inspired much of Westbrook's work and for which he is probably best known. He began articulating this theory in his early articles almost four decades ago. He described the idea in a number of his writings but perhaps no more succinctly than in his 1992 article on the trial scene recorded in the *Iliad*: "The societies of the ancient Near East for which we have written records are diverse in language and culture, but they appear to some considerable extent to have shared a common legal tradition."[1]

It is important to understand what Westbrook meant by "a common legal tradition." The concept has, at times, been misinterpreted to mean that the legal rules of the various ancient Near Eastern societies were entirely

---

1   Westbrook 1992b: 55 (= chap. 12, p. 307 in this volume).

the same. It becomes easy, then, to dismiss his theory out of hand. While many rules across wide spans of both time and space are remarkably similar, Westbrook's theory allows for differences among the ancient Near Eastern legal systems.[2] The key is understanding the *level* at which these differences occur. Although Westbrook himself did not use these terms, we see in his work a distinction between what we call the *micro level* (minor features of a legal system that often distinguish it from others) and the *macro level* (major features of a legal system that are more revealing of its nature, structure, and basic approach to law).[3]

At the micro level, there are indeed differences. An oft-cited example comes from the Covenant Code (CC) in Exodus and the Code of Hammurabi (CH). The former states that a debt-slave may go free after six years of service in the creditor's household (Exod 21:2), whereas CH 117 grants freedom to a debt-slave after only three years of service. It seems quite evident, however, that the basic legal import—the law at the macro level—of both provisions is identical: a limit on the duration of debt-slavery is required. Numerous other examples could be cited, and this volume is replete with them. Eventually, one must come to terms with both the quantity and the quality of data that reveal striking similarities at the level of fundamental law while, at the same time, exhibiting differences in the finer details. The evidence begs for an explanation.

The Law Codes and the Shared Tradition

Westbrook's explanation of the evidence had a mixed reception. The arguments surrounding the possibility of a common legal tradition have often focused on the law codes or law collections, such as CH and CC, that have survived from the ancient Near East. Westbrook argued that these written codes did not function as normative and binding legislation. They were rather the product of groups of scribes who applied their own particular analytical method—essentially the making of lists with individual items formulated in casuistic style (*Listenwissenschaft*)—to a variety of subject

---

2 See Westbrook 2005d: 4–5 (= chap. 13, p. 331 in this volume).

3 Magdalene (2003: 24–27; 2007: 31–33), basing her analysis on much of Westbrook's work, first articulated this distinction in this way.

areas, including that of law. Westbrook then went on to claim that, despite their non-legislative nature, the codes are in fact a reliable description of the law. "After all," he wrote, "the least that one could expect from an academic treatise on law is that it accurately describe the law in practice."[4] These works, therefore, can be compared in many respects to modern legal treatises, which compile known law and, at times, hypothesize what might happen in new situations.[5] Finally, Westbrook posited that the codes give us considerable insight into the substance of the shared tradition. They tell us about the law, and thus, with their correspondences in both content and reasoning, they also tell us about the numerous legal rules, institutions, and practices that were common to ancient Near Eastern societies.

Many scholars, though not all, agree with Westbrook's initial point (the codes are not legislation), but they often take exception to his second (that the codes describe operative law). A relatively common rebuttal highlights discrepancies between, for instance, Old Babylonian documents of practice (contracts, royal orders, etc.) and CH, the primary Old Babylonian code at our disposal.[6] Indeed, there are a few such discrepancies. There are also, however, a number of correspondences.[7]

In addition, there typically exists, even in modern systems, a gap of varying degrees between the stated law and practiced law. All of us who regularly traverse U.S. expressways at exactly ten miles per hour over the posted speed limit can attest to this. A still better example lodges in the sentiments of Oliver Wendell Holmes when he said: "Great cases like hard cases make bad law."[8] The individual circumstances of cases before a tribunal often call for a reshaping of the law in its particular application, which may or may not have long-term consequences for the legal system as a whole. The same was undoubtedly true of ancient systems.

Another common argument that seeks to drive a wedge between the codes and the operative law of ancient Near Eastern societies comes from the failure of contemporary documents of practice (e.g., trial records) to cite the codes. But this failure may be, in fact, a supporting argument for

---

4 Westbrook 1989a: 204 (= chap. 3, pp. 76-77 in this volume).
5 This is not to minimize, however, that the fundamental legal philosophy behind the law and its collection process is quite different in the modern and ancient periods.
6 See, e.g., Fried 2001: 72-84; and Fitzpatrick-McKinley 1999: 96-112.
7 See, e.g., Petschow 1984; and Ries 1984.
8 *Northern Securities Co v United States*, 193 US 197, 400 (1904) (Holmes dissenting).

Westbrook's view that the codes are legal treatises. Treatises are, in many ancient and modern legal systems, a secondary legal authority rather than a primary authority, meaning that they are not the first source of the rule of law for adjudicating individual cases.[9] Although legal treatises have educated lawyers and judges for eons, and, therefore, have had tremendous influence on the shaping of law, in many historical periods, judges have used them sparingly in written decisions.[10] We would not expect to see legal treatises quoted regularly in such systems, even though they articulate actual law. It is our view that, in the ancient Near East, law functioned similarly in this respect.

The more intense disagreement, though, comes with Westbrook's incorporation of the codes into his idea of a common tradition. At least two other models for understanding the nature of the codes currently compete with that of a shared tradition. What can be called the *developmental* model suggests that there was significant growth and expansion in the legal content from one code to the next as ancient Near Eastern societies changed and evolved over the course of time.[11] This sort of development likely took place within the oral legal traditions that undoubtedly existed and reveals only certain manifestations of itself in the written codes. Even the Code of Eshnunna (CE) and CH, both Old Babylonian codes no more than about forty years apart, exhibit sufficient differences, it is argued, to support this conclusion. According to this view, the similarities that one might encounter in the codes are ultimately more apparent than real. The second model can be called the *textual-dependence* model. It proposes that, because the codes were literary compositions, any similarities that one might encounter are most likely due to the reliance by the authors of one code on the actual text of another. The codes may or may not give us any access to the practiced law of the time; therefore, a similarity between two codes separated by centuries points only to the likelihood that the authors of the later of the two had access to copies of the earlier, not that the law in the two respective societies was anything alike.[12]

---

9 Cf. Black, et al. 1990: 133.

10 On the pedagogical value and legal consequences of legal treatises, see, e.g., de Bracton and Thorne 1968-1977; Basile 1998; Downer 2006; and Claeys 2009.

11 See, e.g., Greengus 1994 and Otto 1994, though both differ from each other in certain details.

12 See, e.g., Wright 2003.

We know that common legal traditions have existed and still do exist in the world, some over considerable time. This situation has sometimes arisen through the intentional acts of countries to create a shared tradition[13] or through imperial-colonial aggression and control.[14] How does one begin, however, to resolve this debate with regard to the ancient Near East? A number of questions loom. Are the similarities between the codes real or superficial? Do they span all of the codes or only a select few? Even if one comes to the conclusion that the codes do share a substantial amount of content and reasoning, does this mean that the legal systems of the scribes who produced the codes also shared a great deal in common? To answer any of these questions, at least two important aspects of the codes have to be examined. First, the individual provisions of the codes require close analysis to determine what they mean and how they relate to provisions in other codes. Second, it is necessary to incorporate a broad range of legal documents of practice into this analysis. Such documents can help to illuminate more clearly the relationship between the codes and the societies from which they come. It is the work of Raymond Westbrook found in this collection of his writings—and particularly in this volume—that carries out precisely those two tasks.

The Hebrew Bible and the Shared Tradition

Then there is the question of the Bible. The debate that we have just described has taken on a somewhat more intensive form when it touches on

---

13   In discussing the development of law in Europe from the medieval to the early modern period, Donlan (2008: 4) explains: "European jurists created a *ius commune*, a body of doctrine or 'law' common across the frontiers of the continent, in contrast to particular laws specific to a place. They acted as teachers and scholars, and served as advisors, diplomats, record-keepers, administrators, and judges across the continent, paving the way for receptions of the canon and civil laws."

14   As Marcks (2000: 266) states in his work regarding the use of law in British colonization of Hong Kong: "[L]aw played an essential role as a means for achieving colonial ends by fortifying European control over the colonized, facilitating commerce, and legitimizing colonial rule. Typically, the Europeans would begin their colonizing efforts by instituting a system of criminal law in order to strengthen their hold over the territory. Then they would implement contract, commercial, land, and labor law in order to advance their commercial ambitions."

the relationship between the legal texts of the Hebrew Bible and those from elsewhere in the ancient Near East. Even if one concedes to Westbrook the idea that the cuneiform law codes share in something akin to a common tradition, the fundamental question regarding the Bible still remains. Do the features and content of the biblical codes—primarily the Covenant Code in Exodus and the Deuteronomic Code—warrant inclusion within this same tradition? As one might expect, Westbrook answered strongly in the affirmative.

While there are those who would disagree, from our perspective, it is becoming increasingly evident that the shared material between biblical and cuneiform law is abundant—so much so that recent studies have posited direct dependence by the biblical authors on Mesopotamian legal texts.[15] A look at some of the more obvious examples helps to confirm this.

- limitations on terms of debt-slavery (see above)
- rights of persons injured in a fight to receive compensation for damages and medical costs (Exod 21:18-19; CH 206; HL 10)
- laws on when pregnant women are struck and then miscarry (Exod 21:22-25; CL 25; CH 209-214; HL 17; MAL A 50-51)
- the rule to split the meat and proceeds from a dead ox and a live ox after the latter killed the former (Exod 21:35; CE 53)
- the right to kill a burglar at night but not during the day (Exod 22:1-2; CE 12-13)
- sanctions for the negligent management of one's own field that results in damage to a neighbor's (Exod 22:4-5; HL 106-107)
- the requirement that seducers of unmarried young women marry them (Exod 22:15-16; MAL A 56)
- a type of talionic punishment for false accusers (Deut 19:16-21; CL 17; CH 1-4)
- guilt for a betrothed maiden if taken sexually by a man in a town but innocence if in the countryside (Deut 22:23-27; HL 197)

---

15 E.g., Wright 2003, 2006. Though we disagree with Wright's conclusion regarding direct textual dependence, his work throws into relief the degree of overlap between the codes.

- the requirement that rapists of unmarried young women marry them (Deut 22:28-29; MAL A 55)
- rules for when a woman grabs a man's genitals during a fight (Deut 25:11-12; MAL A 8)

This list of examples could easily be expanded. Thus, however one may understand the tradition that gave rise to the cuneiform law codes—according to Westbrook's theory or otherwise—interpretations of the biblical material must take that tradition into account.

In his understanding of the law-code tradition, Westbrook found warrant for the application of a particular method within his analysis of biblical law, as well as of ancient Near Eastern law in general. The law codes are, by their very nature, only partial reflections of their respective societies' legal systems. Despite even the presence of numerous documents of practice, there will inevitably be gaps in the knowledge of any one of these systems. Westbrook saw it as legitimate, when attempting to reconstruct the law of a particular society, to draw upon the law from other ancient Near Eastern societies as a means of filling in such gaps. One does not, however, merely select at random rules or practices from one system that might seem to fit neatly within another. It is necessary to see how the larger tradition is at work. Regarding his own efforts to complete the lacunae in the Bible's law of adultery, Westbrook stated:

> Acceptance of the fact that the biblical law is a component of a wider tradition raises the broader question of what the tradition is and how the individual legal systems relate to it. It is only by understanding the nature of that tradition that we may elucidate the complexities of the ancient Near Eastern law of adultery and their reflection in the individual systems of the area.[16]

This methodological process of elucidating a legal topic or a set of legal issues by means of "understanding the nature of [the] tradition" is, we believe, the essence of the works of Raymond Westbrook found in this book and throughout this collection.

---

16 Westbrook 1990b: 546-47 (= chap. 10, p. 250 in this volume).

This Volume

There are sixteen articles contained in this volume. We believe that these sixteen, when read together, present a forceful articulation of Westbrook's theory regarding a shared tradition. The first six come in Part I ("The Tradition in the Law Codes") and focus on the nature of the law codes, how they should be understood, and how they contribute to our understanding of ancient Near Eastern legal tradition. Westbrook wrote these articles over the course of fifteen years, and one can see how he developed and enhanced his argument during that time.

Part II ("The Tradition in Legal Practice") contains five articles in which Westbrook selected a particular topic of legal significance and conducted an investigation of the topic across the various time periods and geographical regions of the ancient Near East. It is in these studies that Westbrook demonstrated important connections between the legal theory, as it were, of the law codes and the legal praxis of the societies that produced the codes. Finally, in Part III ("The Tradition in Greco-Roman Law"), we present five of Westbrook's articles that consider certain aspects of early Greek and Roman Law. In these studies, he pointed to problems of interpretation within scholarship on the law of the classical world and examined these problems within the context provided by ancient Near Eastern law. He was able to show that such a context helps to resolve a number of conundrums and that the influence of the common legal tradition of the ancient Near East made its way into the heart of the Mediterranean world.

Several, though not all, of Westbrook's articles were originally accompanied by abstracts. As we began to edit this volume, we decided that these abstracts were sufficiently valuable to be retained. In order to bring uniformity to the volume, we therefore decided to compose abstracts for those articles that did not originally have them. The articles that have original abstracts are: "Biblical and Cuneiform Law Codes" (chap. 1), "Codification and Canonization" (chap. 5), "Patronage in the Ancient Near East" (chap. 9), and "Adultery in Ancient Near Eastern Law" (chap. 10). The remaining articles are accompanied by abstracts written by the editors of this collection.

With respect to more technical matters, we have attempted to make consistent matters of spelling, grammar, and punctuation according to

American standards. We have also made one particular change to the footnotes of the articles. All articles still possess the same number of footnotes as they did in their original publications, but we have adopted the author-date style of citation for the footnotes. Additionally, we have included at the end of the book a comprehensive list of all of the scholarly literature cited in these sixteen articles.

While the production of this collection and the uniformity of format that it seeks to achieve should help to make Westbrook's writings more accessible and usable, the more important purpose is to give his views a full airing and to reinvigorate the conversations that his scholarship originally stimulated. In sum, we believe and hope that this volume will make a significant and lasting contribution not only to the study of its more immediate topic—the legal systems of the ancient Near East—but also to the study of the larger history of law.

Part One

The Tradition in the Law Codes

1

Biblical and Cuneiform Law Codes

Abstract

This article examines the nature and purpose of the so-called "law codes" of the ancient Near East. It concludes that they formed part of a common scientific tradition, which nonetheless had a practical purpose, as a guide to royal judges in difficult cases.

The Law Codes

A particular genre of ancient Near Eastern literature is the so-called "law code." To date, nine separately identifiable law codes have come down to us, in whole or in part. Seven of them are in the form of cuneiform documents:[1] Codex Ur-Namma (CU), Codex Lipit-Ishtar (CL), Codex Eshnunna (CE), Codex Hammurabi (CH), the Middle Assyrian Laws (MAL), the Hittite Laws (HL), and the Neo-Babylonian Laws (NBL). The other two are to be found in the Bible. Exod 21:1-22:16 is part of the Covenant Code and has long been recognized as an independent source.[2] Likewise in Deuteronomy the remains of, or extracts from, an

---

* Originally published in *Revue Biblique* 92 (1985): 247-65. Copyright © J. Gabalda et Cie, Éditeurs. Used by permission.

1 There are also various fragments too small to be of use in this discussion. Note that the so-called "Sumerian Family Laws" in *ana ittišu* are not normative provisions at all, but contractual formulae (edition in Landsberger 1937). Also to be excluded are the "Sumerian Laws" of YBC 2177. As J. J. Finkelstein points out, they are a scribal exercise executed by a student, which combines various legal phrases and contractual formulae with normative provisions (*ANET*[3] 525). The two types of material are never combined elsewhere: there is a strict separation by the scribes between the lexicographical tradition as exemplified by *ana ittišu* and the law code tradition.

2 See, e.g., Eissfeldt 1964: 33-37.

independent legal source can be discerned, especially in chapters 21-25, in spite of being heavily re-worked for their present purpose and interspersed with a great deal of hortatory and other non-legal material.[3]

All nine codes are remarkably similar both in form and content, They are predominantly formulated in a casuistic style (albeit in varying degrees), that is to say, a particular set of circumstances is given, followed by the legal ruling appropriate to that case.[4] The subject matter is problems of practical law: in many cases the same or related problems are considered by different codes, and in some cases whole paragraphs have been copied by one code from another.[5]

This similarity is evidence at least of a common type of intellectual activity. The purpose of this study is to examine whether this factor can help to explain the nature and purpose of these "codes."

The Law Code as a Royal Apologia?

Our starting point is the classical (and most complete) example of the genre, Codex Hammurabi. It has long been recognized that the term "code" as applied to it by Scheil in the *editio princeps* is a misnomer; CH lacks the comprehensiveness that would make it a law code in the same sense as the Code Napoleon, for example. Thus, G. R. Driver and J. C. Miles wrote: "The Laws must not he regarded as a code or digest, but as a series of amendments to the common law of Babylon,"[6] a statement expanded a few pages later to: "a series of amendments and restatements of parts of the law in force."[7] There was no doubt in the learned authors' minds, however, that they were dealing with a source of positive law, any

---

3 The Priestly Code in Leviticus and Numbers has for the most part a different subject matter from the two Biblical codes mentioned or the cuneiform codes. It is more aptly compared with cuneiform series concerning priestly functions such as *Šurpu*. See Geller 1980.

4 The casuistic style is usually introduced by a conditional beginning "If . . .," but other forms are possible. See Yaron 1962a.

5 E.g., CL 29 and CH 160, CE 53 and Exod 21:35.

6 Driver and Miles 1952: 41.

7 Driver and Miles 1952: 45

more than there had been in the earlier commentaries of D. H. Hiller[8] or P. Koschaker.[9]

Doubts on this point were expressed by B. Landsberger, who pointed out that Codex Hammurabi is never cited as authority in judgments, nor does it state that the judges must in future decide according to these laws.[10] Since Landsberger's article two cases have been found which appear to refer to the text of a *narûm*, but they are too obscure to resolve the question of practical application.[11]

These doubts were taken up by J. J. Finkelstein in an entirely new approach to the problem.[12] Finkelstein pointed out, firstly, that Codex Hammurabi could not have been compiled except in the last years of Hammurabi's reign, after he had accomplished all of the conquests enumerated in his prologue, and secondly, that the code concluded with an epilogue addressed primarily to posterity, especially to future kings.[13] He concluded that the code's purpose was not legislative at all. It was representative of a literary genre, namely the royal *apologia,* and its primary purpose was to lay before the public, posterity, future kings, and, above all, the gods, evidence of the king's execution of his divinely ordained mandate: to have been "the Faithful Shepherd" and the *šār mīšarim.*[14]

Finkelstein applied his theory to two earlier law codes, Codex Ur-Namma and Codex Lipit-Ishtar, both of which had prologues and epilogues in the same spirit, and concluded that Hammurabi was following a traditional genre of royal inscription. Our question is whether this understanding of Codex Hammurabi can be used to explain the general phenomenon of law codes in the ancient Near East: was there a literary, rather than legal, tradition shared by the monarchs of that region?

The answer must be in the negative. The prologue and epilogue, which are vital to the purpose of the royal inscription, are missing in the cuneiform codes later than Codex Hammurabi, and probably also in Codex

---

8   Hiller 1903.
9   Koschaker 1917.
10 Landsberger 1939: 221-22. On the meaning of *ṣimdat šarrim*, see de Jong Ellis 1972.
11 Cited by Kraus 1960: 292.
12 Finkelstein 1961.
13 Finkelstein 1961: 101.
14 Finkelstein 1961: 103

Eshnunna (which slightly antedates it).[15] Since we possess copies of these codes that originally provided a complete version of the text, and not an extract (with the possible exception of the Neo-Babylonian Laws), there is no reason for them to have omitted the prologue and epilogue if they existed. We must therefore agree with S. Paul in concluding that this traditional literary pattern was not continued after Codex Hammurabi, if indeed it existed at all outside the central Mesopotamian cultural sphere represented by the three codes that were modeled upon it.[16] Paul does claim to see in both Deuteronomy and the Book of the Covenant the same tripartite division of legal corpus within a prologue-epilogue frame,[17] but the two biblical codes are in a literary context too different from that of their Mesopotamian counterparts to allow any meaningful comparison. The content and purpose of the framework bear no relationship to that of the Mesopotamian codes: by no stretch of the imagination can the chapters following the legal corpus (however widely defined) in Exodus and Deuteronomy be described as an *apologia* of the lawgiver; there is therefore no evidence from their present textual context that the codes originated in a royal inscription. If, in the alternative, it is suggested that the biblical structure is patterned on that of the Mesopotamian codes, the additional difficulty is faced that there exist other models for the biblical version to copy, in particular ancient Near Eastern treaties.[18]

If the activity of writing law codes could be engaged in without the addition of a prologue and epilogue to the legal corpus, it suggests that a royal *apologia* was not the primary purpose in the composition of the latter. This is confirmed by the remarkable dichotomy in style between the Mesopotamian codes' prologues and epilogues and their central legal corpus. It has even been suggested[19] that they were formulated by two different sets of authors: the legal corpus by jurists and the prologue and epilogue by temple or court poets. It seems to us evidence rather that the legal corpus already existed as an independent unit with an independent purpose and was sometimes inserted into a frame, as in Codex Hammu-

---

15 A date-formula appears to precede the laws. The end of both extant copies is not preserved.

16 Paul 1970: 11 n. 5.

17 Paul 1970: 27-36.

18 See Weinfeld 1972: 146-57.

19 Klíma et al. 1971: 244.

rabi, in order to be applied to a new purpose, that of the royal *apologia*. This is a recognized process in the case of the biblical codes, which were inserted into a religious-historical framework.[20]

The Law Codes as a Scribal Exercise?

The nature and purpose of the central legal corpus is the subject of the theory proposed by F. R. Kraus in respect of Codex Hammurabi.[21] Kraus begins with Hammurabi's own definition of his laws: *dīnāt mīšarim*,[22] which he translates *gerechte Richtersprüche* (just judicial decisions).[23] The legal corpus is therefore *prima facie* a list of the king's decisions in his capacity as a judge.[24] Closer examination, however, reveals that by no means all the "judgments" recorded in the code are real. They are organized in groups wherein a single case is expanded by logical extrapolation, i.e., various theoretical alternatives are considered and the appropriate solution given by *a priori* reasoning.[25] For example, paragraphs 229-231 read:

229 If a mason builds a house for a man and does not reinforce his work and the house that he built collapses and kills the owner of the house, that mason shall be killed.

230 If it kills a child of the householder, they shall kill a child of that mason.

231 If it kills a slave of the householder, he shall give slave for slave to the householder.

Similar gradation of penalties occurs elsewhere in the code, in paragraphs 209-211, for example. We are therefore in the presence of a type of

---

20 Weinfeld 1972: 283-96.
21 Kraus 1960.
22 Col. XLVII (= reverse XXIV), lines 1-2.
23 Kraus 1960: 285. First proposed by Landsberger 1939: 223.
24 Although they translated the phrase "just laws" (1955: 95), Driver and Miles in fact noted that these laws resembled English case-laws rather than statute (1952: 52).
25 Kraus 1960: 289. In other passages, the composition of the Code is more complex, although the same principle obtains. See Westbrook and Wilcke 1974-1977.

academic method. Now, this same method is found in a seemingly unrelated group of texts—the omen collections. For example, in the omen series *šumma izbu* a typical sequence is:[26]

> 5 If a woman gives birth, and the right ear (of the child) is (abnormally) small, the house of the man will be scattered.
> 6 If a woman gives birth, and the left ear (of the child) is (abnormally) small, the house of the man will expand.
> 7 If a woman gives birth, and both ears (of the child) are (abnormally) small, the house of the man will become poor.

The connection, according to Kraus, is that the law codes and omen collections are both representatives of a particular type of literature, namely scientific treatises. Divination was regarded as a science by the Mesopotamians and the compiling of omens the equivalent of scientific research. By the same token, the casuistic style in which both texts are couched was the "scientific" style par excellence—transferring the concrete individual case to the sphere of the impersonal rule.[27]

This scientific activity is the work of the scribes and takes place in the scribal schools. Codex Hammurabi itself exists in the form of school copies already in the Old Babylonian period. It borrows extensively, often verbatim, from the text of the earlier codes of Ur-Namma and Lipit-Ishtar (as one would expect if it were a literary genre), which in turn exist in the form of Old Babylonian school copies. Likewise, both extant copies of Codex Eshnunna are school texts.[28] In Kraus' view, therefore, it is Hammurabi the scribe rather than the judge who is represented by the legal corpus of his code. It is a work of theoretical literature designed to illustrate his wisdom—"wise" (*emqum*) being a typical epithet of the scribe.[29]

---

26 Tablet III, lines 5-7. See Leichty 1970: 54.

27 Kraus 1960: 288-90. The same argument is given by Bottéro 1982: 426-35, using the example of the medical texts, another form of scientific treatise. Bottéro points out that Babylonian science sought to achieve exhaustive treatment of a subject by listing examples not only of the commonly observed and the exceptional, but also of the possible.

28 Kraus 1960: 293-94.

29 Kraus 1960: 290.

The notion of the law codes as an activity of the scribal schools provides a ready explanation for their appearance among the Hittites, in Assyria, and as far afield as Israel. Cuneiform scribal schools existed throughout the ancient Near East in the second millennium, including the cities of Canaan prior to the Israelite conquest.[30] They were not merely places for learning the cuneiform script; such schools were the universities of the ancient Near East where the cultural and literary inheritance, both Babylonian and local, was preserved and developed. Codex Hammurabi itself continued to he copied and re-copied in scribal schools both in Babylonia and elsewhere for more than a millennium after its promulgation.[31] It would be no surprise, therefore, to find similar codes compiled from the local law by Canaanite or Hittite scribes who were inspired by contact with Hammurabi's *magnum opus*.

Attractive as this picture is, in our view it requires correction in one important respect: Kraus' basic assumption that the intellectual activity of collecting legal decisions, expanding them by the addition of logical variants and formulating them in scientific style resulted in a work of pure science, a monument to scribal wisdom and no more.[32] Our reasons for questioning this assumption emerge from a closer examination of the parallel adduced by Kraus himself—the omen series.

Law Codes and Omen Series: Practical Application

The omen series were compiled for a very practical purpose: to be used as reference works by diviners when they sought to determine the significance of an ominous feature (as in extispicy) or event. For example, if a lamb were born with but a single horn, the diviner (*bārû*) would consult the series dealing with unusual births, *summa izbu,* select and excerpt the pertinent omens and prepare a report. Then, if necessary, an appropriate ritual would he performed in order to expiate the evil effects of a bad omen. Presumably the report would usually be presented orally, but in the library of Assurbanipal have been preserved a number of written reports

---

30 See Tadmor 1977.
31 See Laessoe 1950; Nougayrol 1951, 1957, 1958; Finkelstein 1967, 1969a.
32 To be fair, Kraus does hint at their possible use: ". . . gibt es ein Handbuch, so greift man zu ihm" (1960: 290), but no specific application is suggested.

from diviners to an Assyrian king, upon which our knowledge of this procedure is based.[33] The diviner did not directly cite the name of the series that he was consulting but would differentiate his sources by drawing a line between omens from different tablets of the series or else by placing them on opposite sides of the tablets.[34] There is evidence of the consultation of omen series as far back as the Old Babylonian period.[35] The activity of compiling the lists of omens together with their meanings was therefore not merely a scribal exercise; it was "applied science."

We suggest that the compiling of lists of legal decisions basically served a similar purpose. They were a reference work for consultation by judges when deciding difficult cases. In view of the association of most of the law codes with a king, it is reasonable to suppose that it was the king as judge, or at least the royal judges, that these lists were intended to serve. The royal courts, as supreme courts, would be called upon to decide difficult points of law and would therefore be most in need of precedents to assist them.[36]

There is no direct evidence from cuneiform sources for the consultation of law codes as there is for the omen series.[37] This is not a decisive consideration, nor even surprising, for three reasons. Firstly, the selection of cuneiform sources available to us is notoriously arbitrary, depending on the fortunes of the archaeologist's spade, and argument from silence is therefore inappropriate. Secondly, the interpretation of omens played a far more important and common role in Mesopotamia than did lawsuits. The king consulted diviners because, like the rest of his subjects and perhaps more so, he was a potential victim of the divine judgment signified by the

---

33 Leichty 1970: 7-11. For reports based on excerpts from an astronomical omen series, see Parpola 1983: nos. 324-326.

34 Leichty 1970: 8.

35 Leichty 1970: 7-8, citing an Old Babylonian letter.

36 On the role of the royal courts as a final court of appeal in difficult cases, see Weinfeld 1977; and Leemans 1968.

37 See note 11 above. An express, if later reference to the use of a law code by royal judges is found in a land which so far has yielded no law codes, namely Egypt. According to the Greek historian Diodorus Siculus (*Bib. Hist.* I 75 [6]), at a trial in Egypt all the laws lay before the judges, written down in eight books. Seidl (1957: 19) claims that this account is confirmed by a picture in the tomb of Rekhmireh, a vizier of the eighteenth dynasty, which shows the vizier sitting in judgment with forty leather scrolls before him.

omens, and because he needed the advice of the diviners before undertak-
ing any significant act and, irrespective of his own initiative, whenever a
natural phenomenon of ominous portent occurred. On the other hand, the
king was never party to a lawsuit, only the judge in a restricted number of
cases, and his need for consultation of legal precedents, whether personally
or through experts, would be much more circumscribed. Inevitably, the
number of recorded omens would be far greater than that of legal precedents, and in fact in the library of Assurbanipal's omen series formed by
far the largest category of texts.[38] This in turn would affect the chances of
finding material evidence of their application. Finally, there is the question
of oral and written procedure. Direct evidence for the consultation of omen
series exists only for a short period of time covering two Neo-Assyrian
kings,[39] and only due to the fortuitous circumstance that the diviners in
question did not live in the palace, so that consultation was by letter.[40] It
would require equally unusual circumstances for consultation of legal reference works during or at the conclusion of a trial to be by letter and not
oral.

The cuneiform sources do, however, provide some indirect evidence of
the use of law codes that we have postulated. Firstly, there is the archaeological evidence concerning the Middle Assyrian Laws. This vast
collection, originally numbering 14 tablets, is, as we have noted, not a
royal inscription. Nor is it a school text. Most of the tablets recovered were
found in a gate-house identified as the "Gate of Shamash," which is the
normal location of the courthouse in Mesopotamia (Shamash being the god
of justice), and already E. Weidner referred to them for this reason as a
legal library for judges.[41]

Secondly, there is the nature of the Hittite Laws. These are likewise
neither a royal inscription nor a school tablet. They are part of the royal
archives, but more interesting than their location is the historical development that they betray. The collection was recopied over several centuries,

---

38 The omen series *šumma izbu* alone, as preserved in the library of Assurbanipal con-
    tains more than two thousand omens, arranged in a series of twenty-four tablets.
    Leichty 1970: 2.
39 Parpola 1983: xvii.
40 Leichty 1970: 9-10.
41 Weidner 1937.

and the later copies still retain some archaic language.[42] On the other hand, there is evidence of an updating not only of language[43] but also of the substantive law. In some cases this is implied and in others in the form of an express reference to an amendment.[44] And a fragment of an even later version (KBo VI 4) substitutes new penalties for those of the principal text. Regular changes to keep abreast of developments in the law would not have been necessary if the text were merely academic,[45] as a comparison with the subsequent fate of Codex Hammurabi shows.

As we have seen, Codex Hammurabi continued to be copied for more than a millennium after its promulgation, both within and outside of Babylonia. The copies are remarkably faithful to the original; certainly no changes whatsoever were made to the substantive law. The reason is that it became a piece of canonical literature, a part of the scribal school curriculum that was copied for its own sake.

This illustrates the difference between school texts and scientific texts. The local scribes saw no reason to alter Codex Hammurabi, because for them it was only a scribal exercise and not part of their positive law. Their own law codes, however, had a practical purpose and therefore had to reflect the local law, which meant also regular amendment to take account of changes in the law. This is not to say that "foreign" codes copied in the scribal schools were not without influence. The codes under discussion contain many similar provisions, because the societies themselves and therefore their substantive law were so similar.

An earlier law code therefore provides an obvious model when drafting one's own, particularly in terms of the legal problems to be addressed, but its provisions are not binding. It has rather what modern lawyers from independent systems with a common tradition call "persuasive authority," as, for example, with United States precedents cited in English courts.[46] The process of adoption is selective. Thus the Sumerian codes of Ur-

---

42 Goetze 1957: 110-11.

43 Hoffner 1981.

44 E.g. Paragraph 94: "If a free man steals in a house, he shall give (back) the respective goods; they would formerly give for the theft 1 mina of silver; now he shall give 12 shekels of silver" (*ANET³* 193). See also Korošec 1957: 99-100.

45 "KBO VI 4 schleppt die veralteten Bestimmungen nicht mehr mit; der Text gibt nur das geltende Recht" (Goetze 1957: 111).

46 Compare Cardascia's theory of the "reception" of Codex Hammurabi, drawing on the analogy of the Continental law experience (1960: 47-48).

Namma and Lipit-Ishtar exist in school copies in the Old Babylonian period and some of their provisions re-appear in Codex Hammurabi in almost verbatim translation.[47] Other paragraphs of Codex Hammurabi, however, depart fundamentally from their parallels in the earlier codes, for example, where physical injury is punished by talio instead of monetary compensation.

Again, the later codes did not reproduce the provisions of Codex Hammurabi verbatim, but a curious use of terminology illustrates how they took note of it as a source. The dowry that a bride brings from her parent's house is consistently called *šeriktum* in Codex Hammurabi, and the gifts that she receives from her husband, *nudunnûm* (paragraph 172). This terminology does not reflect the documents of practice, where *šeriktum* does not appear at all, gifts from the husband have no special appellation, and the *nudunnûm* in all periods refers to the dowry. All the evidence points to an innovation which was not taken up in practice.[48] Nonetheless, the Middle Assyrian Laws in their discussion of questions of marital property use the same scheme—*šerku* for dowry (MAL A 27) and *nudunnû* for gift from the husband (MAL A 29, 32)—suggesting a conscious imitation of Codex Hammurabi, although the laws in which these terms appear are not directly parallel to the provisions of the earlier code. The same tradition even makes its way into the Neo-Babylonian Laws (paragraphs 8-13), with this difference, that the author of the later code found the traditional scheme too illogical and simply reversed it—*nudunnû* for dowry, as in practice, *šeriktu* for gift from the husband, the latter use being a complete innovation. Again, the content of the laws in which these terms appear are not the same as in the earlier codes.

Finally, the practice of selective adoption can be seen in the relationship between the cuneiform and the biblical codes. Codex Eshnunna exists as a school text and in some form must have reached the Israelite cultural sphere, since Exod 21:35, concerning the ox that gores another ox, is virtually a translation of CE 53. However, whereas CE 54 imposes a monetary penalty on the previously warned owner of a goring ox that kills a man, Exod 21:29 in the same circumstances requires the death penalty.

---

47 See n. 5 above.
48 See the discussion by the author in Westbrook 1982a: vol. 2, 257-68 (since published as Westbrook 1988b).

To summarize: in our view the ancient Near Eastern law codes derive from a tradition of compiling series of legal precedents in the same manner as omens, medical prognoses, and other scientific treatises. The purpose of these series was to act as reference works for the royal judges in deciding difficult cases. Probably this began as an oral tradition and only gradually became a systematic written corpus.[49] The clearest examples of such series are the Middle Assyrian Laws and the Hittite Laws; the other law codes are evidence that such series could he adopted to other purposes. Three types of secondary purpose appear from the extant codes: (1) royal inscriptions designed to praise the king's activity as a judge (CU, CL, CH), which were characterized by the addition of a prologue and epilogue; (2) school texts (CU, CL, CE, CH, NBL), which would take on independent existence as part of the scribal curriculum; and (3) part of a religio-historical narrative (Covenant and Deuteronomic Codes) where the deity replaces the king as the source of the law.

The final piece of evidence for this thesis comes from an unexpected source, but in order to evaluate it we must first analyze the process by which the law codes were created.

Law Codes and Omen Series: The Cycle of Creation

The example given earlier in which the diviner, when called upon to interpret the ominous significance of an unusual birth, would select the pertinent omens from the series *šumma izbu,* is but one step in the cycle of creating precedents and applying them.

The first step theoretically will be the case where a birth occurs for which there is no precedent—a mare gives birth to a hare. If the diviner interprets this, whether by analogy with known omens or some other process of logic, as meaning that the king will flee from the battlefield, and in the event the king in question does flee, the diviner's decision will then become a precedent for future omens of the same kind.

The second step is for the omen to pass through what we may call the "first stage of generalization." This stage is evidenced in the cuneiform sources by the "*tamītu*" texts.[50] These are questions put to a god, e.g., *tamīt*

---

49   On the analogy of the omen literature, see Leichty 1970: 23.
50   Lambert 1966.

alāk ḫarrāni, "a *tamītu* concerning going on a campaign." In most cases the name of the person for whom the question was being put is replaced by "so-and-so, son of so-and-so" (*annanna apīl annanna*). W. Lambert explains: "the suppression of the names suggests the reason for the handing down of these documents which at first glance would seem to have no practical use after they were originally employed by the appropriate priest. Just as in law a case once decided can become a precedent so that future parties having the same problem can find the answer without recourse to the expensive and time-consuming processes of the law, so the *tamītus,* once answered, were preserved in case any one should wish to find the gods' answer to that particular question again."[51]

The third step represents the second stage of generalization, whereby the anonymous precedent is put into casuistic form, and the fourth step is the compilation of lists of these casuistic rules with the addition of their logical variations by analogy so as to form a series. This "scientific" treatment is necessary because in Mesopotamian eyes it makes the series universally applicable (by exhausting all possible alternatives) and therefore authoritative.[52]

The fifth step is then one already familiar to us, namely consultation of the series by the diviner who excerpts the relevant omens. If the occurrence contains some new element not directly covered by the existing omens, then the new omen may itself become a precedent, undergo the two stages of generalization, and be taken up into an omen series, thus repeating the cycle.

The above cycle will have a familiar ring to lawyers, for it accurately reflects the development of general legal rules from individual cases in legal systems where judge-made law predominates. The only difference is that in the modern systems the process of generalization consists in creating abstract principles of law rather than variants of the precedent. It is reasonable to suppose, therefore, that the same process took place in moving from individual judgment to law code and back again. A decision of the king (or royal judge) in a difficult case would be turned into a casuistic rule of general application and, expanded with the necessary variants by

---

51 Lambert 1956: 121.
52 See Bottéro 1982: 431-33. In the alternative, precedents might be compiled first and then turned into casuistic form—there are some examples of large tablets containing a number of collected *tamītu*'s (Lambert 1966: 119-20).

extrapolation, would eventually become part of a canon of such rules, which in turn were consulted in deciding new cases, and where a new decision was made it eventually would be added to the canon, and so forth, Accordingly, Hammurabi could speak truthfully in his code of the just decisions that *he* had made, for the central part of that code represents those parts of the received canon of legal rules that he chose to adopt and apply in his own court, supplemented by his own judgments (and perhaps the logical variants thereof).

The cuneiform sources are not, however, so forthcoming with evidence of the legal steps described above as they are with the omen literature. The only step recorded is the first one—the king and his judges giving judgment in a particular case—without any indication of the decision's value as a precedent.[53] Even in the few full trial reports that exist, the *ratio decidendi* is not given.[54] Bottéro refers to one decision of Hammurabi that appears to be based on the same principle as an article of his code.[55] According to CH 32: "If a merchant ransoms a soldier who is taken prisoner on a royal campaign and brings him back to his city, if there are the means for redemption in his house he shall redeem himself. If there are not the means in his house for redeeming himself, he shall be redeemed from (the resources of) his city temple. If there are not the means in his city temple, the palace shall redeem him."

The following order is given by Hammurabi in a letter: "Speak to Luštamar-Zamama and Belanum: Thus says Hammurabi. (As to) Sinanadamru-lippalis, the son of Maninum, whom the enemy took: give his merchant ten shekels of silver from the temple of Sin and redeem him."

---

53 See Leemans 1968 and the examples given therein.

54 A possible exception is the trial report edited by Jacobsen 1970. The legal issue appears to be whether a wife, who is informed by her husband's assassins of his murder but keeps silent, is herself guilty of murder. The case was remitted by the king to the Assembly of Nippur, and the report contains a debate before the Assembly, followed by the Assembly's reasoned decision as to her guilt. The report exists in duplicates from the reign of King Rim-Sin of Larsa and in later copies (unpublished) from the time of Samsu-iluna (Jacobsen 1970: 196). This suggests that it had value as a precedent, although of course it may merely have been a cause célèbre. The same legal issue does not occur in any of the extant law codes. It is interesting to note that according to Jacobsen, the later copies of the report also contain reports of a number of other trials before the Assembly of Nippur (1970: 196).

55 Bottéro 1982: 421.

From the name of the prisoner it could be assumed that the temple of Sin was his city temple. What then is the connection between the king's order and CH 32? Was it the precedent from which at least part of the legal rule was constructed? Or was it given in application of the rule? Indeed, were the conditions for redemption laid down in the rule, namely the lack of funds in the soldier's household, fulfilled in this case? No answer can be derived from the laconic terms of the order. To find evidence of the intervening legal steps we must turn to our one non-cuneiform source: the Bible. The process in question is illustrated not by the biblical law codes themselves but by the reports made of five difficult cases, four of which were decided by recourse to a special procedure (the oracle) and one by the special order of a military leader.

The first case that we wish to consider is reported in Num 15:32-37. A man was found gathering wood on the Sabbath. The case must have been without precedent, for he was held while Moses consulted God. The decision was that the man was to be executed by stoning. As it stands the report is no more informative than Hammurabi's order. The grounds for the decision and the fact that it is intended as a precedent are indeed implicit, but neither received express mention.

The second case is reported in two places. In Numbers 31, after a war against the Midianites, Moses is ordered by God to divide the spoils of war between those who went out to battle and all the "congregation" (*'ēdâ*, vv. 25-28). As in the previous case, there is no specific indication that this decision is to serve as a precedent for future battles. However, the same principle at least (of division between combatants and noncombatants)[56] is the ratio of the decision attributed to David in 1 Samuel 30. The background here is a victory over the Amalekites. The victory was achieved with only part of his forces, the rest being left behind at Nahal Besor (vv. 9-10), but David decides nonetheless that the spoil is to be divided equally between those who actually took part in the engagement and those who remained behind. The decision in this report is formulated in terms of an anonymous rule: "For as his share is who goes down into the battle, so shall his share be who stays by the baggage; they shall share alike" (v. 24). Furthermore, we are expressly informed that this ruling had the force of

---

56 The two rulings differ as to the details of the division: David's decision gives an equal share to each, whether warrior or not; the order in Numbers is to divide the spoil equally between two groups of presumably unequal size.

precedent: "And from that day forward he made it a statute (*ḥōq*) and an ordinance (*mišpāṭ*) for Israel to this day" (v. 25). The terms *ḥōq* and *mišpāṭ* are, of course, familiar from the biblical law codes.

The third case is even more explicit. In Num 27:1-11, the daughters of Zelophehad, who died without sons, approach Moses and claim a share of their father's estate. Following the same procedure as in the case of the man who gathered wood on the Sabbath, Moses consults God, and the specific decision is given to share Zelophehad's estate among his daughters (v. 7). There then follows a re-formulation of that same decision as a casuistic rule, with the addition of possible alternatives (vv. 8-11):

> If a man dies, and has no son, then you shall cause his inheritance to pass to his daughter. And if he has no daughter, then you shall give his inheritance to his brothers. And if he has no brothers, then you shall give his inheritance to his father's brothers. And if his father has no brothers, then you shall give his inheritance to his kinsman that is next to him of his family, and he shall possess it. And it shall be to the people of Israel a statute and ordinance (*ḥuqqat mišpāṭ*).

There thus begin to emerge some of the steps in the creation of a code that we have already seen in the case of the Mesopotamian omen series and postulated for the cuneiform law codes.

The problem of inheritance when a man dies leaving daughters but no sons could not have been a rare one, and in fact we find exactly the same solution in a Sumerian fragment probably belonging to Codex Lipit-Ishtar:[57] "If a man died and he had no son, (his) unmarried daughter [shall become] his heir . . . ." The extra condition of being unmarried fits the case of Zelophehad's daughters perfectly, since in a postscript to the story (Numbers 36) we discover that they were unmarried and had to marry within the clan in order to preserve the family estate. Without wishing to enter into the intricacies of biblical compositional history, it seems to us that if this rule had already entered the law codes as early as the reign of Lipit-Ishtar, then it must have been in a canon of legal rules in Israel as well. If, therefore, as is claimed, the story is the projection back to the time

---

57 CL b; edited by Civil 1965.

of Moses of an incident designed to explain a later political phenomenon,[58] the technique must have been to take the well-known rule from a code and present it as an early precedent, the association being obvious to the contemporary reader familiar with the way that law codes developed from precedents.

The fourth example adds another element. In Num 9:6-14, the oracle is consulted by Moses in the case of persons who were unable to keep the passover on the appointed day. The divine decision is that they are given a second date, but far from being specific to the persons concerned, it is formulated directly as a general casuistic rule: "If any man of you or of your descendants is unclean through touching a dead body or is afar off on a journey, he shall still keep the passover . . . . In the second month on the fourteenth day in the evening they shall keep it . . ." (vv. 11-12). The intermediate steps between case and code are obvious to the reader and can therefore be omitted. The actual wording of the casuistic introit *'îš 'îš kî* is in fact already known in Codex Eshnunna[59] and employed throughout the Neo-Babylonian Laws (*awīlum ša*). But there is, as we mentioned, an additional element. Verse 13 goes on to consider the opposite case: "But the man who is clean and is not on a journey, yet refrains from keeping the passover, that person shall be cut off from his people." Here is the technique familiar from all the law codes and identified by Kraus as the universal thought-process of Mesopotamian science. It is not at all necessary to the decision in this particular case but has been added as the drafters of the codes added theoretical examples. And v. 14 adds a further variant, concerning the applicability of the passover law to the *gēr*. We have thus seen in these four examples: (1) the initial decision; (2) the first stage of generalization (anonymity); (3) the second stage of generalization (casuistic form); and (4) the creation of a code (academic variations). The picture is completed by our final example: the case of the man who in the course of a fight cursed in God's name (Lev 24:10-23).

The case begins with the now familiar pattern of oracular consultation, specific decision (vv. 10-13), and execution in the particular case: "Bring out of the camp him who cursed; and let all who heard him lay their hands

---

58 Snaith 1966. The character of the precedent as a source of law was recognized by Weingreen 1966.

59 CE 12, 13, and 19. It is also found in the Edict of Ammi-ṣaduqa and in the Middle Assyrian Laws, paragraphs A 40 and B 6. See Yaron 1969: 65.

upon his head, and let all the congregation stone him" (v. 14). There then follows the repetition of the same decision in the general casuistic form (vv. 15-16): "Whoever curses his God shall bear his sin. He who blasphemes the name of the Lord shall be put to death; the sojourner as well as the native, when he blasphemes the Name, shall he put to death." Thus far the pattern is the same as in the earlier examples. The ruling continues, however, with the following variants: "He who kills a man shall be put to death. He who kills a beast shall make it good, life for life. When a man causes a disfigurement in his neighbor, as he has done it shall be done to him; fracture for fracture, eye for eye, tooth for tooth; as he had disfigured a man, he shall be disfigured. He who kills a beast shall make it good; and he who kills a man shall be put to death" (vv. 17-21). The relevance of these variants is not all apparent. Only the vaguest association of ideas would link them to the actual decision in the case which concerned the using of God's name in a curse.

On the other hand, if we consider all the circumstances of the case, namely that there was a fight between two men when the one man cursed, then the reference to rules on unlawful death or wounding is understandable. In a modern context, a lawyer giving an opinion on the case—*prior to the decision*—would naturally wish to cover those aspects as well. In the ancient Near Eastern context, the method involved becomes clear if we refer once again to our Mesopotamian parallel, the practice of the diviner (*bārû*) when consulted on an ominous event. It will be recalled that the diviner's report consisted of omens excerpted from the omen-series. But, as Leichty points out, "It is interesting to note that the *bārû*-priest never filed just one omen as a report, but rather attempted to include all omens which might in some way pertain to the case."[60] The very same technique has been used in our passage in Leviticus, and just as the *bārû*-priest would excerpt quotations from *šumma izbu* or some other omen-series, so excerpts from a law code have been quoted here—to all appearances from that same collection upon which the present Covenant Code is based. In the light of the cuneiform material then, the biblical source can be seen to provide the missing piece of evidence that the law codes were applied in practice. And thus the cycle is completed.

---

60 Leichty 1970: 8.

2

The Nature and Origins of the Twelve Tables

Abstract

This article establishes a link between the early Roman code, known as the Twelve Tables, and the ancient Near Eastern law codes. The relationship between the two is evident both in the form of the codes and in their content. Both appear to derive from the Mesopotamian scientific tradition and to deal with similar legal issues that likely formed part of the curriculum in scribal training. A detailed examination of how issues such as minor physical assault and theft are treated in the Roman and Mesopotamian material supports this line of reasoning.

Introduction

The Nature of the Twelve Tables

The various accounts from classical sources agree that the Twelve Tables were a *lex*, a normative statute of the type familiar from the late Republic, promulgated after due deliberation by a legislative body. Indeed, the Twelve Tables were "the *lex*," the archetypal piece of legislation that initially at least constituted a comprehensive codification of the law in force—*fons omnis publici privatique iuris*, as Livy puts it (3.34.6). And like any *lex* its formulation arose out of specific historical

* Originally published in *Zeitschrift der Savigny-Stiftung für Rechtsgeschichte (Romanistische Abteilung)* 105 (1988): 74-121. Used by permission. A new numbering system for the Twelve Tables is set forth in Crawford 1996. This article retains the older system.
* My thanks are due to Professor Peter Birks of Edinburgh University, who read the first draft of the article and made many useful comments and criticisms. Responsibility for the opinions expressed herein rests, as usual, with the author.

circumstances (the struggle between the patricians and the plebeians), the problems of which their provisions were designed to resolve (by removing the plebeians' grievances).

Modern scholarship, while discounting the incidental legends of the traditional account, has been singularly uncritical in assessing its basic premises. Since the universal rejection of Pais' and Lambert's heresy as to the date and authorship of the Twelve Tables,[1] the scholarly consensus has been that the code was indeed the product of conscious intellectual effort on the part of a commission of ten individuals, duly confirmed by a constituent assembly (as legislation ought to be), at about the date ascribed by tradition, namely the mid-fifth century B.C.E., and designed to impose a sweeping reform upon the existing law, a new order that would improve the lot of the plebeians.[2]

Problems arise, however, when we try to apply this view of the Twelve Tables to its actual provisions, as known to us from the surviving fragments. Firstly, there is the question of form. As Daube points out, the predominantly casuistic style of the Twelve Tables ("If a man does X, he shall be subject to Y punishment") is not the form used by classical legislation.[3] But this, it may at once be countered, is scarcely a problem at all. The Twelve Tables are the product of a primitive society; they cannot be expected to have developed the sophistication of the later laws, and any differences may therefore be attributed to normal historical development. This all too obvious explanation, however, leads one to wonder whether the elaborate machinery of the Decemvirs, etc., while eminently suitable for legislation of the classical period, is not also too sophisticated for such a primitive society?

The form of the text gives rise to a further problem. Wieacker discerns two basic stylistic forms: laconic imperatives in parataxis and (the more dominant) the conditional sentence. Even the occasional use of a relative sentence reveals the same thought structure: rules such as *Qui malum*

---

1 For a summary of the controversy, see Schiller 1978: 153-55.
2 E.g., Crifò 1972: 118-121, 123; Kunkel 1973: 23-35; Jolowicz and Nicholas 1972: 14; Wieacker 1956: 472; Wieacker 1966: 299; and especially Westrup 1950: 168-69, 176-82: ". . . a Magna Charta of the plebeian rights and liberties."
3 Daube 1956: 5-7. This difference is not affected by Daube's later argument (1956: 57-61) that the third-person singular forms in the Twelve Tables may have an impersonal sense.

carmen incantassit (VIII 1) could equally well be formulated as a conditional sentence.[4] The result is a series of specific solutions to narrow sets of circumstances; lacking are abstract norms, general principles, or definitions.[5]

In consequence, the Twelve Tables could not have been a comprehensive code, even of the private law to which the surviving fragments seem mostly to confine themselves.[6] Here at least, some modern scholars break ranks with the orthodox Roman view. Gioffredi suggests that the provisions allude to the unwritten principles of the law which, being generally known, there is no need to state expressly,[7] thus admitting the existence of a customary law with equal validity as the written text. Kaser, following the same line of thought, regards the Roman view as a fiction which arose some time after the Twelve Tables' promulgation.[8] The bulk of the law was based on unwritten tradition (*mos maiorum*), while the Twelve Tables affected only a relative small number of rules, which they confirmed or amended.[9] It is to be noted that Kaser's explanation, in denying comprehensiveness to the Twelve Tables, at the same time assumes that they had the character of a classical *lex*, the point being that in later history *lex* was only a sporadic source of law alongside the all-embracing *ius*.[10]

We thus come to the final and most serious problem: the apparent lack of reference in the extant rules to the events which were supposed to be their "raison d'être." Commentators have made great efforts to discover in the terse provisions on private law reforms for the benefit of the plebeians, but all such interpretations are based on *a priori* reasoning. If we did not know of an external tradition concerning patricians and plebeians, would

---

4 Wieacker 1966: 321-22.

5 Gioffredi 1947-1948: 7-140, esp. 44.

6 This is not merely a question of their present fragmentary condition. As Wieacker points out, the impossibility of comprehensiveness can be seen from the near-contemporary Laws of Gortyn, the text of which has been preserved almost in its entirety (1956: 467). In 1966: 299 on the other hand, Wieacker speaks of comprehensive legislation by the Decemvirs, but without giving grounds for this change in his position.

7 Gioffredi 1947-1948: 7-140, esp. 44.

8 Kaser 1973: 523-46, esp. 539.

9 Kaser 1973: 524, 527-28, 533.

10 Kaser 1973: 524.

we conclude from the text of the Twelve Tables alone that they were designed to reform the law in favor of plebeians? Hardly.

1. The text contains only one express reference to the two social classes, namely the prohibition on intermarriage (XI 1), which suggests quite the opposite.[11]
2. In the rules on debt, the right of the creditor to take the debtor "bound with fetters or shackles of 15 pounds, not less, or more if he wishes" (III 3) does not suggest social legislation in favor of the debtor, always assuming the latter to be identifiable with the plebeian class.
3. The bulk of the rules deals with very ordinary aspects of private law, such as procedure, inheritance, and delict. They could apply to almost any period or society.
4. A small number of rules apply to religious practice such as funerals, and are as such of no social immanence.[12]

Furthermore, the very simplicity of the rules belies the notion that the plebeians' ignorance of the law was an evil removed by the legislation. The law was bound to be revealed to them by the precedents that they

---

11 It can be argued that the provision is in one of the supplementary Tables, added against the will of the plebeians. But this again relies on an external story rather than the text, and it could equally be argued that the elaborate tale of the last two Tables, found in certain authors, was designed to cover their embarrassment at the content of the text so flagrantly contradicting their account of its formation.

12 The argument that the prohibition on sumptuous funerals (e.g., Wieacker 1966: 313) was aimed against the high living of the aristocracy is an example of the dangers of uncritically accepting classical Roman interpretation. The claim is based on Cicero's remarks (*de leg.* 2.23.59-24,61), but the picture given from those provisions preserved in the original is somewhat different. The prohibitions are on smoothing the funeral pyre with an axe (X 2), female mourners tearing their cheeks or making a certain type of lamentation (X 4), collecting the bones for a subsequent funeral (X 5), adding various things to the corpse, including gold (X 8). Apart from the gold, none of these prohibitions could possibly have anything to do with luxury. *Prima facie* they represent religious practices, the significance of which would have been lost on Cicero. One has only to compare the prohibition on Canaanite practices in Lev 19:28: "You shall not make any cuttings in your flesh for the dead nor print any marks upon you . . . ." Compare further A. Watson's more sober assessment of all the evidence (1975b: 180-186).

themselves experienced; only its subtleties could be hidden from them, and these would rely on a level of sophistication or a mass of detailed exceptions of which there is no trace in the published text. The most ignorant plebeian could hardly have been unaware that it was forbidden to bury or burn bodies in the city, if that rule had been enforced but once. And by the same token, if there were subtleties concealed from the plebeians, then the provisions of the extant text are singularly inapt for removing them. As Watson admits:[13] ". . . would the XII Tables have enabled the plebeians to know what the law was, and to exercise their private law rights? No! Law remained a mystery. Though the code is explicit on how to summon a defendant to court, on appropriate sureties and so on, there is not a word on the forms of action. One would not learn from the code how to frame the appropriate legis actio."

We conclude, therefore, that the form of the Twelve Tables does not bear the unequivocal marks of a legislative process and that their content is not necessarily explicable by reference to particular historical events. The hypothesis that we shall present in this study is that originally the Twelve Tables, far from being a *lex* in the classical sense, were not normative legislation at all and certainly not a comprehensive code. They represent a work of an entirely different character, a character which is intimately connected with the question of their origins.

The Origins of the Twelve Tables

The classical account with its story of a mission to Greece does at least hint at some foreign influence in the laws. Modern scholarship, on the whole, has taken a much more chauvinistic attitude. Thus Westrup claims:[14] "The Laws of the XII Tables are beyond any doubt whatever as a whole essentially of national Roman origin, even though the composition of a single precept may have had a provision in Solon's laws for its

---

13 Watson 1975b: 185. Ignorance should not be confused with uncertainty in the law, which would work to the detriment of patricians and plebeians equally. It is impossible to tell whether the extant rules resolved uncertainties, since all rules do so by their very existence. Neither comprehensive legislation nor even writing is necessary to establish certainty.

14 Westrup 1950: 108.

prototype." Westrup would look to Rome's own Indo-European heritage for the origins of its law.[15]

The foremost representative of the contrary opinion remains the thesis of Müller in 1903.[16] Having noted that a number of provisions in the newly-discovered Code of Hammurabi bore a close resemblance to provisions of the Covenant Code in Exodus and in some cases also to those of the Twelve Tables, Müller concluded that the first two derived from a common Semitic "Urgesetz,"[17] while some parts thereof were further incorporated into the Twelve Tables through the medium of Greece, where the decemviral mission had become acquainted with that same document.[18]

Müller's hypothesis has been universally rejected, often in the strongest terms. The last detailed refutation was by Volterra in a long essay on the originality of the earliest Roman law.[19] Volterra compared the early Roman and ancient Near Eastern legal systems by an analysis of institutions and concluded that they were incompatible.[20] There is little point in discussing the details of Volterra's comparisons, for two reasons.

The first is one noted by Volterra himself: that future archaeological discoveries might invalidate his conclusions.[21] It is not any particular discovery but the constant addition of new source-material, including a vast quantity of legal sources, that has rendered Volterra's prediction accurate. This material, together with equally extensive advances in the science of cuneiform studies, has rendered the learned works on ancient Near Eastern Law upon which Volterra relied mere milestones in the history of research.[22] Very little of their conclusions remains valid today: in terms of philology alone, many legal terms which were previously mistranslated or untranslatable have been clarified, leading in turn to a radically different interpretation of the legal context in which they appear.[23]

---

15 Westrup 1950: 186.
16 Müller 1903.
17 Müller 1903: 191-204, 210-211.
18 Müller 1903: 205-206.
19 Volterra 1937.
20 Volterra 1937: part II, 85-173.
21 Volterra 1937: 86.
22 E.g., David 1927; Koschaker 1917.
23 For example Volterra's translation (1937: 99) of a key phrase in Codex Hammurabi 185 (*ina mēšu*) as *in suo none* is now known to be incorrect; see Yaron 1965: 171-83.

The second reason is that Volterra's comparison reveals what in our opinion is a fundamental error of method. Volterra took as his point of departure early Roman law as traditionally interpreted, in other words, more or less as seen through the eyes of classical Roman commentators.[24] Now, it may be readily accepted that the classical law was a unique product of Roman civilization, and on this basis it is easy to conclude, when comparing the "classical version" of early Roman law with ancient Near Eastern law, that there is no connection between the two.

It did not occur to Volterra that our understanding of early Roman law might be open to re-interpretation in the light of the ancient Near Eastern material. After all, it is not as if our present understanding of early Roman law removes all obscurities or inconsistencies. It is a methodological error therefore to use the classical interpretation as if it were a constant. Nonetheless, the approach implied in Volterra's method has recently received emphatic expression in Watson's study of the Twelve Tables:[25] "When the direct evidence for archaic Roman law is inconclusive we often have a safer guide than that provided by unconnected systems, namely, developed Roman law. There is really very little connection between early Roman law and, say, the law of Babylon, but the law of the later Roman Republic and of the classical period is the immediate descendant of the law of the early Republic and the XII Tables."

We would argue that the position is by no means so clear. It is well known that much of the early text was obscure to the Romans themselves: the meaning of some terms had already been lost.[26] In the case of the jurists, their interpretation was by definition a distortion, since they were not interested in seeking historical truth but in establishing a rule that would

---

Likewise Volterra's assumption that *riksātu* in CH 128 means a written contract (1937: 117): see Greengus 1969: 505-32. Volterra's statement that ancient Near Eastern law (as opposed to Roman law) used written modes of transfer (1937: 145) was inaccurate even when he wrote: see San Nicolò 1931: 162-63.

24 E.g., that early Roman law placed no restrictions on the right of the *paterfamilias* to alienate property (Volterra 1937: 138-39), or that it had execution against the person, not against his goods (Volterra 1937: 148).

25 Watson 1975b: 8.

26 See, e.g., Cicero, *de leg.* 2.23.59 (*lessus*).

work for their own, vastly different, conditions.[27] But even the so-called "historians" cannot be relied on: being unaware of the conditions of early Roman society, they could only interpret the ancient texts in the light of their own experience. Far from trying to penetrate the thought-process of their ancestors, they imposed their own conceptions upon them.[28] Needless say to, many traditions were preserved, but they must be treated with caution, and not regarded as inherently reliable.

We shall attempt to show in the course of this study examples of where the ancient Near Eastern material can be used, on the one hand to confirm a native Roman tradition and, on the other hand, to clarify a misunderstanding of the law arising from it where that tradition results in an apparent internal contradiction. Such cases in themselves raise a presumption of some connection between the legal systems, but they are insufficient without a proper framework within which the existence of such connections can be accounted for. This framework we hope to provide in demonstrating the common derivation of the Twelve Tables and its counterparts from the ancient Near East.

We thus return to Müller's thesis. The rejection of criticism such as Volterra's does not automatically rehabilitate the former's approach. For Müller, no less than the rest of modern scholarship, assumed in his comparisons that he was dealing with normative statutes. The "Urgesetz" postulated by him was assumed to have been a single piece of legislation[29] which was reproduced more or less faithfully by Moses, adapted by Hammurabi,[30] and adopted in part by the Decemvirs. Müller even surmised that a legal commission might have been responsible for Hammurabi's version.[31] Modern research on the ancient Near Eastern law codes has

---

27 E.g., the reinterpretation of *malum carmen* (T. VIII 1) into the delict of *famosus libellus*. Cf. Paulus *Sent.* 5.4.6: *introducta est lege XII tab. de famosis carminibus . . . .*

28 See n. 12 above.

29 ". . . nicht einzelne Bestimmungen, die da und dort in gleicher Weise entstehen können, sondern das schon feststehende in bestimmte Formen und Gruppen gebrachte Gesetz, das nur an einem Orte in der Fassung und Redaktion entstanden sein kann" (1903: 218).

30 Müller's suggestion that this "Urgesetz" was brought by Abraham to Canaan and thence to Egypt, where Moses became acquainted with it (1903: 219), might seem a little naive to us today. It appeared less so in the then state of biblical research.

31 Müller 1903: 188.

rendered the idea of an "Urgesetz" untenable. Indeed, it is our different understanding of the nature of these law codes that provides the key to the connection between them. But by the same token, this new understanding may be applied equally to the Twelve Tables, so that Müller's researches can be said to have pointed in the right direction. We therefore turn now to examine the ancient Near Eastern material.

The Ancient Near Eastern Law Codes

The Framework: Ancient Near Eastern Civilization

Little more than a century ago virtually the only native evidence that existed for the ancient Near East before the conquest of Alexander was the Hebrew Bible. This document, standing in isolation, provided an obscure and often incomprehensible record of the culture from which it arose, and a highly distorted view of the surrounding civilizations. The archaeological and epigraphical evidence provided since then by excavations in the region has revealed that biblical Israel was but a minor part of a much wider civilization. The various kingdoms of the region were in constant contact throughout millennia, through trade, diplomacy, and at times by direct conquest. Through these channels passed not only men and goods but also ideas: wholesale literary, religious, and scientific traditions.

The pattern of diffusion of ideas was generally from Mesopotamia outwards.[32] The main reason seems to have been the system of writing. Cuneiform script, invented by the Sumerians in the early third millennium, was adopted by their Akkadian-speaking[33] neighbors and thence spread to other areas where it was adapted to the local languages. Already in the third millennium Ebla, in Syria, was using cuneiform for its language.[34] and in the second millennium cuneiform scribal schools were to be found as far afield as Armenia (Urartu), Anatolia (Hittites), Palestine (Canaan),

---

32 Though not exclusively, at least by the 1st millennium.

33 Akkadian was a Semitic language, better known by the names of the two main dialects that developed from it: Babylonian and Assyrian.

34 See Pettinato 1979: chap. 3.

and Egypt.[35] In this process, of particular interest to our inquiry is the position of the Hittites and of ancient Israel.

a) The Hittites spoke an Indo-European language and were never incorporated into any of the Mesopotamian empires.[36] Thus the existence of Mesopotamian traditions in their records can neither be due to some presumed common Semitic heritage[37] nor to the forcible imposition of a foreign culture. Assyrian merchants were active in Anatolia in the early second millennium (before the rise of the Hittite empire),[38] while the later Hittite Empire appears to have imported Babylonian scholarship on a larger scale.[39]

b) The main record of ancient Israel, the Hebrew Bible, is thoroughly pervaded with Mesopotamian influences while at the same time manifesting extreme ideological hostility to Mesopotamian culture.[40] Thus the absorption of outside traditions was not altogether a conscious act of will.[41] Furthermore, the Bible is not written in cuneiform script, showing that the traditions in question could survive the demise of the script in which they were originally expressed. Indeed, such was the tenacity of

---

35 The influence on Egypt was less, since the Egyptians had their own script and highly developed civilization. By the same token, Egyptian influence outside of its own territory was remarkably small, except in the small area of Western Asia that it intermittently held under its control. In the 2nd millennium, Akkadian was the language of diplomatic correspondence, and the Egyptians used it even for communication with their own vassals in Canaan, having a scribal school at El-Amarna for this purpose.

36 The Hittite Empire flourished between the 18th and the end of the 12th century B.C.E., when it was destroyed by the Sea Peoples. For a summary description, see Goetze 1957: 82-178.

37 Also, many of these traditions are found first in Sumerian—a non-Semitic language.

38 For a summary of the relations, see Goetze 1957: 64-81. Our documentation is mainly from the 19th century B.C.E.

39 See Goetze 1957: 171-74.

40 E.g., Jeremiah's objections to the cult of Ishtar (Jer 7:18) and Ezekiel's disgust at women weeping over the death of Tammuz in the temple in Jerusalem (Ezek 8:14).

41 E.g., Ezekiel uses categories known from a Babylonian reference work for priests. See Westbrook 1988d: 29 n. 102.

these traditions that many survived into post-biblical rabbinic literature, even when not mentioned in the Bible.[42]

The spread of Mesopotamian traditions was therefore only in small part due to conquest or ethnic factors. It appears to have occurred mostly through political and commercial interchange, fostered by the use of the cuneiform script. It manifests itself in every field of ideas, most notably in literature, religion, and science.

a) In the literary sphere the best-known example is the Flood story, derived from a Mesopotamian original, which finds its way into the biblical creation account in Gen 6:9-9:17.[43] But there are other examples that follow other patterns of diffusion, for example the Harab myth, which passes from a Babylonian version into the Hittite sphere.[44] Often we find preserved not the whole myth but elements thereof, as with the *apkallu*'s, the seven Mesopotamian sages, who were said to have pre-dated the Flood and who have recently been identified in Prov 9:1.[45] On the other hand, it may be not the content of the literature that is transmitted, but the literary genre, for example "city-laments" or "building stories."[46]

b) The diffusion of traditions in the religious sphere is evidence of even deeper influence. Although they worshipped different gods, the peoples of the ancient Near East shared many cultic practices and concepts, including the classification of sins.[47]

c) A third significant sphere was that of the sciences, but we shall postpone our discussion of the scientific tradition for the moment, and deal first with the position of the law codes in this general picture.

42 See, e.g., Weinfeld 1983: 95-129, esp. 119; and Westbrook 1986b: 393-398.
43 The oldest version is in Sumerian, and an Akkadian version was implanted into the Gilgamesh Epic. See *ANET³* 42-44 (Sumerian version), 93-95 (Akkadian version).
44 Jacobsen 1984: 17-20.
45 Greenfield 1985: 13-20.
46 For "city-laments," see Gwaltney 1983. For "building stories," see Kapelrud 1963; and Hurowitz 1985.
47 See nn. 41 and 42 above; and Moyer 1983.

The Law Codes

The so-called "law codes" from the ancient Near East form a literary genre in which the common tradition is particularly evident. Nine such documents are known to date, seven in cuneiform script and two from the Pentateuch. They are as follows:

1. Codex Ur-Namma (CU), from the city of Ur in southern Mesopotamia. It is written in Sumerian and dates from ca. 2100 B.C.E.[48]

2. Codex Lipit-Ishtar (CL), from the city of Isin in southern Mesopotamia. It is also in Sumerian and dates from ca. 1930 B.C.E.

3. Codex Eshnunna (CE), from the eponymous city in northern Babylonia. It is written in Akkadian and dates from ca. 1790 B.C.E.

4. Codex Hammurabi (CH) from Babylon, is written in Akkadian and dates from ca. 1750 B.C.E.

5. The Middle Assyrian Laws (MAL), from the time of Tiglath-Pileser I (end of the twelfth century B.C.E.). They are written in the Assyrian dialect of Akkadian.

6. The Hittite Laws (HL) are written in Hittite and date from between the sixteenth and twelfth centuries B.C.E.

7. The Neo-Babylonian Laws (NBL) date from the seventh century B.C.E. They consist of a small tablet apparently copied from a larger corpus.

The two biblical codes are:

8. The Covenant Code from the book of Exodus (Exod 21:1-22:16). It is impossible to date this code with any certainty, but

---

48 This and the following dates are very approximate. The law codes cannot be dated to a specific year, only to the reign of the king in whose name they were promulgated or by other external evidence. Furthermore, the chronology itself has not yet been settled. For convenience, we follow the chronological schema of the Cambridge Ancient History. For one view on whether Codex Ur-Namma should be attributed to his son, Shulgi, see Kramer 1983.

it may be one of the earliest strata of biblical literature, probably dating from the first third of the first millennium B.C.E.

9. The Deuteronomic Code from the book of Deuteronomy (Deut 21:10-25:16). This is generally dated to the 7th century B.C.E.

All these codes share certain characteristics which immediately mark them as belonging to a single literary genre:

1. Their content is a collection of legal rules dealing with everyday problems of non-sacral law, i.e., the settlement of legal disputes arising from delict, contract, and the like; the establishment of rights in respect of property, status, etc., procedural rules, or simply norms with a socially immanent sanction.[49]

2. The form is casuistic. The law is expressed as a series of individual cases, the circumstances of which are put into a hypothetical conditional sentence ("If a man does X, . . ."), followed by the appropriate legal response in the particular case (". . . his punishment shall be Y"). While there is some variation within the framework of this form, e.g., the protasis can begin "a man who . . .," or the whole rule can be cast as a direct order ("no credit shall be given to . . . a slave"), the approach is always the same.

As significant as their form is what is missing from all these codes. Two features of classical and modern law codes are notable for their absence: division into abstract legal categories and legal definitions.[50]

---

49 The biblical codes present a somewhat more complicated picture in that the original codes have been transplanted into another literary context and combined with material from sources of a different genre: thus they also contain moral exhortation, norms without sanctions, or with divine or sacral sanctions, and narrative. But this material is easily separated from the pure legal matter which formed the original code.

50 The Middle Assyrian Laws are a good illustration. They consist of a series of 14 tablets divided by subject matter, but the division is material, not legal. Tablet "A" (the only tablet fully preserved) is a collection of the most diverse laws, ranging from theft to witchcraft through marriage, inheritance, and murder, the only common denominator being that all relate in some way to women.

To understand the nature of these codes, we must review the research that has been conducted upon the most famous among their number, Codex Hammurabi. It has long been recognized that the term "code," applied to it in the *editio princeps*, is a misnomer. Large areas of the law are not touched upon, and even in those that are there is not the slightest pretension to completeness,[51]—a task which, given its casuistic form, would require an almost infinite number of paragraphs.

Could these individual paragraphs be understood each as a reform of some specific point of law? At one point Driver and Miles, in their commentary on CH, seem to take this view: "The laws must not be regarded as a code or digest, but as a series of amendments to the common law of Babylon . . . ."[52] This position, however, is too difficult to maintain. Too many of the rules already appear in earlier codes,[53] and too many of them deal with matters so central or banal that it is difficult to imagine that the law would have been otherwise previously. Accordingly, a few pages later, Driver and Miles expand their original statement to: "a series of amendments and restatements of parts of the law in force . . . ."[54] Nonetheless, there was no doubt in these learned authors' minds that they were dealing with a source of positive law, any more than there had been in the earlier commentaries of Müller or Koschaker.[55]

Doubts on the issue were first expressed by Landsberger, who pointed out that CH is never cited as authority in judgments (of which many contemporary examples have been preserved).[56] Landsberger's suspicions were finally confirmed in a seminal article by Kraus.[57] Kraus takes as his starting point Hammurabi's own statement in the epilogue to the code, where the foregoing paragraphs are described as the "just judgments (*dināt mīšarim*) that I made." The legal corpus is therefore *prima facie* a list of the king's decisions in his capacity as a judge.[58]

---

51 Thus the code discussed a false accusation of murder, but not murder itself.
52 Driver and Miles 1952: 41.
53 See below.
54 Driver and Miles 1952: 45.
55 See above, nn. 16 and 22.
56 Landsberger 1939: 219-34, esp. 227.
57 Kraus 1960.
58 Kraus 1960: 285. Kraus rendered *dināt mīšarim* "gerechte Richtersprüche." The word *dīnu* is a standard Akkadian term for the decision of a judge in a lawsuit.

The paragraphs are, it is true, not recognizable as judgments in their present form, having been denuded of the names of the parties and all other details that might connect them with an actual case, and having been put into the form of a hypothetical set of circumstances. On the other hand, this might be all the better for casting them in the role of precedents, since something akin to the *ratio decidendi* now stands stripped of irrelevant details and ready to be applied in analogous circumstances.

Closer examination, however, reveals that by no means all the "judgments" recorded in the code are actual decisions in real cases. They are organized in groups wherein a single case is expanded by logical extrapolation, i.e., various theoretical alternatives are considered and the appropriate solution given by *a priori* reasoning.[59] For example, paragraphs 229-231 read:

229 If a builder builds a house for a man and does not make his work strong and the house that he built collapses and kills the owner of the house, that builder shall be killed.

230 If it kills a child of the owner of the house, they shall kill a child of that builder.

231 If it kills a slave of the owner of the house, he shall give slave for slave to the owner of the house.

Similar gradation of penalties occurs elsewhere in CH, in paragraphs 209-211, for example. We are therefore in the presence of a type of academic method. Now, this same method is found in a seemingly unrelated group of texts—the omen collection. For example, in the omen series *šumma izbu* a typical sequence is:[60]

5 If a woman gives birth, and the right ear (of the child) is (abnormally) small, the house of the man will be scattered.

6 If a woman gives birth, and the left ear (of the child) is (abnormally) small, the house of the man will expand.

7 If a woman gives birth, and both ears (of the child) are (abnormally) small, the house of the man will become poor.

59 Kraus 1960: 289.
60 Leichty 1970: 5-7

The connection, according to Kraus, is that the law codes and omen collections are both representative of a particular genre of literature, *scientific treatises*.[61] Divination was regarded as a science by the Mesopotamians and the compiling of omens the equivalent of scientific research. By the same token, the casuistic style in which both texts are couched was the "scientific" style par excellence—transferring the concrete individual case to the sphere of the impersonal rule.[62] The implications of Kraus' insight into the intellectual context of CH are:

1. CH is not legislation as we understand it; it is not new law created by a process of theoretical reasoning that will apply prospectively to hypothetical situations conceived through that reasoning. The basis of CH is judge-made law: a series of retrospective decisions concerning existing situations which acquire a prospective character only through their eventual application as precedents.[63] The "scientific method" employed seeks to enhance their prospective character somewhat by adding theoretical variants to the existing decisions. But being only logical extrapolation, these variants do not create new law; they merely discover the law.

2. So far from being legislation, CH is not even prescriptive; it is descriptive. It is essentially a record of the common law, that is, the traditional corpus of unwritten law built up mostly through precedents, together with the occasional intervention of administrative measures.[64] The text of the code is not itself authoritative, since the legal rules that it describes are already so in their own right. The nearest modern analogy would be a legal textbook.[65]

---

61 Kraus 1960: 288-89.
62 The "scientific" nature of CH has been further elucidated by Bottéro, using the analogy of Mesopotamian medical treatises, which employ the same technique (1982: 425-35).
63 There are also administrative decisions, fixing the prices of commodities, services etc.
64 It should be noted that the description is not always neutral; it can be phrased so as to emphasize a particular point of view. See Westbrook 1988d: 76-77.
65 This does not mean that it was purely an academic exercise. Mesopotamian science was applied science. For the use of law codes by the royal courts, see Westbrook

CH, as we have seen, does not stand in isolation. It is only one (and not the earliest) in a series of documents found scattered throughout the ancient Near East that share the characteristics of a separate literary genre. Consequently, it may be postulated that the other "law codes," which all use the same casuistic approach, are likewise scientific treatises rather than prescriptive measures, and further that these codes are dependent upon a scientific tradition emanating from Mesopotamia.

This hypothesis is confirmed by two factors. The first is the general context of ancient Near Eastern civilization of which we have spoken. We mentioned the role of cuneiform script as a medium of transmission and the existence of scribal schools throughout the region. The transmission of Mesopotamian scientific traditions alongside literature and religion is comprehensible when it is realized that these schools taught not only the difficult art of writing cuneiform; they were the "universities" of the ancient Near East. On the one hand they were the bearers of Mesopotamian culture: literary monuments such as the Epic of Gilgamesh were part of the scribal curriculum, as was Codex Hammurabi.[66] It continued to be copied and re-copied in scribal schools both in Babylonia and elsewhere for more than a millennium after its original composition. On the other hand, the schools were centers of "scientific" research, where lists of omens, medical texts, etc., were compiled and refined. As a scientific subject, law would give rise to the same research and could expect to enjoy the same pattern of diffusion.[67]

The second factor is the content of the law-codes themselves. While each of the codes contains a fair proportion of original matter (at least in as far as no parallel has yet been discovered), certain material seems to recur again and again. This is discernible on three levels:

1985a: 247-64. For the close connection of the provisions of CH with the law in practice, see Petschow 1984: 181-212. CH was a secondary use of this scientific material for a work of royal propaganda. See Finkelstein 1961: 91-104.

66 CH continued to be copied and re-copied in scribal schools both in Babylonia and elsewhere for more than a millennium after its original composition, but as a literary text. See the references in Westbrook 1985a: 253 n. 31.

67 On the diffusion of the omen-lists, see the most illuminating discussion and chart by Leichty 1970: 20-21.

1. In a very few instances, there appear to be verbatim copies (or rather, translations) of paragraphs from one code to another. This is the case with CH 161 and CL 29[68] and with Exod 21:35 and CE 53.[69]
2. More frequently, the same rule is found in several codes, albeit expressed in a somewhat different manner.[70]
3. Most common are cases in which the same problem is found, either with a somewhat different solution or with attention paid to different aspects of the problem.[71]

It has been argued in the past with regard to specific parallels between the codes that these are mere coincidence or the inevitable response of different societies faced with similar problems. Given the cultural context that we have described, and within this context the sheer quantity of parallels, such a view is no longer tenable.[72] Where parallels occur in the different codes of the ancient Near East, the most reasonable explanation is

---

68 CL 29:
> If an inchoate son-in-law enters the house of his father-in-law and gives the marriage-gift, and later they make him leave and give his wife to his friend, they shall give him double the marriage-gift that he brought. His friend shall not marry his wife.

CH 161:
> If a man causes the *biblum*-gift to be brought to the house of his father-in-law, gives the bride-money, and his friend slanders him and then his father-in-law says to the fiancé "You shall not marry my daughter," he (the father-in-law) shall return double everything that he brought to him. His friend shall not marry his wife.

69 CE 53:
> If an ox gores an ox and causes its death, both ox owners shall divide the price of the live ox and the carcass of the dead ox.

Exod 21:35:
> If a man's ox gores his neighbor's ox and it dies, they shall sell the live ox and divide its price and also divide the dead ox.

70 See below.
71 See below.
72 For the earlier view see, e.g., David 1950: 149-78, and van Selms 1950: 321-327 (whose main argument was later shown to be based on an incorrect reading of the cuneiform text). For the current view, see Yaron 1966: 396-406, and especially Paul 1970: 102-105, where some of the traditions are collected, illustrating what the author calls "a vast juridical canvas which extended throughout the ancient Near East."

that there was some contact between them. But what form of contact? The answer is much more complex than Müller's assumption of an "Urgesetz" and constitutes a central plank of our wider thesis. Let us reconsider for a moment the nature of Mesopotamian science.

Modern scientific method, derived from Greek philosophy, is a vertical system. The material is first organized into general abstract categories, the terminology of these categories defined so that it can at once be seen what material is included and what excluded, then the general categories broken down into successively smaller categories, with appropriate definition of the terminology, until the individual case is reached.

All this was beyond the reach of Mesopotamian science. It was incapable of creating abstract categories or of defining terms. Consequently it was forced to proceed horizontally, to present concrete examples of the topic under discussion, and to exhaust that topic by the accumulation of ever more examples pertaining to different facets thereof. The result is an extremely fragmentary picture, since an infinite number of examples would be necessary to cover the whole of any given topic. In an attempt to overcome this limitation, the science developed certain techniques.[73] These can be illustrated by the method whereby the law codes were constructed.

The starting point was a judgment in an individual case. Preferably a borderline case was taken, since the law in the ordinary case could also be derived from it by implication. For example, in a discussion of rape, a case involving a girl who was betrothed but not married would theoretically inform one also of the position of a fully married woman. The facts and the judgment were then re-cast in the anonymous, objective form of the casuistic sentence that, as we have seen, is the hallmark of the Mesopotamian scientific style: "If a man rapes a betrothed woman, his punishment is Y."[74]

This hypothetical case can then be examined more deeply by the technique of variation. Firstly, the circumstances can be changed in some details: if the girl were willing, if she were unwilling but unable to call for help, etc.; or a vital circumstance can be changed that reverses the judgment from liability to non-liability, or vice versa. Secondly, a further set of

---

73 For a somewhat different, but excellent, exposition of this point, see Bottéro 1982: 431-32.

74 For the detailed steps in this process, see Westbrook 1985a: 258-64.

variations that follow a fixed pattern may be imposed, such as attributing different grades of status to the parties.

The examples that constitute the law codes were not, therefore, cumulated at random, but result from the application of a scientific method. They have not been taken directly from original legal sources but have passed through a stage of processing in an academic school where the traditions of Mesopotamian science were taught.

The basic building blocks for the codes were thus "scholarly problems"—cases that may have begun life as a "cause célèbre" but then became the object of a theoretical discussion in the scribal schools, where all manner of hypothetical variations to the actual circumstances were considered so as to build up a series of precedents grouped around a single theme. A proportion of these problems will have been derived from local judgments and decisions. But where the same problems recur from code to code, it is not because they were re-discovered by each legal system. They formed a canon that was received by each school as part of the scientific tradition.[75]

The existence of a canon of scholarly problems helps to resolve certain anomalies in the parallels between codes that could not be satisfactorily explained by the idea of simple copying from one text to another or of an "Urgesetz." Thus the parallels do not appear in the same order in the different codes, as one might have expected: the same rules may be expressed in very different ways, and the same problems may result in different solutions or may contain aspects which appear in one code and are omitted in another. Nor does the flow of parallels between codes follow any consistent pattern; it certainly does not all pass through CH.[76]

No single code manages to cover every aspect of the traditional problem; instead each selects such facets as it deems germane to its own

---

75 The tradition was probably oral: there is evidence that scholars traveled, but none that cuneiform texts (apart from letters) did. Texts found in provincial locations are invariably written in the local epigraphy. Our account is probably also something of a simplification. There may well have been more than one canon and the canon or canons would have been organic entities subject to change and growth over the centuries, although it should be emphasized that the traditions, where they recur, reveal a remarkable conservatism.

76 While CH was copied outside of Babylonia as a scribal exercise, none of its provisions are reproduced literally in the other extant law codes.

discussion. The rest are not consigned to oblivion; they are part of the common law and their existence is assumed. Moreover, the discussion is a creative process: one code may choose to propose a different solution (although, it must be emphasized, this will not be radically different but within the terms of reference of the received discussion), or to develop the discussion by considering new aspects, using the same method of variation and logical extrapolation.[77] It is in fact by assembling the parallel and not-quite-parallel provisions of the different codes that we are able to reconstruct the full problem and to identify differences in approach between the codes, if any.

To illustrate the above process, we have selected two fairly simple examples. The first is the case of the rape of a betrothed maiden, which is dealt with by four codes.

CU 6
> If a person proceeds with force and deflowers a young man's wife who has not yet been deflowered, he shall kill that man.

CE 26
> If a man brings the bride-price for the daughter of a man, but another, without asking her father and mother, abducts her and deflowers her, it is indeed a capital case; he shall die.

CH 130
> If a man binds a man's wife, who has not known a male and is living in her father's house, and is caught lying in her lap, that man shall be killed; that woman shall be let free.

Deut 22:23-26
> If there is a nubile girl[78] betrothed to a man and a man finds her in the city and lies with her, you (pl.) shall bring them both out to the city gate and stone them to death: the girl because she did not cry out in the city and the man because he took advantage of his neighbor's wife; you (s.) shall remove the evil from your midst. But if the man found the betrothed girl in the

---

77 As Bottéro elegantly expresses it, ". . . comme l'on fait tourner entre ses doigts une babiole qu'on veut examiner sous tous ses angles" (1982: 431).

78 The Hebrew term (*bĕtûlâ*) might mean "virgin." This is an age-old crux. For a detailed discussion, see Locher 1986: 117-238.

country and seized her and lay with her, the man who lay with her shall die alone; you (s.) shall do nothing to the girl.

The act is described in roughly the same terms in all four cases, but the status of the girl is not. The connection becomes clear, however, from the substantive law of betrothal in the ancient Near East. Betrothal was in two stages: the first, a simple contract between the groom (or his parents) and the parents of the bride. The second stage was begun by payment of the agreed bride-price, which made the bride a wife vis-à-vis third parties, even though the relationship between the parties remained contractual and could be terminated without the need for divorce.[79] Both Sumerian and Akkadian lack a technical term for this stage and therefore use various circumlocutions. The terse Sumerian law emphasizes the woman's virginity and the fact that she is the wife of a guruš, a technical term rather inadequately translated "young man" here, but which probably refers to the fact that the man is not yet a father.[80] Akkadian lacks even this term, so CH focuses on the fact that the wife has also not yet left her father's house, as a bride would do on completion of the marriage. Hebrew, on the other hand, does have a technical term for this stage of betrothal and can therefore dispense with circumlocution.

Note that only two codes give any hint as to the identity of the executioner: CU's formulation probably refers to the wronged fiancé (although it could be the father), while Deuteronomy seems to indicate a public body. Here, then, may be a difference between the two systems.

Deuteronomy differs from the other codes in the range of its discussion. It includes the possibility that the girl was willing, in which case she also is punished. This, however, is hinted at in the final provision of CH that the girl is to go free—suggesting that in other circumstances she would not. There is therefore an inference here of a wider oral discussion that did not find its way into the final text.

Furthermore, Deuteronomy applies an evidentiary test in deciding whether the case was rape or seduction. This same test occurs in HL 197:

79 See Westbrook 1988b: chap. 2.
80 See Westbrook 1984: 753-54.

If a man seizes a wife in the mountains, it is the man's crime; he shall die. If he seizes her in the house, it is the wife's crime; she shall die. (If the husband finds them and kills them, it is not an offense.)

In other words, Deuteronomy has broadened the discussion without changing its terms of reference by applying an evidentiary test from another context, that of the rape or adultery of a married woman, which logic would have admitted as appropriate anyway.

Finally, it is important to note how the same legal distinction (betrothed, as opposed to single or married) has been transmitted from code to code in a context where it is not absolutely necessary (rape), despite differences in language and culture, not to mention distances of time and space.

The second example is a case of non-permanent injury which is dealt with in three of the law codes.

CH 206-208

If a man (*awīlum*)[81] strikes a man (*awīlum*) in an affray and inflicts a wound on him, that man shall swear "I did not strike knowingly" (i.e., with malice aforethought) and shall pay the doctor. If he dies of his blow, he shall swear, and if he (the victim) is the son of an *awīlum* he shall pay 1/2 mina of silver; if he is the son of a commoner (*muškēnum*) he shall pay 1/3 mina of silver.

HL 10

If someone wounds a man and makes him ill, he shall nurse him. He shall give a man in his place, and he (the latter) shall work in his house until he is well. When he is well, he shall give him 6 shekels[82] of silver and pay the doctor's fee. (A later

---

81 The terms *awīlum* and *muškēnum* are still the subject of dispute. Not least of the difficulties is that they are used relatively. The term *awīlum* can therefore mean a man (i.e., anybody), a head of household, or a "gentleman" (whether by wealth or social status is not clear). The term *muškēnum* can mean an ordinary citizen (as opposed to the king) or a "commoner" (as opposed to an *awīlum*), or simply a poor man. See Kraus 1973: 95-125.

82 A mina was worth 60 shekels.

> version adds: . . . When he is well, he shall give him 10 shekels of silver and pay the doctor's fee. If it is a slave, he shall pay 2 shekels of silver.)

Exod 21:18-19

> If men fight and a man strikes his neighbor with a stone or a fist and he does not die, but falls to his bed: if he rises and walks abroad on his stick, the striker is clear; he shall pay only his idleness and his (medical) treatment.

Let us begin by noting what the three texts have in common. Firstly, they all concern injury which is non-permanent but results in a period of incapacitation. Secondly, they all mention a doctor's fee. This is quite an unusual feature: nowhere else in the discussion of personal injury is such an expense mentioned, nor for that matter is there any such correlation between the penalty and the expenses suffered by the victim.

Thus we have a traditional scholarly problem with its traditional solution adopted by three different systems. But from this point onwards variations begin to appear on the basic theme. We may list them as follows, using CH as our point of departure.

a) CH expressly deals with the question of intention, stressing the absence of malice. The other two codes do not, but both HL and Exodus locate the injury in the context of a fight, thereby indicating that this is not a case of pre-meditated assault. Exodus adds the further detail of "a stone or a fist" (as opposed to a deadly weapon), suggesting a spontaneous reaction. The latter two codes may therefore be applying the same test as CH, but arrived at by a different path.

b) The total payments vary between all three, CH mentioning only the basic doctor's fee, Exodus a doctor's fee and compensation for loss of work, while HL's approach is yet more generous: doctor's fee plus a substitute for his work plus a lump sum payment. Note that the later version of HL even increases the latter payment.

c) CH expands the discussion to cover the case where the blow results in death. The other two codes do not do so in this context.

d) CH, in discussing death, adds the further dimension of the victim's status. The first sequence is: man wounded, son killed.[83] The intermediate cases of son wounded and man killed are omitted; we are expected to be able to deduce them from the examples given (although in practice it assumes knowledge of the common law). This is a common device in the codes for economizing on variations. It would normally go on to the third member of the sequence, the slave. This happens in the later version of HL, which adds the slave to the discussion of injury.

e) CH discusses a distinction not found in other codes, between *awīlum* and *muškēnum*, the latter apparently being a member of the poorer classes.[84] This does not point to a fundamental difference between the law of CH and the other two codes or to any reforming zeal in the latter omitting the distinction. It is rather a special concern of CH which it introduces into cases in many different areas of law.

Thus on the premise of a scholarly problem, we are able to follow the same tradition from one system to another. The principle remains the same throughout; only on the secondary question of the level of compensation do they differ.[85]

The Ancient Near East and the Twelve Tables

The Framework

From the Persian Gulf to the shores of the Mediterranean, we have outlined the influence of Mesopotamian civilization, and within that

---

83 The distinction in status is significant because of the practice of vicarious punishment. See Westbrook 1988d: 55–64.

84 See n. 81 above.

85 It must be stressed that the two examples presented here were chosen *inter alia*, for their relative simplicity; they do not require a detailed exposition of intricate substantive law or of textual or philological problems. For more complex problems, such as the goring ox or the death of a distrainee, see Westbrook 1988d: chap. 2. The examples used here are themselves, one should note, only part of wider scholarly problems.

civilization the influence of its scientific tradition, and within that scientific tradition again the influence of its legal science. Can that influence be shown to have spread even further, across the Mediterranean basin to Rome itself?

Three intermediaries immediately present themselves. The Etruscans have been assigned an oriental origin by one school of thought,[86] but the matter remains so obscure and controversial that no reliance can be placed upon this possibility for the purposes of our discussion.

The Greeks certainly had contacts with both worlds, but the oriental influence on their early culture is a problem in itself which cannot be pursued here, let alone the question of its further transmission.[87]

The Phoenicians present a far more promising intermediary, being direct bearers of ancient Near Eastern culture. There is ample evidence of their contact with early Rome, and it is on this evidence that we shall concentrate.

Of the three channels for the passage of ideas that we noted in the ancient Near East—trade, diplomacy, and conquest—only the first two could apply to connections with early Rome. The existence of Phoenician trade in central Italy has been well attested from at least the 8th century, with the orientalizing period from about 700 B.C.E., bringing in works of art from as far away as Syria and Mesopotamia, together with a corresponding influence on the local material culture.[88] The Phoenicians set up trading colonies in Etruria and possibly even on the site of Rome itself.[89]

On the diplomatic front, Polybius records the terms of a treaty with Carthage as the first of such acts by the new Republic (3.22.4-13). Without entering into the question of the accuracy of its details or the precise date,

---

86 For a general discussion of the problem of Etruscan origins, see Scullard 1967: 34-57.

87 Note, however, the point made by Ducos (1978: 60-61) that all concrete cases of Greek influence on the Twelve Tables are also found in the ancient Near Eastern codes. Ferenczy's thesis (1984: 2001-2012, esp. 2009) that the Twelve Tables were modeled on the code of Zaleucus of Locri is based on the merest generalities: (1) the tradition that the latter had been adopted by other cities in Magna Graecia; (2) both codes are concerned mostly with private and criminal law; (3) procedural law plays a large role in both; (4) the use of *talio*; and (5) both were concerned to uphold decent behavior (e.g., prohibition on luxury).

88 See, e.g., Ferron 1972: 189-91 and the literature cited therein.

89 Van Berchem 1967: 326-30; and Rebuffat 1966: 7-15.

the feasibility of such diplomatic contacts at that period has been demonstrated by the Pyrgi inscription, which we shall discuss below. Diplomatic contacts between Etruria and Carthage, it should be noted in passing, are mentioned by Aristotle (*Politica* 1280a) as if common knowledge.

Evidence that these contacts functioned as the channels for significant Phoenician influence on Roman thought is provided firstly by the sphere of religion. Van Berchem has argued that the Ara Maxima at Rome, the site of temples and an altar to Hercules, was originally a Phoenician temple to Melqart, the God of Tyre.[90] According to the same author, it was the oldest cult in Rome, practiced before the foundation of the city itself.[91] The significance of Van Berchem's theory lies not only in the existence of such a temple but in the fact that much of the evidence adduced by him comes from peculiar features of the later Hercules cult which are survivals from its oriental origins.[92] The temple was not therefore a closed facility for foreign merchants alone; it entered the religious life of the host nation and its influence remained long after their departure.

In 1964, excavations of a temple at Pyrgi revealed three metal plates with inscriptions in Phoenician and Etruscan.[93] Pyrgi was one of the seaports of Caere, an Etruscan city known to have had an alliance with the Phoenicians,[94] but also enjoying close connections with Rome.[95] The first plate of gold contains an inscription in Phoenician wherein the Etruscan ruler dedicates a temple[96] to Astarte. The second, also of gold, appears to be a translation or equivalent dedication in Etruscan, and the third plate, of

90 Van Berchem 1967: 307-38.
91 Van Berchem 1967: 308.
92 Van Berchem 1967: 317-26. Hercules was represented dressed in the garments of an oriental priest; women were excluded from the cult; only bulls and heifers were sacrificed; it was forbidden to associate other gods with the sacrifice, contrary to the normal Roman practice of *generalis invocatio*; there was a holocaust sacrifice; neither dogs nor flies dared enter the sacred precincts, only priests; the god received a tithe as patron of trade (*pars Herculanea*).
93 For an edition of the Phoenician inscription, see Donner and Röllig 1973: 330-32 (Supplement). For an edition of the Etruscan inscriptions, see Heurgon 1966: 1-15. But see further Ferron 1972: 201-207.
94 They were allies in the battle of Alalia in 535 B.C.E. (Herodotus 1,1966).
95 Rebuffat 1966: 18-19.
96 Or *cella*, according to Ferron (1972: 201).

bronze, also in Etruscan, seems to refer to a later commemoration of the dedication.

The Pyrgi inscription gives to a foreign cult an even stronger role than that which we postulated for the temple of Melqart at Rome. It reveals more than "direct, immediate contacts with the Semitic world";[97] it demonstrates penetration of the local culture by the latter civilization. As Heurgon points out, in these parallel inscriptions it is the Phoenician text which dictates all the minutest details of the ceremony, while the Etruscans have only to translate them as best they can and follow their precepts.[98]

The second sphere for which we have evidence of influence is that of law itself, thanks to a series of researches by Yaron. The first of these that we wish to consider derives from international diplomacy: in a treaty between Rome and the Latins, the Foedus Cassianum of 493 B.C.E., the text of which is given in Greek translation by Dionysius of Halicarnassus,[99] the phrase occurs "And let it not be permitted to add anything to, or take anything away from these agreements . . . ." Yaron points out that this phrase reflects a practice of ancient Near Eastern treaties and suggests that the Romans may have adopted it from the Carthaginians, with whom they and the Etruscans had already made treaties at an earlier date.[100]

The next shows international relations affecting internal constitutional law. According to Yaron the early use of the term *iudex* (judge) as title of the Chief Magistrate at Rome and the curious feature of there being two concurrent holders for a one-year tenure is a copy of the Carthaginian practice with their Chief Magistrate, also called "judge" (*sufes*).[101]

But Yaron's researches lead us even further into the realms of internal law and beyond the point where any specific connection can be shown. Yaron demonstrates that the phrase *vitae necisque potestas* has parallels in equivalent terminology throughout the ancient Near East, referring to a king's power of pardon: "power to put to death —power to keep alive." He concludes that the Latin phrase must originally have referred to a father's

---

97 Yaron 1974: 347-38.

98 Heurgon 1966: 15.

99 6.95.2. Mentioned also in Cicero *pro Balbo* 53 and Livy 2.33.9.

100 Yaron 1974: 348-51. We might add that a further phrase in the *foedus Cassianum*— "so long as heaven and earth have the same place"—is reminiscent of the phrase in the Pyrgi inscription that the statue should stand "as long as these stars."

101 Yaron 1974: 351-54.

power of pardon when his son was guilty of some capital offense, and not to an arbitrary right to kill as later authors assumed.[102]

It is true that Yaron is careful to disclaim a connection between the Eastern concept and the Roman phrase: ". . . not because it is in itself impossible or unlikely, but rather because there is no evidence available to establish it."[103] Such scholarly caution is certainly called for in an isolated case,[104] but if the parallel in question can be seen to be part of a wider pattern,[105] and if a context exists in which the transmission of legal ideas is known to take place, then it is no longer necessary nor is it satisfactory to ascribe the phenomenon to mere coincidence or some presumed deterministic development.[106]

Form

Were one unaware of their provenance, then one would have no hesitation in assigning the Twelve Tables, with their casuistic style and their lack of any abstract categories or definitions, to the same literary genre as the ancient Near Eastern law codes. At most, it might be argued that with their somewhat mixed style, they are more akin to the provincial codes such as the Covenant Code and Codex Eshnunna than to the classical works of the Mesopotamian heartland such as Codex Hammurabi.

We have seen that the factor connecting the ancient Near Eastern codes is a common scientific tradition, which is ascertainable from internal evidence when the evidence is set in the context of the diffusion of Mesopotamian civilization.

102 Yaron 1962b: 243-51.
103 Yaron 1962b: 248.
104 The Chinese T'ang Code (10th century A.D.) contains provisions for the control of goring oxen and vicious dogs which are very similar to those of certain ancient Near Eastern Codes. In such an isolated case, the explanation of two systems independently reaching the same solution to a common problem is obviously preferable to a search for possible connections. See MacCormack 1983: 132-150, esp. 147.
105 Yaron elsewhere provides two more examples, from the Twelve Tables themselves. See below.
106 As Watson puts it (1975b: 17): "It has never been shown that early law everywhere develops in the same way."

Early Rome lay on the periphery of this civilization, was in contact with it, and was subject to its intellectual influence in such spheres as religion and law. Given this context, we submit that the Twelve Tables were a product of that same Mesopotamian scientific tradition.[107] In consequence:

a) Like the other codes, the Twelve Tables were initially a scientific treatise on law; that is to say, it was descriptive, not prescriptive. It was not legislation in the classical sense and certainly not a reform measure called into being by particular historical events.[108]

b) The method of logic employed will have been the same as in the other codes. The individual provisions should be interpreted in this light, i.e., as aspects of scholarly problems, and not as general principles or as the response to putative evils in a previous system.

c) It is doubtful whether a specific date can be assigned to their composition. The Mesopotamian tradition was in essence an oral one transmitted through discussion and learning in schools,[109] and the oriental influence on Rome, whether via

---

107 It is interesting to note at this point Leichty's remarks (1970: 14): "The closest parallels to Mesopotamian birth divination are to be found in the Hittite, Etruscan, and Roman civilizations. The Hittites borrowed their divination techniques directly from the Babylonians and many texts are simply copies or translations of the Babylonian originals." He continues (1970: 16): "There appears to be a strong cultural continuity from Mesopotamia to Rome via the Etruscans in the matter of birth divination. This same continuity is evident in extispicy and could be investigated with regard to other forms of literature with great rewards."

108 Our conclusion, albeit arrived at by a different route, is therefore similar to that of Stein (1966: 9-25), who considers the Twelve Tables to have been declaratory of *ius*. Nonetheless, there is still a difference between descriptive and declaratory. According to Stein (1966: 19), "Once a lex has been enacted, it recorded the law authoritatively and was intended to be as permanent as the ius which it stated." In our view, terms such as "enactment" and "authoritative" suggest a replacement of the common law rather than a guide to it and therefore seem to us less appropriate to the original nature of the Twelve Tables, although they undoubtedly came to assume this character later.

109 A faint echo of this tradition may be contained in Cicero's remark that the Twelve Tables had been part of the school curriculum (*de leg.* 2.4.9 and 2.23.59).

Etruria, Greece, or Carthage, had existed since before the Republic. The idea of a specific mission or teacher seems to us more akin to the spirit of later times. It is possible that the actual writing down of the code in its final version was a datable event, as in the case of Codex Hammurabi.[110]

d) It is most unlikely that Mesopotamian science would have determined the form of the code alone, without influencing its content. While some of the content will have been the product of local intellectual activity and based upon local legal traditions, some will have been taken from the canon of scholarly problems. If such cases can be identified in the Twelve Tables, it would serve to confirm our thesis. It is to this aspect, therefore, that we now turn.

Content

Yaron has already pointed to two cases where reference to ancient Near Eastern sources elucidates an obscure phrase in the Twelve Tables. Thus the phrase *res suas sibi habeto* in IV 3 does not regulate the formalities of divorce but, on the basis of parallel provisions in divorce settlements from widely scattered *loci* in the ancient Near East, the property rights of the wife ancillary to divorce.[111] And the phrase *si adorat furto* in VIII 1 refers

---

110 Not too much store should be set by the tradition of the Twelve Tables being drafted in response to popular pressure for publication of the law; it may reflect a literary topos rather than an historical event. Hammurabi in the epilogue to his code boasts of the salutary effect of its publication (Col. XLVIII 8-19): "Let the oppressed man who has a case come before my statue, 'the king of justice,' let him have read to him my inscribed stela, let him note my precious words, and may my stela make the matter clear to him; may he recognize his case and set his mind at ease!" Likewise in the books of Exodus and Deuteronomy banal legal statements such as the prohibition of theft and murder are given special authority by their being written down on stone tablets in dramatic circumstances which purport to signify their origin as positive law (i.e., the Ten Commandments).

111 Yaron 1960: 1-12.

not to the theft itself but to a false accusation of theft, a legal problem which is found in CH 1-4 and Deut 19:16-21.[112]

We wish to consider two further cases, where a tradition can be traced through several ancient Near Eastern codes and can elucidate the Roman law on the assumption of its continuation into the text of the Twelve Tables. They are, it must be emphasized, both fragments of larger problems which could equally be used for this purpose but whose size and complexity would require a separate study.

T. VIII 4 reads: *Si iniuriam faxsit, viginti quinque poenae sunto*—"If he does *iniuria*, the penalty is 25 (*asses*)." The term *iniuria* causes considerable difficulty. In the classical law it refers to the delict of outrage—an insulting attack on a person's honor whether physically or by some other means. In the original text of the Twelve Tables, it was but the third of a triplet of delicts, the first two involving serious physical injury (*membrum rup[s]it* and *os fregit*) and carrying the considerably heavier penalties of *talio* and 300 *asses* (150 for a slave) respectively. Gaius (*Inst.* III 223) interprets *iniuria* to include these two, explaining that the penalty of 25 applies to "other outrages" (*ceteras . . . iniurias*), but this is clearly a re-interpretation, not least because it involves re-phrasing the text.

What, then, was the original delict? Like most provisions of the Twelve Tables, this problem has attracted a large body of scholarly literature. The dominant view seems to be that *iniuria* referred to minor physical assaults, if only to make the triplet of delicts cover the whole field of physical injury.[113]

This interpretation causes two problems vis-à-vis the classical meaning of *iniuria*. Firstly, the developed delict was understood as outrageous insult, an attack on a person's character or feelings, whether by physical assault or some other means. Secondly, *iniuria* in adverbial use already in the Lex Aquilia had the much wider meaning of any unlawful or wrongful act.

Attempts have been made to resolve the second problem by attributing the wider meaning to the provision in T. VIII 4. Thus Simon argues that

---

112 Yaron 1967: 510-24. For a different reconstruction, see Watson 1975c: 193-96. Without entering into the merits of the case, we would suggest that Watson's reconstruction imposes on the Twelve Tables reasoning more suitable to the time of Gaius.

113 E.g., Simon 1965: 163; Watson 1975a: 216.

the early legal system knew only acts of violence, self-help, which were qualified either as justified (*ius*) or unjustified (*iniuria*).[114] By the time of the Twelve Tables *iniuria* is the residue of violent acts which has not received a more specific designation (i.e., *membrum ruptum, os fractum*) and thus by a process of elimination minor acts of physical violence.[115] Halpin[116] suggests similarly that the phrase *iniuria alteri facere* meant "to do wrong to another," but that in the unsophisticated conceptions of that early period wrong was understood only as a direct physical assault.[117] Birks,[118] relying on the wider meaning of *iniuria*, goes so far as to deny the general consensus as to physical assault. The provision rather refers back to the two previous delicts and imposes the light penalty of 25 *asses* on a victim of one of those delicts who retaliates "*unlawfully*" (*iniuria*), i.e., not within the bounds of revenge or ransom[119] laid down by the statute.[120] Little attention, by contrast, is given to the discrepancy between the delict's early meaning of injury and later one of insult. This is presumed to be a natural development in the law from a primitive to a more sophisticated stage. Only Simon reflects that an unjustified act of violence contained an element of *hubris* which might be of more significance than the injury done.[121]

We shall not enter into a detailed discussion of the various theories, since it is their approach with which we would take issue. The method that they share can be described as follows: having gleaned a particular interpretation of the early rule from hints and allusions in the classical sources, conjectures are made as to the character of "primitive" law. It is then shown how the particular interpretation advocated would fit a system of that character. The difficulty with this method is that it lacks any empirical basis. The primitive systems described are hypothetical constructions with no demonstrable basis in reality. Thus Simon postulates a system concerned solely with classifying acts of violence as offenses or

---

114 Simon 1965: 145-47, 160-62.
115 Simon 1965: 169-75.
116 Halpin 1976: 344-54.
117 Halpin 1976: 351-53
118 Birks 1969: 163-208.
119 On understanding the penalties of 300 and 150 *asses* as such, see Birks 1969: 187-88.
120 Birks 1969: 188-90.
121 Simon 1965: 174-75.

remedies,[122] Birks a system of retaliation and counter-retaliation with appropriate sums by way of ransom for the two stages,[123] while Halpin assumes that indirect harm "would have been alien to the primitive jurisprudence of that time."[124]

The systems thus created are usually internally consistent and reasonable[125] and may in some details have reflected primitive reality, but it is impossible ever to know for certain since they contain no shred of evidence from that reality. Consequently, one theory can follow another, each re-arranging the "classical" evidence[126] according to a new model of primitive law, without ever breaking out of the circle of unsubstantiated hypothesis.

The evidence for the ancient Near Eastern legal systems comes for the most part from sources that are both primary and contemporary with the law that they describe.[127] They provide us from the outset with working models of "primitive" law from which we can draw empirical evidence and thus reduce the scope of hypothetical models. But they do more than this. For the theory that we have proposed is not one of comparative law but of an actual connection between the ancient Near Eastern codes and the Twelve Tables. Where a tradition can be traced through the former into the latter, it will also provide an objective criterion for determining which elements in the later sources, if any, reflect the early law. It enables us in short to follow a chronological method, rather than the practice of the authors discussed above, which is the opposite.

In the case of *iniuria*, at least, the ancient Near Eastern sources enable us to confirm a later tradition. We have noted that the classical law associ-

---

122 Simon 1965: 160-62.

123 Birks 1969: 187-89.

124 Halpin 1976: 351.

125 Although as Birks points out (1969: 167-70), Simon's reconstruction does not work even within its own terms of reference.

126 Where the classical evidence is inconsistent, this often involves value judgments. Thus Simon dismisses the evidence of Gellius in one instance (1965: 156-57), while praising his accuracy in another (1965: 132-133). Birks is forced to question Labeo's reliability on the story of L. Veratius (1969: 174-78), although he appears subsequently to have modified that position (1974).

127 The exception is the Bible, but even there the received text shows all the signs of faithful transmission.

ated *iniuria* with the idea of insult. This notion has been rejected for the early law, both because early Romans were supposedly impervious to insult[128] and on the more weighty grounds that the context is one of physical assault. But there is one case where physical assault results not in injury but only in insult: a slap in the face. And this is exactly the meaning given to the delict in the famous story of Lucius Veratius (as told by the jurist Labeo)[129] who went around slapping people's faces with the flat of his hand and promptly paying them the sum of 25 *asses* demanded by the Twelve Tables, relying on the effects of inflation which had made a mockery of the penalty. It is generally assumed by modern scholars that this story gives but one example of a minor assault, but this type of assault is special in that no injury results for which compensation should be paid, and we see no reason to extend the bounds of the delict beyond the bare facts of the story.

All the ancient Near Eastern codes that discuss physical injury at length do so in the form of lists of the more serious injuries classified either by the part of the body affected (ear, nose, bone, etc.) or by the type of injury inflicted (e.g., burning, cutting). To each injury is assigned the appropriate penalty, which is either talionic or a tariff of fixed payments.[130] Non-permanent injuries are treated differently, as we have seen, the main consideration being compensation for work lost and medical fees. Two codes, however, include with the list of permanent injuries a slap in the face. CH, after considering the gouging of an eye, the breaking of a bone, and the knocking out of a tooth, continues:

> 202 If an *awīlum* slaps the face[131] of an *awīlum* who is older than
> he, he shall be struck with 60 strokes of an ox-hide whip in
> the Assembly.

---

128 Jolowicz and Nicholas 1972: 171.

129 Gell. *NA* 20.1.13.

130 The difference between these two types of penalties is not as profound as it seems. See Westbrook 1988d: 45-47.

131 The Akkadian idiom is "strikes the cheek." Cf. the Latin formula of the *ao. iniuriarum* in the Edict: Quod Auli Agerii Pugno Mala Percussa Est, a formula which is already reflected in Plautus *Asin.* II, 2, 104: *pugno malam si tibi percussero.* See further Lenel 1901-03: 398.

203 If the son of an *awīlum* slaps the face of the son of an *awīlum* who is like him (in age), he shall pay 1 mina of silver.

204 If a *muškēnum* slaps the face of a *muškēnum*, he shall pay 10 shekels of silver.

205 If an *awīlum*'s slave slaps the face of the son of an *awīlum*, they shall cut off his ear.

Since this is an offense against honor, the relative social standing of the parties is a significant factor and allows CH to give free rein to its obsession with status, developing the discussion through ever more subtle gradations. (The basic distinction between *awīlum* "a gentleman" and *muškēnum* "a commoner" has been noted above, n. 81.) The general approach that emerges is that slapping the face of a superior is a serious matter; slapping an equal less so.

CE is less concerned with such distinctions and anchors the offense firmly in the context of permanent injuries:

42 If a man (*awīlum*) bites the nose of a man and severs it, he shall pay 1 mina of silver; an eye—1 mina; a tooth—1/2 mina; an ear—1/2 mina; a slap in the face—he shall pay 10 shekels of silver.[132]

43 If a man severs a man's finger, he shall pay 2/3 mina of silver.

44 If a man knocks a man down in a . . . and breaks his arm, he shall pay 1/2 mina of silver.

45 If he breaks his leg, he shall pay 1/2 mina of silver.

46 If a man strikes a man and breaks his collarbone, he shall pay 1/3 mina of silver.

It should be noted that although the offense does not occur in the biblical codes, it was probably also part of that scholarly tradition. The Mishnah, although a post-biblical source, preserves many oral traditions that failed to find written expression in the Bible.[133] In *Bava Qamma* 8.6, in the context of personal injury, it discusses the same question with a piquant variation: "If he slaps him (in the face), he pays him 200 *zuz*; with

132 1 mina = 60 shekels.
133 See n. 42 above.

the back of his hand—he pays him 400 *zuz*." Thus there existed in the ancient Near Eastern codes a tradition whereby a mere slap in the face was included in the list of injuries which made up the scholarly discussions of assault. The level of the penalty varied from code to code, but at least as between equals it was regarded as less serious than actual injury.

T. VIII 2-4, with its list of serious injuries plus *iniuria*, was a continuation of the same tradition. *Iniuria* already then meant insult, but insult in the physical form then recognized by law[134]—a slap in the face.[135] It was therefore a technical term, different in meaning and use from the adverbial form. If in the result T. VIII 2-4 does not cover the whole range of physical injury, then it is in perfect accord with the other codes.[136] One of the main points of our argument, it will be recalled, was that it is anachronistic to seek comprehensive statements of the law in the Twelve Tables.[137]

The second case that we wish to consider is that of *furtum conceptum*. The problem is well known: according to Gaius, the *actio furti concepti* lay against a person on whose premises stolen goods had been found after a search in the presence of witnesses, even if that person was not the thief (*Inst.* III 186).[138] The Twelve Tables provided a three-fold penalty under this action (*Inst.* III 191).[139] Equally according to the Twelve Tables, however, if stolen goods were found on a person's premises after a ceremonial

---

134 This has nothing to do with the primitive character or otherwise of the legal system: modern English law gives no remedy for verbal insult as such (as opposed to defamation).

135 The other two cases listed, *membrum ruptum* and *as fractum*, may also have constituted an affront to one's honor, but if so it was insult added to injury.

136 CH, for all its sophistication relative to the other law codes, has only eye, bone, and tooth.

137 Da Nobrega (1967: 250-270), who refers to a variety of comparative ancient systems, appears to recognize the specificity of the provisions in T. VIII 2-4 (1967: 268-269), but his conclusion that "iniuria était bien plus une offense morale que physique" (1967: 270) remains a trifle too unspecific. From the comparative material adduced (1967: 259-263), he appears to consider that any insult would be included. Watson (1975a: 216) notes that *iniuria* to a slave is not covered by Chapter III of the Lex Aquilia and must therefore have meant injuries so minor as not to affect his market value or even give rise to medical expenses. It may equally be pointed out that a slave has no honor to be damaged by a slap in the face.

138 But with the possibility of recovery from the person who passed it to him under the *ao. furti oblati*.

139 And the same under the *ao. furti oblati*.

search *lance et licio*, it was regarded as manifest theft, with the appropriate penalties for that offense (*Inst.* III 193-194). By Gaius' time only the *actio furti concepti* existed, but it cannot be concluded that this action was a subsequent replacement for the search *lance et licio*, in view of Gaius' express statement that the action was included in the Twelve Tables. Since he was familiar with the text of the Twelve Tables, Gaius could not have made such an obvious error.[140]

How then is the existence of two different searches in the Twelve Tables, with two different penalties, to be explained? There are three leading theories.

According to De Visscher,[141] there was only one search at the time of the Twelve Tables (*lance et licio*), but with two consequences, depending on whether the householder was the thief (*furtum manifestum*) or an innocent receiver (*conceptum*). This in turn depended on whether there had been an immediate hue and cry leading to the premises or some comparable indication of guilt.[142] When *lance et licio* was later abolished, the penalties of *furtum manifestum* disappeared with it.[143]

Daube, on the other hand, considers that there were two searches.[144] The first was informal and led to three-fold damages if stolen goods were found. If, however, the householder refused to allow a search, recourse was had to the more ceremonial form, *lance et licio*, with a corresponding escalation in the potential penalty.

Pugsley agrees that there were two searches but offers a different rationale.[145] *Furtum manifestum* originally depended not on the mode of theft but on its object, namely *res mancipi*. A search for *res mancipi* required a ceremonial form, *lance et licio*, in view of the seriousness of the consequences. The search for *res nec mancipi* need only be informal and the potential penalty was correspondingly lower.

Our remarks above as to method apply equally here. All three theories rely in varying degrees on the combining of allusions in the classical

---

140 De Zulueta 1946-53: 202. For the original meaning of *lanx et licium*, see Wolf 1970: 59-79.

141 De Visscher 1931: 217-253.

142 ". . . traces, délai, dissimulation . . ." (De Visscher 1931: 249).

143 De Visscher 1931: 223.

144 Daube 1947: 282-83.

145 Pugsley 1969a: 139-52.

sources with conjectures as to the "primitive" law. De Visscher, at least, does bring some comparative evidence for the primitive state of the law (from medieval statutes),[146] although none of his sources involving hot pursuit, etc., mention anything about ritual search. Nor does he explain why the dual penalty should not have survived the abolition of the search *lance et licio*, since under his system it was the hot pursuit and not the form of the search which was decisive as to the penalty. Daube assumes that in the primitive law the householder who had resisted an informal search would not have dared to resist the ceremonial one or if he did, that the state would at this point intervene.[147] But he offers no empirical evidence to support these conjectures. Pugsley's conjecture as to the primitive law may have some basis, since there is plenty of evidence from early systems (not only in the ancient Near East) that the penalty for theft could vary with the object stolen (although Pugsley himself does not refer to this evidence). But that is far from making the theft of *res mancipi* "a heinous offense," a proposition for which he offers no evidence.[148]

The ancient Near Eastern legal tradition contained a classic scholarly problem on theft. The solution differed from system to system, but the problem remained essentially the same. Let us begin with the exposition in CH 9-12:

> 9 If a man whose property is missing seizes his lost property in the hands of a man, (and) the man in whose hands the lost property is seized says: "A seller sold it to me (and) I bought it in front of witnesses," while the owner of the lost property says, "I shall bring witnesses who know my lost property"— then the buyer shall bring the seller who sold it to him and the witnesses in whose presence he bought it, while the seller shall bring the witnesses who know his lost property. The judges shall examine their case. The witnesses in whose presence the purchase was made and the witnesses who know the lost

---

146 De Visscher 1931: 232-42.
147 Daube 1947: 282-83.
148 Pugsley 1969a: 140. Acceptance of Pugsley's theory also requires us to dismiss all the classical sources as unreliable—which in itself is not impossible—but on the sole grounds that they do not comply with the theory.

property shall declare their knowledge before the god. The seller is a thief; he shall be put to death. The owner of the lost property shall take his lost property. The buyer shall take the money he paid from the estate of the seller.

10 If the buyer does not bring the seller who sold it to him and the witnesses in whose presence he bought it, while the owner of the lost property brings the witnesses who know his lost property, the buyer is a thief; he shall be put to death. The owner of the lost property shall take his lost property.

11 If the owner of the lost property does not bring witnesses who know his lost property, he is a liar; he has made a false accusation. He shall be put to death.

12 If the seller had died, the buyer may take five-fold the claim of that very case from the estate of the seller.

To begin with, it is necessary to explain an obvious contradiction within the text. According to paragraph 9, the innocent purchaser receives back only his purchase price from the seller/thief, whereas in paragraph 12, the apparently irrelevant circumstance of the seller/thief having died in the meantime results in his receiving five-fold damages.

This contradiction is compounded when we look at the other paragraphs on theft in CH. According to CH 8:

If a man steals an ox or a sheep or an ass or a pig or a boat, if it belongs to a god or to the palace he shall restore thirty-fold; if it belongs to a subject he shall restore ten-fold. If the thief has not the means to pay, he shall be put to death.

The penalty for theft is multiple damages instead of death, which applies only if the thief is unable to pay.[149] The resolution of these discrepancies lies in part in the substantive law of theft and in part in the techniques of Mesopotamian science.

---

149 Ten-fold damages is also the penalty in CH 265 for a dishonest shepherd who steals sheep by changing their brand and selling them.

Throughout the ancient Near East, theft (like other serious delicts) gave rise to a two-fold right for the victim.[150] In principle, he could take revenge on the thief by having him killed,[151] or, in the alternative, accept ransom for the thief's life. In practice, however, the courts had long since intervened to bar this type of revenge in all but a few aggravated cases such as kidnapping or armed robbery. Instead, they imposed a fixed ransom, usually a multiple of the stolen thing (according to the nature and circumstances of the theft), and only if the thief failed to pay the ransom did the residual right of revenge revive, as in CH 8.

CH 9-11 bears all the marks of a theoretical discussion. A triangular situation, between owner, purchaser, and thief/seller, is reduced to its simplest form, with three basic variations being dealt with in turn: if the seller/thief is guilty, if the purchaser is guilty, if the owner is guilty. The solution is neatly balanced and altogether too ideal, particularly in the first case. The two innocent parties are able to recoup their loss, the owner from the purchaser and the purchaser from the seller/thief. In practice of course, the situation is seldom so convenient: the thief will have disappeared or be insolvent, and one of the innocent parties will have to bear the loss.

The discussion is so theoretical because CH is trying to convey a point of principle, namely that where there are two innocent parties who stand to lose, the primary loss will fall on the purchaser. He is strictly liable to the owner for the consequences of the purchased goods being stolen and bears the risk of being unable to recoup his loss from the seller. Since it could not express this principle except by way of examples, CH tried at least to make the discussion as abstract as possible by removing all extraneous details. Thus the question is discussed in paragraphs 9-11 in terms of the theoretical law (death for the guilty party) and not the law in practice.

---

150 The following is a summary of the more detailed discussion to be found in Westbrook 1988d: chap. 4.

151 It cannot be sufficiently emphasized that this had nothing to do with self-help. In all serious delicts, the court, having heard the case and decided on guilt and the appropriate penalty (where not obvious), then handed the guilty party over to the plaintiff for that revenge alone. Self-help was only justifiable as an *ex-post-facto* defense in certain limited cases, such as flagrant murder, armed robbery, and night burglary. Self-help (and the concomitant unrestricted revenge) was regarded as the antithesis of legal order. See Westbrook 1988d: 45-46.

The moment the discussion moves away from the question of principle to its practical application, then the multiple penalties reappear. CH 12 reflects the combination of the principle of purchaser's strict liability vis-à-vis owner (tempered by his right to recover from the seller) with the rule of multiple damages. The innocent purchaser is being allowed to recoup the payment of multiple damages which he himself has had to make to the owner. "That very case" is the one in which the owner has succeeded in extracting from the purchaser not only restitution of the stolen goods but also multiple damages.

Thus the multiple damages system applied as much to the purchaser of stolen goods, albeit innocent, as to the actual thief. And the documents of practice provide us with evidence of this very system at work. According to MVN 3 219:[152]

> Bukanum the merchant bought from DINGER.E and Idi-ilum 3 sheep, their purchase price being 1½ shekels 15 grains of silver. Nahshubal was the guarantor. These sheep were "turned into" stolen sheep. Bukanum and Nahshubal were "turned into" thieves. Seven shekels of silver were paid for the crime committed regarding the sheep. 1½ shekels 15 grains of silver were paid as purchase price for the sheep. DINGER.E and Idi-ilum have been made obligated to Nahshubal to restore (the money paid). (To do so they have sworn by the life of the king.) (Witnesses, date.)

Bukanum, the merchant, is very clearly an innocent purchaser of sheep, which are later found to be stolen property. He has been found guilty of "theft" in this extenuated sense and has had to restore the sheep to their owner. Most probably he, or rather his guarantor, also had to pay the fine of seven shekels of silver. As the document is not at all interested in this stage of the case, it is simply summarized by the words "turned into a thief." The second stage is that the purchaser recoups from the guarantor the price he had paid and perhaps the seven shekels if the guarantor did not pay it directly. The machinery of payment is not described, since the document is only interested in the fact that the sums have been paid. The

---

152 Edition in Westbrook and Wilcke 1974-1977: 114-15.

third stage, that with which the document is actually concerned, is the obligation of the sellers to restore the money to the guarantor.

The innocent purchaser has had to pay multiple damages to the owner, albeit at a rate (5x) lower than that imposed on a thief (10x). He now seeks to recoup this sum from the seller, only to discover that the seller has died in the interim. He can nonetheless recover his payment from the seller's estate, a right which still leaves him with the risk of the latter's insolvency.

In summary, theft is presented in the above scholarly problem as a three-cornered affair, involving the owner, the thief who is also the seller, and the receiver of the stolen goods from him. The law applied is that the latter is strictly liable to the owner for multiple damages but may recover the same amount from the seller.[153]

The three-cornered presentation of theft is continued in the Middle Assyrian Laws, Tablet A, paragraphs 3-6. It is all the more noticeable, since these paragraphs are not concerned with theft in general but with the special position of a married woman.[154]

Paragraphs 3-4 concern the case of a woman who steals from her husband and passes the stolen goods to a receiver. The laws consider the liability of both wife and receiver;[155] indeed a certain linkage is established between their punishment. Paragraph 5 considers the case of a wife who

---

153 The distinction between innocent and fraudulent receiver lay not only in the amount payable but in the alternative to payment: for the innocent receiver a simple debt; for the fraudulent receiver revenge, as for a thief. Hence the innocent receiver would sometimes still try to establish the identity of the seller, not to avoid all liability, but to avoid the consequences of fraudulent possession. See the cases in Westbrook and Wilcke 1974-77: 116-118, as reinterpreted in Westbrook 1988d: 153 n. 60.

154 See n. 50 above.

155 §3: "If a man is sick or dead and his wife steals something from his house and gives it to a man or a woman or any third party, they shall put to death the wife and the receiver. If a married woman whose husband is well steals from her husband's house and gives it to a man or a woman or any third party, the man shall charge his wife and impose a punishment on her; the receiver who received the stolen property from the man's wife shall restore it, and they shall impose upon the receiver the same penalty as the husband imposed on his wife."

§4: "If a slave or slave woman receives anything from a married woman, they shall cut off the nose and ears of the slave or slave-woman, and they shall restore the stolen property in full. The husband shall cut off his wife's nose, but if he pardons his wife and does not cut off her nose, they shall not cut off those of the slave or slave-woman, nor shall they restore in full the stolen property."

steals from another man.[156] Here there is no mention of any passing of the goods, but the paragraph is nonetheless shown to be but one side of the coin by that following,[157] which considers the strict liability for theft of a mere depositee from the wife. Even when the theft is dealt with from this oblique angle, therefore, the three-cornered pattern is imposed upon it.

Although it plays a key role in the relevant provisions, the three-cornered pattern is less evident in the Hittite Laws. This is due to two factors. Firstly, these laws use a slightly different technique to CH: where CH attempted to compress the problem into the most theoretical examples, adding only a few practical examples at the end, HL expands the problem into the most detailed discussion, considering every variation both by type of goods stolen and the nature of the receiving. Secondly, HL shares a stylistic characteristic of the provincial codes (as opposed to the central Mesopotamian codes such as CH and CL), namely an extreme terseness in identifying the parties involved, often omitting to indicate change of subject from one clause to another.

HL 57-71 deal with theft of animals and related offenses and may be divided into several categories:

1. Ordinary theft. This is characterized by the phrase "if someone steals . . . ." There are three levels of penalty, depending purely on the type of animal stolen. The somewhat complex provisions as to type of animal may be schematized as follows. Paragraphs 57-59 deal with the most valuable animals, the examples given being a bull, a stallion, and a ram. The penalty is fifteen-fold restitution. Paragraphs 63-65 deal with less valuable animals, a plow-ox, a cart-horse, a goat, and certain species of sheep. The penalty here is ten-fold restitution. Para-

---

156 §5: "If a married woman has stolen something from another man's house exceeding 5 mina of lead in value, the owner of the stolen goods shall swear: 'I did not let her have possession of it' and 'there has been a theft from my house.' If her husband agrees, he shall restore the stolen goods and redeem her, and cut off her ears. If the husband does not agree to redeem her, the owner of the stolen goods shall take her and cut off her nose."

157 §6: "If a married woman makes an outside deposit, the receiver shall be liable for the stolen goods."

graphs 67-69 deal with a cow, a mare, and certain other species of sheep. The penalty is six-fold restitution.

2. The fraudulent finder. Here a different act is described: "If someone finds a . . . and 'cleans' it (i.e., removes the marks of ownership) and its owner identifies it . . . ." Paragraphs 60-62 mention a bull, a stallion, and a ram, i.e., animals in the first category of theft, and impose a penalty of seven-fold restitution, which is approximately half of that for stealing the same animals. Although the finder committed a fraudulent act designed permanently to deprive the owner of his property, he did not actively take away the property, and this is apparently regarded as a mitigating circumstance. Note that the owner here has succeeded in proving that the animal is his and that the ownership marks were removed by the present possessor.

3. The negligent finder. This category is represented by paragraph 71, which begins "If someone finds a horse, a donkey, an ass . . . ." His duty is to report it to the authorities, in which case "if its owner finds it he may rightfully (*sakuwassar*) take it, but he may not seize him as a thief." The owner's proprietary right is therefore established, but a right to multiple damages is denied. On the other hand, if the finder does not inform the authorities, the text declares him to be a thief.

The text does not say what the consequences are of being a thief in these circumstances, but this and other significant details are provided by a later version of the same paragraph. There the finder must have the find witnessed, or else he will be considered a thief if the owner finds it. His penalty in that case is three-fold restitution. This version adds to the list of lost property an ox, a sheep, and even utensils, which shows that the list is meant to indicate any lost property: the size of the penalty does not depend on the nature of the property as in ordinary theft or fraudulent finding.

4. Innocent possession. Paragraph 66 concerns various types of animals, large and small, which wander over to another herd. The owner of the herd is entirely innocent and accordingly, "if its owner finds it he may rightfully take it, but he may not seize him as a thief."

5. Paragraph 70 reads: "If someone steals an ox or a horse or a mule or an ass (and) its owner identifies (*kanes*) it, he may rightfully take it. In addition he shall pay two-fold."

In spite of appearances, the person paying the two-fold damages is not the thief. The penalty for theft is much higher: six-, ten-, or fifteen-fold. And the list of animals is the same as for the negligent finder, where we noted that the content of the list is of secondary importance.[158]

Closer analysis of paragraph 70 reveals that it has this special characteristic: it combines the phraseology of the theft paragraphs with that of the finder/possessor paragraphs. From the former it has "if someone steals" and the multiple restitution provision. On the other hand, "If its owner identifies it" comes from the realm of the fraudulent finder, not the thief, while the statement "he may rightfully take it" is altogether out of place in theft, where there could be no doubt as to the owner's right vis-à-vis the thief. The phrase is only found in cases of innocent possession, where the dispute is rather as to ownership between two innocent parties than as to culpability for theft or fraud.

The unidentified person who has to pay two-fold is therefore the innocent receiver of the stolen animals. The thief stole them, removed their identifying marks and sold them to an innocent purchaser. The owner nonetheless manages to identify them as his property and is therefore entitled to their return, even though their present possessor can equally prove innocent acquisition. And in addition, the latter must pay multiple damages.

The principle is therefore the same as in CH. The innocent purchaser is strictly liable to the owner for the penalty for theft, and must recoup his loss from the seller/thief as best he can. And as in CH, the multiple damages paid by the innocent purchaser are lower than those payable by the original thief—his innocence is admitted as a mitigating factor. The possibility of his recouping this payment from the seller/thief is not mentioned, but it is reasonable to assume that some similar rule to this effect existed.

Our final source for this problem is the Covenant Code, which shares the terse provincial style of the Hittite Laws but is drastically more sparing

---

158 A further difference is that all the paragraphs on ordinary theft record the fact that the penalty has been reduced (". . . formerly they gave 30 . . . now he shall give 15 . . .").

in detail. Exod 21:27 reads: "If a man steals an ox or a sheep and slaughters or sells it, he shall pay five oxen for the ox and four sheep for the sheep." Exod 22:3 continues:[159] "If the stolen item—from ox to ass to sheep—is found alive in his hand, he shall pay two-fold."

In Exod 21:27, where the thief has slaughtered or sold the animal, he faces multiple damages according to the type of animal, as in HL 57-59, 63-65, and 67-69. The point of the slaughter or sale is to show that the original thief is meant: the animal is no longer in his possession, and his crime has been proved by circumstantial evidence, such as the testimony of the buyer, as in CH 9.

In Exod 22:3 it is not the same original thief who is the subject but the innocent possessor. As in HL 70, he is not expressly named but may be identified from the pattern of the discussion. Note that Exod 22:3 shares two further features with HL 70: there is a longer list of animals than in the law on original theft, formulated in such a way as to indicate that the type of animal is unimportant since the penalty is uniform; and the penalty itself is a lower level of multiple damages than for original theft. As in HL, the possibility may well have existed of recouping the payment from the seller/thief, although omitted in the text.

We have thus managed to trace a scholarly problem through four law codes and to show that the same basic law underlay them all. That this would not at all be apparent from a superficial reading of the texts is due to the vagaries of Mesopotamian scientific technique and the local variations in its application.

This same problem, we submit, continues into the Twelve Tables, in the form of the *actio furti concepti* and *oblati*, and reflects the same law, namely the strict liability of the receiver of stolen goods, albeit innocent, to pay multiple damages to the owner, tempered only by his right to recover the same from the seller/thief, as in CH.

The element that is missing from all four examples from the ancient Near East is the search. It may have been a possibility, but all these laws are unconcerned with the question of how the owner found his stolen goods; it is the fact that he can identify them in the possession of the

---

159 We have omitted the intervening law on the thief caught breaking in. This was another classic scholarly problem that the Covenant Code combined with the present problem. For the logic of the Covenant Code's presentation see Westbrook 1988d: 154.

receiver which is important. The same, in our view, applies to the *actio furti concepti*. Contrary to the impression given by Gaius, there was only one search in the Twelve Tables, *lance et licio*, which was directed against the thief himself, probably after a hue and cry, as De Visscher surmised.[160] *Furtum conceptum* was a different problem, that of strict liability for receiving stolen goods, to which the search procedure was irrelevant.[161]

In this light, Gaius' description of the law is perfectly understandable. Gaius states (*Inst.* III 191) that a penalty of three-fold damages for a *furtum conceptum* is found in the Twelve Tables, as it undoubtedly was. Gaius' account can be accepted as accurate on this point, since he had access to the actual text. The same is not true, however, of Gaius' account of the legal practice forming the substance of *furtum conceptum*. A little earlier (*Inst.* III 186) he describes the content of that action "as it was in his day," i.e., including a search. It does not follow (and to his credit Gaius does not actually say so expressly) that the "content" was the same at the time of the Twelve Tables, when the search *lance et licio* existed. The obvious time for the change in content was when the search *lance et licio* went out of use. To fill the gap a more modern procedure, *quaestio* before witnesses, became attached to the *actio furti concepti*, which thus lost some of its original rationale.[162]

---

160 Note also that the two biblical parallels adduced by Daube (1947: 257-259), Laban's pursuit and search of Jacob's possessions and Joseph's of his brothers' (Gen 31:22-35; 44:3-13), involve a hue and cry, and the search is directed against the original thief.

161 Daube in fact showed some awareness of this point in his analysis of the terminology (1947: 267-269). He surmised that the *ao. furti concepti* originally meant "an action because of stolen goods received" as the logical parallel to the *ao. furto oblati* "an action because of stolen goods brought," i.e., that the essence of the offense was receiving the stolen goods. Daube ultimately rejected this interpretation, however, because of the weight of tradition (that of the classical Roman jurists) against it.

162 An interesting question, though not strictly relevant to our discussion, is why the innocent possessor should be punished more severely than a common thief. (It arises whether our interpretation is accepted or not.) Pugsley's suggestion that it covers the extra expense and trouble of a search (1969a: 146) is not at all convincing: we know of no legal system where such considerations play a part in the level of punishment, and in any case catching the original thief and proving the case against him could be equally troublesome. We would provisionally suggest that here again is a case where Gaius' interpretation is misleading. His division of theft into two exhaustive categories, one (*manifestum*) being specific and the other (*nec manifestum*) residual, is anachronistic. The Twelve Tables certainly discussed *furtum manifestum*, but the men-

The disparity between the original nature and meaning of the Twelve Tables' provisions on the one hand, and later Roman jurists' understanding of them on the other, was not simply the result of the passage of time or of development in the law. The Twelve Tables were the product of Mesopotamian science, then the dominant intellectual force in the Near East and Mediterranean basin. At some point in the history of the Republic, however, Mesopotamian science was replaced by a scientific method developed by the Greek philosophers, and the Roman jurists, having once adopted this new method, became divided from the old texts by an unbridgeable intellectual gulf. They could no longer look at the Twelve Tables with the same eyes as those who had drafted them.

An instructive example can once again be gleaned from oriental sources; this time not because of any connection, direct or indirect, but merely by way of comparison. The two biblical law codes, the Covenant Code and the Deuteronomic Code, were, as we have seen, part of the Mesopotamian scientific tradition. In the eyes of post-biblical Rabbinic jurists, however, they were something entirely different. They and the other rules found in the Pentateuch were regarded as legislation, enacted at a particular historical juncture in response to charismatic events (by divine proclamation on Mount Sinai after Israel's exodus from Egypt). Together with other law supposedly promulgated orally at the same occasion, they formed a comprehensive code which was to be the fount and origin of all Jewish law.

Unconsciously applying Greek scientific method, the Rabbis proceeded to interpret the content of the biblical codes accordingly. The Covenant Code contains a series of laws on damage to persons or property. Exod 21:28-32 reads:

---

tion of *furtum nec manifestum* in VIII 16 was not to a general category, but to a specific case where the theft was not manifest, as the Mesopotamian scientific method would lead us to expect. The less serious cases of dishonesty in the Twelve Tables (VIII 19, 20) with two-fold damages were taken by Gaius and others as illustrations of a general category of *furtum nec manifestum*. Hence the attribution of two-fold damages to all cases of common theft. In our view, the original penalty for common theft was a higher multiple. It may have varied according to the object stolen, but the most likely figure would be four-fold, i.e., that to which the penalty for *furtum manifestum* was later commuted. The grounds and the evidence for this proposition must await a more detailed study.

If an ox gores a man or a woman and they die, the ox shall be stoned and its flesh not eaten, but the owner of the ox shall be clear. But if the ox has been accustomed to gore in the past, and its owner has been warned but has not guarded it, and it kills a man or a woman, the ox shall be stoned, and its owner shall also be put to death. . . . If it gores a son or a daughter, it shall be done to him according to this rule. If the ox gores a male slave or a female slave, the owner shall give their master 30 shekels of silver and the ox shall be stoned.

Here is a typical scholarly problem dealt with according to the techniques of Mesopotamian science. The original question of liability is expanded by changing the status of the victim: man, woman, son, daughter, slave.[163] The following law also considers oxen, but the association is material not legal. Exod 21:33-34 reads:

If a man opens a pit or a man digs a pit and does not cover it, and an ox or an ass falls into it, the owner of the pit shall make it good; he shall give money to its owner, and the dead beast shall be his.

The next law (vv. 35-36) returns to the question of the goring ox, but where the victim is another ox.[164] The discussion is again, expanded by imposing the *scienter* test on the owner. There then follows a series of provisions on theft, after which the question of damage to property is raised again in two laws concerning responsibility for damage to crops. Exod 22:5-6 reads:

If a man causes a field or vineyard to be grazed over, or lets his beast loose and it feeds in another man's field, he shall make restitution from the best in his field and in his vineyard. If fire breaks out and catches in thorns so that the stacked grain or the standing grain or the field is burned, he that lit the fire shall make full restitution.

163 For a discussion of this particular scholarly problem, see Westbrook 1988d: 70-75.
164 See n. 69 above.

The same principle of liability for negligence can be discerned in these two laws, but it is expressed, as usual, only through isolated examples that give no hint of the limits of that principle.

Now let us compare the treatment of these disparate provisions at the hands of the Rabbinical jurists. The Mishnah, in *Bava Qamma* 1.1, reads:

> The four "fathers" (i.e., primary causes) of injuries are the ox and the pit and the grazing beast and the outbreak of fire. The ox is not like the grazing beast, nor is the grazing beast like the ox; nor is either of these, which have life in them, like fire, which does not have life in it; nor is any of these, whose way it is to go forth and do injury, like the pit, whose way it is not to go forth and do injury. What they have in common is that it is the way of them to do injury and that guarding them is your responsibility; and if one of them did injury, whoever did the injury must make restitution for the injury with the best of his land.

The scattered examples of the ancient text have been transformed into general categories which divide between them the whole field of injury, while common principles of liability and compensation are elucidated.

Not only would this reasoning be beyond the capacity of the original draftsman of the Covenant Code, but it changes the substantive meaning of the biblical text. As we have the original text we are in a position to compare, but were we forced to reconstruct it from the Mishnaic commentary, the result would, for all our efforts, be bound to look very different.

The method of reasoning reflected in the Mishnaic commentary may already have pervaded the *tripertita* of Sextus Aelius. It would certainly have been the basis of Gaius' commentary on the Twelve Tables. Small wonder then, that although he himself may have had the text before him, Gaius (and his fellow jurists alike) cannot reproduce for us its original meaning.[165]

---

165 In conceding Gaius accurate knowledge of the text we may even be going too far, since any version before him will not have been in the language of the fifth-century original. See Nörr 1976: 497-604, esp. 535.

3

Cuneiform Law Codes and the Origins of Legislation

Abstract

Recent scholarship has argued that the ancient Near Eastern law codes constituted legislation. This study takes exception to that view. Even though the codes appear to be fairly accurate *descriptions* of the law, they did not function as *prescriptive* legislation, nor did their provisions serve as legislative reforms. The ancient Near Eastern royal edicts, on the other hand, were a type of legislation. It was not until later biblical and Greek sources combined aspects of both the law codes and the royal edicts that the concept of written normative legislation began to develop.

When first discovered, the cuneiform law codes were assumed by scholars to be legislation in the classical or modern sense of the term. The only discussion was as to whether they were a codification or a reform.

Doubts, however, were expressed by scholars such as Eilers[1] and Landsberger,[2] and a contrary thesis was formulated by Kraus,[3] namely that the codes were an academic exercise, part of the proto-scientific activity of the scribes, on a par with the omen lists and medical treatises. This thesis, further expanded by Bottéro,[4] has gained wide acceptance among Assyriologists.

---

* Originally published in *Zeitschrift für Assyriologie* 79 (1989): 201-22. Used by permission.

1 Eilers 1932: 8-9. Note that P. Koschaker, for whom the legislative character of CH was without question, by the same token concluded that MAL was a private academic work without legislative force, by reason of the contrast in style between it and CH: *apud* Ehelolf 1922: 12-15.

2 Landsberger 1939: 221-22.

3 Kraus 1960.

4 Bottéro 1982. See also Finkelstein 1961 and Renger 1976.

Recently, however, the "academic" view of the law codes has come under attack by a number of legal historians who specialize in the field of cuneiform law. Both new and old arguments have been brought to bear in an attempt to show that the codes were indeed normative legislation, as earlier commentators had assumed. The debate, it should be added, has centered mainly around Codex Hammurabi, but its conclusions are assumed to apply to the codes in general.

Before we examine the arguments of this juridical school, it is necessary to explain the significance of the difference between an academic and a normative interpretation of the codes.

Legislation is an authoritative source of law; the courts are bound to obey its precepts. That binding quality begins at a certain point in time, when the legislation is promulgated. And once promulgated, the text of the legislation takes on a life of its own—the text is the exclusive source of the law. For this reason, the courts must pay great attention to the wording of the text, interpret its meaning, and cite it in their decisions. Even if the legislation does not change the existing law but merely codifies it, the effect is to exclude reliance on the earlier sources.

An academic treatise on the law may be good evidence of what the law is, but it is not an authoritative source. The treatise in describing the law in effect refers the court to the real authoritative sources thereof, whether they be statute, precedent, or custom. The date of the treatise is therefore of less significance; there is no particular point in time at which it comes into effect. And its text has no independent value. Courts need not cite it or pay attention to its wording, since they are essentially looking beyond it to the source that it reflects.

The arguments of legal historians in favor of the former interpretation of the cuneiform codes are the following. Firstly, certain remarks in the epilogue to CH are taken to show that the text of the code was intended to be cited in court.[5] The section in col. XLVIII, lines 3-17, reads:

A man oppressed who has a plaint,[6] let him go before my statue "king of justice," read my inscribed stela, and hear my precious

---

5   Petschow 1986: 21-22.

6   *awātam irašśû*. Not, apparently, a technical term of litigation. In the OB period it occurs in letters rather than legal documents: *JCS* 17 77, no. 5:6; AbB 1 50:20.

words. May my stela reveal to him the matter; may he see his
judgment . . . .

According to Petschow, this invitation presumes that the plaintiff would be
able to rely on the judges applying the relevant provisions in his lawsuit.[7]
That presumption may well be correct, but it does not make the provisions
legislation. They could equally be an earlier judgment of the king which
the stela *describes*, since what the plaintiff has revealed to him is *dīnšu*—
"his judgment"—and elsewhere the provisions as a whole are termed "the
just judgments that (king Hammurabi) established" (*dīnāt mīšarim ša . . .
ukinnu*).[8]

Such judgments would have authority in their own right as precedents,
unless the law code replaced them, and of that step there is no indication in
the text. It can only be supplied by importing modern conceptions of law,
which of course is to beg the question. For the text goes on to describe not
the citation of the judgment found by the plaintiff in the stela, but his joy at
the discovery and the need for him then to praise Hammurabi and to pray
for him. And all this takes place not in the court but in the temple, where
the stela is situated.

On the same subject, Klíma[9] and Démare-Lafont[10] argue that the provisions of the stela are made binding on the courts by the curse formulae
upon anyone disregarding the content of the stela or tampering with the
inscription itself. But these curses are clearly directed against a future ruler
after Hammurabi,[11] not to his own administration. Indeed, the curse against
one who erases Hammurabi's name and inserts his own on the stela[12]
shows that the binding authority of the provisions was not uppermost in
the promulgator's mind, since that action by a future king would not de-
tract from their authority and might even enhance it.

---

7 Petschow 1986: 22. Contra Renger 1976: 234, who considers the invitation to have
   moral rather than legal force, being intended to reassure one seeking justice.
8 Col. XLVII, lines 1-5.
9 Klíma 1972: 308.
10 Démare-Lafont 1987b: 345.
11 Col. XLVII, lines 59-63.
12 Col. XLVII, lines 33-35.

The second main argument put forward is that the political context reveals CH to have been normative legislation. As Klíma puts it:[13]

> Le dynamisme de la politique hammurabienne qui menait à la centralisation et l'unification de l'empire . . . met hors de doute l'intention du souverain de munir son empire d'un droit unifié, obligeant toute la population sans distinction d'origine, de race et de nationalité.

The idea is that an act of legislative codification was necessary to replace conflicting local systems.

Unfortunately, there is no evidence whatsoever that such noble sentiments were abroad in the eighteenth century B.C.E. There is nothing in the sources to suggest either that the legal systems of the region differed to the point of conflict or that there was any awareness that unification of the law was necessary or desirable, or that CH did anything in this regard. The only clear difference between regions known to us is the firstborn son's right to a privileged share of the inheritance, which amounts to ten percent of the total estate in Southern Mesopotamia but to the equivalent of one ordinary heir's share in the North and in peripheral areas.[14] The question is not dealt with at all in CH.

The third argument is that, contrary to the earlier findings of Eilers,[15] there are no discrepancies between the rules of CH and those found in documents of practice.[16] This is a finding that may be accepted without further discussion, for it proves nothing about the legislative effect of the code (except that it was not impossible). It does not prove that practice conformed with the code, since it could equally well have been the code that was conforming with practice. After all, the least that one could expect from an academic treatise on law is that it accurately describe the law in

---

13 Klíma 1972: 306-307. Cf. Petschow 1986: 21 and Démare-Lafont 1987b: 346.

14 See O'Callaghan 1954: 139-140. On the other hand, references to talionic punishment in some codes and to payments in others do *not* point to conflicting legal systems, as we have argued in Westbrook 1988d: 45-77. Hammurabi, at least, regarded the judgments of his defeated neighbors as valid and still binding on the parties, as Jean *Tell Sifr* 58 shows; see Kraus 1958: 208.

15 Eilers 1932: 8, no. 3. Cf. San Nicolò 1932: 189-92.

16 See esp. Petschow 1984. Also U. Sick 1984.

practice. In this respect, the findings of the juridical school are to be com-
mended as a useful qualification to the "academic exercise" theory.[17] It is
not to be supposed that those who drafted the codes invented rules out of
their own imagination; they described the positive law.[18]

The same considerations apply to arguments based on innovations in
the codes.[19] The Hittite Laws in particular make express reference to
changes in the law, e.g., paragraph 59: "If someone steals a ram, formerly
they used to give 30 sheep. Now he shall give 15 sheep; 5 ewes, 5 rams, 5
lambs." Such paragraphs may show that the code is linked to the law in
practice, but they do not necessarily mean that the code is the source of the
reforms mentioned. It could as well be describing changes in the law made
by some other process. An example of such a process is given in paragraph
55 of the same code:

> When the Hattian feudal tenants came and bowed down to the
> king's father and said, "No one pays us a wage, and they belittle
> us (saying), 'You are feudal tenants,'" then the king's father [. . .]
> in the assembly and sealed a document (saying), "Go! Be like your
> colleagues."

The final argument is a more subtle one. It is suggested that the content of certain provisions in the codes indicates that they must have been
legislative reforms. The first instance relates to paragraph 12 of the NBL,
which reads:

> A wife, whose husband has received her dowry, who has no son or
> daughter, and whose husband has died, shall be given a dowry to
> the value of her dowry from her husband's estate.
>   If her husband gave her a marital gift, she shall receive her
> husband's marital gift together with her dowry and is paid.

---

17 Bottero (1982: 435) argues that, as in the omen-texts, the law codes contain cases that
are conceivable but not in the realm of the practical. While the omens do contain fantastic cases, such as a woman giving birth to six, seven, eight, nine, ten and so forth
children at one time, one should not take the analogy too far. Omens are by definition
extraordinary occurrences; the circumstances of legal disputes are not.

18 This is not to exclude some variation or idealization, as in any modern treatise on law.

19 Von Schuler 1959: 436; Preiser 1969: 26-27.

> If she has no dowry, the judges shall consider her husband's estate, and something shall be given her from her husband's estate."

In discussing a Neo-Babylonian trial document in which the widow receives back the value of her dowry, Ries comments that one has the impression that the court had paragraph 12 before it in making its decision.[20] He distinguishes between a trial document in which, for example, the death penalty is imposed for homicide, which need not be based on a provision to that effect in a code, since in the nature of things that would be the appropriate penalty, and the present case, where the provision of the code is so technical that the same result in the trial can be no coincidence.[21] In our view, the opposite is the case. One of the innate functions of the dowry is to provide for the wife during widowhood. The dowry is always to be restored to the wife, and if she dies childless, it is returned to her father's estate; it does not devolve upon her husband's. These principles are already recorded over a thousand years earlier in the Old Babylonian codes[22] and are the rationale for the dowry lists found in documents of practice in which quantities and values are recorded with painstaking detail.[23] It seems to us, therefore, that NBL 12 was not a technical innovation but a banal recapitulation of customary law, and the court in this instance had no need to refer to the text of a code in order to reach its decision.

The second instance relates to differences between CU and CH. In CU 28, if a man floods his neighbor's field, he must pay a fixed amount of

---

20 Ries 1984: 358.

21 Ries 1984: 358-59: "Die Bestimmung ist so sehr technischer Art, daß die Entscheidung nicht auf Zufall beruhen kann, wie etwa, wenn die Anwendung eines Gesetzes über vorsätzliche Tötung in Frage stünde, dessen Rechtsfolge die Todesstrafe ist. Könnte man in diesem Fall ein Dokument der Rechtspraxis entdecken, wonach der Täter zum Tode verurteilt wurde, so wäre das kein zwingender Nachweis dafür, daß das Gericht die Norm bewußt angewandt hat. Anders als im vorliegenden Fall könnte sich dieses Ergebnis auch aus der Natur der Sache ergeben."

22 CE 18, CH 171-172, CH 176. Discussed in Westbrook 1988b. For the widespread application of this principle, see Westbrook 1986b.

23 For examples, see Westbrook 1988b (BE 6/1 84, BE 6/1 101, CT 8 2a).

grain per area unit in compensation. In §29, if a lessee fails to cultivate the land under lease, he must pay the lessor the same fixed amount.

According to Cardascia,[24] CU's system is a primitive one. The fixed amount—in itself a crude measure—is applied indifferently where the whole crop is at issue, as in §28, and where only the rent (one-half or two-thirds of the crop) is at issue. In the parallel provisions in CH a different measure appears—"like his neighbor," i.e., the yield of a neighboring field—and to Cardascia this signals a legislative innovation, a new and more sophisticated concept introduced by CH.

The situation, however, is considerably more complex. CH in fact uses both measures, the fixed as well as the neighboring. It does so, as Cardascia recognized,[25] in different types of circumstances, which suggests to us that the difference is not historical but utilitarian.

The fixed measure is used in CH in three paragraphs. For Cardascia, the common factor is that (on his interpretation of the text) in all these cases the field has been reduced to a totally barren condition. Accordingly, the archaic Sumerian system was applied here or rediscovered by CH for technical reasons, namely the difficulty of estimating the future crop on the basis of the neighboring field's production.[26]

We cannot see the logic in this reasoning. The neighboring fields' production is an equally usable criterion whether part or the whole of a field's crop has been lost. The potential crop will be the same in either case. Moreover, the neighboring field measure is used in CH also where the total crop is lost, in CH 43. The negligent lessee there has to do the same preliminary work on the field before returning it to its owner (hoeing, etc.) as in CH 44, where the fixed measure applies. In our opinion, therefore, the field's reduction to a barren condition was not the factor that determined CH's employment of the fixed measure. The difference between the two measures is to be sought elsewhere.

---

24 Cardascia 1985.
25 Cardascia 1985: 179.
26 Cardascia 1985: 179: "Dans ces trois espèces le forfait serait appliqué, non pour des raisons d'equité—qui militeraient plutôt en sens inverse—mais pour un motif technique: la difficulté que l'on rencontrait à estimer la future récolte (ou le futur fermage) d'après la production des champs contigus. Pour cette raison contingente, Hammurabi aurait, soit conservé, soit retrouvé de façon indépendante, la méthode forfaitaire, seule pratiquée à l'époque sumérienne."

The provisions of CH that use these measures apply them to two types of wrong: where a tenant-farmer through negligence fails to fulfill his contract with the owner and where the owner of a field through negligence floods his neighbor's field.

Let us first consider the contractual provisions. From the documents of practice, we know that a tenant-farmer might pay rent in one of three ways, according to his lease: a fixed quantity of grain (or other crop) for the area leased, a fixed quantity per acre, or a fixed proportion of the harvest (i.e., share-cropping).[27] An example of share-cropping is given in CH 64:

> If a man gives his (date-)palm grove to a gardener for pollination, as long as he holds the grove, the gardener shall give two-thirds of the grove's yield to the owner and shall take one-third himself.

CH 65 continues:

> If the gardener does not pollinate the grove and reduces the yield, the gardener shall measure out to the grove's owner a yield of the grove like his neighbor.

In a share-cropping arrangement, the rent received by the owner is variable, depending on the total yield produced by the tenant's efforts. If the tenant through negligence fails to produce a reasonable yield, he is in breach of contract. The obvious measure of reasonable yield is the production of the neighboring fields. Indeed, it is *only* in a share-cropping situation that this measure is appropriate. If the rent were fixed, whether in total or per acre, that would be the amount payable by the tenant whatever the total yield produced from the rented land. CH 42 reads:

> If a man leases a field for cultivation and does not produce grain in the field, they shall prove that he did not do the husbandry of the field, and he shall give the field's owner grain like his neighbor.[28]

---

27 See Driver and Miles 1952: 131-35.

28 In CH 43, if the tenant did not even plow the field, he must do this and relinquish the lease in addition to paying the owner rent by the same measure.

Although it is not mentioned expressly then, here also the lease must be a share-cropping arrangement, and the payment must thus be the owner's proportion of a reasonable yield.[29]

Turning to the provisions of CH where a fixed measure is applied to breach of contract, we see that the lease is of a different nature. It is for development of waste land (*ana teptītim*). CH 44 reads:

> If a man leases a waste field for three years for development but was negligent and did not develop.the field, in the fourth year he shall plow, hoe, and harrow the field and return it to the field's owner and shall measure out 10 *kor* of grain per *bur*.

The same contract is found in contemporary documents of practice. While there is considerable variation in the terms, the basic condition is that the tenant be allowed a period rent-free or at a reduced rent until the field comes to full production. In some contracts it is only in the final year of the lease that the tenant "enters into rent" (*ana biltim irrub*), i.e., pays the full rent.[30] It is not usually stated what the full rent is, but apparently it may be on any one of the three bases mentioned above, since in one case it is stated as 8 *kor* per *bur*[31] and in another as "like his neighbors,"[32] suggesting share-cropping. Another variation of this contract is for the tenant to pay no rent at all for the period of the lease, but to be obliged to return the land in a developed condition.[33]

In our opinion, it is with the latter arrangement that CH 44 is concerned, for if rent were payable in the final year of the lease, that in itself would provide the measure of compensation for breach. There being no share-cropping arrangement, however, the "like his neighbor" measure is

---

29 Cf. the lease agreement in VAS 8 62-63 (= Schorr 1913: no. 130): A has leased a field, as far as it extends, from B for cultivation. He will do the work like his right (neighbor) and his left (neighbor). If he does not do the work, he (the lessor) will (still) take his half-share of the grain.

  In a very indirect way the document reveals that it is a share-cropping agreement in which the owner is entitled to a share based on the yield from neighboring fields.

30 E.g., CT 2 8, CT 33 36, VAS 7 22.

31 Waterman Bus. Doc. 48 (= AJSL 29 295):15.

32 VAS 7 22.

33 VAS 7 21.

not appropriate, especially since no particular proportion has been agreed upon. An average rent for developed land would therefore seem in order, and that is almost exactly what 10 *kor* per *bur* represents. The contemporary documents that stipulate rent by *kor* per *bur* vary from 6 to 18 *kor*, the average being around 9 *kor*.[34]

In CH 62-63 the two rival measures of compensation are again contrasted, but the situation is quite different, and so is their application. A gardener has contracted to plant a (date-)palm grove on the owner's land, an enterprise that will require four years rent-free occupation, with the parties dividing the field (not the crop) in equal shares in the fifth. CH 62 continues:

> If he did not plant the field given him with a palm grove, if it is developed arable land, the gardener shall measure out to the owner the yield of the field for the years that he was negligent like his neighbor and shall make it a worked field and return it to the owner.

In our opinion, the payment here does not represent rent, which would be inadequate compensation.[35] On the total failure of the investment, the owner is restored to the best position that he would have been in had he retained control of the field, namely its full grain production as developed land.[36] To ascertain that production, the measure "like his neighbor" is the most appropriate. CH 63, however, continues:

34 Driver and Miles 1952: 133.
35 The term GUN (*biltum*) can mean yield or rent, according to context. The latter meaning might apply in the context of a share-cropping agreement, but the context here is explicitly not one of share-cropping: according to §60, if the contract to plant an orchard is successfully completed, the owner and the gardener will physically divide the land as absolute owners.
36 The fact that this optimum standard is used points to some of the difficulties felt by the Babylonian jurisprudence in grappling with the question of fair compensation. In awarding damages for breach of contract, a modern court of law would seek to compensate for loss of expectations: it would seek to put the plaintiff—in financial terms—in the position he would have been had the contract been performed. The quantification, however, is difficult and complex, involving speculation as to the future performance of the investment. It is not surprising therefore that the Babylonian court followed a more attainable goal: the position the plaintiff would have been in

If it is waste land he shall make it a worked field and return the field to the owner and measure out 10 *kor* of grain per *bur* for each year.

Again, the resemblance to rent is purely superficial. The measure of compensation is based on the assumption that the owner would otherwise have developed the waste land as grain-bearing land. The results would have varied, as variations in the development contracts show, but a reasonable average would have been for the owner to have had perhaps a small crop in the second year and a full crop in the third or at least the fourth year. A recent study has shown the average yield at this period to have been about 20 *kor* per *bur*,[37] so that from waste land four years' development would yield on average about 40 *kor*. This is the sum of 10 *kor* per *year* for the four-year lease and may therefore have been the unexpressed aim of this measure.[38] It could have been computed differently, but this was a round measure at hand and was presumably borrowed from the waste land rent case on the same analogy as the "like his neighbor" measure for rent of development land.

Finally, in CH 55–56, the two measures of compensation are again used out of their original context. The situation is no longer contractual, but concerns damage caused by negligence.

55 If a man opens his canal for irrigation and is negligent and lets the water carry away his neighbor's field, he shall measure out grain like his neighbor.

56 If a man opens the water and lets the water carry away the workings (*epšētim*) of his neighbor's field, he shall measure out 10 *kor* of barley per *bur*.

---

had there been no contract and no breach. But there must have been awareness, albeit inarticulate, that this was insufficient, that some allowance for reasonable expectations must be given. Hence the optimistic assessment of the plaintiff's likely earnings in the absence of a development lease.

37 Butz and Schroeder 1985: 189–90.

38 Our remarks in n. 36 as to the optimistic assessment of the owner's putative income apply equally here.

In §55, the rationale for use of the "like his neighbor" measure is clear. The crop has been washed away, and the neighbor is therefore entitled to the quantity that his field would have produced, as evidenced by the production of the surrounding field. In §56, on the other hand, as Driver and Miles point out, "the damage done is merely to the preparatory work on his neighbor's field, such as the fencing and ditching, and this work can be done again and a late crop may be raised."[39] The "like his neighbor" measure would therefore be inappropriate, since there may be no loss of production at all; the loss is rather in extra trouble and expense. Fixed average rent per acre may not be the most sophisticated measure, but given the difficulty of assessing trouble and expense in pecuniary terms, it is a reasonable one.

For good measure, it should be added that there is a third measure of compensation for flooding in CH 53, namely the amount of grain lost. In this case, the negligent farmer has flooded the whole district (*ugārum*), so that presumably there are no neighbors left by whose crop the lost production can be judged. On the other hand, there is no explanation of how the quantity lost is to be assessed.

To summarize, CH discusses a wide variety of cases where agricultural production is disrupted through negligence, some founded in contract and some in what today would be called tort. The code applies several criteria for measurement of compensation, in particular a fixed rate of 10 *kor* per *bur* and "like his neighbor," both of which derive from the practice in different types of lease. There is nothing to suggest that the latter is more sophisticated than the former; rather they are each confined to the circumstances where they would be most appropriate.

With these considerations in mind, we may return to the provisions of the earlier CU. In contrast to the plethora of detail in CH, the Sumerian code presents only two brief paragraphs. The tablet breaks off at that point, however, and it may well be that treatment of the topic was more extensive.

> 28 If a man caused water to carry away the crop-bearing field of a
> man, he shall measure out 3 *kor* of grain per *iku* of field.

---

39 Driver and Miles 1952: 154.

29 If a man leased a crop-bearing field to a man for cultivation, and he did not cultivate it but turned it into an "empty place,"[40] he shall measure out 3 *kor* of grain per *iku* of field.

Although the same general situation is evidently being described, it is impossible to ascertain from these terse and enigmatic provisions which of the several lease or flood cases considered in CH are being adumbrated, if any. It may indeed be none of them, for in the apodosis the whole basis for comparison breaks down. Cardascia notes with astonishment that the measure here of 3 *kor* per *iku* is more than five times higher than in the parallel provisions of CH, but attributes it to the much-reduced yield of the Babylonian fields due to the effects of salinization.[41] Butz, however, has shown that salinization had little effect on yield between the Neo-Sumerian and Old Babylonian periods.[42]

A similar severity is found twice in CH, where the payment required is 60 *kor* per *bur*, i.e., six times higher than the fixed measure under discussion. In §58 it concerns a shepherd who has left his sheep in a field during a period when this is forbidden,[43] and in §255 an employee who dishonestly hires out his employer's ox or who steals his employer's seed-grain. In the latter case at least, the payment can be clearly seen to be penal. We must therefore assume the same for the payments in CU.

Consequently, either CU took a different attitude to CH over the offences in question, or the circumstances of the protasis are not as parallel as they appear. Whatever the case, the payment required by CU cannot be interpreted as a measure of compensation, primitive or otherwise. Neither from internal evidence, therefore, nor from comparison with the provisions of an earlier code, can the "like his neighbor" measure of compensation be seen as a legislative innovation by CH to replace a more primitive fixed rate of payment.

The final argument for the legislative nature of the law codes concerns a question first raised by Landsberger.[44] Why are the law codes never

---

40   šà.sù.ga, see *CAD* Ḫ 249, *ḫurbū* (lexical discussion); and *AHw* 987-88, *rīqu*.
41   Cardascia 1985: 177. 1 *bur* = 18 *iku*.
42   Butz and Schroeder 1985: 197-98.
43   See Dossin 1972: 77-80.
44   Landsberger 1939: 220.

referred to in documents of practice? Two answers are given by legal historians: firstly, citation was not required in ancient legal procedure,[45] and secondly, cuneiform trial records never give the legal grounds for the decisions recorded.[46]

There is some substance in these points. It is not to be expected that the ancients shared the obsession of modern lawyers with citing chapter and verse for every rule applied, and an argument from silence is to be treated with the utmost reserve given the haphazard circumstances upon which we depend for our sources. Nonetheless, they must both be rejected in the light of the following facts.

> 1. In the post-cuneiform period of classical antiquity, it *was* the practice to cite statutes, by name and by direct quotation of

---

45   Klíma 1972: 308.

46   Démare-Lafont 1987b: 344. A different approach has been to claim the existence of citations of legislation in the cuneiform literature. See e.g., Szlechter 1965: 64-74; Preiser 1969: 33-34; and Leemans 1988: 233. As we shall see, there are cases where the king's acts as a lawmaker are cited, but there is no evidence to identify these acts with law codes in the sense of CH, MAL, etc. The nearest candidate is UET 5 420:

> *a-lu-ú-um* / DUMU *a-at-ta-a* / ᵈEN.ZU-*ú-ba-li-iṭ-sú* / *a-na* UGU A.ŠÀ-*šu* / *a-na e-eb-bu-tim* / *iš-ku-un-šu* / *i-na* U₄.1.KAM / ⌜2⌝ SÌLA! NINDA *ù* 3 SÌLA KAŠ / ⌜x⌝ *iš-ku-un-šu* / *še-a-am i-na ka-ba-si-im* / 3 ŠE.GUR *i-na* KAR ÚRIᵏⁱ / *i-na-ad-di-iš-šum* / *a-na ḫi-ṭi-im ša ib-ba-aš-šu* / *ki-ma pí-i* NA₄.RUᵉ / *i-ip-pu-šu-šu*

> Sin-uballissu has established Alum son of Attaya as guardian(?) over his field. He has established 2 *qa* of bread and 3 *qa* of beer per day for him. When the grain is trampled, he will give him 3 *kor* of grain at the quay of Ur. For any shortfall that may be, they will treat him according to the word of the stela. (4 witnesses; date: Samsu-iluna 5).

Since the CH, *inter alia*, is written on a stela, this could be interpreted as a reference to such a law code. It is precisely in a contract, however, that one would *not* expect reference to a law code. If the code constituted positive legislation then there would be no need to refer to the rule in the contractual conditions since it would apply automatically. At most, one might expect a paraphrase of the rule. A possible exception would be where the stela contained a tariff, perhaps not yet fixed at the time of concluding the contract. Since any shortfall would be relative to the size of the harvest, the clause may refer to a tariff posted after the outturn of the harvest is known. The two other similar references to a stela both refer to tariffs—of wages and interest: see *CAD* N/1 364-65, *narû* A.

paragraphs, if not by number.[47] The practice is not, then, a modern innovation, and the difference between classical and pre-classical antiquity in this regard is of great significance.

2. There does exist a comparable type of cuneiform legal source for which contemporary references abound: the royal edict. There are many examples, the most complete of which are the edicts of Uru-inimgina of Lagash (25th century),[48] Ammi-ṣaduqa of Babylon (17th century),[49] Telipinu of Hatti (16th century),[50] and Horemheb of Egypt (14th century).[51] They all take the form of solemn proclamations by a king declaring the reform of some aspect or aspects of the existing law. Evidence external to the texts themselves leaves no doubt as to their practical application; indeed, the existence of most of the edicts is known only from evidence of their effect in practice. The same evidence shows them to have been a widespread phenomenon, common not only to the cuneiform sphere but to the whole of the ancient Near East.[52]

47　Examples are countless. To take two at random:
　　　1. In the Mishnah, *Ketubot* 3.5: "If there be found in her unchastity or if she is not fit to enter the congregation of Israel, he is not permitted to marry her, as it is said: 'And she shall be to him for a wife.' (This means:) a wife who is fit for him." (The citation is of Deut 22:29.)
　　　2. Demosthenes, *In Aristocratem* 51: "This statute, men of Athens, like all the other excerpts from the law of homicide which I have cited for comparison, is a statute of Draco; and you must pay attention to his meaning. 'No man is to be liable to prosecution for murder for laying information against manslayers who return from exile illegally.' Herein he exhibits two principles of justice, both of which have been transgressed by the defendant in his decree" (translation from Vince, in *Loeb Classical Library*, 1978).

48　Edited by Lambert 1956: 169-84. Recent translation and notes in Cooper 1986: 70-78. The king's name was formerly read Urukagina.

49　Edited by Kraus 1984: 163-214. See also the text of fragments of two further edicts from the same period; edited in Kraus 1984: 152-62.

50　Edited by Hoffmann 1984. A fragment of an Edict by Tudhaliya IV of Hatti is edited by Schuler 1959: 435-72. Middle Assyrian edicts concerned with palace protocol are edited by Weidner 1954-56b: 257-93. A recently published fragment may have had wider application: George 1988: 25-30.

51　Edited by Kruchten 1981.

52　The overall picture is discussed by Weinfeld 1985: esp. chapters 4-7 (in Hebrew).

The effect of the edicts can be seen from changes in contemporary economic documents,[53] and they are referred to indirectly in contracts, where it is necessary to emphasize that the transaction in question post-dated the edict.[54] They are the subject of lawsuits[55] and petitions,[56] and their promulgation is recorded in year names[57] and in historical narratives.[58]

The reason for all this evidence is quite simply that, unlike the law-codes, the reform edicts *were* normative legislation. The text lays down a series of rules that come into force at a specific point in time[59] and have to be obeyed by the courts.[60] If the law codes had had the same effect, we

---

53   Maekawa 1973-74: 114-36.

54   E.g., TCL 10 40 (Old Babylonian document from Larsa); edited by Kraus 1984: 31-33. Cf. the clause in a Neo-Assyrian contract ("If a release is established, PN may claim his silver") discussed by Lewy 1958: 30-31.

55   Oliver 1984.

56   Finkelstein 1965.

57   E.g., two year names of king Kaštiliaš, of Hana:
      a) "Year: king Kaštiliaš established a *mīšarum*."
      b) "Year: king Kaštiliaš established a second *mīšarum*."
      See Kraus 1984: 99-100. The numerous examples from the OB period are collected in Kraus 1984: chapters 2-5.

58   Jer 34:8-11, recording an edict by King Zedekiah of Judah releasing debt-slaves.

59   CE is preceded by a date-formula, which might suggest that the code came into force at a specific point in time. (The incongruity with a law code has been noted by Kraus, 1984: 94-96.) What follows the date-formula, however, is a tariff, which appears to have been incorporated from an independent source without any changes. (It has not been put into the casuistic style characteristic of the law codes.) In our view then, the date belongs to the tariff and originally marked the point in time from which the prices were valid.

60   It is a moot point whether the text of the edicts was in itself authoritative. This must have been the case with tariffs, but were the actual words of an edict interpreted by the court? The extant texts of Uru-inimgina's Edict are not the original version and not authoritative. They are dedicatory inscriptions from later in his reign in which the king boasts of his various achievements and in so doing quotes extensively from the re-forms that he had instituted at the beginning of his reign (see Edzard 1974: 147-49). The role of the text in the Old Babylonian *mīšarum*-edicts is not clear (see Kraus 1958). Paragraph 30 of the Edict of Telipinu instructs the nobles to tell a future king planning to kill his siblings to "see the matter of blood *from the tablet.* Formerly blood (= murder) was frequent in Hattusa, and the gods placed it (the bloodguilt) on the great

would expect similar references to them as to the edicts, at least in the Old Babylonian period, when there is ample source-material. Instead, there is silence. The name of king Hammurabi's second year refers to a reform edict, and that of year 22 to his statue "Hammurabi, King of Justice," which is also mentioned in the epilogue to CH, but the promulgation of the great code itself does not even merit a year name. The process of legislation appears to have stopped short at the edicts. And this is no accident.

For legislation, the edicts are remarkably narrow in scope. The earliest, that of king Uru-inimgina of Lagash, contains three types of provisions, which mark the parameters also of the three other major extant examples and to all appearances of those preserved only in fragmentary form or in passing reference. The three categories are:

1. Adjustments to royal administrative machinery. Offices are created or abolished; malpractices of officials are forbidden and their future repetition punished; the administration of state institutions is regulated.[61] The edicts of Telipinu of Hatti and Horemheb of Egypt fall exclusively into this category. The former is concerned mostly with regulating an orderly succession to the throne and with administration of the royal granaries, while the latter is concerned with abuses by military and civilian officials and the provision of supplies for the itinerant royal court.

   The substantive law of the land is untouched by this type of legislation. The king reorganizes his own household and the general population is affected only insofar as they come into contact with the royal bureaucracy.[62]

(= royal) family." This could be a reference simply to the historical preamble, where the gory deeds of Telipinu's predecessors are recounted.

61 E.g., "He installed Ningirsu as proprietor over the ruler's estate and the ruler's fields; he installed Ba'u as proprietor of the estate of the woman's organization and fields of the woman's organization; and he installed Šulšagana as proprietor of the children's estate" (Sollberger *Corpus* Ukg. 5; transl. Cooper 1986: 72). All three are gods—the reference is to a reorganization of public administration, which included the temples.

62 But note that paragraphs 49 and 50 of the Telipinu Edict appear to contain procedural regulations concerning the palace's role in the prosecution of murder and witchcraft.

2. Fixing of tariffs for certain activities such as interest on loans and the price of goods and services.[63] Such tariffs are clearly designed to intervene indirectly in private transactions and will therefore affect the whole population, but they raise no theoretical issues of law. The fixing of prices is a mechanical act, requiring no consideration of issues of principle.

3. Debt-release decrees. This category is the most widespread, to judge from the indirect evidence. A major example is preserved in the Edict of Ammi-ṣaduqa of Babylon (17th century). The king proclaims "equity" (*mīšarum*) for the land, which consists in annulling all non-commercial debts and the transactions based thereon, such as debt-slavery. Here, at least, is an act of general application which intervenes directly in private legal transactions and thus has the potential to affect the principles of the substantive law itself. But the intervention is always *retrospective*; it affects existing and not future contracts. This is in strong contrast to modern legislation, for which the norm is prospective rules.[64]

In short, the principal areas of substance in a legal system: property and inheritance, family law, contract, and delict—areas that receive the full attention of the cuneiform law codes—are virtually ignored in the only true legislative instrument of the cuneiform sources, the royal edict.[65]

---

63   E.g., "When a corpse is brought for burial the *uḫmuš* takes his 3 jugs of beer, his 80 loaves of bread, one bed, and one 'leading goat,' and the *umum* takes 3 *ban* of barley" (Sollberger *Corpus* Ukg. 5; transl. Cooper 1986: 72). Similar lists are found in §§1-11 of the Code of Eshnunna, §§268-277 of the Code of Hammurabi, and §§176B-186 of the Hittite Laws. They appear to have been drawn from independent sources, but no such source has been recovered to date. Nonetheless, there is indirect evidence that tariffs were posted at the city-gate. See n. 46 above on *narû*; and KAH 1 2 iii 16-iv 3.

64   Some secondary rules punishing those who disobey the decree by their nature govern future conduct. Paragraphs 5 and 7 of Ammi-ṣaduqa's edict, which punished complicated attempts to evade the edict, must have been based on court decisions arising from earlier edicts. The same would seem to apply to §§10, 17, 18, and 22, contrary to the interpretation of Finkelstein (1961: 100-102), who saw them as impractical reforms (citing the same paragraphs as 8, 15, 16 and 20, following an earlier edition).

65   The reverse is not true. The law codes contain material from all sources, including royal edicts. See esp. Finkelstein 1961: 103.

The reason for such timidity is in our opinion an intellectual one. Let us consider for a moment the difference between the two great sources of authoritative law: precedent and statute.

Precedent derives from the decisions of a court in a particular case. Initially, the court's judgment looks backward; it resolves a past or existing situation that is presented to it. What precedent does is to make the same judgment look forward, by rendering it applicable to potential future situations where the facts are analogous but not necessarily similar. The key to this process is the extraction of the reasoning behind the decision and its re-formulation as an impersonal rule.

Statute already begins life as an impersonal rule. With the exception of retrospective legislation, its attention is directed exclusively to the future. It may be based on past or present experience but essentially it must *predict* potential situations and formulate rules to resolve them. Clearly, there is a great danger of such rules having unexpected results. It is a danger that is easier to avoid with precedent, where the consequences can already be seen in the case upon which the decision is made. The more widely the precedent is formulated, therefore, the further it departs from the narrow facts upon which the original decision was based, the greater the danger of unpredictable results, and the closer its formulation resembles statute. By the same token, statute may lessen this danger by narrowing its formulation to resemble more that of a precedent, although with a corresponding loss of effectiveness.

In short, the formulation of general principles of law is a difficult intellectual task, in which there is a rising gradation between precedent and statute. Being an intellectual discipline, therefore, law cannot go beyond the philosophical and scientific attainments of the society that has produced it.

The limitations of Mesopotamian science are well known. It was incapable of experiment or of formulating   abstract   categories.[66] These limitations had their effect also in the sphere of law.[67]

Being reluctant to depart from present experience, cuneiform law was based essentially on precedent (for the most part, in fact, it was custom dressed up as precedent). Its legal science hesitantly expanded the scope of

---

66   See Bottéro 1987: 160-69.
67   Bottéro 1982: 425-35; Westbrook 1988a: 86-93.

precedents by logical extrapolation, but this method could lead only to descriptive treatises that "discovered" the law, not to consciously new rules. These were the cuneiform law codes.

Being unable to engage in speculative experiments, its legislation was equally tied to the past. The most radical of reforms acted, like judicial decisions, upon existing situations—they were retrospective. Measures for the future were confined to the mechanical: price-lists and administrative orders. Thus the system produced decrees, but not yet statutes.

The transformation to true prospective legislation was achieved not in the cuneiform sphere but on its periphery. In the second millennium, bronze age Canaan and Mycenaean Greece were still a patchwork of minor provincial kingdoms on the fringe of high civilization, as represented by Egypt, the Hittites, and the Mesopotamian powers. By the early first millennium, however, these two areas had become the foci of new forms of literature and of thought: the prophets in Israel and the pre-Socratic philosophers in Greece. These changes in the intellectual climate find their reflection in the law.

The earliest legal code in the Bible is the Covenant Code (Exod 21:1-22:19). Although it is impossible to date the code with any certainty, it can most probably be assigned to the early monarchy or even pre-monarchical period, and the 10th century is as reasonable a supposition as any.[68] In content and form, the code is very closely related to the cuneiform codes of the second millennium[69] and shares their limitations. It can be characterized as a provincial reflection of the cuneiform legal tradition.

The book of Deuteronomy, on the other hand, can be dated with reasonable confidence to the 7th century. Its ideology is identifiable with the religious reforms of king Josiah, and it reflects the attitudes and concerns of the 8th and 7th century prophets.[70] Its legal provisions use the same material as the Covenant Code and the cuneiform codes, but in its open advocacy of reform[71] (albeit projected back to the time of Moses), it is the

---

68　See the discussion by Noth 1962: 173-75.

69　The parallels are summarized by Paul 1970: 102-105. Cf. Westbrook 1988d: 89-91.

70　It is generally associated with reforms in the reign of king Josiah (ca. 622 B.C.E.). For a summary of the research, see Sellin and Fohrer 1965: 182-92.

71　E.g., Deut 24:16, which inveighs against the system of vicarious revenge still operative in the Covenant Code (Exod 21:20-21). See Westbrook 1988d: 98-99.

expression of a different intellectual climate. The new possibilities that result can be seen in the provisions of Deut 15:1-2:

> At the end of seven years you shall make a release. This is the matter of the release: every creditor shall release his loans that are owed him by his neighbor; he shall not claim them from his neighbor.

Verses 9-10 continue:

> Beware lest there be a word of wickedness in your heart, saying, "The seventh year, the year of release, draws near," and you look ill upon your poor brother and do not give him (a loan); and he calls to the Lord about you, and there is sin in you. You shall surely give to him and not think ill in giving, for because of that the LORD your God will bless you in all your deeds and enterprises.

The content of the law is a debt-release decree, such as we have seen were common throughout the ancient Near East. But in this version there is a significant difference; the effect of the law is prospective, not retrospective. The release has been changed into a cyclical event, and the consequences thereof have been taken into consideration. The resultant appeal to the creditor's conscience may not be very practical,[72] but the method of thinking reveals a fundamental innovation. It is speculation as to the future consequence of rules formulated to apply to a future event.[73]

At the same time in Athens,[74] a law of Drakon presents a discussion of homicide. As we have seen, this subject is within the realm of the

---

72 The law was almost certainly utopian and never applied in practice. Westbrook 1971a and 1986c.

73 If Aristotle is to be believed, a similar process took place a little later in the case of Solon, whose most famous measure was his *seisachtheia*, a retrospective cancellation of debts and debt-slavery on the universal Near Eastern pattern, but who in addition, "made the people free both at the time and *for the future* by prohibiting loans secured on the person" (Aristotle, *Ath. pol.* 6.1).

74 This is not the forum in which to discuss the vexed question of cultural connections between the ancient Near East and pre-classical Greece. Suffice it to say that from the

cuneiform law codes, rather than the edicts, except insofar as administrative aspects are concerned.[75] Drakon's law[76] concentrates heavily on administrative matters such as court procedure,[77] but there are also some provisions that appear to go to the substance of the law of homicide. In lines 13-19 the right to pardon a killer is assigned to various groups in order of priority. If correctly restored,[78] the provision following reads (lines 19-20): "And let those who killed previously [be bound by] th[is ordinance]." It would seem that the concept of a point in time at which the law comes into effect, so lacking in the law codes, is applied in an area formerly reserved to the latter.

Confirmation of the restoration and its interpretation comes from the Great Code of Gortyn, dated by scholars to the fifth century.[79] The code is preserved almost in its entirety, and in its form and content the traditional pattern of the cuneiform law codes can be recognized: a series of casuistic

---

Near Eastern perspective, early legal sources like Drakon's law and the Great Code of Gortyn are immediately recognizable as the culmination of a two-thousand-year-old tradition, rather than creations *ex nihilo* as some modern classicists (e.g., Gagarin 1986: esp. 62) seem to assume.

75   Cf. Telipinu 49: "And the matter of blood is as follows: he who does blood, it is what the owner of the blood (= avenging relative) says. If he says 'Let him die!' then let him die. If he says 'Let him pay ransom!' then let him pay ransom. But to the king, nothing." The paragraph is a banal recapitulation of the basic principles of homicide law as known not only in Hatti but throughout the ancient Near East (see Westbrook 1988d: 45-55). Only the last sentence, in which the king foregoes some privilege, possibly the right to a share of the ransom, is the operative section.

76   Edited by Stroud 1968. For the purposes of this argument it is assumed, with Stroud (1968: 60-64), that the extant text is an authentic copy of the original.

77   In surveying the early Greek inscriptional evidence, Gagarin perceptively notes (1986: 81) that "procedural concerns predominate in laws enacted before 500 B.C." The term "procedural" is perhaps too wide: the inscriptions discussed by Gagarin (1986: 81-96) concern the administration of justice—powers and duties of officials and courts—not, for example, how the parties are to conduct their case. IC 4.1-40 (see Gagarin 1986: 95) may be a price list. In other words, these early Greek laws reveal the same limitations in subject matter as the Near Eastern edicts.

78   Stroud (1968) follows earlier scholars in restoring on the basis of Demosthenes, *Contra Markartatum* 43.57.

79   Discussed by Willetts 1967: 8. As Willetts notes, however, the inscription could be sixth century, and the law of Crete seems to be more conservative than that of contemporary Athens.

provisions deal mostly with property and family law, discussing the alternatives to each hypothetical situation in the systematic method of Mesopotamian science.[80] In col. XI 19-23, however, after a series of provisions on adoption, the following is stated:

> And the rules shall be thus from the time this inscription is written, but as regards matters of previous date, in whatever way one holds (property), whether by adoption or from an adopted son, there shall still be no liability.

As in the case of Drakon, there is a consciousness of a point at which the law comes into effect, but here the context is unambiguously a traditional law code and the subject matter substantive law. Just as the Deuteronomic law extended the scope of the edict, therefore, so these Greek laws extend the scope of the law code, by grafting onto it one of the central characteristics of the edict. It is this combination of the two ancient sources of law that turns the law code into a statute whose text may be cited as authoritative in a court of law.

A further step, outside the scope of our inquiry, was still needed to achieve legislation in the modern sense, namely the analytical method of classical Greek philosophy, which enabled lawmakers to express the rules in abstract general categories and to define terms.[81] These early Greek and Hebrew statutes therefore represent an intermediate stage, and in some respects a direct link, between the cuneiform and classical systems of law.

In conclusion, it should be stressed that the importance of the cuneiform law codes must not be underestimated. They represent a considerable intellectual achievement, and as such made a vital contribution to the process that led to the law codes of late antiquity and thence to modern western statutes. At the same time, if we are to interpret their provisions correctly, their limitations should be recognized. The most salient of these is that they were not normative legislation.

---

80 In fact, as Ducos points out, it is slightly more sophisticated in its method, attempting to provide a general rule followed by a series of particular cases (1978: 67-68).

81 See Westbrook 1988a: 119-21. On the transformation in general, see Lloyd 1970: 1-15.

4

What Is the Covenant Code?

Abstract

Many biblical scholars tend to see the Covenant Code as the result of a process of literary revision and editing. This process, they say, corresponds to the development of law in ancient Israel from a primitive, family-based structure to a more sophisticated legal system in the monarchical period. This approach, however, fails to account for the literary-legal tradition in which the Covenant Code finds its heritage—namely, the cuneiform law-code tradition. When seen within that context, the ostensible discrepancies within the code do not require the kinds of source- and form-critical explanations previously offered. Rather, the Covenant Code presents itself as a coherent document, which scholars should expect to contain clear and understandable laws.

It has long been recognized that the "Book of the Covenant" (Exod 20:22-23:19) forms a separate entity that has been inserted into the surrounding narrative. While the whole entity consists of normative provisions, it is easy to recognize a further section within it which may more properly be described as a law code, in that its norms are justiciable in a human (as opposed to divine) court and carry sanctions enforceable by such a court. The section in question is usually taken to extend from Exod 21:1 to 22:16, but I would include the provisions of 22:17-19 since, although religious in character, they are likewise amenable to normal human jurisdiction, with corresponding sanctions. It is this section, the "Covenant Code" strictly so called, that is the subject of this study, although many of

* Originally *published* in *Theory and Method in Biblical and Cuneiform Law: Revision, Interpolation and Development* (ed. B. M. Levinson; JSOTSup 181; Sheffield: Sheffield Academic Press, 1994 [repr. Sheffield: Sheffield Phoenix Press, 2006]), 13-34. Copyright © Sheffield Phoenix Press. Used by permission.

the opinions that will be considered have been expressed in terms of the wider entity.

Legal interpretation of the code's provisions is fraught with difficulties. Contradictions appear to abound between the various laws and even within them, while abrupt changes of form and syntax seem to break the thread of discourse. Even distinctions made by the laws themselves are hard to appreciate: why should the penalty for theft of an animal vary according to whether the thief has it alive in his possession or has slaughtered or sold it? Traditional commentaries employed numerous devices and rationalizations to arrive at a logical and systematic legal corpus; but the consensus of modern scholars is that the explanation for these discrepancies is historical. They are the result of a long and complex legislative process whereby the original text suffered repeated amendments and accretions in order to take into account developments in the law. Numerous studies of both the code as a whole and of individual provisions have adopted this approach, which may be illustrated by the following examples.

Biblical scholars have, inevitably, applied to the Covenant Code the methods developed with respect to other genres of biblical literature such as psalms and narratives, in particular that of form criticism.[1] The fundamental study remains that of Alt, who distinguished between two types of laws on the basis of form: casuistic and apodictic.[2] The former, characterized by an if-clause ("If men fight . . .") were taken to derive from the cuneiform law code tradition, via putative Canaanite codes, whereas the latter, characterized by concise commands ("Whosoever strikes a man and he dies shall be put to death"), were the indigenous product of ancient Israel. The two types of laws differed not only as to source but as to character, casuistic laws being dry, practical, and secular, apodictic laws being emotional imperatives dealing with religious and moral issues. More important still is their difference in substance. For example, the casuistic law of homicide took into account the culprit's intention; the apodictic law imposed talionic punishment.

Alt's claim of Israelite uniqueness for apodictic law has not been universally accepted, but his basic distinction has, together with the notion

---

1   See Baentsch 1892; Jepsen 1927; Jirku 1927.
2   Alt 1934.

that the two forms are somehow different in source and content.[3] Further-more, the existence in the Covenant Code of both forms closely intermingled and sharing features that were supposedly unique to one or the other (as, for example, the use of YHWH in a casuistic law in Exod 22:10) obliged Alt to assume a complex process of redactional fusion, with secondary insertions and with deletions.[4] Again, this "patchwork quilt" image of the law code has remained a necessary element in the historical explanation of its provisions.

Thus Otto in a recent monograph attributes to the two forms different origins within the internal history of Israelite law.[5] Apodictic law arises from the jurisdiction of the *paterfamilias* within the family or clan. He has power to punish individual members, if necessary with the death penalty. The apodictic form, then, reflects the curt commands of the *paterfamilias*.

Casuistic law, on the other hand, arose from disputes between families within a tribe. It was not concerned with individuals although the dispute may have been triggered by individuals. Jurisdiction was that of the local court, which acted as an arbitrator. It had no coercive powers, since set-tlement of the dispute ultimately depended on the agreement of the two families. Accordingly, all judgments were compensatory in nature, with the exception of blood vengeance, where the parties took justice into their own hands. The casuistic form, then, reflects a series of precedents as to when compensation is appropriate.

With the advent of the monarchy, society became more complex, and according to Otto, this led to two developments. Patriarchal jurisdiction was taken over by the courts, which thereby developed a casuistic criminal law. The law of theft, for example, moved from simple compensation to two-fold to four- and five-fold payment as the courts' jurisdiction became more penal. Secondly, casuistic law, which formerly had dealt with dis-putes between families on an equal footing, now had to deal with vertical disputes between rich and poor, which it achieved by developing a social law to protect the latter.

At the end of the process, therefore, there existed several independent bodies of law—casuistic civil law, casuistic criminal law, apodictic

---

3 See, e.g., T. Meek in *ANET³* 183 n. 24; Mendenhall 1954: 30; Williams 1964: 484-89.
4 Alt 1934 (1959): 294, 302-11.
5 Otto 1988c; see also Otto 1988a.

criminal law, and casuistic social law—which came together under the jurisdiction of the local court. Their ultimate fusion is reflected in the Covenant Code, which interweaves these various sources.

For example, the group of laws from Exod 21:33 to 22:14, which all contain the phrase "he shall pay" (*yĕšallēm*), can be seen to alternate between simple compensation and multiple compensation (= penalty).[6] An even more complex scheme of editing is proposed by Otto for 21:18-32.[7] Its core comprises two laws concerning a fight (vv. 18-19 and vv. 22-25). Both originally ended with payment, reflecting the early casuistic law's function as a compromise settlement. The interpretation of "life for life" in v. 23, however, gave v. 22 a new role: it introduced the death penalty into casuistic law, giving the local court the power of punishment. The interpolation of rules on the killing and the wounding of slaves (vv. 20-21 and vv. 26-27 respectively) after the two core laws added the dimension of social law. The interpolation of the talionic wounding rules (vv. 24-25) replaced compensation with punishment in all but a few special cases such as v. 18.

Other scholars have drawn different conclusions from the logic of legal development. In considering the theft provisions of Exod 21:37-22:3, Daube points out that the passage comprises three rules which are not in their logical order: (a) the thief who slaughters and sells, (b) the right to kill a thief breaking in, (c) the thief who has not yet slaughtered and sold.[8] The logical order would have been for (c) to precede (b).

The logical order was not followed, however, because originally the law consisted of the two provisions: (a) and (b), while (c) is a later amendment. It was appended and not inserted, as logic would require, because the law was too well known in its traditional order.

The reason for adding the later provision, according to Daube, was a development in the law of evidence. The original law contained a crude, objective test—theft was not proven until the stolen object had been used. Later, a more sophisticated test developed whereby the subjective intentions of the thief were considered. If it could be ascertained that he had the intention to misappropriate, then possession alone would be sufficient to establish theft.

6   Otto 1988c: 12-14.
7   Otto 1988c: 28-30.
8   Daube 1947: 74-101.

Similarly, Jackson attributes various features of the law concerning a pregnant woman to the incorporation by editors of reforms in the general law.[9] Thus the singular form "you shall give" in v. 23 was interpolated to restrict liability to a single individual, *wěnātan biplilîm* in v. 22 was interpolated to restrict the husband's claim by assessors, and, most subtly of all, the talionic wounding provisions in vv. 24-25 were added to change the context of the word *'āsôn* and thus shift its meaning from the death of the fetus to the death of the mother, without changing the original wording.

Finally, in his recent monograph dedicated to the Book of the Covenant, Schwienhorst-Schönberger proposes for the Covenant Code the model of a pristine casuistic code, the provisions of which underwent expansion at three stages by different redactors, the first being secular, the second religious, and the third Deuteronomistic.[10] Each stage reflects legal and social developments but is achieved only by interpolation in the previous text, not by amendment.

Thus, for example, in the deposit law (22:6-14), the pristine provision dealt only with injury or death to an ass, ox, or sheep entrusted or loaned (vv. 9, 10, 13).[11] The first redactor added the question of theft of goods deposited and a divine verdict procedure that included the aforementioned animals (vv. 6-8), while in v. 11 he covered for both categories the unresolved case of the depositee's responsibility where he is not the thief. The second redactor replaced the divine verdict with the YHWH oath (vv. 9-10), adding (*inter alia*) the generalizing words "any animal" so as to change the meaning of v. 8 from divine verdict to oath by giving it a new context. As with Jackson, Schwienhorst-Schönberger ascribes great subtlety to the biblical redactors.

The above authors and the many others who espouse a historical explanation of the Covenant Code differ greatly as to the details of historical development and its reflection in the text. Their method, however, is uniform. It is based on no empirical evidence but upon identification of allusions in the text itself by the application to it of certain basic premises. Those premises are difficult to formulate because they are more usually

---

9   Jackson 1975: 75-107.
10   Schwienhorst-Schönberger 1990: 234-38.
11   Schwienhorst-Schönberger 1990: 194-211.

assumed than stated, and they are not shared to the same degree by all scholars.

I would suggest that the following three represent the widest consensus:

1. The Israelite legal system underwent radical development from "primitive" law to a relatively sophisticated model.
2. The process is visible in the Covenant Code because the forms of its provisions are indicative of their content and/or source.
3. The process is also visible because of the manner of the code's editing. The pristine text, although it reflected primitive law, was clear and logical. The present text is neither, because the radicalism of its redactors in matters of content was matched by their conservatism in matters of form. It was possible to add to, or rearrange, existing laws, but difficult to delete any part of their text, and simply to redraft them was out of the question.

Let us now consider whether, in the light of evidence available, these premises are justified.

Primitive Law and Development

Legal historians of the nineteenth century attributed various "primitive" features to early law.[12] The most salient of those features were:

a) law exists between families, clans or tribes, but not between individuals;
b) redress for individual wrongs took the form of feud between the groups to which the culprit and victim belonged;
c) the courts acted as arbitrators between such groups, seeking to find a just settlement, but without the power necessary to enforce their judgments;
d) liability was strict, with no consideration of the culprit's intentions (so-called *Erfolgshaftung*).

12 Maine 1861.

Propositions of this kind constantly recur in scholars' analyses of the Covenant Code, without discussion of the evidence for them; they are taken as axiomatic.

It is not my purpose to enter into a general discussion of their validity, but merely to question whether the picture of early law that they present is at all applicable to the Israelite legal system, at least within the termini for composition of the Covenant Code.

Thanks to cuneiform records, evidence for the history of law in the ancient Near East now extends back to the early third millennium. The very earliest records, however, already reveal a highly organized legal system, whose courts have full coercive power and whose individuals have the capacity to make contracts. Nor are third millennium sources ignorant of the significance of intention in determining liability.[13] As is well known, the Sumero-Akkadian civilization that produced this legal system spread throughout Western Asia through the medium of cuneiform writing. Its influence is already attested in Syria in the third millennium, at Ebla, and legal documents drafted in Akkadian from Alalakh and Hazor show that not merely the writing but the legal culture itself was established in Syria-Palestine by the early second millennium.[14]

The implications for Israelite law are clear. Any primitive stage must either have predated the second millennium (at the very least) or reflect early Israel's total isolation from the surrounding societies. The first is a chronological impossibility, and the second, inherently improbable, is all the more so in the context of the Covenant Code.

Some earlier commentators such as Morgenstern sought to deny any connection between the Covenant Code and the cuneiform law codes, but their position has become untenable in view of the accumulation of parallels.[15] More than half of the Covenant Code's provisions have some parallel in one or more of the cuneiform codes, whether in the form of the same problem addressed or distinction applied, a similar rule, or an identical rule.[16] It is difficult to see how provisions that are so closely associated

---

13 CU 7 (edited by Yildiz 1981: 92, 96). The adulterer's ignorance of the woman's married status relieves him of liability.
14 Wiseman 1953; Hallo and Tadmor 1977.
15 Morgenstern 1930: 68 n. 70.
16 Paul 1970: 43-105.

with an outside source can at the same time be the product of internal development from an earlier primitive version.

The difficulty is seen by Otto, who by way of answer suggests that the cuneiform element in the Covenant Code is due not so much to direct influence as to the fact that Israelite law was part of a common legal culture of the ancient Near East. That culture merely forms the framework within which the Israelite and other legal systems develop.[17]

Otto's answer raises the whole question of legal development in ancient Near Eastern law. At first sight, it may seem obvious to assume that legal systems would change and develop considerably over hundreds, indeed thousands, of years. That, however, is an attitude derived from our own culture, where constant changes in technology, social structure, and ideology raise concomitant demands for reform of the law, demands which are met by the investment of considerable intellectual effort on the part of trained specialists.

The most striking feature of the cuneiform legal material, on the other hand, is its static nature. The basic pattern of contractual transactions found in Sumerian legal documents of the third millennium survives, differences of detail notwithstanding, throughout the cuneiform record.[18] Some contractual terms, indeed, survive even longer, passing into Aramaic and Demotic documents.[19] Continuity is no less evident in the law codes, where the same rules, tests, and distinctions recur in codes separated by hundreds of years. Of course, there are also discrepancies between the codes, but discrepancies do not necessarily betoken a significant development in the law.

It should be remembered firstly that the codes do not give anything approaching a complete account of their legal system or even of any given area of law. It is dangerous, therefore, to argue from the silence of a code on a particular point of law for its absence from that legal system.

Secondly, the circumstances of two cases are seldom the same. In applying rules to an amorphous set of facts, a court will have any number of

17 Otto 1988a: 366-67.
18 See *SRU* 43 (24th century); CT 8 22c (18th century; = Schorr 1913: no. 79); Petschow *MB Rechtsurkunden* 1 (14th century); SAA 6 98 (7th century); San Nicolò-Petschow *Bab. Rechtsurkunden* 17 (6th century).
19 Muffs 1969.

distinctions to make, as to status, wealth, intention, causation, remoteness of damage, etc. Casuistic codes cannot put into their paradigmatic cases every possible circumstance and will inevitably tend either to blur all distinctions if they are too general or to emphasize one distinction to the neglect of others if they are more specific. Patterns of emphasis may be seen in certain codes: between classes of society in Codex Hammurabi, between classes of animal in the Hittite Laws. Rudiments of the same distinctions can be seen in all the codes; differences between them are a matter of degree of emphasis.

Thirdly, differences between the codes may be more apparent than real. As an example I would cite the difference between physical and pecuniary punishments, which has long been seen as signaling the dividing line between primitive and developed law. The earlier view was that a change from physical to pecuniary punishments marked the crucial development from feud to law.[20] It was supported by the appearance of the former in Codex Hammurabi and the latter in the Hittite Laws. It was challenged when earlier codes than Codex Hammurabi were discovered, Codex Ur-Namma and Codex Eshnunna, which contained only pecuniary punishments. The development was then said to be from civil law (pecuniary) to criminal law (physical).[21]

There remained, however, the question of what line of development was followed. A general development of ancient Near Eastern culture could not apply because the movement was not chronological—the Hittites retained the "older" system of civil law. For the same reason, there could be no question of a slow and imperceptible development (as opposed to deliberate reform). In any case, the Hittites undoubtedly knew the text of Codex Hammurabi, and Codex Eshnunna predates Codex Hammurabi by about forty years only.[22] The answer was to make value judgments upon the civilizations in question: the Sumerians, Eshnunnans, and Hittites were more "primitive" than the Babylonians or the Assyrians.[23] Such judgments, however, were based solely on this one difference in their respective law codes; our knowledge of those cultures would demand no such conclusion.

---

20   Driver and Miles 1952: 501-502.
21   Diamond 1957.
22   Cardascia 1960.
23   Diamond 1957: 154-55. Cf. Finkelstein 1961: 96-99.

Imposing a developmental model on apparent differences between law codes entails assumptions about the surrounding culture and society that are not warranted by the empirical evidence. There is empirical evidence, however, that (in the guise of revenge and ransom) physical and pecuniary punishments could be two sides of the same coin, and on this basis we have argued elsewhere that the societies in question all enjoyed the same system of punishment throughout.[24] Where they differed was in the exact limits to be imposed on revenge and ransom—as represented in the codes by physical and pecuniary punishments respectively—and whether the latter was to take precedence over the former in the particular case. No evolution was involved, therefore, but an exercise of discretion that could vary from case to case, from court to court, and from system to system.

Fourthly, consideration must be given to the nature of the law codes themselves. If they were legislation in the modern sense, then they could be expected to furnish reforms as part of their intrinsic purpose. It has been persuasively argued, however, by Kraus and others that the law codes were essentially academic documents, which may accurately have described the law but did not prescribe it.[25] They were, therefore, conduits of tradition rather than of change.

Furthermore, with one important exception (the Hittite laws, to be discussed below), there is no consciousness of reform in the law codes. The kings who are their supposed authors do not boast of changes made in the system by the codes, nor is there any indication of their rules being valid from a particular point in time. The codes have a timeless quality, as perhaps befits an academic document. External evidence likewise gives no hint of awareness of the code's impact. The often monumental reforms posited by scholars find no echo in inscriptions, letters, or legal and administrative documents.

Given the fragmentary state of textual evidence, the preceding statement might be considered an unacceptable argument from silence were it not for the fact that we have ample evidence that a different genre of legal text was consciously seen as reforming the law. The royal edicts both proclaimed themselves as reforms, changing legal rules from a particular point in time, and were regarded in contemporary documents as having

24 Westbrook 1988d: 39-77.
25 Kraus 1960; Bottéro 1982.

such an impact, with corresponding reactions from persons affected by them.[26] Such edicts, however, were remarkable for the narrowness of their scope. Only three categories of reform are recorded in them: retrospective cancellation of debts, reorganization of the royal administration, and the fixing of prices (which in this context also means pecuniary penalties, including fixed limits on ransom). Any reforms, therefore, that are attributed to differences between law codes will only be credible if they fall within those three categories, pending further empirical evidence to the contrary.

This hypothesis as to the limits of reform can be tested by reference to the Hittite Laws, which contain two special features. Firstly, unlike the other codes, they do exhibit some consciousness of reform. The most common expression thereof is the much-repeated phrase—"formerly they gave x shekels; now he shall give y shekels"—in respect of payments by way of penalty.[27] It thus falls within the category of price-fixing and may possibly be recording the provision of an edict or edicts to that effect, especially in view of the other expression of reform, which actually narrates the legislative history of the measure.[28] In paragraph 55 we are told that the king's father in the assembly had altered the status of certain feudal tenants in response to their petition. This reform falls squarely within the category of administrative reorganization.

Secondly, we possess one tablet of the law code (KBo VI 4) that, by its language, appears to be later than the version recorded in the other copies. It contains numerous differences from the main version, and the

---

26 See the literature cited in Westbrook 1989a: 214-16.

27 See paragraph 9, where the king also relinquishes his share of the payment. Cf. the Edict of Uru-inimgina (Sollberger *Corpus* Ukg. 6; transl. in Cooper 1986: no. La 9.3).

28 Paragraph 92 replaces revenge for theft of bee-hives (by stinging) with a fixed ransom. This combines price-fixing with the court's function of setting a limit on revenge and ransom, which may sometimes lead it to give fixed ransom precedence over revenge. On the other hand, §166 replaces a ceremony whereby a man and oxen are killed with a sacrifice of sheep as substitutes. This would appear to be a purification ritual, unconnected with revenge, and the reform is therefore of a religious nature (cf. §196 and §199). The scope of reform in the religious sphere is a question that requires separate study. It should be noted, however, that the possibility of substitution of an animal for the culprit in the sacrifice was an integral part of the system, as attested in the biblical scapegoat ritual and even in early rabbinic sources. See Segal 1989: 107-18.

question thus arises whether those differences represent substantive reforms.[29]

The major difference again lies in the scale of payments by way of penalty. In some cases, the medium of payment has also been changed—from slaves or land into silver—but that is a matter of accountancy rather than law, since it must always have been possible to pay in silver as well as in kind. Where the amount of silver payable has been changed, however, we might seem to be in the presence of a substantive reform. Nonetheless, it is no more than price-fixing.

The second difference takes the form of additional circumstances not covered by the original protasis. They consist of variations, such as in the type of property lost,[30] the type of tax payable,[31] the type of victim,[32] or the type of land on which the offense was committed,[33] or of distinctions, such as those between provocation and negligence[34] or between temporary and disabling injury.[35] These variations and distinctions are not reforms at all, but scholarly refinement, using the characteristic academic method of the codes, of extrapolating variants from the original cases. Some of these variants, indeed, are themselves found elsewhere in the earlier version.

The third difference consists of omissions. Such is the fate of the phrase *parnassea suwaizzi* ("he shall push/peep(?) to his house"), which occurs frequently in the apodosis of paragraphs in the earlier version, but only once in the later version.[36] Both the meaning of the phrase, however,

---

29   In an earlier study, following (uncritically) the opinion of Goetze (1957: 110-11), I did indeed assume that the references to reduction of penalties in the Hittite Laws and the existence of KBo VI 4 in particular indicated substantive law reforms (Westbrook 1985a: 255-56). While rejecting that assumption here, I retain the view espoused by my earlier study that the law codes could have a practical application. I would only emphasize that they functioned as consultative documents rather than authoritative legislation. For the latter distinction, see Bottéro 1982: 435-38 and Westbrook 1989a: 202.

30   §XXXV (= §45 of the older version); cf. §III (= §5).

31   §XXXVII (= §47).

32   §IX (= §10).

33   §IV (= §6).

34   §III (= §5), §§V-VII (= §§7-8).

35   §§X-XI (= §§11-12).

36   §XII (= §13).

and the rationale for its being appended to specific laws remain obscure.[37] No conclusions can therefore be drawn as to the legal import of its omission from later parallels. In two instances an alternative circumstance is omitted from the protasis, thereby eliminating a distinction made by the earlier version. In the first instance, the case of a merchant killed abroad (as opposed to one killed in Hatti),[38] it is of no legal significance, but the second, concerning the month of pregnancy in which a miscarriage was caused, might signal a change in the law.[39] Since the sole consequence of the distinction, however, lay in the amount payable by way of penalty, we are once more in the realm of price-fixing.

The fourth difference consists in additional legal consequences. Thus where the earlier version mentions only that the offender is deemed a thief, the later version adds the penalty applicable.[40] For all we know, the same penalty may have been applicable in the earlier version, and if not, it is again a question of price-fixing. In the second example of this type, the king is granted a discretion over the amount of a certain type of feudal due.[41] If this were an innovation, then it falls within the sphere of administrative reform.

In summary, the Hittite Laws, which afford us a unique diachronic view of a cuneiform legal system, provide little evidence of substantive change, and such evidence as they do provide lies within the narrow categories of reform found in royal edicts.

This image of a static legal system should be less surprising if regard is had for the nature of the society that produced it. From the mid-third millennium to the end of the Bronze Age, the Near East saw no major advance in technology nor any radical change in social or political structure. Intellectual expression was dominated by Mesopotamian "science," a form of logic severely handicapped by inability to define terms, create general

---

37 Haase suggests that the phrase gives the judgment creditor the right to "look into the house" of the judgment debtor, i.e., to distrain upon his property (1980: 93-98). This theory does not explain, however, why a procedural facility, which should in principle be available to any judgment creditor, is expressly mentioned in only a limited number of delicts, nor why any law reform should wish to remove it in some, but not all, cases.

38 §III (= §5).

39 §§XVI-XVII (= §§17-18).

40 §XXXV (= §45).

41 §XXXIXb (= §47b).

categories, or reason vertically from the general to the particular.[42] A legal system cannot be more advanced than its social and intellectual environment: the social environment was hostile to change, while the intellectual environment lacked the tools to give legal expression to anything more than superficial reforms.

Beginning in the seventh century, the intellectual revolution documented in the Greek sources led to sweeping changes in the way that law was conceived and ultimately provided it with the intellectual tools for reforms to match the radical changes in social and political structures. The system that emerged remains the norm for us today. Its Near Eastern predecessor, on the other hand, was already a mature system when it first becomes accessible to us in Sumerian sources of the third millennium. The intellectual revolution that produced it lies further back in time, at a turning-point about which we can only speculate, whether it was the smelting of bronze, urbanization, or even the agricultural revolution. The common legal culture of the ancient Near East would not, then, have provided a framework for legal development in the Covenant Code.

The later biblical codes—the Deuteronomic and Priestly codes—share something of the intellectual ferment of contemporary Greek sources and thus some taste also of their new legal conceptions. The Covenant Code, on the other hand, although it cannot be dated with any confidence, looks back to the cuneiform codes of the second and third millennia. It is in the light of that long and stable tradition that the two remaining premises as to its form and composition are to be judged.

Forms in the Covenant Code

The predominant form in the Covenant Code is casuistic, as is characteristic also of its cuneiform predecessors. Seven laws are in apodictic form, grouped in two blocks: 21:12, 15-17, and 22:17-19. The question that concerns us is whether the difference in form is of *legal* significance, either because the laws derive from a different jurisdiction

---

42   For the application of Mesopotamian science to law, see Bottéro 1982: 425-35; and Westbrook 1988d: 2-5.

(foreign, patriarchal, sacral, etc.) or because they represent different stages of legal development.

It has been pointed out by scholars that apodictic forms, as defined by Alt, do occur in the cuneiform codes, albeit rarely.[43] Alt's hypothesis of a purely Israelite origin for apodictic law cannot, therefore, stand. Furthermore, it is hard to discern any pattern in the isolated instances of apodictic form in the cuneiform codes. In Codex Hammurabi, it occurs in paragraphs 36-40, all of which concern limitations on the rights of tenants over their feudal holdings. It might, therefore, be argued that its use is connected with its original function—administrative orders from the palace concerning its feudal tenants, especially since the only apodictic form in the Hittite Laws (paragraph 56) also concerns feudal tenants.[44] On the other hand, there are many similar provisions in the two codes which concern feudal tenants but are drafted casuistically. Codex Eshnunna, paragraphs 51-52, concerning slaves entering and leaving the city, might have some connection with the city administration, but no such connection is apparent in paragraphs 15-16, which place restrictions on the commercial activities of slaves and sons. The same can be said of the only apodictic provision in the Middle Assyrian Laws (A 40), listing the classes of woman who must or must not veil themselves in public. In sum, there is no obvious common factor in these diverse provisions in source or content and certainly no indication that they might represent types of jurisdiction or levels of legal development.

If the apodictic forms furnish no special rationale for their occasional use in the law codes, perhaps our inquiry should be in the opposite direction, namely as to why the *casuistic* form came to be the dominant form of the codes. It is not, after all, a natural form for a source of law. Judgments are based on actual, not hypothetical, facts and are rendered with reference to the parties in the case, in the form of a specific order. Such is the case, for example, in the various literary accounts of trials from Nippur, which, it has been suggested, may be sources for the law codes.[45] Royal decrees

---

43 See n. 3 above.
44 Cf. Yaron 1988b: 108. Mainly on the basis of form, Yaron divides the provisions of Codex Eshnunna into two groups: those derived from a decree and those based on precedent, while admitting the speculative character of the enterprise (1988b: 106-13).
45 Locher 1986: 93-109.

would also tend to be in the form of direct, if more general, orders. That is indeed the dominant form in administrative and debt-release edicts and in instructions to officials.[46] Price-fixing, on the other hand, would simply be by lists of the goods or services and their corresponding price, usually expressed as a statement of fact. Apart from the latter then, all sources of law would tend to be expressed in some kind of apodictic form.

The casuistic form was the quintessential "scientific" type of Mesopotamian literature, as attested in the omen and medical texts. It was the means whereby raw data could be cast into a generalized, objective form, stripped of any connections with circumstances irrelevant to their universal application. It was the nearest Mesopotamian science could come to expressing principles. The casuistic form, therefore, far from reflecting any particular source of law, was itself a process of editing, creating a uniform body of rules indifferent to their origins.

It would be naive, however, to conclude that a non-casuistic form always betokens an original legal source. The bulk of law in ancient Near Eastern societies was traditional law handed down from time immemorial. It was, however, regarded as having come from specific judgments, orders or the like, an assumption that could be expressed by giving a traditional rule the form of one of those sources.[47] This is why the apodictic rules of the cuneiform codes cannot be assigned to legal categories. The choice of form for the individual paragraphs of what was essentially a literary document, belonging (as we have argued above) to the genre "academic treatise," was not a legal one but depended on other factors, perhaps pedagogical or rhetorical. The casuistic form, for all its scientific credentials, was not always the ideal vehicle for the latter purposes, nor did all the cuneiform codes share the same desire for uniformity. Codex Hammurabi is the most extreme, placing even price lists in casuistic form, although the result is clumsy and unsuitable (§§268-277), while Codex Eshnunna (§§1-4, 7-8, 10-11, 14) and the Hittite Laws (§§178-185) present their tariffs as bald statements. At the other end of the spectrum, Codex Eshnunna pre-

---

46 See, e.g., the Edict of Ammi-ṣaduqa (edition in Kraus 1984: 168-83) and the Hittite Instructions to the Commander of the Border Guards (edition in von Schuler 1957: 41-52).

47 See Codex Hammurabi, epilogue, col. XLVII, lines 1-5; and compare Exod 21:1 itself, which attributes the code to judgments (*mišpāṭîm*) given by God.

sents a mixture of styles, which may more accurately represent the "peripheral" tradition to which the Covenant Code belongs. In contrast to the "core" tradition of southern Mesopotamia, which is a direct heir to Sumerian civilization, the Akkadian-speaking areas of northern Mesopotamia share with the rest of the fertile crescent, where cuneiform learning was acquired primarily through the medium of Akkadian (Susa, Nuzi, Hatti, Emar, Ugarit, Hazor, etc.), a tradition of legal drafting that is less austere and more heterogeneous.[48]

Turning to the apodictic laws of the Covenant Code, we see that they are no less diverse in content than their cuneiform counterparts, covering murder, striking or cursing parents, kidnapping, witchcraft, bestiality, and heretical sacrifice. The only unifying factor is that they are all very serious offenses, requiring the death penalty, but then so does the casuistically formulated case of the goring ox (Exod 21:29). Two of the offenses involve inner-family relations, which is a slim basis on which to conclude, as Otto does, that the apodictic form had its origins in inner-family jurisdiction.[49] The first group comprises private delicts involving a victim, while the second consists of victimless crimes, in which the public interest is engaged.

A further test of their unique status is whether these provisions have an equivalent in the cuneiform codes, and if so, whether those equivalents form any special category. Two laws, cursing parents and heretical sacrifice, have no equivalent, which might give them special status were it not for the other five.

The homicide rule of Exod 21:12, "He who strikes a man and he dies shall be put to death," is directly paralleled by the casuistically formulated paragraph 1 of Codex Ur-Namma: "If a man kills, that man shall be put to death."[50] The Sumerian law is couched in the same stark tones as the biblical law, with no mention of the question of intention—which is, I hasten to add, no evidence that intention was not taken into consideration.[51] Much has been made of the fact that the question of intention in the biblical law

---

48 See Muffs 1969: 17-23.
49 Otto 1988c: 31-33.
50 Edition in Yildiz 1981: 91, 95.
51 Codex Ur-Namma is particularly laconic, leaving out details that are supplied by parallels from later laws. For an example, see Westbrook 1990b: 550.

is couched in casuistic form immediately following upon the above apodictic rule, thereby opening the door to a distinction between the "primitive" strict liability of the apodictic law and the more enlightened casuistic law.[52] I would view the proposed distinction with skepticism, in the light of the *casuistic* cuneiform law above and in the light of paragraph 40 of Tablet A of the Middle Assyrian Laws. The latter begins with a series of apodictic commands concerning the veiling of women, which reveal themselves, however, to be no more than the necessary preamble to the casuistic part of the law, which lays down punishments for men who fail to report infringements of the veiling regulations. In the same way, the apodictic rule of Exod 21:12 can be seen as the necessary preamble to the casuistic rules of vv. 13-14, which distinguish between intentional and non-intentional homicide.

The cuneiform codes likewise furnish casuistic parallels for kidnapping (Codex Hammurabi 14: death), striking a parent (Codex Hammurabi 195: cut off hand), witchcraft (Middle Assyrian Laws A 47: death), and bestiality (Hittite Laws 187-188, 199-200: death or no liability, depending on animal). There is nothing in these parallels to suggest that they come from a special source or contain a special legal content. I conclude that the same must apply to the biblical provisions. As we have seen with the apodictic rules of the cuneiform codes, the reason for their formulation does not lie with legal considerations. Depending on the literary tradition, the same rule may be drafted casuistically, apodictically, or in some other fashion.

The Text of the Covenant Code

The idea of a conservative editing of the text, by exclusion, addition, and interpolation in order to make it comply with changes in the law has one certain historical model, indeed, a model of monumental proportions. The Digest of Justinian, from the sixth century C.E., one of the greatest achievements in the history of law, was just such a compilation. At that time, the writings of classical jurists from some three centuries earlier were cited in court as binding authority, which led to great confusion and incon-

---

52 E.g., Noth 1962: 180; Childs 1974: 470.

venience, since, on the one hand, much was no longer applicable to the conditions of the Byzantine empire and, on the other, they contained innumerable disputes and contradictions. Several committees were, therefore, charged with excerpting from those writings such material as could produce a relevant and coherent body of law. Under the guiding hand of a law professor, Tribonian, they completed the massive task in a mere three years but only at the cost of considerable tampering with their sources. Each excerpt was cited by author, work, chapter, and verse, but by editing, in particular by interpolation, the passage cited was brought into line with contemporary law. The process inevitably left inconsistencies in style and content which can be identified by modern scholars.

In the early years after the discovery of Codex Hammurabi, king Hammurabi was indeed regarded by some scholars as an early Justinian. An eminent legal historian schooled in Roman law, P. Koschaker, attempted to apply the techniques of that field to the cuneiform code. His approach lacked any historical justification, however; the peculiar circumstances of the late Roman Empire, its legal system, and its intellectual climate that led to the compiling of the Digest could not be reproduced in the second millennium B.C.E. Instead, apparent inconsistencies in the provisions of the cuneiform codes are progressively being dissipated through our growing understanding of their linguistic, cultural, and social background, due not least to the continuous stream of newly discovered cuneiform documents.[53]

By the same token, it is inappropriate and anachronistic to apply, consciously or unconsciously, the model of Justinian's Digest to the editing of

---

53   See Codex Hammurabi, paragraph 164, which Koschaker suggested was an interpolation because of its clumsy and over-elaborate discussion of a set-off mechanism (1917: 87 n. 6, 187-88). It was subsequently discovered, however, that the paragraph was in fact taking into consideration a certain marriage custom, in the light of which (and with a different interpretation of the syntax) the paragraph was well formulated and perfectly appropriate; for discussion and references, see Yaron 1988b: 176-79. The one case where Koschaker's approach is generally thought to have been vindicated is Codex Hammurabi, paragraph 125, where his postulated development of the law is said to have been confirmed by the subsequent discovery of Codex Eshnunna, paragraphs 36-37, containing an earlier, more "primitive" rule (Koschaker 1917: 26-33; see also Goetze 1956: 104; Yaron 1988b: 250-51; Otto 1988b: 4-16). All such comparisons, however, rely on translations that disregard certain difficulties in the text. See Westbrook 1994c.

the Covenant Code. The Bible has no background documentation like the cuneiform codes, but the Covenant Code has a ready substitute for such documentation in the cuneiform codes themselves, since it belongs to the same literary genre and the same intellectual tradition as the latter.

As we have seen, one of the cuneiform codes, HL, has at least two chronologically separate versions and can therefore provide explicit evidence of the process of editing that may be expected in texts of this genre.[54] While the two versions were seen to differ but little in substance, the same is not so for their form, which presents many variants. A good proportion may be dismissed as deriving from the peculiarities of the cuneiform script (variant spellings, use of Sumerograms) or of the Hittite language (use of active instead of medio-passive),[55] but some changes in language are more radical. For example, the earliest version's "strikes and wounds" (*hunikzi . . . istarninkzi,* §10) is replaced by "injures the head" (SAG.DU *hapallasai,* §IX). Of relevance here is Hoffner's discussion of a fragment of a version still earlier than the main text (§§164-166), written in the Old Ductus.[56] Although the two versions contain the same law, Hoffner points to considerable differences of language, which he ascribes to a desire by the later scribe to modernize archaic expressions. A more serious reason for change is provided by §IV of the later version, which extends the circumstances discussed to cover a murder committed on land outside the city. Accordingly the expression "in another city" (*takiya* URU-*ri*) in the earlier version (§6) is changed to "in another field and meadow" (*damedani* A.ŠÀ A.GÀR). Finally a most telling change of style occurs between §48 and §XL—from apodictic to casuistic.

The important point about these changes, and the much more frequent additions and omissions in the later text, is that they are achieved without disrupting the logic of the provision or the thread of their discourse in any way. Were there no extant earlier version of the text, one would scarcely be aware from the later versions that it had ever existed, the presence of scattered archaisms in the language being the only indication. It would

---

54 Among biblical scholars, only Schwienhorst-Schönberger has noticed this possibility. He employs it in a single, isolated instance, without considering the wider implications (1990: 121).

55 §§15, 16 = §§XIV, XV.

56 Hoffner 1981: 206-209.

certainly be impossible to reconstruct anything of the earlier version. The assumption, therefore, that the process of editing the Covenant Code left tell-tale traces in the form of inconsistencies can only be justified by reference to a model far removed from it intellectually and culturally, while a model that stands in the same intellectual tradition supports no such conclusions. At most, the tendency that we have seen in the later version of the Hittite Laws, after the method of cuneiform science, to add new circumstances might justify concluding that in the Covenant Code as well certain rules subsidiary to a main problem, such as the distinction between a warned and unwarned ox in the case of ox goring ox, were secondary accretions.[57] Unless, however, they signify some change in the substantive law, it is an arid exercise to speculate as to which components of a legal problem are "original" and which are a later accretion.

It could be argued that, the Hittite evidence notwithstanding, so special is the character of the biblical law and its role in the religious life of ancient Israel that its texts nonetheless acquired a canonicity that demanded more conservative editing. The Bible itself, however, attests to the contrary. There is a salient example within the Bible of the same law existing in an earlier and later version: the slave-release law of Exod 21:2-6 and Deut 15:12-18. The Deuteronomic version pays no respect to the earlier text, but changes the person of the verb and the identity of the slave and makes the transaction *ex latere venditoris* (from the seller's point of view) rather than *ex latere emptoris* (from the buyer's point of view).

Accordingly, the premise of a conservative process of editing is not supported by empirical evidence, external or internal. The present text must be presumed to be clear and coherent. At most, one might argue for the minor editorial emendations and glosses that could be found in any genre of text.

Conclusions

Conventional wisdom regards the Covenant Code as an amalgam of provisions from different sources and periods, the fusion of which has left tell-tale marks in the form of various inconsistencies in the text. That view is

---

57   Cf. Schwienhorst-Schönberger 1990: 121.

based upon assumptions as to the history of the law and its expression which are unsupported by empirical evidence. At most, they can rely on inappropriate models from the classical and later periods.

Such models may have been acceptable in the last century, but since the discovery of massive quantities of cuneiform sources, they are no longer so. Interpreters of the Covenant Code need to come to terms with the fact that it is part of a widespread literary-legal tradition and can only be understood in terms of that tradition.[58] The starting point for interpretation must therefore be the presumption that the Covenant Code is a coherent text comprising clear and consistent laws, in the same manner as its cuneiform forbears. Apparent inconsistencies should be ascribed to the state of our ignorance concerning the social and cultural background to the laws, not necessarily to historical development and certainly not to an excess of either subtlety or incompetence on the part of their compiler.

---

58   See now Malul 1990: 140-43, arguing for a close literary dependence of the Covenant Code on the Mesopotamian law codes.

5

Codification and Canonization

Abstract

First millennium codes from the Mediterranean basin, such as the Twelve Tables and the Pentateuchal codes, were the product of an ancient proto-scientific tradition from Mesopotamia which produced treatises on the law in the form of lists of casuistic examples. Like their cuneiform forerunners, they were originally read as descriptive and not prescriptive sources of law, because the concept of the legislative text as an autonomous source of law had not yet been developed. However, the intellectual revolution that produced analytical jurisprudence and jurists also led to a change in their character. They were "canonized" by having attributed to them the status of legislation and of autonomy. They could thus be read as if they were a comprehensive and prescriptive body of rules.

Introduction

A law code has two requisites: firstly that it be a law and secondly that it be a code. The first means that the text must be a normative source of law which a court is bound to obey, not merely a source of information about the law, however much respect the court may have for its sagacity. The second requirement means that it must be an exclusive source of the law, at least in the area which it purports to regulate (e.g., civil code, criminal code). Even if some exception is made in practice, the theoretical concept remains necessary to interpretation of the code. Its text is deemed to be a comprehensive statement of the relevant law, so that anything omitted from the text is omitted from the law—a sort of legal *horror vacui*.

* Originally published in *La Codification des lois dans l'antiquité: Actes du Colloque de Strasbourg, 27-29 Novembre 1997* (ed. E. Lévy; Travaux du Centre de Recherche sur le Proche-Orient et la Grèce antiques 16; Paris: De Boccard, 2000), 33-47. Used by permission.

Early "Law Codes"

The earliest known legal systems are those of the ancient Near East, the documentary record of which stretches from the 31st to the 3rd century B.C.E. Scattered through this record, and indeed extending beyond it, is a distinctive genre of texts known to modern scholars as law codes. There are seven extant examples in cuneiform script, and several more from the periphery of cuneiform culture, such as the biblical codes, the Laws of Gortyn, the Laws of Drakon, and the Twelve Tables.[1] Did these documents meet the above criteria? Let us begin with the best-known example, Codex Hammurabi.

In the epilogue to his code, king Hammurabi appears to claim both the properties of law and code for its provisions. He states:

> Any man wronged who has a case, may he . . . have read to him the inscription of my stela; may he hear my words sublime and may my stela reveal the case to him. May he see his judgment and his mind be eased . . . (col. XLVIII, lines 3-19).

And a little further on:

> In the future, may any king who arises in the land keep the just words that I have written on my stela. May he not change the judgments of the land that I judged, the decisions of the land that decided . . . (col. XLVIII 59-72).

---

1   The cuneiform codes were: Codex Ur-Namma (Sumerian, c. 2100 B.C.); Codex Lipit-Ishtar (Sumerian, c. 1900 B.C.); Codex Eshnunna (Akkadian, c. 1770 B.C); Codex Hammurabi (Akkadian, c. 1750 B.C.); Middle Assyrian Laws (Akkadian, 14th century); Hittite Laws (Hittite, various copies from 17th to 12th century); Neo-Babylonian Laws (Akkadian, 7th century). The Pentateuch was regarded by Rabbinical tradition as containing 613 laws, comprising both religious prescriptions and temporal rules. Modern scholars refer to the two main clusters of rules in the narrative as the Covenant Code (Exod 20:22-23:33, esp. chapters 21-22, where laws on temporal matters are concentrated) and the Deuteronomic Code (temporal laws concentrated mostly in chapters 15 and chapters 21-25 of Deuteronomy). The Deuteronomic Code is generally dated to the 7th century B.C.E. and the Covenant Code two or three centuries earlier.

We should be careful, however, not to import our own cultural and juridical conceptions into the text. Let us begin with the idea of exhaustiveness that the first of the above passages appears to claim.

Exhaustive Codes?

The provisions of Codex Hammurabi are formulated as a series of casuistic sentences. This form, characteristic of all the law codes, marks it as belonging to a wider literary genre, namely that of Mesopotamian "science." By the third millennium B.C.E., the Mesopotamians had developed a technique for organizing knowledge by compiling lists of like examples: of flora, fauna, professions, grammatical forms, etc. A more sophisticated type of list consisted of cases: medical symptoms and their diagnosis, omens and their significance, legal problems and their solution.[2] They were expressed in a hypothetical form that for the Mesopotamians was the hallmark of their scientific method: e.g., "if X does Y, his punishment shall be Z."

Mesopotamian science must have been a considerable improvement on whatever system of thought had preceded it, for it came to dominate, along with other aspects of Mesopotamian civilization, the whole of the ancient Near East (with the partial exception of Egypt). The genre of casuistic law codes was one aspect of this domination, and one in which it spread even further, into the Mediterranean Basin. A brief examination of the contents of the Mediterranean law codes, as opposed to native accounts of their origins, immediately reveals their dependence in form and content on jurisprudential traditions that can be traced back to Sumer of the third millennium B.C.E.[3]

Compared with classical or modern methods of organizing knowledge, however, the Mesopotamian approach was primitive, a proto-science. In particular, it lacked the ability to formulate general principles or abstract categories. Hence it was unable to reason vertically; it could only proceed horizontally by cumulating examples. Accordingly, neither Codex Hammurabi nor its fellow codes could ever amount to a comprehensive

2   See Bottéro 1982.
3   See, e.g., Westbrook 1988a.

statement of the law; their lists of casuistic examples could not hope to be exhaustive, except at the point of infinity.

How then, could Hammurabi purport to provide every possible answer to the perplexed litigant? He felt perfectly justified in his claim, because his scientific standards were very different from our own. Certain methods were employed by Mesopotamian science to compensate for its own limitations, so that, in native eyes at least, its lists met the requirements of comprehensiveness. The examples were consciously grouped by topic, as we know from a native edition of Codex Hammurabi, which gives subheadings to groups of paragraphs, such as "Rules of House, Field, and Orchard" and "Rules of Soldier and Fisherman" (types of feudal tenants).[4] Note that the headings themselves are not strictly analytical, but list examples. Within topics, the choice and arrangement of examples was designed to place markers at suggestive points—sometimes at the very center of the topic but most often at its periphery—so as to indicate (if not to delineate) its boundaries.[5]

A good example of this technique is to be found in the opening paragraphs of Codex Hammurabi itself:

1 If a man accuses a man of murder and does not prove it, his accuser shall be killed.

2 If a man accuses a man of witchcraft and does not prove it, the one accused of witchcraft shall go to the river and leap the river. If the river overcomes him, his accuser shall take his house; if the river purifies that man and he is saved, the one who accused him of witchcraft shall be killed, and the one who leapt the river shall take the house of his accuser.

3 If a man in a lawsuit proffered false testimony and did not prove what he said, if that case is a capital case, that man shall be killed.

4 If he proffered testimony on grain or silver, he shall bear the penalty of that case.

5 If a judge judges a case, renders a verdict, and has a sealed document drafted, and subsequently changes his verdict, they

---

4 Edition in Finkelstein 1967.
5 Cf. Eichler 1987.

shall prove that judge to have changed his verdict, and he shall pay twelve-fold the claim in that case . . . .

The topic is clearly procedure in litigation. The five paragraphs cover the topic by the simple technique of chronological sequence: initial claim, trial, judgment. At each stage examples are given which illustrate misconduct, some common, others not so. Although only a small sample of possible wrongdoing and of types of claim is given, the parameters of the topic are set and the principles by which other cases within its ambit will be decided are at least adumbrated, if not expressed.

There is thus a considerable gap between the subjective perceptions of the ancient authors as to the exhaustive nature of their work and our evaluation according to modern criteria. It is in the light of this gap that the second passage from Hammurabi's epilogue, referring to his code as a text to be obeyed by future kings, should be considered.

Normative Legislation?

There has been much debate as to whether the ancient Near Eastern law codes were normative legislation at all.[6] It has been noted that they are never cited in the manner of modern laws, but that argument has been dismissed as an argument from silence.[7] A second argument arises from the "scientific" character of the texts. A scientific work is a work of reference: it may be consulted, but it does not stipulate, as does a law. Again, it may be countered that although the ancient law codes were the product of science, they became legislation by virtue of their publication by a king. I wish to raise a third, more radical, argument against the legislative character of the ancient codes. It relates not to the way they were *written* but the way that they, and all other legal documents, were *read*. In my view, Mesopotamian jurisprudence did not read legal texts in the same way as we do. They did not treat them as autonomous sources.

6 For a recent summary of the arguments, see Renger 1994.
7 Renger 1994: 35.

Legal Interpretation and Textual Autonomy

A vital element in the status of modern legislation is that the words of the text are the ultimate point of reference for its meaning. They can be elucidated with the assistance of *travaux préparatoires* or other evidence of the will of the lawgiver, but the lawgiver could never simply declare, for example, that the text did not properly reproduce his intention and should be disregarded. The reason is that the text is not mere evidence of the order of the lawgiver; once promulgated, it becomes the lawgiver itself, the messenger as well as the message. Consequently, specially trained experts are needed to "read" its provisions correctly and understand its words, to introduce that much-maligned practice of *legalistic* interpretation.

In the ancient Near East, lawyers did not yet exist as a learned profession.[8] This curious absence may be explained in part by the fact that the conceptual basis for their discipline was still lacking. Those same inadequacies of Mesopotamian science that shaped the composition of their law codes also circumscribed their reading of legal texts. In particular, one inadequacy not yet mentioned, namely the inability to *define* concepts, was of vital significance. One of the key instruments of *legal* interpretation of texts—definition—was not available to them. More significant, however, was the status of legal texts themselves within the constitutional structure of ancient states: they had not yet attained sufficient autonomy to require a special discipline for their interpretation.

Let us begin with those documents the status of which we can be relatively certain. It is well established that private legal documents such as contracts and testaments were of evidentiary value only: they were the protocol of an oral transaction.[9] Even the most sophisticated of contractual documents, international treaties, were no more than records of an oral oath ceremony, and their drafting was a triumph of the scribe's, not the lawyer's, art.

---

8   The correspondence of scholars with Assyrian kings of the 7th century B.C.E. names five scholarly disciplines: *ṭupšarru* "astrologer/scribe," *bārû* "haruspex/diviner," *āšipu* "exorcist/magician," *asû* "physician," and *kalû* "lamentation chanter." Parpola 1993: xiii–xiv.

9   Already pointed out by San Nicolò 1931: 162-63.

The same may even have been true of records of unquestionably legislative acts. There is plenty of evidence in letters and contracts of rulers making orders and of courts obeying them. But those orders, even when committed to writing, did not stray far from their author, either in scope or duration. Decrees of kings did not set up general rules of permanent validity affecting the general population, i.e., rules of the type found in the law codes. The reason for this is that they could not establish for themselves an existence that would outlive the king's own will. Ultimately, cases would be referred back to the king, not to the decree. Thus the most sophisticated example of ancient Near Eastern legislation, the royal debt-release decree, which was solemnly proclaimed, affected the whole population, and was recorded in a lengthy text, was retrospective. It demonstrated the king's ability to impose his will on past acts. Subject to the restraints of justice, there was no guarantee that an order of the king relating to the future would not be replaced by a contrary order relating to the past, so undoing all that had been done by the first. In these circumstances, the written text could not be more than evidence of the king's order; it never become independent of that order.

Between these two types of legal source lie the "law codes." Their structure made no pretense of being anything but an academic treatise, the context of their publication, in those texts that provide one, was an *apologia*, and nothing in letters or contracts refers to their being obeyed.[10] It is unlikely, therefore, that their text would have had an independent status.

As was the case with comprehensiveness, the limits of Mesopotamian conceptualization provide the cultural context for understanding Hammurabi's claims. Hammurabi expected future kings to follow the words on his stela because they were evidence of his wise judgments, which resolved every case that could possibly exist, not because the stela was law independent of Hammurabi. On the contrary, the same curses that were heaped upon wicked future kings for erasing the words of the stela applied to a king who merely erased the *name* of Hammurabi and substituted his own.[11]

---

10 On the law as royal apologia, see Finkelstein 1961: 103-104.

11 "If that man pays no heed to my words which I wrote on my stela, disregards my curses, does not fear the curses of the gods, and annuls the judgments that I judged,

If this understanding is correct, the reason for the striking absence of all reference in the ancient Near Eastern sources to citation of the law codes in law courts is not the existence of some oral practice which has not happened to surface in the extant written sources (a perfectly feasible possibility), but a fundamental lack of the necessary conceptual basis: legalism.

The total absence of legalism, being a negative proposition, is impossible to prove and, whatever its heuristic value, may be too extreme. It is possible that, as with other areas of theoretical reasoning, the Mesopotamians had some inkling of a text's potential for semantic manipulation but failed to develop it.[12] A search of the cuneiform sources—not merely the legal ones—for evidence of legalistic reasoning brings to light some straws in the wind. From the early second millennium B.C.E., there are a few references in Babylonian contracts and in Assyrian letters and court verdicts to actions to be taken "in accordance with the words of the stela." The city council of Assur in particular uses this formula to refer to what appear to be orders previously made by it.[13] Nonetheless, the words themselves are never given and are never the subject of dispute. It is impossible to determine from the bare formula whether the written text was anything more than a means of disseminating information.

The copious literature relating to omens might be expected to have provided a focus for legalistic reasoning. The omen lists bear a close formal resemblance to the law codes, they apply the same scientific method, and they are analogous to judgments in the sense that they are predictions by divine rulers as to future events within their control. Furthermore, since gods are eternal, an omen will remain valid forever, i.e., the same ominous sign will always have the same significance. Thus it has the potential for becoming independent of the god whose will it represents. In the seventh century, Assyrian kings consulted experts who in turn consulted canonical lists in order to establish the ominous significance of astronomical or other phenomena. Nonetheless, the closest that the experts came to interpreting

---

replaces my words, removes my engraved image, erases my inscribed name and writes in his name..." (col. XLIX, lines 18-35).

12 Cf. Neugebauer's assessment of the achievements and limitations of Babylonian mathematics in Neugebauer 1969: 29-52.

13 For references, see Veenhof 1995.

the lists as independent sources was to suggest that omens predicting defeat in battle applied to an enemy land rather than the Assyrian king. Even here they showed a lack of confidence, advising the king to take apotropaic measures, as if the god could not be relied upon to follow the diviner's interpretation.[14]

There is, however, one definite reference to the power of the written word. King Esarhaddon wished to rebuild Babylon, destroyed by his father, Sennacherib. He tells us: "He (the god Marduk) wrote the time of its lying waste as 70 years, but quickly merciful Marduk's heart calmed down, and he turned it upside down and ordered its rebuilding within 11 years."[15] Although represented as the god changing his mind, it appears to be an allusion to the Assyrian king turning the tablet round so that the same signs read 10+1 instead of 60+10. If so, the text was regarded as an immutable expression of the god's order and could therefore be reinterpreted, albeit in a crude and mechanical fashion.

New Developments

The Assyrian system of the seventh century B.C.E. represents the ultimate refinement of Mesopotamian science. Although in its final stages it drew close to the creation of analytical categories, it failed to attain them and thus failed to provide the basis for analytical jurisprudence.[16] From the Mediterranean littoral, on the other hand, new ideas were emerging that gave exciting possibilities for the development of law.

14 E.g., SAA 10 362 (see Parpola 1993: no. 362), lines 14-18 : "If Jupiter becomes visible in the path of the Anu stars: the crown prince will rebel against his father and seize the throne. The path of the Anu stars (means) Elam; it pertains to Elam. Nevertheless, they should (strengthen) the guard and perform the relevant apotropaic ritual." Some hint of legalistic interpretation might also lie in the question and answer concerning another omen: "Does (the omen) '(If something) passes between the legs of a man' apply to something that came out from underneath a chariot? It does apply."

15 Borger 1956: 15, no. 10a.

16 A Neo-Assyrian learned commentary on extispicy, *Multābiltu*, finally expresses the rules of association between physical conditions of the entrails and their application to human life. It consists of three columns which read: "If length/fulfillment/(casuistic example); if protrusion/fame/(example); if thickness/strength/(example) . . . ." See Jeyes 1980: 23-24.

Firstly, legislation became detached from the legislator. In the book of Deuteronomy (generally dated to the seventh century), the ultimate prerogative of the king, to decree a cancellation of debts, is made automatic and cyclical (15:1-11). The tradition that Solon, after proclaiming such a decree, precluded himself from doing so again by abolishing debt-slavery, belongs to the same trend.[17] The process of detachment was perfected in the Greek cities, where it went hand in hand with the development of new forms of government. It has been argued that the change in terminology from *thesmos* (the decree of an individual ruler) to *nomos*, which by the fourth century meant written statute, marks the change to a democratic attitude.[18] By then it had become standard practice in Athenian courts for judges and juries to swear an oath to decide according to the *nomoi*, referring to the written texts invoked before them by forensic orators (Demosthenes, *In Timocratem* 149-151). What gave the *nomoi* their status was not their publication by or association with a ruler, but their validation by passage through a legitimate political process.

In this way, the text of legislation came to be regarded as having a life of its own, independent of the human agent who had produced it. Accordingly, Socrates could imagine the laws (*nomoi*) personified asking him, "Are you not intending by what you are trying to do (i.e., escape from custody) to destroy us, the laws . . . ?" (*Crito* 11). The book of Daniel (written in the second century B.C.E.) dramatically projects this new attitude back into the Near East with its description of king Darius' decree, which, "according to the law of the Medes and Persians," once written down might not be changed, even by the king himself (Dan 6:9).

The second, interrelated, development was that Greek philosophy provided the means whereby truly comprehensive laws might be formulated. New methods of analytical reasoning such as division into categories (*diaíresis* and *merismós*) and definition (*lógos tes ousías*) enabled laws to be formulated in a vertical manner, with subsidiary rules being derived from general principles, and categorization ensuring that those principles covered the whole of a given field of law.

---

17   Plutarch, Solon XV.3.
18   Ostwald 1969: 158-60; MacDowell 1978: 44.

Canonization

If the promise of such new methods was not immediately fulfilled, it was because they did not fall upon a vacuum. The societies of the Mediterranean basin not only had a long and settled tradition as regards their substantive law, they also had an equally venerable tradition as regards its theoretical formulation. It looked to a fund of casuistic wisdom, compiled by the methods of Mesopotamian science. Local versions drew in varying measure upon a repertoire of traditional legal problems developed originally by Mesopotamian jurisprudence, e.g., the goring ox, the adulteress caught *in flagranti*, the thief breaking in by night, the talionic response to physical injuries.[19] In some cases parts of this casuistic fund of traditional wisdom existed in written form. The latter, none other than the ancient law "codes," enjoyed great prestige and in some instances may have been regarded as comprehensive, by the less exacting standards of Mesopotamian science. Traditional law, especially if concretized in a law code, could not be swept aside; it could only be reformed and reformulated piecemeal.

The task fell not to philosophers, but to an entirely new learned profession—the jurists. By applying the methods of Greek philosophy, they were able to read old sources "legalistically" and thus turn them into comprehensive legislation. Their approach was therefore to "canonize" existing texts, i.e., to read them as if they were law codes created on the basis of the new legal science. For this purpose, the old code would be given the status of *normative legislation* and a suitable historical pedigree, namely promulgation at a critical juncture in the early history of the nation (not at the very beginning, but at the politically appropriate beginning).

Two parallel examples are the Pentateuch and the Twelve Tables. In the first case, several codes, or more probably fragments of codes or of an oral canon, were inserted into an historical narrative which located its promulgation at a convocation in the desert prior to Israel's occupation of the promised land, by no less than God himself.[20] Rabbinic jurists went further by deeming it the basis of all Jewish law (while admitting the existence of an oral code alongside it). In the second case, the Twelve Tables

---

19 See Westbrook 1988a: 91-118.
20 Cf. the legend reported by Aristotle that Locrian law was first codified by Zaleucus, who received the laws from Athena (Frag. 548 Rose).

were referred to by classical jurists simply as *lex*, "the statute," and (while admitting the existence of an oral tradition) were regarded as the "*fons omnis publici privatique iuris*" (Livy, 3.34). The code was said to have been promulgated at a suitably critical moment in the early Republic (not during the monarchy, of course) for a suitably worthy social cause. Its form and content, it is to be noted, give no hint of any of this; they mark the code as a typical product of Mesopotamian science, in the same peripheral tradition as the biblical codes and Codex Eshnunna.

Being regarded as comprehensive legislation, the casuistic paragraphs of the old codes were interpreted as if they had been drafted by a philosopher. Cicero, who spans the two worlds of philosopher and jurist, unwittingly provides us with an insight into the jurists' attitude when he tries to explain how Greek philosophical discourse may be used for legal argumentation. The examples that he adduces to illustrate *genus* and *forma* (= species), *divisio* (= *diaíresis*), *partitio* (= *merismós*), and *definitio* are not from some current juristic treatise or recent legislation, where their influence might be expected to be at its most compelling, but from that (already in Cicero's day) venerable antiquity, the Twelve Tables.[21]

Too little has been preserved of the text of the Twelve Tables for it to furnish a reliable control of the reverse process, namely extrapolation from casuistic examples to general categories. The parallel Jewish sources, on the other hand, preserve the full text of both the original "code" and its reinterpretation at the hands of the jurists. For example, the so-called "Covenant Code" in Exodus 21-22 contains four different cases of wrongful damage scattered through its provisions: a goring ox, an ox or ass that falls into a pit, cattle that trespass on a neighbor's field, and a fire that spreads to a neighbor's field. In the hands of the Rabbinic jurists these were transformed into a code of the law of wrongful damage:

> The four heads of damage are: the ox and the pit and the devourer and the fire. The ox is not like the devourer, and the devourer is not like the ox, nor are both these, which are living, like the fire, which is not living. Nor are all these, whose nature is to go forth

---

21 *Topica*, esp. 2.9-10; 3.13-14; 4.26-28. The formal application of the Greek classifications by Roman jurists has been studied by Nörr 1972: esp. 45-53. Cf. Mélèze-Modrzejewski 1993.

and cause damage, like the pit, whose nature is not to go forth and cause damage. What is the same in them is that their nature is to cause damage and that you are responsible for guarding them, and when they cause damage, the one who caused it is liable to pay compensation with the best of his land (Mishnah, *Bava Qamma* 1.1).

Individual cases thus became *genera*, under which other traditional cases could be classified as if they were subsidiary rules. In the light of this example, one should perhaps be cautious in assuming that rigid bi-polar distinctions of classical Roman law, such as that between *furtum manifestum* and *furtum nec manifestum*, existed in the same form in the Twelve Tables, and wary of reconstructions based on that assumption.[22] If the fragmentary reference in the Twelve Tables to theft *quod nec manifestum erit*[23] was no more than an isolated allusion to a special set of circumstances, then the classical assumption that it was already then an exclusive category to which two-fold damages always applied might also be questionable.[24]

Once a casuistic rule is regarded as theoretically comprehensive, so that what is omitted is deemed to be excluded, the door is opened to extremely creative readings of the text, which were, indeed, an inevitable consequence of canonization. For the orgy of legalism that characterizes the writings of both the Rabbinical and Roman jurists may be traced to a method that on the one hand reveres the text as the most just lawgiver of all, and on the other strives to make an inadequate text cover (in theory) every possible contingency. Thus, for example, the casuistic rule in the Twelve Tables—"If a father sells a son three times, the son is free of the father"—was interpreted by the classical jurists as follows:

Now a son passes out of parental authority by three mancipations, but all other children, male or female, leave it by a single

---

22 E.g., the putative law "*si furtum manifestum est, ni pacit, verberato transque dato . . .*" based on no reported source and offered with all due reserve by the editors in Crawford 1996: vol. 2, 578 at I, 19 (= VIII 14 in FIRA).

23 VIII 16 (in FIRA) = I, 21 in Crawford 1996.

24 The danger of anachronism applies *a fortiori* to reconstructions of broad statement of principle, such as that proposed by Watson (1991: 309-12) for this fragment.

mancipation. For the law of the Twelve Tables speaks of three mancipations only in the case of a son . . . (Gaius Inst. II 32).

The jurists, faced with the practical problems of their own day, adopted a teleological rather than an historical interpretation of the canonized text. The alternative—to rewrite the text itself on the basis of the same principles that were applied to its interpretation—was not attempted. Nonetheless, the intellectual investment arising from canonization may be regarded as an important stepping-stone toward Justinian's *Digest* and subsequent codifications. It allowed the early jurists an opportunity to control the practical consequences of adopting general principles, by confining them within a framework of pragmatically tested casuistic rules.

Conclusions

We have attempted to trace the history of a legal tradition from Mesopotamia of the third millennium to the Roman Empire of the early centuries of the common era. It is a tale of both continuity and caesura. In the course of the odyssey, awareness of the system of thought with which the tradition originated—Mesopotamian legal science—was lost, as indeed was the whole civilization, lying forgotten for nearly two thousand years.

The process of canonization enabled a few products of that system of thought to survive, from societies on the periphery of its sphere of influence. While canonization served working legal systems well, at the same time it threw a veil over the original meaning of the texts, which were henceforth seen exclusively through the perspective of a radically different conceptual structure. The very success of canonization in this regard demonstrates that codification may be as much a function of reading texts as of their composition.

6

Codex Hammurabi and the Ends of the Earth

Abstract

The Code of Hammurabi claims to contain decisions for any legal conflict that might arise among the king's subjects. But the limited number of actual provisions in the code gives the lie to this claim of comprehensiveness. How, then, could such a claim be justified? In the same way that royal propaganda asserted that the king, by means of various military campaigns, had extended his territorial control to the ends of the earth, so the provisions within the code push the law to its very limits. By treating cases that lie at the edge of possibility or that form opposite extremes, the code seeks to demonstrate the king's control of the outer reaches of the law and, thus, of all existing legal terrain in between.

The Problem of Impossible Claims

In the epilogue to his famous code, Hammurabi boasts: "Any man wronged who has a case, may he come before my statue 'The King of Justice,' may he have read to him the inscription of my stela, may he hear my words sublime, and may my stela reveal the case to him. May he see his judgment and his mind be eased" (col. xlviii, lines 3-19).

The code purports to contain every conceivable case, a degree of foresight in human affairs that is impossible, even to modern lawyers. Modern law, however, can have greater pretension to universality because it has recourse to conceptual tools that the ancient Mesopotamians lacked: abstract categories, definitions, principles, and vertical reasoning. A modern law can, for example, divide the whole of the law of property into

---

* Originally published in *Landscapes: Territories, Frontiers and Horizons in the Ancient Near East* (ed. L. Milano et al.; History of the Ancient Near East Monographs 3; Padova: Sargon, 1999), vol. 3, 101-103. Used by permission.

two categories, real and personal, give a definition of real property, divide it into further sub-categories, and formulate principles that will govern the application of rights and duties at each and every level of categorization, down to the individual case of trespass upon another's land. Mesopotamian science, by contrast, could only proceed horizontally, by the cumulation of examples.[1] All the cuneiform law codes, including Codex Hammurabi, reflect this dearth: at most a few hundred individual cases could be presented, out of an almost infinite number of possible variants.

How then could Hammurabi reconcile his boast in the epilogue of his code with the modest selection of cases that had been offered in the body of the text? The answer, I suggest, lay in the use of the same techniques that were employed in royal propaganda concerning the king's conduct of foreign affairs. These techniques have been analyzed to great effect by Liverani, whose insights are the basis for the following remarks.[2]

The Ideology of Universal Control

One of the ideal roles of kingship was to conquer the whole world, to establish a universal empire, as expressed in the traditional formula "king of the four quarters." By doing so, the king pushed back the forces of chaos, which ever threatened to overwhelm civilization, to their natural habitat, the ends of the earth.[3] In the ancient world view, a universal empire should extend literally to the horizon, the edge of a flat earth, where *terra firma* was replaced by the realm of chaos, personified by a great ocean.[4]

In reality, no king could reach the edge of the earth, let alone control all the territory within its compass. Nonetheless, royal propaganda was able to present the king's real achievements in symbolic terms that satisfied that ideal intellectually, even in the minds of those few who actually had knowledge of lands beyond the narrow confines of the home territory.

---

1 Bottéro 1987: 156-84, esp. 169-77.
2 Liverani 1990.
3 Liverani 1990: 56-57.
4 Liverani 1990: 51-56.

Liverani identifies several techniques by which a sense of universal control was achieved, relating either to the content of the universal empire or to the container which held its territories.

Content

The first of Liverani's examples relating to content that I wish to cite is the "open list," where single items are cumulated to give the impression of a totality, or at least a potential one, e.g., the endless listings of subdued countries or the enumeration of conquered cities, enemies slain, or booty seized. They make an obvious point of comparison with the law codes in general, which are seemingly endless lists of cases decided.

Moreover, an open geographical list can, as Liverani points out, be arranged according to a structural pattern (e.g., by opposing southern and northern sites), in order to show that the listed items are not only many but also distributed in a way that will cover the whole world.[5] In the same way, the list of injuries in Codex Eshnunna 42-46 follows a spatial structure, moving from head to limbs to body, but of course giving examples of only some of the possible injuries to those parts:

> 42 If a man bites a man's nose and severs it, he shall pay one mina of silver. An eye—one mina; a tooth—half a mina; an ear—half a mina; a slap in the face—he shall pay ten shekels of silver.
>
> 43 If a man severs a man's finger, he shall pay two-thirds of a mina of silver.
>
> 44 If a man knocks a man down in . . . and breaks his hand, he shall pay half a mina of silver.
>
> 45 If he breaks his foot, he shall pay half a mina of silver.
>
> 46 If a man strikes a man and breaks his collarbone, he shall pay two-thirds of a mina of silver.

In the law codes, the structure may also be temporal, as in CH 1-5, which give isolated examples of attempts to pervert the course of justice

5 Liverani 1990: 46-47.

on a chronological basis, following a lawsuit systematically through its stages from initial accusation to trial to judgment:

> 1 If a man accuses a man of murder and does not prove it, his accuser shall be killed.
> 2 If a man accuses a man of witchcraft . . . etc.
> 3 If a man produces false testimony in a lawsuit and does not prove what he said, if it is a capital case, that man shall be killed.
> 4 If he produces testimony concerning grain or silver, he shall bear the penalty of that case.
> 5 If a judge judges a case, gives a verdict, and has a sealed document drafted, but afterwards changes his judgment, they shall prove that that judge changed his judgment in the case, and he shall pay 12-fold whatever the claim is in the case. . . .

It may also be hierarchical, following, for example, the axis: head of household, son, slave. For example, in CH 229-231:

> 229 If a builder builds a house for a man and does not make his work strong and the house that he built collapses and causes the death of the householder, the builder shall be killed.
> 230 If it causes the death of the householder's son, they shall kill the builder's son.
> 231 If it causes the death of the householder's slave, he shall give slave for slave to the householder.

A second technique for suggesting totality is through subdivision into opposite parts: interior and periphery, upper and lower land, mountains and plains.[6] This can be compared with the use of positive and negative cases in the law codes, as in CH 155-156, which contrast incestuous relations between a father-in-law and daughter-in-law before and after consummation of her marriage:

---

6 Liverani 1990: 44-46.

155 If a man chooses a bride for his son and his son has had intercourse with her, but he thereafter is caught lying in her lap, they shall bind that man and throw him in the water.

156 If a man chooses a bride for his son and his son has not had intercourse with her, but he lies in her lap, he shall pay . . . .

Sometimes the double presentation seems superfluous, as in CH 30-31 where the ruling, that a soldier who abandons his feudal tenancy for three years will forfeit it, is followed by the self-evident ruling that he will not if he abandons it for a lesser period.[7] The presentation of opposites, however, gives the case a merismatic quality and thus a sense of completeness.

Container

Control may be suggested by reference to the geographical container of the territory: the borders of the universe. The very act of reaching them is symbolic of attaining control of all the areas beyond which they lie. This in turn may be suggested by the king leading an expedition to some body of water (or equally unstable element), which is representative of the ultimate ocean surrounding the earth, and there setting up a stela or carving an inscription which marks his presence.[8]

In the law codes, exact opposites such as CH 30-31 mentioned in the previous section are rare. Far more frequent are what Eichler calls "a polar pair of cases with maximal variation."[9] As Hallo explains, it is a "codification of extremes" whereby "[CH] repeatedly multiplies the criteria of both culpability and innocence as if with the intention of leaving

---

7 CH 30: "If a soldier or a fisherman, faced with feudal service, abandons his field, orchard, and house and absconds, and another after him takes his field, orchard, and house and performs his feudal service for three years, if he returns and demands his field, orchard, and house, it shall not be given to him. The one who took it and performed the service shall continue to do so." CH 31: "If he absconds for one year and returns, his field, orchard, and house shall be given to him; he is the one who shall perform his feudal service."

8 Liverani 1990: 59-65.

9 Eichler 1987: 75.

a large discretionary area in the middle, where neither all the criteria of guilt nor all those of innocence may be satisfied."[10]

For example, CH 129 discusses consensual intercourse with a married woman, and §130 contrasts it with forcible intercourse, but not with the same woman. Instead, the victim is merely betrothed. Thus at least two intermediate cases are omitted: forcible intercourse with a married woman and consensual intercourse with a betrothed woman.

Scholars have tended to see in this technique the medium of a hidden message or agenda. For Finkelstein, it was in pursuit of pure justice: extremes emphasized the unambiguously just decision, unburdened by the nuances inevitable in everyday cases.[11] For Eichler, it is a way of stating legal principles by inference. Thus in CH 129-130, contrasting the consensual intercourse of an experienced woman with the non-consensual intercourse of an inexperienced girl amounts to a legal statement that consent is a decisive factor in determining the woman's liability.[12]

I would be reluctant to read such messages into the text, for fear of imposing upon it, unconsciously, our own cultural criteria. It seems to me that a simpler explanation, and one explicitly attested in the text itself, is the desire for completeness. The use of fantastic examples to give an impression of completeness has already been noted by Bottéro, both for the law codes and for other types of scientific literature, such as medical and omen lists.[13]

Those cases in the codes which feature extreme polarity are applying the technique of the royal expedition to the law. They are the markers of the conceptual edge of a topic, or as far out into its ramifications as the draftsmen could penetrate. Theoretically, the appropriate rulings in all intermediate cases within those markers can be logically deduced by extrapolation from the extremes. In practice, however, extrapolation is possible only to a very limited extent (even applying modern legal reasoning), because there are still too many variables left untreated. This is another reason, apart from cultural bias, to be cautious with modern attempts (including my own) to "fill in the gaps" by inference. It mattered

---

10 Hallo 1964: 99 n. 35.
11 Finkelstein 1966: 364.
12 Eichler 1987: 82.
13 Bottéro 1987: 175-177.

less to the ancient draftsmen or their audience, because the rest of the law was common knowledge anyway, and because the impression of completeness was what counted.

Conclusion

Royal inscriptions boast of the king's successful execution of his royal mission, in which he sought to impose peace and order through conquest abroad and through justice at home. In his perfect execution of justice, the king purported to foresee all possible cases. His law code would suggest as much through the same techniques as were used to suggest his total control of foreign lands. Prime among those techniques was the royal expedition to the ends of the earth. Without a map or even knowledge of the surrounding territory, the heroic leader would follow a narrow path, sometimes that of previous kings, sometimes one blazed by himself. So too did the heroic lawgiver reach the edge of each legal topic, by the use of cases culled from the existing legal tradition, or by the use of new decisions made, or at least postulated, by himself. No metaphor could have been more apt.

Part Two

The Tradition in Legal Practice

7

Social Justice in the Ancient Near East

Abstract

For the societies of the ancient Near East, social justice typically meant maintaining the existing socio-economic hierarchy. Thus, those who had lost some measure of their status within that hierarchy could appeal to the king for redress. Other restorative mechanisms, such as the right of redemption, time limits on debt-slavery, and royal debt-cancellation decrees were of particular use in helping households to regain their financial footing and avoid the most extreme consequences of economic misfortune and oppression.

In this chapter I will deal with the sources in cuneiform from Mesopotamia, dating from the third to the first millennium B.C.E., but I will also consider the sources in cuneiform from Syria and Anatolia in the second millennium, and the Hebrew Bible as evidence of ancient Israel in the first millennium, since all these societies shared a similar social and political structure, a common legal tradition, and a common view of social justice.[1]

The societies of the ancient Near East were organized hierarchically. The basic unit was the household, headed by a *paterfamilias* and containing wives, children, and slaves as its subordinate members. Above the households of the citizens lay those of the nobility, above them that of the king, and above the king the gods, whose pantheon itself was conceived in terms of household and hierarchical structures.

---

* Originally published in *Social Justice in the Ancient World* (ed. K. Irani and M. Silver; Westport, Conn.: Greenwood Press, 1995), 149-63. Used by permission.

1 On the common legal tradition, see Paul 1970; on the common view of social justice, see Weinfeld 1985. Epsztein 1986 is a general survey based on secondary sources.

The structure of the society is illustrated by the native use of the term *slave*.[2] While it denotes real slaves, that is, unfree persons, who were of course at the bottom of the ladder, the term was also used relatively to describe one's relationship to any hierarchical superior. Thus, a free citizen was called a slave of his king, and both were slaves of the gods.

The concept of social justice in such a society was not at all one of equality, nor was it identified with the relief of poverty as such, given that large sections of the population existed at subsistence level. Social justice was conceived rather as protecting the weaker strata of society from being unfairly deprived of their due: the legal status, property rights, and economic condition to which their position on the hierarchical ladder entitled them. The ideal was expressed by such phrases as "that the strong not oppress the weak, that justice be done to the orphan and widow"[3] or "the orphan was not delivered up to the rich man, the widow was not delivered up to the powerful man, the man of one shekel was not delivered up to the man of sixty shekels."[4]

A whimsical tale entitled "The Poor Man of Nippur" (Cooper 1975: 170-74), although fiction, is revelatory of Mesopotamian attitudes as to the sort of poor and weak who were embraced by such high-sounding ideals:

> There was a man, a citizen of Nippur, destitute and poor,
> Gimil-Ninurta was his name, an unhappy man.
> In his city, Nippur, he lived, working hard, but
> Had not the silver befitting his class,
> Nor had he the gold befitting people (of his stature).
> His storage bins lacked pure grain,
> His insides burned, craving food, and
> His face was unhappy, craving meat and first-class beer;
> Having no food, he lay hungry every day, and
> Was dressed in garments that had no change (I 1-10).

Poverty, then, is relative. Our hero was a free citizen down on his luck, who could no longer maintain himself in the style to which his status enti-

---

2 Sumerian ìr; Akkadian (*w*)*ardu*; Hebrew *'ebed*.
3 Codex Hammurabi, col. XLVII (= reverse XXIV), lines 59-61. *ANET*[3] 163-80.
4 Prologue to Codex Ur-Namma, A IV, lines 162-168; translation in *ANET*[3] 523-25.

tled him.[5] The story then goes on to tell how, as a result of his condition, he suffered oppression at the hands of the powerful.

His solution to his hunger is to sell his coat in exchange for a goat. He decides, however, not to eat the goat himself, because it would be no feast without beer and because his neighborhood friends and family would be angry with him for not inviting them. Instead, he presents the goat as a gift to the mayor of the city, hoping thereby to garner a greater favor in return. The mayor, however, behaves churlishly: he orders his servant to give the man a drink of third-class beer and to throw him out. The rest of the story is taken up with our hero's elaborate revenge, whereby he succeeds in administering the mayor not one but three good beatings.

To begin his revenge, the Poor Man of Nippur first approaches the king and asks him for the use, on credit, of a chariot for a day, so that he can play the part of a noble. The kings accedes without hesitation or without inquiry into his motives. Improbable as this scenario may seem, it is true in principle regarding a further aspect of social justice presumed by the story. In real life, it was indeed to the king that oppressed citizens looked to fulfill the demands of social justice. A principal function of the king was to intervene in cases of oppression, for the legitimacy of a king's reign was based upon a divine mandate, the terms of which included ensuring social justice in his realm (Finkelstein 1961: 103). The oppression that he was expected to guard against was abuse of administrative power, as in the story above (albeit resulting in more than mere loss of face), or of economic power.

It is for this reason that widows and orphans were singled out for protection by the king. A widow or an orphan need not necessarily be poor; but on the death of the head of a household there might be no one to defend their rights, especially their inheritance rights, against those who coveted the deceased's property. The king, therefore, being head of the household for the population as a whole, intervened as substitute *paterfamilias*. Thus, king Hammurabi of Babylon (eighteenth century) wished to be remembered by the oppressed for whom he had done justice as "the master who is like the father of a child to his people."[6]

---

5 Dearman (1988: 52-53) finds a similar profile in the Bible for the class of poor for whom the prophets demand social justice.
6 Codex Hammurabi, col. XLVIII (= reverse XXV), lines 20-21.

The vulnerability of the weaker classes in general is illustrated by a paragraph from the earliest recorded legislative act in history, the Edict of King Uru-inimgina, ruler of the Sumerian city-state of Lagash in the twenty-fifth century:[7]

> Should the house of a noble adjoin the house of a commoner and the noble says to him, "I wish to buy it from you"—and he says, "If you wish to buy it from me, pay me a satisfactory price; my house is a basket, fill it with barley!"—if he does not then buy from him, the noble shall not, in his anger, "touch" the commoner.[8]

What measures are involved in "touching" the commoner are not made clear, but it is evident that the noble's action was not benign and was aimed at acquiring the commoner's property without having to pay the asking price. As would be expected with such an archaic text, much of its language is obscure.

The paragraph apparently does not impose a sanction upon the oppressive noble. The versions of the edict that we possess are not contemporaneous with its promulgation; but inscriptions from later in the king's reign boasting of his earlier achievements, and much that is recorded in them, may be no more than propagandistic hyperbole. Nonetheless, they would seem to provide sufficient evidence that on his accession to the throne king Uru-inimgina did institute a number of practical reforms, with particular emphasis on the state administration and its bureaucracy (Maekawa 1973-74: 114-36). Various practices of officials are detailed—the appropriation of property, the receipt of payments, and the use of services—which we are given to understand were regarded as abusive, because the officials in question were removed from those areas of responsibility. One reform is clear: the former charges by different functionaries for expenses connected with funerals were listed and a new tariff

---

7   See Steible 1982: 288-312; English translation Cooper 1986: 70-76.

8   In the edition of Steible 1982: Ukg. 4.11.32-4.12.11 = Ukg. 5.11.1-18; cf. Cooper 1986: 72. The Sumerian term here translated "touch" (tag) is translated by Steible as "(den Zorn darüber) fühlen lassen," and by Cooper as "strike at him."

posted in which some of the payments had been drastically reduced, for example, from 420 loaves for the *Uhmush* to 80.

In paragraph 163 of the law code of king Hammurabi, punishment is explicit and is severe where abuse of power takes the form of maltreatment of a subordinate by an official:

> If a "captain" or a "lieutenant" takes a soldier's possessions, deprives a soldier of his due, gives a soldier out for hire, delivers a soldier into the bands of the powerful in a lawsuit, or takes a gift that the king gave the soldier, that "captain" or "lieutenant" shall be killed.

The ancient legal systems did not strictly separate administrative and judicial powers. An official could act in a quasi-judicial capacity, deciding the legal rights of those subordinate to him without a formal trial, even in cases where the official himself had an interest. The best recourse for the injured party was to the king by way of petition. King Hammurabi writes to a senior official as follows (*RA* 21 15; see Thureau-Dangin 1924: 15):

> To Shamash-hazir, speak! Thus says Hammurabi. Sin-ishme'anni of Kutalla, the orchard keeper of the Dilmun date-palms, has informed me as follows: "Shamash-hazir expropriated from me a field of my paternal estate and gave it to a soldier." Thus he informed me. The field is a permanent estate—when can it be taken away? Examine the case and if that field does belong to his paternal estate, return the field to Sin-ishme'anni.

In this case, apparently, the official had wrongfully exercised his discretion to expropriate land, probably for failure by the landowner to meet certain public obligations.

Not every act of oppression, however, involved illegality. Even while operating within the letter of the law, it was possible to achieve results that were regarded as unjust because of their harmful social or economic consequences. This was the case with the laws regarding debt in the ancient Near East. The law allowed a creditor, if unpaid, to acquire by way of foreclosure not only the debtor's property but also his family and even his own person in slavery. The burden of debt was a serious socio-economic problem, leading to the dispossession and enslavement of the class of small farmers. Several different measures were therefore employed to restore families to their patrimony and debt slaves to their families, in derogation from the strict rights of the creditor under the contract of a loan.

The first measure was the right of redemption. If property was pledged for a loan, by the nature of things that property would be released by the creditor to its owner upon repayment of the loan. The courts, however, extended this principle to property sold outright, where the transaction was in effect a forced sale at undervalue to pay off a debt. The seller was, under certain conditions, allowed to buy back—to redeem—his property at the original price. This equitable principle applied only to certain types pf property, namely members of the family sold as slaves and family land (Westbrook 1991b: 90-117). Paragraph 119 of Codex Hammurabi deals with a case arising in the first category: "If a debt has seized a man and he sells his slave-woman who has borne him children, the owner of the slave-woman may pay the silver that the merchant paid and redeem his slave-woman." By virtue of her having borne her master children, the slave acquires the status of a member of the family insofar as the right of redemption is concerned. Note that she does not gain her freedom as a result; the purpose of redemption is to protect the integrity of the family, not necessarily to improve the lot of the individual.

Paragraph 39 of Codex Eshnunna[9] deals with a sale of family land: "If a man grows weak and sells his house, the day that the buyer will sell, the owner of the house may redeem." The phrase "grows weak" is an indication that a forced sale for debt is meant (Westbrook 1991b: 100-102). The law protects not the poor as a class, but the impoverished, that is, those families who are in danger of losing their place on the socio-economic ladder. It was not intended to bar the normal sale of land at its full market price but was intended for those cases where the "price" was really the amount of the loan and the property was in effect being confiscated for default on that sum. A contract from Emar, a city-state that flourished in

---

9   A kingdom to the north of Babylonia in the eighteenth century. The name of the king responsible for this code is not preserved. Most probably it is to be attributed to King Dadusha, an earlier contemporary of Hammurabi. In that case, it would predate Codex Hammurabi by several decades.

north Syria in the late second millennium, depicts the circumstances contemplated by the law (Arnaud *Emar* 6 123):

> A owed twenty shekels of silver to B and ten shekels of silver
> to C and could not repay. Now A has sold his house to B and C for
> thirty shekels of silver as full price and has handed over to them
> the old tablet of his house that was sealed with the seal of (the
> god) Ninurta.
>
> If in the future A repays the thirty shekels of silver to its own-
> ers in a single day, he may take his house. If not, and if two days
> have passed, whoever in the future claims this house may pay the
> same amount of silver and take his house.

The final clause is an oblique reference to the fact that in default of its exercise by the seller, the right of redemption accrued to the seller's nearest
relative. Again, it is the family (in the sense of extended family or clan)
that this social law is primarily designed to benefit, not the individual. The
order in which the right may be exercised is given in the redemption law of
Lev 25:47-49:

> If a resident alien grows successful among you and your brother
> grows poor with him and he is sold to a resident alien among you
> or to the descendant of an alien clan, after he is sold he shall have
> redemption: one of his brothers may redeem him, or his uncle or
> his cousin or a further relative from his clan may redeem him, or
> he may be redeemed by his own resources.

A further document from Emar shows this right in operation (Arnaud
Emar 6 205):

> A died and his sons entered B's house, and he (B) released the
> 25 shekels of silver. And now B brought the two sons of A before .
> . . the city elders and their father's brothers. He spoke thus: "Take
> your two nephews and give me back my 25 shekels. . . . These two
> nephews entered voluntarily into my slaveship."
>
> Their father's brothers refused to give the 25 shekels
> belonging to B, and they confirmed by a sealed tablet, voluntarily,
> the enslavement of their two nephews to B. Dead or alive, they are

B's slaves. In the future, if C and their father's brothers say: "We will redeem our two nephews," they shall give B two souls for D and two souls for E, the blind one, and they may take their two nephews.

Redemption, therefore, was not a very reliable form of social protection. The seller might be unable to raise the amount necessary to repay his debt, even though it was less than the market price of the property, and other members of the family might be equally unable or unwilling to do so in his stead. In the book of Ruth (4:3-6), Naomi's closest relative decides to forego his right of redemption when Boaz reveals to him that it will trigger the duty of levirate marriage and thus render his investment unprofitable (Westbrook 1991b: 63-67).

If redemption failed, however, all was not lost. A second, more radical, remedy might be available. According to Codex Hammurabi 117, "If a debt seizes a man and he gives his wife, son, and daughter in sale or *ana kiššātim*, they shall serve in the house of their purchaser or holder for three years; in the fourth year their freedom shall be established." The same remedy for debt slavery is provided by Exod 21:2 and Deut 15:12, except that the period of service before release is six years. In all these laws, release from slavery occurred by operation of law; there was no need for any redemption payment. This was a special privilege for members of the family; it did not apply to family land.

It is curious that the period of service varies so radically between the biblical and cuneiform laws. Despite their apparently absolute language, such paragraphs in the law codes may possibly reflect an equitable discretion of the court that was applied in differing measure according to the circumstances of the case. The rationale for release appears to have been that the debt slaves by their period of service had paid off the capital of the debt. This somewhat more flexible criterion is used in Codex Lipit-Ishtar, a Sumerian law code predating Codex Hammurabi by about a hundred years. According to paragraph 14, "If a man has returned his slavery to his master and it is confirmed (that he has done so) two-fold, that slave shall be released." A similar underlying principle is alluded to in the remark of Deut 15:18 that "he has served twice the hire of a hireling in serving you for six years."

In practice then, the actual lapse of time needed for a court to declare the release of debt slaves will have varied. Nonetheless, it was still linked to the contract between the parties and acted upon its terms in a manner that could be anticipated. This was not the case with the third and final measure, which sought to achieve social justice through a sweeping and arbitrary intervention in the normal economic life of the society.

It was the practice of Mesopotamian kings every so often to issue a decree annulling debts throughout the kingdom. The decrees were retrospective: they applied to existing contracts at whatever stage of completion they happened to be at the moment of proclamation. Affected also were those same ancillary transactions that the mechanisms of redemption and limitation of servitude sought to control: the pledge or forced sale of family land or the enslavement of members of the family.

The king, in issuing a decree, was said to "establish equity for the land"—literally, a "straightening out."[10] The normal judicial activity of the king in answering individual petitions was defined in the same way. It was regarded as the correction of imbalances, the restoration of a status quo that had been destroyed temporarily by some act of injustice. "Equity for the land" was the same action on a grand scale, where the imbalance affected whole strata of the population.

The earliest mention of such a decree is in an inscription of a predecessor of Uru-inimgina at Lagash, king Entemena (twenty-fifth century). He boasts that he "caused the son to return to the mother, he caused the mother to return to the son, he established the release ('freedom') of interest-bearing loans."[11]

Entemena is here indulging in a rhetorical game, since the Sumerian term for "freedom" (amar.gi₄) means literally "return to the mother"; but its literal sense had long since given way to a technical legal meaning, as is shown by its use in this inscription for the release of debts.

Debt release also formed part of Uru-inimgina's edict: "He cleansed the citizens of Lagash, who were living in debt for planted acres(?), late grain, theft, and murder—he established their release."[12] The association of murder and theft with debts for crops and commodities may seem strange, but is perfectly logical in the context of the ancient Near Eastern system of criminal justice. I shall postpone discussion of it for the moment,

---

10 Sumerian níg.si.sá; Akkadian *mīšarum*.
11 Entemena 79.4.2-5; see Steible 1982: 269.
12 In the edition of Steible 1982, Ukg. 4.12.13-22 = Ukg. 5.11.20-29.

however, since it is the subject of much more detailed provisions in a later edict.

The Sumerian documents of the third millennium yield few further references to the release of debts and no information on its operation in practice. It is the following period, the early second millennium (usually referred to as the "Old Babylonian Period"), that provides us with an abundance of sources: royal inscriptions, references in letters and private legal documents, and the partially preserved text of three decrees.[13] The sources then decline precipitately in the following periods, but there are sufficient scattered references to establish that the custom had not died out and that our dearth of information is probably due to the random preservation of ancient records.[14] In particular, an edict of a Hittite ruler of the twelfth century has recently been identified as containing debt release provisions (Westbrook and Woodard 1990: 641-59).

The most complete text of a debt release decree is the Edict of King Ammi-ṣaduqa of Babylon, the great-great-grandson of Hammurabi (Kraus 1984: 168-83). The twenty-two paragraphs preserved reveal a complex set of provisions designed to focus the effects of the decree on its intended beneficiaries while limiting disruption of normal commerce. The provisions are of two types, those canceling various categories of debts and those concerned with problems of implementation.

The central provisions are paragraphs 3 and 8, which contain a crucial distinction. According to paragraph 3, "Whoever lends silver or barley to an Akkadian or Amorite at interest . . . and has had a tablet drafted, because the king has established equity for the land, his tablet is broken. He may not collect silver or barley in accordance with his tablet." Silver and barley are the normal media of exchange. Akkadians and Amorites are the two main ethnic components of the population. The wording could be intended to privilege these two ethnic groups in particular, but it is more probably a means of referring to the population as a whole, as opposed to

---

13 Kraus (1984) contains all known Old Babylonian references until that date and an edition of the three extant decrees.

14 See *CAD* A/2, *andurāru*, 116-17, meanings g and h, for references from Nuzi (fifteenth century) and the Neo-Assyrian period (eighth-sixth century). On the latter, see Lewy 1958: 30*-31*.

the citizens of specific towns, who are the beneficiaries of other provisions in the decree.

The paragraph is thus drafted in the most general terms, annulling the normal type of loan that would be made to farmers, who composed the bulk of the population. In contrast, paragraph 8 states: "An Akkadian or an Amorite who has received barley, silver, or goods as a purchase-price, for a (business) journey, for partnership, or as a capital advance: his tablet shall not be broken; he shall pay according to his contract." Trade was thus exempted from the operation of the decree. Various business transactions that involved the giving of credit would continue to be enforced by the courts, as long as the profit element was not derived from interest. Paragraph 9 specifies that if such a contract contains a penalty clause imposing interest after the due date for repayment has passed, that clause is void, but the contract itself remains valid.

A distinction between valid and invalid loans is an open invitation to fraud by moneylenders seeking to preserve their investment, and several paragraphs of the edict contain complicated measures to counter evasion. Paragraph 7 reads:

> If a man has lent barley or silver at interest and has had a tablet drafted but has kept the tablet in his possession and said, "I did not lend at interest; the barley or silver that I gave you was for a purchase-price, for a capital advance, or for another such purpose," the man who borrowed the barley or silver from the merchant shall bring witnesses to the wording of the tablet that the lender denies. They shall make their declaration before the god, and because he distorted his tablet and denied the transaction, he shall pay six-fold. If he cannot pay his penalty, he shall die.

Note that the term *merchant* is synonymous with moneylender. Merchants were the source of capital for both trade and agriculture and thus would be in a position to claim that a transaction belonged to one sphere of their activities rather than another.

A slightly different type of annulment was the cancellation of arrears on unspecified debts that was made in favor of certain sections of the population only. The criterion appears to have been socio-economic: some of the groups named are known to be types of feudal tenants, and it is possible that they may all have been dependants of the palace in one way or another. The intention of the legislation is expressly stated to be "to strengthen them and to deal equitably with them," a statement that is made only with reference to these groups. At least part of the arrears in question, possibly all of them, were owed to the palace itself in the form of feudal dues or taxes. Other paragraphs of the edict (§§11, 12) reveal a complicated arrangement whereby merchants acted as wholesalers to market commodities owned by the palace, part of which the merchants received from palace stores but part of which they had to collect themselves from feudal tenants who owed the commodities by way of taxes.

Special consideration is given in the edict to the position of the taverness. This lady was an important factor in the economic life of the society—and one to whom strict regulations applied to prevent her from engaging in fraud or exploitation.[15] Beer was a staple commodity that was sometimes supplied as rations or wages. The taverness would market the beer of those who had a surplus and would supply beer on credit, or rather beer mash, which could keep for much longer, against payment in barley at the next year's harvest (Kraus 1984: 254). Although not in form a loan at interest, it was one in substance, since the taverness gained her profit by supplying in one commodity and receiving payment in another. Paragraph 17, therefore, bars her directly from claiming payment for this type of transaction.

The last provision from this edict that I wish to discuss is directed, not at the debt itself, but at its consequences. Paragraph 20 reads: "If a citizen of Numhia, Emut-balum, Idamaraz, Uruk, Isin, Kisurra, (or) Malgium has been bound by a debt and has given [hims]elf, his wife, or [his child] in sale, *ana kiššātim,* or in pledge, because the king has established equity for the land, he is released, his freedom is established." Why the citizens of these particular towns should have been singled out is not clear. There is no common link between them, and it is unwise to speculate as to special social conditions or pressures, for reasons that will be explained shortly. What is also remarkable is the similarity of language between this provision and CH 117 discussed above, which released the debtor's family after

---

15 Codex Hammurabi 111 fixes the rate at which the taverness could give beer on credit, and paragraph 108 prescribes the death penalty for a taverness using false weights. A slightly earlier law code, Codex Eshnunna, in paragraph 41, obliges the taverness who sells nonresidents' beer on their behalf to obtain the current market price.

three years. It casts further doubt on the effectiveness—or, at least, the general applicability—of the law code provision.

The following paragraph of the edict contains an important proviso: the release in question is not to apply to house-born slaves of the citizens of those towns. Once again we see that the purpose of the edict is to aid citizens fallen on hard times; its conception of social justice does not extend to the truly weakest strata of society, those born into slavery or poverty.

One type of debt that is not covered by the Edict of Ammi-ṣaduqa but which we have already met in a tantalizingly brief reference in the Edict of Uru-inimgina is that arising from crime. Crimes such as murder, adultery, rape, and theft, which in modern law are prosecuted and punished by the state, were dealt with on an entirely different basis in the ancient systems. Such crimes gave rise to a dual right on the part of the victim or his family: to revenge or to accept payment in lieu of revenge. The payment was therefore neither a fine nor compensation, but composition, whereby the culprit ransomed his own life, limb, or liberty, depending on the nature of the revenge appropriate. The ransom agreement was a contract like any other and, therefore, gave rise to a debt that had to be paid or satisfied in some other way, whether by transfer of the debtor's property, his family, or his own person (Westbrook 1988d: 39-83).

Because a ransom agreement was a kind of forced sale, the question arises whether its consequences might be annulled under the terms of a debt release decree. That question appears to be addressed in the Edict of the Hittite king Tudhaliya IV:[16]

> And if someone has given ransom for blood, and he has purchased himself from you, whether (the ransom be) a field or a person, no one shall release it.
>
> If he (i.e., the holder of the ransom) has taken those things along with his (i.e., the culprit's) wives and sons, he shall release them(?) to him.
>
> And if someone has given ransom for theft, if it is a field, they shall not release it (II 3-10).

16 Westbrook and Woodard 1990: 642-44.

The edict distinguishes between two cases. In the first, a person has committed homicide and has paid a ransom for his own life: he has "bought himself." Can the property that he handed over as the price of his life be released by the decree? The edict answers in the negative, even if the property be land or persons, which could refer to slaves or, possibly, dependent members of his family. In the second case, on the other hand, the creditor (i.e., the avenger) appears to have made a general seizure of the homicide's property and family, and their release is authorized. The edict then goes on to discuss debts arising from theft, along the same lines.

It may seem strange that criminals could be regarded as potential objects of social justice, but it should be remembered that payment of ransom would usually apply to less serious degrees of homicide and that the thief's condition might evoke some sympathy. As the book of Proverbs puts it:

> A thief is not held in contempt
> For stealing to appease his hunger;
> Yet if caught he must pay sevenfold;
> He must give up all he owns (Prov 6:30-31).

Under what circumstances were debt release decrees promulgated? It is clear that, traditionally, a king would be expected to declare a release in the first year of his reign, as part of the pomp and circumstance surrounding his accession to the throne. The copious evidence of the Old Babylonian period, however, reveals that a king in the course of his reign might issue one or more further decrees.

Thus, Hammurabi appears to have issued a decree in the twelfth and again in the thirty-third year of his reign; his third successor, Ammi-ditana, in his twenty-first year; and the latter's successor, Ammi-ṣaduqa, in his tenth year. A contemporary of Hammurabi, king Rim-Sin of Larsa, is thought to have issued at least three extra decrees, in the twenty-fifth, thirty-fourth, and some time after the fortieth year of his sixty-year reign.[17]

According to Bottéro (1961: 152-53), the frequency of these decrees indicates serious economic disorder in the kingdoms of the period. It took

---

17 See Kraus 1984: 16-110 for a full list of all possible edicts alluded to in the Old Babylonian sources.

the form of the disastrous indebtedness of the majority of the population, which paralyzed production or, at least, failed to encourage it sufficiently, for the yield to satisfy the collective needs of the society. The decrees were to some extent acts of desperation, which attempted to cure the worst effects of the economic situation without dealing with its underlying causes.

I regard such conclusions with skepticism. The debt release decree was an ancient custom that formed part of the religious duty of kings. There is no evidence that the economic situation was worse in the Old Babylonian period than at other times nor that indebtedness, however widespread and crushing, would have had a serious effect on overall production. It would, on the other hand, have altered the distribution of land ownership, with a tendency toward the formation of latifundia. Accordingly, we should look to social rather than economic stability as the motive for these recurrent decrees.

The cuneiform records give little evidence of social unrest. It is true that they represent the voice of the establishment, rather than the opposition, but one would still expect to find some echo of widespread discontent in the sources. The "protest" of the individual debtor lay in flight, abandoning his home and family and seeking refuge in a foreign kingdom or perhaps in the lightly populated steppe. It is also possible that the various social measures were effective in keeping economic grievances from becoming too widespread. Tudhaliya IV informs us at the beginning of his edict that it was promulgated as a direct result of a protest by his citizens:

> When I had destroyed Assuwa and returned to Hattusa, I refurbished the gods; the men of Hatti all began to bow down to me, and they spoke as follows: "O great king, you are our lord, a leader of campaigns. Are you not able to judge in matters of justice? Behold, evil people [. . .] have utterly destroyed [. . .] the feudal holdings and the *sarikuwa* tenants [. . .] (I 1-11).

Unfortunately, the broken state of the tablet prevents us from learning what the point of the protest was. Nonetheless, it does show the ability of the citizens as a group to petition the king about a particular abuse—and in fairly bold terms. Similar group petitions are found elsewhere in the Hittite sources. Paragraph 55 of the Hittite Laws records the king's accession to a petition by a certain class of feudal tenants to receive equal treatment to that of other classes. In a document from Ugarit (PRU IV, RS 17.130; see

Nougayrol 1956: 103-105), a vassal state of the Hittites, the king of Ugarit petitions the Hittite emperor on behalf of his free citizens, who have complained that Hittite merchants are "heavy upon the land." The emperor grants a seasonal restriction on the merchants' activities at Ugarit. By contrast, the dire political consequences of failing to heed popular grievances are revealed in the biblical account of king Rehoboam's refusal grant a petition of his citizens led by one Jeroboam (1 Kgs 12:1-20).

The Old Babylonian decrees do not mention any specific occasion for the promulgation; the only motivation given is religious—that it is pleasing to the god of justice.[18] The same motivation, it should be noted, is present in the Hittite decree. Tudhaliya's remark that he refurbished the gods would appear to have no relevance to his account, unless it is to suggest that part of the "refurbishment" was to correct injustices displeasing to the gods.

Fear of the gods may provide a clue to the specific occasion for some of the decrees. It will be recalled that the edict of Uru-inimgina referred to the release of debts as a process of "cleansing." If an accumulation of injustice could, like murder or sacrilege, ritually pollute the land, then the anger of the gods would express itself in general disasters such as crop failure, plague, and defeat in war, and debt release would be a means of assuaging their anger. An example from the Bible is the slave release decree of king Zedekiah, proclaimed when Jerusalem was besieged by the Babylonian army (Jer 34:1-10). While nothing as dramatic can be correlated with any of the Old Babylonian decrees, it is possible that their occasional nature may be linked to natural disasters, such as failure of the harvest, that resulted in a year of famine and provided good grounds political and religious, for relief of debts.

Whatever the occasion for their promulgation, the one character that the decrees from cuneiform sources share is their unpredictability, depending entirely on the discretion of the ruler. The same is true of the decree promulgated in an emergency by king Zedekiah. In contrast, the equivalent measures enshrined in biblical laws—the famous Sabbatical and Jubilee years—are cyclical in occurrence and automatic in operation. Deut 15:1-3

---

18 An example is the following petition to the king: "When my lord raised the Golden Torch for Sippar and established equity for Shamash (the god of justice) who loves him . . ." (BM 80318; see Finkelstein 1965: 236).

directly annuls debts: "Every seventh year you shall make a cancellation. The cancellation shall be as follows: every creditor is to release the debts that he has owing to him by his neighbor; he shall not press his neighbor for payment." Lev 25:9 annuls transactions founded on debt which resulted in the alienation of family land or the enslavement of members of the family: "You shall make the fiftieth year a holy year and declare freedom in the land for all its inhabitants: it shall be a Jubilee for you and each man shall return to his estate and each shall return to his clan."

Now this cyclical aspect changes the whole nature of the debt release and ultimately destroys its usefulness. It was the very unpredictability of the decree that made it effective: it acted retrospectively and without warning on existing contracts. But a creditor, who knows that his loan is bound to be annulled at a certain point in the future and any security taken lost, will simply not give credit or will find some means of evading the release. The effect on debtors will be far worse than before, drying up their sources of credit or driving it underground into a black market. The biblical measures, unlike their cuneiform counterparts, must therefore be regarded as utopian.

The question then arises, why a practical measure, which was used by Israelite kings in the same manner as Mesopotamian and Hittite rulers, was turned into an impractical one. The answer is suggested by the aftermath of king Zedekiah's decree. The decree ordered the release of debt slaves, which indeed occurred, but subsequently the same persons were enslaved again by their former masters (Jer 34:10-11). This breach of faith elicited divine anger, as conveyed through the prophet Jeremiah: "Thus says the LORD: Because you have not obeyed me by declaring freedom, each man to his brother and his neighbor, I hereby declare freedom for you, says the LORD, to the sword, to plague, and to hunger, and I shall make you an object of horror to all the kingdoms on Earth."

In general, the Hebrew prophets repeatedly inveighed against the Israelite ruling class for their failure to do social justice: "Woe to them who make evil decrees and who write documents of suffering; to turn aside the indigent from judgment and to oppress the poor in court, to make widows their booty and orphans their plunder" (Isa 10:2). Like the prophets, but unlike the cuneiform sources, much of Leviticus and Deuteronomy derives from circles representing the voice of the opposition. In their eyes, the Israelite kings had failed in their constitutional duty; they had not taken the necessary measures to ensure the social justice that their divine mandate demanded of them.

Since the king of flesh and blood could not be trusted to proclaim a debt release when needed, these circles advocated its removal from his discretion to the authority of the divine king and—to make sure that it happened—made its occurrence cyclical.

In summary, social justice was regarded in the ancient Near East as the preservation of the status quo—as the privileges owed to each citizen as member of a family unit with a certain recognized socio-economic status. Where those privileges were lost through an act of oppression, certain mechanisms were available to restore the balance.

If due to abuse of administrative power, a petition to the king was expected to result in an order canceling the administrative act and, if necessary, punishing the offender. If due to abuse of economic power, the right of redemption was available to the debtor or his family. If that right could not be exercised, there remained for debt slaves the possibility of release without payment after a period of service. Finally, the king could intervene by a general cancellation of debts and of transactions ancillary thereto.

Ultimately, it was the responsibility of the king, as part of his divine mandate, to ensure that these mechanisms functioned effectively. Mesopotamian kings boasted of having fulfilled their mandate, but evidence from the Bible suggests that the practice of kings sometimes failed to live up to the ideals of social justice.

8

Slave and Master in Ancient Near Eastern Law

Abstract

This study considers the topic of slavery by examining a variety of sources, including law codes, contracts, trial records, narratives, and royal inscriptions, ranging from the third millennium well into the last half of the first millennium B.C.E. The article carefully distinguishes types of slaves and explains what options were available for each type to achieve freedom. Slaves were indeed treated as property by the legal systems of the ancient Near East. Still, they were afforded certain protections due to their humanity, such as restrictions on their excessive abuse and on their sale into a foreign land.

I. Scope of Study

The purpose of this article is to examine the legal aspects of the relationship between slave and master in the world's oldest recorded legal systems.[1] It will concentrate upon the creation and termination of slavery and the transfer and treatment of slaves by their masters. The legal capacity of slaves (marriage, contract, litigation, etc.) and liability to and of third parties in delict must be reserved for a later study.

The geographic area bounded by this study is the Fertile Crescent of the ancient Near East, from Mesopotamia in the East, through Anatolia in the North, to Syria-Palestine in the West, but, for the most part, excluding Egypt. The time period covered extends from approximately the twenty-fifth century B.C.E., when the earliest legal documents concerning slavery

---

* Originally published in *Chicago-Kent Law Review* 70 (1995): 1631-1676. Used by permission.

1 By "master" we refer to private owners of slaves. Slaves could also be owned by public institutions, namely the palace and the temple. Special features attach to public slaves, especially temple slaves; see Dandamaev 1984: 469-584.

were found, to the fourth century B.C.E., when, with its conquest by Alexander, the area became part of the larger Hellenistic world.

II. Historical Background

The sources are mostly written in cuneiform script (in various languages),[2] with the exception of the Hebrew Bible and a few documents in Aramaic. They are very unevenly divided in space and time. As the history of this period is not generally familiar to legal scholars, this article begins with a brief historical survey of the societies and cultures which form the background to the legal institutions that we are about to study.

The sources from the third millennium are mostly in Sumerian, a language with no known cognates, which was spoken by a people who founded an urban civilization in southern Mesopotamia. The sources primarily date from the Old Sumerian period (twenty-fifth century through twenty-second century), characterized by independent city-states, and the Neo-Sumerian period (twenty-first century), characterized by a highly bureaucratic and centralized empire. In between these periods is the Sargonic Empire (twenty-fourth century), whose rulers spoke Akkadian, a Semitic language.

In the first half of the second millennium, Akkadian divided into two dialects, Babylonian and Assyrian. Sources from this period are classified as either Old Babylonian, when their provenance is the city-states of southern and central Mesopotamia, or Old Assyrian, which mostly comprises the records of Assyrian merchants in Anatolia.

The second half of the second millennium was a period of great empires, namely Egypt, Babylonia, Assyria, Mitanni, and Hatti. The population of Mitanni spoke Hurrian, a non-Semitic language, but wrote their legal documents in Akkadian. The inhabitants of Hatti, the Hittites, spoke an Indo-European language which they wrote in cuneiform. Mesopotamian sources from this period are referred to as Middle Babylonian or

---

2   Sigla such as YOS 8 91 are standard abbreviations used by Assyriologists to refer to publications of copies of cuneiform texts (e.g., Yale Oriental Series, Babylonian Texts, Vol. 8 no. 91). Where there exists a published edition or translation of the text, it will be given after an = sign following the siglum.

Middle Assyrian. Syria-Palestine consisted of many small states, divided between the Hittite and Egyptian spheres of influence. Their legal records are mostly in Akkadian.

The early centuries of the first millennium were marked by Assyria's rise to universal dominion. At its zenith in the eighth and seventh centuries, the Assyrian Empire controlled the entire Fertile Crescent. Sources from this period are referred to as Neo-Assyrian. Most of biblical law can be dated to this and the subsequent period. The Assyrian Empire collapsed in 612 B.C.E. and was replaced by Babylonian hegemony. The term "Neo-Babylonian" encompasses sources from the subsequent Persian period (from 539 B.C.E.), since the cuneiform sources from Mesopotamia continued to be written in the same Akkadian dialect, although Aramaic had in fact become the lingua franca of the region.

The legal sources that we shall be applying are of three main kinds: law codes, royal edicts, and documents of practice.

The extant law codes are as follows:

1. Codex Ur-Namma (CU): Twenty-first century, from Ur in southern Mesopotamia. Written in Sumerian.
2. Codex Lipit-Ishtar (CL): Twentieth century, from Isin in southern Mesopotamia. Written in Sumerian.
3. Codex Eshnunna (CE): Eighteenth century, from Eshnunna in central Mesopotamia. Written in Akkadian.
4. Codex Hammurabi (CH): Eighteenth century, from Babylon. Written in Akkadian.
5. Hittite Laws (HL): Fourteenth century, from Anatolia. Written in Hittite.
6. Middle Assyrian Laws (MAL): Thirteenth century, from Assur in northern Mesopotamia. Written in Akkadian.
7. Neo-Babylonian Laws (NBL): Sixth century, from Babylon. Written in Akkadian.
8. Covenant Code, essentially Exodus 21:1-22:16. Ninth century? Written in Hebrew.
9. Deuteronomic Code, mostly in Deuteronomy 21-25: Seventh century. Written in Hebrew.

Although modern scholars call these law codes, I subscribe to the view that these documents are not legislation in the modern sense, but rather academic treatises on law expressed in casuistic form.[3]

Kings occasionally decreed the cancellation of existing debts and related transactions. These are genuine examples of legislation, if somewhat narrow in scope. We shall refer to four such edicts: by King Uru-inimgina (Sumerian, twenty-sixth century), Ammi-ṣaduqa (Babylonian, seventeenth century), Tudhaliya IV (Hittite, thirteenth century), and Zedekiah (Hebrew, sixth century).

The documents are mostly records of legal transactions such as sale, hire, redemption, etc., with a much smaller number of litigation records and miscellaneous records such as letters. Most of those documents date from the Old Babylonian and Neo-Babylonian periods. The Middle Babylonian period contains a number of small but significant archives, from Nuzi in Mesopotamia, a city in the Empire of Mitanni, and from Emar, Alalakh, and Ugarit, cities in Syria. The Neo-Sumerian period has yielded a number of litigation records, a relatively rare genre.

In total, there are, by a conservative estimate, more than twenty thousand such documents already published, any of which might touch upon the question of slavery. A comprehensive view of slavery in the ancient Near East is not attainable in the present state of research. At most, one may hope to ascertain the salient features of that institution's legal framework. On the other hand, the task is made easier by the fact that, in spite of the huge distances of time and space and the many different languages and cultures involved, the societies of the ancient Near East did share a common legal tradition which persisted throughout the period in question with no radical change and is particularly noticeable in the academic tradition of the law codes.[4] We may be confident therefore that throughout the gamut of sources, from Old Sumerian to Neo-Babylonian, we are dealing with essentially the same underlying laws of slavery.

---

3 Argued by Kraus in his seminal article in 1960; and elaborated by Bottéro 1982. For the most recent summary in English of this much-debated question, see Westbrook 1989a.

4 See Westbrook 1988a: 82-97.

III. Definition

In law, a slave may be defined as a person who is owned by another in the manner of a chattel, subject only to special considerations that may arise from his humanity. Such considerations may affect the extent to which the rules of property law are applied and may vary from system to system, but they do not derogate from the basic status. Applying this definition to the systems of the ancient Near East, however, is complicated by two factors: 1) the ambiguity of native terminology; and 2) the plethora of servile conditions that share some of the characteristics of slavery but were nonetheless distinct in law.

A. Terminology

The native terminology can be misleading. In the strongly hierarchical societies of the region, the term "slave" was used to refer not only to a person owned in law by another but to any subordinate in the social ladder. Thus, the subjects of a king were called his "slaves" even though they were free citizens. The king himself, if a vassal, was the "slave" of his emperor, and kings, emperors, and commoners alike were "slaves" of the gods. A social inferior, when addressing a social superior, referred to himself out of politeness as "your slave." Context is the only criterion for determining which nuance of the term is implied, and in a legal context that will normally be the legal meaning. Also, slaves can usually be identified by the lack of a patronymic, but this is by no means always the case. The names of free persons were not always written with a patronymic, while slave names with a patronymic are occasionally encountered.

Akkadian sources also occasionally use the terms "boy" and "girl" for slave and slave-woman, with no indication except context to indicate whether a free child or a slave, who may well be an adult, is meant.[5]

B. Slavery and Servitude

Slavery is a separate status and should be distinguished from the following servile conditions:

---

5 See *CAD* Š 231-34; and Finet 1972.

1. Family

The authority of a head of household over other members of the family gave him powers that were, in some cases, analogous to those of a property owner. He could sell his children into slavery or hire out their labor, or he could hand over his wife or children by way of pledge to secure a debt. A son owned no property while his father was alive, and a wife's dowry was subsumed into the marital assets that were controlled by her husband.

On the other hand, this is one area where terminological differences are maintained. Although a husband is often called the "master" of his wife, neither wives nor children are ever referred to as the "slaves" of the head of household. Furthermore, a son had a vested interest in his father's property, of which he could not be divested except for cause and by a court order (CH 168-169). In addition, if a father chose to allot his son his share in the father's lifetime, the son became present owner of that property and did not lose his status as a son. Similarly, a wife remained the theoretical owner of her dowry, as a fund which was to be restored to her on termination of the marriage, and might have legal possession of certain items of it, such as clothes, jewelry, and personal slaves. A wife who was guilty of certain marital offenses could be divorced without compensation or, if the husband chose not to divorce her, she would dwell in his house "like a slave," i.e., deprived of her status as a wife and of her dowry (CH 141).

Although members of the family other than the head of household held a subordinate status, it was a separate status in law with its own special rules, which only occasionally coincided with those of slavery.

2. Serfdom

At various periods there is evidence of classes of workers attached to an institution (palace or temple) or to an estate, whom modern scholars have classified as serfs.[6] The native terms attributed to this status are manifold

---

6   I. Gelb compares 20 distinct features of slaves and serfs (1970: 81-92; cf. Gelb 1979). Diakonov points out, however, that most of these features are non-essential and lists 18 features himself (1974: 55-63).

and varied greatly from society to society.[7] While economically they may have shared the condition of slaves, it is doubtful that these classes of persons shared their legal status, although it is impossible to state to what degree they lacked freedom.[8] The few references in law codes do not contrast their legal treatment with that of free men, as is regularly the case with slaves.[9]

3. Pledge

Debtors could give themselves or persons under their authority to creditors by way of pledge. The resulting conditions were analogous to those of slavery: the pledge lost his personal freedom and was required to serve the pledgee, who exploited the pledge's labor. Nonetheless, the relationship between debtor and creditor remained one of contract, not property. Since the pledgee did not own the pledge, he could not alienate him, nor did the pledge's property automatically vest in the pledgee. It was in the nature of a pledge that it could be redeemed by payment of the debt, at which point the pledge would go free. During the period of his service, failure by the pledge to fulfill his duties led to contractual penalties, not punishment under the general disciplinary powers of a master. The contract could, however, contain a forfeiture clause whereby the pledge was reduced to slavery. A Middle Assyrian example reads:[10]

> A. and B. have borrowed 5 homers of barley, the property of C., from C. They shall pay the capital, the barley, within x months. When the due date is past they shall pay 2⅔ mina of tin. As pledge (*šapartu*) for this tin, C. holds their field or house or threshing-floors or wells or sons or daughters. When the due date is past,

---

7 E.g., guruš, erin in Sumerian texts; *miqtum, nāši biltim* in Old Babylonian; *hupparas*, LÚ ^{giš}TUKUL in Hittite; *ikkaru, šušānu* in Neo-Babylonian.

8 Diakonoff (1974: 58-59) includes in his list four "legal" features. They are not very revealing. Only "Alienability" differs; slaves are alienable, serfs are not or seldom so. The others are "Freedom of movement" (no), Emancipation (rare), Legal rights (limited/subject to change).

9 CL 15-16 (*miqtum*); HL 40-41 (LÚ ^{giš}TUKUL).

10 KAJ 66 = David and Ebeling 1929: no. 55.

their pledges are acquired . . . . A. and B. have received the tin as purchase price of their pledges.

Any children given as pledge could presumably then be sold. The alienability of the former pledge is made explicit in this contract:[11]

> (Concerning a loan of 6½ shekels) C. wife of B. has been handed over to A. as a pledge (*mazzazzānu*). If he (B.) does not pay the silver in two months, C. wife of B. may be sold.

Pledge frequently had an antichretic character. In other words, the person pledged was employed by the creditor in lieu of payment of interest on the loan. The result could be a form of service that lasted for many years, even for life. An antichretic pledge contract from Nuzi reads as follows:[12]

> Thus says A. son of X. Before witnesses he declared as follows: "I have received 12 mina of tin; I have caused myself to enter the house of B as pledge (*tidennūtu*) and do his work. When I have done his harvest, I shall return 12 mina of tin to B and cause myself to go out of B's house. If I neglect the work of B for a single day, I shall pay one seah of barley to B as a penalty." He who violates the agreement shall pay one ox.

The period of service here is relatively short—until the end of the harvest. In other such contracts, however, the period could be up to fifty years, and it is to be noted that the stated period was a minimum. A. had to wait until after the harvest to free himself. If he did not then pay, he remained in service. Note that the penalty for absence was contractual and that repayment was by the pledge himself.

4. Distraint

Where a debtor was in default, the creditor was entitled to distrain his property, including slaves, as well as members of his family. In the Old

---

11   ARM 8 71 (Old Babylonian).
12   HSS 5 40 = Eichler 1973: 126.

Babylonian period, this power (*nepûtum*) is the subject of letters and of some legal regulations. Persons distrained could be held prisoner and possibly forced to work for the creditor, but the evidence suggests that they could not be sold to satisfy the debt. The purpose of distraint appears rather to have been to put pressure on the debtor to repay:[13]

> After you went away on a journey A. came and, with the statement "He owes me one-third of a mina of silver," distrained your wife and daughter. Come and get your wife and daughter released before they die from being kept in detention. Please!

5. *Kiššātum*

Like distraint, this Old Babylonian term refers to a non-consensual form of servitude, but in this case it arose *ex delicto*. It appears to have been the penalty for certain minor offenses, such as petty theft.

The basic system of retribution for offenses that would be regarded as crimes in modern legal systems was a dual right that accrued to the victim (or his family): 1) revenge against the culprit (or his family), or 2) the acceptance of a payment by way of ransom in lieu of revenge. This right was a legal right, regulated by the courts who intervened to fix not only the appropriate level of revenge but also, in less serious cases, the appropriate ransom. In the latter case, revenge was only available if the ransom was not duly paid. *Kiššātum* reflected this duality, falling at the lower end of the scale. Revenge was loss of freedom; if the culprit could not pay the ransom (fixed or negotiated according to the circumstances of the case), the victim was entitled to take the culprit or members of his family or possibly one of his slaves into servitude.[14] In a sense it was servitude for debt, because if the ransom were ever paid, the person was released. There is indirect evidence, however, that the perpetrator could not be sold to a third party to realize the ransom. According to CH 117, family members given for *kiššātum* were to be released after three years, but CH 118 provides that a slave given for *kiššātum* was not released. Instead, the slave could be sold by the creditor if not redeemed within a three-year period.

---

13   UET 5 9 = Kraus 1959: 28.
14   See Westbrook 1996b.

The permission accorded by CH 118 to sell slaves after a grace period assumes an incapacity to sell free persons in the same condition.

C. Categories of Slavery

The status of slavery itself was not monolithic. The legal regime applied might differ in some aspects as between categories of slaves and even as between individual slaves. Three principal factors were responsible:

1. Social Justice

The legal systems of the ancient Near East contained various laws and measures of social justice for the relief of debtors. They applied not only to persons held by way of pledge, distraint, etc., but often explicitly included persons sold into slavery, where the sale arose from indebtedness. The rationale was that sale in such cases was merely an outward legal form, the true transaction being forfeiture for debt, which should be treated in the same way as pledge or distraint.[15] The effect of these rules was to create in practice two classes of slavery—debt-slavery and chattel-slavery—with different consequences in terms of manumission. A third class was constituted by what we shall term famine-slavery. The law intervened, to a more limited extent than with debt-slavery, to protect persons who entered into slavery under duress due to famine at a time of general calamity. Restrictions on the maltreatment of slaves also differed according to class of slave.

2. Contract

A characteristic feature of legal transactions recorded in cuneiform is the use of contracts ancillary to the creation of a legal status. Although contractual agreements could not directly annul or amend the rules that defined a status, it was possible for contractual terms to achieve the same purpose indirectly. For example, the status of marriage gave a wife the right to divorce her husband at will, but the marriage contract would im-

---

15　See Westbrook 1991b: 90-117.

pose a penalty on the wife for her exercise of that right.[16] Where slavery was created by contract, especially where self-sale was involved, the rules of the status could be affected in an analogous way. The terms of the contract could ameliorate the slave's condition, making it closer to other types of servile condition such as pledge, or they could reduce it, for example by stultifying the effect of rules of social justice.

3. Citizenship/Ethnicity

Foreigners in the ancient Near East were in a precarious situation. They had no legal rights outside of their own country or ethnic group unless they fell under the local rulers' protection. Even their lives were not safe. When the Egyptian envoy Wen-Amon was ship-wrecked on Cyprus, the inhabitants sought to kill him, and he only saved himself by forcing his way through to the local ruler and claiming her protection. Similarly, Genesis 12 narrates that when Abraham and his wife Sarah went down to Egypt, Abraham asked his wife to pretend to be his sister, for fear that the Egyptians, seeing her beauty, would kill him in order to take her from him. Involuntary enslavement was therefore a distinct possibility.

Protection could be acquired in several ways. Between states enjoying friendly relations, the rules of international law obliged the local sovereign to forbid and to punish crimes against the citizens of the other state committed on his territory, and he would be held accountable by the victim's own sovereign. A foreigner who had no allied sovereign to support him would seek to be designated a resident alien, a status that gave him protection against involuntary slavery, but not necessarily the benefit of social justice measures that citizens enjoyed.[17] Many such measures were expressly limited to citizens or to members of the local ethnic group. Furthermore, even within a state, the privileges of residence might have had only local validity. As a Babylonian proverb remarks: "A resident alien in another city is a slave."[18] Inevitably, foreign slaves were heavily represented in the category of chattel-slaves.

16 See Westbrook 1988b: 58–59, 79–85.
17 Akkadian *ubāru*, Hebrew *gēr*. See Kühne 1973: 29 n.128.
18 Lambert *BWL* 259 (= AJSL 28 242); edition in Lambert 1960a: 259.

D. Biblical Law

The slave laws of the Bible offer a special complication because biblical Hebrew does not appear to have had special terminology for servile conditions apart from slavery. As a result, not only debt-relief laws, but all laws protecting pledges, etc., were applied to slaves. The main distinction was between native and foreign slaves, it being assumed for the purposes of social justice measures that all native slaves were debt-slaves.[19]

IV. Creation

A. War

Foreigners captured in war were booty, which could be dealt with as the captor saw fit. They could be held for ransom, exploited as labor, or resettled.[20] They were not automatically slaves, but they were without rights and therefore potential slaves. Indeed, they were without the legal complications of domestically created slaves, since their enslavement was in the nature of acquisition of ownerless property.

Although war might be expected to be a prime source of slavery, there is very little mention of slaves from this source. In the cuneiform writing system, the Sumerian ideograms for slave and slave-woman were originally pictograms composed of the signs MAN+MOUNTAIN and WOMAN+MOUNTAIN, respectively, suggesting that in early times (i.e., the fourth millennium) the mountains to the East of the Tigris-Euphrates Valley, which, in Sumerian eyes, were populated by hostile barbarian tribes, were raided for slaves. At the end of the third millennium, a Neo-Sumerian king, Shu-Sin, boasted:[21]

---

19 The Covenant Code describes a procedure (Exod 21:5-6) whereby a debt-slave voluntarily becomes a chattel-slave, but the parallel slave-regulations of Lev 25 (considered by biblical scholarship to be from a different source) do not appear to recognize this possibility.

20 See *CAD* Š/1 248-50.

21 Kutscher *Brockmon Tablets* 90 iv: lines 15-31.

He blinded the young men whom he captured in their cities and gave them as . . . in the orchard of (the gods) Enlil and Ninlil and in the orchards of the great gods. And the young women whom he captured in the cities he devoted to the weaver's mills of Enlil and Ninlil and to the temples of the great gods.

Such slaves were regarded primarily as a royal resource, the male prisoners being blinded as a security measure, and therefore of limited usefulness. Some Old Sumerian contracts were for the sale, at a discount, of "blinded men" (igi-nu-du$_8$), the sellers being orchard-keepers and in one case a state employee.[22] They may then allude to some traffic of royal prisoners in the private sector. There is more positive evidence for the private acquisition of captured girls, who would obviously be more suited for private domestic service. A contract from Nuzi contains the declaration:[23]

(Ms.) A. of the land of Arrapha I took from the land of Kukapshu-hena as booty(?) to my chariot and sold her to B. son of X.

Similarly, a Neo-Babylonian contract reads:[24]

A. son of X. has voluntarily sold to B. son of Y. his slave-woman C. and her daughter of 3 months, an Egyptian from his booty of the bow, for 2 mina of silver as the full price.

Deut 21:10-14 laid down rules for a soldier wishing to marry a woman that he had captured:

When you go out to war against your enemies and the LORD your God gives them into your hand and you take captives: if you see among the captives a beautiful woman and you desire to marry her, you shall bring her into your house and she shall shave her head and pare her nails and remove the garment of captivity and sit in your house and mourn her father and mother for one month

---

22 *SRU* 40-42.
23 JEN 179 = Saarisalo 1934: no. 28.
24 *Camb.* 334 = Dandamaev 1984: 107.

and thereafter you may consummate the marriage with her. But should she not please you, you shall send her out where she will (i.e., be divorced and leave as a free woman); you shall not sell her, and you shall not reduce her status (*tit'ammēr*) because you have shamed her.

The Hebrew verb here translated "reduce her status" is found elsewhere in the Bible only in Deut 24:7, where it refers to the act of selling a kidnapped free man into slavery. The basis of the present law is therefore that a prisoner was not yet a slave but had the potential to be one. Here the intervening marriage interfered with the normal rights of the captor and rendered it unjust for him to exercise them should he then terminate the marriage.

B. Kidnapping

Involuntary enslavement applied only to foreigners. With respect to one's fellow citizens, the law codes contained stern injunctions against kidnapping free persons for the purpose of reducing them to slavery:

CH 14: If a man steals the young son of a man, he shall be killed.

Exod 21:16: A man who steals a man and sells him, and one in whose hand he is found, shall be put to death.

The safest course was to sell the kidnap victim abroad, as is illustrated by the story of Joseph. Judah urged Joseph's brothers not to kill him but to sell him to a caravan of foreign merchants on their way to Egypt, a transaction which was ultimately made by some passing Midianites (Gen 37:25-28). An Old Babylonian administrative order alludes to the misadventures of a child sold abroad due to the fortunes of war but apparently later acquired in ignorance by a local citizen:[25]

---

25 AbB 6 80. Siegel suggests that her freedom was made possible by reconquest from the Elamites of the area in which she lived (1947: 44, 46).

A free lady, a native of the city of Idamaraz, was deported by the Elamites with the general population but without her family. Her wet-nurse sold her. Her city has attested that she is a free lady. Her present owner, (in) the city of Muti-abala, has not freed her; he has detained her in his house. Judgment should be given according to the order.

C. House-Born

In Old Babylonian slave-sales it was occasionally noted that a slave is "house-born" (*wilid bītim*).[26] In one such document, the slave-girl was said to have been "born on the roof."[27] Such slaves could have been the off-spring of a union of master and slave, as attested in the law codes (CL 25, CH 171) or of slaves. In a Neo-Sumerian court record a slave claimed to be a free man, but was proved to have been born in the late master's house as the son of a slave of the latter and was therefore assigned to the late master's heirs.[28]

D. Debt

If a debt fell due and the debtor was unable to pay, the creditor could seize goods or members of the debtor's family in order to force him to pay the sum owing. In the latter case the Old Babylonian law codes spoke of the creditor detaining the distrainee in his house and imposed severe penalties should the distrainee have been killed there by beating or abuse (CE 23, CH 115-116). The selection of this special situation, rather than slavery in general, as the locus of a discussion of abuse suggests to us that the simple alternative of selling the distrainee to realize the sum of the debt was not available to the creditor. Enslavement for debt required a voluntary act by the debtor, at least in law. Contracts of sale into slavery for debt made efforts to emphasize the voluntary nature of the sale, especially where the debtor was selling himself. In practice, the debtor may have been left with

---

26   E.g., YOS 13 248:2. Further references in *CAD* I/J 71.
27   Sumerian: ù r . r a . tu . ud . d a. YOS 12 74:2.
28   *NSG* 32.

no choice. CH 117 speaks of a loan "seizing" a man, so that he sells his wife, son, or daughter.

The realities of the situation may be reflected in the ambiguous statement in 2 Kgs 4:1:

> One of the wives of the prophets cried out to Elisha: "Your servant my husband has died . . . and the creditor comes to take my two children as his slaves."

Was the creditor acquiring slaves by distraint, something that we have argued was not possible in neighboring legal systems? Given the absence of special terminology in biblical Hebrew, it may indeed be that two legal institutions were fused in law. On the other hand, this non-legal text may merely be alluding to the widow's helplessness in the situation. The same circumstances are described in the opening lines of a court record from Emar:[29]

> Before X. and the city elders: A. owed B. 25 shekels; then A. died and his two children entered B.'s house and he released the 25 shekels. Now B. has produced the two children of A. before X. and the elders and before their (paternal) uncles and declared: "Take your two nephews and repay me my 25 shekels . . . . These two nephews have entered voluntarily into slavery with me."

Where a sale took place, it could be to the creditor himself or to a third party. We have already seen that pledge contracts could contain a foreclosure clause converting the pledge into sale to the creditor or allowing the creditor to sell the pledge. In the absence of pledge, direct reference to the loan could be made in the contract of sale; such reference occurs in a Neo-Assyrian document:[30]

> A. has purchased and acquired B. daughter of C. from C. in lieu of 30 shekels of silver belonging to A. and to (the goddess) Ishtar of

---

29   Arnaud *Emar* 6 205.

30   Kwasman *NA Legal* 401.

Arba'il. In lieu of his debts he has given his daughter to A. That woman is paid for and acquired.

An Old Babylonian document where the purchaser was a well-known financier expresses the same in the case of a self-sale:[31]

Balmunamhe has purchased A. and B., the sons of X . . . from themselves. He has paid one-third of a mina of silver for their loan as their full price.

An Emar document records sale to a third party who effected a purchase of the debtor's loans:[32]

Before the elders of the city of Ur, A. son of X. stated thus: "I was indebted for 100 shekels of silver, and B. son of Y. has paid my debts. In exchange for my debts that he paid for me, I, together with my two wives, . . . have of my own free will entered into the slavery of B." This is the silver for which he entered: 70 shekels of silver given to C., 10 shekels of silver given to D., 20 shekels of silver given to E.

Debt did not only arise from loans. Certain types of delict created a debt in the culprit to the victim or his family which, if not paid, might be satisfied by sale of the culprit into slavery. Thus CH 53-54 ordered that where a negligent farmer had managed to flood the whole district and did not have the means to compensate all his neighbors for their loss, the latter could sell him and his property and divide the proceeds among themselves. Similarly, in Exod 22:2 a burglar caught breaking in had to pay the householder a ransom for his freedom, and, if he could not, was to be sold "for his theft."[33] The same rule would seem to lie behind a Neo-Sumerian trial report which recorded the sale of the culprit's family:[34]

---

31 YOS 8 31 = Mendelsohn 1949: 15-16.
32 Arnaud *Emar* 6 215.
33 For an analysis of this law, see Westbrook 1988d: 124-26.
34 *NSG* 42.

> A. gave B., the wife of C., his (C.'s) daughter D., and E., the slave of C., to F. and G. in slavery because C. had robbed him (A.).

In another of these records, the victims elected to keep the culprit's family for themselves as slaves, after the culprit's death (execution?):[35]

> It was established before the grand vizier that A. son of X. had killed B. Y. was presiding officer when, because A. was killed, his estate and wife and daughter were handed over to B.'s sons. In the fifth year A.'s wife and daughter ran away from B.'s sons, but B.'s sons caught them.

Finally, in a document from Emar, a person accused of theft reached a settlement whereby he avoided slavery for himself:[36]

> A. stole the slave of B. and was caught with that slave. They brought him to judgment before the king, and the king gave the nobles of the town of S. to the oath. The king declared: "If the nobles swear, A. shall remain to B. as a slave." A. did not wish to agree to the nobles swearing; he gave his sister to B. as a slave in exchange for himself. In the future A. may not raise claims against B.

E. Famine

In contracts written in the town of Nippur when it was under siege by Nabopolassar, children were sold into slavery in exchange for their being kept alive and for money for food for their parents:[37]

> A. spoke thus to B.: "Take my . . . daughter C. and keep her alive. She shall be your slave. Give me 6 shekels of silver so that I may eat."

---

35 *NSG* 41.
36 Arnaud *Emar* 6 257.
37 *Iraq* 17 no. 2 (NT 97).

Enslavement for famine was similar to enslavement for debt, but was not always identical. The sale of a child in times of famine could always be regarded as a sale made under duress with the price being a debt. Sometimes, however, there was no price. Rather, free persons gave their children or themselves into slavery in return for being kept alive until the famine was over. A small group of contracts among the Middle Babylonian records from Nuzi, mostly from the business archive of a single financier, Tehip-tilla (and his son Enna-mati), involved persons who voluntarily entered his house as slaves.[38] The reason was not stated and no money changed hands. Some of the contracts describe the subjects as *ḫābiru*, referring to a marginal category of people who would, for the most part, have been landless, or as being of foreign origin.[39] It is reasonable to assume therefore that such contracts concerned self-enslavement by reason of famine. They contained some remarkable clauses, some of which are typical of famine-induced slavery and others which are best explained as attempts to avoid the rules of social justice that applied in that situation. A Neo-Babylonian contract is more explicit:[40]

> In that time, A. spoke thus to B., the scribe of Sippar: "Keep me alive and I will be your slave." B. agreed and established food rations for her.

The question then arose whether such a person was to continue in slavery once the famine was over. If not, how long was he to serve? If he could be redeemed, at what price, since there was no debt to provide a criterion? The legal principles that applied to famine-induced contracts will be discussed below under the heading "Termination."

Famine also resulted in the abandonment of children. If a passerby saved an abandoned child, he might adopt him, as was the good fortune of Moses, or he might take him as a slave. We have little evidence on the latter case, but in an Old Sumerian slave sale the slave's name was "Found-in-a-well" (tul-ta-pad-da) which was a standard mode of describing a

---

38   JEN 446-465, 610, 611, 613. Edited by Bottéro 1954: 43-61; and Greenberg 1955: 23-28, 30-32.

39   For a detailed discussion, see Bottéro 1954 and Greenberg 1955.

40   BM 74652 = *AfO* 16 37 (plate III).

foundling.[41] A slave taken as a foundling would presumably be ownerless property, like a prisoner of war. In the case of adoption, the possibility of the natural parents reclaiming the child under certain circumstances was considered in the law codes.[42] Whether the same applied to an enslaved foundling is an intriguing, but as yet unanswerable, question.

F. Penalty

Slavery also arose from the operation of contractual penalty clauses. A Sumerian-Akkadian dictionary of legal phrases (mid-first millennium) contains the following standard clause:[43]

> If a son says to his father "You are not my father," he will shave him, place the slave-mark (*abbuttu*) upon him and sell him.

The words quoted are the *verba solemnia* dissolving adoption. A wife who pronounced the divorce formula might be visited with the same penalty. An Old Babylonian contract contains the clauses:[44]

> If A says to his wife B, "You are not my wife," he shall pay half a mina of silver.
> If B says to her husband A, "You are not my husband," they will shave her and sell her.

Similar clauses are also occasionally found in commercial agreements. An Old Babylonian labor contract reads:[45]

> A. and his son shall make their labor available to B. Yearly B. shall give them 1 kor of barley, 1 garment, and a shirt. A. and his son have sworn by (the god) Ninurta that if they abandon the work, B. may sell them.

---

41   *SRU* 43.
42   CH 185-186; cf. MSL I 3 III 28-57.
43   MSL I 7 III 23-28.
44   BE 6/2 48 = Westbrook 1988b: 115-16.
45   Kienast *Kisurra* 88.

Such a delinquency clause is even found in a slave sale contract, as part of the seller's warranty:[46]

> A. has purchased a slave-woman named B. from her brothers C. and D. If she abandons (her work), they will become slaves (in her place).

In an unusual case, a Neo-Babylonian document reveals that a young woman called the penalty of slavery upon herself for immoral conduct:[47]

> If A., daughter of X., is seen with B., son of Y., and he leads her to himself under false pretenses . . . but she does not say to the master of the house "Inform Y. the father of B.," then A. will receive the mark of slavery.

V. Termination

A. By Manumission

The Neo-Sumerian records of litigation include a number of disputes between slaves and the heirs of their owners. For example:[48]

> The heirs of A. sued the daughters of B., slave of A. C., daughter of B., brought before the vizier a tablet of A. (stating) that A. in his lifetime had appeared and declared: "By the king's oath! I free the daughters of B., my slave." The daughters of B. severed themselves from the heirs of A.

In spite of the wording of the oath, it appears that manumission was only to be postmortem, leading to disputes when the heirs sought to claim their inheritance.[49] In *NSG* 99:15-51, on the death of the slave-owner, his heirs claimed a slave from their mother, but she was able to prove that their

---

46 Steinkeller *Sale Documents* 45 (Neo-Sumerian).
47 *Cyr.* 307 = Dandamaev 1984: 105.
48 *NSG* 205:27-42.
49 Cf. *NSG* 75, 178:12-23, and the discussion by Falkenstein 1956-57: vol. 1, 94-95.

father had given her the slave as a gift during his lifetime. She then freed that slave's daughters, and the heirs swore an oath not to "change their mother's word." The reference is to respecting her testamentary dispositions when they eventually inherited from her.[50]

The motivation for manumission in these cases is not mentioned, and it may well have been pure liberality on the owner's part. But documents of manumission from later periods for the most part record reciprocal arrangements whereby the slave was freed in return for continuing to look after his master, especially in old age. These arrangements were of two kinds. In the first, the master manumitted the slave upon his death, in return for support during the rest of his life, as in a document from Elephantine:[51]

A. son of X., a Jew of Elephantine the fortress of the Iddinnabu detachment, said to B., his slave-woman who is marked on her right hand "Belonging to A" thus: "I took thought of you in my lifetime. I have set you free at my death, and I have freed C., your daughter whom you bore me. A son or daughter of mine or brother or sister, near or distant (relative) . . . has no right to you or to C., your daughter whom you bore me, has no right to brand you or sell you. Whoever lays claims to you or to C., your daughter whom you bore me, shall be liable to you for a penalty of 50 karsh of silver . . . . You are freed, from shadow to sun, and your daughter C., and another has no right over you and your daughter C.; you are freed to God." And B. and her daughter C. said: "We shall serve you as a son or daughter supports his father during your lifetime, and upon your death we shall support your son D., like a son who supports his father, as we shall have been doing for you during your lifetime. If we arise and say: "We will not support you like a son who supports his father nor your son D. after your death," we shall be liable to you and your son D. for a penalty of 50 karsh of silver."

50 Cf. CL 31: "If a father in his lifetime has made a gift to a favorite son and drafted a sealed tablet for him, after the father's death the heirs shall divide the father's estate, but they shall not claim his share; they shall not . . . their father's word."

51 Kraeling 5 = *TAD* B3.6.

According to CH 171, a master's slave-concubine and his issue by her were to be freed automatically upon his death. That surprising piece of liberality was not widely emulated, and here we see that it had to be achieved through an express contractual clause.

Three further points should be noted with respect to this document. First, the manner of the slaves' service was to be like that of a son caring for his father. Second, the slaves' obligation continued after their master's death with respect to his son even though they were free; they were bound by contract, not status, from that point on. Third, even during their remaining period of slavery, the grant of freedom was irrevocable. Their misconduct would result in a contractual penalty, not in cancellation of the grant. The contract thus mitigated the effects of slavery, at least in law. In practice, however, the impossibility of paying the huge penalty would inevitably lead to their re-enslavement.

The second method was to free the slave immediately and adopt him, thereby ensuring for the manumitter the duties of support imposed by analogy in the Elephantine contract. The duty thus arose from status, but the status of a son, not a slave. According to an Old Babylonian contract:[52]

> A. is the son of B. His mother B., the priestess, daughter of X., has purified him; she has placed his face to the sunrise.[53] If A. continues to support B. as long as she lives, after her death no one shall have any claim upon A; he is purified. No one from among the children of X. or the children of Y. shall raise a claim against him.

Failure to support was a breach that would lead to the loss of his status as son. He would then be liable to be reclaimed as a slave by his mistress's heirs. An Old Assyrian contract provides further details:[54]

> A. son of X. has purified the forehead of his slave B. As long as his father A. and his mother C. live, he shall support them and serve them. After (the death of) his father A. and his mother B., he

---

52   CT 8 48a = Schorr 1913: no. 27.
53   This is a reference to a ritual of manumission; see Malul 1988: 41-51.
54   Kraus *AV* 359-85.

shall receive *x* acres of land and one ox. If A. reclaims him, he shall pay 2 mina of silver, and if B. repudiates A. and C. and leaves, he shall be sold in the town market where he is spotted.

It can be inferred that the slave was adopted upon manumission. The contract was unusually favorable to the slave. He was allotted an inheritance share, which is unusual in this type of manumission. The penalty on his former master for attempting to reclaim him as a slave was very large while the penalty on the former slave was standard for repudiation by an adoptee.

Occasionally, a contract manumitted forthwith and stipulated service without adoption of the freed slave.[55] In such cases, it would appear that the obligation to serve once free was based on contract alone. The consequences of a breach would not have differed significantly, as a Neo-Babylonian document reveals:[56]

A., son of X. descendant of Y., sealed a tablet of free status of his slave B. (in return) for giving food and clothing. After he had sealed the tablet of free status, B. ran away and did not give him food, oil, and clothing. But C. daughter of Z. etc., the wife of D. son of A., served, honored, and looked after him. A. voluntarily annulled B.'s tablet of free status and sealed a tablet assigning (B.) to C. and her daughter F., the daughter of D. son of (A. descendant of) X. C. and her daughter F. shall serve (A.), and after C.'s death he (B.) will pass to F.

A document from Ugarit records a contract wherein an owner manumitted his slave-woman and married her off, receiving from the groom the betrothal payment that would normally be paid to a parent or guardian:[57]

---

55 See e.g., the text cited in Roth 1979: 108-9: "A. has freed [his slave-woman B.]. He has purified her forehead, he has broken the pot of her slavery, and he has executed a document concerning her purification. As long as she lives, she shall serve him. A., the father, while still alive, has sworn by the king that after A. dies, A.'s heirs shall not claim her for slavery."

56 *Nbn.* 697 = Dandamaev 1984: 438.

57 RS 8.208 = Thureau-Dangin 1937: 253-54; and Schaeffer 1955: 110-11 (in part).

As of this day, before witnesses A. has freed B., his slave-woman, . . . (declaring) thus: "I have poured oil on her head and I thereby purify her. As the Sun is pure, so B. is pure for ever." Furthermore, C. has taken her as his wife. C., her husband, has brought 20 (shekels of) silver and has given them to A.

It is not clear from the document whether he received the payment by way of owner or parent (in which case we would need to assume an intervening adoption). In an Old Babylonian document, the mistress manumitted her slave-woman, adopted her, and gave her in marriage. No betrothal payment is mentioned in its very summary text.[58]

B. By Redemption

1. Debt-Slavery

If property was pledged for a loan, by the nature of things that property would be released to its owner upon payment of the loan. The courts of the ancient Near East, however, extended that principle by way of equity to sales, where the sale was in effect a forced sale at under-value to pay off a debt. The seller was, under certain conditions, allowed to buy back, to "redeem," that property at the original price, as if it had merely been pledged. This equitable principle applied only to certain types of property, in particular family land, but also to members of one's family sold as slaves.[59] As Lev 25:47-49 puts it:

If a resident alien obtained means and your brother grows weak with him and is sold to the resident alien . . . after he is sold he shall have (the right of) redemption: one of his brothers may redeem him, or any of his relatives from his clan may redeem him or he may obtain the means and be redeemed.

The circumstances are graphically portrayed in an Emar document:[60]

---

58 CT 2 33 = Westbrook 1988b: 116.
59 See Westbrook 1991b: 90-117.
60 Arnaud *Emar* 6 205, discussed in part IV. D. above.

Before X. and the city elders: A. owed B. 25 shekels; then A. died and his two children entered into B.'s house, and he released the 25 shekels. Now B. has produced these two children of A. before X. and before the elders and before their (paternal) uncles, and he has declared: "Take your two nephews and repay me my 25 shekels . . . . These two nephews have entered voluntarily into slavery with me."

Their father's brothers refused to give the 25 shekels of B., and they confirmed by sealed tablet, voluntarily, the enslavement of their two nephews to B. Dead or alive, they are B.'s slaves. In the future, if C. and their father's brothers say: "We will redeem our two nephews," they shall give two souls for D. and two souls for E., the blind one, to B., and then they may take their two nephews.

In paragraph 119 of Codex Hammurabi, the principle is extended to a slave concubine:

If a debt has seized a man, and he sells his slave-woman who has borne him children, the owner of the slave-woman may pay the silver that the merchant paid and redeem his slave-woman.

Note that in this case the result was not freedom for the slave but return to her former master. A right of redemption based on ownership will return property to its previous owner or to one with a right to inherit it. That is how the system worked with redemption of family land. In the case of a previously free debt-slave, however, the right of redemption in a relative would seem to be based not on ownership or inheritance but on family authority. Thus, a slave who reverted to the authority of the head of household, for example a son redeemed by his father, would thereby be freed but once more be subordinate to his father. It is an open question whether a more distant relative acting as redeemer, such as a cousin, also acquired family authority over the family member redeemed. The redeemer certainly acquired the rights of a creditor, but with a loan that was now unsecured.

If the line of relatives was exhausted, there existed the possibility that the public authorities could intervene. A broken Neo-Assyrian document contains the following clause:[61]

> Whenever . . . his brothers or the prefect or his people or his governor or his prefect or the mayor of his city shall come, he shall pay . . . seventy shekels of copper and cause the man to go out.

Evidently, not every debt-slave was eligible, and the circumstances under which the authorities would choose to intervene are not known. It is reminiscent of the duty of the local authorities in CH 32 to pay the ransom of a captured soldier if he did not have the means to do so himself. Ideologically, the king was the "father of his people" in matters of social justice, a role to which being a redeemer was eminently suitable.[62] In a series of transactions from the Old Babylonian stratum at Alalakh, the king of Alalakh redeemed various debt-slaves from their creditors by paying their debts.[63] It appears that the relation between the former slaves and their new creditor was changed to one of antichretic pledge.[64]

An outside redeemer might be motivated by altogether different considerations. In a remarkable Middle Assyrian case, a slave, with his master's authority (and presumably his funds), redeemed a slave-woman from a different master, manumitted her, and married her. She was to be subordinate to her husband's master in some way, but the contract expressly prohibited the master from enslaving her or her children.[65] Prior to his marriage, the redeemer appears to have had no standing that would have given him a right to redeem, irrespective of the owner's consent. We

---

61 *ARU* 133:4-10. The clause is apparently preceded by a previous redemption and duty to serve for the lifetime (of the redeemer?). The clause is too fragmentary to draw any conclusions.

62 CH Epilogue Col. XLVIII 20-24. It is not surprising that the God of Israel, the ultimate king and father, is referred to as the redeemer of his people, e.g., Psalm 103:4.

63 AT 28-31.

64 This is stated expressly in AT 28 and is inferred in the other documents by the statement that the capital bears no interest.

65 The transaction is recorded in two documents: KAJ 167 = David and Ebeling 1929: no. 7 (redemption); and KAJ 7 = David and Ebeling 1929: no. 1 (marriage). The husband to all appearances remains his master's slave.

must assume, therefore, that this special arrangement was made with the consent of all the parties concerned, including the slave-woman.

The final resort, according to Lev 25:49, was for the slave to find the means to redeem himself. That arrangement was recorded in a Neo-Sumerian contract:[66]

> A., the slave of B., has redeemed herself from B. She has paid him one-third of a mina of silver as her full price. As long as B. and C. live she shall do service with their spouses and children. After B.'s and C.'s death, A. may go where she pleases; no one shall raise claims against her.

What was the source of funds for the slave's redemption? If a slave could own no property of his own, how could he repay his master? In an Old Babylonian document, a slave was manumitted after she had "brought in" ten shekels of silver to her mistress, which suggests an outside source.[67] One can speculate that it might have sometimes been in the master's interest to allow the slave, by his work or through his peculium,[68] to accumulate sufficient funds for his redemption. The paradox of the Neo-Sumerian contract just discussed, namely that the slave has paid the full price of her redemption but must still serve under a contractual obligation in the manner of a manumitted slave, may be explained by supposing that at least a part of the payment was fictitious, being the capitalization of her future work. An Old Babylonian document is even more suggestive of this possibility:[69]

> One slave, A. by name, the slave of B., redeemed himself. He (B.) has purified his forehead and smashed his foot fetters. He established his freedom and gave him towards the Sun. As long as B. lives, A. shall support him. After B. dies, if any of B.'s sons de-

---

66 UET 3 51 = Falkenstein 1956-57: vol. 1, 95.
67 BE 6/2 8 = Schorr 1913: no. 28. Antichretic pledge documents, by contrast, sometimes make express mention of the debtor's land, which may be seized by the creditor if he absents himself from work, e.g., Eichler 1973: nos. 33, 34.
68 On the slave's peculium, see Dandamaev 1970: 35-39.
69 Speleers Recueil 45 = Roth 1979: 110-11.

clare as regards A.: "(He is) my slave," he shall pay two minas of silver.

2. Famine-Slavery

Where a person enslaved themselves in return for sustenance in a year of famine, there was no obvious price for their redemption. HL 172 set a standard tariff:

> If a man saves a free man's life in a year of famine, he shall give his substitute. If it is a slave, he shall give 10 shekels of silver.

The provision of a substitute appears to be the usual contractual practice. In the Middle Assyrian marriage arrangement just described, where the bride had originally been taken into slavery "for keeping alive and for acquisition," the receipt of "a Subarian girl" (i.e., a foreign slave) by her owner is described as "her redemption payment (*ipṭiriša*)."

Other contractual arrangements were, however, possible. A price in silver could be set by the contract, as in an Old Assyrian example:[70]

> A., in a time of famine, gave B. and his wife to C. In a time of famine he kept them alive. B. is his slave; his wife is his slave-woman. If anyone should claim them, he shall pay two mina of silver to C. and cause them to go out.

The document does not provide sufficient background information to explain the basis for the price set. The relationship between A., the couple B., and C. is not specified.

In the small group of contracts of the financier Tehip-tilla from Nuzi that we have identified as famine-induced, several stipulated the provision of a substitute,[71] but others imposed harsher terms. For example, in one

---

70 *AHDO* 1 106-108.

71 JEN 458 = Greenberg 1955: no. 43; JEN 463 = Greenberg 1955: no. 42; JEN 611 = Greenberg 1955: no. 65. Curiously enough, the first two refer to the payment as being for breach of contract.

case a father had to give ten slaves in order to redeem his son.[72] Some contracts sought to delay the possibility of release:[73]

> A. son of X. the scribe, an Assyrian, has caused himself to enter the house of B. son of Y. for slavery. As long as B. lives A. shall serve him, and when B. dies, A. shall give to B.'s son a scribe as his substitute and he may depart. B. shall furnish A. with food and clothing. If A. leaves now, he shall pay 10 mina of silver and 10 mina of gold.

This contract restricted the slave's service to the lifetime of his first owner, entitling him to redeem himself from the latter's heir. In this respect the contract gave slavery features typical of certain types of antichretic pledges. Compare an antichretic pledge from Nuzi not involving slavery:[74]

> Thus A. declares: "I caused myself to enter the house of B. together with my sons and the people of my house." As long as A. lives he shall not leave B.'s house. When A. dies, A.'s sons shall give one boy of 2½ cubits and one girl of the same height, and they themselves may leave. If A. leaves B.'s house, he shall pay B. one mina of silver and one mina of gold. If A. quits the work of B. for one day he shall pay the hire of a slave.

In antichretic pledges from Emar, the resemblance is closer. The pledge typically had to serve for the lifetime of the creditor, after which he could redeem himself from the creditor's heir, and penalties were imposed upon both parties for attempting to end the relationship prematurely.[75]

---

72 JEN 455:8-16 = Greenberg 1955: no. 46.

73 JEN 456:9-13+613 = Greenberg 1955: nos. 59, 60. The translation is a composite of the two sources, which are a shorter and longer version of the same transaction.

74 JEN 312:5ff. = Saarisalo 1934: no. 34; Eichler 1973: 20.

75 Arnaud *Emar* 6 16. Cf. also an innominate form of servitude recorded in a document from Emar which specifically mentions famine (Arnaud *Emar* 6 86): "A. son of X. said thus: 'B. son of Y. kept me alive in a year of famine and paid my debt of 2½ shekels of silver. As long as I live I shall serve you (*apallaḫka*). If in the future A. says to B., 'I will leave your house,' he may pay B. 10 shekels of silver and go where he pleases."

The penalty for premature termination in the Nuzi slavery contract—ten minas of silver and ten minas of gold—is absurdly large and clearly *in terrorem*, but it is still by no means the harshest in this group of contracts. As we shall see, cruel physical punishments were also possible. On the other hand, the contractual penalty could be even milder than the norm set by the Hittite Laws. In one contract, Tehip-tilla's son Enna-mati supplied the person who entered into slavery with him a peculium and a wife. The slave had to serve Enna-mati and his successor, but his penalty for premature termination was nothing more than forfeiture of the wife and property received.[76]

Famine-slavery therefore occupied an intermediate position between debt-slavery, where redemption was a right and the price was predetermined by the original debt, and chattel-slavery, in which a slave could not unilaterally end his slavery and no contractual penalty was necessary, since any attempt by the slave to end his slavery would have no legal consequences. In famine-slavery it appears that a person saved from famine had an underlying right to redeem himself from his benefactor's service. The terms of the right of redemption could be determined by contract. Supplying a substitute was the equitable arrangement, but the enslaver was allowed a great deal of freedom to impose terms. These terms ran the gamut from milder than the standard set in the Hittite Laws to incomparably more severe. The grounds for the terms in a particular case are hidden from us. It is not known whether there was a natural market, even in times of famine, in which the poor and their creditors competed among each other for the best terms,[77] or whether there were restrictions based on the equitable jurisdiction of the king and the courts that could only sometimes be evaded. In many of the contracts with Tehip-tilla, it is stressed that the people entering into slavery with him were foreigners, which may be the reason why their rights could be so drastically curtailed by contractual clauses. Paradoxically, those clauses are at the same time evidence that the

---

76 JEN 610 = Greenberg 1955: no. 64.

77 In an Emar document (Arnaud *Emar* 6 216), the contract relates the statement of a woman that she sold her daughter to another woman in order to keep her other children alive in a year of famine. A second contract, however, (Arnaud *Emar* 6 217) reveals that payment on the first agreement was not made, and so instead of selling one child for 30 shekels, the couple sold all four of their children to another financier for 60 shekels.

protection of social justice measures was to some extent available to foreigners as well, since there would have been no point in inserting in the
contract a penalty for the exercise of a non-existent right.

C. By Debt-Release

If the debtor was so impoverished that he could not find the funds to redeem himself or his family, even at the reduced price of their original debt
or sale, then redemption was a hollow right for him. The social and economic consequences of the debt-burden were such that rulers felt obliged
to intervene with more drastic measures. Not surprisingly, the benefit of
these measures was generally confined to citizens or members of the ethnic group.

First, the courts might decree the automatic release of a debt-slave after a certain number of years of service. According to CH 117:

> If a debt seizes a man and he sells his wife, son, or daughter or
> gives them for *kiššātum*, they shall work three years in the house
> of their purchaser or holder in *kiššātum*; in the fourth their restora-
> tion (*andurārum*) shall be established.

Andurārum is an important term, which is generally translated as "freedom." Charpin has shown, however, that the basic root of the word means
"to return to the point of origin."[78] In terms of slaves, a return to their
original status would generally mean freedom, as is certainly the case here,
but in certain circumstances, it would only mean a return to their previous
master.

The same mechanism is found in the Bible in Exod 21:2 and Deut
15:12-17. The first of these reads:

> If you buy a Hebrew slave, he shall work six years, and in the sev-
> enth he shall go out free for nothing.

The phrase "for nothing" indicates that debt-slavery is at issue because the
slave does not have to pay redemption. A remark in Deut 15:18 justifies

78   Charpin 1987: 36-41.

the measure by suggesting that, as we have seen implied in some redemption documents, the slave's service was deemed to have amortized the loan:

> It shall not seem hard to you to set him free, for he has served you twice the hire of a hired man, six years.

Although the above texts from law codes give the impression of a universal rule that was applied automatically, they are, in my view, to be interpreted as indications of the courts' equitable discretion. The law codes were not normative legislation, and there is some suspicion that rules of this nature were more ideal standards than standard practice. On the other hand, the king did have power to correct injustices even if the acts in question were within the letter of the law. There is copious evidence of the king's exercise of this equitable role in individual cases, usually in response to petitions.[79] We suspect, therefore, that the above limits on the length of debt-slavery represent criteria that the king might have applied in exercising his discretion in response to an individual petition. Indirect evidence for exercise of discretion in this regard comes from the slave contracts of Balmunamhe, a slave-owner of the Old Babylonian period. A number of transactions involving debt-slaves contained clauses making sureties, sometimes identified as the slave's relatives, liable to pay compensation to Balmunamhe if the slave "seeks/turns to the palace or to an influential or important person."[80] In other words, if the slave gained his freedom by petitioning the king or one of his officials, the surety had to compensate the owner for his loss.

When exercised on a universal basis, the king's equitable discretion led to a more drastic solution to the plight of debt-slaves. It was the practice of kings throughout the ancient Near East to decree on their accession to the throne, and occasionally at other times, a general cancellation of existing debts. This retrospective measure—"establishing equity"—also brought to an end the service of persons pledged or sold for non-payment of debts. Thus, in the prologue to his law code, King Lipit-Ishtar boasted:

---

79   The king's equitable powers are discussed in Westbrook 1988d: 9-38.
80   See Van De Mieroop 1987: 7.

> I restored the freedom (literally, "obtained the restoration") of the sons and daughters (i.e., free citizens) of Nippur, of Ur, of Isin, Sumer and Akkad (upon whom) . . . slavery . . . (had been imposed).

Note that the release applied only to the citizens of certain towns. The edict of King Ammi-ṣaduqa of Babylon contained several express provisions concerning release from debt-slavery. According to paragraph 20:

> If a debt binds a son of the cities of Numhia, Emutbalum, Idamaraz, Isin, etc., and he sells himself, his wife, or his children or gives them for *kiššātum* or in pledge, because the king has established equity for the land, he is released; his restoration (*andurārum*) is established.

The wording is very similar to that of CH 117, but whereas the latter applied after a fixed period of debt-service, here the release intervened at an arbitrary point, regardless of how long the individual debt-slave may have served. Note also that those pledged, as well as those sold for debt, qualified for release.

Paragraph 21 provided an exception to the foregoing rule:

> If the house-born slave of a son of Numhia, etc., is sold or given for *kiššātum* or in pledge, his restoration shall not be established.

A house-born slave was apparently not sufficiently a member of the family to qualify for the privileges of the release. His release would, in any case, have returned him to slavery with his former master, which was probably not the equitable result that the decree sought to obtain.

This edict also released debts which arose from *kiššātum*, which was a type of debt *ex delicto* resulting from the system of revenge and ransom. An early reformer, king Uru-inimgina, expressly included such debts:[81]

---

81 Edition in Steible 1982: 308-11 (Ukg. 4.12, 4.13-22 = 5.11, 5.20-29).

The sons of Lagash who were living in debt due to interest . . . he cleared them of . . . barely taxes, theft, murder, of those . . . and established their restoration.

The Hittite king Tudhaliya IV, on the other hand, made certain distinctions in his edict:[82]

And if someone has given ransom for blood and he has purchased himself from you, whether the ransom be a field or a person, no one shall release it. If he (the ransom-holder) has taken those things along with his (the offender's) wives and sons, he will release him/it to him.

The edict distinguished between two cases. In the first, a person had committed homicide and had paid a ransom for his own life: he had "bought himself." This raised the question as to whether the property that he had handed over as the price of his life could be released by the decree. The edict answered in the negative, even if the property was land or persons, which referred to slaves as well as dependent members of his family.

The second case is more difficult to determine because of the ambiguity (for us) of its phrasing. We tentatively suggest that the creditor, the avenger, has made a general seizure of the culprit's property and family. The edict decreed the release of "him/it to him," which presumably referred to the release to the culprit himself of the aforementioned property and of his family.

The Bible also has laws concerning debt-release and the concomitant release of debt-slaves. According to Lev 25:10:

You shall sanctify the fiftieth year and decree a restoration (*dĕrôr*) in the land, for all its inhabitants. It will be a Jubilee for you, and you shall return, each man to his family estate and to his family.

In v. 54 the particular situation of the debt-slave is considered:

---

82   Edition in Westbrook and Woodard 1990: 643, 654-56 (II 3-8).

> If he is not redeemed by any (of the above), he shall go free in the
> Jubilee year, he and his sons with him.

Release in the Jubilee year is emphatically confined to Israelites (vv. 44-
46):

> As for male and female slaves that you have—you may acquire
> slaves from the nations around you. You may also acquire them
> from aliens resident with you and from their families who are with
> them, who have been born in your land. You shall have them as
> heritable property. You shall give them by way of inheritance to
> your children after you, to acquire permanent title in them.

The Jubilee release of debt-slaves differed from the cuneiform edicts in
one vital respect: it was cyclical, coming every fifty years, and thus
amounted to a prospective, as opposed to retroactive, cancellation of debts.
This made it unworkable in practice, since no one would give credit under
those conditions as the Jubilee approached.

Why, then, did the biblical jurists remove the very factors that made a
debt-release workable: its unpredictability and its retroactivity? Precisely
because it was in the hands of kings of flesh and blood, who could not be
relied upon to act when men of religion thought it necessary. The prophets
furiously berated the kings of Israel and Judah for not doing justice and
equity, among which they meant releasing debts and debtors. Just such an
incident occurred during the reign of king Zedekiah (Jer 34:8-11):

> The word that came to Jeremiah from God after king Zedekiah had
> made a covenant with all the people to decree for them restoration
> (*děrôr*): for each man to free his Hebrew slave and slave-woman
> so that no man would enslave his brother in Judah. All the princes
> and people, who entered into a covenant to release etc., agreed and
> freed (them). But afterwards they reneged and took back the slaves
> and slave-women whom they had released and re-enslaved them.

The king at first followed the prophet's advice and decreed a release, using
his prerogative in the customary manner of ancient Near Eastern kings.
But the decree was ineffective and the ruling classes re-enslaved their

debtors. Jeremiah was enraged with the king for breaking his word and predicted divine punishment in consequence:[83]

> Thus says the LORD: "You did not obey me and declare a restoration, each man for his brother and each man for his neighbor; now I declare a restoration for you, says the Lord—to the sword, to pestilence, and to famine . . . ."

It is a small wonder that the circles who were responsible for drafting the Levitical law adopted an approach that avoided the pitfalls of human discretion but nevertheless fell into the trap of utopian economics.

VI. Transfer

A. Alienability

Slaves were treated as ordinary chattels and could be sold, pledged, hired, given as gifts, inherited, and forfeited. Although the law codes and debt-release decrees portray them as leaving the house of the original owner, there is no reason to suppose that debt-slaves, as opposed to other types of slaves, were inalienable. As Yaron points out, there is no theoretical difficulty since any transfer would be subject to the debtor's power of redemption. The creditor would not be able to grant any better title than he himself had.[84] A Middle Babylonian document describes redemption from a transferee:[85]

---

83 Jer 34:17. In his polemic, Jeremiah quotes the seven-year slave release law as if it were the rule to be applied by Zedekiah in this case (v. 14). But that law is inappropriate to a general release, being measured by each individual slave's term of service, and the text cited is a garbled version of the Deuteronomic law. It is probably an editorial gloss designed to harmonize Jeremiah's words with the provisions of the Torah.

84 Yaron 1959: 155-76 at p. 158. Contra Driver and Miles 1956: vol. 1, 218.

85 Gurney *MB Texts* 1 (see Gurney 1983: 17-22).

> A., the prefect, took a slave-woman[86] named X. from B., the pre-
> fect, . . . and later C. took her from A. and gave her to D., the
> weaver, for spinning, and since she is the wife of Y., the brewer,
> Y. approached C., the prefect of the land, and they entered in to E.,
> the prefect, and E. released X. to her husband and gave Z. as re-
> demption-payment for X. to D., the weaver, and gave back X. to
> Y.

This may have been a case of famine-slavery rather than debt-slavery, but
the principle is the same. A Neo-Assyrian contract provides an example of
debt-release affecting transferred slaves:[87]

> A. has sold and delivered to B. 6 persons in total, X., Y., Z., etc.,
> belonging to A., in consideration of 2 minas of silver by the mina
> of the merchants. The full price is paid; the people are paid for and
> acquired. If those people leave in a restoration (*durāri*), A. shall
> return the silver to its owners.

Important, if indirect, evidence on the alienability of debt-slaves comes
from MAL Tablet C+G 3:

> [If a man] sells into a foreign land [either a man's son] or a man's
> daughter who [is residing in his house] by way of sale or anti-
> chretic pledge . . . he shall forfeit his silver [and] he shall pay . . . .
> But if the man whom he sells dies in the foreign land, he shall pay
> a life. He may sell into a foreign land an Assyrian man or an
> Assyrian woman who had been taken for full value.

We have seen that the equitable principle of redemption applied not only
to pledges but also to forced sales at under-value to pay off a debt. It also
applied to forfeiture of pledges, which purported to turn a pledge into a
sale after the due date for repayment of the loan had passed. The natural

---

86 Sumerian SAL.TUR = Akkadian *ṣuḫārtu* which, as we have pointed out, could mean a
    female child, rather than a slave. It is, however, unlikely in this case, since the subject
    is a married woman.

87 CTN 2 248 (see Postgate 1973: 230-32).

corollary is, however, that where full value was given, the principle no longer applied. A pledge for whom the creditor gave full value, either at the time of the loan or (if the contract so allowed) by paying the balance after default,[88] was no longer protected once the forfeiture clause had operated. He was no longer regarded as a pledge or a debt-slave, but as a chattel-slave. Therefore, the underlying distinction is between pledges, who could not be sold at all, and chattel-slaves, who could even be sold abroad. We may conclude that in the intermediate case of debt-slaves, they could be sold domestically but not abroad.

The same rule is applied in Exod 21:7-8, where a girl was sold by her father as a slave-concubine, but the new owner changed his mind as to her attractiveness. He was ordered to allow her redemption but at the same time forbidden from selling her to a foreign people. Again, the intermediate case would have been a domestic sale, which appears to have been allowed and was not affected by the right of redemption.

B. Special Terms

Special features relating to slaves are found in contracts of sale. The earliest slave sale documents (in Sumerian) date to the Sargonic period. A typical example reads:[89]

> A. son of X. has received one-third of a mina of silver as the purchase-price for B. son of Y. C., the Prefect, has paid the silver, he has caused him to climb over the wood.

Payment of the price was followed by a ceremony special to slave sales, whereby the slave was made to climb over a wooden bar.[90] The significance of this symbolic act is not clear. It is generally assumed that it signified a transfer of ownership from the seller to the buyer. Throughout Mesopotamian sale law, however, ownership passed with full payment of

---

88 An example is *ZVR* 44 no. 55 (in pp. 305-81), where in spite of appearances the forfeiture clause only allows the creditor to pay the difference between value of the loan and value of the pledge in order to acquire full title. See Westbrook 1991b: 107-10.

89 *SRU* 49.

90 Edzard 1970: 8-53.

the price, which was always recorded, even when the wooden bar ceremony was not. Two possible explanations are that it either indicated the
transfer of possession or a recognition of the slave's potential volition in
obliging him to submit to the authority of a new master. Its occurrence in
the Sumerian-Akkadian dictionary of legal phrases as a measure taken after recapture of a runaway slave might be taken as evidence in favor of the
latter explanation.[91] In the Neo-Sumerian period, the wooden bar became a
pestle. The phrase continued into the Old Babylonian period, by which
time, however, it had become a frozen formula, not representing an actual
ceremony.[92]

Special warranties applied to slave sales, arising out of the slave's
character as a living creature with volition. We have already seen an example of a warranty against a slave's delinquency. Liability could also fall
on the seller if the slave ran away, as a Neo-Sumerian record of litigation
reveals:[93]

> A. bought from B. and his wife C. one woman, her price being 2⅔
> shekels of silver. Because the slave-woman escaped, C. swore by
> the king's name to deliver (another) slave-woman.

Some of the liabilities of a seller of slaves are set out in CH 278-279:

> If a man purchases a slave or slave-woman and, his month not be-
> ing completed, epilepsy attacks him, he shall return him to his
> seller and the buyer will take the money that he paid. If a man pur-
> chases a slave or slave-woman and he acquires a claim, his seller
> shall be liable for the claim.

These paragraphs are probably intended to indicate fair standards of practice in slave sale agreements and do in fact reflect in part the standard Old
Babylonian contractual warranty (e.g., YOS 13 5):

---

91   MSL I 2 IV 7'-14'.
92   See Malul 1985: 66-77.
93   Steinkeller *Sale Documents* S.3 (see Steinkeller 1989: 333-34).

Three days "search"; one month epilepsy; he (seller) is liable for claims upon him according to the order of the king.

Whereas the legal meaning of the first warranty is not known,[94] the warranty against epilepsy and the warranty of good title match the provisions of the law code.[95]

By the advent of the Neo-Babylonian period, the warranty-clause had expanded considerably. NBL 6 added a rider to the basic statement of liability in CH 279:

A man who has sold a female slave and a claim arises upon her and she is taken away: the seller shall pay the buyer the silver in full according to the promissory note. If she has borne children, he shall give half a shekel of silver for each.

As many as fifteen different warranties are recorded in sale contracts, although almost never together in the same document.[96] The seller had to warranty against false claim, vindication, the slave being sold having the status of a free person, a temple slave, a royal slave or a serf (*šušānu*), or having certain obligations to perform royal service. All of these warranties were stated as being in perpetuity. Additional warranties against flight or sudden death were for one hundred days. A contemporary document recorded a claim before the court by A. that his slave X. had run away and that he had later seen the slave at the home of B., who had given him another name and subsequently sold him to C. The judges ruled that, if A.'s statement was confirmed, he could take his slave away "according to the order (*dātu*) of the king."[97]

---

94 A recent suggestion is that it refers to investigation of the possible free status of the person purchased; see Stol 1993: 134-35.

95 The import of the enigmatic phrase "order of the king" (*ṣimdat šarrim*) is not known. It is tempting to assume that it refers to the rules of the law code, but such an assumption would be anachronistic and does not accord with the many occurrences of the phrase. The most recent study (Kraus 1979), fails to reach a satisfactory conclusion.

96 Dandamaev 1984: 182-94; Mendelsohn 1949: 38-39.

97 *Dar.* 53 = Dandamaev 1984: 223.

A clause found to date in a few Neo-Assyrian sale documents added further conditions:[98]

> Seizure(?),[99] epilepsy up to 100 days, criminal record in perpetuity, madness within months . . . .

The vagueness of the time limit in the final provision is unusual for a legal document—it may have been a question of reasonable delay in determining the condition.

CH 280-281 contained special provisions concerning stolen slaves purchased abroad:

> If a man has bought another's slave or slave-woman in a foreign land, and when he returns home the owner of the slave or slave-woman identifies his slave or slave-woman: if that slave or slave-woman is a native of the land, their restoration (*andurārum*) shall be established without (payment of) silver.
>
> If they are natives of another land, the purchaser shall declare before the god the silver that he paid, the owner of the slave or slave-woman shall give the merchant the silver that he paid and redeem his slave or slave-woman.

The second provision is clear: a merchant traveling abroad innocently purchased a foreign slave. Upon his return home it is revealed that the slave belonged to a local owner. The local owner could not simply reclaim him, however, as he could in a domestic case. The merchant had to be rewarded for his pains with the price of the slave. As Driver and Miles point out, the merchant would normally have had recourse against his seller under the warranty against eviction, but since the seller was in a foreign land and the merchant could not have been expected to suppose that a foreign slave bought in a foreign country had a Babylonian owner, there was a measure of fairness in the law.[100]

---

98 *BaghM* 16 373-374.
99 I.e., a medical condition. See Stol 1993: 136.
100 Driver and Miles 1956: vol. 1, 482-84.

Interpretation of the first provision has been complicated by the word *andurārum*, conventionally translated "freedom," which is certainly its meaning in many other contexts. Earlier commentators were puzzled as to why native slaves would be freed by this chance circumstance of their being taken abroad and back, and why their master would identify them when he had no hope of recovering them. Driver and Miles already suggested, however, that in this context *andurārum* meant only release to the original owner.[101] The basic meaning of the word is restoration to one's previous status, which in this case meant a return to the slave's previous master. A merchant abroad, therefore, should have been on his guard when he bought a fellow countryman as to the possibility that he was stolen goods.[102]

Finally, it is to be noted that slaves could be used as a mode of payment, especially as compensation or penalties for delict. In a Neo-Assyrian contract settling the blood-money payable for a killing, it is provided:[103]

A. son of B. shall give C. the slave-woman, the daughter of D., the scribe, together with her family, in lieu of the blood. He shall wash the blood. If he does not give the woman, they will kill him on top of B.'s grave.

In a Middle Babylonian homicide case, the king ordered one of the parties to pay the other seven slaves.[104] HL 1-4 set tariffs in payment of slaves for homicide in various circumstances.

---

101   Driver and Miles 1956: vol. 1, 482-84, with a review of the earlier commentators.
102   Driver and Miles (1956: vol. 1, 486) saw no reason for discrimination against the merchant in paragraph 280, arguing that it would discourage him from bringing home Babylonian slaves. But merchants faced far higher risks in their domestic purchases—they could be liable not only to return stolen goods, but also to pay the owner a penalty, which they would then have to recoup from the seller (see Westbrook and Wilcke 1974-1977: 111-21). As recouping from a foreign seller was difficult, the law in fact offers some relief in restricting the merchant's liability to restitution.
103   ADD 321 = Kwasman 1988: no. 341. Our interpretation differs slightly from Kwasman's.
104   *BBSt.* 9.

VII. Treatment

A. Principles

MAL A 44 reads as follows:

> If an Assyrian man or woman who is dwelling in the house of a
> man as a pledge for their value is acquired for their full value, he
> may beat, tear out hair, crush his ears, or pierce them.

The principle is that where a pledge was acquired for full value, in this
case evidently by operation of a forfeiture clause in the contract of loan, he
no longer enjoyed the right of redemption. By forfeiture he became a
slave; but so far from being a debt-slave, his status was that of a chattel-
slave, and he could be treated accordingly.

This paragraph illustrates the difference between the permissible
treatment of pledges, slaves, and, by implication, debt-slaves. A pledge
could not be punished by physical maltreatment nor marked as a slave (by
piercing his ear).[105] The same restrictions would appear to apply to a debt-
slave. These measures applied to chattel-slaves only, but at the same time
they acted as limitations, since they marked the limit of what could be
done to such a slave.[106]

Let us now consider other evidence for the two measures taken in the
Assyrian law: marking and punishment.

---

105 This paragraph has generally been understood as a list of punishments, of which
piercing the slave's ear is but one. This is incorrect. Ear-piercing is not especially
painful, nor was it regarded in the ancient Near East as disfiguring or degrading; it
was common for free men and women to wear earrings in pierced ears. Confirmation
of our interpretation comes from paragraph A 59 of the same code, which is explicitly
a list of punishments that a man may inflict on his wife. The list is identical to that of
our paragraph, except for the last verb; instead of "pierce" (*upallaš*) with respect to
her ears, it has a broken verb which cannot be identical and which almost certainly is
to be restored "touch" (*ulappat*). The latter verb in Akkadian is a known euphemism
for "to strike, hurt." See *CAD* L 91.

106 There is no doubt that the purpose of the paragraph is restrictive: the parallel paragraph 59, discussed in the previous note, lists the punishments that a husband is
allowed to inflict on his wife apart from those allowed in specific situations in the
other paragraphs of the tablet.

B. The Slave-Mark

Since wearing earrings was widespread in the ancient Near East, piercing a slave's ear was presumably for the purpose of inserting an ownership tag of some sort. The purpose of the exercise, as we learn from the only other source where piercing is mentioned, was to mark him as a chattel-slave. Exod 21:5-6 discusses the case of a debt-slave due to be released after six years of service but who had received a wife from his master:

> If the slave says, "I love my master, my wife, and my children; I will not go free," his master shall bring him to the door or door-post of the shrine(?)[107] and bore his ear with an awl, and he is his slave for ever.

Other sources mention different types of slave-marks: in Old Babylonian the *abbuttum*, which was a mark or tattoo applied to a slave's shaven head, and in Neo-Babylonian the *šindu*, a tattoo or brand which could mark the status of slavery or the identity of a particular owner.[108] In contractual penalty clauses that imposed slavery, marking was frequently mentioned as well, to emphasize that the person would become a chattel-slave, not subject to redemption. Nonetheless, by no means were all chattel-slaves so marked. It appears to have been used where the status or owner of the slave might be called into question, or where the slave was likely to run away.

C. Punishment: Licit

In the law codes, the only mention of punishment besides MAL A 44 is CH 282, which allowed a master to cut off his slave's ear for denying that he was his slave. Like the Assyrian law, it implies that a master did not

---

107 Literally: "to the god/gods, to the door or doorpost." This is only one explanation among many that have been proffered. See most recently Viberg 1992: 77-81.
108 The exact nature of the Old Babylonian *abbuttum* is disputed. See Driver and Miles 1956: vol. 1, 421-25; and Szlechter 1950: 391-418. *CAD* A/1 48-50 regards it as a hairstyle in the form of a top-knot. The Neo-Babylonian *šindu*, on the other hand, is clearly a brand, sometimes with symbols or writing indicating the owner. It is also applied to cattle. See Dandamaev 1984: 229-34; and Mendelsohn 1949: 42-50.

have a general right to disfigure his slave. For the same offense, however, some of the contracts in the Tehip-tilla archive from Nuzi applied a remarkably severe penalty:[109]

> If A. breaks the contract and leaves B.'s house and declares thus,
> "I am not a slave-woman and my sons are not slaves," B. shall put
> out the eyes of A. and her children and sell them.

The purpose of blinding was so that they could be sold as chattel-slaves, not famine-slaves who would be subject to redemption. But it is not clear what circumstances in these particular cases allowed the slave's owner to change their status in such a drastic manner.

Another contract from the Tehip-tilla archive is milder. It merely allowed the owner to treat the slave who denied his ownership and left "as he pleases." In other words, the owner had the discretion to treat the famine-slave as a chattel-slave.[110] The same clause is found in an Emar contract, with the further provision that the owner "has the *locus standi* of their case" (*bēl dīnišunu šūt*). The reason is that the contract was one of purchase of a slave from a third party and the slave's denial was in favor not of freedom but of the previous owner.[111]

D. Punishment: Abusive

We have seen that the law codes severely punished the killing of a distrainee. In CH 116, if the distrainee was the debtor's son, the distrainer's son was to be killed. In our opinion, Exod 21:20-21, following the tendency of biblical law not to distinguish between slavery—at least debt-slavery—and other servile conditions, applied the same rule. Our translation reads:[112]

---

109   JEN 449 = Greenberg 1955: no. 58; similarly JEN 452 (without denial, "goes to the house of another"; Greenberg 1955: no. 45) and JEN 457 (Greenberg 1955: no. 63).
110   JEN 462 = Greenberg 1955: no. 61.
111   Arnaud *Emar* 6 211. Cf. an Old Babylonian letter (AbB 1 27:16-26), where a correspondent reports to X. that his slave-girl screamed hysterically, "I am the slave of X.! My mistress gave me to him!" She had to be physically restrained from running away.
112   For the supporting philological arguments, see Westbrook 1988d: 89-100.

If a man strikes his slave or slave-woman with a stick and he dies
under his hand, he shall be avenged. But if he survives a day or
two he shall not be avenged, but it is his silver.

The vengeance in question is taken to have been the appropriate vicarious
revenge as in CH 116. The last phrase we understand to mean "it (the revenge) is his silver (the loan)." In other words, the creditor/master
forfeited the right to repayment of the loan for which the slave was security, by way of fixed ransom in lieu of revenge. The same applied to v.
26:[113]

If a man strikes his slave's or slave-woman's eye and destroys it,
he shall set him free for his eye.

If the ransom was fixed at the level of the debt, thereby annulling it, it
would automatically release the debt-slave.

E. Exploitation of Labor

In the context of the Jubilee laws, Lev 25:39-40 enjoins:

If your brother grows weak with you (i.e., becomes insolvent) and
is sold to you, you shall not make him work the work of a slave;
he shall be like a hired man or dependent with you and shall work
with you until the Jubilee.

We have already drawn attention to the fact that the Jubilee slave-release
was a utopian measure. The impractical character of this provision is even
more obvious. It is interesting, however, for the distinction that it drew
between treatment of the Israelite slave—"your brother"—and foreign
slaves. Of the latter, v. 46 states:

You shall make them work, but your Israelite brother you shall not
pursue with harshness.

---

113 Westbrook 1988d: 101.

F. Sexual Abuse

The Hittite laws considered sexual offenses like sleeping with a woman and her daughter to be "abominations," the penalty for which was usually exile or death (§191). But if the women in question were slaves, it was no sin (§194). The Bible, on the other hand, in the curious case of Lev 19:20-22, regarded an act of sexual abuse of one's slave as a sin but no delict. Our translation differs from the accepted one and gives a completely different law:[114]

> If a man has sexual intercourse with a married woman, she being a slave pledged[115] to the man and not redeemed or given her freedom, an action lies for her return. They may not be put to death because she was not freed. But he shall bring a guilt-offering.

Adultery was an offense against the husband for which revenge could be demanded. But where the wife was a debt-slave in the hands of his creditor, the husband had no right to revenge because of her unfree status, which acted in mitigation of the offense. Instead, he was limited again to ransom fixed at the level of the debt and thus to an *in rem* action for her return. As the sexual act remained a sin against God, the creditor nonetheless had to bring an offering to the temple in atonement.

G. Furlough

A number of texts from the archive of an Old Babylonian slave and landowner named Balmunamhe provide evidence that home leave was sometimes possible for slaves.[116] In these transactions, Balmunamhe temporarily released a slave into the custody of a third party, sometimes identified as a relative, who acted as a surety for the slave not absconding

---

114 For a full legal and philological discussion, see Westbrook 1988d: 101-109; and Westbrook 1990b: 564-69.

115 The combination of slavery and pledge is a further example of the special character of biblical slave law that we have noted: its failure to distinguish between slavery and other servile conditions. It is his wife that the man pledged, not his slave.

116 The archive is discussed by Van De Mieroop 1987.

or ceasing work.[117] For example, in YOS 5 141 parents sold their son to Balmunamhe, and in YOS 8 35 (five years later) they received him back on the following terms:

> X., his father, and Y., his mother, received in the capacity of sureties one slave named A., the slave of B., from his owner B. If he absconds, X., his father, and Y., his mother, shall convey their house and orchard to B.

Balmunamhe received no payment for the transfer, but it has been pointed out that most such transactions took place in the winter months when there was insufficient agricultural work on his estate and the price of grain for feeding his slaves was high.[118] It was therefore in the slave-owner's interest during the low season to release some of his slaves to their family, who stood surety for their eventual return to work.

H. Abandonment

Mendelsohn asserts that sick slaves who could no longer perform the duties expected of them were cast out and abandoned to fend for themselves.[119] There is, however, no real evidence on this question. Mendelsohn cites a single source, 1 Sam 30:11-15, where a slave found half-starved by David declared that he was abandoned by his master "because three days ago I fell sick." But the circumstances were anything but normal. The master was a member of an Amalekite raiding party being pursued by David's troops.

I. Flight

As Renger has pointed out, flight was a social phenomenon that affected not only slaves but many of the lower economic strata, where it was seen

---

117 The recurrence of transfers involving the same slave reveals them to be provisional; see Van De Mieroop 1987: 12.
118 See Van De Mieroop 1987: 11-12, 23-24.
119 Mendelsohn 1949: 65.

as an escape from oppressive debt and fiscal or feudal burdens.[120] In the case of slaves, counter-measures were directed both against the slave himself and against third parties from whom he might seek assistance or refuge. A Neo-Sumerian document records:[121]

> A., the slave of B., ran away. They caught him. He appeared and said: "The king's oath! The day that I run away a second time, may I perish!" X., Y., and Z. were the judges. The sons of Nippur. (Date.)

The oath was a powerful deterrent, since breach of it brought down divine sanctions.[122] The difficulty was that it could only be taken voluntarily. On the other hand, it was undoubtedly a preferable alternative to punishment (the procedure in the present document is before a court) or to the physical impediments that were available to an owner. Some are listed in the Sumerian-Akkadian dictionary of legal phrases:[123]

> He fled from the house of his master. After he had fled from his master's house, they brought him back. After they had brought him back, he placed hobbles on his feet, he put him in chains, he caused him to cross the pestle, and he engraved on his face: "Fugitive, seize!"

The normal slave-mark was not so dramatic but still had the purpose of revealing the slave's status to third parties. CH 226-227 imposed severe penalties on a corrupt barber who excised the slave-mark or on an accomplice who tricked an innocent barber into excising it. Even fetters were no guarantee against escape, as CE 51 reveals:

---

120 Renger 1970: 167-82, referring to the Old Babylonian period. For biblical society, compare the malcontents who gathered around the renegade David: "There gathered to him every man in distress and every man who had a creditor and every man who was discontented" (1 Sam 22:2).

121 Çiğ and Kizilyay *NRVN* 1.

122 Cf. Gen 24:2-4, where Abraham uses the same device to ensure that his slave Eliezer will fulfill his mission.

123 MSL I 2 IV 7'-14'.

A slave or slave-woman of Eshnunna, upon whom are placed fetters, shackles, or the slave-mark, may not go out of the city-gate of Eshnunna without his master's permission.

It is not clear to whom this prohibition was directed, but the free citizenry were expected to cooperate in the re-capture of fugitive slaves. According to CH 15-16:

If a man causes a fugitive slave or slave-woman of the palace or of a private citizen to go out through the city-gate, he shall be killed.

If a man conceals a fugitive slave or slave-woman of the palace or of a private citizen in his house, and does not bring him out at the herald's call, that householder shall be killed.

Other law codes were less harsh in their punishment of one who harbored a fugitive slave. According to HL 24:

If a slave or slave-woman runs away, the one at whose hearth his master finds him shall give x shekels of silver as the wages of a man for one year, and y shekels of silver as the wages of a woman for one year.

If the culprit was not caught in possession of the slave, CL 12-13 rules:

If a slave-woman or a slave of a man has run away from the city and it has been proved that she dwelt in the house of a man for one month, he shall give slave for slave. If he has no slave, he shall pay 15 shekels of silver.

By the same token, one who brought back a fugitive slave was entitled to a reward from the slave's master, set by the law codes at between two and six shekels of silver.[124]

---

124 CU 14 (two shekels), CH 17 (two shekels), HL 22-23 (up to six shekels, according to the distance involved).

The fugitive slave's best chance of freedom was to escape the country altogether. If he had been sold abroad, he would have attempted to return home, as in an Old Babylonian case:[125]

> A., whom B., his master, had sold to (the city of) Eshnunna for one-and-a-half mina of silver, after he had served as a slave for five years in Eshnunna, fled to Babylon. C. and D., the army officials, seized A. and said, "You are cleansed; your slave-mark is shaved off. You shall serve in the armed forces." A. replied: "I will not serve with the soldiers; I will perform the feudal service of my father's house." His brothers X., Y., and Z. swore the oath of (the god) Marduk and king Ammi-ditana. There is no claim upon their brother A. for service;[126] as long as he lives, A. will perform the feudal service of their father's house with his brothers.

A slave who fled in the other direction, to a foreign county, could not be sure of the welcome he would receive. His hope for free status rested on being granted the status of resident alien, a privilege entirely at the discretion of the local ruler. There might also have been a treaty between two states, providing for the extradition of fugitive slaves. A Middle Babylonian treaty between king Idrimi of Alalakh and king Pillia of Kizzuwatna provides:[127]

> When Pillia and Idrimi swore the oath of the gods and made this treaty between them:
>   They will always return fugitives between them. If Idrimi seizes a fugitive of Pillia, he shall return him to Pillia, and if Pillia

---

125   CT 6 29 = Yoffee 1977: 57-59. Yoffee suggests that A. had been adopted by B. (post mortem) and B.'s death while A. was in Eshnunna had automatically freed A. This scenario assumes that i) B. is the father of X.,Y., and Z., ii) B. adopted A., and iii) B. died. None of these assumptions can be verified from the text. The content of the brothers' oath is not stated; it may refer to their not contesting A.'s right to a share of the estate in return for feudal service.

126   *ana rešūtim*. It is not clear whether this unusual term means slavery or public service: see *AHw* 976. We incline to the view that it means the latter—in this case, the military service from which A. was excused.

127   AT 3 = Reiner in *ANET³* 532.

seizes a fugitive of Idrimi, he shall return him to Idrimi. Anyone who seizes a fugitive and returns him to his master, if it is a man, he shall be given 500 (shekels of) copper as his reward; if a woman, he shall be given 1000 (shekels of) copper as his reward. If a fugitive of Pillia enters the land of Idrimi and no one seizes him, but his master seizes him, he need not give a reward to anyone; and if a fugitive of Idrimi enters the land of Pillia, etc.

In any town in which a fugitive is concealed, the mayor and five men of good standing shall swear the oath of the gods.

The same reward system was applied as in domestic law, but punishment was collective. A similar treaty between Alalakh and Tunip reveals the context of the oath and specifies the consequences of breach:[128]

The mayor and five elders shall swear the oath of the gods: "Your slave does not live among us, and we do not conceal him." If they are unwilling to take the oath but return his slave (. . . they are not liable . . .). If they swear and afterwards he discovers his slave . . . they are thieves: their hands are cut off; they shall give 6000 (shekels) of copper to the palace.

The last phrase suggests that the palace may have indemnified the foreign owner for the loss of his slave.

The above treaty provisions put in perspective the injunction in Deut 23:16-17:

You shall not surrender to his master a slave who has fled to you from his master. He shall live with you in your midst where he chooses in one of your settlements as he pleases; you shall not oppress him.

It was recognized by early commentators that this provision could not apply to domestic slavery, since it would have undermined the right to recover property upon which the whole institution depended. It makes perfect sense, however, when applied to the international sphere, where no

---

128   AT 2:27-32 = Wiseman 1953: 29; and Reiner in *ANET³* 531.

right of recovery existed unless expressly authorized by treaty. The passage can therefore be seen as a polemic against such treaty provisions, and a prohibition on the authorities in Israel against ever including an extradition clause in their treaties with neighboring states. Mendelsohn suggested that it applied only to a Hebrew slave fleeing a foreign master.[129] The terms of the law which granted the fugitive a choice of dwelling in any city negate this interpretation. A Hebrew slave would have returned to his home, not picked a city to dwell in. By that grant of choice of dwelling and the injunction not to oppress him, the foreign fugitive was being granted the status of resident alien without geographical limitation, which would protect him from being enslaved by an Israelite.

VIII. Summary and Conclusions

The legal systems of the ancient Near East recognized persons as a category of property that might be owned by private individuals. It was pursuant to the normal rights of ownership that a master could exploit the slave's labor, restrict his freedom, and alienate him. Nonetheless, the relationship between master and slave was subject to legal restrictions based on the humanity of the slave and concerns of social justice. In spite of the impression given by certain law codes, those restrictions were not imposed in a systematic manner but derived mainly from the equitable discretion of the courts, in particular the king (or his officials), who, as the font of justice, had the power (and the divine mandate) to intervene in order to alleviate injustice, even where it arose from arrangements that were within the letter of the law. As a result, the "rights" of slaves were uneven in quality, varying from system to system and from period to period, and even as between individual cases within the same society. The basic principles, however, were the same in all the societies in question.

In determining who should benefit from measures of social justice, the legal systems drew two main distinctions: between debt-slave and chattel-slaves, and between native and foreign slaves. The authorities intervened first and foremost to protect citizens who had fallen on hard times and had been forced into slavery by debt. The tendency was to assimilate them for

---

129 Mendelsohn 1949: 63-64.

these purposes into the class of pledges, persons whose labor might be exploited under a contractual arrangement but who remained personally free in terms of status. At the other end of the scale, foreigners who had been acquired by capture or by purchase abroad received very little succor from the local legal system.

The benefits of the law related to (a) enslavement, (b) length of service, and (c) conditions of service. Under the first aspect, enslavement, the prime distinction was between native and foreign slaves. A person who was ethnically or by birth a free member of a particular society could not be enslaved against his will if independent or without the permission of the person under whose authority he was if a subordinate member of a household. The only exception was enslavement by court order for commission of a delict. Although, in practice, economic circumstances would often force a person into slavery, in law his act was voluntary.

The foreigner, by contrast, could be enslaved through capture in war, kidnapping, or force, unless protected by the local ruler, either under the rules of customary international law which applied between friendly states or as a resident alien. In the latter case, protection still might have been only partial.

Under the second aspect, length of service, three means were available for the slave to gain his freedom. First, a slave could gain his freedom through redemption, that is, payment of the original debt. Where found, this appears to have been a legal right, which attached to the slave, binding subsequent purchasers. It vested in both the slave himself and in close relatives, and possibly also the king.

Second, freedom could be attained through manumission after a period of service. The law codes where this means is attested set different periods of service, one as short as three years, which if it had applied automatically would have made all other measures superfluous. We therefore consider that it was not a right like redemption but a discretion of the authorities to intervene in individual cases and free a debt-slave after a reasonable length of service in relation to his debt. The fixed periods in the sources are attempts to set a "fair" standard.

Third, freedom could be achieved through release under a general cancellation of debts. This was the most radical measure but was unpredictable, being entirely dependent on the king's equitable discretion. It was confined to native debt-slaves.

Under the third aspect, conditions of service, the slave was protected against three forms of maltreatment. First, slaves were protected against excessive physical punishment. Even chattel-slaves appear to have benefited to some extent from this protection.

Second, protection was afforded against sexual abuse. Sexual intercourse with a woman amounted to an offense in the ancient Near East when it was an infringement of the rights of the person under whose authority she was, for example, her father or her husband. Ownership of a chattel-slave eliminated that authority, but there is evidence that it did not entirely do so in the case of a debt-slave.

Third, slaves were protected from sale abroad. Only native debt-slaves were protected by this prohibition, which must in any case have been difficult to enforce in practice.

Between the debt-slave and the chattel-slave we have identified a third category, which we have termed the famine-slave, where a person entered into slavery in a year of famine in return for being kept alive. This category shared some of the benefits accorded to the debt-slave, albeit in a lesser measure. There appears to have been a right of redemption after the end of the famine, at a reasonable price set by the law, and possibly even to manumission after a period of service, but it also seems that these rights could be restricted or overridden by contract. The contracts in question often make specific mention of the foreign origin of the person enslaved, which paradoxically both points to their being able to share these rights with natives and suggests a reason why their rights could be restricted by private agreement.

9

Patronage in the Ancient Near East

Abstract

Patronage is generally assumed by scholars to have been a universal feature of ancient Near Eastern societies but has been neglected as a topic of serious investigation. The purpose of this study is to offer, without prior assumptions, textual evidence that establishes the existence of the concept of patronage. The approach is to present case studies from various parts of the region which are best explained by the presence of patronage. For these purposes patronage is narrowly defined on the basis of ancient Roman and contemporary anthropological models.

Methodological Introduction

The term patronage is borrowed from Roman history.[1] In the late Republic, a *patronus* was a powerful aristocrat who gathered around him loyal followers, known as *clientes*. A client would be expected to vote for his patron and to provide him with political support and any other services that might be requested of him, in return for protection from other nobles and legal and material assistance (Scullard 1973: 12-18; Verboven 2002;

*   Originally published in the *Journal for the Economic and Social History of the Orient* 48 (2005): 210-33. Copyright © Koninklijke Brill NV, Leiden. Used by permission.

1   This article was first presented, under the title "À la recherche du patronage dans le Proche-Orient Ancien," to the équipe "Anthropologie et sociologie comparative des institutions" of the Laboratoire d'Anthropologie Sociale in Paris, in their seminar series "Clientèle et Patronage." I am grateful to Prof. Alain Testart and Dr. Valérie Lécrivain for inviting me to participate in the series and to the participants in the seminar for their comments and criticisms. I am likewise grateful to my colleagues and students in the Department of Near Eastern Studies at Johns Hopkins University for their critique of a revised version and their helpful suggestions. The usual caveats as to responsibility apply.

Wallace-Hadrill 1989). Anthropologists have identified patronage and clientship as a widespread phenomenon in both the ancient world and in contemporary traditional societies.[2]

The basic characteristics of patronage as a cross-cultural phenomenon may be summarized as follows:

1. It is a personal relationship, often referred to as "friendship," but is asymmetrical, between a socially dominant and a socially servient party.
2. It is based on the mutual exchange of goods and services. Non-material services provided by the patron include protection and access to decision-making bodies or persons within government. The prime non-material service that the client provides is loyalty. While the patron might appear to give more in goods and services than he receives, he obtains a valuable intangible benefit from the relationship in the form of enhanced prestige.
3. The relationship must be of some duration. A single transaction or exchange of favors would not amount to patronage.
4. The relationship must be voluntary, or at least purport to be voluntary.

Patronage is to be distinguished from other relationships:

1. Legal relations are formal and give rise to rights that are enforceable in a court of law. Patronage gives rise to expectations, not rights. It is an informal tie, based on moral obligations, and the sanctions for breach of those obligations are moral and social.
2. Bureaucracy is supposed to create an impersonal relationship with its beneficiaries based on rules, and thus to ensure equal treatment for all. Patronage is a personal relationship with no fixed criteria for the allocation of its benefits. Far from ensuring equal treatment, patronage gives an advantage to the client

---

2 This is particularly true of the more traditional regions of contemporary Mediterranean countries. The classic study is Pitt-Rivers 1971; see also Campbell 1964; Peters 1968; Waterbury 1977; and Zuckerman 1977.

over other persons in like circumstances. Where scarce resources cannot be obtained by all, it is a way for a few to gain
privileged access to them.

3. Commercial exchanges are impersonal and immediate. The dynamic of patronage is serial rather than reciprocal. Being
notionally based on friendship, each benefit must be deemed
gratuitous, an act of generosity (whether spontaneous or requested). It creates a moral obligation to respond generously at
some point in the future. Although there is an overall accounting, no one counter-gift need exactly equal the value of a
previous gift. The standard is appropriateness, not equivalence.

4. Kinship obligations have many similarities to those of patronage but are based upon an involuntary, indissoluble tie.
Patronage exists only as long as its obligations are met. Serfdom and slavery are analogous to kinship in so far as they are
formalized, coercive relationships that cannot be dissolved at
will, at least by the servient party.

It is important to recognize at this point that our definition of patronage as
a cross-cultural phenomenon is of necessity narrow, excluding atypical
forms that may be found in certain modern societies, such as "spiritual"
patronage[3] or the extended use of the terminology in modern parlance,
such as patronage of the arts, which can refer to charitable donations.

There are three further aspects of patronage that are relevant to this
study:

1. It can co-exist with one of the formal relationships above. In a
sense, patronage will be symbiotic, allowing formal rights and
duties to be tempered or distorted (depending on one's viewpoint) by favoritism.

2. It can be analyzed on an individual level, but patronage can
also exist as a system. Given its symbiotic capacity, it may

---

3 "Spiritual" patronage is a special form deriving from the religious duties of a Christian
godfather. Unlike ordinary patronage, it is indissoluble. Identified in some modern
Mediterranean societies, it has to our knowledge no echo in the ancient world. See
Pitt-Rivers 1971: 107-108; and Campbell 1964: 217-24.

even result in parallel formal and informal systems of govern-
ance within the same state.

3. In the light of the above two aspects, it should be noted that patrons can be primary or intermediary. A primary patron is the
sovereign ruler, who also dispenses the benefits of patronage to
certain of his privileged subjects. An intermediary patron
would be a noble or official who has access to higher levels of
government (whether as a client himself or by virtue of office)
and can act as a broker to give clients the benefit of his influence. Depending on which function he is exercising, the same
patron could be primary and intermediary.

Previous Scholarship and Present Approach

Conditions in the societies of the ancient Near East would seem ripe for
the flourishing of patron-client relationships. Notwithstanding large bu-
reaucracies, governments were highly personalized, with hereditary rulers
surrounded by a court of family members and privileged nobles. The
economies, if not entirely redistributive, were far from offering a free market in goods and services. Although free citizens made up a large part of
the population, society tended to be highly stratified, with rigid hierarchies
and little mobility.

Nonetheless, with one notable exception (discussed below), historians
of the ancient Near East have sometimes assumed the existence of patronage but have otherwise disregarded it. Studies of political and social
structures focus upon bureaucratic systems and kinship. Schloen's analysis
of the society of Ugarit and its neighbors, for example, mentions patronage
in passing, but its focus is the patriarchal household and associated kinship
systems. It assumes patronage to be an intrinsic feature of traditional societies (2001: 72, 110, 310). Matthews and Benjamin in an avowedly anthropological approach to Biblical Israel adduce anthropological literature on
wealthy villagers as patrons of poorer ones. They transpose these models
in a general way onto Israelite village society without citing Biblical references (1993: 120-22, 159-60). Similarly, Kemp speaks of ancient Egyptian
mayors having power which "must have lain in the respect and influence
they commanded by virtue of local landownership and family ties and a

network of patronage and obligation" (1989: 219), without explicating any further.

One reason why scholars have not considered the question seriously is that none of the languages of the region reveals a dedicated vocabulary, the usual starting point for inquiry into social structures. Patronage, however, often adopts terms describing other types of relations, mainly kinship and affect relations, as well as the vocabulary of gift giving. None of them are unfailing markers of patronage, but combined with other evidence they can be a strong indicator, especially when they seem incongruous in the context in which they are used.

A difficulty with such terms in the languages of the ancient Near East is their very wide semantic range. Kinship terms such as "father" and "son" are promiscuously employed outside of the realm of the family for all manner of social, commercial, and legal relations. Terms for "gift" are frequently used in legal fictions to designate a payment that would be illegal or invalid if given its real title of price, fee, or compensation. Terms of affect such as "love" are employed in servant-master/vassal-overlord relations (witness the biblical injunction that Israelites should love their god). Even terms for "friend" may designate a commercial or professional relationship.[4]

The problem of terminology is illustrated by the corpus of letters from the Old Babylonian period. The term "father" is widely attested in these letters as a general mark of respect to the addressee, who in most cases is evidently not the actual parent of the correspondent. Use of the term is often accompanied by effusive wishes for the addressee's welfare. The content of the letters themselves, however, does not provide unambiguous evidence that the "father" is really the patron and the writer the client. Two examples, one positive and one negative, will illustrate the difficulty. AbB 5 166 reads:

> Speak to my father; thus says Sin-magir: May the gods Shamash and Ninurta keep you healthy for many days for my sake! The men whom I sent to you are poor. . . . There is no sustenance. I seized the men . . . and they left. May they constantly pray to

---

4 On the Akkadian term *ibru*, see *CAD* I/J 5-7; on the Sumerian term ku-li, see Wilcke 1969, who questions some of *CAD*'s conclusions.

Shamash for you! . . . As for the ox about which you wrote to me, I was busy and have not sent it to you; as soon as I have some rest, I will send it to you. Regarding the harvest and all that you ordered, I will have men from the Tigris sent to you. They are 5 men who are in my service. There is no sustenance. Let them pray for you constantly! Let them not be lost to me!

The deference shown by the writer, his willingness to take orders from his "father," and his appeal for financial assistance could all point to some form of patronage. The second document, however, paints a different picture (AbB 5 224):

Speak to my father; thus says Zimri-Erah: May the gods Shamash and Marduk keep you healthy for ever! May you be well. I write to you regarding your well-being; write to me whether you are well. I am engaged in opening and damming the canal at Dur-Sin. Where I am situated, I have nothing to eat. I herewith send you one-third of a shekel of silver under my seal. With the said silver, buy me good fish and send them here for me to eat.

This may be a letter from a client to a patron, but the request to purchase food on the writer's behalf, with the purchase money enclosed, does not use the kind of language that would be expected when an inferior speaks to a superior. The request is more in the nature of a mandate that a superior would impose on an inferior, or at least between equals, i.e., that one friend would ask of another.

A further difficulty is the nature of the sources. Most of the primary sources from the region are institutional—from the palace or the temple—and record formalized relationships of dependence. Even private sources tend to be of a purely legal, commercial, or administrative nature, revealing little of the social relations between individuals. There is no theoretical literature and such "scientific literature" as exists, namely lexical lists, does not discuss the topic, in the sense that they present no identifiably dedicated terminology. It is not surprising then that scholars have tended to concentrate on the formal relationships that are so abundantly attested.

The pioneering studies of Lemche are a notable exception to the general silence, arguing trenchantly for the importance of patronage, at least in ancient Israel and its environs.[5] In the most theoretical of his essays (1995a), Lemche berates scholars for not considering patronage as a factor in ancient Near Eastern societies and presents several examples of patron-client relationships in the ancient sources. Unfortunately, his conception of patronage is somewhat misleading. According to Lemche, the very center of the system of patronage is loyalty based on mutual oaths that binds patron and client in an unbreakable relationship. The term *ḥesed* in the Hebrew Bible is indicative of patronage, particularly since a *ḥesed*-relationship can be effectuated by solemn oath. As explained by Glueck, *ḥesed* can only be given and received by people in a binding legal relationship (German: *Rechtspflichtverhältnis*), which for Lemche is the very essence of patronage. On the same basis, Hittite vassal treaties established a patronage relationship between the local kings and the Hittite emperor, and the biblical covenant did the same between God and Israel.

There is very little in this account that a Roman historian or an anthropologist would recognize as patronage. Oaths are not necessary to patronage, which is an informal association, and the tie, being voluntary, is not unbreakable. Most important of all, patronage is the antithesis of a legal relationship. Formal Hittite treaties and the biblical covenant are definitely to be excluded from its ambit.[6]

Lemche also considers the position of rulers as patrons, pointing to the example of Egypt's Canaanite vassals, who in the Amarna correspondence see themselves as clients of the Pharaoh. This is an important insight to

---

5 Lemche 1995a on royal patronage, 1995b on patronage and the law, 1996 on patronage in the early Israelite monarchy.

6 Some confusion has entered discussion of the term due to the nature of the Roman sources. The classical authors created a mythological vision of archaic patronage. Thus the 1st-century historian Dionysius of Halicarnassus attributes the founding of patronage to Romulus, who supposedly laid down various legal and religious obligations for it (*Roman Antiquities* 2.9-11). His account certainly does not reflect the conditions of the late Republic, which is the point of departure for patronage as we now understand it (see Wallace-Hadrill 1989: 66-67). The first modern historians, such as Fustel de Coulanges, uncritically used classical sources like Dionysius, Plutarch, and Livy to depict archaic patronage as a sacred, legal tie and thus helped to perpetuate the myth (1982[1864]: 128-30, 242-45, 267-79).

which we will return below.[7] On the other hand, he regards the kings of Judah and Israel as the personal patrons of all their citizens, or at least of every one who sought their help. Patronage of such a kind would be so diluted as to be meaningless. To be effective, patronage must bestow, or be perceived to bestow, upon the client a privilege over at least some of his peers (cf. Waterbury 1977: 332; Wallace-Hadrill 1989: 72-73).

Finally, Lemche repeatedly refers to patronage as a system. There is, as we have noted, a distinction between patronage at the individual level and at the systemic level.[8] Whether individual patronage relationships amount to a system is a separate question, to be determined by examining the evidence from each society. Lemche deems this unnecessary because he sees patronage as a universal phenomenon in traditional states with only a rudimentary bureaucracy. The states of the ancient Near East (or at least of Western Asia) were "patronage societies" (1995b: 1708-11). Patronage can be assumed to inform virtually all asymmetrical power relations.[9]

While Lemche has performed a valuable service in drawing attention to a neglected dimension of social relations, his account identifies patronage with conceptually different relationships and assumes rather than demonstrates the pervasiveness of a patronage system. The aim of the present study is more modest. We will revisit the basic question of whether the concept of patronage existed at all in the ancient Near East, using the narrow criteria set out in the methodological introduction. We will present several case studies from different parts of the region which are best explained by the existence of patronage, and where recognition of patronage improves our understanding of the text. We will concentrate on relations between individuals and not try to prove the existence of a system, although the existence of a system might be inferred from them.

---

7 Likewise Thompson (1995), following Lemche. Both Lemche (1995a: 128) and Thompson (1995: 64 n. 20) attribute the idea to Liverani (1967 and 1990: 187-202 respectively), but Liverani does not use the term patronage, speaking only of protection, a narrower concept.

8 Note the strictures of Johnson and Dandeker 1989.

9 In 1995b: 1712-14 (see also 1996: 111), Lemche regards patronage as replacing law at the local level, to the point where judicial decisions were unthinkable except as arbitration between peer patrons. The justification given for this assumption—that assertions to the contrary in the biblical text are late ideological concoctions—does not, even if correct, amount to empirical evidence.

A rigorously narrow approach is necessary in order to avoid the temptation to see patronage in every unequal power relationship and in every isolated act of granting a benefit. The pitfalls are illustrated by an existing case study of Thompson, who applies the criteria set out by Lemche to the incident of David and Nabal in 1 Sam 25:2-42. David, a bandit chief, sends his men to Nabal, a wealthy livestock farmer, with the following message (vv. 7-8):

> I hear that your flocks are being shorn. Now, your shepherds were with us and we did not harm them, nor was anything of theirs missing all the time they were on the Carmel. Ask your men and they will tell you. Please oblige my men, for we have come on a feast day: give whatever you can to your servants and to your son David.

According to Thompson, "David sends ten of his 'retainers' to explain to Nabal that he has all along been giving Nabal's shepherds needed protection, and so asks a 'favor' in return. The language of the story makes it very clear that David here seeks to put the 'House' of Nabal under his patronage" (1995: 70).

We would question this interpretation for two reasons. First, if the relationship were patronage, it would in theory be the converse. David would be the client and Nabal the patron, since David is asking for Nabal's generosity and refers to himself deferentially as Nabal's son. Second, the protection mentioned is not against violence from third parties, which would be the office of a patron. The potential violence was from David's men themselves. In other words, it is nothing more than criminal extortion: a thinly veiled threat to rob Nabal if he does not hand over property. It is not inconceivable that a distorted form of patronage could exist between a criminal and his victim, but there is nothing in the present narrative to compel that conclusion from a single instance of exaction by a bandit.[10] Even David himself maintains the fiction that this is a single act of charity

---

10 Lemche (1995a: 119-20) invokes the "Godfather" model to characterize patronage, referring to modern fictional representations of organized crime in the United States. In that model, however, the criminal's patronage consists of protecting those loyal to him from third parties or obtaining benefits for them from the same.

appropriate to a religious occasion, rather than the mark of a continuing relationship.

Primary Patronage

Great Expectations

An Old Babylonian letter from Tell al Rimah illustrates the intangible benefit to the patron of enhanced prestige:[11]

> Speak to my lady: thus says Yasitna-abum your servant. May Shamash and Marduk grant that my lady live forever for the sake of myself, a ghost's son. I am well. No greeting from my lady has ever reached me, so that my heart does not live.
>
> In Andarig you made me trust in a blind gamble (lit. uninspected birds), saying: "Learn to be a scribe and I will make your household that of a gentleman"—in that you made me put my trust. You made me forego both fish and fowl and made me wander about, a ghost's son in the midst of my family. You are not mindful that you once encouraged me and tried hard for me; you have not a woman's pity. Do you not know that a ghost's son is deserving of pity, even more than a corpse?
>
> Now, render Justice (literally, "Shamash") a favor, do an eternal kindness to a ghost's son: because I have nothing, I cannot serve in the palace.
>
> But what more can I write to you? Do I know more of these matters than you? Do you not know that a gentleman whose household members cannot trust him loses face in his own palace and he himself is contemptible? I have written to you often enough.
>
> Just as a father would not look askance at his own son, so may my lady uphold me, the ghost's son. Just as gentlemen trust in their fathers and brothers, so do I trust in my lady. May my lady not let me down!

11   *OBT Tell Rimah* 150. Edited by Foster 1993a.

The letter is addressed to Iltani, queen of Qattara. The writer reveals that he has been the object of his queen's patronage in the past, but no longer enjoys her favor. He recognizes that patronage can be terminated by a unilateral act or even by mere omission, but complains of the special damage that resulted, for it was her encouragement and support in the first place that had led him to give up his livelihood in exchange for a scribal career.

The writer's arguments in favor of renewal are of three different kinds: an appeal to a woman's pity, an appeal to justice, and most tellingly, the suggestion that her prestige as ruler will suffer if she is seen to be unreliable to those under her special protection. The appeal to the addressee's self-interest is a sure sign that the writer acknowledges that he has no legal recourse, even in a divine court. As befits an informal arrangement that created expectations but not rights, he invokes justice and mercy, but not the law.

The Poor Man of Nippur

The Poor Man of Nippur is a satire written in Babylonia in the first millennium.[12] The opening lines (1-22) read:

> There was a man, a citizen of Nippur, poor and destitute,
> Gimil-Ninurta his name, an unhappy man.
> In his city of Nippur in misery he dwelt,
> He had not silver as befits his kind,
> Gold he had not as befits mankind,
> His storage jars were lacking pure grain,
> With a craving for bread his innards burned,
> With a craving for meat and best beer his face was
>   made grim;
> Every day he lay hungry for want of a meal,
> Was dressed in garments that had no change.
> In his gloomy heart, he had a thought:
> "I'll strip off my garments that have no change,
> In my city Nippur's market I'll buy a sheep!"

---

12   Edition in Gurney 1956; Cooper 1975; and Foster 1993: vol. 2, 829-34.

So he stripped off his garments that had no change,
In his city Nippur's market bought a three-year old goat.
In his gloomy heart, he had a thought:
"Supposing I slaughter the goat in my yard—
There could be no feast, for where is the beer?
My neighbors would be outraged to hear of it,
My family and relatives would be furious with me.
So I'll take the goat to the mayor's house,
I'll try (to provide) something good and tasty for his
    stomach!"

These lines tell us a great deal about the social standing of the protagonist. Gimil-Ninurta lacks means but not status. He is not some poor beggar on the margins of society; on the contrary, he is a citizen of Nippur, living among his family and in a neighborhood where he is well known. His dilemma shows that he holds a position of respect in those circles. We might expect that he would look first to family and then to peer group—his neighbors—for aid; instead, it is they who will expect to benefit from him, in spite of his strained finances. Indeed, his standing is such that later in the story he is able to rent a chariot from the king for a considerable sum without being required to pay in advance. The Poor Man of Nippur cannot enjoy a proper meal because he is trapped as much by social convention as by poverty.

Gimil-Ninurta's solution is to give the goat to the local mayor. The mayor likewise recognizes his status: on hearing that a citizen of Nippur is at the door, he chides his doorkeeper for keeping the man waiting. Lines 34-40 then read:

When Gimil-Ninurta entered the mayor's presence,
In his left hand he held the neck of his goat,
With his right hand he greeted the mayor:
"May (the gods) Enlil and Nippur bless the mayor!
May (the gods) Ninurta and Nusku make him prosper
    greatly!"
The mayor spoke to the citizen of Nippur:
"What is the wrong done to you, that you bear me a gift
    (*kadrâ*)?"

The mayor assumes that the visitor is a petitioner with a legal complaint of loss or damage,[13] for which the mayor may give redress if in his judgment the complaint is justified. Dealing with petitions and correcting injustices was a customary function of a Mesopotamian ruler, as the correspondence of Hammurabi makes clear (see Leemans 1968). It was common practice for a petitioner to bring a gift (here called alternately *šulmānu* and *kadrû*) to an official in order that the official should examine his case, even if it were not resolved in his favor. In Middle Assyrian texts such a "gift" (*šulmānu*) was even booked as a debt, with the notation "When he (official) has attended to his (applicant's) affair, he shall receive his *šulmānu*."[14] The gift, in other words, was nothing but a thinly disguised fee. Thus the mayor's understanding of the purpose of the gift of a goat was as a fee for a single service to be rendered. Gurney's surmise (1956: 145-46) that the mayor mistook the gift for a bribe and became incensed can be discounted. If the mayor had been outraged at the offer of a bribe, he would not have accepted it, nor would he have given the culprit anything in return, however derisory.

Instead of making the expected complaint against a third party, Gimil-Ninurta simply repeats the opening lines describing his poverty, the purchase of the goat, his social dilemma, and his decision to bring the goat to the mayor. Evidently, he expects something in return, but does not say what. The text is broken after this point: apparently the mayor has the goat slaughtered and a meal prepared, but then gives the order:

> "Give the citizen of Nippur a bone and a sinew,
> From your flask give him third-rate beer to drink,
> Send him away, throw him out through the gate!" (lines 58-60)

Gimil-Ninurta promises the mayor revenge for this insult:

> "For the one insult[15] that you heaped upon me
> I will repay you three-fold!" (lines 67-68)

---

13 On *ḫibiltu*, see *CAD* Ḫ 179-80.
14 See Finkelstein 1952 and Postgate 1988: xiii-xvi.
15 For the term *pištu*, see Moran 1991: 327-28

The rest of the story is an account of how Gimil-Ninurta manages to get his revenge by administering three beatings to the mayor.

Gimil-Ninurta's motivation in bringing the goat to the mayor remains obscure. Gurney suggested that he hoped that the mayor would arrange a feast for him with beer, although he admitted that the logic was by no means clear (1956: 145). Nor is it clear why this tactic would assuage the wrath of family and friends at being excluded from the feast.

We suggest that Gimil-Ninurta was not seeking an immediate benefit from his gift but had decided to make of it a long-term investment. Hence his reply to the mayor was deliberately vague. The gift was not a payment, disguised or otherwise, for a specific service but a communication of the donor's desire for an ongoing relationship with the recipient, namely patronage. Eventually the patron would reciprocate in more generous measure and ensure the client's maintenance.[16] Gimil-Ninurta wanted to be taken under the mayor's protection.

What benefit did he have to offer to the mayor in return? The goat was the least of it. Let us return for a moment to the Roman model. Patronage did not end with the fall of the Republic, but was continued by the emperors. As a primary patron, the emperor gathered around him a select group of friends (*amici Caesaris*), whom he met on a personal basis at morning audiences (*salutationes*) and banquets (*convivia*). They were the beneficiaries of imperial largesse in the form of offices, honors, and material gifts. In return, the emperor received the loyalty of an influential group of citizens. Despite their awesome power, Roman emperors lived in constant fear of conspiracies and rebellions. Patronal resources were deployed as a tool for the maintenance of political power (Saller 1982: 70-78; Roller 2001: 130, 144-46, 173-82).

On a more modest level, the mayor of Nippur faced the same need to secure loyalty among the more influential members of the populace. Mesopotamian mayors, albeit not elected by modern democratic methods, shared power with the leading citizens, sometimes referred to as an assem-

---

16 In Roman terms a shared meal, a *convivium*, provided by the patron, was one way of reciprocating (see Roller 2001: 135-41), but it was by no means the only benefit that could accrue to the client.

bly (*puḫru*).[17] Gimil-Ninurta's offer of clientship should therefore have been attractive, provided he could show himself to be a man of influence.[18] In his reply to the mayor's query, Gimil-Ninurta emphasizes the problems that purchase of the goat has brought upon him, as one who is expected to give, not to receive (as he had previously informed the audience in his soliloquy). He thus artfully alludes to his high social standing, that same position of respect that put him on the horns of a social dilemma.

The mayor could have simply rejected Gimil-Ninurta's gift, if he deemed the future relationship that it implied insufficiently attractive. Instead, he chose to demonstrate his lack of interest in the most insulting way. He arranged for immediate payment, to show that he regarded this as a relationship of commerce, not patronage. Moreover, he made the payment derisory and threw out the supplicant, without even sharing the meal. He would have been better advised to have adopted the attitude of the indifferent Roman patron satirized by Juvenal. A duplicitous patron will keep his client in expectation of benefits but will reward him with infrequent meals, where he is insulted with cheap scraps, while the patron gorges himself on delicacies.[19]

Adad-šumu-uṣur and His Son Arad-Gula

Where primary patronage overlays an existing relationship of dependency such as that of an official or a vassal, it is not always easy to disentangle

17 Although the mayor was subordinate to the king, Gimil-Ninurta appears to be seeking him as a primary, not an intermediate, patron. Later, Gimil-Ninurta has no difficulty in approaching the king directly.

18 On the personal nature of politics in a society lacking modern ideological parties, see Lenclud 1998.

19 Satire V: A meal is the return which your grand friendship yields you; the great man reckons it against you; and though it seldom comes, he reckons it against you all the same. So if after a couple of months it is his pleasure to invite his forgotten client, lest the third place on the lowest couch be unoccupied, and he says to you, "Come and dine with me," you are in the seventh heaven! What more could you desire? (14-19).

   See now that huge lobster being served to my lord, all garnished with asparagus; see how his lordly breast distinguishes the dish; with what a tail he looks down upon the company, borne aloft in the hands of a tall attendant! Before you is placed on a tiny plate a shrimp hemmed in by half an egg—a fit banquet for the dead (80-85).

the privileges and obligations of being a client from the rights and duties of office. The letters of Neo-Assyrian scholars to the king are a case in point. Occasionally they contain complaints and pleas regarding their treatment. Are these demands within the framework of their remuneration or an attempt to gain extra benefits on the basis of the king's gratitude for their personal services?

The exorcist Adad-šumu-uṣur was the personal physician of Esarhaddon. In an eloquent letter to the king he seeks preferment for his son Arad-Gula at court (SAA 10 226). He contrasts the general contentment that the king has brought about in the population with the unhappiness of himself and his son, and gives the reason:

> Now the king, my lord, has shown his love of Nineveh to the people, saying to the heads of household, "Bring your sons to me; let them attend me" (*ina pāniya lizzizū*). Arad-Gula is my son; let him attend the king, my lord, along with them. Let us rejoice, dance, and bless the king, my lord, with all the people (reverse, lines 6-12).

It is unlikely that the king is supporting the entire youth of Nineveh in his entourage. The writer must be referring to a privileged circle in which his son for some reason has not been included. When the king grants his request, bringing not only his son but other members of his family into the privileged circle, Adad-šumu-uṣur writes an effusive thank-you letter (SAA 10 227) that contains, *inter alia*, the following expression of his feelings:

> The king, my lord, has treated his servants like a father treats his sons. Since mankind has existed, what king has done such a favor (*damiqtu*) for his servants and what friend (*bēl ṭābti*) has returned such a kindness to his friend? (lines 22-29)

The question is whether Adad-šumu-uṣur was entitled to that privilege by virtue of his rank, or whether it was a gift in the discretion of the king as patron. We may compare the language of Arad-Gula himself, after he has attained the position of a royal exorcist. Arad-Gula writes to the king claiming certain benefits, but in very different terms to his father's appeals (SAA 10 294):

When my lord was crown prince I received the "leftovers" with your exorcists. I stationed myself at the windows and kept watch. The whole time that I attended him I observed the taboos sur-rounding him. I did not enter the house of a eunuch or a courtier without his permission. . . . Now the king my lord, after his father, has added to his good name, but I am not treated in accordance with my services (*ina pitti epšētiya*). I have suffered as never be-fore; I have laid down my life (lines 19-25).

If it is fitting that senior scholars and their assistants receive mules, then let them give me one donkey. Furthermore, they ap-portion oxen in the month of Tebet; let [me receive] one ox (lines 31-34).

The contrast is striking. Adad-šumu-uṣur uses the language of affect; Arad-Gula the language of entitlement. The one is a bid for patronage; the other is an assertion of the privileges of office. This distinction between a request for favor and a claim to fair treatment is also an important factor in the Amarna letters, discussed below.

Pharaoh and the Canaanite Kings

The Amarna archive from fourteenth-century Egypt contains diplomatic correspondence between Egypt and other kingdoms of the region. Al-though dealing with matters of state, the letters are always phrased as if they were personal communications between the two rulers. The reason is that kings saw themselves as householders writ large: the theoretical basis of international relations was metaphors of inter-personal relationships such as family ties and individual friendship (Liverani 2000: 18-19).

The letters between equals frequently appeal to personal sentiments of love, brotherhood, and friendship. Since they are between equals, they cannot involve patronage, but in a sense they lay the theoretical ground-work for patronage, in that they reveal an understanding of friendship based upon mutual interest and mutual exchange (cf. Zaccagnini 2000). Patronage is a form of friendship in this self-interested sense, but with the additional mutation of being between unequal partners.

The bulk of the Amarna correspondence is between Pharaoh and the petty kings of Canaan, who were his vassals. "Vassalage" is a term borrowed from medieval history and generally distinguishable from patronage by its formality and permanence. At first sight, the ancient Near Eastern equivalent is expressed in even stronger terms: the overlord is called "master" and the vassal "slave," implying absolute obedience and servitude from the vassal and no reciprocal obligations from the overlord. It would seem that patronage could have no place, even as an accretion, in such a despotic, one-sided relationship. The terminology of servitude, however, has a wide semantic range in the languages of the ancient Near East, indicating anything from proprietary slavery to mere hierarchical subordination. In the field of international relations, vassalage can entail many different degrees of political control, from province to sphere of influence.

In the Hittite empire of the same period, the formal treaty was the instrument of choice for determining the status of individual vassals. The treaty set out the reciprocal rights and duties of overlord and vassal, naturally weighted in favor of the former. Its provisions were so comprehensive and detailed that they left no room for patronage outside of the juridical relationship. The situation within the Egyptian empire in Western Asia was more complex. On the one hand, the language of the Canaanite vassals themselves serves to reinforce an impression of absolutism:

> I fall at the feet of the king, my lord, seven times and seven times.
> I am dust under the sandals of the king, my lord (EA 147: 3-5).

On the other hand, there is an absence of formal treaties. The Egyptians may have taken loyalty oaths from their vassals at the outset, but they did not spell out rights and duties, whether orally or in a formal document. Instead, they left it to district administrators (*rābiṣu*—"commissioner") to regulate ongoing relations with the vassals, on an informal basis. Perhaps in the interests of flexibility, a certain ambiguity was built into the Egyptian system.

Liverani has pointed to a discrepancy between the Egyptian and Canaanite interpretations of certain aspects of vassalage (1967; 1983: 49-56; 2001: 160-65). The Egyptians insist on the vassal kings performing their duties as if they were members of the Egyptian administration, while still regarding them as outsiders and thus denying them any of the emoluments that an Egyptian official would be entitled to. The vassal kings refer to themselves as members of the administration (*ḫazannu*—"mayor") and regard themselves as entitled to be treated as officials.[20]

Liverani's identification of the discrepancy is a great insight. It is not, however, a matter of misunderstanding. The letters reveal a far more subtle dynamic, in which the correspondent's interpretation of terms is in itself a negotiation, as Na'aman has pointed out (2000: 131-38). We would add that Na'aman's analysis applies irrespective of whether the correspondent is Pharaoh or a vassal. The issue is not so much which status is to apply; rather, each side picks out a particular property of one or other status that happens to serve their interest.

Aziru of Amurru ruled a kingdom that stood on the border between the Egyptian and the Hittite spheres of influence. He was therefore in a position to play off one against the other and adopt a more independent attitude toward Pharaoh. He sends Pharaoh "tribute" in the form of timber (EA 160), but it emerges that Pharaoh reciprocates with deliveries of silver and gold (EA 161).

When it suits him, Aziru chooses not only to be a loyal vassal but, like many lesser vassals, to claim insider status within the administration. When accused of entertaining the envoy of a great power, a gesture of independent foreign policy forbidden to a vassal king, Aziru protests (EA 161: 47-53):

> Moreover, the king, my lord, also said, "Why did you provide for the messenger of the king of Hatti, but did not provide for my messenger?" But this is the land of my lord, and the king, my lord, made me one of the mayors!

Aziru does not deny the facts, but suggests that his acts or omissions cannot be interpreted as a political gesture. If he provided food for a foreign messenger, it was as a representative of the Pharaoh, because he is an Egyptian official.

On the other hand, alongside the language of subservience, Aziru adds vague promises more appropriate to patronage:

---

20 In the special dialect of this correspondence, "mayor" is used to mean a member of the Egyptian bureaucracy, not the head of a local authority as in Mesopotamia.

> . . . as to any request that the Sun, my lord, makes, I am your ser-
> vant forever . . . (EA 156: 4-7)

> . . . and whatever the request of the king, my lord, I will grant it
> (EA 157: 17-19)

Such statements should be compared with the language of friendship used
by the Great Kings, Pharaoh's peers:

> Furthermore, whatever my brother wants, let my brother just write
> me so it can be taken from the house (EA 7: 61-62—Babylonia)

> Whatever my brother needs for his house, let him write and take it
> (EA 19: 68-69— Mittani)

Aziru actually uses the language of personal affect in referring to his relationship with Pharaoh (EA 158: 36-38):

> But if the king, my lord, does not love me but hates me, then what
> am I to say?

Pharaoh was accustomed to speak of obedience and duty, not love, in relation to his vassals. Aziru sought to overlay his vassal status with the
special privileges of a client. His efforts were not without result. Pharaoh's
attitude to Aziru is revealed by the copy of a letter sent by him to Aziru,
remarkable for its weakness (EA 162).

> 7-11 Do you not write to the king, my lord, saying, "I am your
> servant like all the previous mayors in this city"? Yet you
> acted delinquently by taking the mayor whose brother had
> cast him away at the gate, from his city. . . .
> 19-21 And if you did act loyally, still all the things you wrote
> were not true. In fact, the king has reflected on them as fol-
> lows, "Everything you have said is not friendly."
> 22-29 Now the king has heard as follows, "You are at peace with
> the ruler of Qadesh. The two of you take food and strong
> drink together." And it is true. Why do you act so? Why
> are you at peace with a ruler with whom the king is fight-

ing? And even if you did act loyally, you considered your
own judgment, and his judgment did not count. You have
paid no attention to the things you did earlier. What happened to you among them that you are not on the side of
the king, your lord?

30-32 Consider the people that are training you for their own advantage. They want to throw you into the fire. . . .

33-40 But if you perform your service for the king, your lord,
what is there that the king will not do for you? If for any
reason whatsoever you prefer to do evil, and if you plot
evil, treacherous things, then you, together with your entire
family, shall die by the axe of the king. So perform your
service for the king, your lord, and you will live.

Although Aziru has performed patently treasonable acts, Pharaoh each
time offers him a way out, settling for a light reprimand. In lines 30-32
Pharaoh himself finds an excuse for Aziru's misconduct, appealing to him
not to be led astray by others seeking to exploit him for their own ends. In
lines 33-38, the threat of punishment for a disobedient servant was to be
expected; what is surprising is the offer of benefits by the king in return for
services. Especially significant is the fact that Pharaoh's offer is couched
in the vague terms of boundless generosity, not an exact quid pro quo or
payment. It creates expectations for the vassal, not categorical legal rights.
It is the pure language of patronage.

Aziru's bid for patronage, apparently successful, should be contrasted
with the correspondence of Rib-Hadda of Gubla. Rib-Hadda repeatedly
sought Pharaoh's aid against his fellow vassals but had no rival patron to
whom he could turn.[21] His letters therefore argue exclusively from the
standpoint of a member of the Egyptian administration and use the language of entitlement, demanding fairness in his treatment (EA 88: 43-48):

---

21 Rib-Hadda tries to give his local rivals the status of foreign enemies, by suggesting
    that they threaten the integrity of the Egyptian empire (EA 137). They represent the
    Apiru, that is, the forces of chaos (EA 88, 90); they are comparable to external threats
    such as the Hittites or the Babylonians (EA 76, 116); they are forming a coalition that
    will challenge Egyptian hegemony (EA 74:30-45); they are in collusion with the Hit-
    tites (EA 126:53-66— perhaps with a grain of truth!).

Gubla is not like the other cities. Gubla is a loyal city to the king, my lord, from most ancient times. Still, the messenger of the king of Akka is honored more than my messenger, for they furnished him with a horse. . . .

Intermediary Patronage

Aziru Again

A classic example of intermediary patronage is the great man at court who will use his influence for the benefit and protection of his client. In EA 198 above, Arasha of Kumidu, seeking military aid, sought to assure Pharaoh of his loyalty:

May the king, my lord, inquire of all his commissioners whether I am a loyal servant of the king, my lord. May the king, my lord, inquire of Hamasha whether I am a loyal servant of the king, my lord . . . (lines 11-17).

The mention of commissioners is no more than a reference to credible witnesses. The mention of Hamasha, a senior Egyptian courtier, is not of the same order. He could just have been a disinterested witness, but it is more likely that Arasha saw him as his patron at the Egyptian court.[22] In EA 158, Aziru of Amurru writes directly to Tutu, a high official at the Egyptian court, with the same purpose:

To Tutu, my lord, my father: Message of Aziru, your son, your servant. I fall at the feet of my father. For my father may all go well. Tutu, I herewith grant the request of the king, my lord, and whatever may be the request of the king, my lord, he should write and I will grant it.

Moreover, as you in that place are my father, whatever may be the request of Tutu, my father, just write and I will grant it.

---

22 On the assumption that Moran is correct in identifying him with Haamashi who had served as an envoy to Mittani (1992: 381).

As you are my father and my lord, and I am your son, the land of Amurru is your land and my house is your house. Write to me any request at all of yours, and I will grant your every request.

And you are in the personal service of the king, my lord. Heaven forbid that treacherous men have spoken maliciously against me in the presence of the king, my lord. And you should not permit them. And as you are in the personal service of the king, my lord, in my place, you should not permit malicious talk against me.

I am the servant of the king, my lord, and I will not deviate from the orders of the king, my lord, or from the orders of Tutu, my father, forever. But if the king, my lord, does not love me but hates me, then what am I to say?

Several points stand out from this letter. First, the writer calls the Egyptian official "my father" and himself "your son." While not necessarily a sign of patronage, it is certainly appropriate to it. Secondly, the writer offers to fulfill any request of the official (and of the Pharaoh). It is the same vague offer made to and by Pharaoh elsewhere in Aziru's correspondence that we have noted as indicative of patronage obligations. Thirdly, his letter has one overriding purpose: to exploit the influence of that official with the Pharaoh. Nothing, from the vassal's point of view, could be more valuable, as he makes clear in the last sentence.

A requirement of patronage is that the personal relationship not be restricted to an isolated transaction. The same Tutu appears several times in Aziru's correspondence (EA 167, 169). He was most probably an established contact at court that the vassal in this letter tries to enlist in his ongoing campaign to neutralize enemies among his fellow vassals and influence Pharaoh in his favor.

Adad-šumu-uṣur Again

In his request to Esarhaddon for preferment of his son, Adad-šumu-uṣur complains that he has no "friend" (*bēl ṭābti*) at court who would accept a *šulmānu*-gift from him in order to present his case to the king (SAA 10 226: reverse 14-19). The "friend" could of course be a colleague who would accept a mandate to intercede on his behalf, but it is difficult to see

why a courtier of equal standing should be more effective than the petitioner himself. It seems more likely to indicate that there are higher
echelons of courtiers, for example princes or generals, among whose ranks
he has no intermediary patron to act as broker for him.

Biblical Prophets

In 1 Kgs 17:8-24, the prophet Elijah is given a curious instruction by God.
He is to request support from a poor widow, in other words, to become her
client. The woman, not unwilling in principle, points out her inability to
fulfill the prophet's request, given that she and her son are on the point of
starving to death. The prophet, by a miracle, provides her with limitless
supplies and thus in one stroke becomes her patron rather than her client.
Her maintenance of him, originally demanded as a gratuitous service, becomes a reciprocal gift for his intervening with the divine ruler to ensure
maintenance of herself and her son. Later, when her son falls ill, her reaction is not to entreat Elijah but to berate him. "What have I to do with you,
man of God? Have you come to me to invoke my sin and kill my son?" she
remarks sarcastically (v. 18).[23] As her intermediary patron, he has failed in
his duty to protect her from adverse decisions of the divine ruler. Elijah is
keenly aware of his failure. His plea to God for the son's life is not for the
boy's sake but rests upon the mother's client status (v. 20): "Will you harm
the widow with whom I lodge by killing her son?" When he succeeds in
reviving her son, her reaction is again logical within the framework of patronage: she affirms his effectiveness as an intermediary with the divine
ruler (v. 24): "Now I know that you are a man of God and that the word of
the LORD in your mouth is true."

2 Kgs 4:8-37 and 8:1-6 repeat the same topos, but in a more complex
and subtle narrative, charged with irony regarding the vicissitudes of fortune. It concerns the relationship of the prophet Elisha with a wealthy
woman in the town of Shunem. Whenever he passes through the town, she
invites him for a meal, and eventually she and her husband construct an

---

23 Following MT. If the manuscripts that insert *kî* are followed, the tone of the widow's
    remarks nevertheless remains the same: "What have I to do with you, man of God, that
    you have come to me to invoke my sin and kill my son?"

extra bedroom in their house that he can use as lodgings. The motivation for their generosity is piety, because the prophet is a holy man. They ask no favors from him, but they do stand to gain from the relationship in terms of social prestige and perhaps favor with God.

Nonetheless, the prophet is determined to reciprocate and instructs his servant Gehazi to ask her: "Would you have a word spoken on your behalf to the king or to the commander of the army?" In other words, he offers his patronage as an intermediary: to use his influence at the royal court on her behalf. Note that his offer comes some time after he has been receiving her hospitality. The relationship demands that his offer not be seen as payment for services, but as a counter-gift in recognition of her generosity. The relationship can thus remain personal, not commercial.

Although phrased as an offer of assistance, its effect will be to shift Elisha's status from client to patron. It is an assertion of his role as the superior in the relationship, and the woman, understanding its implications, rejects it out of hand. Her reply—"I am dwelling among my clan"— stresses that she relies on a different support system, based on kinship, not patronage. Moreover, she is "a great woman" (*'iššâ gĕdôlâ* in 2 Kgs 4:8), i.e., a person of high status. Holding a preeminent position within her clan gives her influence enough, without the need for a patron at court.

Elisha, not satisfied with her reply, discovers that she is lacking in one respect. She has no children. He therefore informs her that she will bear a son, and by doing so he does succeed in reversing their patronage relationship, making himself the dominant party, as in the Elijah story. She does not need his influence in the royal court, but Elisha is a prophet, and has influence in an even higher court, that of the divine king.

The patronage relationship, thus established, continues to function for some years, until events take a dramatic turn. The boy falls ill and dies. The woman hastens to the prophet and grasps his legs—the gesture of a supplicant. Her attitude, however, reveals an ongoing concern with status. Immediately beforehand, she had turned aside the polite inquiry of Gehazi, Elisha's servant, by stating that the boy was well. Unwilling to go through the servant, she approaches Elisha directly, and when she addresses him it is not with words of supplication but of reproach (4:28): "Did I ask a son of my lord? Did I not say 'Do not deceive me'?" It was he who chose to reverse their roles, and now he has failed to fulfill the promises of his patronage. Elisha understands and proceeds to correct his error, praying to God until the child is revived.

Seen against the background of a rich and powerful woman's pride and her earlier rejection of intervention at court, the biblical narrative uses the motif of reversal of fortune to emphasize its message. Not only is the prophet's patronage more effective than kinship or high status; the prophet, albeit intermediary and not primary, is a more powerful patron than even a king because as an official of God, he can use his influence to bestow benefits uniquely within divine power, such as the birth of a child and revival of the dead.[24]

The woman's reversal of fortune continues. Elisha, acting as a good patron, warns her of an imminent famine. The famine is a decision of the divine ruler: the prophet, with insider knowledge of government policy, as it were, is able to protect a privileged client from its effects. She flees the country for seven years, only to find on her return that her land has been occupied by others in her absence.[25] Presumably, she is also by now a widow, since she went out "she and her house" (2 Kgs 8:2), but now petitions the king alone for his aid in restoring "her house and field" (8:3, 8).

In the absence of Elisha, it is his servant Gehazi who helps her by informing the king of Elisha's patronage of her. The woman's circumstances have been reduced to the point where she now needs the prophet's influence in the earthly court, but the narrative leaves the task of intervening at this lower level to the prophet's servant, that same servant whom in an earlier meeting with the prophet she had circumvented.

Conclusions

If our examples have been few, they are drawn from a wide spectrum of societies in the region, in the second and first millennia. They are not evidence of widespread practice on the Roman model, republican or imperial, nor of a parallel system alongside the formal structures of government, as anthropologists have demonstrated for many traditional societies. Further-

---

24   The latter power is described in 1 Sam 2:6: "The LORD puts to death and makes live; he brings down to the Netherworld and he brings up."

25   The assumption by some commentators that the property had been taken over by the crown, in trust or otherwise (e.g., Gray 1970: 527; Jones 1984: 440), is anachronistic.

more, they reveal only the operation of patronage; they give no hint as to its moral ideology.

These limitations are not altogether unexpected, given the narrow criteria that we have adopted on the one hand and the nature of our sources on the other. The former are necessary to dispel unwarranted assumptions but result in a lean harvest. It has not been our intention, however, to multiply examples but, rather, to present a heuristic model which it is hoped other researchers will apply to identify further verifiable cases of patronage in the primary sources and so slowly build up a picture of its true impact on the societies of the ancient Near East.

As regards the sources, it is significant that our cases come from the two genres most apt to reveal informal arrangements, namely literary narratives and letters. By their nature, narratives and letters will not give a systematic picture of the phenomena mentioned in them. Nonetheless, these few cases are sufficient to show that the concept of patronage, although never given distinct expression, was not alien to the ancient Near East. The expectations of patronage can be seen to color interpersonal reactions, in the context of both political negotiations and social courtesies.

Once we eschew the assumption of a "patronage society" and confine ourselves to textual evidence, patronage is bound to remain a shadowy phenomenon, reflected in the sources rather than displayed by them. Nevertheless, it is a useful reminder that ancient Near Eastern societies had available to them more subtle modes of distribution than are dreamt of in the philosophy of ration lists.

10

Adultery in Ancient Near Eastern Law

Abstract

The biblical and cuneiform sources reveal a common legal tradition in the treatment of adultery. Apparent differences are due to the method of presentation used
by the ancient law codes. Adultery was an offense against the husband by two
parties: the wife and the paramour. His legal remedies against them sometimes
coincided or were linked for reasons of policy, but they were on a different basis.
Adultery was at the same time a sin which could result in divine punishment. Pre-
marital infidelity was subject to analogous rules.

Introduction

A dultery is dealt with by a number of the ancient Near Eastern law
codes, both cuneiform and biblical. Provisions are to be found in Codex Ur-Namma (CU) 7,[1] Codex Eshnunna (CE) 28, Codex Hammurabi
(CH) 129, Tablet A of the Middle Assyrian Laws (MAL) 13-16, 22-23, the
Hittite Laws (HL) 197-198, the Priestly Code in Lev 18:20 and 20:10, and
the Deuteronomic Code in Deut 22:22. Evidence for the law in practice is
sparse but can be gleaned from a variety of sources which will be discussed in the course of this article.[2]

---

* Originally published in *Revue Biblique* 97 (1990): 542-80. Copyright © J. Gabalda et
  Cie, Éditeurs. Used by permission.
1 Kramer (1983) has proposed that the code was in fact the product of Ur-Namma's son
  and successor Šulgi.
2 Egypt provides no legal sources on the subject of adultery. There are two stories that
  mention adultery: *The Two Brothers* (translation by Lichtheim 1976: 203-211) and
  King Cheops and the Magicians (translation by Simpson 1973: 16-18 [2nd tale]). The
  first is a fantasy tale which is of doubtful evidentiary value, but the second may

At first sight, these sources present a homogeneous picture. The basic conception of adultery is the same throughout: consensual sexual intercourse by a married woman with a man other than her husband. In contrast to modern western systems, intercourse by a married man with a woman other than his wife was not regarded as adultery, unless of course that woman was married.[3]

Nevertheless, the question of differences between the ancient legal systems has given rise to considerable scholarly debate. A dividing line has been drawn between the biblical system on the one hand, and the cuneiform systems on the other.

Biblical and Cuneiform Law

The theory was proposed by W. Kornfeld[4] and later expanded upon by M. Greenberg[5] that whereas in the other ancient Near Eastern systems adultery is a private wrong against the husband, in biblical law it is an offense against God. Thus whereas in the former case the husband may prosecute the offenders or may waive prosecution at his choice, and may pardon his wife or mitigate her punishment, in the latter prosecution is mandatory and the penalty is invariably death for both the wife and the adulterer, with no possibility of pardon.

Variants on this basic theory have been proposed by H. McKeating[6] and A. Phillips.[7] McKeating accepts that the death penalty is mandatory in biblical law, but only in the Deuteronomic and Holiness codes. Previously, it had been at the husband's discretion, as in the rest of the ancient Near East. Biblical law thus demonstrates an historical development away from the common system.

---

reflect contemporary legal practice (see n. 84 below). A wisdom text, *The Instructions of Any* (translation by Lichtheim 1976: 137) refers to adultery as "a great deadly crime when it is heard" (cf. Prov 7:23).

3   It might, however, be censured as immoral in certain circumstances. See Westbrook 1984.

4   Kornfeld 1950.

5   Greenberg 1960: 12-13; and Greenberg 1986: 1-4.

6   McKeating 1979.

7   Phillips 1981.

Phillips likewise explains the biblical law in terms of historical development. The death sentence was mandatory, but originally this applied only to the adulterer. The wife was either divorced or pardoned by her husband at his discretion, a procedure which lay within the realm of family law and was not a matter for the courts at all. The effect of the Deuteronomic reform (and subsequently the Priestly Code) was to apply the mandatory death sentence to the wife as well.

The above theory in all its variations suffers from the same weakness: it relies not on evidence from the facts but on their silence. Three main arguments are presented:

1. The right of mitigation or pardon by the husband or by the king, which is mentioned in the cuneiform codes, does not occur in the biblical laws.[8] According to Greenberg, the biblical laws provide that the adulterous couple "must be put to death,"[9] but his translation is misleading. The Hebrew verb could equally well be translated "shall" or even "may."[10] Its evidence is therefore neutral on this question.
2. In the incident in Genesis 20, where Abimelech takes Abraham's wife Sarah and almost has intercourse with her, his offense is treated as a sin against God; there is not a word about the wrong done to Abraham.[11]
3. In the same incident, there is no suggestion that Sarah might in any way be liable for her adultery with Abimelech, and the same applies to Bathsheba for her adultery with David.[12]

The second and third points, however, are equally explicable in terms of adultery being a wrong against the husband, to be prosecuted at his discretion. Abraham acquiesced in Sarah's adultery: indeed, he colluded in the deception of Abimelech as to her status, by presenting her as his sister. Bathsheba's husband was dead—killed at David's order—before he could

---

8   Greenberg 1960: 12-13; Kornfeld 1950: 94-95.
9   Greenberg 1960: 12.
10 See Buss 1973: 55-56.
11 Greenberg 1960: 12.
12 Phillips 1981: 14-15.

discover his wife's adultery, and therefore was not in a position to prosecute. In any case, since the adulterer in both these instances was a monarch, the idea of his prosecution in a court of law would be somewhat academic.

On the other hand, the theory is faced with explicit evidence to the contrary, which its proponents are at pains to explain away.

1.   Prov 6:32-35, in warning the foolish against adultery, states:

> The fury of the husband will be passionate;
> He will show no pity on his day of vengeance.
> He will not have regard for any ransom;
> He will refuse your bribe, however great.

The passage assumes that the penalty for adultery was vengeance by the husband, which he could commute to ransom at his own discretion. So far from being ineluctable, therefore, punishment was no more than a private arrangement between the wronged husband and the adulterer. Greenberg feels entitled to disregard this evidence on the ground that it represents an extra-legal agreement, the verb "to avenge" (*nqm*) indicating an extraordinary, usually extra-legal remedy.[13] But *nqm* indicates a strictly legal remedy in Exod 21:20,[14] and the alternative of ransom still remains to be explained. If adultery was a breach of God's law which had to punished with death by an earthly court, then the possibility of the husband taking personal vengeance would be irrelevant, and his agreement to accept ransom in lieu of vengeance would be void and most probably illegal also. The point is well taken by Phillips, who argues that the ransom in question was illegal hush-money to cover up the offense. He points out that the two Hebrew terms used for ransom, *kpr* and *šḥd*, can be used of bribes to pervert justice.[15] So they can, if given to the wrong person, such as a judge or an official. But if given to a litigant, as the husband is, *kpr* is a perfectly

---

13   Greenberg 1986: 4.
14   As Greenberg himself argues (1962: 738) with reference to this passage, stating that the verb referred to the operation of Israelite justice. For a discussion of the legal meaning of *nqm* see Westbrook 1988d.
15   Phillips 1981: 17-18.

legitimate part of the legal process, which is expressly sanctioned by a law code in Exod 21:30, while *šḥd*, when paid by one king to another to persuade the latter to come to the former's aid in pursuance of an existing treaty of friendship (1 Kgs 15:19) or vassalage (2 Kgs 16:8), would seem to be a legitimate instrument of international law.

2.   In Gen 38:24, Judah, having been informed that his daughter-in-law has become pregnant while awaiting marriage to his infant son, orders that she be taken out and immolated. This apparent discretion on the part of the wronged party is explained by Phillips as the paterfamilias exercising his patriarchal powers.[16] But Judah is not the paterfamilias; he is the father-in-law, and his daughter-in-law is not even living in his house, but in her own father's. Given the minority of the groom (Shelah), Judah may clearly be seen to be acting on the latter's behalf. And since Tamar is only betrothed, not married at the time, the groom's rights cannot derive from some informal "family law." (As we shall see below, her offense in these circumstances still falls squarely within the normal rules of adultery.)

The contrary view, that the biblical law is the same as in the rest of the ancient Near East, i.e., an offense against the husband, with prosecution at his discretion, has been proposed by B. Jackson[17] and S. Loewenstamm,[18] mainly on the basis of Prov 6:32-35. As regards the silence of the biblical codes on the question of pardon, Loewenstamm points out that they are equally silent as to the identity of the prosecutor. Prov 6:32-35 shows him to be the husband, who may waive his right or accept ransom in lieu. The situation in adultery is comparable to that in murder, where the death penalty is imposed, but its execution is in the hands of the avenger of blood.[19]

The evidence presented above clearly favors the views of Jackson and Loewenstamm. Nonetheless, the considerations of the opposing school of thought should not be dismissed altogether. The silence of the biblical codes where the cuneiform codes are explicit, as noted by these eminent scholars, while not supporting their hypothesis, is a phenomenon worthy of

---

16   Phillips 1970: 117, n. 34. Phillips offers an alternative argument: that the reference to burning is a priestly gloss (1970: 129). But no ground for excising this section of the text is given other than its inconsistency with the author's theory

17   Jackson 1975: 60.

18   Loewenstamm 1980b.

19   Loewenstamm 1980b: 148-49.

some consideration. Furthermore, acceptance of the fact that the biblical law is a component part of a wider tradition raises the broader question of what the tradition is and how the individual legal systems relate to it. It is only by understanding the nature of that tradition that we may elucidate the complexities of the ancient Near Eastern law of adultery and their reflection in the individual systems of the area.

The Scientific Tradition

The similarity between the adultery laws of the various cuneiform and biblical law codes is not a coincidence. It derives from the nature of the codes themselves. In spite of their modern appellation, the codes were not legislation in the modern sense but scientific treatises on the existing laws, which consisted mostly of customary law with an admixture of more recent precedents and administrative measures.[20] Their scientific method had likewise little in common with modern science; it was based on the Mesopotamian scientific tradition, sometimes contemptuously referred to as a science of lists. Lacking the ability to define terms or create abstract categories, the method employed was to compile long lists of examples illustrating the principles involved, without actually expressing them. To enhance the heuristic value of these examples in the case of law, an actual judgment was taken and cast into the form of a hypothetical set of facts with its accompanying decision, then further hypothetical variations added, usually along certain set patterns. In this way a scholarly legal problem was created which could be used to instruct pupils in the Mesopotamian equivalent of a university, the scribal school.[21]

20 See Kraus 1960; Westbrook 1988a: 84-97. *Contra* Preiser 1969; Petschow 1986: 18-23. Kraus (1984) recanted his original view, making reference to Preiser's article. In our view the article in question does not justify any change of opinion, since it adds nothing new to the debate. It merely summarizes the opposing views and declares *ex cathedra* that one is more convincing than the other. The author apparently has no knowledge of the primary sources or of the cultural context in which those sources are embedded; instead he applies anachronistic analogies. For a rebutter and summary of the debate, see now Westbrook 1989a.

21 Bottéro 1982.

For example, an owner's liability for his goring ox could be considered along a series of different lines: firstly, if the owner had been warned or not of the ox's propensity to gore; secondly, what the status of the ox's victim was (head of household, wife, son, daughter, or slave); thirdly, if the victim was another ox, which raised different questions of liability. Furthermore, combinations of all these different lines of inquiry could be constructed so as to create a discussion that was at least far-ranging, if by its nature it could never be comprehensive.

By the second millennium (if not earlier) a canon of such scholarly problems had been created, and it was upon this scientific tradition that the Mesopotamian law codes drew in committing the law to writing. With the spread of cuneiform writing, the Mesopotamian scientific tradition was carried throughout the ancient Near East and beyond.[22] Local law codes in Hatti, Canaan, and even, to a lesser extent, in early Greece[23] and Rome,[24] applied the same methods and drew upon the same canon of scholarly problems.

Because these law codes could only have a fraction of their discussion committed to writing, each code contains no more than a few aspects of a given scholarly problem, sometimes overlapping with the aspects preserved in other codes, sometimes not. Moreover, a given system may pursue the discussion in a particular direction, considering variants not discussed elsewhere.

It is by combining the similar and not-so-similar provisions of the various codes that the whole problem and thus the underlying law may be revealed and any peculiarities of the individual systems disclosed. This approach is, to be sure, in some sense an argument from silence, but it is a positive argument, that refuses to see contradictions in mere omissions from sources that are by their nature incomplete, when in all other respects they are complementary.[25]

Adultery forms part of a complex of interrelated scholarly problems discussing social offenses such as seduction and rape.[26] And it is itself a

22 Westbrook 1988a: 92-93.
23 For an example of Near Eastern influence in the Law Code of Gortyn, see Muhl 1933: 79-81.
24 Westbrook 1988a: 97-118.
25 Westbrook 1988d: 5-6.
26 For a survey of sexual offenses, see Finkelstein 1966.

complex problem, containing several interrelated cases, upon which the discussions of the law codes are built. We shall consider each case in detail.

The Treatment of Adultery in the Law Codes

1.   The first case sets out the basic crime of adultery and the appropriate sanction. It is found in three codes: MAL, Leviticus, and Deuteronomy.

> MAL 13   If the wife of a man goes out of her house and goes to a man where he is dwelling (and) he has intercourse with her knowing that she is the wife of a man, the man and the woman shall be killed.[27]

> Lev 20:10   A man who commits adultery (verb *n'p*) with the wife of a man, the man who commits adultery with the wife of his neighbor shall be killed—the adulterer and the adulteress.[28]

> Deut 22:22   If a man is discovered[29] to have slept with a married woman, both shall die—the man sleeping with the woman and the woman. You shall purge evil from Israel.

All three laws contain the basic elements of adultery: a married woman, a man (married or not), intercourse, consent. The sanction is death for both, stated in the most categorical terms. There is no mention of the husband in any role or of the possibility of pardon.

Differences between the three are that Leviticus uses a technical term for adultery, Deuteronomy describes the physical act, and MAL does

---

27   Literally: "they shall kill" (*idukkū*), i.e., the 3rd masc. pl. impersonal form.

28   Note the literary structure of the verse, which in its partial repetition creates a "word chain," a device sometimes found in biblical poetry. See Berlin 1987: 141-47.

29   Daube (1971) argued that the verb *yimmāṣē'* indicated that the culprit was caught in the act. But see in refutation Dempster 1984.

likewise but with additional circumstantial material—which is not surprising, as MAL is the most detailed of all the codes, cuneiform as well as biblical.

MAL gives two extra details: the location of the act—which plays an evidentiary rather than a substantive role in the offense (as we shall see presently)—and the paramour's knowledge of the woman's status. The latter point is mentioned because in MAL this case is part of a larger discussion: it is to be contrasted with another set of circumstances where the paramour was totally in ignorance. This brings us to the second case, which is presented in two codes, CU and MAL.

2. CU 7 reads:[30] "If a married woman of her own initiative leads a man and sleeps with him,[31] the man (i.e., the husband) shall kill that woman; he shall let that man go free." The extremely terse formulation, if taken literally, would leave us with an absurd law: the paramour would only have to prove than he was seduced in order to escape entirely the consequences of his adultery. That more lay behind the law than was expressed is shown when we complement it with the details in MAL's treatment of the same case.

> MAL 14 If a man has intercourse with the wife of a man in a tavern or in the square, knowing that she is a man's wife, whatever the husband states is to be done to his wife shall be done to the paramour.
>
> If he has intercourse with her not knowing that she is the man's wife, the paramour is free (of liability). The husband shall establish (the case against) his wife and do with her(!) as he wishes.[32]

---

30 Gurney and Kramer 1965: 13; Finkelstein 1969b: 68; Yildiz 1981: 90, 92. Cf. Lambert 1968: 96. Paragraph number follows Yildiz' edition, but the text presented here is Yildiz C. See note 51 below. The Sumerian text reads: tukum-bi dam-guruš-a / me-te-a-ni-ta / lú ba-an-ús / úr-ra-na ba-an-ná / munus-bi / lú i-gaz-e / nitaḫ-ba / ama <ar>-gi-bi / i-gar.

31 Literally, "lies in his lap."

32 *ki-i lib-bi-šu e-pa-a-[s]u.* For this phrase, cf. the declaration of king Shaushgamuwa of Amurru on agreeing to restore to king Ammistamru of Ugarit his adulterous wife:

A woman has given herself to a man in one of the typical haunts of a prostitute,[33] i.e., in circumstances in which his ignorance of her status is credible. Only if he in fact knew her to be a married woman is he to be punished for adultery.

The principle is, in our view, the same in both the Sumerian and the Assyrian law. A wife plays the part of a single woman in order to initiate intercourse with an outsider: punishment therefore falls entirely upon her and not upon her unwitting partner. The Assyrian law expresses it with a very concrete example; the Sumerian law only alludes to the circumstances with the enigmatic verb "leads." In both the result is the same: death for the wife, freedom for the man.

Thus far we have seen two cases: the statement of principle in which both the wife and the paramour die, and a special circumstance in which only the wife dies. A case where only the paramour dies does not arise, and for good reason. Adultery is an offense against the husband. It is an infringement by a third party of his marital rights over his wife. If the husband acquiesces in that infringement then there cannot have been a wrong against him. Consequently, punishment of the paramour is conditional upon punishment of the wife. All three texts which lay down the principle of adultery emphasize this point, stating that both guilty parties are to be killed. The formulation of Lev 20:10 is of particular note in this regard. Phillips has made much of the fact that the law at first concerns the paramour alone but then adds as a rider "the adulterer and the adulteress," suggesting that this rider was a subsequent amendment to the original law, expanding its scope.[34] But there is no need to assume an historical development expressed through clumsy drafting.[35] The formulation, as McKeating surmised,[36] is designed to show that the paramour's death is dependent upon the wife's.

"Take her and do with her as you wish. If you wish, kill her or throw her into the sea!" (in *PRU IV*, RS 17.228: 10-14 [p. 142]).

33 With reference to a prostitute from the town square; cf. CL 30 and *ana ittišu* 7 II 23-23a (see Landsberger 1937: 96). For the immoral reputation of a tavern, cf. CH 110.

34 Phillips 1981: 6.

35 On the contrary, the laws of the priestly source show a polished, literary quality that stands apart from the traditional law-code formulation. See n. 28 above and compare, for example, the chiastic structure of Lev 24:17-21.

36 McKeating 1979: 58-59.

A further aspect of this dependence is considered by MAL 14a. In the event that the paramour was aware of the wife's true status, his punishment is still linked to that which the husband imposes on his wife. The reason for this linkage has rightly been seen by commentators as a safeguard against collusion between husband and wife.[37] The suspicion is that the husband himself sent his wife out to prostitute herself, and if she is not punished for adultery when her clients are, the corrupt couple can easily blackmail their victims, on a false claim as much as on a real one. The husband's lack of acquiescence in his wife's conduct is therefore tested by this device of linkage. The text also reveals the role of the husband and the possibility that adultery may be punished other than by death, points to which we shall return below. Firstly, however, we must examine more deeply the question of collusion, which is a vital factor in the third case.

3. Where a wife and her paramour are caught *in flagranti delicto*, three possibilities are envisaged.

a) The husband kills the adulterers on the spot. This is discussed in HL, CE, and MAL.

> HL 197 . . . If the husband finds them (the adulterers) and kills them, there is no liability upon him.

> CE 28 If he establishes a contract and *kirrum* with her father and mother and marries her, she is a wife. The day she is seized in the lap of a man she[38] shall die; she shall not live.

---

37 Driver and Miles 1935: 44-45; Cardascia 1969: 118-19.

38 Yaron (1988b: 284-85) has suggested that this clause could refer to the paramour, rather than the wife. Grammatically speaking, this interpretation is possible, since the 3rd singular in the Old Babylonian dialect does not distinguish between masculine and feminine. It seems to us highly unlikely, however. CE 27-28 is concerned with the question of the woman's legal position. As we shall see below, the penalties on the wife and the paramour for adultery were inherently different and did not need to be considered in the same discussion. See also the remarks of Roth 1988: 206.

The phrase "shall die . . . shall not live" is found in CE in other cases where the culprit is caught *in flagranti delicto*[39] and has been explained by Szlechter as the right of the injured party to kill the culprit on the spot.[40]

MAL 15 is a difficult text. To interpret the first part, which concerns us here, it is necessary to consider the whole law, which reads:

> If a man seizes a man with his wife, (and if) it has been established and proved (against) him: (on condition that) both are killed, there is no liability[41] upon him.
>
> If he seizes (him) and brings (him) before the king or the judges, (and if) it has been established and proved (against) him: if the husband of the woman kills his wife, he shall kill the man; if he cuts off his wife's nose, he shall turn the man into a eunuch and his whole face shall be mutilated; but if he frees his wife, he shall free the man.

The problematic clause in the first paragraph reads literally: "they have established him and have proved him; it is both of them that they kill; his liability is not" (*ubta'erūš ukta'inūš kilallišunūma idukkū šunu aranšu laššu*).

According to Driver and Miles, the husband here is inflicting summary vengeance on the couple caught *in flagranti delicto*, but nonetheless some form of trial procedure is needed beforehand, to safeguard from liability the husband and those who joined him in exacting vengeance.[42] Cardascia supports this view, adducing the example of Hephaistos from the Odyssey and the case of killing a burglar in the Twelve Tables, where the neighbors have to be called in to witness the act of summary justice.[43] The difficulty is that the phrase 'establish and prove,' which is found repeatedly in MAL, elsewhere refers to the burden of proving an accusation before the trial

---

39   CE 12-13: the case of a burglar seized in a field or house at night. Cf. Exod 22:1-2.

40   Szlechter 1954: 110, 123. Yaron objects (1988b: 260-62) that the phrase in its literal meaning "does not connect up" with the question of whether the killing was justified. But such is frequently the case with technical legal phrases, and Yaron's own suggestion—that it is a stylistic conceit devoid of legal meaning—is a counsel of despair.

41   *arnu*. Possibly "penalty." See *CAD* A/2 294; and Hengstl 1980.

42   Driver and Miles 1935: 45-46.

43   Cardascia 1969: 121.

court, which then pronounces sentence.[44] But the latter procedure is presented as the alternative option for the husband in the second part of the text. We suggest therefore that the establishing and proving refer to a procedure *ex post facto* of the husband killing the lovers on the spot, in a trial in which he is the defendant. The burden is on the husband to prove the circumstances in which the killing of the paramour took place (since it is the latter's relatives who would be the accusers in a murder trial), as expressed by the third person plural impersonal form of the verbs with the object 'him,' i.e., the paramour. If the husband can discharge this burden and on condition that both the paramour and his wife were killed—again expressed by the impersonal form of the verb[45] but with the emphatic *-ma* on "both of them" to show that it is a condition—it is a complete defense.

Whichever interpretation is adopted, it is clear that it is the husband's liability for homicide that is in issue in this part of the paragraph. HL 197 and MAL 15a therefore represent the same rule, providing a defense to a husband who kills both his wife and her paramour upon catching them *in flagranti delicto*, instead of bringing them before the court. On the evidence of the Assyrian law, the plural object ("them") in the Hittite law may be taken to be a necessary condition for escaping liability and not merely a narrative element.

CE 28 mentions killing only the wife, but again we cannot infer from this that Eshnunna knew a different rule. CE 28 strictly speaking belongs to a different standard problem, concerning the validity of marriage and mentions the right to kill the wife seized in adultery only in passing as a consequence of that validity. It is not surprising, therefore, that the paragraph concentrates on the fate of the wife and does not mention other conditions associated with adultery. For that matter, it may be assumed that a valid marriage was a condition for the husband's defense in HL 197 and MAL 15a, although the point is omitted.

b) The husband, on catching the lovers, hauls them before the court and demands the death penalty for both. This we have already seen in the

---

44 MAL 1, 9, 16, 20, 21, 40, etc. [Editors' note: see now Westbrook 2003c on this phrase in MAL.]

45 The durative tense (*idukkū*) need not express *consecutio temporum*, but may likewise refer to the condition.

second part of MAL 15; it also occurs in HL 198 which we shall discuss below, but for the moment it is important to note CH 129, the first part of which belongs in this category: "If the wife of a man is seized while lying with a man, they shall be bound and thrown into the water . . . ." The continuation of this law brings us to the third possibility where the husband demands death for the paramour alone.

c)   CH 129 continues: ". . . If the wife's master lets his wife live, the king shall indeed let his servant live." The right of the husband to pardon his wife is assumed by this law. Its concern is to link a royal pardon of the paramour to the husband's pardon of his wife as an almost automatic proc- ess. The same concern informs MAL 15 above, which as usual enters into more detail, linking the court's punishment of the paramour with the de- gree of punishment inflicted by the husband on his wife.[46]

The reason for the court's solicitude for the paramour is not merely a sense of equity, although that undoubtedly plays some part. As we have seen above, acquiescence by the husband would nullify the adultery, while failure to punish his wife severely enough might suggest collusion.[47] In the present circumstances there is a further danger: that of entrapment. An in- nocent person is invited to the couple's house, possibly upon what he thinks is legitimate business, and is there entrapped when the husband claims to have seized him *in flagranti delicto.*

An explicit reference to this danger is found in the Law Code of Gortyn. The latter is a Greek code from Crete, usually dated to the fifth century B.C.E.[48] Its style and content reveal it to be an heir to the Mesopo- tamian scientific tradition, retaining the method of the Near Eastern academies and occasionally an echo of their canon of scholarly problems. Such an echo is found in col. II, lines 20-24, 36-46:

---

46 Could the different gradation of penalty also be linked to the alternative jurisdictions, i.e., before the king—death; before the judges—mutilation? Cf. the discussion below on the jurisdiction of the local court in pre-marital infidelity.

47 A further motivation in exacting punishment on the paramour was the amount of ransom that might be elicited from him (see below). The necessity of exacting paral- lel mutilation on his wife would serve to dampen the colluding husband's greed in this respect.

48 Willetts 1967.

If someone is taken in adultery with a free woman in a father's, brother's, or the husband's house, he shall pay a hundred staters; but if in another's, fifty; . . . but if he should declare that he has been entrapped,[49] the captor is to swear, in a case involving fifty staters or more, each calling down solemn curses upon himself . . . that he took him in adultery and did not entrap him.

In this peripheral code the solution is different, but there is the same awareness of the dangers inherent in a claim to have caught someone in the act of adultery.

Returning to the ancient Near East, HL adopts the same solution in principle to this problem but adds a further factor.

198 If he (the husband) brings them to the gate of the palace and says, "My wife shall not die," and he lets his wife live, he shall let the paramour live, and he shall clothe his head.

  If he says, "Let them both die," and they kneel at the wheel, the king may kill them; the king may let them live.

The first part of the law follows the pattern that we have seen in CH and MAL. The husband cannot claim death for the paramour alone. To show that his case is genuine, he must also be prepared to have his wife killed. But the second part, where the husband does claim death for both culprits, introduces a new element—the right of the king to pardon them nonetheless. This has nothing to do with the pardon linked to the husband's action. It is an independent prerogative of the king, which is found elsewhere in HL. According to §§187-188, the king may pardon acts of bestiality, which were otherwise punishable by death. In these cases, the culprit remained ritually impure. It is possible that in §198 the pardoned adulterer did not escape all consequences of his offense. Such a right of pardon may well have existed in other systems, but it only finds expression in the Hittite Laws.

---

49 Verb *dolōsasthai*. As Willetts points out, the verb is in the middle voice because the relatives stand to profit from the deception (1967: 60 *ad* lines 31-37). The allusion is to ransom: see n. 47 above and see further below.

To summarize so far: the discussion of adultery in the ancient Near Eastern law codes is fragmented into a series of standard problems. We have seen the following cases: the basic principle of adultery, the seduction of an unwitting man, and the claim to have caught the adulterous partners *in flagranti delicto*—which in turn contains three sub-cases: justified killing of the culprits on the spot, legal proceedings against both culprits, legal proceedings against the paramour alone.

With the exception of MAL, the individual codes do not cover all the cases that comprised the traditional discussion.[50] CH omits the first two cases, dealing only with seizure *in flagranti delicto* and within that case omitting the possibility of self-help. CU covers no more than the second case, that of the seductress, omitting the first and the third. HL deals with the second and third cases. The two biblical codes cover only the first case.

Furthermore, several of the codes, such as CU and HL, are extremely terse in their treatment of the problems that they do discuss. Vital details from the underlying oral discussion are omitted in the written version or find only the slightest allusion—sufficient for the initiated, of course.[51]

Both these difficulties can be overcome to some extent by combining the versions, using the information from one code to fill in gaps in the others. Genuine differences also come to light in this way, such as the unique royal prerogative of pardon in HL 198.

In the light of this analysis, the failure of the biblical laws to mention the husband's role or the possibility of pardon by him is readily explained. The first case—the basic case of adultery—which they represent, does not traditionally mention these elements. They appear only in the second and third cases, where they are relevant to questions of collusion and entrapment.

---

50 MAL includes two other cases, not discussed here, with further complications involving journeys, procuresses, etc.: see §§22 and 23. Paragraph 16 is broken at a key point and any interpretation is speculative. See Cardascia 1969: 124-26.

51 CU 7 illustrates the pitfalls of our reliance on extant copies. The text exists in three versions. Two versions read: "he shall kill (i-gaz-e) . . . he shall establish (freedom) (i-gá-gá)." The third version (Yildiz C) reveals the subject of the verb: lú i-gaz-e "the husband shall kill." The identity of the subject was so obvious to the contemporary audience that two of the three extant versions dispensed with it. (For references, see n. 30 above.)

Remedies

The victim of adultery was the husband, who was wronged by two parties: his wife and her paramour. So far we have seen cases where the husband's remedies against the two were linked. Nonetheless, they were in essence separate, being based on different principles.

1. Against the wife

The husband's right to punish his wife was based on the character of ancient Near Eastern marriage, which saw the husband as the master of his wife[52] and her adultery as an offense akin to treason.[53] The parallel is well brought out in CH 129, where the husband's pardon of his wife is likened to a king's pardon of his subject.

The husband's rights against his wife did not, however, amount to jurisdiction over her, but were subject to the control of the courts. In particular, the husband was required to prove his charge of adultery, even when he caught the lovers *in flagranti delicto*, as we have seen in MAL 15. In the Odyssey (8.266-359) it is related that Hephaistos trapped his wife Aphrodite in bed with Ares by binding them with invisible fetters. He then summoned the gods to witness the spectacle and hear his claim for damages.[54] This device must have been an old-established literary topos, for in a literary account of an adultery trial from Nippur in the Old Babylonian period, the husband binds the lovers to the bed and then brings them in that condition, bed and all, before the court. Curiously, the husband further charges her with several counts of stealing from his stores.[55] These accusations seem absurdly petty compared to the principal

---

52 Akkadian *bēlum*, Hebrew *ba'al*, *'ādôn*.
53 In Egypt, Israel and Ugarit, the wife's offense against her husband is referred to as the "great sin." See Rabinowitz 1959: 73; Moran 1959: 280-81.
54 Cf. the remarks of Roth (1988: 195) on later Greek law.
55 Following the interpretation of Greengus 1969-1970. The parallel to the Odyssey is noted by Greengus (1969-1970: 37). Van Dijk (1963) had earlier interpreted it as a case of divorce by reason of the husband's homosexuality, but his scenario does not produce a coherent narrative and does not accord with our knowledge of Mesopotamian social conditions. Recently, Durand (1977-1978) has offered a different interpretation of the wife's misconduct. The wife quarreled with her husband (line 12:

offense, but may be connected with matters more evidentiary than substantial. By revealing her bad character, they undermine the wife's credibility as a witness, and thereby any defense that the apparently compromising circumstances were in fact the entrapment of innocents.

If the husband failed to catch his wife in the act, he might still be able to prove her adultery by circumstantial evidence, e.g., her pregnancy during his absence.[56] Where he was unable to bring concrete evidence, the husband might have recourse to divine judgment. According to CH 131 and Num 5:11-31, the suspicious husband could force his wife to take an exculpatory oath (which would bring down divine retribution upon her if she were lying) and in the latter source also to undergo the ordeal of bitter waters.[57]

While the husband was entitled to impose the ultimate sanction on his wife, he could in his discretion choose a lesser penalty, such as mutilation, as we have seen in MAL 15.[58] Since adultery belongs not only to the realm of criminal law but intersects with marriage law, divorce must also have been an option, although not mentioned specifically by the law codes. Certainly, in cases where the wife was guilty of misconduct amounting to less than adultery, such as immodesty, the husband was entitled to divorce her without compensation and to keep her dowry for himself.[59] It may be

---

ugu-lú-ka in-dab₅ = *ina muḫḫi mutim iṣṣabit*) and denied him sexual intercourse (line 13: su-lú inim ᵍⁱˢná-a in-kéš—"she bound the body of the husband with respect to the matter of the bed"). Because the husband became hostile to her (line 16: mu lú ugu.na al.dab₅.ba.aš), he was awarded a divorce without penalty of divorce-money. Durand's interpretation strains the literal meaning of the Sumerian phrases and contains a non-sequitur. The husband is entitled to a penalty-free divorce because of her misconduct, not because he quarreled with his wife. Durand compares the use of the term "hate" in CH 142, but the verb "to hate" (*zêru*) in CH is a technical legal term used solely in conjunction with a verb of action and designed to show that the action in question was taken for subjective reasons and without objective justification (see Westbrook 1986b). On the lesser acts of misconduct, Durand rejects Greengus' "burglarized his storehouse" on the grounds that the wife, as mistress of the house, would have access to her husband's storehouse. But his own translation— "she pierced his wall," i.e., tried to escape, assumes that the mistress of the house was a prisoner in her own home.

56   As in the case of Judah and Tamar (Gen 38:24) discussed below.
57   For a recent discussion of this ceremony, see Frymer-Kensky 1984.
58   And see n. 32 above.
59   See Westbrook 1986b.

presumed that the same course was open to the husband where her misconduct did amount to adultery. Hephaistos' demand for releasing his wife and her paramour is merely that his father-in-law restore to him the marriage payment that he had made for his wife.[60] This is not a penalty confined to the Greek sphere, as can be seen from the Nippur adultery trial discussed above, where it is stated that the court determined his/her divorce-money, which we take to mean money payable by the wife (or her family) to the husband, since she was the guilty party.[61] The connection between the Greek and Sumerian payments is that in Mesopotamia, divorce-money, in the absence of contractual agreement, was customarily fixed at the level of the marriage payment made by the groom to the bride's father, although normally it is the husband who pays the divorce-money.[62]

In the Nippur trial (if Greengus' interpretation of the partially broken and ambiguous terminology is correct), the court imposes further punishment on the wife: her pudenda were to be shaved, her nose was to be bored with an arrow, and she was to be led thus around the city.[63] The divorced

---

60 *Od.* 8.318-319; Greek *eedna* (a payment to the bride's father for the right to marry his daughter) = Akkadian *terḫatu(m)*, Hebrew *mōhar*, Hittite *kuššata*, Sumerian kù.dam.tuku / níg-mí-ús-sá.

61 Line 19: kù.dam.tak₄.ni. For cases of the wife paying divorce money, see Greengus 1969-1970: 39 n. 15. Unfortunately, the rest of the line is badly damaged. The text is published by van Dijk 1963. Van Dijk restores the rest of the line [x ma-na-k]ù-[babbar], but the traces are too slight to give any positive indication. It is nonetheless preferable to Greengus' second suggestion (1969-1970: 39 n. 16), "They decreed [not to pay] her divorce money," since the verb in line 20 (gar) suggests the setting of a price.

62 Cf. CH 138. See Westbrook 1988b: 69-70.

63 Greengus 1969-1970: 34 and 41. Lines 21-26: [. . .] ù⁷.sur.ra gal₄.la.a / um[bi]n in.ku₅.ru.ne / kiri (KA).ni ᵍⁱˢkak.si.sá in.burù.uš / uruᵏⁱ nigin.e.dè / lugal.e [ba].an.sum. The pronouns could be masculine, in which case it is the paramour upon whom these punishments are being inflicted—or at least part of them, since according to Greengus (1969-1970: 39 n. 17) ù.sur.ra refers to female genitalia. Greengus (1969-1970: 40-41) also raises the possibility that the shaving was a preliminary to slavery, rather than for humiliation. But for that purpose one shaves heads, not pudenda. Roth (1983: 278) has read the beginning of line 21 (correctly, according to the copy) ke-ze-er-x, which would suggest that the woman is to be shaved "like (?) a prostitute."

wife was thus subjected to public humiliation, perhaps—if the shaving of the pudenda were to have any effect—being paraded naked.[64]

The association of divorce with stripping the wife naked is also made in BRM 4 52, an Old Babylonian tablet from Hana. Lines 11-14 read:

> And if his wife Bitti-Dagan says to her husband Kikkinu, "You are not my husband," she shall go out naked; they will cause her to go up to the roof of the palace.[65]

This is a penalty clause designed to deter the wife from exercising her right to pronounce the divorce formula. The rationale of the penalty would appear to be that the wife's action is deemed a betrayal on a par with adultery. Contemporary Babylonian contracts often impose as penalty for the same act defenestration or drowning of the wife, the latter at least being the typical mode of execution of an adulteress in Babylonia, as we have seen from CH 129.[66]

More direct evidence of divorce plus stripping naked as a punishment for adultery may be gleaned from the prophetical books of the Bible. Several of the prophets use the metaphor of marriage to describe God's relationship with Israel or Judah.[67] The latter, in worshipping other gods, are like an unfaithful wife, and the terms "adultery" (*n'p*) and "whoring" (*znh*) are used in this context.

---

64   It is no objection to Greengus' interpretation that punishment of the paramour is not mentioned. The text is concerned exclusively with relations between husband and wife. The punishment of the paramour certainly took place, but it was not the issue addressed in this school text (see Greengus 1969-1970: 43-44 and Roth 1983: 279-82).

65   *ù šum-ma* [f]*bi-it-ti-*[d]*da-gan* DAM-*su* / *a-na ki-ik-ki-ni* DAM-*ša* / *u-ul* DAM-*mi at-ta i-qa-ab-bi* / *e-ri-ši-ša ú-ṣi a-na* É *ru-uk-ba-at* / É-GAL *ú-še-el-lu-ši*. The meaning of the last clause is obscure. *CAD* E 320 suggests that the purpose is to expose her.

66   See Westbrook 1988b: 82-83. In some "testaments" from Nuzi, the wife's remarrying after her husband's death was also considered an act of betrayal and was penalized with stripping and expulsion (see Chiera HSS 5 71:34-35, JEN 5 444:19-23). These contractual provisions were concerned to prevent the wife depriving her husband's family of the benefit of her dowry by leaving to remarry. Cf. Westbrook 1988b: 71 n. 13, and see further Wilcke 1984: 303-13.

67   See generally Neher 1954.

An explicit reference to divorce as the penalty for adultery appears in Jer 3:8: ". . . because the unfaithful one, Israel, had committed adultery, I had divorced[68] her and given her her document of severance." No further consequences are mentioned, but if the divorce is an allusion to Israel's conquest and exile by Assyria, then in terms of the metaphor the divorcee was being stripped of her possessions and driven from the matrimonial home. Jer 13:26 does speak of God exposing Jerusalem's hem over her face, so that her shame is revealed, and the following verse refers to her adultery, but whether this reflects the process of a divorce is not clear.[69]

The metaphor is extended in Ezek 16:37-41, where God informs his unfaithful wife, Jerusalem, that he will judge her for adultery and murder (the sacrifice of her children, v. 21), by handing her over to a gathering of her paramours to be stripped of all her clothes and finery until she is naked, and then to be stoned and dismembered with swords. Note that reality intrudes into the metaphor with two further punishments—the destruction of platform and towers (v. 39) and the burning of houses (v. 41)—which regard Jerusalem as a real city, not a wife.[70] They are therefore irrelevant to the question of adultery. The use of the paramours as the executors of the wife's punishment may seem strange, if necessary for the political message behind the metaphor, but it should be remembered that while the husband could not punish the paramour without punishing his wife, the opposite was not true. The husband was perfectly entitled to punish his wife and forego his rights against the paramour.

W. Eichrodt takes the stoning as the judicial punishment for adultery alone[71] but achieves this result by the unacceptable method of excising the reference to murder from the text.[72] The point is that there are two separate offenses and two separate punishments: adultery, for which stripping is appropriate, and murder, for which stoning and dismemberment are appropriate.

---

68 *šlḥ* in this context is the technical legal term "to divorce." Cf. Deut 24:1, 3, and 4.

69 Some commentators (e.g., Carroll 1986: 304) consider that the verse refers to rape. This interpretation may apply to v. 22, where the verbs are in the passive, but cannot apply to the verse under discussion, since the subject of the verb "to expose" is God himself.

70 Greenberg 1983: 287-88.

71 Eichrodt 1970: 209. Cf. McKeating 1979: 61-62.

72 Eichrodt 1970: 198.

There is no mention of divorce in the passage, but it may have been understood as the context of stripping or may have been unnecessary in this case since the wife was to be executed. The connection between divorce for adultery and stripping naked is provided by Hos 2:4-5.

> Take issue with your mother, take issue. For "she is not my wife and I am not her husband." Let her remove her whoring from her face and her adultery from between her breasts. Lest I strip her naked and set her forth as the day she was born, place her like a desert and put her like a waterless land, and cause her to die of thirst.

It was first pointed by C. Kuhl that the phrase "she is not my wife and I am not her husband" is the formula of words whereby marriage is dissolved, as we have seen in BRM 4 52 above, and as is common throughout the ancient Near East.[73] The reference is therefore to a procedure whereby a man divorces his wife on the grounds of adultery and expels her naked from the matrimonial home.[74] The further reference to her dying of thirst is unlikely to be punishment, no such punishment being attested in the Bible or in any other ancient Near Eastern source. We suggest that it is an allusion to the fact that she has no provisions, not even those that proved so inadequate for Hagar in similar circumstances (Gen 21:14-16). CH 141 permits a man whose wife has committed grave marital offenses (not amounting to adultery) to divorce her without paying her anything, not even *ḫarrānša* "her (provisions for the) journey."

In these prophetic passages, therefore, we see a metaphor drawn from everyday life of the husband exercising a right to divorce his adulterous wife and drive her from the matrimonial home penniless and possibly naked. Presumably he could have claimed the ultimate penalty but chose not to do so, which suggests that, as McKeating has argued,[75] divorce and humiliation may have been a more common punishment for adultery than the terse provisions of the codes would imply.

---

73 Kuhl 1934: 102-109. See also Gordon 1936: 277-80. For a discussion of the divorce-formula, see Westbrook 1988b: 69, 80.

74 See further the excursus to this article: "Hosea's Divorce."

75 McKeating 1979: 61-65.

The fate of the adulterous wife actually becomes the subject of a con-tractual clause in a small number of Neo-Babylonian marriage documents discussed by M. Roth.[76] The clause reads: "Should ᶠPN (wife) be caught/seen with another man, she will die by the iron dagger." As Roth points out,[77] a clause that regulates adultery is curious and unexpected in a marriage agreement. Throughout the ancient Near East, the death penalty for adultery was an inherent right deriving from the status of marriage. Unless the death penalty had ceased to be such an automatic right in the society that produced these documents—an unlikely hypothesis—there would seem no reason to include it in a contractual clause. Roth discusses various possible interpretations, such as the right of the husband to exer-cise self-help with his personal weapon, the prescription of a public execution, and a reference to a particular type of trial, and finds none of them conclusive. The legal purpose of the clause therefore remains unre-solved. Our tentative suggestion is that the phrase "caught/seen *with* another man," although Roth rightly associates it with adultery, might al-lude to compromising but ambiguous circumstances where actual adultery would be difficult to prove. The clause deems them adultery by consent of the contracting parties, thus allowing the husband to apply the death pen-alty, rather than divorce without compensation for mere immodest conduct.[78] Roth argues that employment of the verbs "catch" (*kašādu*) or "see" (*amāru*) in the clause explicitly assumes discovery *in flagranti delicto*, pointing out that the phraseology is similar to that found in the law codes.[79] But the phrase indicating *in flagranti delicto* in the law codes is in fact not quite the same; the language is more explicit. In CE 28 the wife is caught "in the lap of a man," i.e., a euphemism for sexual intercourse, and in CH 129, 131, and 132 she is caught (or not caught) "lying together" with another man. Likewise in the Nippur trial the wife was seized "upon" (UGU) a man, and in another Old Babylonian case, UET 5 203, the wife is apparently (the text is partly broken) caught in the lap of her paramour.[80] Only in MAL 15 is the phrasing ambiguous: the husband catches a man

76 Roth 1988.
77 Roth 1988: 187.
78 See n. 59 above.
79 Roth 1988: 194 and n. 19.
80 See Roth 1988: 196-97 and n. 26.

"with" (*ištu*) his wife. According to Cardascia, the man has been surprised in the company of the wife but not in the actual act of adultery, and there is therefore room for doubt.[81] It is in this case, as we have seen, that the husband is expressly required to prove the circumstances, even if he kills the adulterers himself. It should also be noted that where in MAL more explicit language is necessary, it is used. In paragraph 12 of the same tablet, a case of rape, witnesses are required to prove that they either "caught the man on top of the wife" (*ina muḫḫi aššati a'īla ikšudūš*) or that he was having intercourse with the woman. (The point is that the rapist is liable to the death penalty whether he achieved penetration or not.) Use of the term (caught) "with (*itti*) a man" in the Neo-Babylonian clause, therefore, might be the key to its contractual purpose.

Whereas divorce is a personal legal act of the husband, it is not clear that he personally executed the more severe penalties of mutilation or death. *Prima facie*, MAL 15 does give the husband the right to do so in Assyrian law.[82] In the two trial reports from southern Mesopotamia discussed above, however, the task appears to be left to the public authority. In the Nippur Trial (lines 16-26) it is stated that "they (impersonal plural) shaved her pudendum (and) bored her nose with an arrow" and that "*the king* gave her over to be led around the city."[83] In UET 5 203, the husband, having seized the adulterers *in flagranti delicto*, brought them before the king, who "gave them to the stake."[84]

2. Against the Paramour

The husband's rights against the paramour were not on the same basis as those against his adulterous wife. The paramour had committed a serious wrong, an injury to a vital interest of the husband. It is classified by some scholars as an injury to the husband's property, at least as regards the

---

81 Cardascia 1969: 123.
82 MAL 57-59, on the execution of punishments on the wife, are unfortunately badly broken, but they appear to allow the husband to perform them under official supervision. See the reconstruction of Cardascia 1969: 255-58.
83 Or him, i.e., the paramour. See n. 63 above.
84 In *King Cheops and the Magicians* (see n. 2 above), it is the Egyptian king, before whom the husband brings his case, who orders the wife to be immolated.

Mesopotamian systems,[85] but this is too reductionist a view. To plow with one's neighbor's ox, or even to injure or steal it, did not produce penalties anything like as drastic as sleeping with his wife. Nor, for that matter, did defloration of his slave woman.[86] Rather than try to dissect the complex psychological amalgam of honor, status, property, and morality that made up the husband's interest, it is better to think of adultery as *sui generis*, an independent delict comparable but not reducible to other serious delicts such as homicide, wounding, and theft.

For the latter delicts, we have argued at length elsewhere that throughout the ancient Near East the same basic system of remedies existed.[87] In principle the injured party (or his family) had a dual right against the culprit (or his family): to exact revenge or to accept ransom offered in lieu of revenge. This remedy was a judicial remedy, not a measure of self-help. The courts fixed the appropriate revenge in each case, having regard to the circumstances, and their decision represented a limit which the plaintiff might not overstep, although he was always free to accept ransom instead. In what were perceived to be less severe cases the courts would actually set the ransom themselves, so that only if that fixed ransom were not paid would the right to revenge revive. Now this whole structure of remedies, however, is assumed in the law codes; it is not spelled out systematically. Accordingly, the various paragraphs of the different codes sometimes concentrate on one aspect—setting the appropriate revenge (such as talion)— and sometimes on the other—giving a tariff of fixed rates of ransom. In all cases the hidden assumption is that the alternative—ransom or revenge— still exists. But that possibility is revealed only occasionally in the sources, almost by accident, and incidentally to some other concern.

Applying this system to adultery, we would follow Loewenstamm's opinion discussed above that the paramour's offense lay in the most serious category of delicts, such as murder, and thus gave the injured husband the right to take revenge by demanding the death of the paramour himself, or to accept ransom of the latter's life, should a satisfactory sum be offered. The "death penalty" imposed by the codes, biblical and cuneiform,

---

85 Driver and Miles 1935: 37; Kornfeld 1950: 94.
86 CE 31: "If a man has deflowered a man's slave-woman, he shall pay one third of a mina of silver and the slave-woman remains her master's."
87 Westbrook 1988d: 45-46.

is therefore nothing more than the limit, imposed in principle on the husband's right to revenge by the courts. It could in particular circumstances be set lower, as indeed we have seen in MAL 15 (mutilation), and it does not in itself exclude ransom.

Direct evidence for the application of the revenge/ransom system to adultery comes not from cuneiform sources but from the periphery. Both the Greek and Hebrew texts provide us with explicit examples.

In the passage from the Law Code of Gortyn discussed above, the paramour had to pay 50 or 100 staters for his offense. What those sums represent is revealed by lines 28-36:

> Let him (the plaintiff) proclaim in the presence of three witness to the relatives of the one caught in (the house) that he is to be ransomed[88] within five days . . . and if he should not be ransomed, those who caught him may deal with him as they wish.

In other words, they are a fixed ransom payable in lieu of revenge. Likewise, in the incident from the Odyssey discussed above, where the god Hephaistos binds his wife and her paramour to the bed, the issue is resolved by ransom. Another god offers to stand surety for payment by the paramour of "all that is fitting"[89] in return for his release. (As the gods are immortal, there can be no question of killing Ares, the paramour.) Note that this payment is different in nature from the payment demanded by Hephaistos in respect of his wife's offense.

In the Bible, we have already discussed the passage in Prov 6:32-35, where the outraged husband insists on revenge, spurning all offers of ransom. This evidence of practice is complemented by a law from the Priestly Code. In the RSV translation, Lev 19:20-21 reads:

> If a man lies carnally with a woman who is a slave, betrothed to another man and not yet ransomed or given her freedom, an inquiry shall be held. They shall not be put to death, because she was not free, but he shall bring a guilt offering for himself to the LORD.

---

88 Verb *analuō*.
89 *Od.* 8.347-348 (*aisima panta*) and *Od.* 8.355-356.

The passage has been considered by us in detail in an earlier study.[90] The following is a summary of that discussion.

There are two *hapax legomena* in the passage: *neḥĕrepet*, translated "betrothed," and *biqqōret*, translated "inquiry." We translate *neḥĕrepet* "pledged," on the assumption that the root *ḥrp* is connected with *'rb* "security." What is pledged is the slave who is an *'iššâ*, which we translate "wife," not "woman," and this wife is pledged not "to another man" (*lĕ'îš* in the Masoretic text), but by changing the pointing slightly, "to *the* man" (*lā'îš*)—that is, the man who had lain carnally with her. Thus the situation is in our translation: "If a man has intercourse with a wife, she being a slave pledged to the man . . . ." In other words, a husband has been forced to give his wife to a creditor in pledge, and the creditor has slept with her. In the apodosis, we take *biqqōret* to mean "claim *in rem*" like its Akkadian counterpart *buqrum*, and translate ". . . there is a claim *in rem*. They shall not be killed because she was not free."

In other words, the husband can claim back his wife (and thus cancel the debt). Why would it be different if she had been ransomed or freed? The difference is not that it would then have been adultery; it would have been adultery in either case. The difference is one of remedies. If the woman is a slave, then the husband can only claim back his wife. If she is free, the husband can claim from the paramour/creditor the normal penalty for adultery with a free woman—death. The slave status of the wife mitigates the penalty for adultery, and the courts therefore impose a fixed ransom in lieu of revenge. That ransom is fixed, logically enough, at the level of the husband's debt. Thus the death penalty is assumed by this law to be a right in the husband which is commutable to ransom.

Adultery as a Sin

Adultery is not only an offense against the husband but also a sin against the gods, which may be visited with divine punishment.[91] Divine punishment is particularly appropriate for an offense which is typically committed in secret and unlike murder or theft may leave no physical

90 Westbrook 1988d: 101-109.
91 Loewenstamm 1980b: 147-48.

traces. Curiously, in all the relevant sources, divine retribution is directed solely against the paramour.

In the cuneiform sources, several references are contained in *Šurpu*, a compendium of incantations whereby a sinner who is suffering divine punishment (presumably in the form of sickness) seeks relief from the gods.[92] Among the sinners is the man "who entered the house of his companion, (sexually) approached the wife of his companion" (II 47-48) and the man whose sin was "to go in secret to his friend's wife" (IV 6). In a hymn to Ninurta, alongside various types of oppressors who have sinned against the god is the adulterer: "One who has intercourse with the wife of a man: his sin/punishment is grievous."[93] Similarly, in a hymn to Shamash, the adulterer is among those whom the god will punish: "One who casts his [eye] upon his companion's wife will [die] before his appointed time."[94]

From these few references it is impossible to tell whether divine punishment occurs only when the offender has escaped human justice or is a sin to be atoned for in addition to whatever reparation is made to the husband. In the Bible, the latter is the case, at least when reparation is in the form of ransom rather than revenge.

In Lev 19:20-21, it will be recalled that the adulterer had only to return the slave woman to her husband in lieu of ransom. Nonetheless, his act was still regarded as a sin against God, for which he had to make atonement in the form of sin-offering (*'āšām*, v. 21).

Furthermore, a number of instances in the Bible suggest that even where the offense against the husband was negated by his acquiescence, the act remained a sin against God that would receive divine punishment. In Gen 26:6-11, Isaac, while resident in Gerar, represents his wife as his sister. The deception is unmasked by the local king, Abimelech, who bitterly upbraids Isaac, since "someone might have slept with your wife and you would have brought upon us sin" (*'āšām*, v. 10).[95] In an earlier incident in which Abraham practiced the same deception on the Egyptians

---

92 Edition in Reiner 1958.

93 Lambert *BWL* 119 (= KAR 119), lines 3-4: nam.tag.ga dugud.àm = *aranšu kabtumma*. Edition in Lambert 1960a: 119.

94 Lambert *BWL* 130, lines 88-89; edition in Lambert 1960a: 130-31. Cf. Job 31:9-12.

95 Cf. Gen 20:1-14, where the same incident is recounted as between Abraham and Abimelech. The latter in v. 9 rebukes Abraham for bringing "upon me and upon my kingdom a great sin." See n. 53 above.

(Gen 12:10-12), the Pharaoh does actually take Sarah as his wife, in all innocence. Nonetheless, God afflicts Pharaoh and his household with plague, and when Pharaoh discovers the reason, he forthwith expels Abraham and Sarah, likewise upbraiding Abraham for his deceit. In both cases, the concern is with divine, not human punishment.

Abimelech's complaint that unwitting adultery would have brought sin "upon *us*" (Gen 26:10) suggests that the divine punishment might be visited not merely upon the adulterer himself but upon the whole society. The doctrine is canvassed in the priestly source, which places adultery in the context of sexual offenses such as incest and bestiality (Leviticus 18 and 20). The point about the latter offenses is that in the ancient Near East they were conceived of as causing pollution, which was likely to bring divine wrath down upon the whole area in which the polluting event took place. Drastic measures therefore had to be taken to kill or expel the culprits and ritually purify the scene of their sin.[96]

The priestly source deals with adultery in two laws, and at first sight seems needlessly repetitive. In Lev 20:10, as we have seen, the technical term for adultery is used, and the punishment is death for both partners. In Lev 18:20, however, there is no punishment; merely an admonition not to do a polluting act which is described in the following terms: "You shall not give your lying to your companion's wife for seed, to pollute yourself with her." The reason for this strange mode of describing adultery is, we suggest, that it is *not* adultery in the strict legal sense. The paramour agrees to sleep with his companion's wife *with the consent of the husband*, evidently in order to provide "seed," i.e., offspring for a childless couple. There is therefore no prospect of legal proceedings by the husband or of the matter ever coming to light. Nonetheless, the priestly source warns, it is a sin and likely to be punished by God.[97] Indeed, since it causes pollution, it may bring about calamities on the whole nation (Lev 18:28).

Finally, a curious form of divine punishment inflicted upon the paramour relies on the principle of vicarious talion. This version of talionic

---

96 See Finkelstein 1981: 28; Frymer-Kensky 1983; and Westbrook 1988d: 77-83.

97 Cf. the cases of incest in Lev 18:14-16 and 20:20-21 which involve the wife of a relative. Such cases would have been adultery and would therefore seem not to require any further prohibition, unless the question of adultery had been rendered nugatory by the husband's consent and collusion. (I thank Dr. Peretz Segal for drawing my attention to the possibility of collusion here.) Note that the punishment is childlessness.

punishment, well attested in the law codes, is applied when the victim was a subordinate member of a family and the offender a head of family. The offender is punished by having the same injury that the victim suffered inflicted on an equivalent member of his own family.[98] In terms of adultery, it means having the paramour's own wife handed over to others for sexual purposes. In 2 Sam 12:11-12, after king David has committed adultery with Bathsheba (and had her husband killed), he is informed by Nathan of the various divine punishments which are to befall him, including the following:

> Thus says God: I shall cause evil for you from your own house. I shall take your wives before your eyes and give them to another, and he will lie with them in the light of the sun itself. For you did it in secret, but I shall do this before all Israel and before the sun.

Although the allusion is to coming political events, they are interpreted in a legal framework, in which the sexual abuse of David's wives is justified as being his legitimate punishment imposed by a divine tribunal. The phrase "light of the sun" (although it also is given a literal meaning here) is a legal term signifying a legitimate act, as its use in land-sale documents from Ugarit demonstrates.[99]

The same sentiments are echoed by Job (31:9-11) :

> If I was tempted to a married woman[100] and lurked at my neighbor's door, may my wife grind for another, may others crouch over her. For it is a defilement; it is an offense solely my own.[101]

---

98 E.g., in CH 230, where a house collapses due to the builder's negligence and kills the householder's son, the builder's son is put to death. See Westbrook 1988d: 55-64, 89-100.

99 E.g., *PRU III*, RS 15.119, reverse lines 6'-11' (pp. 86-87): ". . . Yaheshar has acquired a watchtower from Iddaranu son of Astehe for 20 (shekels) of silver. The watchtower is bound in the sun of the day (*ina šamši ūmi*) to Yaheshar and his sons forever."

100 The context demands this translation of Hebrew *'iššâ*. Cf. the discussion of Lev 19:20-21 above.

101 For this interpretation of *'āwōn pĕlîlîm*, see Westbrook 1986a: 58-61. *Contra* Berlin (1989): "an offense for which one is legally accountable."

Job would expect God to punish him for adultery by delivering his wife to others for sexual abuse, apparently as a slave-concubine.

Strange as this type of vicarious talion may seem to modern eyes, according to MAL it was even to be applied by a human court. In paragraph 55, where a man rapes a virgin, the girl's father may take the rapist's wife and hand her over for sexual abuse, and not return her.[102] Again, the reference, is probably to slave-concubinage.

Pre-Marital Infidelity

Pre-marital infidelity is dealt with in three laws in the codes (CH 142, Deut 22:13-21 and 22:23-24), each representing different, but very closely related, scholarly problems or cases. In two of them (CH 142, Deut 22:23-24) the litigation actually takes place before the marriage, so that a preliminary question arises of the potential husband's interest at this point.

Once the marriage payment (Hebrew *mōhar*, Akkadian *terḫatu(m)*, Hittite *kuššata*) had been made by the groom or his father to the bride's father, it created a status very close to marriage in its legal effects, and therefore most accurately described by Driver and Miles as "inchoate marriage."[103] The bride usually remained in her father's house and either side might still refuse to complete the marriage (subject to payment of compensation), but as far as third parties were concerned the couple were already married and are referred to as husband and wife. In Hebrew the verb *'rś* is used to denote this status, and in Hittite the verb *hamenk*, but Akkadian lacks any technical term and must use circumlocutions.[104]

In these circumstances, it is to be expected that the law of adultery would apply, *mutatis mutandis*, to the inchoate wife. The fact that she lives with her father does not decrease her inchoate husband's interest in her fidelity: perhaps it even increases it, since there is the factor of her virginity to consider. Where the inchoate husband is a minor and payment

---

102 See Cardascia 1969: 251-52.
103 Driver and Miles 1952: 248-49.
104 CH 130: "the wife of a man who is a virgin and is living in her father's house." CE 26, describing the same circumstances, merely refers to the bringing of the marriage payment. For the effects of inchoate marriage see Westbrook, 1988b: 34-36.

was made by his father, it is the latter who will represent his interests at law.[105]

The first case to be considered very closely parallels adultery in marriage. It concerns intercourse during inchoate marriage with a known paramour.

> Deut 22:23-24
>
> If there be a young maiden inchoately married (*mě'ōrāśâ*) to a man and a man finds her in the city and sleeps with her, you (pl.) shall take them both out to the city gate and stone them to death— the girl for not crying out in the city and the man for dishonoring his neighbor's wife. You shall purge evil from Israel.

The law goes on to consider the alternative of the same incident occurring in the open fields where the girl's cries would be of no avail, in which case it is rape. The rape of an inchoately married girl is a canonical scholarly problem which is recorded in several codes (CU 6, CE 26, CH 130). The Deuteronomic law extends the discussion to include consensual intercourse, but there are indications that this was part of the original scholarly problem.

Firstly there is the structure of the discussion in CU 6-7. Two extremes are considered: a man rapes an inchoately married girl; a married woman seduces an unwitting man. It is standard method for the law codes, in the interests of economy, to pick one or two examples that reveal the range of the discussion, while assuming knowledge in the reader of the intermediate examples.[106] Among the intermediate examples here must have been the rape of a wife and the seduction of an inchoately married girl.

Secondly, the rape of a wife is in fact considered in the Hittite Laws, but using the same evidentiary test for consent as is applied to the inchoately married girl in Deuteronomy.

> HL 197 If a man seizes a woman in the mountains: it is the man's guilt and he shall be killed. But if he seizes her in the

---

105 This form of inchoate marriage is called *kallūtum* in Akkadian. See Westbrook 1988b: 36-38.
106 See Westbrook 1988b: 46, 81, discussing CH 142-143.

house, it is the woman's guilt and the woman shall be killed. If the husband finds them, he may kill them; there shall be no punishment for him.

Thirdly. in CH 130, the rapist of an inchoately married woman is to be killed, while "that woman shall go free." This last phrase infers that there are circumstances in which she would not, the most obvious being where she was a willing partner.

It is likely therefore, that all these systems adopted a similar approach to the inchoately married girl and her paramour. The elements of the Deuteronomic law, then, are as follows:

a) the unfaithful woman is inchoately married;
b) both parties are killed, as in adultery, with the same implications for acquiescence by the inchoate husband;
c) the jurisdiction appears to be that of a local court. The law is addressed to a body of persons, who are to execute judgment at the local city gate;
d) execution is public. No role is assigned to the inchoate husband, either in punishing or pardoning the inchoate wife. This is not surprising, since at this stage she is not under his control and the question of collusion does not arise. On the other hand, the paramour's offense is stated to be against the latter's interest ("for dishonoring his neighbor's wife"), and discretion to demand punishment in pursuit of that interest also lay in his hands, as an example from practice illustrates.

In Genesis 38, Judah, having seen his first two sons die after marriage to Tamar, tells the latter to remain in her father's house until his third son, Shelah, should be old enough to marry her in accordance with the levirate rule. Suspecting that Judah will not keep his word, however, Tamar arranges to have herself impregnated by the unwitting Judah. The narrative continues (v. 24):

After three months Judah was told "your daughter-in-law Tamar has been fornicating (verb *znh*) and she is pregnant as the result of her fornication." Judah said, "Take (pl.) her out and let her be burnt."

Tamar is inchoately married to Shelah by reason of the levirate bond, and accordingly is expressly referred to as Judah's daughter-in-law and he as her father-in-law (v. 13).[107] She is not living in his house and is therefore not under his authority. Accordingly, Judah's right to punish her can only arise from the fact that he is the injured party, representing the interest of his son, the inchoate husband, who is still a minor. Since it was his right and his decision, Judah could, theoretically, have refrained from insisting on her punishment or have claimed a less severe punishment.

The next case from the codes also provides an example of the inchoate husband's right. It concerns the *ex post facto* discovery of infidelity with a paramour (or paramours) unknown.

CH 142   If a woman hates her (inchoate) husband and says "You shall not marry me," her case shall be decided in her local court, and if she is chaste and has no sin and her husband is going out and greatly deprecating her, that woman has no fault; she shall take her dowry and go off to her father's house.

    143   If she is not chaste and is going out, scattering her house, deprecating her husband, they shall cast that woman into the water.

The elements of the law are:

a) the woman is inchoately married.[108] Her offenses are in the past and need not necessarily have all been within the period of the inchoate marriage. The law does not contemplate a distinction, which would be impossible to establish in practice, and may have regarded her deception as turning any previous act of fornication into one of infidelity against her later acquired inchoate husband;

107   Any marriage payment originally made by Judah on behalf of his son Er would have remained valid for Onan and then for Shelah. Cf. MAL 30, 43.

108   The question whether the woman is inchoately or fully married has been the subject of much debate. We have argued for the former (Westbrook 1988b: 14-16, 45-46), *inter alia* because of the difficulty of explaining otherwise how a woman can refuse to marry her "husband." For criticism, see Locher 1986: 290-95.

b) if guilty of infidelity, she is killed;

c) the jurisdiction is that of a local court;

d) execution is public, by the same method prescribed by CH for adultery (§129);

e) the question of infidelity emerges from litigation between the woman and her inchoate husband, in which each of the parties charges the other with misconduct ("deprecating," verb *šumṭû*). If the woman's charges are justified, she is entitled to refuse marriage with no financial loss. If they are not, she will lose her dowry to the husband.[109] If, however, it emerges, as in §143, that the woman's refusal to marry is due to some illicit liaison, i.e., the husband's charges are justified, she suffers death, which should therefore be understood as a right in the inchoate husband. The infidelity is nonspecific: she is said to be "unchaste" (*lā naṣrat*) and to be "going out" (*waṣīat*), a verb which, as Finkelstein has noted, has in the appropriate context connotations of promiscuity.[110] The further mention of her "scattering her house," i.e., of being financially irresponsible, recalls the misdemeanors in the Nippur adultery trial and may have served the same purpose of undermining her credibility.[111]

For the final case we return to Deuteronomy and move forward in time, to litigation after completion of the marriage. As in CH 142, however, it refers to the *ex post facto* discovery of pre-marital infidelity with a paramour unknown.

---

109   See Westbrook 1988b: 46-47.

110   Finkelstein 1966: 362-63.

111   Koschaker (1924: 206 n. 1) suggested that in CH 142-143 the girl's virginity would be checked by a physical examination, but curiously enough, although it would seem to us the most obvious method of proof, there is no evidence of such a procedure in the ancient Near East. The Talmud, which discusses the question of virginity in connection with the law of Deut 22:13-21 (discussed below), might be expected to provide details of just such a practice. Instead, we are told (*Ketubot* 10b) that Rabban Gamliel tested for virginity by seating the girl on a cask of wine. If she was no longer a virgin, one could smell the wine on her breath!

Deut 22:13-21

If a man marries a woman and has intercourse with her and hates her and slanders her with false accusations, saying, "I married this woman and had intercourse with her and did not find in her signs of virginity," but the girl's father and mother take the signs of the girl's virginity and bring them to the city elders at the gate and the girl's father says to the elders, "I gave my daughter to this man in marriage and he hated her and has made false accusations, saying, 'I did not find the signs of virginity in your daughter,' but these are the signs of my daughter's virginity," and they display the sheet before the city elders:

The city elders shall take the man and whip him and impose a penalty of a hundred (shekels of) silver upon him and give it to the girl's father because he slandered a virgin of Israel. She shall be his wife: he cannot divorce her all his life. But if the accusation is true—the signs of virginity were not found in the girl—they shall bring the girl out to the door of her father's house, and men of her city shall stone her to death because she did a shameful thing in Israel to fornicate (verb *znh*) *in* the house of her father. You shall purge evil from your midst.[112]

a) It is most likely that the woman had been inchoately married at the time when she committed fornication, since this would be the standard practice for a maiden being given by her father in marriage for the first time. The ruling does not, however, rely on that contingency, and in any case, her fornication (with person or persons unknown) could have been prior to any period of inchoate marriage. Nonetheless, the law's indifference to the wife's previous status is not an extremist moralistic innovation of the Deuteronomist, as Rofé surmises.[113] The distinction between an inchoately married and unattached virgin would thereby be eliminated, and the distinction is expressly preserved by Deut 22:23-29, with a corresponding mitigation for the rapist of the unattached virgin. Mere seduction of the latter

---

112   The pericope is discussed in exhaustive detail by Locher 1986.
113   Rofé 1986: 3-5.

is not mentioned, but logic and the parallel of Exod 22:15-16 suggest that his penalty would be compulsory marriage. It is hardly to be supposed, then, that the seducer of an unbetrothed virgin was forced to marry her while at the same time the girl herself was to be executed.

The point is that, as in CH 142, when an unchaste girl marries (or becomes inchoately married for that matter), there is the added element of deception which aggravates her offense, turning it into one of infidelity.

b) If guilty of infidelity, she is killed.

c) The jurisdiction is that of a local court. The emphasis on the local court in all three cases is curious and indicative of their belonging to a closely-related complex of scholarly problems. Possibly it signifies that, in contrast to adultery, where the death penalty was within the jurisdiction of the king, with premarital infidelity the local court had jurisdiction to award the death penalty.[114] The reason for such a distinction, if it existed, is obscure.

d) Execution is public, with the extra provision that it is to take place at the door of her father's house. It seems to us that the purpose of the latter provision was to shame the father, who was a party to the litigation and who can be said to have failed in his responsibility toward the future husband, with whom he had made the marriage contract.

Some enigmatic but suggestive evidence comes from a small group of Old Babylonian marriage contracts, in which a guardian has been appointed over the bride.[115] In one of these (CT 48 56) the guardian is said to be responsible, *inter alia*, "for her sins" (*ana . . . gullulīša*)—presumably to the other contracting party, i.e., the groom, and, since the marriage is completed from the standpoint of the document and the bride is therefore under her husband's guardianship, probably with

---

114   Cf. CE 48, in the context of homicide and wounding: "And for . . . from one third mina to one mina, they shall cause him to submit to the jurisdiction, but a capital case is for the king." And see n. 46 above.

115   Discussed in Westbrook 1988d: 33-34 and translated in the Appendix thereto.

reference to pre-marital conduct. The nature of the responsibility is not specified, but whatever responsibility a guardian has by contract, a natural parent would have by virtue of his status.

e) The question of infidelity arises during litigation between the husband and the wife's father. As in CH 142, two results are contemplated: that the husband's accusations are untrue, in which case he loses the suit and suffers a penalty; that they are true, in which case the wife suffers death. Some scholars have commented on the lack of symmetry between the results, in contradiction with the talionic rule that the false accuser is to suffer the penalty contemplated for the accused.[116]

This is to assume too mechanical an application of the talionic principle by the ancient jurists. Talion only applied where appropriate, and here it was not. The different status of husband and wife and the impracticality of forcing the wrongly accused wife into widowhood militate against it. The husband who wrongly accuses his wife of adultery, forcing her to vindicate herself by oath or ordeal, it is to be noted, suffers no consequences whatsoever.[117]

The reason why the litigation is between the husband and the wife's father, not the wife herself, has already been adumbrated. It is the father's failure in his responsibility to the husband to safeguard his daughter's honor until marriage which is at issue, a point which suggests that here also the husband's interest may have arisen out of inchoate marriage.

In all these three cases (and in the example from practice) then, pre-marital infidelity is treated on the same principle as adultery, namely as an injury to the interest of the (inchoate) husband. His remedy against the (inchoate) wife may include some remedy against her father, who was responsible for her at the time the offense was committed. His remedy against the paramour, where known, is the same as for adultery, and although the sources give no indication thereof, we would deduce from that

---

116   Reviewed by Locher 1986: 315-23, 373-80.
117   CH 131, Num 5:11-31. See Démare-Lafont 1987a: 49-52.

parallelism that it was in substance a right to revenge with the concomitant alternative of ransom.

Summary and Conclusions

The law of adultery in the ancient Near East was a complex affair. It was at the same time an offense against the husband, for which he could claim certain remedies, and a sin, which might bring down divine punishment. Acquiescence by the husband would nullify the offense but not necessarily the sin. The husband's remedies against his wife and her paramour were often coordinated for reasons of public policy but were in essence different. The husband was entitled to punish his wife for a breach of her marital duty of fidelity to him. He was entitled to seek revenge against the paramour up to the (very ample) limit allowed by law and could, in his discretion, accept ransom in lieu of revenge.

The inchoate husband was entitled, on the same principles as for adultery, to remedies for pre-marital infidelity during the period when the wife was still under her father's authority.

The above principles were common to all the legal systems of the ancient Near East for which we have evidence. That evidence, however, comes from sources that are fragmentary both in preservation and in their very nature. They were written for the initiated and assume knowledge of most of the matters which the modern researcher seeks to discover. To extract from them the substantive law, it is necessary to look beyond the surface of the texts: to take into account the conceptual world of the ancient Near Eastern jurists and to appreciate occasional inferences and oblique allusions to the underlying reality.

Excursus: Hosea's Divorce (Hos 2:4-22)

The idea that divorce is involved in these verses has been strongly attacked by F. I. Andersen and D. N. Freedman.[118] They present two main arguments. Firstly, the consequences are not consistent with the biblical law of

118 Andersen and Freedman 1980: 218-90.

adultery, according to which adultery was a capital crime with no possibility of pardon. That, of course, is an issue which this study has sought to resolve, and it is hoped that by this stage sufficient evidence has been adduced to show that such an absolute position is incorrect for biblical law. In particular, the argument ignores the clear evidence of the parallel metaphor in Jer 3:8 that divorce was a possible consequence of adultery.

Their second argument is that the husband's exhortations to and continued dealings with the wife after pronouncement of the formula are not consonant with her having been divorced. The immediate answer to this argument is that in vv. 16-22 the parties remarry, which assumes an intervening divorce. Andersen and Freedman's reply is that in general the legal background to the chapter is not realistic and that "Hos. 2:16-22 requires miraculous transformation into a first marriage 'as in the time of her youth' (v. 17). Here we go beyond historical realities."[119]

Apart from being a counsel of despair, there is an inherent improbability in such reasoning. If God's relationship with Israel is to be explained by a metaphor drawing upon the everyday life of the audience, then that metaphor, to be effective, must reflect accurately the reality known to the audience. If the narrator were to invent the legal rules on which the metaphor is based, it would cease to be a valid metaphor.

Furthermore, although it is beyond the scope of this study to address all the problems of Hosea's marriage, even in an excursus, there seems to us no overwhelming difficulty in interpreting the events of chapter 2 in the light of a divorce at its inception, providing two factors are borne in mind. Firstly, as in the previous example from Ezekiel, it must be recognized that reality sometimes intrudes into the metaphor.[120] Secondly, as R. Gordis has shown, there is in the chapter a process of "identification" whereby God and Israel replace Hosea and his wife as the paradigmatic couple.[121] We would add that as a result of this identification, the threat of divorce ceases to be a contingency and becomes instead a plan of future action, ultimately resulting in reconciliation. The chapter can then be schematically analyzed into a number of incidents:

---

119   Andersen and Freedman 1980: 222.
120   See n. 70 above.
121   Gordis 1954: 19-20.

I. v. 4: Hosea cites a formula which is strikingly similar to those used to effect divorce throughout the ancient Near East. In the cuneiform sources, the formula is "You are not my wife," and at Elephantine, "She is not my wife." Apart from being more prolix,[122] the difference lies in its being phrased in the third person, a variation which is not surprising in view of the fact that it is addressed to the prophet's children rather than to his wife. It is therefore a reference to the formula rather than the formula itself. As such, it is in our interpretation an allusion to the possibility of divorce, subject to the contingency provided by the following clause, namely that the children take issue with their mother to make her desist from her adulterous conduct. The reference to the familiar divorce formula is thus a statement that her present conduct is a matter for divorce.

II. v. 5: Hosea goes on to threaten particular consequences for such a divorce. Normally, the divorced wife would receive a financial settlement, but if the husband claims grounds, the most serious of which is adultery, then he may inflict upon her harsh punishments instead, as we have seen in this study.

III. vv. 6-7a: A further consequence would be repudiation of the children of the marriage, as the illegitimate product of adulterous unions.[123]

IV. vv. 7b-9: The wife has previously declared her plan to avoid the consequences of a divorce with grounds by seeking shelter with her paramours. The husband therefore declares that he will frustrate such efforts, to the point that she will

---

122 Prolixity in itself does not signify any difference in meaning. Cf. the Elephantine divorce formula, which occurs in both brief and prolix forms: "I hate my wife X" (Cowley 15 [= TAD B2.6] and Kraeling 2 [= TAD B3.3]); and "I hate my wife X; she shall not be my wife" (Kraeling 7 [= TAD B3.8]). On the other hand, the biblical phrase is directly parallel to the Elephantine marriage formula "She is my wife and I am her husband," to which divorce is but the *contrarius actus*.

123 Gordis claims that the process of identification with God starts in v. 6 with the punishment inflicted on the children. But it would be a right of the husband, where the children are found not to be his offspring.

eventually wish to return to him. It is important to note that the husband's actions in this regard have no legal content and do not require any legal relationship between the parties. Furthermore, the husband at this point has become identified with God—hence the supernatural means employed.

V. vv. 10-11: The husband explains that he was the real provider, and he will take back his marital gifts. This would be his right under divorce for grounds, but here reality intrudes, since the image is one of agricultural fertility being withdrawn. The consequences will therefore only be felt after divorce, at the appropriate agricultural seasons.

VI. v. 12: The husband will also expose her faults to her paramours, so that none will come to her aid. Here again is an action without legal content (but which is not absent even from present-day divorces).

VII. v. 13: The husband will put an end to her festivals and celebrations. This may be the result of her destitute condition or possibly an act of God, i.e., an intrusion of reality. In either case the act again has no legal content.

VIII. v. 14: The husband will destroy the vines and fig trees that she obtained as wages from her paramours. This would be in pursuit of the husband's rights over her property (he would be able to confiscate her dowry and assets acquired during the marriage),[124] but reality intrudes with the image of crops destroyed by wild beasts.

IX. v. 15: The husband will thus punish her for her misdeeds during the marriage.

X. v. 17: The husband will then effect a reconciliation with his ex-wife and offer her courting-gifts.

---

124 Cf. The Law Code of Gortyn II 45-55, in which the proceeds from the wife's labors are included in the property settlement pursuant to divorce:

> If a husband and wife should be divorced, she is to have her own property which she came with to her husband and half of the produce, if there be any from her own property, and half of whatever she has woven within, whatever there may be, plus five staters if the husband be the cause of divorce (Willetts 1967: 40).

XI. vv. 18-19: The two parties will agree to remarry.

XII. v. 20: Intrusion of reality. God will make an agreement bringing peace and security. The beneficiaries of the agreement are not stated, but Andersen and Freedman's suggestion that they are the children of the original marriage[125] is attractive. In Babylonian marriage contracts involving a woman with children from a previous marriage, the second husband often makes property arrangements for the benefit of those children.[126] If Hosea's children had been expelled with their mother, such an arrangement would be apposite here.

XIII. vv. 21-22: The husband rebetroths his ex-wife, with various virtues as the marriage payment (*mōhar*). Andersen and Freedman object that these attributes must be promises for the marriage and not once-for-all payments at the time of engagement.[127] But herein lies the key factor that proves this betrothal to be a second marriage. When a girl is married for the first time, it is her father who receives the marriage payment. But a widow or divorcee who remarries is *sui iuris* and could only receive the payment for herself (unless she had returned to her father's house, which obviously did not happen in the present case).[128] Such receipts would become part of her marital property, which in turn is subsumed into the marital assets of the couple during the subsistence of the marriage. The virtues of righteousness, justice, mercy, pity, and faithfulness would thus be shared by both.

XIV. vv. 23-25: Consummation of the marriage and acceptance back of the children.

---

125 Andersen and Freedman 1980: 281.

126 See Westbrook 1988b: 63.

127 Andersen and Freedman 1980: 283.

128 See Westbrook 1988b: 61-62.

11

Witchcraft and the Law in the Ancient Near East

Abstract

This article examines how the problem of witchcraft was handled in the law codes and in other legal texts. A fairly coherent picture emerges. The amateur practice of witchcraft was treated as a serious crime against an individual such as homicide, with the right of restitution or revenge. Like homicide it created some pollution in the society. Violations by professional practitioners, typically women, were treated as polluting crimes as against the gods, such as incest and bestiality.

Introduction

It is a great pleasure to dedicate this modest study to Professor Haase, whose contributions have done so much to improve our understanding of cuneiform law.

Witchcraft is an almost universal phenomenon, deeply rooted in folk culture. In the first millennium B.C.E. in Mesopotamia it was the subject of a major learned treatise, called *Maqlû* ("Burning"), but there are many references to witchcraft throughout cuneiform literature, going back at least as far as the late third millennium.[1]

Witchcraft is seldom mentioned in the legal sources, but the spread of references is wide enough to show that the legal systems of the region were concerned with its effects, and did occasionally intervene. It is a recurring theme in the cuneiform law codes, albeit in sparse measure: the

* Originally published in *Recht gestern und heute: Festschrift zum 85. Geburtstag von Richard Haase* (ed. J. Hengstl und U. Sick; Wiesbaden: Harrassowitz, 2006), 45-52. Used by permission.
1 For witchcraft in Mesopotamia, see Thomsen 2001: 23-35; among the Hittites, Haas 1994: 882-88; in the Bible, Kuemmerlin-McLean 1992: 468-71.

laws of Ur-Namma (CU), Hammurabi (CH), the Middle Assyrian Laws (MAL), the Hittite Laws (HL), and the Neo-Babylonian Laws (NBL) all have one or more paragraphs dealing with diverse aspects of witchcraft. The Edict of Telipinu devotes a paragraph to witchcraft, which is also the subject of several records of litigation. Outside the cuneiform sphere, the Hebrew Bible has a few pertinent regulations.

In view of the paucity of legal sources, I will not attempt to reconstruct the law of a single system or trace its development. The purpose of this brief essay is rather to gain an overview of the legal measures recorded and to see if they exhibit any general pattern.

Witchcraft and Legality

Magic can be white or black, according to whether its purpose was to benefit or to harm. Witchcraft was black magic directed against an individual. It was considered capable of bringing sickness or even death. The victim had several means of defense (or counter-attack):

1. He could invoke the aid of the gods through prayer, or seek a judgment by the gods against the sorcerer.
2. He could use magic to counter magic, e.g., by amulets, apotropaic figurines and the like.
3. He could employ the services of a specialist, namely an exorcist, to destroy or render ineffective the magic directed against him.
4. He could sue the perpetrator in a human court.

The first incantation in *Maqlû* (I 1-36) describes a petition of a victim of witchcraft to the gods to judge his case. As Abusch rightly notes, the case turns upon a witch's false accusation of the victim before the gods, which has led them to inflict him with certain injuries (1987: 138-39). The opening lines read:

1 I have called upon you Gods of the Night . . .
4 Because a witch (*kaššaptu*) has bewitched me (*ukaššipanni*),
5 A deceitful woman (*elēnītu*) has accused me (*ubbiranni*),

6 Has (thereby) caused my god and goddess to be estranged from me (and)

7 I have become sickening in the sight of those who behold me,

8 I am therefore unable to rest day or night . . .

13 Stand by me ye Great Gods and give heed to my suit,

14 Judge my case and grant me an (oracular) decision! . . .

18 Because evil did she perform against me, and baseless charges has she conjured up against me,

19 May she die, but I live![2]

Abusch argues that the opening lines do not constitute an indictment of the witch.

> The speaker's description of the witch's activities (lines 4-12) carries no legal force beyond that of setting out the grounds for his request; it is intended, that is, to explain and justify the plaintiff's request to the divine court that it convene and hear his case. The description simply presents the facts of the case as they appear at the beginning of the trial. These facts constitute neither proof of the witch's guilt nor an accusation against her. In fact, the witch would not deny these facts. She and the speaker would differ solely on their interpretation, and she would claim that her actions were legally justified and that he was guilty of an undefined crime (2002: 9).

Abusch' analysis reveals a certain confusion as to the nature of pleas in litigation. The fact that the defendant would deny the harm or claim that it is the plaintiff's fault is irrelevant. Denial of a claim in no way invalidates it (nor does a counter-claim); only the judgment can do that. There is no reason to treat the opening part of the plea as neutral by severing it from the demand for justice in lines 13-14 or the remedy sought in lines 18-19. The victim opens his case with the claim, formulated in parallelism,

2 Edition in Meier 1937. Translation in Abusch 2002: 8-9; also in Abusch 1987: 99.

that the person who has caused him harm has done so by witchcraft and deceit.[3]

Witchcraft is thus a form of harm no less than homicide or wounding, for which redress can be claimed in the divine courts. As *Maqlû* I also informs us, the plaintiff may bring a figurine of the witch before the gods just as he would bring a defendant before the human court:

> 15 I have made a figurine of my sorcerer and of my sorceress (*kaššapīa u kaššaptīa*),
> 16 of my wizard and of my witch (*ēpišīa u muštepistīa*),
> 17 I have laid it at your feet and stated my case (*adibbub dīnī*).

Witchcraft as a Public Danger

Figurines are a stock accessory of both magic and exorcism, but the reason for using a figurine in what is supposed to be a lawsuit is probably that the identity of the sorcerer was unknown to the plaintiff. The problem of identifying sorcerers also exercised the human authorities, as exemplified by the Edict of Telipinu (§50):[4]

> (As regards) sorcery in Hatti, you shall keep purifying things of it. Whoever practices sorcery within a family, do you seize him/her out of the family and bring him/her to the palace gate. Whoever does not bring him/her, it will come out badly for that man and his house.

Hoffner translates: "Whoever in the royal family practices sorcery" (1995: 237-38), but the word "royal" is added gratuitously. It is true that the earlier part of the Edict concerns crimes committed within the royal family, but thereafter the focus of attention widens, to palace officials, then to matters in which the palace has a concern, such as the security of the

---

3 According to Abusch, even black magic "was not necessarily objectionable from a legal point of view; that is, a witch or sorcerer could perform magical activities (later associated with black magic) without being culpable" (2002: 8). The victim's claim, however, equates black magic with perjury before the gods.

4 Edition in Hoffmann 1984.

royal granaries. The last two regulations, after the space of nearly a whole column in which the text is too broken for the meaning or the context to be established, deal with homicide and witchcraft. The first provision establishes the customary rule for any homicide not specifically within the royal family and makes the point that the palace will take no payment in addition to the penalty exacted by the victim's family. The final provision concerns witchcraft outside the royal circle, as confirmed by the provision that the perpetrator be brought to the palace gate.[5]

The interest of the palace in suppressing witchcraft is confirmed by MAL A 47, where the king intervenes to force an eye-witness to witchcraft who has been denounced by a hearsay witness to present his testimony. King, prince, and royal exorcist are all involved in the case. The paragraph gives the impression that witchcraft was seen as a public danger, requiring mobilization of government power in order to suppress it.

In a recent survey of criminal law in the Ancient Near East, I distinguished between three broad categories of offence: wrongs against a hierarchical superior; serious wrongs against the person, honor, or property of an individual; and minor harm to an individual's person or property (2003b: 75-82). The third category is a matter for compensation and does not concern us here.

Where the first category is an offence against a god, it creates impurity which may endanger the surrounding area or even the whole society. The remedy is therefore death or banishment of the offender and possibly his family, and purification rituals. Offences in this category include breach of taboos and sexual aberrations such as incest and bestiality.

The second category comprises crimes such as homicide, injury, theft, rape, and adultery. The remedy was a private right in the victim or his family to revenge or ransom to buy off revenge. The level of revenge and of ransom could sometimes be fixed by the courts. Some of the more morally serious offences, in particular homicide and adultery, might involve a certain degree of pollution, at least of the parties involved.

On the basis of the Telipinu Edict and MAL A 47 discussed above, and of certain biblical texts, I included witchcraft in the first category as an

---

5   The mention of a family as the context probably refers to the duty to denounce one's own relatives: cf. Deut 13:6-11.

offence against the gods. Certainly, it was associated with impurity.[6] Indeed, unlike homicide or adultery, where impurity was a side-product, the very essence of witchcraft was to create impurity. As Haas puts it: "Behexungen mobilisieren und stören dämonische Schadenstoffe auf, die den Behexten in den Zustand der Unreinheit versetzen" (1994: 884). In the light of other sources, however, it may be necessary to qualify that categorization somewhat.

Witchcraft as a Private Wrong

In CH 2, a man accuses another of sorcery, but is unable to bring evidence (of a normal, rational nature). They are therefore sent to the river ordeal. If the one accused of sorcery fails the ordeal (and dies), his accuser takes his house; if he passes the ordeal, the accuser is killed and he takes the accuser's house.

The law does not state any relationship between the accuser and the accused, which might lead to the conclusion that he could be an officious member of the public. This would be in accord with the public nature of the offence and the need to encourage its suppression. On the other hand, a parallel law in CU 13 demands only 3 shekels as the penalty for false accusation, which seems remarkably light in view of the seriousness of the offence. Another possibility, therefore, is that the accusation is made in the heated exchange between parties to a dispute, even litigants in an existing lawsuit over some other matter.

In his political autobiography, Hattusili III recounts that before he became emperor, Arma-Tarhuntašša, a relative and political enemy, together with his wife and son, began to use witchcraft (*alwanzatar*) upon him, and "he even filled Samuha, city of the god, with witchcraft" (II 74-79).[7] Hattusili responds by bringing a lawsuit against Arma-Tarhuntašša in the court of the king, his brother. The court found all three guilty of witchcraft and "my brother turned him over (*piran naiš*) to me together with his house, his wife and his son" (III 20-21). Hattusili, however,

---

6   Hittite *papratar*; see Hoffner 1973: 84; Hutter 1988: 30-31 (line 18). Deut 18:8-12 refers to witchcraft as an abomination (*tō 'ēbâ*) that provokes divine anger.
7   Edition in Otten 1981.

decided to be merciful: "because Arma-Tarhuntašša belonged to my family and was old, I let him go" (*arha daliyamun*). He also returned to him half his property and released a son who was not involved, but sent the wife and guilty son into exile (III 22-30).

Although Hattusili is careful to mention the defilement of a holy city, it would seem that the court regarded the offence as being against him alone, and gave the culprits into his hands to do with as he thought fit. The judgment fits the pattern of a second category offence, where the punishment is the victim's right of revenge. It would fit into the highest level of culpability in that category, since the whole family of the culprit is handed over to the victim, including an innocent member (although with a recommendation for mercy: III 21-22) and no limitation is placed on his revenge. The significance of banishment is ambiguous here: on the one hand, it was used for crimes of pollution and regarded as equal in measure to execution;[8] on the other, it was a recognized way of dealing with political opponents. As regards mercy, in crimes like adultery it is the prerogative of the victim, whereas in first category crimes like bestiality it is the prerogative of the king.[9]

In his account of the affair of the Tawananna, Mursili II accuses his stepmother, the Queen Mother, of having killed his wife by means of witchcraft. Although king, he refrains from exercising his prerogative as judge. Instead, he refers the question of her punishment to a higher court, that of the gods "my masters" (*be-lu*[meš]*-ia*), through oracular consultation. "And she was determined by oracle for me to execute; she was determined by oracle for me for removal from office."[10] Mursili did not then have the Tawananna executed; he only removed her from the office of high priestess and, indeed, gave her an estate for her sustenance. Again, the court determines the limits of the victim's rights and hands the culprit over to the victim for implementation at his discretion.

---

8 "As the rule for sexual abominations has been from olden times in the lands: in a town where they customarily executed, let them continue to execute, and in a town where they customarily banished, let them continue to banish. The town should purify itself afterwards" (*Bēl Madgalti* III 11-14).

9 For adultery, HL 197-198, but the king has a further prerogative of mercy if the husband refuses to pardon the offenders. For bestiality, HL 187, 199.

10 *CTH* 71 (KBo IV 8 + "Izmir" 1277): lines 7-8. Edition in Hoffner 1984: 187-92. See also the edition and commentary of Cornelius 1975: 27-45.

The classification of witchcraft as a second category offence on a par with homicide and adultery also explains the penalty imposed in HL 170:

> If a free man kills a snake and speaks the name of another, he shall give 40 shekels of silver. If it is a slave, he himself shall die.

As Hoffner points out, the death penalty is not prescribed for a free man, but the penalty is relatively high (1997: 189 *ad* §44b). It makes sense if regarded as a fixed ransom imposed by the court in lieu of revenge. It is a measure of mitigation justified by the fact that no actual harm to the intended victim has yet occurred. The right of the victim to have the culprit executed, however, would revive if the culprit were unwilling or unable to pay the sum demanded.[11] In HL 44b and 111 (leaving the residues from a purification ritual on a person's property and making a figurine, respectively) the performing of acts of sorcery without proof of actual harm is deemed sufficiently serious to be referred to the king's jurisdiction, presumably because the royal court has the authority to impose the death penalty. If the same system applied to the slave, it would have worked in the reverse order, in that the victim was in principle entitled to have him executed but might spare him if the slave's owner offered a sufficient sum to ransom his life. The slave's offence was more serious because it was against a hierarchical superior (assuming the victim always to be a free man).[12]

The discrepancy between CH 2 and CU 13 may also be explained by this analysis: CH emphasized the revenge aspect and parity of punishment for the offence itself and for a false accusation (death plus forfeiture of property), whereas CU, focusing solely on a false accusation in the course of a dispute, regarded it as a less serious offence meriting a low fixed

---

11 See Westbrook 2003d: 78.

12 The law codes did not always articulate aspects of the law that would have been self-evident to a contemporary. The dichotomy between free man/payment and slave/death is, however, typical of their reasoning by "polar cases with maximal variation" (Eichler 1987: 72-75). It suggests intermediate categories of free man/death and slave/payment. It should also be noted that the phrase "he himself shall die" suggests that the same fate would apply to the free man if he did not make the payment, which could in fact have been in slaves (cf. HL 1-4).

ransom, without indicating what measure of revenge was allowed as the alternative.

At the same time, the highly toxic nature of witchcraft gives it strong affinities with first category offences. HL 44b is an apt illustration: leaving the polluted residues from a purification ritual (*kuptar*) elsewhere than in a designated incineration dump is regarded as so serious a matter that it could result in death for the culprit.

Professionals and Amateurs

The involvement of the palace that emerges from sources like the Telipinu Edict and MAL A 47 goes beyond what would be expected in a case of homicide or adultery. Perhaps another distinction is at play here that is not articulated in the sources: between professional sorcerer and amateur. In the case of Arma-Tarhuntašša discussed above, the culprit was a politician; he was not a sorcerer by profession, nor were the members of his family. They resorted to witchcraft as part of their political campaign against Hattusili. The same is true in the Tawananna affair, when Mursili accused the Queen Mother of causing his wife's death by witchcraft. Again, she was an amateur, but in this case she also hired a professional, a woman who pronounced spells (*hukmaeš*-incantations) against Mursili's wife.[13] Similarly, *Maqlû* (III 121-122) raises the possibility of someone commissioning a professional witch (*ēpištu*) or sorceress (*sāḥirtu*).

Sefati and Klein note that "Whereas the law codes, as a rule, do not distinguish between men and women in the laws pertaining to sorcery (i.e., black magic), in the cultic-ritual and other sources the role of women in sorcery far exceeds that of men" (2001: 570). They find that women are the archetypal sorcerers from the Old Babylonian period onward, with men only slowly emerging alongside them during the first millennium and never with more than a subsidiary role. Many of the first-millennium sources mention men alongside women as a formulaic merism.

---

13 KUB XIV 4 Rs III 7-8; edition in Cornelius 1975. See Bin-Nun 1975: 186. The only legal record of a witchcraft trial, Bo. 557 (edition in Werner 1967: 64-67), is unfortunately too broken to determine the status of the parties.

I would place a slightly different emphasis on these conclusions, namely that anyone can practice witchcraft, but that as a profession, it was regarded as essentially a female reserve, into which men would occasionally enter. A modern analogy, apart from the word "witch" itself, is the English use of "nurse" in pre-feminist parlance of the twentieth century. Although originally gender-neutral, it came to refer exclusively to women, so that a man practicing the profession of nursing was called a "male nurse." Where men and women are mentioned together, therefore, it is a marker of professional sorcerers.

An Old Babylonian correspondence concerning a bitter lawsuit between father and son over a straightforward commercial dispute shows how the image of a female witch served as a stereotype. The father refers to the son's wife and mother-in-law as "your witches" whom he will have imprisoned, and the son responds with a like threat.[14] It is more than doubtful that the good ladies were professionals, but they could be called witches by way of insult.

A closer look at the law codes shows that they do distinguish between men and women, on a logical basis. Where the culprit is unequivocally male, the sorcery is amateur, as in CU 13 and CH 2, where one party to a dispute has resorted to sorcery, and HL 170, where a man, even a slave, can perform a simple magical procedure against an enemy.[15] Where it is ambiguous, as in HL 111 (someone: *kuiški*), it is likely to be amateur, as anyone can form a clay doll, the most basic of magical practices. In HL 44b the subject is again ambiguous (*kuiški*) and presumably professional, but not a professional sorcerer. Rather, the culprit is an exorcist who has performed a legitimate purification ritual but then acted improperly in disposing of the resulting polluted residues.[16]

---

14 AbB 9 268 and 269. See Walters 1970: 27-38.

15 Vgl. Haas: "Behexung und Enthexung geschieht, falls professionell ausgeführt, nicht durch eine singuläre, sondern durch eine Kette magischer Handlungen" (1994: 889).

16 NBL 7 apparently concerns a similar problem, involving a woman who is a professional but not, apparently, a witch: "A woman who performs *nēpešu* or a ritual purification (*takpirtu*) in a man's field or boat or oven or anything, (concerning) the trees (literally, 'wood'—what is growing in the field) on which she performs, she shall give the owner of the field three times its yield. If she does the purification on a boat, in an oven, or anything else, she shall give threefold the losses caused to the object (text: 'field'). If she is seized in the doorway of a man's house, she shall be killed."

The one law code provision that expressly mentions men and women is MAL A 47. The reason, I suggest, is to make it clear that the law is directed against professionals. As in the couplets of *Maqlû*, the female practitioner indicates a professional witch and the male is added as a merism, for the sake of completeness. It is also this law that involves the palace in the suppression of witchcraft. In the public interest, the palace was concerned to catch professional witches before they could do harm.

Outside the law codes, the Edict of Telipinu, as we have seen, also prescribes preventive measures by the palace. It is directed against a person who "knows witchcraft" (*alwanzatar šakki*), which would indicate an expert rather than an isolated attempt.[17] The person to be denounced as a practitioner of sorcery is usually translated "him," but the Hittite enclitic pronoun denotes common gender, and so could apply to a male or female.

Finally, it is worth comparing three biblical texts. Deut 18:9-11 gives an exclusively male list of forbidden professions ("one who passes his son or daughter through fire, a diviner, soothsayer, augur, sorcerer, charmcaster, medium, or necromancer"), some of whom, however, would be regarded as legitimate forms of magician elsewhere.[18] On the other hand, Lev 20:27 prescribes public stoning for a type of professional medium, whose gender is identified as "a man or a woman," whereas the only known example of this type of medium in the narratives is a woman: the "witch" of Endor (1 Sam 28:7ff.). Finally, Exod 22:18 orders the local authority to execute without the possibility of pardon a witch, without doubt a female professional.[19]

Summary and Conclusions

The classification of crimes in the Ancient Near East into three categories is a modern heuristic tool, which should not be applied too rigidly to the ancient sources. Likewise, the distinction between professional and amateur sorcerers is not made explicitly in the sources and is likely to have had

---

17 Hoffman translates "sich auf Zauberei versteht" (1984: 55).
18 Discussed by Kuemmerlin-McLean 1992: 468-69.
19 For the interpretation of the law as a directive to the local authority, see Westbrook 1986a: 62-66; and Westbrook 1997: 66-67.

shades and gradations rather than a sharp dividing line. Nonetheless, applying both distinctions to the legal sources does produce a coherent picture. Amateur, opportunistic acts of sorcery tended to be treated as a serious crime analogous to homicide or adultery, which gave the right of revenge or ransom to the victim, while creating some pollution which might have public repercussions. The work of professional sorcerers, typically women, was a source of public concern and could lead to repressive measures analogous to the treatment of polluting crimes like incest and bestiality.

Part Three

The Tradition in Greco-Roman Law

12

The Trial Scene in the *Iliad*

Abstract

The trial on Achilles' shield is typically understood in one of two ways: as a *fac-tual* dispute (has the killer paid the ransom money or not?); or as a *legal* dispute (is ransom money allowed in this case?). This article opts essentially for the *legal* interpretation but contests the idea that the courts of this period were forums of arbitration and made no binding decisions. Instead, these courts likely functioned much like their ancient Near Eastern counterparts, who had coercive powers. One such power was the establishment of limits on the revenge or ransom that victims of a crime (or their families) could demand. It is the question of just such a limit that forms the core of the dispute in this trial.

The description of the homicide trial depicted on the shield of Achilles is one of the most disputed passages in the *Iliad*, both as to its transla-tion and the legal significance of the trial. A typical modern translation reads:[1]

In the assembly place were people gathered. There a dispute had arisen: two men were disputing about the recompense (*poin*) for a dead man. The one was claiming to have paid it in full, making his statement to the people, but the other was refusing to receive any-thing; both wished to obtain trial at the hands of a judge. The

* Originally published in *Harvard Studies in Classical Philology* 94 (1992): 53-76. Copyright © Department of the Classics, Harvard University. Used by permission.
* My thanks are due to Prof. R. Wallace, who read the first draft and made many useful criticisms, and to Profs. J. Russo and R. Woodard for their helpful comments. Respon-sibility, as usual, rests with the author.
1 MacDowell 1978: 19.

people were cheering them both on, supporting both sides; and heralds quieted the people. The elders sat on polished stones in a sacred circle, and held in their hands sceptres from the loud-voiced heralds; with these they were then hurrying forward and giving their judgments in turn. And in the middle lay two talents of gold, to give to the one who delivered judgment most rightly among them (18.497-508).

The same translator admits that lines 499-500 could be rendered: "the one was claiming to have paid it in full . . . , but the other was denying that he had received anything."[2] Therein lies the crux of the dispute.

The traditional view, following the latter translation, is that the litigation concerns a question of fact: whether the blood-money for a homicide (*poin*), i.e., the ransom payable by the killer to the victim's family in lieu of revenge, has been paid or not.[3] The other view is that it is a legal question: whether the blood money is acceptable or not.[4] In legal terms, the second hypothesis seems immediately preferable. As already pointed out by Leaf, it is difficult to see why there should be such popular ferment, with heralds and councilors and prizes for forensic eloquence, about a simple matter of the payment of a debt, which could only be settled, if at all, by oaths and witnesses.[5] And as Andersen remarks, there does not seem to be much room for difference of opinion among the elders on a mere question of fact.[6] It must be an issue of principle that taxes the wisdom of the court.

The question then arises, however, what is the precise legal issue before the court? Gagarin supposes that a disagreement exists between the relatives of the victim. One relative has agreed to accept compensation and has done so, but another disagrees with this decision and takes the dispute to a public forum.[7] But then we would expect the dispute to be between the

---

2 MacDowell 1978: 19.
3 E.g., Calhoun 1927: 18; Bonner and Smith 1930: 32-35; Hommel 1969: 16; Primmer 1970: 11-13; Cantarella 1976: 73-74.
4 Leaf 1887: 122-32; Benveniste 1969: 240-42; Andersen 1976: 12-15; MacDowell 1978: 19-20; Gagarin 1981: 13-16; Gagarin 1986: 32-33; Hammond 1985: 80-81.
5 Leaf 1887: 123, followed by Benveniste 1969: 241-42.
6 Andersen 1976: 12-15.
7 Gagarin 1981: 13-16; Gagarin 1986: 31-33.

two relatives, or at least for the other relative to be joined. Gargarin's explanation that Homer's comments "only hint at the full complexity of the case"[8] may be questioned on methodological grounds. In the absence of their explicit mention in the text, circumstances cannot be assumed because the case described was never a real event. It is a fiction, a work of literature that has no reality (however realistic the description may be) outside the mind of the author who created it.[9] The more commonly accepted viewpoint is that the issue is simply the lengths to which revenge may be taken,[10] or as Muellner puts it, whether the murdered man's kinsman has the right actually to *refuse* the murderer's offer of *poin*.[11] But *poin* is a sum offered by the murderer as ransom for his life, to stave off the revenge to which the victim's kinsman is entitled. Its level is therefore what is acceptable to the kinsman or, more realistically, what may be arrived at by bargaining between the parties. How did the court intervene in this process and impose one party's terms on the other (or did it impose its own terms on both)? In what circumstances would it intervene and on what criteria? Although there are frequent references to homicide, revenge, and ransom in the Homeric poems, they give no hint of the exercise of such judicial powers.

To answer these questions, we propose to look beyond the Homeric literature itself to the neighboring societies of the ancient Near East. Their copious sources provide the detailed working model of a legal system in which revenge and ransom are an integral part of the judicial process. In the context of that model, the legal issues in the trial will, it is hoped, become clear, and the details of the scene form a coherent picture.

The Ancient Near Eastern Model

The societies of the ancient Near East for which we have written records are diverse in language and culture, but they appear to some considerable extent to have shared a common legal tradition. The underlying structure

8 Gagarin 1986: 33.
9 See Waldock 1966: 11-24; and Wallace and Westbrook 1989: 364-65.
10 MacDowell 1978: 20.
11 Muellner 1976: 106.

of their legal systems was the same, while the content of the law drew upon a canon of traditional learning that had originated in Mesopotamia in the third millennium or earlier and spread across the fertile crescent to Anatolia and the Mediterranean coast.[12] This tradition was very tenacious, lasting well into the first millennium, when new ideas from the Eastern Mediterranean began to create a different conception of law.[13]

Already in the earliest records from the third millennium, the states of the ancient Near East are revealed as tightly organized societies, with a complex bureaucracy to support the process of government and a system of courts to administer justice.[14]

The courts dealt with private wrongs and offences against the collectivity, and in both cases handed down judgments that could involve harsh punishments such as mutilation and death. Their jurisdiction could hardly have been voluntary under the circumstances but must have relied on some powers of coercion.

The problem of coercion arises at two stages: bringing one's opponent to court and enforcement of the court's judgment. The former would appear to have been the harder task. We have no evidence of any summons mechanism by the local courts (although it may have existed) or of any powers of arrest, and often the plaintiff would have had to rely on his own powers or the help of family and neighbors. Petitions to the king do appeal to his coercive power, which is also executive, and the king's response is sometimes to summon the parties before him,[15] sometimes to judge in the absence of the defendant,[16] a power which the local courts may also have

---

12 See n. 25 below.

13 See Westbrook 1989a: 218-22.

14 For a survey of the early materials, see Kramer 1963: chapter three, and the literature cited thereto.

15 E.g., in a letter from king Hammurabi to a royal official in a provincial town (ca. 18th century: "To Sin-iddinam, speak: thus says Hammurabi: concerning Ili-ippalsam, the overseer of the bakers, who is engaged in a claim for a field against Sin-gimlanni, son of Bitum-rabi the chamberlain, and Lipit-Ishtar, scribe of Tarbatum's steward, and about whom you wrote; I have just sent Ili-ippalsam the overseer of bakers on a mission to Ur to make sacrifice. As soon as he has completed the sacrifice at Ur, send him to me at Babylon together with his opponents Sin-Gimlanni and Lipit-Ishtar so that their case may be concluded" (AbB 2 9 [Frankena 1966: no. 9]).

16 E.g., AbB 2 24 (Frankena 1966: no. 24), where a merchant petitions Hammurabi over an unpaid loan of grain, outstanding for three years. Hammurabi examines the loan

had, and which would provide a powerful incentive to the defendant to come to court in the first place. For we do have plentiful evidence of the court's power to enforce its judgments.[17]

Refusal to obey the court's judgment is severely punished by the Hittite Laws:

> 173 If anyone rejects the judgment of the king, his house shall be razed. If anyone rejects the judgment of a district official they shall cut off his head.[18]

The courts of the ancient Near East were therefore more than mere arbitrators of disputes voluntarily submitted to them. They formed a coercive framework, and it is within this framework that the criminal law recorded in the sources is to be interpreted.

The types of wrong which in modern systems would be subject to criminal law, such as homicide, wounding, rape, and theft, also formed a separate category in the ancient Near Eastern systems, but with very different consequences. These wrongs (together with adultery) were not subject to punishment by the State; instead, they gave rise to a dual right in the victim or his family: to take revenge on the culprit and/or his family, or to accept ransom in lieu of revenge. Paragraph 49 of the Edict of the Hittite King Telipinu illustrates the principle in the case of homicide:

---

document and gives orders to his official that the grain plus interest be collected from the debtor and given to the merchant. In 2 Sam 12:1-6, the prophet Nathan informs king David that in a provincial town a rich man has committed an abuse of power, taking a lamb from a poor man. David is outraged and immediately pronounces sentence on the offender. See further Westbrook 1988d: 30-35.

17 The court of the city of Nippur in the early second millennium, for example, handed down a judgment in an adultery case whereby the guilty lovers were stripped, mutilated, and paraded around the town. They had been brought to the court strapped to the bed on which they had been caught *in flagranti delicto*: Greengus 1969: 33-44. At the royal level, in an Old Babylonian letter, for example, the king dispatches a soldier with the successful plaintiff to help her recover property from the defendant's house: YOS 2 25 (edition in Westbrook 1988b: 136-37).

18 Cf. Deut 17:12: "The man who willfully disobeys the priest . . . or the judge—that man shall die."

A matter of blood is as follows. Whoever does blood, whatever the owner of the blood says. If he says, "Let him die!" he shall die. If he says, "Let him pay ransom!" he shall pay ransom. But to the king, nothing.

The "owner of the blood" is the closest male relative of the victim. He is known by the same name in neo-Assyrian,[19] as the "owner of the life" in the Middle Assyrian Laws (B 2), and in the Bible as the "redeemer of the blood," i.e., the one who brings it back within the family. The theory is that the blood of the victim has been lost to his family and must be returned. This can be achieved by killing the culprit. As a letter from the Babylonian king to the Pharaoh puts it: ". . . the men who killed my subjects—kill them! Return their blood!"[20]

If, on the other hand, the victim's family opts for ransom, the amount will be negotiated with the culprit and an agreement thereon drafted in the form of a legal contract, as illustrated by a neo-Assyrian document (ADD 321):[21]

A son of B shall give C daughter of D, the scribe, in lieu of the blood. He shall wash the blood. If he does not give the woman, they will kill him on B's grave. Whichever of them breaks the contract shall pay ten mina of silver.

Thus far, the criminal law gives the impression of being very much a private affair between the affected families. How did it fit into the structure of a coercive judicial system? The answer is that revenge was conceived of as a *legal* remedy, not the mere expression of a personal vendetta. Paragraph 49 of the Telipinu Edict above gives only the theoretical principle; in practice, the rights of the parties were subject to the jurisdiction of the law courts.

With homicide and other serious crimes, the court determined not only the facts of the case but also the legal questions:

---

19   Assyrian *bēl dāmi*. Contra *CAD* B 80, but see Roth 1987: 363-65.
20   El-Amarna no. 8:25-29 (14th century). Edition in Knudtzon 1907-15 (1964): 84-88.
21   Edition in Kwasman 1988: no. 341.

a) whether the plaintiff was entitled to revenge at all;
b) the appropriate revenge or ransom to which the plaintiff was entitled.

The plaintiff was not entitled to revenge if the killing was justified. According to Exod 22:1, the burglar who is killed breaking in at night "has no blood," i.e., there is no blood to be returned to his family through revenge.[22] Where a husband kills his wife and her lover caught *in flagranti delicto*, HL 197 rules that "there is no penalty on him."

If the plaintiff is entitled to revenge in principle, its measure is not left to his discretion but is fixed by the court in accordance with the gravity of the crime. Indeed, the idea of unbridled revenge was regarded with aversion. Two passages from the Bible are indicative of this point.

First, there is the boast of Lamech in Gen 4:23-24: "I have slain a man for a wound on me, a boy for a blow on me. Cain shall be avenged sevenfold, but Lamech seventy-sevenfold." The second passage is the account of Samson's revenge on the Philistines for the wrong that his betrothed's father had done him in giving his bride to another. He burns their crops and commits a great slaughter among them (Judg 15:1-8).

In both cases, revenge is enforced by self-help and limited only by the avenger's discretion. But both passages are legends describing what was perceived to have been the unsatisfactory situation before the advent of civilized society: Lamech was one of the wicked generation before the Flood, and Samson lived in what was regarded as a period of anarchy, when "each man did what was right in his own eyes."

The court's role was therefore to limit revenge to what was just in the circumstances of the case.[23] At its worst, revenge could be collective, on the culprit and his family, but this would be rare. The more usual choice would be between revenge on the culprit himself and vicarious revenge on a subordinate member of his family, which was regarded as a mitigated penalty. It also needed to be determined what form the revenge was to take: death, mutilation, pain (beating or whipping), humiliation, etc. In this

---

22 See Schoneveld 1973: 335-40. The rule concerning the burglar killed at night recurs in several law codes: CE 13 and Twelve Tables VIII 12.

23 For a detailed discussion of the courts' role in the revenge/ransom system, see Westbrook 1988d: 39-83.

connection the famous talionic rule was but one criterion by which the just limitation on revenge was determined.

It will be recalled, however, that the plaintiff's right was a dual one: to revenge or ransom. In principle, it was the plaintiff's free choice, but here again the courts intervened, imposing a fixed ransom where they considered that the gravity of the offence did not merit free bargaining. The plaintiff's right to revenge was not thereby extinguished, but it was rendered secondary. It was only realizable if the defendant was unable or unwilling to pay the ransom set by the court. The formulae for the fixing of ransom are various: a number of slaves, a weight of silver, a multiple of the thing stolen in case of theft, the whole of the defendant's property, or the whole of a debt owed by the plaintiff to the defendant. The appropriate limitations on revenge or ransom in a large variety of cases are discussed in the law codes. In order to understand that discussion, it is necessary first to appreciate the particular nature of the law codes themselves. The seven extant cuneiform codes and two biblical codes[24] form a special genre of literature through which transmission of the common legal tradition, in all its vagaries, can be seen.

Although referred to by modern scholars as law codes, they were not legislation. Rather, they were scientific treatises on the law, albeit not scientific in the modern sense. They comprised mainly judicial decisions which had been reformulated and expanded for heuristic purposes to make scholarly legal problems. A canon of such problems formed a repository of wisdom upon which all the ancient Near Eastern law codes drew. In this sense, the codes represent a literary tradition rather than a direct description of their respective legal systems. The individual problems may have begun life as real judgments, but they had long since been divorced from their original context. Where such a problem appears in a code, it signifies neither that it is a common case nor that it is a central rule of law; rather, it illustrates some principle of justice which a wise judge would follow. Indeed, many of the original decisions must have found their way into the

---

24   Codex Ur-Namma (CU), Codex Lipit-Ishtar (CL), Codex Eshnunna (CE), Codex Hammurabi (CH), Hittite Laws (HL), Middle Assyrian Laws (MAL), Neo-Babylonian Laws (NBL), Exodus 21-22, Deuteronomy 21-22.

canon precisely because they dealt with some particularly unusual or diffi-cult legal problem.[25]

The difficulty with these scholarly problems from the modern point of view is that they do not express the principles that they embody; ancient jurisprudence was incapable of doing that. The ancient court would draw wisdom from them as it sought to do justice in the case before it, but being isolated examples with complex fact situations they could seldom, if ever, act as direct precedents. Furthermore, no single law code reproduces the whole of a particular scholarly problem. Different fragments are scattered across the various codes, so that the original problem has to be recon-structed like a vase from the remaining shards.

On the subject of homicide, five classic examples from the canon of scholarly problems are recorded in the codes: the maltreated distrainee, the pregnant woman, the goring ox, the tragic accident, and the violent quar-rel. For the sake of brevity, we shall confine ourselves to two examples.

1.   The responsibility of the owner of an ox that has caused a person's death by goring is discussed by CE 54-58, CH 250-252 and Exod 21:28-32. In all three the possibility is considered that the owner had previously been warned by the local authority of his ox's propensity to gore, but the consequences differ radically. CE and CH set fixed ransoms at the very low rate usually associated with vicarious revenge (CH 251: ". . . if it gores the son of a man and causes his death, he shall pay half a mina of silver"), whereas Exodus insists that the culprit be killed, or "if ransom be imposed upon him, he shall pay all that is imposed upon him to redeem his life"—i.e., ransom is limited only by the plaintiff's discretion, as in aggra-vated homicide. Furthermore, vicarious revenge is excluded even when the victim is a subordinate member of the family: "if it gores a son or a daugh-ter, the same rule shall be applied to him."

---

25   For a detailed discussion of the nature of the law codes, see Westbrook 1988a: 82-97. The academic character of the law codes has been strongly disputed by legal histori-ans, but in our view their arguments ignore the cultural context of the codes. For a summary of the arguments and our latest contribution to the polemic, see Westbrook 1989a and the bibliography cited therein.

2. The violent quarrel that leads to injury or death is discussed in four passages:

CH 206-207

> If a man strikes a man in a brawl and inflicts a wound on him, the man shall swear "I did not strike knowingly," and he shall pay the doctor. If he dies from being struck, he shall swear; if it was the son of a man, he shall pay half a mina of silver.

HL 1

> If someone kills a man or a woman as the result of a quarrel/fight, he shall . . . him and give four slaves, male or female.

HL 10

> If someone wounds a man and makes him ill, he shall nurse him. He shall give a man in his place who will work in his house until he is well. When he is well, he shall give him six shekels of silver, and he shall pay the doctor's fee.

Exod 21:18-19

> If men quarrel and one strikes his neighbor with a stone or fist and he does not die but falls to a bed, if he rises and walks out and about on his stick, the striker is free of liability. He shall only pay for his not working and heal him.

The first point to note is the leniency of the penalties. In the case of injury it is based on the principle of indemnifying the injured party for his actual loss. This is in total contrast to the treatment of injury elsewhere in the codes, where it invariably is subject to talionic revenge or fixed ransom in lieu of revenge. It is this difference in the basis of payment to which Exodus refers when it states that the striker is "free of liability." The exception is HL 10, which adds a fixed payment to the indemnity. But it is an exception that proves the rule, as this paragraph, unlike the others, omits the element of quarrel—a significant omission, as we shall see.

The penalty for causing death in these circumstances is also relatively low: in HL, less than for kidnapping,[26] and in CH, a sum which evidently represents fixed ransom in lieu of vicarious revenge.

---

26 Six slaves for the kidnapping of a free man, according to HL 19b.

Accordingly, there must be mitigating factors in the circumstances described in the protasis of these laws. We can identify two:

i) A violent quarrel. The examples cover a fairly wide range: CH talks of a brawl (*risbatum*), while the Exodus text uses a term associated with verbal abuse rather than physical blows (*rîb*). HL uses a term which can refer to a quarrel or a fight (*sullatar*). The impression therefore is of a violent quarrel which can erupt into fighting. It does not at first sight appear the most obvious choice for a mitigating circumstance, but as Driver and Miles have discerned, the point seems to be that it is a situation for which both parties may be blamed.[27] In modern terms we would say that the culprit suffered provocation; the ancient jurisprudence expressed it by referring to a concrete example. This can be illustrated by the report of an actual trial from Nuzi, a town in northern Mesopotamia, from the fifteenth century:[28]

> Unaya son of Hampizi went before the judges in a lawsuit with Aqawatil son of Tarmiya. Unaya said: "Aqawatil struck me in the open fields." The tongue of Aqawatil stated to the judges: "Yes, we fought with one another." Because their statements were in agreement, saying "We fought each other," the judges examined the injuries of both. The head of Unaya with one blow and blood had been let. . . . their blows . . . . Unaya won the case, and the judges made Aqawatil pay in accordance with his statement a penalty of 30 shekels of silver: one ox, one ass, and one sheep.

ii) The mental state of the culprit. This is expressly stated by CH to be the fact that the culprit struck "not knowingly." The phrase cannot mean that the culprit did not intend to strike the blow, since in the context of a fight his act could hardly be

---

27 Driver and Miles 1952: vol. 1, 412.
28 SMN 2131. Edition in Pfeiffer and Speiser 1936: 47.

accidental. It must mean, as Driver and Miles rightly point out, that he did not intend the injury or death that resulted.[29] It was, from the culprit's point of view, an unforeseen consequence. The other law codes do not directly mention the mental element, but Exodus refers to the blow being struck "with a stone or a fist." The reason for this apparently superfluous detail is, we suggest, to distinguish the present case, where the consequences of the blow were not expected to be serious, from the use of a deadly weapon, where the consequence would be predictable.

Accordingly, where both mitigating factors are present, revenge for homicide is limited, being subordinated to a fixed ransom. But the burden of proving their existence lies with the culprit who would benefit from this limitation.[30] CH requires him to take an oath to establish the second factor;[31] the other systems may have relied on the credibility of his evidence combined with presumptions raised by the surrounding circumstances. Where the culprit cannot discharge the burden of proof, the plaintiff will be entitled to the option of revenge, as is illustrated by the story of the widow of Tekoah in 2 Sam 14:6-7.

The story is related to king David by a woman who represents herself as a widow from the village of Tekoah:

Your servant had two sons and they both fought together in the open field, and there was no one to separate them and the one struck the other and caused his death. Now the whole clan has risen up against your servant, saying: "Hand over the one who

---

29 Driver and Miles 1952: vol. 1, 412.
30 In modern criminal law, the burden is in principle on the prosecution to prove the defendant's guilty mental state, but there are some instances, e.g., a defense of insanity, where the burden may be on the defendant. This is the established rule in English law since McNaghten's Case (1843): see Cross 1974: 85. In U.S. jurisdictions, attitudes to the McNaghten rule are more ambiguous: see Gard 1972: vol. 3, 13.
31 Taking the oath was not an easy option. The consequences of divine wrath were feared, and litigants would often settle rather than face the procedure. See Loewenstamm 1980a: 341-45.

struck his brother that we may put him to death for the life of his
brother whom he killed."

The widow and the clan offer conflicting versions of the facts. The widow
asserts that there was a fight and implies that the culprit did not intend to
kill with his blow ("struck . . . caused death"—*ymt*),[32] whereas the clan
claims that he did ("struck . . . killed"—*hrg*). As the alleged fight took
place away from the village and there were no witnesses, the widow cannot discharge the burden of proof on behalf of her son, and no mitigation is
possible. Her only recourse therefore is to petition the king to exercise his
prerogative of mercy. The king does so, thereby incidentally demonstrating his authority over the revenge system.

The Mycenaean Context

Can the ancient Near Eastern model be applied to the trial scene in the *Iliad*? It is not a question of some distant parallel applied for didactic
purposes. The sources in question derive from Greece's neighbors and
span both the time of Homer and the era in which his poems are set. The
traditions carried by those sources are not those of a particular society or
societies but were widespread, covering all the legal systems of the area
for which pertinent records are preserved (with the possible exception of
Egypt). It is not impossible therefore that these traditions could have entered the Greek sphere, just as Near Eastern myths and, later, the alphabet
are known to have done.[33] Their ability to elucidate a Greek source would
not then be coincidental.

A specific instance from a different area of law has recently been provided by Russo and Knox, who explain Agamemnon's decision to test his
troops in *Il.* 2.73-75 by reference to the rule in Deut 20:8 that cowards are
to be dismissed before a battle. This is the traditional rule (*thémis*) that

---

32 Cf. Exod 21:18 discussed above: "Struck . . . not die."
33 For reception of the alphabet, see Naveh 1982: 175-86; Bernal 1990: esp. 53-70. For
    the reception of myth, see Burkert 1979: 7-10, 20-22, 80-83, 99-142; and Jacobsen
    1984: 20-22. For a more general (and controversial) view of the West Semitic impact
    on Mycenaean Greece, see Astour 1965.

Agamemnon is applying.[34] The Deuteronomic law, however, mentions other categories who are released from military service. In particular, "the man who has betrothed a wife and not married her shall go and return to his home, lest he die in war and another marry her" (v. 7). In the myth of Keret from the Canaanite city of Ugarit (ca. fourteenth century), Keret musters a huge army for his divinely ordered campaign. So total is the conscription that "the sick man is carried in bed, the blind man gropes his way. Even the newly betrothed goes forth; he leads his wife to another, his beloved to a stranger."[35] In the list of unlikely conscripts, the place of the newly betrothed is comprehensible because of the traditional legal rule that allowed his exemption in normal circumstances.

If we combine these three sources, then—a seventh-century biblical text, a fourteenth-century Canaanite myth, and the *Iliad* verse—we can discern the existence of a widespread and long-standing legal tradition common to the Greek and Near Eastern spheres, whereby various categories of men might be exempted from a military campaign. It is significant that the tradition finds its way into a law code in Deuteronomy, while in the *Iliad* it is referred to as a *thémis*. That a collection of the latter existed for reference by judges[36] is implied by *Il.* 1.236-238: ". . . the sons of the Achaeans who give judgment . . . who keep the *thémistes* in Zeus' name."

While no date could be placed on the process of reception posited by us, the evidence of the Linear B documents shows that it was feasible at least as early as the Mycenaean period. The latter attest to an administrative structure which would provide a suitable context for the ancient Near Eastern model and at the same time indicate specific connections with the text of the trial scene.

The Linear B tablets reveal a highly centralized society with a large, bureaucratic administration, on the same general pattern that we have seen in the states of the ancient Near East. Ucitel has shown close parallels with the administration of Ur in the neo-Sumerian period (end of third millennium), without, of course, supposing any particular connection.[37] The

---

34   Russo and Knox 1989: 174-80. Dumezil (1985: 26-29) points out that this is to be the first major engagement of the war.
35   Col. II, lines 98-103; col. IV, lines 186-191. Edition in Ginsberg 1946.
36   For the suggestion that the ancient Near Eastern law codes may have had the same function, see Westbrook 1985a: 253-58.
37   Ucitel 1988: 19-30.

central authority of the Mycenaean state is represented by palace and temple, but there is also a local administration called the *dāmos*. Lejeune has shown that while *dāmos can* refer to a section of the population, in the administrative context it has a legal personality and as such possesses land, part of which it appears to hold as communal land, and the rest of which it assigns to individual usufructuaries.[38] The nature of the archive is such that we learn nothing of the substantive law, but the organized society that it reveals is likely to have had an equally well-organized administration of justice, especially when one remembers that the rigorous separation of legal and executive powers is a relatively recent invention. It certainly is a context in which the courts could have had the same role with respect to homicide as in the ancient Near East.

Furthermore, Muellner has identified the *dāmos* in the sense of a collective legal entity with the word *dmos* in the trial scene (line 500).[39] The legal implications of this identification, into which Muellner does not enter, will be discussed below. For present purposes, suffice it to say that, if Muellner is correct, then we have in the trial scene an addition to the small number of attestations to Mycenaean culture so far discovered in the Homeric poems.[40]

The Trial Scene and Homeric Homicide Law

Before we apply the ancient Near Eastern evidence to the trial scene, there is a major objection that needs to be considered. There are many other references to homicide in the Homeric poems, and the consensus among scholars is that the underlying legal system reflected in them is one of arbitration. Disputes were submitted voluntarily to the court, whose judgments could not be binding against the will of the parties.[41]

In this context, the law of homicide was one of private vendetta. The relatives of the victim were entitled to revenge, and although they might

38 Lejeune 1965: 3-16.
39 Muellner 1976: 104.
40 Discussed by Page 1959: 218-51; and Kirk 1975: 833-37.
41 E.g., Biscardi 1982: 275-78; Bonner and Smith 1930: 11-19, 29-31; Calhoun 1927: 17-18; Gagarin 1986: 42-43; Hommel 1969: 30-31; Steinwenter 1925: 29-30.

accept ransom instead, they were in no way obliged to do so. Once ransom had been accepted, however, they could not continue the vendetta. If they did so, they committed a wrongful act which justified a new vendetta. The external constraints in this system of private vengeance were not legal but at most social, through the expression of public opinion.[42] The killer, therefore, could not look to the courts for protection, but if the offer of ransom were unacceptable, his only safety lay in flight, a course of action frequently mentioned in Homer in connection with homicide. It is the "factual" rather than the "legal" interpretation of the trial scene—i.e., the issue is whether ransom *was* paid or not rather than whether it is *payable* or not—that best fits this system. For if ransom is purely within the discretion of the victim's relatives, what is there to litigate about? There seems no reason for the relatives to refer the matter to a court.

Steinwenter has attempted to overcome this difficulty by arguing that the relative's rejection of the killer's offer in the trial scene is a mere formality, necessary to found the litigation, which in fact will be nothing more than arbitration.[43] But what need is there for arbitration when one of the parties has no bargaining power whatsoever? Steinwenter's suggestion[44] that pressure of public opinion forced the victim's relatives to lay the dispute before the court is contradicted by his own insistence that the verdict will be a proposal for composition that is not binding in itself, but only because it is acceptable to both sides.[45] It must therefore be admitted that the trial scene, on the "legal" interpretation, seems inconsistent with the other references in Homer.

The traditional approach to reconciling these references is to suppose a historical development. On this view the trial scene belongs to the later strata of the *Iliad*.[46] It represents a transitional stage[47] between the old private vendetta and the transformation of the law under Drakon into true criminal law.[48]

---

42 Cantarella 1976: 5-6.
43 Steinwenter 1948: 13.
44 Steinwenter 1948: 13.
45 Steinwenter 1948: 15.
46 Steinwenter 1925: 34-36.
47 Andersen 1976: 12.
48 Cantarella 1976: cf. 7-8 and 73-74.

The resolution of apparently conflicting laws by arranging them historically should be treated with a certain degree of skepticism. There is no external evidence for the process postulated, and it is noteworthy that the evidence of the copious Near Eastern sources, with a history of nearly three thousand years, is also negative. Furthermore, there is the problem of where exactly to place these stages in the course of Greek history. The Mycenaean age, on the evidence of the Linear B texts, would seem less suitable for the earlier stage than the following Dark Age, which would suggest a reverse development. Of course, the earlier stage could be projected back into the pre-Mycenaean period, but then we begin to leave the sphere of Greek history proper and enter the murky depths of an Indo-European tradition. It is not surprising that the protagonists of historical development are vague as to its absolute chronology.

We would therefore propose a different approach, namely, that the trial scene and the other Homeric references indeed represent the same law, but seen from different perspectives.

a)   The trial scene is part of a tableau of events from everyday life, depicted on the shield of Achilles. It takes its place alongside such banal occurrences as a wedding procession and agricultural labor. It is set at the level of the local village, not of the royal court, and concerns the lot of the common man. All this is in strong contrast with the normal course of the epic genre, which focuses upon the affairs of the upper stratum of society—of kings and princes, or at least of nobles.

Kings and princes are not necessarily above the law, but they are usually in a better position to avoid its consequences than ordinary mortals. Where they are involved in homicide, the results may not reflect the ordinary workings of the law. For example, flight was undoubtedly an option to which an ordinary killer might have recourse (as he did in the ancient Near East), but it is unlikely that many would follow the example of Prince Tlepolemus who, after killing his uncle, builds a navy and raises an army before fleeing to escape the revenge of his fellow princes.[49] Clearly, his whole conduct and the potential sanctions against him are in the realm of the political, not the legal.

---

49   *Il.* 2.661-666.

It is worth comparing at this point the case of Absalom in the Bible. Enraged at the rape of his sister Tamar, he arranges for his retainers to kill the culprit, his half-brother Amnon, and then flees with them, taking refuge with king Talmi of Gashur.[50] If this were our only evidence for homicide in the Bible, we might conclude that it was a reflection on the legal system, or lack of one. It is only because we have a control in the form of the different literary genres within the Bible, such as the laws and narrative accounts of litigation in practice, that we can recognize the Absalom incident for the unusual case that it is. The operation of the characters outside the bounds set for ordinary men is emphasized by the fact that king David is finally induced to pardon his son by the case of the widow of Tekoah, through which he is forced to compare his attitude to his own son with his willingness to pardon a stranger in a banal case involving commoners, where the possibility of flight does not even arise.[51] Indeed, given the striking similarity of Absalom's actions to those of Tlepolemus, it seems to us that the motif of killing, flight, and refuge is an old-established literary topos, whose frequency in Homer reflects less the statistics of social reality than the usefulness of a literary device which adds background to the poem's characters and explains their transfer from one location to another.

b)   A seemingly unambiguous statement of the law is made by Ajax in his argument with Achilles in *Il.* 9.632-636:

> . . . a man accepts ransom from the slayer of his brother, or for his
> dead son; and the slayer remains in his own land for the paying of
> a great price, and the kinsman's heart and proud spirit are re-
> strained by the taking of ransom.

Ajax's words would at first sight appear to make the question of ransom purely one for the avenger's discretion, with flight as the only alternative, and no role for the courts. In their context, however, they are not a comprehensive statement of the law of homicide; they merely express the theoretical principle, as does the Edict of Telipinu, to which they bear a

---

50   2 Samuel 13
51   2 Sam 14:19-21, and see above.

close similarity. And as in the Edict of Telipinu, they cover in practice only aggravated homicide. As Vatin points out, Ajax is using *a fortiori* reasoning.[52] Ajax's point is that *even* for the most serious of crimes, deliberate murder, ransom is an honorable alternative that is voluntarily accepted, and therefore Achilles should voluntarily accept ransom for Agamemnon's offence, which was certainly less serious, albeit deliberate. If Ajax's statement were to cover mitigated homicide, such as accidental death, it would lose all its impact.

c) For aggravated homicide, the choice of revenge or ransom is purely in the hands of the avenger. The question of some limitation being imposed only applies if there is some gradation of homicide. That possibility has been raised with reference to the killer's volition. The orthodox view, as expressed by Latte, is that there was no distinction in Homeric law between intent and accident in homicide. The principle was one of "Erfolgshaftung," i.e., strict liability.[53]

Already Leist, however, argued that for involuntary homicide the relatives could be forced to accept *poin*,[54] and Daube has more recently poured scorn on the theory of Erfolgshaftung as romantic mythology derived from a nineteenth-century belief in the steady progress of mankind and a notion of ancient heroes as elemental force of nature, hitting back without question.[55] The controversy centers on the meaning of the term *ouk ethélōn*, which occurs twice in the Homeric poems.

In *Il.* 23.86-90, Patroclus recalls how as a boy he fled his homeland because in his folly he killed another boy over a game of dice, *ouk ethélōn*, "not willingly," but *kholōtheís*, "in anger." Since Patroclus was still obliged to flee, it has been argued that lack of intention played no role in his culpability.[56] The situation is comparable rather to the scholarly problem from the Near Eastern law codes where one person kills another "not knowingly." As we have seen, there must be two elements in mitigation, a threshold situation for which the killer was not entirely to blame, i.e., a

---

52   Vatin 1982: 276.
53   Latte 1933: cols. 280-81.
54   Leist 1884: 328-34.
55   Daube 1969: 171-72.
56   Latte 1933: cols. 280-81; Bonner and Smith 1930: 21; and Cantarella 1976: 33-34.

fight or a quarrel in which he was provoked, and lack of intention to strike a fatal blow. Patroclus hints at both: he killed because of anger over some incident in the game, and while he certainly must have wished to strike the other boy, he did not wish his death, i.e., he did not intend the consequence of his blow. But again, as we have seen in the case of the widow of Te-koah, all this may be insufficient to escape liability. The burden is on the defendant to prove these mitigating circumstances. Patroclus' case is therefore more than uncertain, and flight a sensible course. Nonetheless, Patroclus' very mention of his lack of intention shows an awareness of the distinction between intended and unintended homicide and may have been designated to lessen his moral, if not his legal, culpability. It may well have been the grounds on which he was granted asylum and an honorable place at the court of Achilles' father. Of course, one can also dismiss his statement as a mere personal remark without any legal implication, but it is curious that Patroclus should raise the very two factors that are regarded as mitigating in the Near Eastern legal tradition on homicide.

In *Od.* 22.31, Odysseus, acting the part of a drunken beggar, takes his bow and, declaring that he will hit an unusual target, shoots and kills Anti-nous, leader of the Suitors. The latter assume that he killed *ouk ethélonta*, "not willingly." Nonetheless, they declare that he will die for it (25-30). Again this example is taken to show that intention plays no legal role.[57]

Daube interprets the passage as meaning that they believed him to have acted not without intent but without set purpose. They *do* attribute intent to him, but intent that is the result, not of rational planning, but of a drunken fit, just as Patroclus' killing was the result, in Daube's view, of uncontrolled anger.[58]

While agreeing with Daube on the invalidity of the Erfolgshaftung theory, we cannot follow his interpretation in this particular instance. It places a heavy burden on the term "not willing" and attributes to the Suit-ors some very hair-splitting distinctions on the subject of volition. In their context, the words *ouk ethélonta* refer to the Suitors' perception of the danger to themselves, or rather, lack of danger. They think that the stranger, being drunk did not intend the consequences of his act, and there-fore the most they have to fear is another wild shot from him. Lack of

---

57   E.g., Gagarin 1981: 11.
58   Daube 1969: 171-72.

intention is irrelevant to Odysseus' liability for homicide, however, first because there are no other mitigating circumstances, such as provocation, and second because it was caused by inebriation, which serves to negate mitigation, as he has earlier been warned by the Suitors, citing the case of the drunken centaur who raped the bride at a wedding feast (21.228-310).[59] Accordingly, they condemn him to death (22.27-30).

In summary, neither of these two cases provides a firm basis for the Erfolgshaftung theory. In spite of their lack of volition, Patroclus is in danger of being held liable because of the burden of proof, and Odysseus is considered liable because of the absence of mitigating circumstances. The possibility of some gradation of homicide based on the mental condition of the offender therefore remains open.

The Trial

Let us re-examine the terms used in lines 499-500. We would translate as literally as possible:

The one was claiming (*eúkheto*) to pay (*apondoûnai*) all (*pánta*) expounding (*piphaúskōn*) to the *dmos*; the other was refusing (*anaíneto*) to take (*helésthai*)[60] anything.

Note that we have not translated either of the aorist infinitives with the past tense, as is often done. As the aorist is an aspect, not a tense, it is

---

59 The connection is noted by Daube 1969: 171-72. It is disputed by Gagarin (1981: 12) on two grounds: (1) the incident of the drunken centaur is more than a hundred lines earlier; (2) it does not imply that the same degree of intentionality underlines a drunken rape and a drunken accident. But however many lines separate Odysseus' act from the centaur's, they are part of the same scene. Indeed, the mention of the centaur has no point, unless it is to lay the groundwork for Odysseus' culpability for a drunken act. If inebriation goes to the question of mitigation rather than of intention, as we have argued, then any difference in intentionality between rape and homicide is irrelevant.

60 Muellner 1976: 102 suggests that *helésthai* cannot have the sense of "to accept." But the verb is used in the *Iliad* in the sense of accepting something offered, as in 7.482 and 9.709: ὕπνου δῶρον ἕλοντο—"they took the gift of sleep."

unnecessary to do so, unless one wishes to assign a chronological order to the actions.

Muellner has pointed out that the verb *eúkhomai*, used only here in the Homeric corpus in a legal sense, has a direct parallel in what appears to be a record of litigation over land in a Linear B tablet from Pylos.[61] Lines 5-6 of PY Ep 704 read:[62]

> Erita the priestess has and claims (*e-u-ke-to-qe*) to have *etonijo* land for the god, but the *dāmos* says that she has a holding from the common land in usufruct.

According to Muellner, the parallelism of *eúkheto* and *phasí* shows that the verb *eúkhomai* in a legal context must mean "to state, assert, claim."[63] We would add that since the facts are not in issue in this case (the priestess is expressly stated to be holding the land), her claim may rather be one of right than of fact. She claims the right to hold the land in question absolutely as a temple prebend rather than in usufruct.

On the basis of this parallel, the killer in our Homeric passage is claiming the right to pay ransom (*poin*) in full (*pánta*). This cannot refer simply to any amount that the killer chooses to offer. The concept of a full payment assumes the possibility of a sum fixed by objective criteria, which would constitute the *whole* amount payable. Applying the Near Eastern evidence, we would expect: (a) that the ransom would be fixed by the court, in accordance with the objective criteria of traditional law; and (b) that the basis for such a claim by the killer would be that the case is one of mitigated homicide. If his claim is accepted, then the right to avenge will be subordinated to the payment of ransom, only becoming available again if the killer cannot or will not pay the amount so fixed.

Our expectations are confirmed by the following phrase. The killer, in making his claim, is expounding (*piphaúskōn*) his case to the *dmos*. This is

---

61 Muellner 1976: 102-104.

62 *e-ri-ta i-je-re-ja e-ke e-u-ke-to-qe e-to-ni-jo e-ke-e te-o da-mo-de-mi pa-si ko-to-na-o ke-ke-me-na-o o-na-to e-ke-e*. Edition in Bennett and Olivier 1973: 126.

63 Muellner 1976: 104. Muellner also prays in aid use of the verb in Homer for assertions of pedigree (e.g., *Il.* 14.113-114), rejecting as artificial Benveniste's attempt (1969: 237, 240) to interpret such assertions as self-consecrations in the manner of Roman *devotio*.

usually translated "the people," identifying it with the rowdy mass of spectators gathered in the town square.[64] But the latter are consistently referred to in this passage as *laoí* (479, 502). As we have seen, Muellner has identified the *dmos* here with the *dāmos* of the Linear B texts, where besides meaning the common people it sometimes refers to a unit of local administration which holds and assigns common land.[65]

In the Pylos litigation the *dāmos* would appear to have this role, and in a parallel record of the same case the term *kotonooko* (literally: "plotholder") is substituted, referring to a body of local notables.[66] We would therefore translate *dāmos* in the Pylos document and *dmos* in the trial scene as "village" or "commune," referring not to the population but to the community as a legal entity represented by a body of notables.

The killer thus expounds his case to the "village," represented by the college of elders who in lines 503-508 are called upon to give judgment in the case. The reason why the killer and not the other party is said to be arguing before this court is that *the burden of proof is upon him* to establish the existence of mitigating circumstances, as we have seen from our discussion of the Near Eastern sources.

The other party, the avenger, has the dual right to ransom or revenge. By refusing to take ransom, he asserts that the case is one of aggravated homicide and that he therefore has a free choice between ransom and revenge, and he chooses the latter.[67]

---

64 Wolff in particular (1946: 41-42) constructs a scenario in which the people's applause of each speech by an elder is decisive of the outcome. But this requires the people to listen in silence, which they are obviously not doing; they are cheering on the rival parties (not the judges!) and having to be held back by the heralds while the elders speak.

65 Muellner 1976: 102-104.

66 PY Eb 297: *i-je-re-ja e-ke-qe e-u-ke-to-qe e-to-ni-jo e-ke-e te-o ko-to-no-o-ko-de ko-to-na-o ke-ke-me-na-o o-na-ta e-ke-e.* Edition in Bennett and Oliver 1973: 94. See Lejeune 1965: 11-16. From PY Ep 301.2-4, Lejeune concludes that the college of notables was twelve in number. The term *geronsiā* ("council of elders"?) also appears at Pylos (PY An 261). The relationship between the two bodies is not clear.

67 Cf. the Gibeonites in 2 Sam 21:4-6 who, when asked by king David what remedy he can offer them for the massacre perpetrated upon them by his predecessor king Saul, reject ransom and demand instead vicarious revenge: the execution of Saul's seven sons.

The dispute therefore is about what limit the court should impose on the right of revenge or ransom in order to ensure that its exercise will be appropriate to the gravity of the wrong. This is the archetypal role of a court, as we have seen from the Near Eastern law codes, where finding the appropriate limit is the epitome of legal wisdom. It is an ideal choice for representing a model lawsuit.[68]

Our interpretation has been arrived at by placing the trial scene in the context of our knowledge of other legal systems, Mycenaean and Near Eastern. The terms of the dispute can be seen to fit that context exactly. But our conclusions do not rest entirely upon analogy. On the contrary, the text itself states explicitly what we have implied. For the following line (501) reads: "They both wished to obtain from a judge[69] a *peîrar*."

The term *peîrar* is usually translated here "judgment," "decision," or the like, but that is no more than a guess based on context, and an unlikely one, since in no other reference does *peîrar* have anything like this meaning.[70] The term is a problematic one, it is true, but one meaning is

---

68   The Near Eastern idea that such limitation represents the triumph of civilization over chaos (i.e., unbridled revenge) is graphically reflected in the detail of the heralds holding back the noisy crowd, i.e., forming a boundary within which the elders can give their judgments in good order. Cf. the different descriptions of the opposing armies in *Il.* 3.1-9: the Trojans are a noisy rabble, clamoring like cranes, while Achaeans advance in disciplined silence. I am grateful to Professor J. Russo for drawing my attention to this passage.

69   *istōr*, literally "one who knows" (see Nagy 1990: 250-52, 258-59). Without entering into a discussion of the meaning of this difficult term, which would take us beyond the bounds of our topic, we regard as most plausible the view that the *istōr* was that one of the elders whose opinion was ultimately adopted as the judgment of the whole body, and who thereby gained the two talents of gold put up by the litigants as a court fee. See H. H. Pflüger 1942: 146-48. On this view, the *istōr* would naturally be the judge most knowledgeable of the traditional law.

70   Nothdurft (1978: 25-40) proposes a radical new interpretation: that *peîrar* refers to the means rather than the end. To turn this interpretation into "judgment" in the trial scene, however, Nothdurft is forced to supply an extra word (*peîrar*) *dikēs* ("means of achieving judgment") and then assume that it had dropped out of the phrase at some earlier stage (1978: 33-34). More reasonable is Hommel's translation (1969: 16): "Nun begehrten beide, vor dem (Rechts)-kundigen zu einem *Ende* (ihres Streits) zu gelangen," although the result is a somewhat banal and unnecessary statement.

undisputed, that of a "limit," as in *peírata gaiēs*, "the limits of the earth."[71]
Thus both parties literally wished to obtain from the judge a limit.[72]

---

71 E.g., *Od.* 4.563. On etymological grounds, Heubeck (1972: 139-40) proposes a basic
    meaning of "(äusserstes) Ende, Grenze."

72 It might be argued that the plaintiff sought the absence of any limit, but this is incor-
    rect. The court's judgment would set a limit on his rights by the very act of defining
    them; he wishes that limit to be revenge, not fixed ransom. His revenge would still be
    limited: to the culprit himself or perhaps a member of his family. It is worth noting
    here the difference between judicial revenge and revenge in war in the *Iliad*, where no
    limits apply. As Cantarella points out (1976: 18-20), the battles in the *Iliad* are pre-
    sented as a series of related acts of revenge. Legitimate vengeance in these
    circumstances, however, was not confined to the original killer, but was satisfied by
    striking indiscriminately at all members of his group (e.g., *Il.* 14.449-474). See further
    the discussion of revenge in war and within the legal system in Westbrook 1988d: 92-
    99.

13

Penelope's Dowry and Odysseus' Kingship

Abstract

A great deal of difficulty surrounds any attempt to reconstruct a legal system from the disjointed allusions to law within Homeric poetry. By understanding these allusions in the light of ancient Near Eastern legal traditions, however, a coherent system can be reconstructed. This study of Penelope's dowry and its attendant arrangements presents a case in point. Moreoever, it demonstrates that a proper legal understanding of how a dowry functioned helps to explain certain actions on the part of Odysseus, his son, and Penelope's subsequent suitors.

Introduction

The Homeric poems contain references to legal rules and practice but in the form of fragmentary, unconnected allusions. Attempts to recreate a system from these references alone are doomed to failure. They will inevitably create an imaginary legal universe, where literary topos is identified with legal rule, and legal institutions are artificial constructs.

Fragmentary references can only be understood when placed in the context of a working legal system. In exposing the underlying principles that they represent, the proper context not only enables us to judge whether the visible fragments are internally consistent but also reveals the application of hitherto unrecognized rules in the narrative. The proper context, however, is lacking. There are virtually no contemporary sources of Greek law, at any time from the Mycenaean period, in which the poems are set, to the seventh century, when the process of composition is presumed by most scholars to be complete.

* Originally published in *Symposion 2001* (eds. R. W. Wallace and M. Gagarin; Wien: Österreichischen Akademie der Wissenschaften, 2005), 3-23. Used by permission.

The nearest well-documented system is classical Athenian law. Scholars are understandably reluctant to force its sophisticated technicalities upon the very different society described in the Homeric poems. Instead, recourse is had to ethnographic data which, having no historical connection whatsoever, can only serve to support the feasibility of putative structures. It cannot serve as confirmation that imagined laws existed in reality.

I propose as a more satisfactory substitute not a single system; rather, a whole legal tradition. The societies of the ancient Near East were diverse in language and culture, but they appear to some considerable extent to have shared a common legal tradition.[1] The underlying structure of their legal systems was the same, while the content of the law drew upon a canon of received wisdom that had originated in Mesopotamia in the third millennium or earlier and had spread across the fertile crescent to Anatolia and the Mediterranean coast. The tradition was very tenacious, lasting well into the first millennium.[2]

---

1   There is no fixed criterion for determining what constitutes a "society." If we separate Near Eastern sources by political units (i.e., by kingdom and reign, or even dynasty), then over the course of three thousand years the number runs into hundreds. At the other end of the scale, intelligible records are confined to no more than a dozen or so languages: Sumerian, Akkadian (which divides into Assyrian and Babylonian), Elamite, Persian, Hurrian, Hittite, Luwian, Urartian, Aramaic, Ugaritic, Phoenician, Hebrew, Egyptian. There was, however, no necessary correlation between society and language. A more practical, if rough, guide is by archives: the sources tend to cluster into archives covering not more than three generations. A few examples will illustrate the complexity of the situation. 1) Old Assyrian archives (18th century) come almost exclusively from Assyrian merchant colonies in Anatolia, mainly Kanesh. Written in Assyrian, they inform us of the community of expatriate merchants, of the local Anatolian kingdom (language unknown), and of the capital city, Assur. 2) The city of Alalakh on the Orontes in Syria has produced two archives, from the 18th and 15th centuries, with several layers of destruction in between. The earlier layer uses the Old Babylonian dialect and the later Middle Babylonian with an admixture of Hurrian, reflecting its position as a vassal of Mitanni. The native language, unrecovered except for isolated terms, was a West Semitic dialect. 3) The archives from Elephantine represent a Persian garrison town in 5th-century Egypt. They are the records of Egyptians, Arameans, Jews, Persians and sundry other ethnic groups, written in Aramaic and Demotic.

2   See Malul 1990; Muffs 1969; Westbrook 1990b, 1994e, and 2000b.

The ancient Near Eastern legal tradition was thus contemporary with Homeric society, whichever period is taken as applicable, and in close geographical proximity. At all material times there were extensive contacts between the two areas and demonstrable cultural influences.[3] I have argued elsewhere that those influences included elements of legal culture.[4]

When seen in the context of ancient Near Eastern law, Homeric law presents a coherent, viable system that fits into the mainstream tradition. The variants that it displays are no greater than those exhibited by any individual system within the ancient Near East. Furthermore, the tradition acts as a control for classical Athenian law, identifying elements that already existed in earlier periods.

As an example, I propose to examine the case of Penelope's dowry. Using the Near Eastern legal tradition and Athenian law as a framework, I hope to show the legal coherence of her dowry arrangements, their wider constitutional significance, and how they were used to subtle effect in the narrative. The results will be further evidence, I hope, that the widespread ancient Near Eastern legal tradition did not stop dead at the shores of the Eastern Mediterranean.

Marriage and Marital Property in the Ancient Near East

One of the advantages of the huge amount of legal material available from the ancient Near East is that we can avoid reliance on isolated parallels. This survey, being concerned with a common tradition, is based either on rules that recur in more than one system or on principles or concepts that are illustrated by rules from different systems, even though individual solutions may vary and even conflict.

Marriage, which created a relationship of status between husband and wife, was preceded by betrothal, a contract normally between the groom and the father of the bride. Betrothal could be sealed by a payment—the so-called "bride-price"—by the groom to the bride's father. Marriage and purchase were in fact two distinct institutions, and the payment had nothing to do with a price. It would be better to refer to it as a betrothal

---

3 E.g., Burkert 1992 for the area of myth.
4 Westbrook 1992b. See also Westbrook 1988a, 1990b, 1999f; and Yaron 1974.

payment, since it inaugurated a special state of betrothal.[5] To avoid confusion, however, the conventional term will be retained here. The "bride-price" was not necessary, but it was desirable, because it secured for the groom an exclusive right to the bride. As far as outsiders were concerned they were already married, pending the groom's exercise of his right to claim the bride from her father's house.[6] The various languages of the region all have a special technical term for bride-price, e.g., *terḫatu* (Akkadian), níg.mí.ús.sá (Sumerian), *mōhar* (Hebrew, Aramaic), *kussata* (Hittite). Some languages (e.g., Hebrew, Ugaritic) also have a verbal form from the same root.

The dowry was in essence a gift from the bride's father to the bride, which could be enhanced by gifts from other sources. Economically, it represented her share of the inheritance, but legally it differed fundamentally from male inheritance. As in Athenian law (and exactly as in *Od.* 14.208-209), sons had a vested right to their father's estate, which they divided by lot after his death, but a father was not obliged in law to provide his daughter with a dowry; it was theoretically a voluntary gift.[7] The terminology reflects the distinction. Technical terms for dowry are derived from words for gift or in some cases are simply a word for gift, e.g., *nudunnû*, *šeriktu* (Akkadian), sag.rig$_7$, níg.ba (Sumerian), *iwaru* (Hittite), *šilluḥîm* (Hebrew), *tlḫ* (Ugaritic). Frequently, no special term at all is used, the context supplying the special purpose for the transfer of property.

The dowry entered the husband's house with the bride and was thus transferred to him. It disappeared into his assets for the duration of the marriage. The duality of the transfer is reflected in a slight ambiguity of language. Sometimes the father is said to give it to his daughter, the bride, who brings it with her to the husband's house. At other times he is said to give it to the husband with his daughter.[8]

---

5 The legal principles are discussed in Westbrook 1988b: 53-60.

6 Called "inchoate marriage" by Driver and Miles 1952: 249-50. LE 26: "If a man brings the 'bride-price' for the daughter of a man and another abducts her and deflowers her without asking her father and mother, it is a capital offense—he shall die."

7 See Kraus 1969; Westbrook 1994b: 273-75; cf. MacDowell 1978: 91-93.

8 Compare the following clauses: "All this is the dowry of A daughter of B, which her father B has given to her and caused to enter the house of C for his son D [groom]" (BE 6/1 84:32-39; edition in Westbrook 1988b: 113); "A has given to B [groom] the dowry of his daughter C with C . . ." (*Nbn.* 243:10-12; edition in Roth 1989: no. 12);

Except for a small and significant part, to which I shall return, the husband had control and management of the dowry property. What the wife had was a right to restoration of the dowry on termination of the marriage. Her right was not to the return of specific items but to their full value. If she could be said to retain ownership in the dowry, it was only in the sense of a contingent ownership in a fund. If by the end of the marriage the husband had dissipated dowry assets, the shortfall had to be made good from his own property.[9]

If a wife survived her husband, the dowry served to provide for her during her widowhood. On her death, it would be inherited by her children and her children only. The sources emphasize that neither the husband, his family, nor his children by another marriage were entitled to inherit the dowry.[10] If, on the other hand, the widow remarried, her children from both marriages were entitled to share after her death. In the meantime, the second husband controlled the dowry assets just like the first. It is important to note that if she predeceased her second husband, her children would have to wait until his death in order to inherit her dowry.[11]

The "bride-price" has no equivalent in Athenian law, but the contours of the law of dowry will be very familiar. The Athenian *proix* had the same legal basis and followed the same devolution.[12] So also did the wife's

---

"A [bride's mother] has given as dowry to B [groom] torques and rings (worth) 20 shekels of silver belonging to her daughter C" (VAS 6 61:5-8; edition in Roth 1989: no. 8); "[Groom speaking:] 'Your daughter A has brought into me in her hand . . .'" (Porten and Yardeni 1989: B2.6 [= Cowley 15], line 6).

9   NBL 12: "A wife whose husband took her dowry and she has no sons or daughters and her husband dies: a dowry as much as the dowry shall be given to her from her husband's estate."

10 LH 162: "If a man marries a wife and she does not provide him with children and the woman dies . . ., her husband shall have no claim to the woman's dowry; her dowry belongs only to her father's house." Cf. LE 17-18; MAL A 27. MAL A 29: "If a woman enters her husband's house, her dowry and whatever she brings from her father's house, or her father-in-law gave her upon her entry, are reserved for her sons; her father-in-law's sons have no claim."

11 LH 167: "If a man marries a wife and she bears him children and the woman dies, and after her death he marries a second woman and she bears children: after the father's death, the sons shall not divide according to mothers; they shall take the dowries of their (respective) mothers and divide equally the property of the father's house."

12 Harrison 1968: 46-49, 55-57.

marital property at Gortyn.[13] The most notable difference with Athens is that the ancient Near Eastern widow seems to have had somewhat more independence, becoming head of household if her children were still young, not necessarily being obliged to return to her father's house (except in some cases where childless), and having control over her dowry and her own remarriage.[14]

Homeric Marital Property

References to marital property in the Homeric poems fit neatly into the above pattern. The "bride-price," which is designated by the term *hedna* (see below), is normally given by the groom to the bride's father (*Od.* 8.318-319).[15] Payment secures the bride against third parties (*Od.* 6.159; 15.16-18; 16.390-392; 21.160-162) and entitles the groom to claim the bride at the father-in-law's house (*Il.* 22.471-472). It is not a necessary item; some marriages are said to be "without 'bride-price'" (*anaednon*).[16]

---

13 III 17-20 (see n. 14 below); III 31-34: if a wife dies childless, (the husband) is to return her property to the relatives (*epiballontes*).

14 The position of the widow at Gortyn seems to have been closer to the Near Eastern model. According to III 17-20: if a man dies leaving children, if the wife so desires, she may marry, keeping her own property and whatever her husband may have given her.

15 In the case of Penelope it is unclear whether the recipient is herself, Telemachus, or her father and brothers, in the event that she returns to the family home. See Lacey 1968.

16 Lacey suggests that these were all uxorilocal marriages, "bride-price" applying only to virilocal marriages. The division of marriages into two rigid categories on the basis of a limited sample illustrates one of the problems that arise from creating a system out of the Homeric references alone: the danger of equating literary topos with legal category. The many references from the ancient Near East show that the connection between uxorilocal marriage and the absence of "bride-price" is legally speaking fortuitous. It is obviously more likely to occur in such a marriage, where the groom tends to be poorer and his father-in-law is more interested in his services. It is a favorite topos of heroic stories, but even there the absence of "bride-price" is more apparent than real. When Saul offers his daughter in marriage to David, he informs him: "the king has no desire for 'bride-price' (*mōhar*) but for a hundred foreskins of the Philistines, to have revenge on the king's enemies," i.e., a deed of heroism (1 Sam 18:25). David obliges and duly takes up residence in Saul's palace with his bride. Some years

Dowry is not designated by a technical term; instead words for gift are used (*meilia, doron*), with the context revealing that the gift in question was a dowry, namely that the bride's father is giving it to the groom. The father is said to give it either directly to the groom (*Il.* 6.191-193; *Od.* 7.311-315; cf. *Hymn to Aphrodite* 139-140) or indirectly through his daughter (*Il.* 9.147-148; 22.51), hence the epithet *alochos poludoros* for Penelope (*Od.* 24.294; and for Andromache: *Il.* 6.394). The dowry is subsumed into the husband's assets and is used by him. A clear example is Priam's decision to ransom two sons of his who have been captured: "We will certainly ransom them with bronze and gold, for there is much of that in my house; for many gifts did the old Altes, of glorious name, give to his daughter" (*Il.* 22.51). Priam's policy is to limit the amount available for ransom to the value of the son's mother's dowry (a sensible approach, given the number of wives and sons that he has). The funds, however, are in his possession. The first person plural verb could refer to Priam and his wife jointly but could equally be unspecific or (the most likely hypothesis) refer to Priam and Hector, whom Priam is addressing at that moment. There is no evidence as to the devolution of the dowry after termination of the marriage.

Penelope and Marital Property

There are two passages where the term *hedna* is used regarding Penelope, on the contingency of her returning to her father's house and the latter giving her in marriage to one of the suitors. In *Od.* 1.276-278 (= 2.196-197) it is stated:

---

later, however, when he is embroiled in civil war with Saul's son, he is able successfully to claim that the latter hand over to him "my wife . . . whom I betrothed for a hundred foreskins of the Philistines" (2 Sam 3:14). David's heroic deed thus had the legal effect of a "bride-price." Closer examination of the examples in Homer show that where the term "without 'bride-price'" is used, there is in fact a *quid pro quo*: Othryoneus offers Priam military service in exchange for Cassandra (*Il.* 13.363-382), and Agamemnon makes his offer to Achilles in anticipation of the same (*Il.* 9.144-148). Nor would the latter arrangement appear in any case to be uxorilocal.

Let her go back to the hall of her powerful father, and there they will prepare a wedding feast and make ready the gifts (ἄρτυνέουσιν ἔεδνα) in their abundance, all that should go with a beloved daughter.[17]

According to *Od.* 2.52-54:

They (the suitors) shrink from going to the house of her father, Icarius, that he may himself see to his daughter's bride-gifts (*eed-nosaito*), and give her to whom he will.

The possibility that in the context the term should be interpreted as dowry, or at least as a gift from the bride's father to the groom (as Murray's translation suggests), has led to a lively debate on the nature of marital gifts.

According to Finley, *hedna* was a general term for gifts accompanying marriage in either direction. The system was one of gift-exchange, in which the groom's gifts to the girl's father were intended to provoke a counter-gift commensurate in value, together with the girl herself.[18] Snodgrass rejects Finley's schema, pointing out that there are no cases in Homer (with one dubious exception) of parity between the groom's gifts and the bride's father's gifts that would suggest gift-exchange. Instead, there are at least two forms of marital gift, bride-price and dowry. Anthropological evidence adduced by Snodgrass shows that their coexistence in the same legal system is unlikely. His conclusion is that Homer does not present a coherent system but describes a mixture of practices, derived from a diversity of historical sources.[19]

Against Snodgrass, Morris argues that the marriage practices described by Homer are consistent, but he reaches this conclusion only by denying the existence of dowry altogether in Homeric society. In his analysis, *hedna* are in all cases gifts from the groom; *dora* are gifts exchanged in

---

17 Unless otherwise stated, the English translation of all passages cited from the *Iliad* and the *Odyssey* is that of Murray (revised by Wyatt and Dimock, respectively), *Loeb Classical Library*, 1995.

18 Finley 1955.

19 Snodgrass 1988.

both directions, a distribution apparently found also among the Trobriand Islanders.[20]

From the Near Eastern perspective, a debate centered on reservations about the compatibility of "bride-price" and dowry is bemusing. A typical marriage involved both, not to mention the possibility of gifts from other relatives to the bride, from husband to wife, from groom to members of the bride's family—even a settlement by the groom's father on the groom.[21] In marriage negotiations between the rulers of Egypt and Babylonia (14th century), for example, the Babylonian king shamelessly tries to bid up the "bride-price" for his daughter ("If during this summer, in the months of Tammuz or Ab, you send the gold I wrote you about, I will give you my daughter"), while the Pharaoh tries to shame his counterpart by suggesting that he has a mercenary attitude to marriage ("It is a fine thing that you give your daughters in order to acquire a nugget of gold from your neighbors!"). Nonetheless, when the marriage takes place, it is accompanied by a sumptuous dowry, not to mention further gifts from the Egyptian side.[22] There was also a non-binding custom whereby the bride's father would return the "bride-price" to the groom as a supplement to the dowry.[23]

In assuming a contradiction, Finley and Snodgrass confuse the economic and legal aspects of marital gifts. The dowry is a share of the paternal estate and has essentially an economic function: its purpose is to

---

20 Morris 1986. It seems to me that this is an abuse of ethnographic material, pressed into service to support an artificial construct. Morris admits the existence of a trousseau, an archaic version of later *pherne*, but wrongly attributes it to Laothoe in *Il.* 22.51. An archaic form of *pherne* does in fact exist in the poems and is discussed below.

21 If the wife dies childless, dowry and "bride-price" are to be returned to source. The law codes even provide for the one sum to be set off against the other, e.g., LH 164: "If his father-in-law has not returned the 'bride-price' to him, he (the husband) shall deduct the value of her 'bride-price' from her dowry and return her dowry to her father's house. For gifts from relatives, see Renger 1973. For gifts from the husband, see Ezekiel 16. For settlement on the groom, see NBL 8: "A man who gives his daughter to the son of a man and (the latter's) father assigns and gives his son property in his tablet, and the father-in-law assigns the dowry of his daughter and they write tablets in mutual agreement, they shall not alter their tablets."

22 EA 4:36-50; EA 1:61-62; EA 13, 14. Translations in Moran 1992.

23 E.g., CT 48 50:15-20: "A [bride's father] has received 10 shekels of silver, her 'bride-price,' has kissed (it/her?) and bound it in the hem of his daughter B—it has (thus) been returned to C [groom]" (translation from Westbrook 1988b: 122).

help set up a household for the new couple, to maintain the wife during widowhood, and to provide the issue of the marriage with an inheritance. The essential function of the "bride-price," in contrast, is legal: its purpose is to secure the bride against the claims of outsiders. There is no reason for them to be equal in value or to be compared on that basis.

If the "bride-price" has a specific legal function, then it is understandable that it would be described by a dedicated technical term. In the Homeric poems, the term *hedna* in all cases except the two passages under discussion unambiguously describes a payment from the suitor to the bride's father.[24] In the context of the Near Eastern parallels, this fact suggests that *hedna* is indeed a technical legal term, not a vague description of marital gifts going in either direction. In interpreting these two ambiguous passages, therefore, we agree with those scholars who regard *hedna* as a "bride-price" that Penelope's father demanded for her rather than dowry that he gave with her.[25]

There is a further reason for rejecting the notion that Penelope's father was about to dower her. The marriage in question was Penelope's second, and she would already have a dowry from her first marriage. It might well have been acceptable for a widow (or her family) to demand a "bride-price" from her subsequent spouse(s),[26] but it could not be expected of her family that they provide her new husband with what was in practice an inheritance share every time she remarried. Following both the Near Eastern and the later Athenian pattern,[27] we would expect Penelope to take her dowry from her first marriage with her when she left the matrimonial home to enter her second marriage.

Given Penelope's high status and the fact that she is called *poludoros*, we may assume that she brought a substantial dowry into her marriage to Odysseus. We can immediately identify two items.

In the ancient Near East, a small part of the dowry did not follow the normal path described above. Instead, the wife retained control of the

---

24 The term *anaednos* has the same function, indicating that the bride's father foregoes payment of *hedna* from the suitor; see Finley 1955: 182.
25 Perysinakis 1991; Wagner-Hasel 1988.
26 The ancient Near Eastern sources provide no direct evidence on this point. At Elephantine the father of a lady named Miphtahiah receives a bride-price for what appears to be her second marriage. See Porten and Yardeni 1989: 15 *ad* B2.6.
27 See Harrison 1968: 56-57.

property. By the same token, she bore the risk of it perishing, the husband or his heirs having no duty to reimburse her on termination of the marriage. In Rabbinic law it is called *melog*. The same term is found in Ugaritic in 13th century Syria (*mlg*) and in Akkadian at Nuzi, in eastern Mesopotamia, in the 15th century (*mulūgu*).[28] It is clearly also comparable to Athenian *pherne*. The latter, however, seems to have been regarded as something entirely separate from the dowry, a trousseau of purely personal items.[29] In the Near East, it was regarded as a component of the dowry, although sometimes listed separately, and devolved together with the rest of the dowry. Furthermore, it could include any property, even land, although most commonly it consisted of slaves. The personal slaves Dolius and the daughter of Actor, who, we are told, were given to Penelope by her father before she entered Odysseus' house, fit into this category. Penelope's gift of a brooch to Odysseus before his departure may adumbrate further personal wealth from the same source (*Od.* 19.256-257). At the same time, these items could only account for a fraction of her dowry.

The content of the rest of the dowry is bound to remain speculative, in the absence of direct evidence. I suggest, however, that from the logic of its legal context we may deduce the presence of one very substantial asset. A slight hint emerges from the epithet given to Icarius. Although a shadowy figure, who does not appear to be present in Ithaca nor to have any interest in his grandson's welfare, he is described as her greatly powerful father (*Od.* 1.276: *patros mega dunamenoio*). I would postulate that the power in question was political and that the primary asset of the dowry that Icarius gave Odysseus through his daughter Penelope was the kingship of Ithaca.

Odysseus' Kingship

The nature of Odysseus' rule over Ithaca has long been regarded as problematic. He is called a king (*basileus*) and his son Telemachus is acknowledged to have an hereditary right to the throne (*Od.* 1.386-387). Yet even when Odysseus is believed to be dead, Telemachus is unable to

28 See Levine 1968; Westbrook 1994b: 274-75.
29 Harrison 1968: 46-47; cf. Finley 1955: 183.

assume power. The position of Laertes is even stranger. It is not clear why and when he relinquished the throne to Odysseus, nor why he should not return to it in Odysseus' absence. Notwithstanding the emphasis on his old age, he is by no means incompetent to rule: he still manages the estate (*Od.* 16.138-145) and he would be able to address the assembly (*Od.* 4.739-741).

Odysseus' absence has left a power vacuum in Ithaca. In the words of Laertes: "wanton and reckless men now possess it" (*Od.* 24.282). These are the suitors, whose behavior Eurymachus in a key passage reveals to have had ulterior motives:

> But he now lies dead who was to blame for everything, namely Antinous; for it was he who set on foot these deeds, not so much through desire or need of the marriage, but with another purpose, that in the land of . . . Ithaca he might be king (*basileuoi*), and might lie in wait for your son and kill him (*Od.* 22.48-53).

Finley described the situation as follows: "The king is dead! The struggle for the throne is open! Not, however, by straight violence; the suitors give Penelope the right to choose Odysseus' successor by choosing her spouse."[30] Therein lies the difficulty, not in the suitors' goal, but in the curious means that they adopt to achieve it. Finley found it strange that such a power should have been placed in the hands of a woman. There is nothing about Penelope, he noted, that could have won her this right as a personal triumph. In the absence of a rational explanation, Finley concluded that Homer is neither clear nor quite consistent about the legal picture.[31]

Halverson, on the other hand, denies that Odysseus had the functions of a king at all. In his view there was no throne, no office of king, indeed no real Ithacan state. It is true that Odysseus is called *basileus*, but "king" is a mistranslation. Odysseus was the leading man of the region, but his position was one of status, not an office, a position based above all on wealth. As others in Ithaca are called *basileus* (in particular two of the suitors, Antinous and Eurymachus), he was merely the greatest *basileus* of

---

30 Finley 1979: 97.
31 Finley 1979: 101-102.

the area. There was therefore no succession struggle; the suitors were con-
tending for Penelope herself and nothing more. At most, acquisition of
Odysseus' wife (and his wealth) would give the successful suitor something of Odysseus' prestige and Eurymachus' statement has to be
interpreted in this light.[32]

Before considering these opposing positions, some remarks are in order on the nature of Homeric kingship, against the Near Eastern
background. First, monarchy was the standard form of government
throughout the ancient Near East, including Anatolia and the eastern Mediterranean. Oligarchies did exist but were rare and were generally regarded
as a more primitive form of government.[33] Secondly, the same term was
applied to any political ruler from a petty chieftain to an emperor.[34]
Thirdly, that term still applied to a ruler when he himself was subordinate
to another ruler. In a world of empires based often on loose vassalage or
spheres of influence, there existed political hierarchies of kings.[35] As the
dispatch of a diplomat from Mari in the 18th century cynically reports:[36]

---

32 Halverson 1986; cf. Drews 1983: 129.

33 For example, among the semi-nomadic Kaskean peoples of Anatolia, whom the Hittites noted as not having kingship (Goetze 1967: 88.). For the biblical narrator, the pre-
monarchic period was a time of anarchy, when "each man did what was right in his
own eyes" (Judg 21:25). Oligarchy was characteristic of local, rather than central,
government.

34 The earliest term, in Sumerian, is LUGAL, literally "big man." It continues to be used as
a logogram in later cuneiform texts in other languages, e.g., Akkadian, Hittite. As an
alternative, the logogram LÚ "man" is sometimes used, in the sense of head of household, the concept of king being of a householder writ large (e.g., Hammurabi is called
"the man of Babylon"). The Akkadian term is *šarru*, Hittite *hassu*, West Semitic *mlk*,
all explicitly made equivalent in lexical lists. In Old Babylonian legal documents,
LUGAL is sometimes used as the logogram for "owner" (Akkadian *bēlu*). The Akkadian term *šarru*, however, is never used to mean private owner.

35 A clear terminological distinction is made between king and mayor (Akkadian
rabiānu, *hazannu*), who was an official within the administrative hierarchy with a limited term of office, albeit head of the local council. The distinction is blurred in a
significant manner in the Amarna Letters (14th century), in correspondence between
the Egyptian ruler and his vassals, the petty kings of Syria-Palestine. He refers to them
as kings, while they often refer to themselves as his mayors (*hazannu*), in an attempt
to suggest that they are a part of the internal Egyptian administration, which is patently
not the case.

36 Dossin 1938: 117.

There is no king who is powerful by himself: ten to fifteen kings follow Hammurabi, the man of Babylon; as many follow Rim-Sin, the man of Larsa; as many follow Ibal-pi-el, the man of Eshnunna; as many Amut-pi-el, the man of Qatna; and twenty kings follow Yarim-Lim, the man of Yamhad.

Thus there is no problem in the existence of other kings (*basileis*) in Ithaca or in two of the suitors, Antinous and Eurymachus, being called kings. They could still be subordinate to king Odysseus.[37] Indeed, a hierarchical structure is the only possible explanation of Eurymachus' claim that Antinous was scheming to become *basileus*, when both Antinous and himself already have that title (22.48-53; 18.64-65). A relationship of overlord and vassal also explains how the remote but powerful Icarius could have had Ithaca, together with its kings, in his gift.[38]

Homeric kingship is conceived of as monarchy: the incumbent rules alone, not as part of an oligarchy, and permanently, not for a limited term of office.[39] His function as a war leader is emphasized, of course, but he also has peacetime functions, which are listed in Agamemnon's offer of territory to Achilles:

And seven well-peopled cities will I give him . . ., and in them dwell men rich in flocks and rich in cattle, men who will honor him with gifts as though he were a god, and beneath his scepter will bring his ordinances to prosperous fulfillment (*Il.* 9.149-156).

37 The poem ends with a solemn oath between the suitors' relatives and Odysseus confirming Odysseus as king for ever (24.482-486, 546). This is the typical pattern of a vassal treaty from the ancient Near East. See e.g., Parpola and Watanabe 1988: *passim.*

38 The *Odyssey* gives no other clues as to what the contemporary audience knew of Icarius. He was certainly not an invention of the poem but must already have existed independently in myth. Later legends about him, which connect him with Sparta or Acarnia, are unreliable. Of the many children that they attribute to him, only Penelope is mentioned in the *Odyssey*, while the later legends fail to include Penelope's sister, Iphthime, who is mentioned in the poem (4.797).

39 Agamemnon's leadership of the Trojan expedition is not relevant, being an ad hoc arrangement necessarily limited in duration and without territory. Agamemnon was, of course, a king in his own right, with his own kingdom.

Behind the poetic hyperbole lie two very prosaic functions of government: the receipt of revenues and the administration of justice. The same two functions are attributed to Odysseus: in 2.230-234 we are informed that he did justice as a sceptered king, and in 23.354-30 he looks forward after his restoration to receiving revenues from the Achaeans. Odysseus' kingship may have been modest, but he had real political authority.

The question remains whether Odysseus' kingship is the true target of the suitors' machinations. Halverson argues that, notwithstanding Eurymachus' statement, the suitors cannot be after the kingship, since (a) they contemplate dividing Odysseus' *oikos* among all 108 of them, and (b) Penelope's marriage entails her departure from the house and thus her separation from Odysseus' estate.[40] Both arguments confuse personal property, Odysseus' *oikos*, with political privileges, Odysseus' kingship. Telemachus expressly distinguishes between them:

> It is no bad thing to be king (*basileuemen*). Straightway one's house grows rich and oneself is held in greater honor. However, there are other kings of the Achaeans in plenty in seagirt Ithaca, both young and old. One of these, it may chance, will have this honor, since noble Odysseus is dead. But I will be lord (*anax*) of our own house and of the slaves that noble Odysseus plundered for me (*Od.* 1.392-398).

Eurymachus makes the same distinction:

> Telemachus, this matter surely lies on the knees of the gods, who of the Achaeans shall be king (*basileusei*) in seagirt Ithaca; but as for your possessions (*ktemata*), keep them yourself, and be lord (*anassois*) in your own house (*Od.* 1.400-402).

In the same way, when Odysseus in Hades asks after his property, the answer he receives distinguishes between his lands (*temenea*), which Telemachus holds unchallenged, and his *geras*, which no one has (*Od.* 11.174-185). *Geras* in Homer is an entitlement: a benefit received as one's due either by way of reward for services rendered or by reason of one's

---

40   Halverson 1986: 122-23.

position or status. The distinction is thrown into relief by Achilles' bitter criticism of Agamemnon (*Il.* 1.158-168). Whenever the Achaeans sack a city, Achilles receives as a reward for fighting in the battle a small share of the booty, whereas Agamemnon receives a much larger share, simply by reason of being the leader of the expedition. Both shares are called *geras*. Other examples of a reward are the command of the Trojan armies, which Achilles mockingly suggests that Aeneas hopes to receive from Priam in return for slaying him (*Il.* 20.178-183), and the payment expected by a bath attendant (*Od.* 20.296-298). Entitlements arising from status or office are, for example, offerings to the gods (*Il.* 4.49) or the portion of meat due to a king (*Od.* 4.65-66). When Odysseus wishes for the nobles dining at Alcinous' court that each may hand down to his children his property (*ktemata*) and the *geras* that the people have given him (*Od.* 7.149-150), the former must refer to their personal estates and the latter to the feudal dues that they receive by virtue of their status. Accordingly, I interpret the *geras* in our passage simply as Odysseus' royal revenues.[41] He had expected Laertes and Telemachus to receive them on his behalf, but evidently they have been in abeyance since his departure.

The fate of the kingship is not therefore dependent upon the fate of Odysseus' personal estate. Failure to obtain Odysseus' personal estate would not prevent a suitor from exercising kingship from his own estate. Nevertheless, if the kingship were heritable in the same way as the *oikos*, we would expect whoever acquires Odysseus' *oikos* at the same time to acquire his kingship. Marriage to Penelope would be an irrelevancy. As Halverson points out, a departing widow would not take with her her late husband's estate, to which she had no inheritance claim.[42] She would, however, take with her her dowry. For this reason I consider that the dowry, rather than the line of male succession, was the source of Odysseus' kingship.

The transfer of political power through the medium of a dowry is attested both in ancient Near Eastern and Homeric sources. The Bible

---

41 Wagner-Hasel similarly interprets *geras* in this context as a material privilege, the right to receive honorific gifts and to exploit labor for work on the *temenos*, like the *time* of which Bellerophon received a share (1988: 54-55). See below for her reasons for drawing this analogy.

42 Halverson 1986: 122.

contains a striking example: in 1 Kgs 9:16 we are told that when king Solomon married an Egyptian princess, the Pharaoh captured the city of Gezer and gave it as a dowry to his daughter. In the same way, Agamemnon offers seven cities as the main part of a munificent dowry that is to accompany whichever of his three daughters Achilles chooses to take in marriage (*Il.* 9.147-156).[43] A slightly different but equally cogent example is where Bellerophon marries the daughter of the Lycian king, who shares half the *time* of his kingship with him (*Il.* 6.191-194). *Time* cannot be honor in the abstract here; as Wagner-Hasel points out, it must refer to material privileges. The offer in this case is not separate territory, but co-regency.[44]

The Devolution of Penelope's Dowry

In both ancient Near Eastern sources and later Athenian law, we have seen the same general pattern of devolution of a dowry. It is subsumed into the husband's assets; it resurfaces on his death; if the widow remarries the process is repeated; on the wife's death (or her husband's, if later) it is inherited by her children from both marriages. If we place Odysseus' kingship in the context of that pattern, a coherent picture emerges of the events on Ithaca and the actions and motivations of the principal protagonists.

The first question to be resolved is the curious position of Odysseus' father and son, neither of whom seems able to exercise kingship in his absence. Finkelberg explains their lack of a role—and the dependence of the kingship on marriage to Penelope—by positing an ancient tradition of dynastic succession through the female line, from mother to daughter. In each generation the only way a man can become king is by marrying the incumbent queen's daughter. The incumbent king's son can never qualify as his father's successor for reasons of incest. This would disqualify both

---

43 Murray's translation (see n. 17 above)—"And seven cities will I give him"—might give the impression that this was a separate gift offered directly to Achilles, but there is in fact no (dative) pronoun in the Greek. The passage immediately follows (linked by *de*, not *kai*) the offer of dowry at large (lines 147-148). Of course, the dowry will pass into Achilles' possession on marriage.

44 Wagner-Hasel 1988: 54-55.

Laertes and Telemachus.[45] Unfortunately, Finkelberg's logic is not supported by the text, which explicitly concedes to Telemachus at least a hereditary right to the kingship (*Od.* 1.386-387). There is in any case no need to presume the existence, or survival, of some anomalous, otherwise unattested system of succession alongside agnatic inheritance. The attested rules of dowry permit a different approach, which differentiates between the status of Laertes and that of Telemachus.[46]

If Odysseus had received the kingship of Ithaca as dowry from Penelope's father, then the inaction of Laertes is simply explained. Laertes cannot exercise kingship. He has no claim to reoccupy the throne, because he never was king. Laertes states that he once acted as lord (*anasson*) of the Cephallenians (*Od.* 24.375-378), but it is clear that he was only a military commander on that occasion.[47] *Anax* is a more flexible term than *basileus*, covering everything from a king to the owner of a dog (*Od.* 10.216, cf. 9.440). Elsewhere, Laertes is referred to as having been one of the elders (*Od.* 21.20), which would exclude a higher office.

Laertes was thus a military commander and a high-ranking member of society, but not a king. There are many references to him being wealthy (*Od.* 1.430; 15.483; 24.137; 24.206-207). His son Odysseus was also a military commander and gained great wealth in terms of herds of animals (*Od.* 14.96-108). Part of his wealth derived from booty, as Odysseus himself states: "Thus my house (*oikos*) at once grew rich" (*Od.* 14.230-234). Telemachus refers to the slaves that Odysseus plundered for him (*Od.* 1.398). The potential sources for the rest of Odysseus' personal property were capitalized revenues from his kingship and his father's estate. Since Laertes appears to have only one farm remaining from his great wealth (*Od.* 24.206-207), it is reasonable to presume that he had transferred the

---

45   Finkelberg 1991: 307.

46   Postulating the remnants of an archaic matrilineal succession creates almost as many problems as it resolves. Finkelberg constructs a highly complex schema for heroic sources outside of Homer, involving a kingship by marriage rotating among patrilineal clans. Discussion of her system is beyond the scope of this article, but it might be worth investigating whether dowry could provide a solution to some of the cases she presents.

47   Cf. *Il.* 20.180-182: Achilles mocks Aeneas for hoping that by killing Achilles he will become *anax* of the Trojans: Priam will never grant him that privilege (*geras*), since the latter has sons and is not stupid. See also Wender 1978: 53-54.

residue to his son *inter vivos* (cf. *Od.* 24.337-344).[48] We are informed that Laertes was still overseeing the work on Odysseus' farmland in his absence (*Od.* 16.138-145), but apparently he had left the house to Penelope's management while Telemachus was still a child.

The role of Telemachus is more complex. Initially, his age holds the key to his position. Homeric kingship was based upon two conditions: strength and legitimacy. The former is exemplified by military leadership, often, as Finley points out, associated with the term *iphi* ("by force").[49] The second derives from rightful succession, symbolized by the scepter.[50] Odysseus had fulfilled the first condition by being a hero and military leader and the second from possession of his wife's dowry as husband and head of household.[51] Telemachus fulfilled the condition of legitimacy, as Antinous expressly acknowledges: "which thing (kingship) is by birth your heritage (*patroion*)" (*Od.* 1.386-387). Use of the term *patroion* might suggest that it was inherited from his father, but the term is used in the *Odyssey* in a general sense of property to which one is entitled (and may pass on to one's own issue), not in the strict sense of an inheritance from the father, as opposed to one from the mother. *Od.* 17.79-80 shows that it can include property acquired other than by inheritance, i.e., the gifts that Telemachus received from Menelaus. As will be seen below, a better explanation of the unfolding events is legitimacy based on Telemachus being heir to the kingship through his mother Penelope. Nonetheless, being a child, Telemachus could not yet fulfill the other condition, however legitimate his claim to the throne.

---

48   This is a well-known procedure in the ancient Near East, if rare, for obvious practical reasons. One has only to think of the case of the Prodigal Son in the New Testament. More frequent is the assignment of an irrevocably fixed inheritance share, with actual possession postponed until after the testator's death.

49   Finley 1979: 96.

50   Cf. Agammemnon, *Il.* 2.100-108; Achilles, *Il.* 9.155-156.

51   In the false autobiography he gives to Eumaeus, Odysseus hints at his true situation: his own ancestry, not being the direct line of succession, got him only a small portion of land and a dwelling. "But I took to me a wife from a house that had wide possessions, winning her by my valor: for I was no weakling, nor a coward in battle" (*Od.* 14.199-212). At the end of the poem, Zeus reestablishes Odysseus' kingship on a new basis: an oath of loyalty sworn to him by the nobles (*Od.* 24.482-486, 546-547). This constitutional practice also has strong ancient Near Eastern parallels: see n. 35 above.

In Odysseus' absence, any one of the suitors might be able to seize the throne by force, but he would then be faced with 107 powerful opponents, each with an equal claim. To settle the matter among themselves, the suitors had to resolve the question of legitimacy. Their plan was as follows. Telemachus was heir to Odysseus' personal fortune and to the kingship through his mother, Penelope. He was, however, still a child. If a suitor married Penelope, he would become head of that household and would be entitled to control of her dowry, i.e., the kingship. Penelope's dowry was in theory heritable by her heirs, namely Telemachus and any issue of her second marriage with the successful suitor, but only on the death of the second husband (not of Penelope if she predeceased him). Furthermore, unlike an ordinary estate, kingship was indivisible—only one son could inherit it.[52] Consequently, the suitor who married Penelope would have a good chance of excluding Telemachus in his own lifetime and thereafter in favor of his own son. Telemachus would inherit only his father's personal assets.

This is the suitors' plan—summarized by Telemachus himself when he wryly notes that the suitors are eager, and Eurymachus most of all, to marry Penelope and so acquire the *geras* of Odysseus (*Od.* 15.518-522). Wagner-Hasel notes the importance of this passage in showing that the transfer of *geras* must involve the female line. She considers, however, only two possibilities. The first is that it was inheritable through the female line, which she rightly rejects. The second is that Odysseus' marriage must have been uxorilocal, as in the case of Bellerophon, creating a quasi-familial relationship that enabled Odysseus to share in the privileges of the host household.[53] There is no indication whatsoever that Odysseus' marriage was uxorilocal nor, in my view, would it make the slightest difference if it were. Bellerophon was not absorbed into the privileges of his father-in-law's household in some mysterious way; he was assigned a

---

52 The co-regency of Bellerophon and his father-in-law is an exception made possible by their belonging to different generations. Bellerophon will ultimately succeed to the old king's throne anyway. Telemachus and the suitors, in spite of differences in age, belong to the same generation. They can only be rivals. In the ancient Near East, co-regency is not attested, except possibly between Amenhotep III and Amenhotep IV (Akhenaten), i.e., father and son. Division between brothers meant division of the territory into two kingdoms.

53 Wagner-Hasel 1988: 56-58.

discrete share, exactly in the manner of a dowry. *A fortiori* Odysseus on Ithaca, his homeland.

When the poem opens, the plan is in disarray. The suitors have two problems. First, Penelope by her deception over Laertes' shroud has successfully stalled them for three years. The suitors are attempting to counter her delaying tactics by devouring her son's inheritance—Odysseus' personal estate—thereby forcing her hand.

Secondly, Telemachus has reached manhood. He asserts himself before the suitors, ostensibly about their depredation of his personal estate, but all understand the implications for the kingship, hence Antinous' furious reaction:

> May the son of Cronos never make you king in seagirt Ithaca,
> which thing is by birth your heritage (*Od.* 1.386-387).

Antinous makes clear that Telemachus lacks the necessary strength for kingship, at which point Telemachus retreats, ceding his right to the kingship and asserting his claim only to the paternal estate (*Od.* 1.392-398).

Telemachus' concession, however, turns out to lack credibility. For even if he excludes himself from the kingship, he remains able and willing to bar others from it, as long as Penelope refuses to marry and he allows her to stay in the house in which he is now head of household. The suitors' new tactic is therefore to separate Penelope from Telemachus. She must be persuaded to leave his house, taking her dowry, the kingship, with her.

Penelope, however, refuses to leave, a right accorded to a woman in her situation by both Near Eastern and Athenian law.[54] Telemachus, for his part, refuses to send her away. His excuse is that he would suffer a penalty payable to Icarius, divine wrath, and general censure, if he were to send her away against her will (*Od.* 2.132-137).[55] From the suitors' viewpoint, it

---

54 MacDowell 1978: 88-89; LH 172: "If her sons harass her (the widow) to make her leave the house, the judges shall investigate her case and impose a penalty on the sons; the woman shall not leave her husband's house."

55 As Wagner-Hasel points out, the sum payable is a penalty, not return of the dowry (1988: 45). The dowry would be returnable even if she left of her own free will. In LH 172 (see n. 54 above) the court imposes a penalty on sons who try to drive out their widowed mother; if she leaves of her own accord, however, she takes only her dowry with her.

looks like collusion between mother and son. For their mutual refusal once more gains time, which Telemachus could use to garner military support in order to end the occupation of his house.[56]

Such is the state of affairs when Odysseus makes inquiry of his mother in Hades (*Od.* 11.174-196). While purporting to ask about each of his family in turn—his mother, Laertes, Telemachus, and Penelope—Odysseus alludes to the political situation in Ithaca. He first posits two alternative scenarios:

a) His *geras* (which I have interpreted as his royal right to revenues) is still with Laertes and Telemachus. Their joint role does not presume political power; quite the contrary. The two together can only be acting as his representatives to receive or collect the revenues due, on the basis that his absence is temporary.[57] They would not be able to perform the other main peacetime role of a king—dispensing justice—on his behalf.

b) A stranger has his geras, because he has been given up for dead. Odysseus does not explain how a stranger, not acting as his representative, could have access to the royal revenues, without usurping his throne or Telemachus' right to it.

The process that he assumes, however, emerges from the second set of alternatives that he posits. Ostensibly concerning Penelope's marriage, they might be taken as regarding her personal status alone. In my view, however, they merely repeat the first set of alternatives as to the political situation, from the point of view of Penelope. Odysseus posits that:

i) Penelope remains head of household in his absence, and guardian of Telemachus. The assumption is that Odysseus' return is expected and the implication is that his throne is safe.

---

56 He has two potential sources of support against the nobles: from the populace and from abroad (*Od.* 2.60-79, 314-317). His first attempt to garner support in the assembly is a failure—he does not even get a ship and crew in order to seek news of his father: *Od.* 2.1-257. Nonetheless, the threat to the suitors remains, particularly when they learn that he has assembled a crew after all.

57 Collecting debts for the government may have been a typical task allotted to a callow youth on his way to manhood: cf. Odysseus' mission in *Od.* 21.16-21.

ii) Penelope has remarried. The new spouse would become head
of household and thus be entitled to the royal revenues,
through her dowry. Telemachus' ultimate right to the throne
would not necessarily be excluded, because he is still
Penelope's first heir.

Odysseus' questions thus reveal a naive optimism about the constitutional machinery of Ithaca. He supposes that Penelope's second husband
will play the role of regent accorded to him by possession of her dowry,
taking its income without prejudice to Telemachus' prospects of succession. He could not be expected to guess that a far uglier situation has
developed, an oligarchic conspiracy to usurp the throne that will give the
usurper the power to exclude Telemachus altogether. Nor does his
mother's answer tell him the full truth, although it drops strong hints that
all is not well. His mother answers his questions chiastically, dealing with
each member of the family in turn: Penelope, Telemachus, Laertes, his
mother. She reveals that:

a) Penelope remains loyal to him and unmarried. This good news
should mean that his throne is safe.
b) No one has his *geras*. Here is an unexpected turn of events
which hints at anarchy.
c) Penelope is no longer head of household, because Telemachus
has reached manhood. He holds Odysseus' estate (*temenea*)
unchallenged (*hekelos*), which is strictly speaking the truth,
since the suitors have publicly conceded his right to inherit
Odysseus' personal property, while consuming his inheritance.
It implies that he is not so secure elsewhere, in particular in the
matter of *geras*.
d) Laertes has withdrawn from public life altogether.

Faced with this impasse, the suitors decide once more to change their
tactics. With some hesitation, they agree upon a more drastic step—the
assassination of Telemachus. Although an unlawful act, it will not
delegitimize their bid for the throne, since they regard legitimacy as a
matter between themselves, not relevant vis-à-vis an outsider to their

group.[58] Their first attempt proves unsuccessful, but it achieves the desired result. Penelope finally gives in to their demands and agrees in principle to marry one of them. Her motive is to save Telemachus' life, by removing him as a bar and potential rival for the kingship.[59]

Summary

Odysseus' kingship is mentioned explicitly only twice in the poem but in a way that frames the whole narrative of events in Ithaca. At the beginning, Telemachus' challenge to the suitors is interpreted as a bid for the kingship, and at the end, Eurymachus, on the point of death, reveals that marriage to Penelope was really a tactic to gain the kingship. In between, there is an indirect allusion when Odysseus inquires whether Laertes and Telemachus have his *geras*, which we have interpreted as royal revenues, and is informed that no one has them. Telemachus, however, reveals his awareness of the suitors' plan when he states that Eurymachus is the most eager to marry his mother and to have the *geras* of Odysseus (*Od.* 15.518-522).[60]

Otherwise, the issue of kingship is not raised. The protagonists give the impression that the suit is entirely about the charms of Penelope. Nonetheless, it is my view that kingship was the hidden agenda behind the struggle for Penelope, which remains the underlying, unspoken assumption

---

58 For this reason also they can contemplate the illegal act of dividing the dead Telemachus' estate among themselves or awarding his house to the winner (by an ironic reversal in one version, as a dowry for Penelope: *Od.* 2.335-336). Nonetheless, some have scruples about killing a legitimate heir to the throne (*Od.* 16.400-401). There is also the fear that if Telemachus tells the assembly of the failed first attempt, he will be able to stir the people to act against them (16.371-386), thus fulfilling the condition of strength that earlier he had failed to meet. Eurymachus falsely denies Penelope's accusations (16.434-447).

59 Penelope engages in one final ruse: to recover some of the losses to Odysseus' personal wealth by beguiling precious gifts from the suitors. It is for this reason that Odysseus, observing her incognito, approves of her action (*Od.* 18.281-283).

60 Ironically, Eurymachus is the only suitor to enjoy any of Penelope's dowry, but it is the wrong part. He seduces Penelope's maid, Melantho, the daughter of her personal slave, Dolius (*Od.* 18.320-325).

of all until Eurymachus finally blurts it out.[61] The reason is that the king-ship of Ithaca was not a direct, automatic consequence of marrying Penelope. Rather, marriage was an essential pre-condition, a gateway to legitimacy that would enable a powerful noble to gain the acceptance of his fellow nobles and to push aside the legitimate but impotent heir to the throne.[62] The rules of dowry were well understood by Homer's contempo-rary audience; there was no need to spell out the implications. Devolution by dowry, however, was less direct and less certain than normal agnatic inheritance. Its vagaries provided convolutions for the plot, opportunities for moves and countermoves that added to its dramatic tension.

---

61   It is noteworthy that Penelope's suitors are frequently described as the suitors "of the glorious queen" (*agakleites basileies*).

62   The order of events in Eurymachus' accusation of Antinous is significant: "that he might rule as king (*basileuoi*), yet might lie in wait for your son and kill him" (*Od.* 22.52-53). Interestingly, Athene urges on Telemachus a similar sequence: if his father is dead, he should marry off his mother and then kill the suitors (1.289-296).

14

The Coherence of the Lex Aquilia

Abstract

A longstanding crux among legal historians has been the thematic relationship between Chapters I, II, and III of the Lex Aquilia. By analyzing the Lex Aquilia against the background of ancient Near Eastern law codes, this article argues that its chapters follow a standard organizational technique found in these codes. Further, the chapters are structured around a single theme: points in time upon which assessments of damages can be based. It was only later that the Lex Aquilia took on the aura of fundamental law on liability for wrongful damage.

Introduction

When in 1816 Niebuhr's discovery of the Gaius palimpsest also brought to light the missing second chapter of the Lex Aquilia, the newly revealed text should have laid to rest centuries of speculation and argument.[1] It did not. For, contrary to all expectations, the second chapter as summarized by Gaius did not form a bridge between the killing of Chapter I and the wounding of Chapter III; it dealt with a totally unrelated topic, the fraudulent *adstipulator*.[2]

---

* Originally published in *Revue Internationale des Droits de l'Antiquité* 42 (1995): 437-71. Used by permission.

1 An earlier version of this paper was presented in Oxford to the 1993 meeting of the Société Internationale de l'Histoire des Droits de l'Antiquité (SIHDA). It was read in manuscript by Professor P. Birks and Dr. A. Wygant, for whose comments and criticisms I am grateful. Responsibility for the content rests as usual with the author.

2 For a review of earlier theories as to the content of Chapter II, see Cannata 1994: 151-52.

Speculation as to the relationship between the three parts of this law has therefore continued. According to Daube, their order is the result of an historical accident.[3] The law originally consisted of the first two chapters only, on different topics. When the third was added to supplement the first, the text of the existing law was already too familiar and too fixed, in inscription or in people's minds, for the new chapter to be inserted between its members, and it was therefore tacked on the end. Daube cannot adduce examples of this process, although he applies his reasoning elsewhere, to explain the apparently curious order of the laws in a number of biblical passages.[4]

In fact, there exists one example not mentioned by Daube which would seem to support the feasibility of his hypothesis. In the Great Code of Gortyn, the provisions are organized by topic, but at the end there are two sets of supplementary provisions, the first being independent and the second relating to various rules already formulated in the main body of the text.[5] The reason for this order would appear obvious: the Code being inscribed on a stone wall, it was not physically possible to insert later provisions in their logical place among the earlier ones. The supplementary provisions, however, are separated from their earlier counterparts by a great deal of text; the third chapter of the Lex Aquilia by but a single short provision. A change of order would not therefore meet any comparable practical obstacle. Daube surmises that the first two paragraphs constituted only a small fraction of the earlier statute from which they were taken to form the present version through the addition of a third.[6] In those circumstances, however, the problem of rearranging an existing text carved on stone no longer applies.

The underlying difficulty with Daube's thesis is that, while it seeks to provide a plausible explanation for the separation of Chapters I and III, it

---

3 Daube 1936: 266-68; 1948: 154-56; and 1947: 74-85.
4 Daube 1947: 85-98. In our view, the order of the biblical examples yields to a far different explanation. See the discussion of the organization of ancient Near Eastern law codes below (under "The Background to the Lex"). As regards the theft laws of Exod 21:37–22:3, discussed by Daube (1947: 91-95), we have offered an entirely different interpretation; see Westbrook 1988d: 111-28.
5 Col. IX 24–Col. X 32 and Col. XI 24–Col. XII 19, respectively. Edition in Willets 1967.
6 Daube 1947: 84-85.

fails to account in any way for the connection between Chapters I and II. Daube can only suggest the model of a *lex satura*,[7] a statute comprising miscellaneous reforms—which begs the question why these two provisions, unrelated in substance, should have been thrown together, and in such intimacy that they could not then be parted by a provision with a better claim.

The difficulty is equally acute in Pringsheim's proposal, which claims to see in our textual witnesses the traces of a highly systematic process of historical evolution.[8] Pringsheim suggested that the law passed through no less than six stages of amendments by successive legislators. Chapter I was first followed by a new statute, Chapter II, and then by four other enactments, which were ultimately combined to form Chapter III: i) wounding slaves and fourfooted *pecudes*, ii) killing and wounding fourfooted animals who are not *pecudes*, iii) killing and wounding other animals, iv) damage to inanimate objects. While many objections could be made to his treatment of Chapter III, such as its failure to distinguish between legislation and juristic interpretation, at least it may be said that the stages represented by Chapters I and III follow a logical pattern of expansion. Not so the insertion of Chapter II as stage two, which as Pringsheim admitted is "rather odd."[9] His explanation, that it is easier to understand on the assumption that there were six independent enactments, of which it formed one, effectively undermines his own logic, since it abandons the idea of rational expansion on which his division of Chapter III into chronological steps depends.

In this regard Pugsley is more consistent. He takes the model of the *lex satura* to extremes, denying a connection between any of the three chapters.[10] Again, we are not concerned with his interpretation of Chapter III (although it does depend on an approach that we regard as methodologically unacceptable, namely emendation of the text on the basis of the author's theory rather than of independent criteria). Our objection is to the assumption, common to all these three authors, that because the organization of the Lex Aquilia is not immediately apparent, it did not exist. Given

7 Daube 1936: 267-68.
8 Pringsheim 1959.
9 Pringsheim 1959: 238.
10 Pugsley 1969b.

the amount of effort that has been expended by modern scholars to arrange the fragments of the XII Tables in a rational order, it is remarkable how readily the opposite has been assumed for the Lex Aquilia, whose order is known to us and was regarded as fixed by the Roman jurists themselves.

The Text

It is of course impossible to reconstruct the original text itself from our present sources, not least because the language in them has undergone a process of modernization.[11] The best we can hope to attain is its most faithful representation in the extant sources, by relying on the most direct textual witnesses.[12]

Chapter I presents the least difficulty, since it is reproduced in similar versions in Gaius' Institutes and in the Digest, where Gaius is purported to quote the text directly:

> D. 9.2.2 pr. (*Gaius ad edictum provinciale*): *<si quis>*[a] *servum servamve alienum alienamve quadrupedem vel pecudem iniuria occiderit, quanti id in eo anno plurimi fuit, tantum aes dare domino damnas esto.*

> [a] Gaius *Inst.* III 210: *«ut qui»*.

For Chapter II we have only a paraphrase by Gaius, which will have to serve as our text:

> Gaius *Inst.* III 215: *Capite secundo <adversus> adstipulatorem qui pecuniam in fraudem stipulatoris acceptam fecerit, quanti ea res est, tanti actio constituitur.*

---

11 For example the term *eras* has been replaced by *dominus*: *Dig.* 9.2. 11.6. Attempts at reconstruction inevitably rely on substitution of the author's words for those of the extant sources. See Kelly 1964: 73-83; and 1971: 235-41.

12 Cf. the remarks of Crook (1984: 67-77) and his proposed text for Chapters I and III.

Chapter III exists in several conflicting versions, but only *D*. 9.2.27.5 purports to be a direct quotation by Ulpian of the whole text:[13]

> *D*. 9.2.27.5 (*Ulpianus ad edictum*): «   »[a] *si quis alteri damnum faxit quod usserit fregerit ruperit iniuria, quanti ea res erit in diebus triginta proximis, tantum aes domino dare damnas esto.*

> [a] *ceterarum rerum praeter hominem et pecudem occisos*

Following Lenel, we have omitted the opening clause.[14] The phrase *praeter hominem et pecudem occisos* has long been regarded as suspect, not least because it is ungrammatical.[15]

Lenel rejected *ceterarum rerum* on the grounds that "other things" could not refer hack to Chapter II, since it concerned a debt, not a thing. Honoré, however, regards these words as genuine, referring not to things other than slaves and animals but to "matters other than those comprised under the first two chapters of the statute."[16] In the absence of a substantive link between Chapter I and Chapter II, however, the phrase is meaningless. Any provision would be bound to deal with "other matters" than the first two chapters because they deal with entirely different matters themselves. It only makes sense on the assumption either that Chapter II has been omitted, which was of course the situation in Justinian's day, or at least is to be disregarded, which seems to have been the attitude of Gaius.[17]

---

13 Gaius *Inst.* III 217-218 and Justinian *Inst.* 4.13.14 are paraphrases.

14 Lenel 1922.

15 See already Pernice 1867: 14. For a summary of the arguments, see Honoré 1972: 138-41.

16 Honoré 1972: 141-45.

17 Gaius states: "*Capite tertio de omni cetero damno cavetur*" (*Inst.* III 217), but fails to give other examples of loss by fraud, even though this sentence immediately follows his discussion of Chapter II. His examples are all extensions of the principle in Chapter 1 (on *damnum* = "loss," see Daube 1948: 93-156).

As evidence for the antiquity of the phrase, Honoré adduces *Dig*. 21.1.42, citing the aedilician edict *de feris*. The edict contained two specific provisions, dealing with killing and wounding a free man, followed by a residuary clause introduced by *ceterarum rerum* dealing with all other cases (Honoré 1972: 144). It may equally well be argued, however, that this edict provided the compilers with the model for interpolat-

The special feature of this version is the verb *erit*; G. III 218 has *fuerit* and *D.* 9.2.29.8 (Ulpian) has *fuit.* Although the latter two represent the classical jurists' understanding that damages were to be assessed by reference to the preceding thirty days, the form *erit* is still to be preferred, without reference to the content of the clause,[18] because it is both a direct quotation and the *lectio difficilior.* It would have been unthinkable to a jurist in Ulpian's day or subsequently that the third chapter could refer to a future period of time. At the same time, the discussion among classical jurists of Sabinus' proposal to imply the term "highest" in the third chapter and their attempt to justify it by an historical fiction reveals a certain disquiet which may point to an innovative interpretation, changing the direction of the clause, as Daube surmised.[19]

Nonetheless, Ankum argues that the word *erit* is no more than a scribal error in the manuscript that now constitutes our primary witness.[20] His grounds are threefold. Firstly, he points out that while the passage in Gaius' Institutes is admittedly a paraphrase, *D.* 9.2.29.8, containing *fuit,* purports to be a direct quotation of Ulpian no less than in the passage under discussion.[21] They are not *pari passu,* however. Our passage cites the whole law; 29.8 only the offensive clause—in the context of Sabinus' tendentious interpretation! It should be added for good measure that the exact same limitations, i.e., discussion of the one clause and acceptance of Sabinus' interpretation, characterize Gaius' paraphrase in III 218.

Secondly, Ankum argues that it is *fuit* or *fuerit* that should be regarded as the *lectio difficilior,* since the phrase *quanti ea res erit* is far more common in the Digest and the scribe was therefore likely to write *erit* in

---

ing the phrase in 9.2.27.5, since "other cases" is obviously restricted to other cases of damage by wild beasts kept contrary to the edict. It is thus parallel to a Lex Aquilia untrammeled by an intervening provision on an entirely different matter. The question is not whether the compilers invented the phrase but how it is used in the particular context. This distinction applies *a fortiori* to the other examples of *ceterarum rerum* adduced by Nörr 1986: 213-16, which are not genitives of respect.

18 The theory that the law originally referred to the next thirty days, propounded by Daube (1936), has been the subject of much debate. See Ankum 1983: 172-80, for a summary of the copious literature.

19 Daube 1936: 262-63.

20 Ankum 1983.

21 Ankum 1983: 178.

error instead of *fuit*, rather than the other way round.[22] The term *lectio difficilior* used in this way is a misnomer. Properly speaking, it indicates a writing against the accepted meaning of the passage, which *erit* clearly is (and was at all material times: of the Florentine manuscript and of Justinian's and Ulpian's compilations) and *fuit* and *fuerit* are not. Ankum's argument amounts to no more than a possible rationale for scribal error. That possibility is not strong enough to overcome the stringencies of the *lectio difficilior*: the phrase *quanti ea res erit* is frequent but not universal, and its use is therefore not inevitable. It does explain, however, how the interpretation of "last thirty days" could have prevailed among the classical jurists in spite of the express wording of the *lex*. It was possible to relate *erit* to the idea of what the facts at the coming trial would prove to be (as regards the highest value in the thirty days preceding the damage), which is the meaning the phrase *quanti ea res erit* has in the *condemnatio* of a classical formulary action,[23] but which is irrelevant to the question of the point in time to which the value should be imputed.[24] The use of such reasoning would account for Gaius' choice of *fuerit* in his paraphrase, namely "the highest it shall turn out to have been in the preceding thirty days."[25]

22   Ankum 1983: 177.
23   As e.g., in Gaius *Inst.* IV 47. See Buckland and Stein 1966: 658.
24   The same reasoning has been used by some scholars to suggest that the phrase originally related to purely procedural matters connected with the trial. Thus Iliffe suggests: "The thirty day period in the third chapter may have referred to the period between the first appearance *in iure* and the second. The parties may have been required to make an *aestimatio* on the first appearance and then have been allowed to prove extra damage when the case was heard by the *iudex*. Alternatively, they may not have needed to do more than, as we should say, 'show cause' on the first appearance" (1958: 503-505). Similarly, for Kelly the thirty days represent "the time within which compensation—on the perfectly simple basis of *quanti ea res erit*—shall be payable" before the judgment debtor became liable to *mantes iniectio* (1971: 239-41). It is not clear to us why procedural provisions that must have been of general application under the *legis actio* should be linked to one particular action. It is certainly not the case with comparable provisions in the Twelve Tables, such as *in ius vocatio*.
25   As Pernice (1867: 15) put it in arguing for Gaius' *fuerit* as the original verb: ". . . und sodann erhielten wir damit den vollkommen sachgemessen Sinn: wieviel die Sache werth gewesen sein wird, d.h. wieviel der Richter finden wird, daß die Sache werth gewesen sei." (It would also account for Gaius' gratuitous use of *fuerit* over *fuit* in his discussion of Chapter I in *Inst.* III 214.)

Ankum's final argument is that the sixth-century Greek translation of
D. 9.2.27.5 in the *Basilica* has the verb in the past tense (ἦν) and the translator therefore had the word *fuit* before him. It should be remembered,
however, that the *lectio difficilior* is no less valid an approach to translations than to original transcriptions. As with ancient copyists, there was a
tendency for ancient translators to harmonize "difficult" words or phrases
in the original with the accepted interpretation of the passage in their day.[26]
For a Byzantine translator of this text, to use the future tense would be to
mistranslate, since the resulting law would have made no sense to him.

The Structure of the Lex

A formal analysis of the text thus established gives rise to two simple ob-
servations. Firstly, it presents two casuistic laws, beginning *si quis*. It does
not necessarily follow, but it is reasonable to suppose that the middle law
originally had a similar form, at least casuistic, if perhaps beginning *si adstipulator*, rather than *si quis*.[27]

Secondly, there is one feature that all three laws have in common,
namely a clause beginning *quanti*. In the successive clauses, however, the

---

26 See e.g., Barthélemy (1979: IX): "When a text was particularly difficult, there was a
    tendency for ancient scribes and translators to simplify the text by employing more fit-
    ting lexical, grammatical, and stylistic forms (these modifications are often spoken of
    as 'facilitating')." Nörr (1986: 217) suggests that *erit* might have been a mistranslation
    of an archaic Latin verb, especially since archaic Latin lacked precision in dealing
    with *consecutio temporum*. Be that as it may, the *concept* of past, present, and future
    time was certainly not lacking in early Rome, and it is pointless to speculate about the
    ambiguities of a putative Urtext that we do not have, when *consecutio temporium* is
    clearly expressed by the received text that we do have.

27 Cf. the reconstruction of Cannata 1994: 151. Gaius mentions two further provisions of
    the Lex Aquilia, a double penalty against one who denies the accusation (*Dig.* 9.2.2.1,
    Inst. III 216, cf. Ulpian *Dig.* 9.2.23.10 and Paulus *Dig.* 9.2.24) and noxal liability
    (*Inst.* IV 76, cf. Ulpian *Dig.* 9.4.2.1). It is difficult to know what form these provisions
    took, whether separate chapters like the first three or sub-clauses within those chapters
    or suggestive terms in the three chapters that were interpreted as laying down these
    rules. Since both are secondary rules, not special to the Lex Aquilia, the first possibil-
    ity is the least likely. On the insertion of subordinate rules, see n. 36 below.

tense of the respective verbs follows a strict chronological order: *quanti id fuit, quanti ea res est, quanti ea res erit.*

In our view, that sequence is the key to understanding the structure of the Lex Aquilia. The connection between the three laws lies not in their protasis, in the circumstances to which they apply. It lies in the apodosis. The purpose of the apodosis in all three laws is to establish not liability for the wrongs described in the protasis but the point in time upon which assessment of damages is to be based. In the first and third laws, the element of time (and the rationale for the tense of the verb) is clear. Express reference is made to a point in time preceding commission of the wrong (up to a year) and to one following it (thirty days).

In the second law, the element of time is not so evident, since the time of the offence would naturally be the moment at which to assess damages in most laws. It could be of significance only if there were something in the circumstances of the protasis that could give rise to a claim that the time of the offence was *not* appropriate. Given the emphasis on time in the two surrounding laws, it is reasonable to suppose that there was such a claim, and circumstances can be posited to which it would apply. (It should be stressed that we have insufficient information about the nature of the fraud and the loss occasioned by it to establish more than the feasibility of a time-conditioned assessment.) *Adstipulatio* was used to ensure the performance of a promise in the absence, or after the death, of the principal stipulator.[28] Gaius informs us that *acceptilatio* was a sort of imaginary payment (III 169), which means that it could be used for remission of obligations not performed. Thus if *acceptilatio* of an obligation were made by the *adstipulator* before its due date, for example, the question might arise whether damages should be assessed as of the time of the *acceptilatio* or as of the due date.[29]

---

28 G. III 117; see Buckland and Stein 1966: 443-44.

29 This conventional view of *acceptilatio* has been challenged by Lévy-Bruhl, who argued that *acceptilatio* in Chapter II meant receipt of a real payment and that the fraud was therefore nothing more than failure to pay over to the debtor the sum received (1958: 507-17). His reasoning is that the phrase *acceptum facere* "ne décèle aucune idée de fiction. Elle désigne le comportement du créancier qui se déclare satisfait" (1958: 510). The second proposition, however, does not complement the first. The phrase describes the creditor's state of mind, not an objective state of facts. Precisely because it will apply whether the debt has actually been paid or not, it is an

To summarize so far: the Lex Aquilia has a logical structure. Three examples are given of different circumstances which give rise to a different point in time for assessment of damages: prior to the wrong, at the same time as the wrong, and subsequent to the wrong.

The Background to the Lex

To a scholar trained in classical Roman law, the appearance of these three clauses in chronological sequence would seem to be nothing more than coincidence. When placed against the background of ancient Near Eastern law codes, however, it can be seen in an entirely different light.

The nine extant law codes from the ancient Near East, seven preserved in cuneiform script and two found in the Hebrew Bible, show, in both form and content, the marks of a common intellectual tradition.[30] As to form,

---

ideal vehicle for a fictional payment. Cf. Watson, who points out that *acceptum facere* is a technical legal term, which always means "to make an *acceptilatio*" (1991: 196). Real payment is a possibility, it is true, but for the purposes of the *acceptilatio* it is irrelevant. Furthermore, the existence of such a fiction has a clear rationale: it is sometimes expedient for creditors to remit obligations. In the context of *adstipulatio*, the most obvious example of fraud that springs to mind is remission of an obligation in pursuance of a corrupt bargain. This is dismissed by Lévy-Bruhl as "rarissime" (1958: 511), an assessment that we would question, but in any case the validity of legal rules does not depend on statistics, and, however rare, the possibility is a real and present danger of the sort that laws exist to guard against. Failure to pay over the debt to the principal creditor, on the other hand, is fraud not in respect of the *acceptilatio* but of a collateral contract (cf. Cannata 1994: 154). Both aspects will be covered by the classical contract of mandate, but the one that is likely not to have been covered in an earlier period (unless one believes that mandate sprang into existence overnight and fully grown) is the fraud wherein the *adstipulator* acts legally in form but not in substance. It will only be caught by the principles of good faith developed by the jurists of the late Republic.

30 The seven cuneiform codes are: Codex Ur-Namma (Sumerian, 21st century B.C.E.), Codex Lipit-Ishtar (Sumerian, 20th), Codex Eshnunna (Akkadian, 18th), Codex Hammurabi (Akkadian, 18th), Hittite Laws (Hittite 16th–13th), Middle Assyrian Laws (Akkadian, 12th), Neo-Babylonian Laws (Akkadian, 6th). A recent translation of all these codes is to be found in Borger et al. 1982 and Roth 1997. The two Hebrew codes are found inserted into the narrative of the Pentateuch. They are (part of) the "Covenant Code" (Exod 21:1-22:19) and the Deuteronomic Code, which consists of

they all consist of endless lists of individual cases, formulated casuistically, for the most part after the pattern: "if a man does x, the legal
consequence is y."

When first deciphered, the codes were regarded as little more than
random concatenations of such cases, a *satura legum*, but more recent
research has shown them to be endowed with a tight organizational
structure, in which various techniques are used to draw several disparate
examples together so as to mark the parameters of a given theme.
Rhetorical devices include chiasm, progression, and what may be called
"extreme opposites."[31]

A particularly popular form of progression is the chronological sequence. Thus Codex Eshnunna 25-35 discusses the theme of marriage by
culling examples from its various stages: betrothal, marriage, and children,[32] while contractual provisions in Codex Hammurabi 241-272 follow
the rhythm of agricultural work, from planting to harvest.[33] In a sequence
in Deut 20:1-21:9 on the theme of war, four laws deal successively with
the mustering of the army, declaring war, conduct of a siege, and banditry
after the supposed cessation of hostilities.[34] An example brief enough to be
cited in full is furnished by Codex Hammurabi 1-5:

1 If a man accuses a man of murder and does not prove it, his accuser shall be killed.
2 If a man accuses a man of witchcraft and does not prove it, the
   one accused of witchcraft shall go to the river and "leap the
   river." If it overcomes him, his accuser shall take his house; if
   the river clears the man of guilt, the one who accused him of
   witchcraft shall be killed. The one who "leapt the river" shall
   take his accuser's house.

---

provisions scattered through the book of Deuteronomy, with the main concentration in
chapters 15, 21, and 22. The Deuteronomic Code is usually associated with the reign
of king Josiah (7th century), and the Covenant Code is thought to be somewhat earlier,
although not even an approximate date can be assigned with confidence.

31 See esp. Petschow 1965; 1968; and Eichler 1987.
32 Petschow 1968: 137-38.
33 Petschow 1965: 166.
34 Westbrook 1995d: 168-72.

3   If a man comes forward to give false testimony in a lawsuit and does not prove what he said, if it is a capital case that man shall be killed.

4   If he comes forward with evidence concerning barley or silver, he shall bear the penalty of that case.

5   If a judge gives a judgment, renders a decision, and has a sealed document drafted but afterwards changes his judgment: they shall prove that the judge changed the judgment he gave, and he shall pay 12-fold whatever claim is in that case and be expelled from his judge's seat in the assembly. He shall not sit again with the judges in a lawsuit.

The unit discusses the topic of litigation by choosing examples from the three chronological stages of a lawsuit: accusation, testimony, and judgment.

In the sequences discussed so far, the theme linking the individual rules is found in the circumstances to which they apply. The common factor of a group of laws need not, however, be confined to the facts in their protasis. In Exod 21:12-17 we find the following four laws:

12-14   He who strikes a man so that he dies shall be put to death. As for him who did not lie in wait, but God forced his hand, I shall establish for you a place to which he may flee. But if a man plots against his neighbor to kill him with cunning, you shall take him from my altar to die.

15   He who strikes his father or mother shall be put to death.

16   He who steals a man and sells him or in whose hands he is found shall be put to death.

17   He who curses his father or mother shall be put to death.

The only link between these laws is in their legal consequence: they are all cases involving the death penalty.

The tradition exemplified by these scattered examples that we have considered so far was not confined to the Near Eastern codes but appears to have cast its shadow further westward. The Great Code of Gortyn was referred to above as a possible model for Daube's theory of subsequent additions. It also may serve as a model for our thesis, since it not only shares the basic casuistic form of the Near Eastern codes but also shows signs of similar structural patterns.[35] Thus we find the chronological sequence:

Seduction (II 16-20)
Adultery (II 20-45)
Divorce (II 45-III 16)
Widowhood (III 17-37)
Children (III 44-IV 23).

It is interesting to compare a sequence from the Laws of Eshnunna that we have already mentioned:

Seduction/rape of betrothed (§§25-26)
Adultery (§§27-28)
Desertion (§§29-30)
Children (§§32-35).

In both cases, it should be noted that there is a gap in the paragraphs that constitute the sequence. The reason is the same: the chronological sequence is broken by another familiar sequence: that of free/slave (III 37-44 and §31 respectively).[36]

At Rome, the only law of greater antiquity than the Lex Aquilia is (by conventional dating) the Twelve Tables. For the most part, the order in which the individual provisions of the Twelve Tables are arranged in modern editions exists only for the purposes of convenience; it has no claim to historical authenticity. One sequence that could be regarded as authentic is that of the provisions on personal injury now found in VIII 2-4. Although the text given by Gaius in III 223 is not a direct quotation, its accuracy is confirmed by direct quotations of its individual laws by other authors.[37] If the order given by Gaius is correct, then, it follows a familiar pattern in the

---

35 On the structural coherence of the Gortyn code, see Gagarin 1982.
36 Free/slave sequences usually concern the status of the victim, but in the provisions of the Hittite Laws 93-100 we find the sequence: burglary of house, burglary of granary, arson of house, arson of barn, on which is imposed a free/slave sequence concerning the culprit which lays down noxal liability. Noxal liability might possibly have been dealt with in the Lex Aquilia in a similar way. See n. 27 above.
37 E.g., Festus 550.3; Gell. *NA* 20.1.12, 14; Paulus, *Collatio* II 5 5.

Near Eastern codes, namely a list of injuries by body part in the protasis and a (generally) declining severity of penalty in the apodosis, with intervening sub-sequences of free man, slave, as victim.[38]

We have argued elsewhere (on grounds of form and substance, but not of structure) that the Twelve Tables belong to the same scholastic legal tradition as that of the ancient Near Eastern codes.[39] The evidence for the Lex Aquilia also belonging to this tradition seems to us as strong if not stronger. Three laws in casuistic form are organized in a pattern that is not identical to any particular law from the ancient Near Eastern codes, but matches exactly the type of structures in which the latter are organized. Structure is all the more significant because it is purely a product of intellectual effort; it cannot be dismissed as the coincidental recurrence of an everyday legal problem, as is sometimes claimed with regard to similarities of content between laws in different codes.[40]

The Nature of the Lex

The interpretation here proposed for the Lex Aquilia faces an immediate objection in respect of function. It is difficult to believe that a legislative reform, even a technical reform of the assessment of damages, would have been structured in this way. The assembly of three different cases as examples of different means of assessment and their arrangement in a chronological order is more appropriate to an academic discussion than to a statutory enactment.

The reason, in our view, is precisely that: the text of the Lex Aquilia was in origin an academic document. To return to the law codes of the ancient Near East, a series of studies in recent years has shown that they were not, as first assumed, legislation of any sort, but scholarly treatises on the law which were purely descriptive in character. They belong to a wider tradition of Mesopotamian science whereby intellectual inquiry was pur-

---

38 See e.g., Codex Eshnunna 42-47, esp. 42, Codex Hammurabi 196-205, and Hittite Laws 7-9 and 11-16. Cf. Westbrook 1988a: 106-108.

39 Westbrook 1988a.

40 E.g., David 1950: 153-54. Cf. the response of Yaron 1966. The nature of possible connections between similar laws is discussed by Malul 1990: esp. 133-39.

sued by the compilation of lists—lists of legal cases and their resolution, of omens and their meaning, of medical symptoms and their prognosis, of words and grammatical forms.[41]

The casuistic formulation is both characteristic of this genre of literature and marks its limitations. Lacking all-embracing categories, definitions, or any of the analytic tools at our command, Mesopotamian science could only compile endless lists of examples and relied on structure, on its organization of those examples, to give some analytical shape to the discussion. As Eichler concludes with regard to the organization of the paragraphs of Codex Eshnunna, "This structure would rather seem to add further support for placing the Eshnunna law compilation within the orbit of Mesopotamian tradition. The features of the structure suggest a legal textbook, featuring a 'socratic' methodology, designed for the teaching of Mesopotamian legal thought and the appreciation of the complexities of legal situations."[42]

The Lex Aquilia, if it derives from this background, would have begun life as part of a body of learning, a scholastic document or oral tradition. Its classification as a *lex* is a reflection of subsequent events which removed it from its original context and gave it a new role as the basis of the law of wrongful damage. To understand the process involved, we may refer again to the Near Eastern sources, and to the one ancient legal system that continued in use in Hellenistic times.

The Bible, as we have noted, contains two law codes which are based on the tradition of Mesopotamian science, having strong connections in content with earlier cuneiform codes and being cast in its characteristic "scientific" style, the casuistic formulation. They were, therefore, originally independent sources or oral traditions but were incorporated into a historical narrative that attributed their origin to an act of divine legislation in the Sinai desert prior to settlement of the Israelites in the promised land. The process of incorporation is a complex and much disputed problem but

---

41 See our earlier discussion of this question in Westbrook 1988a: 82-97, and further in Westbrook 1989a, with a summary of the opposing views. Two recent studies take up more extreme positions in favor of the legislative character of the codes on the one hand and of their scholastic character on the other: respectively, Leemans 1991: 409-20, and Malul 1990: 105 n. 13.

42 Eichler 1987: 81. See also Westbrook 1995d: 159-63.

must have been complete by the 4th century B.C.E., before the closing of the biblical canon.

The Mishnah is a compilation, committed to writing in the early 3rd century A.D., of the jurisprudence of the Tannaim, Rabbinical jurists who were active from the mid-first century B.C.E. The Mishnah regards the biblical laws as still valid, indeed as holy writ, but its use of them completely transforms their meaning. Casuistic laws applying to very narrow cases are reinterpreted as broad basic statements of the law which they touch upon. From then on the old laws are interpreted as if they were recent, general legislation, often in complete contradiction with their earlier meaning or with an entirely new emphasis. For example, Deut 24:1-4 presents a complicated case of divorce and remarriage:

1 If a man marries a woman and it happens that she finds no favor in his eyes because he found something of unseemliness in her and he writes her a bill of divorce and gives it into her hand and sends her from his house,
2 and she goes forth from his house and goes and becomes the wife of another,
3 and the latter hates her and writes her a bill of divorce and gives it into her hand and sends her from his house, or the latter husband who marries her dies:
4 her first husband cannot take her again as his wife, after she has been made unclean to him . . . .

The purpose of the law is to prevent remarriage by the original husband when there has been an intervening marriage by the wife. The rationale of this prohibition and the exact circumstances to which it applied have been much debated.[43] It is clear, however, that the question of divorce is subsidiary to the main point of the law: the divorce procedure is mentioned in passing, in the recital of circumstances in the protasis; it is not regulated in the apodosis. In the Mishnah and later jurisprudence, on the other hand, this text is taken to be the basic law on divorce as such. Its opening clause, "If a man marries a woman and it happens that she finds

---

43   The literature is summarized by Pressler 1993: 45-62, to which should be added Otto 1991: 290-306.

no favor in his eyes because he found something of unseemliness in her" is interpreted by the Tannaitic jurists as follows (*Giṭṭin* 9.11):

> The School of Shammai say, A man may not divorce his wife un-less he has found in her something improper, as it is said, *because he found something of unseemliness in her*. But the School of Hil-lel say, Even if she spoiled a dish for him, as it is said, *because he found something of unseemliness in her* (i.e., understanding the phrase to mean "unseemliness or something else"). Rabbi Akiba says, Even if he found another more beautiful than she, as it is said, *And it happens that she finds no favor in his eyes*.

The background to this transformation is an intellectual revolution in which ancient Israel was caught up when it became part of the Hellenistic world: the replacement of Mesopotamian scientific thought by Greek phi-losophy.[44] The ability that the latter gave to define terms and create universal categories allowed jurists to create a new legal system, but not *ex nihilo*—rather by placing existing legal material in an entirely different intellectual framework, so as to change in effect its substantive meaning.

The same process was, we suggest, at work at Rome during the late Republic, where the influence of Greek thought is too well known to require demonstration.[45] In the case of the Lex Aquilia, this meant that a

---

44 See Westbrook 1988a: 119-21; and 1989a: 218-22. Daube has demonstrated the reli-ance of Tannaitic jurisprudence on Greek systems of logic in their interpretation of biblical texts (Daube 1992). It is important to understand that our thesis proposes a more fundamental change than does Daube's. Being unaware of the earlier phase rep-resented by Mesopotamian science, Daube assumes that the biblical codes were legislation and that Rabbinical interpretation was merely a more sophisticated version of existing canons of statutory interpretation.

45 For an overview, see Rawson 1989: 448-76. We would draw particular attention to Rawson's discussion of the unconscious infiltration of Greek thought on the one hand (1989: 448-49) and the influence of Greek scientific method on the other: "A Greek treatise on almost any subject, a *techne* or, as the Romans were to say, an *ars* (as both subject and treatise were known) first defines its subject, and then subdivides it, going on to deal separately and in order with the various parts, kinds or aspects. This is a method that goes back through the great philosophers to the sophists, who first taught the Greeks to think and speak in an orderly fashion. In the first century B.C. at Rome Varro treated agriculture on this model, criticizing all his predecessors, including

very specialized rule on the assessment of compensation was elevated to the status of a basic statement on the law of wrongful damage.

The Origins of the Lex

The assumption that the Lex Aquilia was a legislative reform raises the question, what was the object of the reform? Two answers have been proposed.

The first is associated with the date found most frequently in textbooks (albeit with varying degrees of skepticism) for promulgation of the *lex*, namely 287/6 B.C.E.[46] According to Beinart, the law was passed by the *plebs* after their third secession in order to exact reparations from the patricians.[47] Beinart surmises that the secession was attended by disorders, during which plebeians suffered undue attacks on their property at the hands of the patricians. Since it was difficult to prove who had been the author of particular attacks, the retrospective provisions of the law (if one assumes both Chapters I and III to be retrospective) served as a sort of collective fine for any previous damage inflicted by the defendant's brothers-in-arms.

Beinart's theory has not found acceptance, for two reasons. Firstly, as von Lübtow points out, there is nothing in the law's provisions of a political character or of substantive connection with secession of the *plebs*.[48] Nor, we would add, is there anything to suggest that the law had any bearing whatsoever on the struggle between the orders.[49]

Cato, for not starting with an accurate definition of the subject and for including irrelevant material. In fact, it seems pretty clear that it was only from the start of the first century that Greek method was used by the Romans for organizing treatises on any subject—rhetoric, grammar and the rest" (1989: 456-57).

46 Tellegen-Couperus 1993: 50-51; cf. Lee 1956: 393.

47 Beinart 1956: 70-80.

48 Von Lübtow 1971: 15-16.

49 In attempting to find some social dispute to explain the origin of the Lex Aquilia, however, von Lübtow appears to adopt the very approach that he has just rejected in Beinart's theory. He suggests that the occasion for the law was disputes between patricians and wealthy plebeians over *ager publicus*, "bei denen gegenseitige Gewaltakte stattgefunden hatten, deren zivilrechtliche Sühne eine zusammenfassende, abschlieβende Regelung verlangte" (1971: 16).

Secondly, the sources that suggest a connection, namely the assertions of certain Byzantine jurists, are not to be relied upon.[50] They have been dismissed as historical fantasies, concocted from scraps of information such as Ulpian's remark (*D.* 9.2.1.1) that the Lex Aquilia was a plebiscite and Pomponius' account (*D.* 1.2.2.8)[51] of how plebiscites became binding on the whole people by the Lex Hortensia after a secession of the *plebs.*[52] We would add that Cicero at the end of the Republic seems to know nothing of a tradition linking the Lex Aquilia with civil strife and general destruction; on the contrary, he contrasts its provisions, suited to ancient times when killing was a rarity, with provisions enacted in his own day against the background of civil war to give a remedy against armed hands, for which the Lex Aquilia was inadequate.[53] It is unlikely therefore that the Lex Aquilia was a measure of political reform.

The second object proposed for the Lex Aquilia's reforming zeal is to protect the interests not of disaffected plebeians but of wealthy creditors. According to Honoré, the main point of the legislation was to substitute for the fixed penalties of the earlier law an assessment of damages based on the value of the thing killed or the actual loss suffered through burning, breaking, or tearing another's property.[54] Fixed penalties such as those in the Twelve Tables of 150 *asses* for breaking a slave's bone and 25 *asses* for cutting down a tree ceased to be of use to property owners when inflation destroyed their value. Honoré accordingly attributes the passing of the Lex Aquilia to the period of high inflation at the end of second Punic war.

---

50 Theophilus states that the law was passed at the time of the dissension (*diastasis*) between the *plebs* and the patricians (*Paraphrasis* 4.3.15), and the scholiast to the *Basilica* that it was the work of Aquilius, who was the *plebs*' leader when they rebelled against the patricians and seceded from them (*Schol. ad Bas.* 60.3.1).

51 Cf. Livy III 55; Gaius *Inst.* I 3; Justinian *Inst.* 1.2.4.

52 Gordon 1976: 315-21; Honoré 1972: 145-46; and von Lübtow 1971: 15-16.

53 9. *et cum sciret de damno legem esse Aquiliam, tamen hoc ita existimavit, apud maiores nostros, cum et res et cupiditates minores essent et familiae non magnae magno metu continerentur, at perraro fieret, ut homo occideretur, idque nefarium ac singulare facinus putaretur, nihil opus fuisse iudicio de vi coactis armatisque hominibus . . .* 10. *his temporibus, cum ex bello diuturno atque domestico res in eam consuetudinem venisset, ut homines minore religione armis uterentur, necesse putavit esse . . . et poenam graviorem constituere, ut metu comprimeretur audacia, et illam latebram tollere DAMNUM INIURIA (pro Tullio, 4).*

54 Honoré 1972: 147-50.

The difficulty with Honoré's proposal is that the provisions of the Lex Aquilia are singularly ill-suited to the purpose of compensating for the effects of inflation. It is pointless to look back to the previous year for the highest value of a slave when inflation ensures that his value will always be highest at the latest possible date.[55] Even the next thirty days provision of Chapter III will be of little help: the only fair measure in a time of high inflation is value at the time of judgment. Ironically, Chapter II appears the most suited to the task attributed by Honoré to the *lex*, but only perhaps because of our uncertainty as to the details of that provision.

Birks suggests that Chapter II was indeed promulgated to deal with the effects of inflation, albeit of a different kind. It was designed to prevent corrupt bargains between debtor and *adstipulator* to accept repayment of a loan made in *asses* in silver coins of a higher denomination, such as *denarii*, at less than the going commercial rate of exchange between the silver and bronze coins. This could only have occurred during the inflationary conditions of the Punic wars, when the exchange rate was "floating," i.e., a matter for free bargaining. Thereafter, return to currency stability made the law obsolete.[56]

Stipulatio, however, was an obligation *stricti iuris*, with all the rigor in favor of the creditor thereby implied. Even assuming that a situation existed wherein the exchange rate was a matter for bargaining between creditor and debtor *at the time of repayment*[57] and further that the *adstipulator* had a discretion to bargain with the debtor over repayment in terms that did not amount to *datio in solutum*,[58] then it is still not clear why legis-

---

55 Inflation is to be distinguished from seasonal fluctuation of prices, which is identified by Cardascia (1974: 62-64) as the rationale for the retrospective highest value in Chapter I.

56 Birks 1994: 181-88.

57 Birks (1994: 184) imagines the following scenario: "The debt of 5000 *asses* in this state of affairs might require a payment of only, say, 300 *denarii*, though the exact number will not be discoverable except through a bargain between the parties. . . . The honest debtor will offer what he perceives to be the going rate, say 300 *denarii*, and he will insist that, if he pays that sum, the debt must also be artificially discharged. . . . The discussion will very likely end in compromise. The debtor will pay 325."

58 "The conscientious *adstipulator* will do his best to defend his principal's interest. He will try to push the debtor up to, say, 350. . . . If these same parties are less than perfectly honest they will see that the unstable currency conditions leave room for secret advantage to themselves. The *adstipulator* will be easily tempted to do a deal with the

lation would have been necessary to remedy a wrong that any intelligent creditor could have avoided by formulating his *stipulatio* more tightly, so as to bar payment in unfavorable coinage.

To return to Chapters I and III, it is true that, even without the factor of inflation, the Aquilian measure of damages appears to be more sophisticated than that of the Twelve Tables, and certainly by Ulpian's day it had superseded the latter in areas where they were deemed to overlap.[59] It would be rash to assume however, as for example Daube does,[60] that the one was necessarily a reform of the other. The relationship between the two laws can be put in perspective by recourse once more to sources from the ancient Near East.

The example that served Daube as a model for the idea of emerging damage in Chapter III is the case in Exod 21:18-19, where a man injured in a fight is paid compensation, after his recovery, for his medical expenses and loss of work. That case is a standard scholarly legal problem that recurs in other ancient Near Eastern law codes, namely paragraph 206 of Codex Hammurabi and paragraph 10 of the Hittite Laws.[61] Those same law codes, however, contain another legal problem on wounding, which takes the standard form of a list of injuries with either talionic punishment or a tariff of fixed payments according to the part affected: eye destroyed, bone broken, face slapped, etc. We have argued elsewhere that the fixed payments are not by way of compensation, but just as *talio* represents a limit on permissible revenge, so fixed payments set a limit on the ransom payable in lieu of revenge.[62]

Thus two measures of damage coexist in the same law code.[63] The reason, we suggest, is that they are concerned with separate offences. The one deals with injury where there is a low level of culpability or damages or

---

debtor. He will discharge the debt at a not wholly implausible 280 *denarii*, so long as he receives 20 into his own pocket" (Birks 1994: 184).

59 *Dig.* 9.2.1. Note, however, that Ulpian merely says *derogavit*; he does not suggest that the passing of the statute abrogated existing laws.

60 Daube 1936: 255.

61 Westbrook 1988a: 95-97.

62 Westbrook 1988d: 39-77.

63 Paragraph 10 of the Hittite Laws for good measure adds a small fixed payment to the compensation. §104, incidentally, sets a fixed payment for cutting down trees, while §98 applies indemnification of loss where the culprit burns down a house.

some mitigating circumstance, and the other with assaults that represent an affront to the victim's dignity, as the case of the slap in the face graphically illustrates.[64] The one therefore emphasizes indemnification as the measure of damages, while the other emphasizes revenge, as exemplified by *talio*. In our view it is no accident that the same dichotomy (expressed by the terms *contumelia* and *culpa*) is found in the developed actions of *iniuria* and *damnum iniuria datum*; it represents the original scope of apparently overlapping provisions of the Twelve Tables and the Lex Aquilia, with *talio* and fixed payments on the one hand, and indemnification on the other.

To summarize: the view that the Lex Aquilia was a legislative reform is unsupported by evidence linking it to any historical object of reform. In particular, there is no basis for supposing that it embodied a political reform such as might be implied by the use of a plebiscite.

The evidence for the latter proposition is, as we have seen, a statement attributed to Ulpian in the Digest. Ulpian's statement is of an antiquarian character. On the one hand, it may reflect a long-standing tradition. On the other, it is possible that the tradition itself is no more than a historical fiction, that at some point the law's origins had been attributed to a plebiscite as a sort of pedigree, a way of accounting for its authority by reference to the customary mode of legislation in the late Republic.[65]

---

64 Our arguments are set out in Westbrook 1992b: 61-64. On the voluntary nature of the second category, see Cardascia 1985: 200-207.

65 Methodologically, a distinction should be made between the received text of a law and an historical notice about a law. The former is a primary source which has been transmitted because of its function, namely its use by succeeding generations of lawyers as a source of law. Even if we question the authenticity of parts of the present text, there is no reason for us to dismiss the whole as a fabrication. The historical notice, on the other hand, is not a primary source, nor can it claim any ongoing legal function.

Ulpian's statement about the legislative pedigree of the Lex Aquilia is of no legal significance: it was not necessary for citation or for establishing the validity of such an old law, which Ulpian in any case examined through the prism of the praetorian edict. It therefore falls within the second category: it is an historiographical assertion about an *event* that took place more than five hundred years earlier. We must judge it by the same criteria by which we judge the works of native Roman historians (one of which was possibly the source of Ulpian's statement). Those works can certainty not be read uncritically, as if their sources were primary, their purpose objective, and their under-

Assuming, nonetheless, that at some point during the Republic a plebiscite was promulgated at the instance of one Aquilius, there is no need to suppose that it was a reform *ex nihilo*. For on the one hand the use of the plebiscite mode in this case lacks any demonstrable political or economic implications, and on the other the narrow technicality of its contents and the pedantry of its formulation are unequal to the role of a considered innovation. Rather, they evoke the adoption of an existing scholarly text or oral tradition. Honoré points out that the *terminus post quem* for the plebiscite could theoretically be as early as 449 B.C.E.,[66] but it is unnecessary to seek an early date if the plebiscite is not itself the origin of its provisions. They go back to an indefinable point in early Roman history, being an element of traditional legal learning that for some reason had not been canonized in the Twelve Tables.[67]

Conclusion

The Lex Aquilia is a source that goes back to a shadowy period of Roman law for which native historiographical traditions are unreliable. We do however possess a text which, if not entirely in its original form, retains enough thereof to discern the original focus of the law and the sequence of its clauses. That sequence has generally been regarded as arbitrary, but when placed against the background of far more copiously documented scholastic legal traditions from the ancient Near East, attests to a coherent set of provisions. They follow an organizational pattern widely employed in the ancient Near Eastern law codes, namely the chronological sequence.

The organization of the ancient Near Eastern law codes is predicated upon the fact that they were not legislation in the modern sense but academic treatises, a part of a more general scientific tradition in which the same type of organizational patterns prevailed. While some of those patterns would not be inconceivable in a legislative reform, the sequence

---

standing of former times not tainted by the projection backwards of conditions prevailing in the writer's own time.

66 Honoré 1972: 146; see also Thomas 1976: 19. Biscardi (1967: 75-88) argues for an early date on the basis of Gaius *Inst.* IV 37.

67 Ulpian provides a *terminus ante quem* by citing an interpretation of the consul M. Iunius Brutus (*Dig.* 9.2.27.22), a jurist of the 2nd century B.C.E.

found in the Lex Aquilia is too pure an example of this type of academic discourse. Its structure was a consequence of its academic character.

The Lex Aquilia of classical Roman law was therefore the culmination of a two-fold process of transformation. On the one hand it developed from three technical rules on a narrow question of the point in time to which the assessment of damages should be referred to the general basis of liability for wrongful damage. On the other, it acquired the status of normative legislation, through insertion into a known legislative form and by juristic interpretation within that conceptual framework. Neither development affected the integrity of the original text; rather, they were achieved by a change in attitude to the ancient source, a shift in the way the text was read.

In this respect Roman law reflects the same process that was undergone by the one ancient Near Eastern system to acquire a classical form, namely biblical law. For behind both cases lay an intellectual revolution, in which Greek philosophy replaced Mesopotamian science as the basis of jurisprudence. The original coherence of the Lex Aquilia, therefore, and its subsequent rereading, are emblematic of Roman intellectual as well as legal history.

15

Restrictions on Alienation of Property in Early Roman Law

Abstract

This article seeks to demonstrate how an understanding of ancient Near Eastern law can help to elucidate early Roman law. Two conundrums from the Twelve Tables are solved by analyzing them within the context provided by Near Eastern legal practices involving redemption of land and release of slaves.

The starting point of this paper is a premise—the premise that certain legal traditions that were widespread throughout the ancient Near East found their way into the earliest Roman law.[1] To justify such a premise a great deal of evidence would be required, far beyond the scope of this paper, whose aim is therefore more modest. We intend only to show through two examples how the application of our premise can help to elucidate some of the more enigmatic provisions of the Twelve Tables and thereby demonstrate its feasibility.

The ancient Near Eastern traditions to which we are referring concern the law of property. The legal systems of that region contained special rules protecting the family (in the extended sense) from the danger of permanently losing its principal assets due to temporary economic

---

* Originally published in *New Perspectives in the Roman Law of Property: Essays for Barry Nicholas* (ed. P. Birks; Oxford: Oxford University Press, 1989), 207-13. Copyright © Oxford University Press. Used by permission.

1 On the reception of ancient Near Eastern law into early Roman law, see Yaron 1974; and Westbrook 1988a. The particular connection predicated here was the subject of a paper given by the author to the annual conference of the Société Internationale de l'Histoire des Droits de l'Antiquité (SIHDA) in Stockholm in September 1986.

difficulties.[2] Their purpose was to preserve the family as an economic unit by safeguarding its primary sources of income. Therefore only certain types of property were protected and the beneficiary was the family as a whole, rather than their immediate owner.

As to the types of property involved, we have positive evidence in the case of land, temple prebends, and slaves.[3] There is indirect evidence that large farm animals and boats were also included in this category, at least on occasion.[4] All these items, it will be noted, make up the core of the male inheritance.[5] The beneficiary of the rules might well be the original owner but was not necessarily so. If he were unable to realize his rights, then they passed to his potential heirs—sons, brothers, cousins—and in any case survived his death.

Two examples of these rules will serve: redemption of land and release of slaves. The former right was a conditional one: if land had been sold for less than its real value, a member of the seller's family could later force the present owner to resell it to him at the same low price.[6] Only purchase at the full value would allow permanent alienation of the land, because it would not prejudice the economic survival of the family. The important point for the law was to maintain the distinction between sale and pledge. If the owner of land pledged it against a loan, he retained the possibility of its return on repayment; if he sold it outright, this possibility was lost. If failure to repay the loan resulted in forfeiture of the land, the creditor had in effect bought the land at less than its true value, since the loan would seldom amount to anything like the full value of the land pledged to secure

---

2   For a detailed account of these rules, see Westbrook 1985b.

3   For land and slaves, see below. Temple prebends were treated like land for the purposes of sale and inheritance, and at least one redemption-purchase of a prebend is recorded (BE 6/2 66).

4   Sale documents in the same formulation as those for land, slaves, and prebends are occasionally also found for oxen, cows, and boats. In our view these documents record a ceremony designed to overcome rules restricting transfer of ownership. See Westbrook 1985b: 119-24.

5   The female equivalent of inheritance, the dowry, consists mostly of inanimate moveables, albeit sometimes of considerable worth. Land, slaves, etc., are a rarity confined to the rich.

6   See Westbrook 1985b: 109-11.

it. The right of redemption, however, gave forced sale by a debtor the status of pledge.

The buyer who purchased at the full price, on the other hand, needed evidence thereof in order to prevent the seller or his heirs from claiming the right to redeem at a later date. This was achieved at a ceremony in which the full price was weighed out and handed over before witnesses, and their testimony in turn was given greater longevity by a sealed document recording the ceremony and the witnesses present, which could ensure security of tenure for generations to come. As a sale document from Susa (MDP 22 44) puts it: "Not redemption, not pledge; full price. Like a father buys for his son, A has bought . . . [this property] for generations [i.e., for ever]."[7]

In the case of slaves, the right to redeem existed as with land, at least for certain categories of slave, and on the same conditions. But here there was an added factor: the slave might be a member of the seller's own family, or the seller himself. Accordingly, additional rules are found which effect the automatic release of such slaves after a certain number of years' service, when the debt was deemed to have been paid off by the slave's labor.[8] Again, the point was to distinguish between pledge, for which antichretic contracts were common,[9] and outright sale in which all hope of freeing the slave would be lost. In the case of close members of the family or of self-sale, the laws assume that they would only be sold under dire circumstances of indebtedness.

We may now set out our premise in detail: the category of *res mancipi* in early Roman law was distinguished from all other property in that it was subject to similar restrictive rules as we have seen from the ancient Near East. The ceremony of *mancipatio* was designed to overcome these rules by evidencing sale *at the full value*, which as we have seen, nullified the rights of the seller and his heirs. Failure to use *mancipatio* would not invalidate a sale but would leave the buyer without a guarantee of ownership in perpetuity, since there existed in theory at least the possibility of redemption, release, or the like at some future date. By classical times these

---

7 Westbrook 1985b: 109-11.
8 See below and cf. Deut 15:18: "It shall not seem hard to you to free him [the slave], for he has worked double the hire of a hired man for you for six years."
9 See Eichler 1973: 37-46.

restrictive rules had entirely disappeared, leaving only the *mancipatio* ceremony as an empty shell, an irksome formality that was applied automatically and without any rationale.

Now we turn to two examples from the Twelve Tables where this premise may be applied. The first is VI 1: *cum nexum faciet mancipiumque uti lingua nuncupassit, ita ius esto.*

It has justifiably been called a "strikingly clear yet strangely and intractably obscure clause."[10] A literal translation would be: "When he does *nexum* and *mancipium*, as the tongue shall have declared, so be the right." To take this as affirming the legal validity of whatever ceremony is used is not only too banal, but it offends against the literal sense, expressed by the enclitic *–que*, that *mancipium* and *nexum* are cumulative, not alternative. For on the face of it, they are not two possible examples from a long list, but the two components of a particular legal act.[11] Reluctance to regard them as such derives not from a close reading of the text but from considerations of legal logic. From the sparse information available we can conclude at least that *nexum* at the time of the Twelve Tables was a real obligation involving the pledging of a person as security for a loan. The person pledged was obliged to work for the creditor until the loan was repaid.[12] *Mancipium*, by contrast, was the outright alienation of property to a buyer. A slave thus sold would remain the buyer's property, and the seller could have no legal influence over his subsequent fate. Our literal rendering, then, would appear to contemplate the legally impossible: a transaction which combines pledge with outright alienation.

The paradox may be resolved, however, if we return to our basic premise and examine the ancient Near Eastern sources. There we find special types of contract which actually combine pledge and sale, but which are explicable in the context of the rules protecting family property that we outlined above.

The most explicit examples come from the Middle Assyrian Period (15th to 12th century B.C.E.). Loan contracts are secured by various types

---

10   Watson 1975b: 144.

11   The classical explanation, that the clause authorizes the insertion of subordinate clauses in the *mancipatio* (see Buckland and Stein 1966: 237), is more jurisprudential than historical. It gives the term *nexum* a general meaning more suitable to classical law (following Manilius: Varro *L.* 7.105).

12   Cf. Watson 1975b: 118-19.

of pledge, namely land, members of the debtor's family, slaves (e.g., *ARU* 46),[13] and in one instance an ox (*ARU* 59). For example, *ARU* 24 reads:

> A has received *x* talents of tin as a loan from B. He will repay the capital, the tin, within seven months. If the due date passes, the tin will bear interest. . . . His field, sons, and house are security for the tin. He will pay the tin to the bearer of his tablet.

Other such contracts contain a further clause explicitly stating the fate of the pledge should the debtor fail to repay the loan by the due date. They are classified by Koschaker[14] into two types, depending on the consequences stipulated. In the first, termed *Verfallspfand*, ownership in the pledge passes automatically to the creditor. Thus, in *ARU* 55 we read:

> A and B have borrowed *x* homer of barley from C. [They will repay the capital, the barley, within *y* months]. If [the due date] passes, they will repay [. . .] *z* mina of tin. C will hold their field, house, threshing-floors, wells, sons, or daughters as pledge. If the due date passes, their pledges are acquired. There is no withdrawal or claim. A and B have received the tin, the purchase-price of their pledges: they are paid, quit. They will clear their pledges of claims, measure with the royal line, and write a "firm" tablet before the king.

Forfeiture of the pledge is expressed here in terms of sale, with typical sale clauses including a payment clause, although the only express payment that the document records is the sum of the original loan. It looks very much then as if the creditor has obtained what the law of redemption was supposed to prevent: the outright purchase of land or persons for the mere price of the loan for which it was security. That the law was not so, however, is shown by a further tablet that was drawn up at the stage of forfeiture itself.[15] The text relates that a specified area of land was pledged

---

13   Published in David and Ebeling 1929.
14   Koschaker 1928: 102-108.
15   KAJ 150, edited and discussed by Koschaker (1928: 103) and by Westbrook (1985b: 117).

as security for the relatively small sum of 30 mina of tin, the due date passed, and the field was duly alienated to the creditor. But it continues: "He [debtor] claimed the price of his field, and he received the balance of his tin: he received 100 mina apart from the contents of his tablet."

In other words, the creditor did indeed "purchase" the pledged land by way of forfeiture, but he still had to pay the full price for it, by giving the debtor the difference between the value of the loan and that of the field.

An express statement of this rule is found in the contemporary Middle Assyrian Laws. Paragraph C + G 7 reads:

> [If a slave(?) an ox(?)][16] or anything taken as a pledge is dwelling in the house of an Assyrian, and the due date passes, [after it has p]assed, if the loan amounts to as much as his price, he is acquired and taken; if the loan does not am[ount] to as much as his price, [the creditor] may acquire and take him but may not reduce [the price(?)]—he shall ded[uct] the capital of the loan . . . .

In other words, the creditor must pay the debtor the difference between the loan and the pledge's full value if he is to gain full ownership of the pledge, unless the loan and the pledge are already equal in value.

The second type of contract is called by Koschaker *Lösungspfand*. *ARU* 46 is an example thereof:

> A has borrowed *x* mina of tin and *y* homer of barley . . . from B. He shall repay the capital, the tin, and the barley, within 6 months. If the due date passes, the tin will bear interest. If he does not repay the barley, he shall pay tin for barley at the going rate. If he does not pay tin, the tin will bear interest.
>
> B will take and hold A's slave C and a house of his in his town as pledge. On the day that he repays the tin and its interest, he redeems his pledges.

Here then we have a clause allowing the debtor to redeem his pledge even after the due date on payment of the loan capital plus interest. It is not clear that this clause was inserted entirely for the benefit of the debtor.

---

16 Restorations proposed on the basis of context. Cf. Cardascia 1969: 307.

Possibly the creditor did not wish to make the extra capital expenditure in order to acquire the pledge in perpetuity. While the creditor could not claim full ownership of the pledge, therefore, the debtor equally could not claim the balance of its value from him. And while awaiting redemption, the creditor still had a profitable investment. This consideration is illustrated by *ARU* 38, a *Lösungspfand* where the debtor does not have to pay interest but at the same time must wait six years to redeem the land pledged.

To summarize, in both types of pledge, contract ownership in the pledge passes to the creditor on expiration of the term for repayment. The difference is that in *Lösungspfand* the pledge is acquired at the price of the loan and therefore remains redeemable, while *Verfallspfand* contains a mechanism for acquisition of the land in perpetuity by paying its full value. In our submission it is this mechanism, this grafting of outright sale on to pledge, that forms the background to VI 1 in the Twelve Tables and resolves the paradox of two incompatible transactions, pledge and sale, being lumped together in the protasis. The situation contemplated is where the creditor is prepared to turn *nexum* into *mancipium* either by giving a loan equal in value to the pledge[17] or by paying the difference if the pledge is not redeemed by the due date.

The meaning of the apodosis of VI 1, that is, the purpose of the law, is more difficult to ascertain, since the ancient Near Eastern sources provide us with a context but no direct parallel. Our remarks on this point, therefore, are bound to be more speculative and are offered with due reserve.

To begin on relatively sure ground, we know that the active party in the ceremony of *mancipatio* was the buyer, who made a formal declaration of acquisition. It is therefore reasonable to suppose that the subject of the verb *faciet* and of the declaration is the creditor/buyer, and from this to conclude that the law is regulating his actions in some way, possibly defining his rights by reference to the terms of his declaration. The most plausible form that this would take, it seems to us, would be a regulation preventing the creditor from claiming the right to buy the pledge definitively (on payment of the balance) where the debtor has defaulted,

---

17 In the extant sources *nexum* is a pledge of persons, but there is no intrinsic reason why it could not have applied to other pledgeable items such as land or animals.

unless the transaction had expressly been declared a *Verfallspfand* at the outset.

Our second example from the Twelve Tables is IV 2: *si pater filium ter venum duit, filius a patre liber esto*. Here again, a literal translation produces an apparently inescapable contradiction. "If a father sells a son three times, the son is free of the father." How could the father, having sold his son, get him back not once but twice in order to be able to resell him?

Watson suggests that pledge, in the form of *nexum*, is behind the transaction, and the son could thus return to his father's *potestas* in spite of having been sold by *mancipatio*.[18] He does not explain, however, how pledge can be identified with sale or why the transaction was not simply called *nexum*. Yaron assumes the existence of a regulation by law or legal custom, whereby the *mancipium* relationship is limited in time, and mentions ancient Near Eastern parallels.[19] Kelly argues that *venum duit* does not refer to *mancipatio*, but to sale in a limited sense of to lease, but can cite only a weak parallel from a non-legal source.[20]

Instead of choosing between these conflicting suggestions we wish to combine the leading elements in them: that the background to the transaction was the satisfaction of debts, that the sale in question is of the same nature as the slave-sales regulated in ancient Near Eastern laws, but that it is not *mancipatio*. If we place this composite hypothesis in the context of our foregoing discussion, a coherent picture emerges.

In the ancient Near East when a man sold members of his family into slavery, it was not a commercial transaction for the full value but a necessity brought about by debt, and the right of redemption could therefore be invoked. For example, Codex Hammurabi 119 reads:

> If a man is seized by a debt and gives his slave-woman who has borne him sons for sale,[21] the owner of the slave-woman may pay the silver that the merchant paid and redeem his slave-woman.

18   Watson 1975b: 118-19.
19   Yaron 1968: esp. 71 n. 34.
20   Kelly 1974: 183-86, citing Cato, *De Agr.* 149.
21   The Akkadian phrase is literally "to give for silver" (*ana kaspim nadānum*), a standard expression for sale.

The point here is that the slave-woman is regarded as a member of the family in these circumstances and her sale deemed non-commercial.

But some legal systems, at least, went further. According to Exod 21:2:

> If you buy a Hebrew slave, he shall work six years and in the seventh go free for nothing (i.e., without repaying the debt).

Similarly in Codex Hammurabi 117:

> If a man is seized by a debt and gives his wife, son, and daughter for sale[22] or in *kiššātum*, they shall serve the household of their buyer or holder in *kiššātum* for three years; in the fourth year their emancipation shall be established.

The term *kiššātum* is still unclear but appears to refer to some sort of pledge with a right of redemption limited in time.[23] It is important to note that it is in parallel with straightforward sale; both are equally affected by the emancipation rule. Clearly, for persons in such straits as to be forced to sell their own family, even redemption might remain a hollow right and more radical measures were needed.[24]

The situation in IV 2 is, we submit, that a father has likewise had to sell his son into slavery under pressure of debt. The unusual terminology—*venum duit*—is used advisedly; the sale was not at full value and therefore in this early period was not *mancipatio*, in spite of the nature of its object. Accordingly, the right of redemption still existed, but possibly also, as Yaron surmised, a rule effecting automatic emancipation (and cancellation of the debt) after a fixed period. We know from the ancient Near Eastern sources that even such drastic measures were sometimes ineffective: in Jeremiah 34:8-11 it is related that king Zedekiah decreed a general release

---

22 The phrase is the same as in CH 119 (see previous note), but the verb "to give" has a double predicate "for silver" and "for *kiššātum*."

23 See the discussion by Kraus 1984: 266-77.

24 A further measure was a general, retrospective cancellation of debts. This was typically proclaimed by a king on his accession to the throne or in a national emergency. For a Babylonian example see *ANET³* 526-28, and the literature cited therein.

of slaves,[25] but that subsequently the same persons were re-enslaved for debt. Emancipation had brought only temporary relief. The same is true, it would appear, of the father in IV 2, from the very circumstances of his having to resell his son. It is therefore more likely that the son had returned to him by automatic emancipation than by redemption. Where such a sale recurs three times, it is obvious that the family must be totally impoverished. There is therefore little point in the son remaining in his father's *potestas*. He has no prospect of an inheritance, only of being exploited by his father's creditors. A rule releasing him from *potestas* will at least ensure that his emancipation will not again be nullified by his father's chronic indebtedness.

25   See previous note.

16

Vitae Necisque Potestas

Abstract

The Latin expression *vitae necisque potestas* means "power of life and death" and is used in a variety of classical legal and literary texts. This article locates the origins of this phrase in legal language from the ancient Near East. It also attempts to demonstrate how the transmission of scholastic traditions from the Near East to the Mediterranean world may have led to the incorporation of this phrase in early Roman law.

The purpose of this article is to trace the vicissitudes of a notorious phrase and its congeners. The Latin phrase *vitae necisque potestas*, "power of life and death," is replete with paradox. It was intimately associated with Roman law but at the same time was so beloved of Roman poets, historians, and philosophers that its legal meaning has become lost in a tangle of figurative and metaphorical usages.[1]

The essential feature of the phrase, which gives it its dramatic appeal, is its duality: "life and death" or more precisely "life and killing" (*nex*). But that duality reveals an inherent imbalance. It accords the right to change another's state from live to dead (*necis potestas*), but there appears to be no concomitant right to change from dead to live, for the obvious reason that it is impossible to raise the dead. Our objection may seem not only pedantic but unnecessary, for, it will be argued, the duality surely refers to the element of choice: to kill or not to kill. From a legal point of view, however, the duality of expression is superfluous in such a case,

---

* Originally published in *Historia* 48/2 (1999): 203-23. Copyright © Franz Steiner Verlag. Used by Permission.

1 E.g., Livy 2.35; Manilius *Astr.* 4.24; Pliny *Nat.* 29.11; Sen. *Ep. Mor.* 4.8, *Phoenissae* 103; Tac. *Hist.* 4.62.

because every legal right in the form of a power by definition involves that same element of choice—to do or not to do. The right to kill in itself gives the right-holder the choice between killing and not killing.

The phrase is used in Roman sources primarily in respect of three relationships: master and slave, ruler and subject, and father and son (or daughter). In the first of these, master and slave, both law and practice are straightforward. The standard statement of the law is found in a passage of Gaius, a jurist of the 2nd century A.D., which is repeated in later legal sources:[2]

In potestate itaque sunt servi dominorum. quae quidem potestas iuris gentium est. nam apud omnes peraeque gentes animadvertere possumus dominis in servos vitae necisque potestatem esse . . . sed hoc tempore neque civibus Romanis nec ullis aliis hominibus, qui sub imperio populi Romani sunt, licet supra modum et sine causa in servos suos saevire. nam, ex constitutione sacratissimi imperatoris Antonini, qui sine causa servum suum occiderit non minus teneri iubetur quam qui alienum servum occiderit.

Gaius' understanding of the phrase is clear: a master may kill his slave without cause, at a whim, and not be answerable at law for his action. He also informs us that this principle was valid law until fairly recently, when it was moderated by express legislation. That Gaius' account conformed to practice is confirmed by a tale told by Seneca in his essay *On Anger* (3.40.1-3). A certain Vedius Pollio, while the emperor Augustus was dining at his house, ordered a slave boy who had broken a cup to be fed to his lampreys. The boy took advantage of the emperor's presence to beg not for his life, but that he be given a less horrible death. The interest of the story for us is the assumption of Vedius Pollio that even in the presence of his

---

2 "Slaves are under the power of their masters. This power is part of the law of peoples, for it is observable that among all peoples alike masters have power of life and death over their slaves. . . . But at the present day neither Roman citizens nor any other persons subject to Roman rule are allowed to treat their slaves with excessive and causeless harshness. For by a constitution of the late emperor Antoninus it is laid down that one who kills his own slave without cause is as much amenable to justice as one who kills another's" (I 52-53 = *Dig.* 1.6.1.1; Justinian *Inst.* 1.8.1-2).

ruler he could with impunity kill his slaves for no cause other than his own anger.

It is not surprising therefore that the phrase when used of rulers does not generally have a positive sense. A phrase that characterizes political power as arbitrary and unlimited is consonant with absolutism rather than with constitutional authority. For Cicero it is the essence of tyranny:[3] *sunt enim omnes, qui in populum vitae necisque potestatem habent, tyranni, sed se . . . malunt reges vocari.*

Far be it, then, from Roman authors to associate the phrase with their own constitutional machinery; it was regarded rather as characteristic of barbarian rulers. According to Sallustius, the deposed Numidian ruler Adherbal bewailed the fact that in seeking to exercise his royal functions, his power of life and death depended on the assistance of others.[4] Caesar, who has a predilection for the phrase in describing barbarian customs, attributes it to the Haeduan *vergobretus* and to German leaders appointed to conduct a war (*Bell. gall.* 1.16; 6.23). At Rome, the only named ruler to whom the power is attributed is Nero, and for good reason:[5] *et usque ad Neronem quidem senatus auctoritas valuit, qui sordidum et impurum principem*

---

3   ". . . for all who have the power of life and death over a people are tyrants, but they prefer to be called kings" (*Rep.* 3.23). The image of the tyrant is behind two examples of a fanciful adaptation of the phrase. Quintilian (*Decl. min.* 309) raises the imaginary case of a deflo
wered virgin to whom the law gives the right to choose between having her ravisher executed and having him marry her. The girl first chooses marriage but, the ravisher having denied the charge and lost his case, changes her mind and opts for execution. The unhappy young man protests: *potestatem tibi vitae ac necis lex dedit; ultra regnum omne, ultra tyranidem omnem est hoc diu licere.* Pliny (*Nat.* 29.11), with scathing sarcasm, applies it to the power of fashionable doctors over their patients: *imperatorem illico vitae nostrae necisque fieri.*

4   . . . *incertus . . . an regno consulam, quoius vitae necisque potestas ex opibus alienis pendet* (*Bell. Iug.* 14.23). Cf. the reproach addressed to kings in Seneca's *Thyestes*: *vos quibus rector maris atque terrae ius dedit magnum necis atque vitae, ponite inflatos tumidosque vultus* (607-609).

5   "Even as late as the time of Nero, the power of the Senate prevailed, and the Senate did not fear to deliver speeches against a base and filthy emperor and condemn him who held the power of life and death and imperial authority" (*SHA* 13.8). Seneca, addressing the youthful Nero, puts the following reminder into his head: *ego vitae necisque gentibus arbiter.* As the following lines confirm, however, this does not refer to power over Roman citizens but over foreign nations (Sen. *Clem.* 1.1.2).

damnare non timuit, cum sententiae in eum dictae sint, qui vitae necisque potestatem atque imperium tunc tenebat.

It is significant that the text distinguishes constitutional authority (*imperium*) from the arbitrary *vitae necisque potestas*. Seneca, in his essay *On Anger*, appears to attribute the latter power to a judge, but on a level of abstraction that precludes direct connection with a Roman judicial office.[6]

The content of the phrase in the third relationship, that of father and son, is less clear. On the one hand, the phrase is deeply rooted in the legal relationship between them, as is shown by the formula used in the ancient ceremony of *adrogatio*, a type of adoption. The *Pontifex Maximus* proposed to a council of the people (*comitia curiata*) that the adoption be approved in the following words:[7] *velitis, iubeatis, uti L. Valerius L. Titio tam iure legeque filius siet, quam si ex eo patre matreque familias eius natus esset, utique ei vitae necisque in eum potestas siet, uti patri endo filio est.*

On the other hand, the extent of that power was not necessarily the same as that of a master over his slave. It is true that Dionysius of Halicarnassus attributes to Romulus a law giving a father total power over his son (2.26.4; cf. Dio Chrys. 15.20), including the right to kill him, but a legal source is rightly puzzled by the resulting inconsistency, even in early law. According to the Theodosian code:[8] *libertati a maioribus tantum inpensum*

---

6   Seneca's discussion follows an example of abusive exercise of the death penalty which has as its subject a named Roman commander (1.18.3-19.8), presumably acting under the much wider discretion afforded by military discipline. It is not clear that the example is intended as an illustration of arbitrary power: the commander provides due grounds, albeit specious in Seneca's eyes, for the death sentences that he orders. Also beyond the constitutional sphere are Manilius' references to laws (*leges*) and scales (*examen*) of life and death. These powers are in the celestial sphere, belonging to Fate and the constellation Libra respectively. They assume judgments that are logical, equitable, and well-founded, even if from the perspective of humans they appear arbitrary (*Astronomica* 4.24; 5.49-50).

7   "By your permission and order, may Lucius Valerius be a son to Lucius Titius in law and statute, as if he had been born from that father and mother, and may he (Titius) have the power of life and death over him (Valerius), as a father has over a son" (Gell. *NA* 5.19.9; cf. Cicero *Dom.* 77.11; Seneca Major *Controv.* 3.3).

8   "So much importance was attached to freedom by our forbears that fathers, to whom was granted the right of life and the power of death over their children, were not allowed to rob them of their freedom" (4.9[8].6.pr.). The fragmentary Autun

est, ut patribus, quibus vitae in liberos necisque potestas permissa est,
eripere libertatem non liceret.

For later law, the power was a dead letter, although abrogated by no
specific statute, unlike the power of a master. A constitution of
Constantine includes within the ambit of parricide the case of fathers killing sons (*Cod. Theod.* 9.15.1), which had been notably absent from the
earlier *Lex Pompeia de Parricidiis.*[9] Not all killing was parricide, however.
A text in Justinian's Digest attributed to Ulpian (3rd A.D.) states:[10] *inaudi-*
tum filium pater occidere non potest, sed accusare eum apud praefectum
praesidemve provinciae debet.

Even if it is, as has been suggested, an interpolation by Justinian's
compilers,[11] it attests to the persistent idea that a father could kill his son
for cause, arrogating to himself the jurisdiction of a court of law for this
purpose. Although the principle that a son's serious crimes were under the
jurisdiction of the courts, not the family, may have been established by the
time of Constantine (*Cod. Theod.* 9.13.1.), a residual right of the father to
kill his son for cause appears to have survived even in the later law. The
Digest records with approval a decision recorded by Marcianus:[12]

Divus Hadrianus fertur, cum in venatione filium suum quidam ne-
caverat, qui novercam adulterabat, in insulam eum deportasse,

---

commentary on Gaius first equates the powers of master and father, but then appears
to distinguish them. Apparently, the author considers that in the case of a father, just
cause is needed, but it is not clear from the broken context whether he regards this requirement as stemming from the Twelve Tables or from subsequent reform: *domino*
vel parenti et occidere eum et mortuum dedere in noxam . . . patria potestas potest . . .
n . . . cum patris potestas talis est ut habeat vitae et necis potestatem. de filio hoc trac-
tari crudele est, sed . . . non est post . . . r . . . occidere sine iusta causa, ut constituit
lex XII tabularum (Gaius *Augustod.* 4.85-86).

9 *Dig.* 48.9.1 (Marcianus). It is curious that Justinian's compilers failed to update the
   law in this case by interpolation.
10 "A father cannot kill his son without a hearing but must accuse him before the prefect
   or provincial governor" (*Dig.* 48.8.2).
11 Sachers 1953: col. 1087.
12 "It is said that when a certain man had killed in the course of a hunt his son, who had
   been committing adultery with his stepmother, the late emperor Hadrian exiled him to
   an island, because he killed him more by the law of a brigand than by the right of a father; for paternal power ought to depend on compassion not cruelty" (*Dig.* 48.9.5).

> *quod latronis magis quam patris iure eum interfecit: nam patria potestas in pietate debet, non atrocitate consistere.*

It is implied that the father had a right to kill his son because of the son's offence and was only punished because he went about it in an unacceptable way. Indeed, when we look back at the earlier accounts of fathers killing sons, the question of justified punishment for an offence is always the key element. In an imaginary case used by Quintilian as material for a declamation, the same offence, actually incest with his natural mother, leads to the son's death in the family home at his father's hands, after torture to ascertain the truth, the father invoking *vitae necisque potestas* (*Decl. mai.* 19.5).

Likewise, three famous historical cases, reported in multiple sources, purport to reflect practice during the Republic. Our concern is not with the genuineness of the reports but with the assumptions on which they operate.[13] Disregarding the conflicting details of the different versions, then, the three stories are:

a) a tribune of the plebs, Spurius Cassius, after he had relinquished his office, was tried and executed by his own father for the crime of seeking the kingship (Val. Max. 5.8.2; Livy 2.41.10);

b) Aulus Fulvius was killed by his own father when he went to join the Catiline conspiracy (Val. Max. 5.8.5; Sallust. *Bell. Cat.* 39.5; Dio Cass. 37.36.4);

c) Quintus Fabius Maximus had his son killed, apparently for some sexual misconduct (Val. Max. 6.1.5; Oros. 5.16.8).

---

13 For this reason we have excluded from consideration isolated late accounts, such as Oros. 4.13.18. Other sources cited by Sachers 1953: col. 1086-87, as evidence of the father's right to kill his son, all concern a consul, dictator, military commander, etc., carrying out his public duty to punish a culprit in spite of the fact that the latter happens to be his son, e.g., Livy 4.29.5; 8.7.8; Cic. *Fin.* 1.7.23-24. Harris (1986: 82-87) adduces several further incidents where *vitae necisque potestas* might have been in issue. He attempts to assess the historicity of the incidents reported—in our view an impossible task. All of them were literary topoi that served a purpose in relation to the author's contemporary audience.

Only in the third case is it reported that the father suffered punishment for his act (Livy 2.41.10; Oros. 5.16.8). The assumption in all cases is that the father had the right to kill his son for the commission of an offence for which he would otherwise have been tried and executed by the public authorities. The father's right is called into question only where it is less clear that the offence or the evidence justified the father's action.[14]

Daughters were presumed by later writers to have been subject to the same *vitae necisque potestas* as sons in early law,[15] but the few accounts of early practice as there are place the father's action in the context of preserving his daughter's chastity. One Aufidianus is supposed to have killed his daughter for unchastity with a slave, along with the slave himself (Val. Max. 6.1.3), and one Philiscus is likewise said to have killed his daughter for illicit intercourse (Val. Max. 6.1.6). In Livy's dramatic account, Verginius slew his daughter to save her from being raped by the tyrannical decemvir Appius Claudius (3.48.4-7). Livy has him ask the revolutionary mob not to regard him as a parricide, assigning guilt for the deed rather to Claudius himself (3.50.5-7).

Control over the daughter's sexuality through *vitae necisque potestas* raises the question of a husband's power over his wife. Although the phrase is never used of husband-wife relations, at least not at Rome,[16] tradition had it that in early law a husband could kill his wife for drinking wine, otherwise a public offence, or for adultery (Dion. Hal. 2.25.6; Gell. *NA* 10.23.3-5; Pliny *Nat.* 14.14.89-91). The significance of the latter right will become evident when we examine ancient Near Eastern sources.

Nothing in the law and practice discussed above serves to resolve the imbalances that we noted in the phrase itself: that one can only kill, not bring alive, and that the choice of killing or not killing does not require the duality of expression. In spite of its legal functions, which tend to require terminological rigor, the dual phrase seems to be no more than a pleonasm.

---

14 Cf. Seneca's account of a relatively recent case in which a father tried his son for parricide by family council and condemned him to exile rather than opting for the usual form of execution for parricides (Sen. *Clem.* 1.15.2-7). The preceding story of a father who was almost lynched for flogging his son to death lacks sufficient details to draw conclusions as to *vitae necisque potestas* (Sen. *Clem.* 1.15.1).

15 *Coll.* 4.8.1 (Papinian) attributes the father's power to the *leges regiae*. See the discussion of adultery below.

16 Cf. Caes. *Bell. gall.* 6.19 on Gallic husbands.

Harris claims that its duality is nonetheless significant and can be explained by connecting the phrase with two practices: exposure of infants at birth and a father's recognition of his new-born child (*filium tollere*).[17] By recognition in the first few days during which an infant might be exposed, the father was giving it life. There are at least three objections to this.

1. The phrase is never associated with exposure of infants. Indeed, its most established legal use in the father-son relationship is in the ceremony of *adrogatio*, the adoption of an adult. Harris' response—that the phrase was never thought of as applying exclusively to infants—raises the question whether it was thought of as applying to infants at all. The question of infant exposure or recognition could not be more irrelevant to the legal relationship being created by the ceremony.
2. Exposure was not necessarily the prerogative of the father. In *Dig.* 40.4.29, for example, it was carried out by the mother. Mothers are never endowed with *vitae necisque potestas*.
3. The phrase does not apply only to fathers, but, as we have seen, applies equally to slave owners, who could have no possible connection with the decision to expose or recognize infants; and *a fortiori* to political rulers.

Accordingly, Harris' explanation must be rejected as too speculative, since it is based on no evidence but merely on a situation to which the wording of the phrase might logically apply. Nevertheless, Harris' approach is valuable, in that it points to the necessity to find a separate function for *vitae necisque potestas*. No evidence for such a function has been found in Roman sources, but, as we shall see, there is abundant evidence from the ancient Near East.

*   *   *

In a short article published more than thirty years ago, Yaron drew attention to the similarity between the phrase *vitae necisque potestas* and a

---

17   Harris 1986: 93-95.

widespread expression from the ancient Near East.[18] It is often said of a king that "he kills; he makes live." For example, Hittite Laws 187 reads: "If a man sins with a bull, it is an abomination; he shall die. They shall bring him to the royal gate. The king may kill him; the king may make him live.[19] But he shall not come near the king."

Through this and the many other examples of the phrase, the true content of its second leg, "make live," is revealed. It refers to the king's prerogative of pardon. The reason for the dual character of the phrase thus becomes apparent. It expresses a choice, not between action and inaction but between two different types of action: to execute the criminal or to pardon him. The two acts are theoretically independent of each other, and, as in modern legal systems, might be in the hands of different persons. For example, a letter to king Ashurbanipal praises the benefits of his rule:[20] "He for whose crime death had been ordered, my lord the king has made live; he who had been a prisoner for many years, you have redeemed; he who had been ill for many days has recovered."

There still remains the inherent imbalance that we noted in the Latin phrase, namely that in spite of its wording, the power is only to cause death, not to bring to life. Again, closer scrutiny of the ancient Near Eastern sources provides this missing element.

The first point to note is that there exists one type of ruler for whom aspects of the power are perfectly feasible. The Bible tells us (1 Sam 2:6): "The LORD puts to death and makes live; he brings down to the Netherworld and he brings up."

Mere mortals, on the other hand, cannot make the dead live. Or can they?[21] The law has remarkable powers: it can make a man a woman or a

---

18 Yaron 1962b: 243-51.

19 *huišnuzzi*, the causative form in Hittite from the verb "to live." In the Semitic languages, the intensive stem of the verb (a form that does not exist in Hittite) is used.

20 ABL 2; edition in Pfeiffer 1935: no. 160. Lines 21-22: *ša ḫīṭašuni ana muāte qabûni šarru bēlī ubtallissu.* Cf. *CAD* B 61-62 and Q 38. The separate nature of the two acts also emerges from the distributive use of the phrase, e.g., Esarhaddon's Succession Treaty (SAA 2 6), lines 193-194: "he shall put to death him who is worthy of death (*ša duāki*); he shall pardon him who is worthy of pardon (*ša balluṭi*)." Edition in Parpola and Watanabe 1988: 36.

21 The letter to Ashurbanipal cited above gives the ruler only an indirect role in the curing of the sick, for which the intransitive verb "to live" (= to recover) is used.

woman a man, a live man dead or a dead man live—in law, that is. Consider the following law in Deut 17:6: "The dead man shall be put to death on the word of two or three witnesses; he shall not be put to death on the word of one witness."

The apparent absurdity of this literal translation disappears once we realize that it is legal death that is in issue.[22] A man who has been found guilty of a capital offence is deemed dead in the eyes of the law; his physical death must await his execution, which is not a foregone conclusion. For, as the prophet Ezekiel puts it (18:32): "Do not desire the death of the dead, says the Lord GOD; so repent and live."

The concept is illustrated by a letter to king Ashurbanipal from one of his officers. The letter begins by reporting success in a minor skirmish, but it then emerges that the officer is in disgrace due to an earlier military disaster:[23] "Since Birat was sacked and its gods carried off, I am dead (*mītu anāku*). Had I but seen the golden ring of my lord the king, I would have lived (*abtaluṭ*). But behold, when I sent my messenger to my lord the king, I did not see the ring of my lord the king, and I did not live (*ul abluṭ*). I am dead (*mītu anāku*); let my lord the king not forsake me!"

Clearly, the death in question is figurative, referring to the officer's disgrace. The king has punished him in some way, and the officer seeks a reversal of that order. There is hyperbole in the officer's statement in that he compares his punishment to a death sentence, but the principle is not affected. The sequence of events narrated is: 1) punishment; 2) petition for remission of punishment (messenger, see the king's ring); and 3) rejection of petition (not see the king's ring). "Dead" refers to the original punishment, whereas "live" and "not live" refer to the petition and its failure. Of course, as a result of that failure, the officer remains in his previous status, hence repetition of the term "dead."

In Isa 38:1 (= 2 Kgs 20:1) king Hezekiah falls seriously ill. God informs him through the prophet Isaiah: "Put your house in order, for you are dead and you shall not live." As in the letter of the Assyrian officer,

---

22 Standard translations ignore the word "dead man" (*mēt*) in the Hebrew text, even though the Septuagint tries to take account of it (*apothnēskōn*: "dying man"). E.g., "the death sentence shall be executed" (Oxford Bible); "a person shall be put to death" (JPS); "on ne pourra être condamné à mort" (Bible de Jérusalem). Note that the Hebrew root *mt meaning "man" is not attested in the singular.

23 ABL 259; edition in Pfeiffer 1935: no. 22: reverse 1-10.

"dead" refers to Hezekiah's status as a condemned man. Sickness was regarded in the ancient Near East as, *inter alia*, divine punishment for sin,
and a mortal illness was therefore a death sentence.[24] "You are dead" thus
means that Hezekiah has been found guilty of a capital sin by the divine
judge. "You shall not live" means that he can expect no mercy. Hezekiah,
however, refuses to take God at his word and begs for mercy (vv. 2-3),
with the result that God eventually relents somewhat and grants Hezekiah
another fifteen years of life (vv. 4-5). The message is that prayer and re-
pentance may soften even the harshest decision, at least where the divine
king is concerned.

In the light of these examples, we see that the notion "make live" is a
perfectly logical counterpart to "kill." The condemned man is, legally
speaking, dead, and the effect of pardon is to bring him back to life
again.[25] It should be noted in passing that we have moved in these examples from transitive to intransitive verbs, from "kill" and "make live" to
"die" and "live." All this means is that death sentence and pardon are being looked at from the condemned man's point of view, rather than that of
the judge.

So far we have been examining the *dual* phrase, but there is no reason
why "live" or "make live" should not be used alone to indicate pardon, or
even to indicate by ellipsis the whole process of condemnation and pardon,
if the context is sufficiently suggestive. In the "Nippur Homicide Trial," an
account from the early second millennium B.C.E. of a trial for murder before the Assembly of the city of Nippur, three men conspired to kill a
fourth and, when they had done the deed, informed the victim's wife.[26] She
kept her silence. All four were brought to trial. One group in the assembly
argued as follows: "As men who have killed a man they are not live men
(lú.lú.ù in.gaz.eš.àm lú.ti.la nu.me.eš). Those three males and that
female shall be killed before the chair (of the victim)." Another group,
however, argued that mercy should be shown to the wife: "Even if Ninda

---

24 See e.g., *Šurpu* (edition in Reiner 1958), a series of incantations designed to remove
sin from a sick man by means of confession and ritual purification. Cf. Num 27:3 and
2 Kgs 5:20-27.

25 Yaron already surmised this possibility: "by his god-like intervention [the sovereign]
'keeps alive,' perhaps even 'restores to life,' the offender who has been condemned to
death" (1962b: 248).

26 Edition in Jacobsen 1970: 193-214.

daughter of Lu-Ninurta may have killed her husband, a woman, what can she do, that she should be killed?"

The Assembly then considered the wife's case and decided that she should be executed with the others. In this account, the facts had been proven; the only issue before the court was the possibility of clemency. It is therefore appropriate that the culprits are referred to by the group arguing against mercy not as "dead" but as "not live," i.e., not worthy of mercy.[27]

More than a thousand years later, a striking illustration of this elliptical usage is given in a report of a trial for high treason.[28] King Nebuchadnezzar II, having discovered a plot against him by a certain Babu-aḫḫa-iddina, "proved against him in the popular assembly the crimes that he had committed and looked upon him angrily and pronounced his not-living (*lā balāssu iqbi*), and his throat was cut" (lines 17-20). The narrative omits mention of the death sentence, which is self-evident in a case of treason, and focuses on the king's prerogative of pardon, which presupposes a death sentence. The death penalty for treason resulted from a conviction by a court (the popular assembly, not the king); "not-living" resulted from the king's decision to deny mercy.

Finally, the same metonymy explains an enigmatic biblical law. Exod 22:17 reads: "You shall not make a witch live." The law, in our interpretation, is addressed to the local authorities.[29] It is understood that witchcraft is a capital offence. The purpose of the law is to forbid the local authorities to exercise a prerogative of mercy with regard to witches.

The effect of elliptical usage of one part of the dual phrase is to cast emphasis on that aspect. In certain contexts, when used as a speech formula, that emphasis is such as to give the phrase a slightly different nuance.

In 2 Kgs 10:19, king Jehu issues an order summoning the priests of Baal, without exception, and adds: "Anyone who is missing shall not live." We understand from this that the penalty for disobedience is death, but it adds little to emphasize that the king will not pardon the offender. The

---

27 Cf. ABL 620 (edition in Waterman 1930-36: no. 620): "I am one of killing; I am not one of making live."

28 *AfO* 17 2; edition in Weidner 1954-56a.

29 Westbrook 1986a: 62-66.

emphasis lies rather in its focus on the final stage of judgment to the exclusion of the preceding stages. In the context of a speech formula expressing a peremptory order, truncation of the legal phrase is symbolic of truncation of the judicial process. The offender will be put to death summarily, without trial, without being able to offer an explanation or excuse. Failure to appear is proof of his guilt; there is no need for legal niceties and no question of pardon. The same is true in Gen 31:32 when Jacob, accused by Laban of stealing his household gods, accepts a search of members of his household, declaring: "With whomever your gods are found shall not live."

The use of the truncated phrase as a peremptory order is not confined to the Bible. In a letter from Mari dating to the 18th century, an official reports,[30] "I assembled the sheikhs of the cities of the Binu-Yamina and I gave them the following strict order:[31] 'Whoever you are, if a single individual leaves your city and you do not seize him and bring him to me, in truth you shall not live.'"

Finally, returning to the Bible, in Exod 19:12-13, we find the full dual phrase but separated in a way that changes its emphasis. Moses, about to ascend Mount Sinai, is instructed to warn the people: "Do not go up onto the mountain or touch its edge. Anyone who touches the mountain shall be killed. No hand shall touch him, but he shall surely be stoned or shot. Whether beast or man, he shall not live."

There is to be no trial but instant death for trespassers, as postponement of the element "shall not live" until after the mode of execution indicates. It is not clear who was to carry out the stoning or shooting. The order seems to allude to the posting of guards, but another possibility, that we shall now examine, is that it entitled ordinary Israelites to take law into their own hands.

In all the examples that we have examined from the ancient Near East the power of life and death is vested in the hands of the king or his delegates. The phrase is never used in connection with masters of slaves nor

---

30 ARM 2 92; edition in Jean 1950:122.

31 *ašpuṭšunuti. CAD* translates *šapāṭu* "to issue orders" (Š/1 450) but for no apparent reason creates a second lemma (Š/1 451) with three examples—one uncertain, one in broken context, and this passage, which it translates "I informed(?) them . . . ." In my opinion, the first meaning applies here also. Confirmation is provided by examples of the noun *šipṭu*, "ruling, strict order, reprimand" given in *CAD* Š/2 93.

with fathers (with one partial exception that we shall discuss below). In cuneiform sources there is no hint that a master had the right to kill his slave under any circumstances.[32] The one explicit biblical law on the subject, Exod 21:20-21, punishes a master whose slave dies in consequence of legitimate punishment, unless death was not reasonably foreseeable. In the case of a father, the law is explicit: Deut 21:18-21 requires a father desiring the execution of his wicked son to apply for a court order, and Codex Hammurabi 168-169 has the same requirement even for disinheritance.

There are, however, two key texts where the phrase is used in connection with private individuals. The first is a passage in the book of Zechariah (13:3):

> "But if a man continues to prophesy, his father and mother who bore him shall say to him, 'You shall not live, for you have spoken falsehood in the name of the Lord,' and his father and mother who bore him shall pierce him through because of his prophesying."

False prophesy was a form of apostasy, a serious public offence for which the death penalty is prescribed in the laws of Deuteronomy (18:20, cf. 13:5, 9-10; 17:2-5). According to those laws, execution was to be by the community and only after a public trial, with procedural safeguards for the defendants, or after a formal inquiry by the public authorities (13:1-16; 17:2-7). In the prophetic passage, however, the situation is considered so serious that the culprit's parents are given the right to execute summary justice themselves, without going through the normal procedures. They assert that right by means of the speech formula "You shall not live," which as we have seen is normally used by rulers when they order summary execution.[33] For a brief moment, and in special circumstances, the

---

32 In the Hittite Instructions for Temple Officials, there is mention of killing a slave (lines 29-30): "If a slave should anger his master, either they kill him, or they harm his nose, his eyes, his ears." The unexpected shift to third person plural in the verbs of punishment shows, however, that the punishment was to be carried out by someone other than the master. (A full translation of the complete text is available in *ANET*[3] 207-10.)

33 The difficulty of this phrase for commentators, and the strained rationalizations that result, are illustrated by a recent example: ". . . the sentence here is expressed somewhat less directly, perhaps to ameliorate the harsh and extraordinary circumstances

parents are given the authority of a ruler or judge over a criminal: their own son.

The second text consists of three paragraphs of Codex Eshnunna, a law code from a kingdom to the north of Babylonia that slightly predates the Codex Hammurabi:

12 A man who is seized in the field of an ordinary citizen, in the sheaves at noon, shall pay 10 shekels of silver. He who is seized in the sheaves at night: he shall die, he shall not live.

13 A man who is seized in the house of an ordinary citizen, in the house at noon, shall pay 10 shekels of silver. He who is seized in the house at night: he shall die, he shall not live.

28 . . . If he makes the contract and libation with her father and mother and marries her, she is a wife. The day she is seized in the lap of a man she shall die, she shall not live.

Two situations are described which are familiar from the many parallels in laws from not only the ancient Near East but also Greece and Rome. The first is the burglar caught at night, and the second is the wife caught in adultery. All the parallels share a common feature—the culprit is caught *in flagranti delicto*—and offer the same legal solution: the victim is entitled to kill the culprit on the spot without trial and is not liable for murder. The case of the burglar is found in the laws of Exodus,[34] of Solon,[35] and of the Roman Twelve Tables.[36] In all three the distinction is made between seizure by day, when the victim is not entitled to kill the burglar but only to claim the normal penalties for theft, and seizure by night, when he can kill

---

whereby parents are called upon to execute their own children" (Meyers and Meyers 1993: 374).

34 "If the thief is caught breaking in and is struck dead, he has no blood. If the sun has risen on him, he has blood. He shall surely pay. If he cannot, he shall be sold for his theft" (Exod 22:1-2).

35 "For a theft in day-time of more than fifty drachmas a man might be arrested summarily and put into custody of the Eleven. If he stole anything, however small, by night, the person aggrieved might lawfully pursue and kill or wound him, or else put him into the hands of the Eleven, at his own option" (Demosthenes, *In Timocratem* 113).

36 *SI NOX FURTUM FAXSIT, SI IM OCCISIT, IURE CAESUS ESTO. LUCI . . . SI SE TELO DEFENDIT, . . . ENDOQUE PLORATO* (VIII 12-13).

with impunity. The case of adultery is found in the Hittite Laws[37] and the Middle Assyrian Laws.[38] In both, the husband has the right to kill his wife and her lover should he catch them *in flagranti delicto*, provided he kills both.

At Rome, the right of the husband in early law is described by Aulus Gellius, quoting M. Cato, thus:[39] *in adulterio uxorem tuam si prehendisses, sine iudicio inpune necares*. Augustan legislation (*lex Julia de adulteriis coercendis*) shifted the right from the woman's husband to her father but retained the old (i.e., ancient Near Eastern) learning on the circumstances, namely that he was entitled to kill the lover provided he killed the woman at the same time.[40]

In our view, these parallels are no accident. The two cases are scholastic legal problems from Mesopotamian scribal schools, part of a body of learning that spread across the ancient Near East and even found its way into the Mediterranean countries.[41] The solution that we would expect in the Eshnunna laws is summary execution by the householder or husband, and by now we can see that the enigmatic formula "he shall die, he shall not live" is entirely appropriate. Here the formula is not truncated, but that is not surprising, as it is not a speech formula and the context in itself does not explain the right. Theft and adultery are not public offences that have

---

37 "... if the husband finds them (the adulterers) and kills them, there is no liability upon him" (§197).

38 MAL A 15 is a difficult text, the interpretation of which is the subject of debate among scholars. I translate as follows: "If a man seizes a man with his wife (and if) it has been established and proved with respect to him: (on condition that) both are killed, there is no liability upon him." See further Westbrook 1990b: 551-54.

39 "If you should take your wife in adultery, you may with impunity kill her without trial" (Gell. *NA* 10.23.5).

40 *Coll.* 4.2.3-4, 6-7 (Paul); *Dig.* 48.5.21(20) (Papinian); *Dig.* 48.5.24(23).pr.-4 (Ulpian). In *Coll.* 4.8.1, Papinian is asked the following question: *cum patri lex regia dederit in filia vitae necisque potestatem, quo bonum fuit lege conprehendi, ut potestas fieret etiam filiam occidendi*. Many commentators have assumed *lex* to refer to the Twelve Tables (e.g., Watson 1975b: 42 n. 12), but since the extract is from Papinian's book *On Adulteries* and since it is given in the context of a discussion of the *lex Julia*, it would seem much more reasonable to conclude that it is the Augustan statute that is meant. See Rabello 1979: 36 n.39.

41 The influence of ancient Near Eastern intellectual traditions on early Roman law is discussed in detail below.

to be stopped at all costs, in which action might be expected of a private person.[42] If a private person is to be given the authority of a ruler, a reference to the full formula is necessary. "Shall die" establishes that the culprit is liable to the death penalty; "shall not live" establishes the modalities of its execution, namely summarily at the hands of the victim. Were the victim to spare the culprit and bring him or her before a court, it is not clear that the result would be the same in both cases. The comparative evidence suggests that the adulterous wife might still suffer the death penalty but that the thief would receive a lesser punishment.[43]

To summarize the Near Eastern evidence: the dual formula was used in three situations. Firstly, and primarily, it was used to describe the dual right of rulers to condemn to death or to pardon a person guilty of a capital offence. In this situation, however, the right had one vital feature which has yet to be been mentioned. As Yaron emphasizes, the phrase refers not to some tyrannical whim but to a proper judicial discretion, the exercise of mercy as part of the normal, and desirable, functions of a sovereign subject to the rule of law.[44] This is only to be expected since ancient Near Eastern sovereigns were thought to have received a divine mandate to do justice

---

42 Compare the case of Pinhas in Num 25:7-8, who brought to an end a plague by summarily killing apostates.

43 The continuation of Middle Assyrian Laws A 15 cited above reads: "If he (the husband) seizes (the lover) and brings him before the king or the judges, (and if) it has been established and proved with respect to him: if the husband of the woman will kill his wife, he shall kill the man; if he cuts off his wife's nose, he shall turn the man into a eunuch and his whole face shall be mutilated; but if he frees his wife, he shall free the man." Codex Hammurabi 129 contains a similar rule. Yaron in a recent article claims antonymic use of the phrase "he shall die; he shall not live" is an empty flourish (Yaron 1993b). While admitting that the right to kill the culprit caught *in flagranti delicto* is the most satisfactory legal explanation of the phrase in the Eshnunna provisions, he finally rejects that solution because the wording of the phrase "does not connect up." Curiously, Yaron fails to cite his earlier article on *vitae necisque potestas*, which provides the basis for our attempt in this article to demonstrate a connection between law and phraseology. It is true that the antonymic repetition could well be merely for emphasis in many of the texts in which it is used, but in a legal context we are entitled to look for a legal meaning, to assume more than a rhetorical flourish. This aspect of the problem is discussed by us in Westbrook 1997.

44 Yaron 1962b: 248.

and the legitimacy of their rule depended upon fulfillment of their divine mandate.[45]

The second situation is where a ruler in the proper context uses a truncated version of the formula as a speech formula denying mercy. From that context, the formula may be understood to refer to the ruler's right to impose summary execution for manifest infringement of a law or order.

Thirdly, in exceptional circumstances, the phrase may indicate the right of a private person to execute summary justice by killing a criminal himself. In those cases the right will constitute a defense to a subsequent charge of murder.

*   *   *

What then was its relationship with the Latin phrase and the very different institution attested at Rome? Yaron issues the following disclaimer: "A connection between the Eastern notions and Roman *vnp* is not suggested,—not because it is in itself impossible or unlikely, but rather because there is no evidence available to establish it. Since that is so, our case rests simply on the existence of similar notions in similar situations."[46]

On the face of it, however, neither the notions nor the situations are so very similar. The symbol of a legitimate king in one sphere is the symbol of tyranny in the other. A legal function attributed to Near Eastern kings is matched by a different legal function attributed to Roman masters and fathers. In the ancient Near East, the phrase is not associated with masters, who are not endowed with the right to kill their slaves, whether at will or for cause. With one partial exception that we have seen, the same applies to fathers. On the other hand, a key element of the institution in ancient Near Eastern sources, the right to pardon, is totally absent from the Roman sources.

---

45 King Hammurabi, for example, states in the prologue to his law code: "(the gods) Anu and Enlil, in order to ensure the welfare of the people, named me, Hammurabi, the pious prince who fears the gods, to make justice in the land, to destroy the evil and the wicked, that the strong might not oppress the weak." (Col. I, lines 27-49). See Wiseman 1962.

46 Yaron 1962b: 248.

Yaron suggests[47] that the sovereign nature of early Roman *patria potestas* provides a sufficient analogy, but to what? Not to early Roman kings, of whom the phrase is never used. Comparison between the two institutions can be drawn only on the basis of a historical development, which presupposes a historical connection. In our opinion, Yaron's caution is unwarranted and detracts from the importance of his insight. The key similarity of the phrases is in their form—that curious duality, illogical in Roman usage but logical in Near Eastern usage, through which the missing element in the Roman usage is revealed. That combination of similar form and complementary meaning is in itself evidence of a literary dependency.

The literary dependency indicated by the dual phrase strongly correlates with the influence of ancient Near Eastern intellectual traditions on early Roman law as attested in the phenomenon of "law codes."[48]

In the ancient Near East, there was a recognizably distinct genre of literature that modern scholars refer to as law codes. In spite of being widely scattered in time (from the third to the first millennium) and place (Sumer, Babylonia, Assyria, Hatti, and biblical Israel), the nine extant examples show a striking similarity on several levels.[49]

The most immediate resemblance is in style: all are casuistic collections, that is to say lists of hypothetical cases ("If a man does X . . .") followed by an appropriate legal ruling ("his punishment shall be Y"). At a second level, they all share the same method of reasoning. Paragraphs are not concatenated at random but are organized in groups that follow certain set patterns. For example, a single case will be considered over the course of several paragraphs by varying the circumstances so as to alter the legal ruling, with frequent use of certain standard variations, e.g., if the victim

---

47   Yaron 1962b: 248-49.

48   The following discussion summarizes our previous, detailed studies of this topic: Westbrook 1985a; 1988a; 1990b: 547-56; 1995a. See also Yaron 1974.

49   Codex Ur-Namma, from the city of Ur in southern Mesopotamia (21st century); Codex Lipit-Ishtar, from the city of Isin in southern Mesopotamia (20th century); Codex Eshnunna, from the eponymous city in central Mesopotamia (18th century); Codex Hammurabi, from Babylon in central Mesopotamia (18th century); Middle Assyrian Laws, from Assur in northern Mesopotamia (11th century); Hittite Laws, from Hattusas in Anatolia (various versions from 17th to 12th century); Covenant Code = Exod 21:1-22:16, from Israel (9th century?); Deuteronomic Code = Deut 21:1-25:16, from Israel (7th century).

were free or slave, male or female, etc. Thirdly, the same content is repeated from code to code, in varying degrees. Most frequently, the same
basic case is found, albeit with different variants; sometimes the same
variants are found; occasionally the very same legal ruling; and in a few
instances the phraseology is so close as to be virtually a translation, leaving no doubt as to their dependency on a common literature.[50]
Furthermore, crucial legal distinctions and evidentiary presumptions are
also repeated, showing dependency on a common jurisprudence.[51]

The connection between these codes did not lie in the realm of legal
systems or institutions but of ideas. The Near Eastern codes were not legislation as we understand it today. They belonged to a wider genre of
"scientific" literature, which included divinatory, medical, and lexical
texts.[52] All were presented in the form of lists of examples—in the case of
the omens and their meaning and medical symptoms and their diagnosis, in
casuistic form like the codes. This was Mesopotamian science: the attempt
to understand phenomena by listing them in endless groups of associated
examples. The law codes were lists of legal problems with their solutions,
based upon a core of precedents expanded by extrapolation to theoretical
variations. A canon of standard problems, such as the goring ox, the burglar caught at night, the wife caught in adultery, were used for didactic
purposes and transmitted (orally) from generation to generation, which
explains their recurrence in various law codes. As part of the wider scientific tradition, the legal canon spread from Mesopotamia across the ancient
Near East, occasionally finding written expression in documents such as
those that we call law codes.[53]

---

50 The most striking example is the rule concerning an ox goring an ox, which results in
    virtually identical texts in Codex Eshnunna 53 (in Akkadian) and Exod 21:35 (in He-
    brew). See Malul 1990: 113-52.

51 For example, the distinction between day and night in guilt for killing a burglar, dis-
    cussed above; the distinction between town and countryside in presuming
    acquiescence of a woman in intercourse (Hittite Laws 197 and Deut 22:23-26); the
    status of a woman who is betrothed but not married in cases of sexual misconduct
    (Codex Ur-Namma 6, Codex Eshnunna 26, Codex Hammurabi 130, Deut 22:23-4).

52 See Bottéro 1992: 156-84.

53 The law codes of necessity contain only a small part of the body of knowledge that
    must have existed in the scholastic legal tradition. The reason for creating written
    codes varied. Codex Hammurabi, for example, was a royal apologia, designed to dem-

The characteristic features of the Near Eastern codes are shared by early Roman laws such as the Twelve Tables and the Lex Aquilia. Examples from the canon of standard legal problems are found both within the law codes and in other sources recording traditions of early law. We have seen in our discussion above two such examples—the burglar caught by night and the woman taken in adultery—that relate directly to rights associated with the dual phrase. We therefore consider the Roman codes to have been a manifestation of the same scholastic tradition that lay behind the Near Eastern codes. Accordingly, we suggest that the various rights conceptualized by the dual phrase *vitae necisque potestas* may initially have entered Roman law as part of that scholastic tradition.

Quite apart from the evidence of the law codes, the time for reception of the dual phrase must be located in early Roman history, for two reasons. Firstly, the hoary antiquity attributed to the phrase by Roman tradition is confirmed by its role in the archaic ceremony of *adrogatio*.[54] Secondly, whereas the Near Eastern institution shows a clear and logical development by analogy from the royal prerogative, Roman usage is confused and contradictory, pointing to an inner-Roman development, or rather distortion, which may be linked to the vicissitudes of Roman history. For the central aspect of the Near Eastern institution, the prerogative of the ruler to pardon, would be most appropriate to the period of the kings, and by the same token the absence of this central aspect in the Roman version is accounted for by the caesura in Roman history that replacement of monarchy by the republic represents.[55]

The period of the kings is notorious for the predominance of legend over historical evidence. Moreover, if the connection was through an intellectual tradition, it would be unwise to seek a specific point of reception. Nonetheless, it can be said that the period of the last kings, with their

---

onstrate primarily to the gods that Hammurabi had fulfilled his divine mandate to be a just king; see Finkelstein 1961: 91-104.

54 The *comitia curiata*, which was responsible for *adrogatio*, goes back to the period of the kings. See Heurgon 1993: 216-18; and Linke 1995: 56-63.

55 It is no objection to say that the Twelve Tables and the Lex Aquilia are located by later tradition in the Republican period. The traditional dates for their promulgation can in no way be relied upon, and even if they are accurate, they do not preclude the possibility, highly likely in our view, of the legal traditions that they contain going back to a much earlier date.

Etruscan background, provides especially propitious conditions. On the one hand, the Pyrgi inscription attests to the penetration of Near Eastern elements into the constitutional structure of neighboring Etruscan kingdoms.[56] On the other, several scholars have identified the last Roman kings, of Etruscan origin, as the conduit through which the central elements of an ancient Near Eastern religio-political institution, the New Year Festival, were introduced into Rome.[57] The reason, according to Cornell, was that the sixth-century kings, in their search for legitimacy and charismatic authority, adopted Greek and Near Eastern models of kingship.[58] The dual formula, embodying a ruler's prerogatives of punishment and pardon, would have furnished just such a model.

*   *   *

A reconstruction of the early history of the dual phrase at Rome can, in the absence of contemporary native evidence, only be speculative. If it is descended from the Near Eastern institution, however, then evidence from the latter sphere places our speculations on a slightly firmer footing. We tentatively suggest the following scenario.

1. The prerogative of the kings of early Rome to execute and pardon, conceptualized in a dual phrase of ancient Near Eastern origin—*vitae necisque potestas*—disappeared with the Republic, under which an entirely different system of appeal (*provocatio ad populum*) prevailed.[59]

---

56   For a recent translation of the Phoenician text, see Schmitz 1995.

57   Versnel sees the *ludi Romani* as an Etruscan New Year Festival of Near Eastern origin in which the king acted the part of Iuppiter (1970: 255-84). Cornell identifies the central ritual of the New Year festival—the "sacred marriage" between the king and a goddess—in the legend of Servius Tullius' relationship with the goddess Fortuna (1995: 146-48). For a recent study of the Babylonian New Year Festival, see Black 1981. On the sacred marriage ritual by Near Eastern kings, see Renger 1975.

58   Cornell in fact denies that the rule of the so-called Etruscan kings resulted in Etruscan political or cultural domination of Rome (1995: 151-72), but this does not affect our argument, since he still attributes to those same kings the introduction of Near Eastern institutions into the Roman kingship.

59   The history of *provocatio* in the Republic is the subject of scholarly controversy, but it is agreed that purported instances in the regal period are fictions. See Bleicken 1959: esp. 333-39; and Lintott 1972.

2. A right of summary execution by private citizens, conceived under the same rubric, existed in certain narrow circumstances, such as the thief caught by night, the wife caught in adultery, and those guilty of serious crimes caught by their parents. The right of parents became institutionalized, as evidenced by the use of the dual phrase in the formula of the *adrogatio* ceremony, and a faint echo of this right to kill for cause still existed in later law.[60]

3. A right of summary execution must also have existed for masters of slaves, but it is doubtful that originally it could be exercised without cause. One of the main factors tempering the harshness of slavery in ancient Near Eastern law was that a major source of slaves was citizens selling themselves or their children for debt. A curious feature of classical Roman law, by contrast, was the virtual absence of debt slavery.[61]

Early law had recognized the sale of children of citizens into slavery, probably for debt, as the protasis of IV 2 in the Twelve Tables reveals: *si pater ter filium venum duit* . . . .[62] There had also existed the widespread practice of taking citizens into debt bondage (*nexum*) which, if it was not slavery in strict law, in social reality amounted to the same.[63] *Nexum*, however, was abolished by the Lex Poetelia towards the end of

---

60 Compare the case reported by Valerius Maximus (6.3.8): *publicia autem . . . item Licinia, quae . . . viros suos veneno necaverunt, propinquorum decreto strangulatae sunt. Non enim putaverunt severissimi viri in tam evidenti scelere longum publicae quaestionis tempus exspectandum. itaque quarum innocentium defensores fuissent, sontium mature vindices extiterunt.*

61 The statement of principle for classical law is found in Paulus, *Sent.* 5.1: *qui contemplatione extremae necessitatis aut alimentorum gratia filios suos vendiderint, statui ingenuitatis eorum non praeiudicant: homo enim liber nullo pretio aestimatur.* Codex Theodosianus, as we have seen, projected this view back into early history (4.9[8].6.pr.). An exception, however, remained for the sale of newborn babies; see Buckland 1908: 421-22; and Yaron 1965.

62 On the connection between this provision and debt slavery, in the light of ancient Near Eastern sources, see Westbrook 1989b.

63 On the social reality behind *nexum* and the background to its abolition, see Richard 1986: 124-27; and Raaflaub 1986: 208-17. On the legal nature of *nexum*, see MacCormack 1967: 350-55.

the fourth century, and by the late Republic the sale of children had become a mere fiction to effect emancipation from *patria potestas* (Gaius *Inst.* I 132). Instead, expansion of the empire from the third century on radically changed the nature of slave-holding. The main source of slaves became foreign captives (and later their offspring), thereby opening the way to a much harsher attitude to slaves and the abandonment of all restraint on masters' powers.[64] For the classical jurists, the prisoner of war was the archetype of a slave and his captive status the legal basis of slavery, by a mode of reasoning which brings us full circle to the rationale for the power of life and death in ancient Near Eastern jurisprudence.

Florentinus takes it as axiomatic that the origin of slavery was captivity in war:[65] *servi ex eo appellati sunt, quod impera-tores captivos vendere ac per hoc servare nec occidere solent: mancipia vero dicta, quod ab hostibus manu capiantur.* On the other hand, according to Ulpian "slavery is equated with death."[66] The resolution of the apparent contradiction between these two statements lies in the concept which we have seen was central to the dual prerogative in the ancient Near East, that of legal death. For Ulpian elsewhere states:[67] *in omnibus partibus iuris is, qui reversus non est ab hostibus, quasi tunc decessisse videtur, cum captus est.* Although Roman law was interested only in Roman citizens captured by foreign enemies, the same principle would be equally valid for foreign captives of Roman arms. As Bradley puts it, the enslaved captive was

---

64 Bradley 1987; and 1994: 13-14, 31-33, 39-42.

65 "Slaves (*servi*) are so called because generals have a custom of selling their prisoners and thereby *preserving* rather than killing them; and indeed they are said to be *man-cipia*, because they are *captives* in the hand (*manus*) of their enemies" (*Dig.* 1.5.4.2).

66 *servitus morti adsimulatur. Dig.* 35.1.59.2. Cf. *Dig.* 50.17.209 (Ulpian).

67 "In every branch of the law, a person who fails to return from enemy hands is regarded as having died at the moment when he was captured" (*Dig.* 49.15.18). The doctrine of *postliminium* may therefore be regarded as the equivalent of pardon in that it brought back to life a person who was legally dead.

regarded as being in a condition of suspended death at the discretion of his captor.[68]

4. By the late Republic, the master-slave relationship was the only legal relationship in which *vitae necisque potestas* was still a living institution. Based on the experience of that relationship, the phrase became a metaphor for unbridled tyranny in the political sphere, being now understood as the right of summary execution without cause.

68   Bradley 1994: 26.

Abbreviations

A	tablets in the collections of the Oriental Institute, University of Chicago
AAASH	*Acta Antiqua Academiae Scientiarum Hungaricae*
AASOR	*Annual of the American Schools of Oriental Research*
AB	Anchor Bible
ABAW	Abhandlungen der Bayerischen Akademie der Wissenschaften
AbB	Altbabylonische Briefe im Umschrift and Übersetzung
ABL	Harper, R., ed. 1892-1914. *Assyrian and Babylonian Letters Belonging to the Kouyunjik Collections of the British Museum.* 14 vols. Chicago: University of Chicago Press.
ADD	Johns, C. H. W. 1898-1924. *Assyrian Deeds and Documents.* 4 vols. Cambridge: Deighton, Bell.
AEM	Archives Epistolaires de Mari
ÄF	Ägyptologische Forschungen
AfK	*Archiv für Keilschriftforschung*
AfO	*Archiv für Orientforschung*
AfO Beiheft	Archiv für Orientforschung Beiheft
AHDO	Archives d'histoire du droit oriental
AHw	Soden, W. von. 1965-1981. *Akkadisches Handwörterbuch.* 3 vols. Wiesbaden: Harrassowitz.
AION	*Annali dell'Istituto Universitario Orientale di Napoli*
AJSL	*American Journal of Semitic Languages and Literature*
AnBib	Analecta biblica
ANET[3]	Pritchard, J. B., ed. 1969. *Ancient Near Eastern Texts Relating to the Old Testament.* 3d ed. with supplement. Princeton: Princeton University Press.
AnOr	Analecta orientalia
AnSt	*Anatolian Studies*
AOAT	Alter Orient und Altes Testament
AoF	*Altorientalische Forschungen*
AOS	American Oriental Series

Aristotle *Ath. Pol.*   Aristotle, *Athenain politeia*

ARM   Archives Royales de Mari

Arnaud *Emar* 6   Arnaud, D. 1986. *Recherches au pays d'Aštata, Emar VI.* Vol. 3: *Textes sumériens et accadiens.* Paris: Éditions Recherches sur les civilisations.

Arnaud *Textes*   Arnaud, D. 1991 *Textes syriens de l'âge du bronze récent.*
   syriens   AuOrSup 1. Barcelona: Editorial Ausa.

ArOr   *Archív Orientální*

ARU   Kohler, J., and A. Ungnad. 1913. *Assyrische Rechtsurkunden, in Umschrift und Übersetzung nebst einem Index der Personen-Namen und Rechtserläuterungen.* Leipzig: Pfeiffer.

AS   Assyriological Studies

ASAW   Abhandlungen der Sächsischen Akademie der Wissenschaften

ASJ   *Acta Sumerologica*

ASOR   American Schools of Oriental Research

ASORSup   American Schools of Oriental Research Supplement Series

AT   Alalakh Tablets

AuOr   *Aula Orientalis*

AuOrSup   Aula Orientalis Supplement Series

Authorized Version   Authorized Version. See Hall, F., et al., eds. 1924. *The Holy Bible, Reprinted according to the Authorized Version, 1611.* London and New York: Nonesuch Press; Lincoln MacVeagh; Dial Press.

AV   Anniversary Volume

b. B. Qam.   Babylonian Talmud *Bava Qamma*

b. Git.   Babylonian Talmud *Gittin*

b. Sotah   Babylonian Talmud *Sotah*

BA   Babylonische Archive

BA   *Biblical Archaeologist*

BaghM   *Baghdader Mitteilungen*

BASOR   *Bulletin of the American Schools of Oriental Research*

BASP   *Bulletin of the American Society of Papyrologists*

BBB   Bonner Biblische Beiträge

BBSt.   King, L. W. 1912. *Babylonian Boundary Stones*, London: British Museum.

BE   Babylonian Expedition of the University of Pennsylvania, Series A: Cuneiform Texts

Beckman and   Beckman, G. M., and H. A. Hoffner, Jr. 1996. *Hittite*
   Hoffner 1996   *Diplomatic Texts.* SBLWAW 7. Atlanta: Scholars Press.

Beckman *Emar*	Beckman, G. M. 1996. *Texts from the Vicinity of Emar in the Collection of Jonathan Rosen.* HANEM 2. Padua: Sargon.
Bib	*Biblica*
Bible de Jérusalem	École Biblique et Archéologique Française. 1974. *La Bible de Jérusalem: La Sainte Bible.* Paris: Éditions du Cerf.
BICSSup	Bulletin of the Institute of Classical Studies Supplement
BiMes	Bibliotheca Mesopotamica
BIN	Babylonian Inscriptions in the Collection of J. B. Nies
BISNELC	Bar-Ilan Studies in Near Eastern Languages and Culture
BM	tablets in the collections of the British Museum
BO	*Bibliotheca Orientalis*
Bo.	field numbers of tablets excavated at Boghazköi
Boyer *Contribution*	Boyer, G. 1928. *Contribution à l'histoire juridique de la 1ère dynastie babylonienne.* Paris: Geuthner.
BRM	Babylonian Records in the Library of J. Pierpoint Morgan
BT	Kutscher, R. 1989. *The Brockman Tablets of the University of Haifa.* Vol. 1. *Royal Inscriptions.* Haifa: Haifa University Press; Harrassowitz: Wiesbaden.
BWANT	Beiträge zur Wissenschaft von Alten und Neuen Testament
BZ	*Biblische Zeitschrift*
BzA	*Beiträge zur Assyriologie*
BZAR	Beihefte zur Zeitschrift für altorientalische und biblische Rechtgeschichte
BZAW	Beihefte zur Zeitschrift für die alttestamentliche Wissenschaft
c(a).	circa
CAD	Oppenheim, A. L., et al., eds.1956-. *The Assyrian Dictionary of the Oriental Institute of Chicago.* Chicago: Oriental Institute of the University of Chicago.
Caesar *Bell. gall.*	Caesar, *de bello gallico = Gallic War*
Camb.	Strassmaier, J. N. 1890. *Inschriften von Cambyses, König von Babylon (529-521 v. Chr.).* Leipzig: Pfeiffer.
Cato *de agr.*	Cato, *de agri cultura origins*
CBS	tablets in the collections of the University Museum of the University of Pennsylvania, Philadelphia
CC	Covenant Code
CE	Code of Eshnunna
CH	Code of Hammurabi
CHANE	Culture and History of the Ancient Near East
chap(s).	chapter(s)

CHD	Güterbock, H. G., and H. A. Hoffner, Jr. 1980-. *The Hittite Dictionary of the Oriental Institute of the University of Chicago.* Chicago: The Oriental Institute.
Cicero *Att.*	Cicero, *Epistulae ad Atticum*
Cicero *de leg.*	Cicero, *de legibus*
Cicero *Dom.*	Cicero, *de domo sua*
Cicero *Fin.*	Cicero, *de finibus bonorum et malorum*
Cicero *pro Balbo*	Cicero, *pro L. Balbo*
Cicero *pro Tullio*	Cicero, *pro M. Tullio*
Cicero *Rep.*	Cicero, *de re publica*
Cicero *Verr.*	Cicero, *In Verrem*
CL	Code of Lipit-Ishtar
Claud. *Rap. Pros.*	Claudian, *de Raptu Proserpinae*
aCM	Cuneiform Monographs
Cod. Theod.	Theodosian Code; Codex Theodosianus
col(s).	column(s)
Coll.	*Mosaicarum et Romanarum legum collatio*
ConBOT	Coniectanea Biblica Old Testament Series
Cowley	Cowley, A. 1923. *The Aramaic Papyri of the Fifth Century B.C.* Oxford: Oxford University Press.
CQ	*Classical Quarterly*
CRRAI	Compte-rendu de la Rencontre Assyriologique International
CSA	Cahiers de la Société Asiatique
CT	Cuneiform Texts from Babylonian Tablets in the British Museum
CT Nebraska	Forde, N. W. 1967. *Nebraska Cuneiform Tests of the Sumerian Ur Dynasty.* Lawrence, Kansas: Coronado Press.
CTH	Laroche, E. 1971. *Catalogue des textes hittites.* Études et commentaires 75. Paris: Klincksieck.
CTN	Cuneiform Texts from Nimrud
CU	Code of Ur-Namma
Cyr.	Strassmaier, J. N. 1890. *Inschriften von Cyrus, König von Babylon (538-529 v. Chr.).* Leipzig: Pfeiffer.
D.	Corpus Juris Civilis, *Digesta* (author as applicable)
Dalley *Edinburgh*	Dalley, S. 1979. *A Catalogue of the Akkadian Cuneiform Tablets in the Collections of the Royal Scottish Museum, Edinburgh, with Copies of Texts.* Royal Scottish Museum Art and Archaeology 2. Edinburgh: Royal Scottish Museum.
Dar.	Strassmaier, J. N. 1890. *Inschriften von Darius, König von Babylon (521-485 v. Chr.).* Leipzig: Pfeiffer.

Demosthenes *Timocr.*	Demosthenes, *In Timocratem*
Dig.	Corpus Juris Civilis, *Digesta* (author as applicable)
Dio Cass.	Cassius Dio
Diodorus Siculus *Bib. Hist.*	Diodorus Siculus, *Biblioteca Historica*
Dion. Hal.	Dionysius (of) Halicarnassus
DN	divine name
EA	El-Amarna Letters, as edited in Knudtzon, J. A., ed. 1907-1915. *Die El-Amarna-Tafeln.* 2 vols. Vorderasiatische Bibliothek. Leipzig: Hinrichs.
Ea	lexical series ea A = *nâqu*; published in MSL XIV
ed(s).	editor(s)
EI	*Eretz-Israel*
Ent.	Entemena
Erimhuš	lexical series erimḫuš = *anantu*; published in MSL XVII
FAOS	Freiburger Altorientalische Studien
ff.	and following
FIOL	The Formation and Interpretation of Old Testament Literature
FIRA	Riccobono, S., and J. Baviera, eds. 1968. *Fontes iuris Romani anteiustiniani.* 3 vols. Florenz: Barbèra.
Florentinus *Dig.*	Corpus Juris Civilis, *Digesta* (Florentinus)
G.	Gaius, *Institutiones*
GAG	Soden, W. von. 1969. *Grundriss der Akkadischen Grammatik.* 2 vols. Analecta Orientalia 33 and 47. Rome: Pontifical Biblical Institute.
Gaius *Augustod.*	*Fragmenta interpretationis Gai institutionum Augustodunensia*
Gaius *Dig.*	Corpus Juris Civilis, *Digesta* (Gaius)
Gaius *Inst.*	Gaius, *Institutiones*
Gaius *Prov. Edict*	Gaius, *Ad Edictum Praetoris Provinciale* = *Commentary on the Provincial Edict*
Gell. *NA*	Gellius, *noctes Atticae*
GN	geographic name
GRBS	*Greek, Roman, and Byzantine Studies*
GRBM	Greek, Roman, and Byzantine Monographs
Gurney *MB Texts*	Gurney, O. R. 1983. *The Middle Babylonian Legal and Economic Texts from Ur.* London: British School of Archaeology in Iraq.

HAL³	Köhler, L., Baumgartner, W., and Stamm, J. J. 1967-96. *Hebräisches und Aramäisches Lexikon zum Alten Testament*. 3d ed. Edited by W. Baumgartner. Leiden: Brill.
HANEM	History of the Ancient Near East Monographs
HANES	History of the Ancient Near East Studies
HdO	Handbuch der Orientalistik
HG	Kohler J., A. Ungnad et al. 1904-23. *Hammurabis Gesetz*. 6 vols. Leipzig: Pfeiffer.
Hg.	lexical series ḪAR.gud = *imrú* = *ballu*; published in MSL V-XI
Hh.	lexical series ḪAR.ra = *ḫubullu*; published in MSL V-XI
HL	Hittite Laws
HSCP	*Harvard Studies in Classical Philology*
HSM	Harvard Semitic Monographs
HSS	Harvard Semitic Studies
HTR	*Harvard Theological Review*
HUCA	*Hebrew Union College Annual*
IBHS	Waltke, B. K., and M. O'Conner. 1990. *An Introduction to Biblical Syntax*. Winona Lake, Ind.: Eisenbrauns.
IBoT	Istanbul Arkeoloji Müzelerinde Bulunan Boğazköy Tabletleri
ICC	International Critical Commentary
ICK	Hrozný B. 1952-62. *Inscriptions cunéiformes du Kultépé*. Translated by M. David. 2 vols. Archív Orientální Monografie 14. Praha: Státni pedogogické nakl.
IEJ	*Israel Exploration Journal*
Il.	Homer, *The Iliad*
IM	tablets in the collections of the Iraq Museum, Baghdad
IOS	*Israel Oriental Society*
ITT	Constantinople Arkeoloji Müzeleri [Constantinople Archaeological Museum]. 1910-21. *Inventaire des tablettes de Tello conservées au Musée impérial ottoman*. 5 vols. Paris: Leroux.
J. Westenholz Emar	Westenholz, J. G. 2000. *Cuneiform Inscriptions in the Collection of the Bible Lands Museum Jerusalem: The Emar Tablets*. CM 13. Groningen: Styx.
JANES	*Journal of the Ancient Near East Society of Columbia University*
JAOS	*Journal of the American Oriental Society*
JBL	*Journal of Biblical Literature*
JCS	*Journal of Cuneiform Studies*

Jean *Tell Sifr*	Jean, Ch.-F. 1931. *Tell Sifr textes cunéiformes conservés au British Museum*. Paris: Geuthner.
JEN	Joint Expedition with the Iraq Museum at Nuzi
JEOL	*Jaarbericht van het Vooraziatisch-Egyptisch Genootschap "Ex Oriente Lux"*
JESHO	*Journal of the Economic and Social History of the Orient*
JHS	*Journal of Hebrew Scriptures*
JJP	*Journal of Juristic Papyrology*
JJS	*Journal of Jewish Studies*
JLA	*Jewish Law Annual*
JNES	*Journal of Near Eastern Studies*
JNSL	*Journal of Northwest Semitic Languages*
Jones and Snyder	Jones, T. B., and J. W. Snyder. 1991. *Sumerian Economic Texts from the Third Ur Dynasty*. Minneapolis: University of Minnesota Press.
JPS	Jewish Publication Society. 1985. *Tanakh*. New York: Jewish Publication Society.
JPS Torah Comm.	Jewish Publication Society Torah Commentary
JQR	*Jewish Quarterly Review*
JRS	*Journal of Roman Studies*
JSOT	*Journal for the Study of the Old Testament*
JSOTSup	Journal for the Study of the Old Testament Supplement Series
JSS	*Journal of Semitic Studies*
Justinian *Inst.*	Justinian, *Institutiones*
KadmosSup	Kadmos (Zeitschrift für vor- und frühgriechische Epigraphik) Supplement
KAH	Keilschrifttexte aus Assur historischen Inhalts
KAJ	Keilschrifttexte aus Assur juristischen Inhalts
KAR	Keilschrifttexte aus Assur religiösen Inhalts
KAV	Keilschrifttexte aus Assur verschiedenen Inhalts
KBo	Keilschrifturkunden von Boghazköi
KḪ	Kodex Ḫammurabi = Code of Hammurabi
Kienast *Altass. Kaufvertragsrecht*	Kienast, B. 1984. *Das altassyrische Kaufvertragsrecht*. FAOS 1. Altassyrische Texte und Untersuchungen 1. Stuttgart: Steiner.
Kraeling	Kraeling, E. 1953. *The Brooklyn Museum Aramaic Papyri: New Documents of the Fifth Century B.C. from the Jewish Colony at Elephantine*. Publications of the Department of Egyptian Art. New Haven: Yale University Press. Reprinted New York: Arno Press, 1969.

Kramer *AV*	Eichler, B. L., J. W. Heimerdinger, and Å. W. Sjöberg, eds. 1976. *Kramer Anniversary Volume: Cuneiform Studies in Honor of Samuel Noah Kramer*. AOAT 25. Kevelaer: Butzon & Bercker.
Kraus *AV*	Driel, G. van, et. al., eds. 1982. *Zikir Šumim: Assyriological Studies Presented to F. R. Kraus on the Occasion of His Seventieth Birthday*. Leiden: Brill.
KTS	Keilschrifttexte in den Antiken-Museen zu Stambul
KUB	Keilschrifturkunden aus Boghazköi
Lambert *BWL*	Lambert, W. G. 1960. *Babylonian Wisdom Literature*. Oxford: Clarendon.
LAPO	Littératures anciennes du Proche Orient
LCL	Loeb Classical Library
LHB/OTS	Library of Hebrew Bible / Old Testament Studies
LIH	King, L. W. 1898-1900. *The Letters and Inscriptions of Ḥammurabi, King of Babylon*. London: Luzac.
Livy	Titus Lilvius, *Ab urbe condita libri*
LQR	*Law Quarterly Review*
LSJ	Liddell, H. G., R. Scott, H. S. Jones et al., eds. 1996. *A Greek-English Lexicon*. Oxford and New York: Clarendon Press; University of Oxford Press.
LTBA	Soden, W. von, and Staatliche Museen zu Berlin, Vorderasiatische Abteilung. 1933-. *Die lexikalischen Tafelserien der Babylonier und Assyrer in den Berliner Museen*. 2 vols. Berlin: Vorderasiatische Abteilung der Staatliche Museen zu Berlin.
Lucilius	Gaius Lucilius, *The Twelve Tables*
LXX	Septuagint
m. Giṭ.	Mishnah *Giṭṭin*
m. Ketub.	Mishnah *Ketubbot*
m. Yebam.	Mishnah *Yebamot*
m. Yoma	Mishnah *Yoma* = Mishnah *Kippurim*
MA	Middle Assyrian
MAL	Middle Assyrian Laws
MAL A	Middle Assyrian Laws, Tablet A (and so forth through N)
MANE	Sources and Monographs. Monographs on the Ancient Near East
Manilius *Astr.*	Manilius, *astronomica*
MAOG	Mitteilungen der Altorientalischen Gesellschaft
Marcianus *Dig.*	Corpus Juris Civilis, *Digesta* (Marcianus)
MB	Middle Babylonian

MDP	Mémoires de la Délégation en Perse
MEFR	*Mélanges d'archéologie et d'histoire de l'école français de Rome*
Meissner *BAP*	Meissner, B. 1893. *Beiträge zum altbabylonischen Privatrecht*. Leipzig: Hinrichs.
Mek.	*Mekhilta*
MIO	*Mitteilungen des Instituts für Orientforschung*
MKNAW	Mededelingen der Koninklijke Nederlandse Akademie van Wetenschappen
MSL	Materialien zum sumerischen Lexikon
	I = Landsberger 1937
	VI = Landsberger 1958
	VIII/1 = Kilmer, Gordon, and Landsberger 1960
	VIII/2 = Kilmer and Landsberger 1962
	IX = Civil and Landsberger 1967
	XII = Civil 1969
	XIII = Civil 1971
	XIV = Civil 1979
	XVI = Finkel and Civil 1982
	XVII = Cavigneaux et al. 1985
MT	Masoretic Text
MVAG	Mitteilungen der Vorderasiatisch-Ägyptischen Gesellschaft
MVN	Materiali per il vocabolario neo-sumerico
n(n).	note(s)
N.A.B.U.	Nouvelles Assyriologiques Brèves et Utilitaires
NA	Neo-Assyrian
Nabnitu	lexical series SIG₇ + ALAM = *nabnītu* published in MSL XVI
NB	Neo-Babylonian
NBL	Neo-Babylonian Laws
Nbn.	Strassmaier, J. N. 1889. *Inschriften von Nabonidus, König von Babylon (555-538 v. Chr.)*. Leipzig: Pfeiffer.
NCB	New Century Bible
NCBT	tablets in the Newell Collection of Babylonian Tablets, Yale University Library
ND	field numbers of tablets excavated at Nimrud (Kalhu)
New English Bible	Joint Committee on the New Translation of the Bible. 1970. *The New English Bible with the Apocrypha*. London and New York: Oxford University Press; Cambridge University Press.
NF / n.F.	Neue Folge
no(s).	number(s)

NRVN	Çiğ, M., and H. Kizilyay. 1965. *Neusumerische Rechts- und Verwaltungsurkunden aus Nippur I*. TTKY 6/7. Ankara: Türk tarih kurumu basimevi.
NS / ns	New Series
NSG	Falkenstein, A. 1956-1957. *Die neusumerischen Gerichtsurkunden*. 3 vols. ABAW philosophisch-historische Klasse n.F. 39, 40, 44. Munich: Bayerische Akademie der Wissenschaften.
NT	field numbers of tablets excavated at Nippur by the Oriental Institute and other institutions
OA	Old Assyrian
OB	Old Babylonian
OBC	Orientalia Biblica et Christiana
OBO	Orbis Biblicus et Orientalis
OBT Tell Rimah	Dalley, S., C. B. F. Walker, and J. D. Hawkins. 1976. *Old Babylonian Texts from Tell al Rimah*. London: British School of Archaeology in Iraq.
Od.	Homer, *The Odyssey*
OECT	Oxford Editions of Cuneiform Texts
OIP	Oriental Institute Publications
OLA	Orientalia Lovaniensia Analecta
OLZ	*Orientalische Literaturzeitung*
Or (NS)	*Orientalia (Nova Series)*
OrAnt	*Oriens antiquus*
Oros.	Orosius
OTL	Old Testament Library
OtSt	*Oudtestamentische Studiën*
Ovid *Fast.*	Ovid, *Fasti*
Ovid *Metam.*	Ovid, *Metamorphoses*
Oxford Bible	May, H. G., and B. M. Metzger, eds. 1962. *The Holy Bible: Revised Standard Version*. London and New York: Oxford University Press.
Papinian *Dig.*	Corpus Juris Civilis, *Digesta* (Papinian)
Paulus *Dig.*	Corpus Juris Civilis, *Digesta* (Paulus)
Paulus *Sent.*	Paulus, *Sententiae*
PBS	Publications of the Babylonian Section, University Museum, University of Pennsylvania
Petschow *MB Rechtsurkunden*	Petschow, H. 1974. *Mittelbabylonische Rechts- und Wirtschaftsurkunden der Hilprecht-Sammlung Jena*. ASAW philosophisch-historische Klasse 64/4. Berlin: Akademie-Verlag.

Philo *Spec. Laws*	Philo of Alexandria, *On Special Laws*
PIHANS	Uitgaven van het Nederlands Historisch-archeologische Instituut te Istanbul
pl.	plate
Plautus *Asin.*	Plautus, *Asinaria*
Plautus *Merc.*	Plautus, *Mercator*
Plautus *Pseud.*	Plautus, *Pseudolus*
Plautus *Rud.*	Plautus, *Rudens*
Pliny *Nat.*	Pliny (the Elder), *Naturalis historia*
PN	personal name
Pomponius *Dig.*	Corpus Juris Civilis, *Digesta* (Pomponius)
PRU	Le Palais Royal d'Ugarit
PY	Pylos (site where numerous Linear B texts were discovered; on additional sigla, see Bennett 1953).
Quintilian *Decl. mai.*	Quintilianus, *Declamationes maiores*
Quintilian *Decl. min.*	Quintilianus, *Declamationes minores*
Quintilian *Inst.*	Quintilian, *Institutio oratoria*
RA	*Revue d'Assyriologique et d'Archéologie orientale*
RAI	Rencontre Assyriologique Internationale
RB	*Revue Biblique*
RHA	*Revue hittite et asianique*
RHPR	*Revue d'Histoire et de Philosophie Religieuses*
RIDA	*Revue internationale du droit de l'antiquité*
Riftin	Riftin, A. P. 1937. *Staro-Vavilonskie iuridicheskie i administrativnye dokumenty v sobraniiakh SSSR*. Moscow: Izd-vo Akademii nauk SSSR.
RlA	*Reallexikon der Assyriologie*. Edited by E. Ebeling, et al. 16 vols. Berlin: de Gruyter, 1928–.
RN	royal name
RS	field numbers of tablets excavated at Ras Shamra
RSO	Rivista degli studi orientali
RSV	Revised Standard Version. See Burrows, M., et al., ed. 1952. *The Holy Bible: Revised Standard Version*. Toronto and New York: T. Nelson.
SAA	State Archives of Assyria
SAAS	State Archives of Assyria Studies
Sallust. *Bell. Cat.*	Sallustius, *Bellum catilinae*
Sallust. *Bell. Iug.*	Sallustius, *Bellum iugurthinum*

San Nicolò- Petschow *Bab.* *Rechtsurkunden*	San Nicolò, M., and H. Petschow. 1960. *Babylonische Rechtsurkunden aus dem 6. Jahrhundert v. Chr.* ABAW philosophisch-historische Klasse n.F. 51. Munich: Bayerische Akademie der Wissenschaften.
SANE	Sources from the Ancient Near East
SBH	Reisner, G. A. 1986. *Sumerisch-babylonische Hymnen nach Thontafeln griechischer Zeit.* Königliche Museen zu Berlin. Mitteilungen aus den orientalischen Sammlungen 10. Berlin: Spemann
SBLDS	Society of Biblical Literature Dissertation Series
SBLSymS	Society of Biblical Literature Symposium Series
SBLWAW	Society of Biblical Literature Writings from the Ancient World
SBS	Stuttgarter Bibelstudien
SCCNH	Studies on the Civilization and Culture of Nuzi and the Hurrians
Schol. ad Bas.	Scholiast on the *Basilica*
SDHI	*Studia et documenta historiae et iuris*
SDIOAP	Studia et documenta ad iura orientis antiqui pertinentia
Sen. *Clem.*	Seneca minor, *de clementia*
Sen. *Controv.*	Seneca maior, *controversiae*
Sen. *Ep. Mor.*	Seneca minor, *epistulae morales ad Lucilium*
SHA	*scriptores historiae Augustae*
Sigrist *Kutscher Mem. Vol.*	Rainey, A., et al., eds. 1993. Kinattūtu ša dārâti. *Raphael Kutscher Memorial Volume.* Tel Aviv Occasional Publications 1. Tel Aviv: Institute of Archaeology of Tel Aviv University.
Sigrist *Messenger Texts*	Sigrist, M. 1990. *Messenger Texts from the British Museum.* Potomac, Md.: Capital Decisions.
SJLA	Studies in Judaism in Late Antiquity
SLB	Studia ad tabulas cuneiformes collectas a F. M. Th. de Liagre Böhl pertinentia.
SMEA	*Studi Micenei e Egeo-Anatolici*
SMN	tablets excavated at Nuzi, in the Semitic Museum, Harvard University, Cambridge, Mass.
SNATBM	Ozaki (Gomi), T., and S. Sato. 1990. *Selected Neo-Sumerian Administrative Texts from the British Museum.* Soken kenkyu shiryo 7. Abiko: Research Institute, Chuo-Gakuin University.
Sollberger *Corpus*	Sollberger, E. 1956. *Corpus des inscriptions "royales" présargoniques de Lagaš.* Geneva: Dros.

SR	*Studies in Religion/Sciences religieuses*
SRU	Edzard, D. O. 1968. *Sumerische Rechtsurkunden des III. Jahrtausends aus der Zeit vor der III. Dynastie von Ur.* ABAW philosophisch-historische Klasse n.F. 67. Munich: Bayerische Akademie der Wissenschaften, with Beck.
Statius *Theb.*	Publius Papinius Statius, *Thebaid*
StBoT	Studien zu den Boğazöy-Texten
Strabo *Geo.*	Strabo, *Geographica*
StudBib	Studia Biblica
Studies Landsberger	Güterbock, H. G., and T. Jacobsen, eds. 1965. *Studies in Honour of Benno Landsberger on His Seventy-Fifth Birthday.* AS 16. Chicago: University of Chicago Press.
SubBi	Subsidia biblica
Szlechter *TJA*	Szlechter, E. 1963. *Tablettes juridiques et administratives de la IIIe dynastie d'Ur.* Publications de l'Institut de droit romain de l'Université de Paris 21. Paris: Recueil Sirey.
T.	(Twelve) Tables
Tac. *Hist.*	Tacitus, *Historiae*
TAD	Porten, B., and A. Yardeni, eds. 1989. *Textbook of Aramaic Documents from Ancient Egypt.* 2 vols. Texts and Studies for Students. Jerusalem: Hebrew University, Department of the History of the Jewish People; Winona Lake, Ind.: Eisenbrauns.
TAPA	Transactions of the American Philosophical Society
TCL	Textes cunéiformes du Louvre
TCM	Textes cunéiformes de Mari
TCS	Texts from Cuneiform Sources
Theophilus *Para.*	Theophilus, *Paraphrasis*
TIM	Texts in the Iraq Museum
TLB	Tabulae cuneiformes a F. M. Th. de Liagre Böhl collectae
trans.	translated by
transl.	translation
TTKY	Türk Tarih Kurumu Yayinlari(ndan)
TUAT	Texte aus der Umwelt des Alten Testaments
TuM	Texte und Materialien der Frau Professor Hilprecht Collection of Babylonian Antiquities im Eigentum der Universität Jena
TvR	*Tijdschrift voor Rechtsgeschiedenis*
UCP	University of California Publications in Semitic Philology
UET	Ur Excavations, Texts

UF	*Ugarit-Forschungen*
Ukg.	Urkagina = Uru-inimgina = Irikagina (the preferred reading of this name)
Ulpian *Dig.*	Corpus Juris Civilis, *Digesta* (Ulpian)
Urk. IV	Sethe, K., and Helck, W., eds. 1906-09; 1955-58. *Urkunden des ägyptischen Altertums IV: Urkunden der 18. Dynastie.* 22 vols. Leipzig: Heinrich (vols. 1-16, 1906-1909); Berlin: Akademie-Verlag (vols. 17-22, 1955-1958).
US	United States (Supreme Court) Reporter
v(v).	verse(s)
Val. Max.	Valerius Maximus, *Factorum et Dictorum Memorabilium Libri Novem*
Varro *L.*	Varro, *de lingua latina*
VAS	Vorderasiatische Schriftdenkmäler
Vienna Convention on the Law of Treaties	United Nations, International Law Commission. 1969. Vienna Convention on the Law of Treaties: drafted 1969, revised and adopted 1980.
Virgil *Aen.*	Virgil, *Aeneid*
VS	= VAS
VSAW	Verhandlungen der Sächsischen Akademie der Wissenschaften
VT	*Vetus Testamentum*
VTSup	Supplements to Vetus Testamentum
Waterman, *Bus. Doc.*	Waterman, L. 1916. *Business Documents of the Hammurapi Period. Ancient Mesopotamian Tests and Studies.* London: Ams Press (= *AJSL* 29-30 [1912-1914])
Westenholz *OSP*	Westenholz, A. 1975 & 1987. *Old Sumerian and Old Akkadian Texts in Philadelphia Chiefly from Nippur* (1 = BiMes 1, Malibu, Calif.: Undena Publications; 2 = Carsten Niebuhr Institute Publications 3, Copenhagen: Carsten Niebuhr Institute of Ancient Near Eastern Studies).
WMANT	Wissenschaftliche Monographien zum Alten und Neuen Testament
WO	*Die Welt des Orients*
WVDOH	Wissenschaftliche Veröffentlichungen der deutschen Orientgesellschaft
WZKM	*Wiener Zeitschrift für die Kunde des Morgenlands*
Xenophon *Cyn.*	Xenophon, *Cynegeticus*
YBC	tablets in the Babylonian Collection, Yale University Library

YNER	Yale Near Eastern Researches Series
YOS	Yale Oriental Series
YOSR	Yale Oriental Series, Researches
ZA	*Zeitschrift für Assyriologie*
ZAH	*Zeitschrift für Althebräistik*
ZÄS	*Zeitschrift für die Ägyptische Sprache und Altertumskunde*
ZAW	*Zeitschrift für die alttestamentliche Wissenschaft*
ZDMG	*Zeitschrift der Deutschen Morgenländischen Gesellschaft*
ZSSR (Rom. Abt.)	*Zeitschrift der Savigny-Stiftung für Rechtsgeschichte (Romanistische Abteilung)*
ZVR	*Zeitschrift für vergleichende Rechtswissenschaft*
ZVS	*Zeitschrift für vergleichende Sprachforschung*

Bibliography

Abusch, I. T.
1987   *Babylonian Witchcraft Literature: Case Studies.* Atlanta: Scholars Press.
2002   *Mesopotamian Witchcraft: Toward a History and Understanding of Babylonian Witchcraft Beliefs and Literature.* Ancient Magic and Divination 5. Leiden: Brill/Styx.

Alt, A.
1934   *Ursprünge des israelitischen Rechts.* VSAW philologisch-historische Klasse 86/1. Leipzig: Hirzel. Reprinted as pages 278-332 in vol. 1 of *Kleine Schriften zur Geschichte des Volkes Israel.* 3 vols. Munich: Beck, 1959. English edition: "The Origins of Israelite Law." Pages 81-132 in *Essays on Old Testament History and Religion.* Translated by R. A. Wilson. Oxford: Blackwell, 1966.

Andersen, F. I., and D. N. Freedman
1980   *Hosea.* AB 24. New York: Doubleday.

Andersen, Ø.
1976   "Some Thoughts on the Shield of Achilles." *Symbolae Osloenses* 51: 5-18.

Ankum, H.
1983   "QUANTI EA RES ERIT IN DIEBUS XXX PROXIMIS dans le troisième chapitre de la *lex Aquilia*: un fantasme florentin." Pages 171-83 in *Religion, Société et Politique. Mélanges en hommage à Jacques Ellul.* Edited by E. Bravase, C. Emeri, and J.-L. Seurin. Paris: Presses universitaires de France.

Arnaud, D.
1986   *Recherches au pays d'Aštata, Emar VI.* Vol. 3: *Textes sumériens et accadiens.* Paris: Éditions Recherches sur les civilisations.

Artzi, P.
2005   "EA 42, the Earliest Known Case of *parşu*, 'Correct International Custom.'" Pages 462-79 in *An Experienced Scribe Who Neglects Nothing:*

Ancient Near Eastern Studies in Honor of Jacob Klein. Edited by Y. Sefati, P. Artzi, C. Cohen, B. L. Eichler, and V. A. Hurowitz. Publications of the Samuel Noah Kramer Institute of Assyriology and Ancient Near Eastern Studies, The Faculty of Jewish Studies, Bar-Ilan University. Bethesda, Md.: CDL.

Asper, M.
2004   "Law and Logic: Towards an Archaeology of Greek Abstract Reason." *AION* 26: 73-94.

Astour, M. C.
1965   *Hellenosemitica: An Ethnic and Cultural Study in West Semitic Impact on Mycenaean Greece*. Leiden: Brill.

Baentsch, B.
1892   *Das Bundesbuch*. Halle: Niemayer.

Barthélemy, D., et al., eds.
1979   *Preliminary and Interim Report on the Hebrew Old Testament Text Project*. Vol. 1: *Pentateuch*. 2d ed. New York: United Biblical Societies.

Basile, M. E., ed. and trans.
1998   *Lex Mercatoria and Legal Pluralism: A Late Thirteenth-Century Treatise and Its Afterlife*. Cambridge, Mass.: Ames Foundation.

Bemal, M.
1990   *Cadmian Letters*. Winona Lake, Ind.: Eisenbrauns.

Bennett, E. L.
1953   *A Minoan Linear B Index*. New Haven: Yale University Press.

Bennett, E. L., and J.-P. Olivier, eds.
1973   *The Pylos Tablets Transcribed*. Incunabula Graeca 51. Rome: Edizioni dell'Ateneo.

Benveniste, E.
1969   *Le vocabulaire des institutions indo-européennes*. Vol. 2: *Pourvoir, droit, religion*. Paris: Éditions de Minuit.

Berchem, D. van
1967   "Sanctuaires d'Hercule-Melqart. Contribution à l'étude de l'expansion phénicienne en Méditerranée." *Syria* 44: 73-109, 307-38.

Bergel, J. L.
1988   "Principal Features and Methods of Codification." *Louisiana Law Review* 48: 1073-97.

Berlin, A.
1987   "On the Interpretation of Psalm 133." Pages 141-47 in *Directions in Biblical Hebrew Poetry*. Edited by E. R. Follis. JSOTSup 40. Sheffield: Sheffield Academic.
1989   "On the Meaning of *pll* in the Bible." *RB* 96: 345-51.

Bin-Nun, S. R.
1975   *The Tawananna in the Hittite Kingdom.* Texte der Hethiter 5. Heidelberg: Winter.
Birks, P. B. H.
1969   "The Early History of Iniuria." *TvR* 37: 163-208.
Biscardi, A.
1982   *Diritto Greco Antico.* Milan: Giuffrè.
Black, H. C., J. R. Nolan, J. M. Nolan-Haley, M. J. Connolly, S. C. Hicks, et al.
1990   *Black's Law Dictionary.* 6th ed. St. Paul: West Publishers.
Black, J.
1981   "The New Year Ceremonies in Ancient Babylon: 'Taking Bel by the Hand' and a Cultic Picnic." *Religion* 11: 39-59.
Bleicken, J.
1959   "Ursprung und Bedeutung der Provocation." *ZSSR (Rom. Abt.)* 76: 324-77.
Bonner, R. J., and G. Smith
1930   *The Administration of Justice from Homer to Aristotle.* Vol. 1. Chicago: University of Chicago Press. Reprinted Union, N.J.: Law Book Exchange, 2000.
Borger, R.
1956   *Die Inschriften Asarhaddons Königs von Assyien.* AfO Beihefte 9. Graz: Wiedner.
1982   "Der Kodex Hammurapi." Pages 39-80 in *Rechtsbücher.* Edited by R. Borger et al. TUAT 1/1. Gütersloh: Gerd Mohn.
Borger, R., and O. Kaiser, eds.
1982   *Texte aus der Umwelt des Alten Testaments.* Vol. 1: *Rechts- und Wirtschaftsurkunden, historisch-chronologische Texte.* Lieferung 1: *Rechtsbücher.* Gütersloh: Mohr.
Bottéro, J.
1954   *Le problème des Ḫabiru à la 4ᵐᵉ Rencontre Assyriologique Internationale.* CRRAI 4; Cahiers de la Société Asiatique 12. Paris: Imprimerie Nationale.
1961   "Désordre économique et annulation des dettes en Mésopotamie à l'époque paléo-babylonienne." *JESHO* 4: 113-64.
1982   "Le 'Code' de Hammu-rabi." *Annali della Scola Normale Superiore di Pisa* 12: 409-44. English edition: "The 'Code' of Ḫammurabi." Pages 156-84 in *Mesopotamia: Writing, Reasoning, and the Gods.* Translated by Z. Bahrani and M. van de Mieroop. Chicago: University of Chicago Press, 1992.
1987   *Mésopotamie: L'écriture, la raison et les dieux.* Bibliothèque des Histoires. Paris: Gallimard.

1992   *Mesopotamia: Writing, Reasoning, and the Gods.* Translated by Z. Bahrani and M. van de Mieroop. Chicago: University of Chicago Press.

Boyer, G.
1958   *Textes Juridiques.* ARM 8. TCL 29. Paris: Geuthner.

Bracton, H. de, and S. E. Thorne, trans.
1968-77   *Bracton De Legibus et Consuetudinibus Angliae (Bracton on the Laws and Customs of England).* 4 vols. Cambridge, Mass.: Harvard University Press.

Bradley, K.
1987   "On the Roman Slave Supply and Slavebreeding." Pages 42-64 in *Classical Slavery.* Edited by M. I. Finley. London and Totowa, N. J.: Cass.
1994   *Slavery and Society at Rome: Key Themes in Ancient History.* Cambridge and New York: Cambridge University Press.

Brugman, J., M. David, F. R. Kraus, P. W. Pestman, and M. H. van der Valk
1969   *Essays on Oriental Laws of Succession.* SDIOAP 9. Leiden: Brill.

Buckland, W. W.
1908   *The Roman Law of Slavery: The Condition of the Slave in Private Law from Augustus to Justinian.* Cambridge: Cambridge University Press. Reprinted Union, N.J.: Lawbook Exchange, 2000.

Buckland, W. W., and P. Stein
1966   *A Textbook of Roman Law from Augustus to Justinian.* 3d ed. Cambridge: Cambridge University Press.

Burkert, W.
1979   *Structure and History in Greek Mythology and Ritual.* Sather Classical Lectures 47. Berkeley: University of California Press.
1992   *The Orientalizing Revolution: Near Eastern Influence on Greek Culture in the Early Archaic Age.* Translated by W. Burkert and M. E. Pinder. Revealing Antiquity 5. Cambridge, Mass.: Harvard University Press.

Buss, M. J.
1973   "The Distinction between Civil and Criminal Law in Ancient Israel." Pages 51-62 in *Proceedings of the 6th World Congress on Jewish Studies, 1973.* Edited by A. Shinan. Vol. 1. Internationaler Kongreß für Studien zum Judentum 6. Jerusalem: World Union of Jewish Studies.

Butz, K., and P. Schroeder
1985   "Zu Getreideerträgen in Mesopotamien und dem Mittelmeergebiet." *BaghM* 16: 165-209.

Calhoun, G. M.
1927   *The Growth of Criminal Law in Ancient Greece.* Berkeley: University
        of California Press.
Campbell, J. K.
1964   *Honour, Family and Patronage. A Study of Institutions and Moral
        Values in a Greek Mountain Community.* Oxford: Clarendon. Re-
        printed 1970, 1973.
Cannata, C. A.
1994   "Considerazione sul testo e la portata originaria del secondo capo della
        'lex Aquilia.'" *Index* 22: 151-62.
Cantarella, E.
1976   *Studi sull' omicidio in diritto greco e romano.* Università degli studi di
        Milano, Facoltà di giurisprudenza. Pubblicazioni dell'Istituto di diritto
        romano. Milan: Giuffrè.
Cardascia, G.
1960   "La transmission des sources juridiques cunéiformes." *RIDA* 7: 31-50.
1969   *Les Lois Assyriennes.* LAOP 2. Paris. Éditions du Cerf.
1985   "La réparation des dommages agricoles dans le Code de Hammurabi."
        RA 79: 169-80.
Carroll, R. P.
1986   *Jeremiah.* OTL. Philadelphia: Westminster.
Charpin, D.
1987   "Les decrets royaux à l'Epoque Paleo-Babylonienne." *AfO* 34: 36-44.
Childs, B. S.
1974   *The Book of Exodus: A Critical Theological Commentary.* OTL.
        Philadelphia: Westminster.
Çiğ, M., and H. Kizilyay
1965   *Yeni Sumer çagina ait Nippur hukukî ve idarî belgeleri* [*Neusu-
        merische Rechts- und Verwaltungsurkunden aus Nippur*]. Türk tarih
        kurumu yayınlarından 6/7. Ankara: Türk tarih kurumu basimevi.
Civil, M.
1965   "New Sumerian Law Fragments." Pages 1-12 in *Studies in Honour of
        Benno Landsberger on His Seventy-Fifth Birthday.* Edited by H. G.
        Güterbock and T. Jacobsen. AS 16. Chicago: University of Chicago
        Press.
Claeys, E.
2009   "Property, Morality, and Society in Founding Era Legal Treatises."
        Paper presented at the annual meeting of the American Political Sci-
        ence Association Boston, Massachusetts, 28 August 2002.
        <*http://www.allacademic.com/meta/p66626_index.html*>

Cooper, J. S.
1975   "Structure, Humor, and Satire in the Poor Man of Nippur." *JCS* 27: 163-74.
1986   *Sumerian and Akkadian Royal Inscriptions*. Vol. 1: *Presargonic Inscriptions*. New Haven: The American Oriental Society.

Cornelius, F.
1975   "Ein hethitischer Hexenprozess." *RIDA* 22: 27-45.

Cornell, T.
1994   *The Beginnings of Rome*. London and New York: Routledge.

Coulanges, N. D. Fustel de
1982   *La Cité Antique: Étude sur le culte, le droit, les institutions de al Grèce de Rome,* Edited by G. Dumézil. Paris: Albatros. Reprint of original 1864.
1993   "Letters and Literature: A Ghost's Entreaty." Pages 98-102 in *The Tablet and the Scroll: Near Eastern Studies in Honor of William W. Hallo*. Edited By M. E. Cohen, D. C. Snell, and D. B. Weisberg. Bethesda, Md.: CDL Press. Original date unavailable.

Crawford, M. H., ed.
1996   *Roman Statutes*. 2 vols. Bulletin of the Institute of Classical Studies Supplement 64. London: Institute of Classical Studies, School of Advanced Studies, University of London.

Crifò, G.
1972   "La legge delle XII Tavole. Osservazione e Problemi." Pages 115-33 in *Aufstieg und Niedergang der römischen Welt: Geschichte und Kultur Roms im Spiegel der neueren Forschung*. Vol. 1/1. Edited by H. Temporini. Berlin and New York: de Gruyter.

Crook, J. A.
1984   "Lex Aquilia." *Athenaeum* 62: 67-77.

Cross, R.
1974   *Evidence*. 4th ed. London: Butterworths.

Dalley, S., C. B. F. Walker, and J. D. Hawkins
1976   *Old Babylonian Texts from Tell al Rimah*. London: British School of Archaeology in Iraq.

Dandamaev, M. A.
1972   "The Economic and Legal Character of the Slave's Peculium in the Neo-Babylonian and Achaemenid Periods." Pages 35-39 in *Gesellschaftsklassen im Alten Zweistromland und in den angrenzenden Gebieten. 18. Rencontre Assyriologique Internatonale. München. 29. Juni bis 3. Juli 1970*. Edited by D. O. Edzard. CRRAI 18; ABAW philosophisch-historische Klasse n.F. 75. Munich: Bayerische Akademie der Wissenschaften.

1984   *Slavery in Babylonia: From Nabopolassar to Alexander the Great (626–331 B.C.).* Edited by V. A. Powell and D. B. Weisberg. Translated by V. A. Powell. De Kalb, Ill.: Northern Illinois Press. Original 1974.

Daube, D.

1936   "On the Third Chapter of the Lex Aquilia." *LQR* 52: 253-68.

1947   *Studies in Biblical Law.* Cambridge: Cambridge University Press.

1948   "On the Use of the Term *Damnum.*" Pages 93-156 in *Studi in onore di Siro Solazzi nel cinquantesimo anniversario del suo insegnamento universitario.* Edited by V. Arangio-Ruiz. Naples: Jovene.

1956   *Forms of Roman Legislation.* Oxford: Clarendon.

1969   *Roman Law: Linguistic, Social and Philosophical Aspects. The J. H. Gray Lectures, 1966-67.* Edinburgh: Edinburgh University Press; Chicago: Aldine.

1971   "To Be Found Doing Wrong." Pages 1-13 in vol. 2 of *Studi in Onore di Edoardo Volterra.* 6 vols. Università di Roma Facoltà di giurisprudenza 45. Milan and Rome: Giuffrè.

David, M.

1927   *Die Adoption im altbabylonischen Recht.* Leipziger rechtswissenschaftliche Studien, Leipziger Juristen-Fakultät 23. Leipzig: Weicher.

1950   "The Codex Hammurabi and its Relations to the Provisions of Law in Exodus." *OtSt* 7: 149-78.

David, M., and E. Ebeling

1929   "Assyrische Rechtsurkunden." *ZVR* 44: 305-81. Reprinted *Assyrische Rechtsurkunden.* Stuttgart: Enke.

Dearman, J. A.

1988   *Property Rights in the Eighth-Century Prophets.* SBLDS 106. Atlanta: Scholars Press.

Deller, K.

1985   "Köche und Küche des Aššur-Tempels." *BaghM* 16: 347-76.

Démare-Lafont, S.

1987a   "L'interprétation de *Nb* 5,31 á la lumière des droits cunéiformes." Pages 49-52 in *La Femme dans le Proche-Orient Antique. Compterendu de la 33ᵉ Rencontre Assyriologique International (Paris, 7-10 juillet 1986).* Edited by J.-M. Durand. CRRAI 33; Éditions Recherches sur les civilisations. Paris: ADPF.

1987b   "La valeur de la loi dans les droits cunéiformes." *Archives de philosophie du droit* 32: 335-46.

Demosthenes

1978   "Against Aristocrates." Translated by J. H. Vince. Vol. 3. LCL 209. Cambridge, Mass.: Harvard University Press.

Dempster, S.
1984   "The Deuteronomic Formula *KI YIMMĀṢĒ'* in the Light of Biblical and Ancient Near Eastern Law." *RB* 91: 188-211.

Diakonov, I. M.
1974   "Slaves, Helots and Serfs in Early Antiquity." *AAASH* 22: 45-78.

Diamond, A. S.
1957   "An Eye for an Eye." *Iraq* 19: 151-55.

Dijk, J. J. A. van
1962   "Neusumerische Gerichtsurkunden in Bagdad." *ZA* 55: 70-90.

Donlan, S. P.
2008   "'Our laws are as mixed as our language': Commentaries on the Laws of England and Ireland, 1704-1804." *Electronic Journal of Comparative Law* 12.1: 1-19.

Donner, H., and W. Röllig
1973   *Kanaanäische und aramäische Inschriften.* 3d ed. Vol. 2. Wiesbaden: Harrassowitz.

Dossin, G.
1938   "Les Archives epistolaries de Mari." *Syria* 19: 105-26.
1972   "A propos de l'article 58 du Code de Hammu-rapi." *RA* 66: 77-80.

Downer, L. J., ed. and trans.
1996   *Leges Henrici Primi.* Oxford: Clarendon.

Drews, R.
1983   *Basileus: The Evidence for Kingship in Geometric Greece.* New Haven: Yale University Press.

Driel, G. van, et al., eds.
1982   *Zikir Šumim: Assyriological Studies Presented to F. R. Kraus on the Occasion of His Seventieth Birthday.* Leiden: Brill.

Driver, G. R., and J. C. Miles, eds.
1935   *The Assyrian Laws.* Oxford: Clarendon. Reprinted Aalen: Scientia, 1975.
1952   *The Babylonian Laws.* Vol. 1. Oxford: Clarendon.
1955   *The Babylonian Laws.* Vol. 2. Oxford: Clarendon.
1956   *The Babylonian Laws.* Reissued with revisions. Vol. 1. Oxford: Clarendon.
1960   *The Babylonian Laws.* Reissued with revisions. Vol. 2. Oxford: Clarendon.

Ducos, M.
1978   *L'influence grècque sur la lois des Douze Tables.* Travaux et recherches de l'Université de droit, d'économie et de sciences sociales de Paris. Paris: Presses universitaires de France.

Dumézil, G.
1985   *L'oubli de l'homme et l'honneur des dieux et autres essais: vingt-cinq esquisses de mythologie.* Bibliothèque des sciences humaines. Paris: Gallimard.

Durand, J.-M.
1977-78   [Title unavailable.] *Annuaire de l'École Pratique des Hautes Études. IVe Section: Sciences historiques et philologiques* 110: 144-52.
2002   "La vengeance à l'époque Amorrite." Pages 39-50 in *Recueils d'études à la mémoire d'André Parrot.* Edited by D. Charpin and J.-M. Durand. Florilegium Marianum 6; Mémoires de N.A.B.U. 7. Paris: Société pour l'Étude du Proche-Orient Ancien.

Ebeling, E.
1919-23   *Keilschrifttexte aus Assur religiösen Inhalts.* Leipzig: Hinrichs.

Edzard, D. O.
1968   *Sumerische Rechtsurkunden des III. Jahrtausends aus der Zeit vor der III. Dynastie von Ur.* ABAW philosophisch-historische Klasse n.F. 67. Munich: Bayerische Akademie der Wissenschaften, with Beck.
1970   "Die *bukānum*-Formel der altbabylonischen Kaufverträge and ihre sumerische Entsprechung." *ZA* 60: 8-53.
1974   "'Soziale Reformen' in Zweistromland bis ca. 1600 v.Chr.: Realität oder literarischer Topos?" *AAASH* 22: 145-56.

Ehelolf, H.
1922   *Ein altassyrisches Rechtsbuch.* Berlin: Curtis.

Eichler, B. L.
1973   *Indenture at Nuzi: The Personal Tidennutu Contract and Its Mesopotamian Analogues.* YNER 5. New Haven: Yale University Press.
1987   "Literary Structure in the Laws of Eshnunna." Pages 71-84 in *Language, Literature and History: Philological and Historical Studies Presented to Erica Reiner.* Edited by F. Rochberg-Halton. AOS 67. New Haven: American Oriental Society.

Eichrodt, W.
1970   *Ezekiel: A Commentary.* OTL. Philadelphia: Westminster.

Eilers, W.
1932   *Die Gesetzstele Chammurabis: Gesetze um die Wenden des dritten vorchristlichen Jahrtausends (= Der alte Orient* 31 nos. 3-4). Leipzig: Hinrichs.

Eissfeldt, O.
1964   *Einleitung in das Alte Testament.* 3d ed. Neue theologische Grundrisse. Tübingen: Mohr. Translated into English as *The Old Testament: An Introduction.* Translated by P. R. Ackroyd. New York: Harper & Row, 1965.

Ellis, M. de J.
1972   "*Ṣimdatu* in the Old Babylonian Sources." *JCS* 24: 74-82.
Epsztein, L.
1986   *Social Justice in the Ancient Near East and the People of the Bible.* Translated by J. Bowen. London: SCM Press.
Falkenstein, A.
1956-57   *Die neusumerischen Gerichtsurkunden.* 3 vols. ABAW philosophisch-historische Klasse n.F. 39, 40, 44. Munich: Bayerische Akademie der Wissenschaften.
Ferenczy, E.
1984   "La Legge delle XII Tavole e le codificazione greche." Pages 2001-12 in vol. 4 of *Sodalitas: Scritti in onore di Antonio Guarino.* Edited by G. Vincernzo. 10 vols. Biblioteca di Labeo 8. Naples: Jovene.
Ferron, J.
1972   "Un traité d'alliance entre Caere et Carthage contemporain, des dernier stems de la royauté étrusque à Rome ou l'évènement commémoré par la quasi-bilingue de Pyrgi." Pages 189-215 in *Aufstieg und Niedergang der römischen Welt: Geschichte und Kultur Roms im Spiegel der neueren Forschung.* Vol. 1/1. Edited by H. Temporini. Berlin and New York: de Gruyter.
Finet, A.
1972   "Le *ṣuhārum* à Mari." Pages 65-72 in *Gesellschaftsklassen im Alten Zweistromland und in den angrenzenden Gebieten. 18. Rencontre Assyriologique Internatonale. München. 29. Juni bis 3. Juli 1970.* Edited by D. O. Edzard. CRRAI 18; ABAW philosophisch-historische Klasse n.F. 75. Munich: Bayerische Akademie der Wissenschaften, with Beck.
Finkelberg, M.
1991   "Royal Succession in Heroic Greece." *CQ* 41: 303-16.
Finkelstein, J. J.
1952   "The Middle Assyrian *šulmānu*-Texts." *JAOS* 72: 77-80.
1961   "Ammiṣaduqa's Edict and the Babylonian 'Law Codes.'" *JCS* 15: 91-104.
1965   "Some New *Mīšarum* Material and its Implications." Pages 233-51 in *Studies in Honour of Benno Landsberger on His Seventy-Fifth Birthday.* Edited by H. G. Güterbock and T. Jacobsen. AS 16. Chicago: University of Chicago Press.
1966   "Sex Offenses in Sumerian Laws." *JAOS* 86: 355-72.
1967   "A Late Old Babylonian Copy of the Laws of Hammurapi." *JCS* 21: 39-48.

1969a   "The Hammurabi Law Tablet *BE* XXXI 22." *RA* 63: 11-27.

1969b   "The Laws of Ur-Nammu." *JCS* 22: 66-82.

1981   *The Ox that Gored*. TAPA 71/2. Philadelphia: American Philosophical Society.

Finley, M. I.

1955   "Marriage, Sale and Gift in the Homeric World." *RIDA* 2: 177-86.

1979   *The World of Odysseus*. 2d ed. New York: Penguin.

Fitzpatrick-McKinley, A.

1999   *The Transformation of Torah from Scribal Advice to Law*. JSOTSup 287. Sheffield: Sheffield Academic.

Foster, B.

1993   *Before the Muses*. 2 vols. Bethesda, Md.: CDL. 2d ed., 1996.

Frankena, R.

1966   *Briefe aus dem British Museum (LIH und CT 2-33)*. AbB 2. Leiden: Brill.

1974   *Briefe aus dem Berliner Museum*. AbB 6. Leiden: Brill.

Freeman, M. D. A.

1979   "The Concept of Codification." *JLA* 2: 168-79.

Fried, L. S.

2001   "'You Shall Appoint Judges': Ezra's Mission and the Rescript of Artaxerxes." Pages 63-89 in *Persia and Torah: The Theory of Imperial Authorization of the Pentateuch*. Edited by J. W. Watts. SBLSymS 17. Atlanta: Society of Biblical Literature.

Frymer-Kensky, T.

1983   "Pollution, Purification and Purgation in Biblical Israel." Pages 399-414 in *The Word of the Lord Shall Go Forth: Essays in Honor of David Noel Freedman in Celebration of his Sixtieth Birthday*. Edited by C. L. Meyers and M. O'Connor. Special Volume Series, ASOR Research 1. Philadelphia: American School of Oriental Research; Winona Lake, Ind.: Eisenbrauns.

1984   "The Strange Case of the Suspected Sotah (Numbers v 11-31)." *VT* 34: 11-26.

Gagarin, M.

1981   *Drakon and Early Athenian Homicide Law*. New Haven: Yale University Press.

1982   "The Organization of the Gortyn Law Code." *GRBS* 22: 129-46.

1986   *Early Greek Law*. Berkeley: University of California Press.

Gard, S. A.

1972   *Jones on Evidence*. 6th ed. 4 vols. Rochester, N.Y.: Lawyers Cooperative. 7th ed., 2008.

Gelb, I. J.
1972   "From Freedom to Slavery." Pages 81-92 in *Gesellschaftsklassen im Alten Zweistromland und in den angrenzenden Gebieten. 18. Rencontre Assyriologique Internatonale. München. 29. Juni bis 3. Juli 1970.* Edited by D. O. Edzard. CRRAI 18; ABAW philosophisch-historische Klasse n.F. 75. Munich: Bayerische Akademie der Wissenschaften.
1979   "Definition and Discussion of Slavery and Serfdom." *UF* 11: 283-97.

Geller, M. J.
1980   "The Šurpu Incantations and Lev. V.1-5." *JSS* 25: 181-92.

Gellner, E.
1977   "Patrons and Clients." Pages 1-6 in *Patrons and Clients in Mediterranean Societies.* Edited by E. Gellner and J. Waterbury. London: Duckworth; Hanover, N.H.: Center for Mediterranean Studies of the American Universities Field Staff.

George, A. R.
1988   "Three Middle Assyrian Tablets in the British Museum." *Iraq* 50: 25-37.

Ginsberg, H. L.
1946   *The Legend of King Keret: A Canaanite Epic of the Bronze Age.* ASORSup 2-3. New Haven: American Schools for Oriental Research.

Gioffredi, C.
1947-48   "Ius, Lex, Praetor." *SDHI* 13-14: 7-140.

Goetze, A.
1956   Laws of Eshnunna. AASOR 31. New Haven: American Schools for Oriental Research.
1957   *Kleinasien.* 2d ed. Handbuch der Altertumswissenschaft 3.1.3.3.1. Munich: Beck.
1963   "Babylonian Letters in American Collections II-VI." *JCS* 17: 77-86.
1967   *Die Annalen des Mursilis.* Darmstadt: Wissenschaftliche Buchgesellschaft. Reprint of MVAG 38. Leipzig: Hinrichs, 1933.

Gordis, R.
1954   "Hosea's Marriage and Message." *HUCA* 25: 9-35.

Gordon, C. H.
1936   "Hos. 2, 4-5 in the Light of New Semitic Inscriptions." *ZAW* 13: 277-80.

Gray, J.
1970   *I & II Kings.* 2d ed. OTL. London: SCM Press; Philadelphia: Westminster.

Greenberg, M.
1955   *The Ḫab/piru.* AOS 39. New Haven: American Oriental Society.

1960   "Some Postulates of Biblical Criminal Law." Pages 5-28 in *Studies in Bible and Jewish Religion: Yehezkel Kaufmann Jubilee Volume*. Edited by M. Haran. Jerusalem: Magnes.

1962   "Crimes and Punishment." Pages 733-44 in vol. 1 of *The Interpreter's Dictionary of the Bible*. Edited by G. A. Butterick. 4 vols. Nashville: Abingdon.

1983   *Ezekiel 1-20*. AB 22. Garden City, N.Y.: Doubleday.

1986   "More Reflections on Biblical Criminal Law." Pages 1-17 in *Studies in Bible*. Edited by S. Japhet. Scripta Hierosolymitana 31. Jerusalem: Magnes.

Greenfield, J. C.

1985   "The Seven Pillars of Wisdom (Prov. 9.1): A Mistranslation." *JQR* 79: 13-20.

Greengus, S.

1969   "The Old Babylonian Marriage Contract." *JAOS* 89: 505-32.

1969-70 "A Textbook Case of Adultery in Ancient Mesopotamia." *HUCA* 40-41: 33-44.

1979   *Old Babylonian Tablets from Ishchali and Vicinity*. PIHANS 44. Istanbul: Nederlands Instituut voor het Nabije Oosten.

1994   "Some Issues Relating to the Comparability of Laws and the Coherence of the Legal Tradition." Pages 60-87 in *Theory and Method in Biblical and Cuneiform Law: Revision, Interpolation and Development*. Edited by B. M. Levinson. JSOTSup 181. Sheffield: Sheffield Academic.

Günbatti, C.

2004   "Two Treaty Texts Found at Kültepe." Pages 249-68 in *Assyria and Beyond: Studies Presented to Mogens Trolle Larsen*. Edited by J. G. Dercksen. PIHANS 100. Leiden: Nederlands Instituut voor het Nabije Oosten.

Gurney, O. R.

1956   "The Sultantepe Tablets (continued). V. The Tale of the Poor Man of Nippur." *AnSt* 6: 145-64.

1972   "The Tale of the Poor Man of Nippur and Its Folktale Parallels." *AnSt* 22: 149-58.

1983   *The Middle Babylonian Legal and Economic Texts from Ur*. London: British School of Archaeology in Iraq.

Gurney. O. R., and S. N. Kramer

1965   "Two Fragments of Sumerian Laws." Pages 13-19 in *Studies in Honour of Benno Landsberger on His Seventy-Fifth Birthday*. Edited by H. G. Güterbock and T. Jacobsen. AS 16. Chicago: University of Chicago Press.

Gwaltney, W. C.
1983   "The Biblical Book of Lamentations in the Context of Near Eastern
          Lament Literature." Pages 191-211 in *Scripture in Context II*. Edited
          by W. W. Hallo, J. C. Moyer, and L. G. Perdue. Winona Lake, Ind.:
          Eisenbrauns.

Haas, V.
1994   *Geschichte der hethitischen Religion*. HdO 15. Leiden and New York:
          Brill.

Haase, R.
1980   "Gedanken zur Formel *parnasseia suwaizzi* in den Hethitischen
          Gesetzen." *WO* 11: 93-98.
2003   "The Hittite Kingdom." Pages 619-56 in vol. 1 of *A History of Ancient
          Near Eastern Law*. Edited by R. Westbrook. 2 vols. HdO 72. Leiden
          and New York: Brill.
2005   "Darf man den sog. Telipinu-Erlass eine Verfassung nennen?" *WO* 35:
          56-61.

Hallo, W. W.
1964   "The Slandered Bride." Pages 95-105 in *Studies Presented to A. Leo
          Oppenheim, June 7, 1964*. Edited by R. Biggs and J. Brinkman. Chi-
          cago: Oriental Institute of the University of Chicago.

Hallo, W. W., and H. Tadmor
1977   "A Lawsuit from Hazor." *IEJ* 27: 1-11.

Halpin, A. K. W.
1976   "The Usage of Iniuria in the Twelve Tables." *Irish Jurist* 11: 344-54.

Halverson, J.
1985   "Social Order in the 'Odyssey.'" *Hermes* 113: 129-45.
1986   "The Succession Issue in the 'Odyssey.'" *Greece and Rome* 33: 119-
          28.

Hammond, N. G. L.
1985   "The Scene in Iliad 18.497-508 and the Albanian Blood-Feud." *BASP*
          22: 79-86.

Harper, R.
1892   *Assyrian and Babylonian Letters Belonging to the Kouyunjik Collec-
          tions of the British Museum*. 14 vols. Chicago: University of Chicago
          Press.

Harris, W.
1986   "The Roman Father's Power of Life and Death." Pages 82-87 in *Stud-
          ies in Roman Law in Memory of A. Arthur Schiller*. Edited by R. S.
          Bagnall and W. V. Harris. Columbia Studies in the Classical Tradition
          13. Leiden: Brill.

Harrison, A.
1968   *The Law of Athens.* 2 vols. Oxford: Clarendon.
Hengstl, J.
1980   "Zur rechtlichen Bedeutung von *arnum* in der altbabylonischen Epoche." *WO* 11: 23-34.
Heubeck, A.
1972   "Nochmal zur 'inner-homerischen Chronologie.'" *Glotta* 50: 139-40.
Heurgon, J.
1966   "The Inscriptions of Pyrgi." *JRS* 56: 1-15.
1993   *Rome et la Méditerranée occidentale jusqu'aux guerres puniques.* 3d ed. Paris: Presses universitaires France.
Hoffmann, I.
1984   *Der Erlass Telipinus.* Texte der Hethiter 11. Heidelberg: Winter.
Hoffner, H. A., Jr.
1973   "Incest, Sodomy, and Bestiality in the Ancient Near East." Pages 81-90 in *Orient and Occident: Essays Presented to Cyrus H. Gordon.* Edited by H. A. Hoffner, Jr. Kevelaer: Butzon & Bercker.
1981   "The Old Hittite Version of Laws 164-166." *JCS* 33: 206-9.
1984   "A Prayer of Muršili II about His Stepmother." Pages 187-92 in *Studies in Literature from the Ancient Near East: Dedicated to Samuel Noah Kramer.* Edited by J. M. Sasson. AOS 65. New Haven: American Oriental Society. Reprint of *JAOS* 103 (1983): 187-92.
1995   "Hittite Laws." Pages 213-47 in *Law Collections from Mesopotamia and Asia Minor.* Edited by M. T. Roth. 1st ed. SBLWAW 6. Atlanta: Scholars Press. 2d ed., 1997.
1997   *The Laws of the Hittites.* Leiden: Brill.
Hommel, H.
1969   "Die Gerichtsszene auf dem Schild des Achilleus: Zur Pflege des Rechts in homerischer Zeit." Pages 11-38 in *Politeia und Res Publica: Beiträge zum Verständis von Politik, Recht und Staat in der Antike.* Edited by P. Steinmetz. Palingenesia 4. Wiesbaden: Steiner.
Honoré, A.
1972   "Linguistic and Social Context of the *Lex Aquilia.*" *Irish Jurist* 7: 138-41.
Hopwood, K.
1989   "Bandits, Elites and Rural Order." Pages 171-87 in *Patronage in Ancient Society.* Edited by A. Wallace-Hadrill. Leicester-Nottingham Studies in Ancient Society 1. London and New York: Routledge.
Hurowitz, V. A.
1985   "The Priestly Account of Building the Tabernacle." *JAOS* 105: 21-30.

Hutter, M.
1988   *Behexung, Entsühnung und Heilung: Das Ritual der Tunnawiya für ein Königspaar aus mittelhethitischer Zeit (KBo XXI 1-KUB IX 34— KBo XXI 6)*. OBO 82. Freiburg: Universitätsverlag; Göttingen: Vandenhoeck & Ruprecht.

Iliffe, J.
1958   "Thirty Days hath Lex Aquilia." *RIDA* 5: 495-506.

Jackson, B. S.
1975   *Essays in Jewish and Comparative Legal History*. SJLA 10. Leiden: Brill.

Jacobsen, T.
1970   "An Ancient Mesopotamian Trial for Homicide." Pages 193-214 in *Toward the Image of Tammuz and Other Essays on Mesopotamian History and Culture*. Edited by W. L. Moran. HSS 21. Cambridge, Mass.: Harvard University Press.
1984   *The Harab Myth*. SANE 2/3. Malibu: Undena Publications.

Jacobsen, T., ed.
1970   *Toward the Image of Tammuz and Other Essays on Mesopotamian History and Culture*. Edited by W. L. Moran. HSS 21. Cambridge, Mass.: Harvard University Press.

Jean, Ch.-F.
1931   *Tell Sifr texts cunéiforms consérves au British Museum*. Paris: Geuthner.

Jean, Ch.-F., ed.
1950   *Archives royales de Mari*. Vol. 2: *Lettres diverses*. Paris. Imprimerie Nationale.

Jepsen, A.
1927   *Untersuchungen zum Bundesbuch*. BWANT 3/5. Stuttgart: Kohlhammer.

Jeyes, U.
1980   "The Act of Extispicy in Ancient Mesopotamia." Pages 13-32 in vol. 1 of *Assyriological Miscellanies*. Edited by I. M. Diakonoff et al. Copenhagen: The Institute of Assyriology.

Jirku, A.
1927   *Das weltliche Recht im Alten Testament: Stilgeschichtliche und rechtsvergleichende Studien zu den juristischen Gesetzen des Pentateuchs*. Gütersloh: Bertelsmann.

Johns, C. H. W.
1898-1924 *Assyrian Deeds and Documents*. 4 vols. Cambridge: Deighton, Bell.

Johnson, T., and C. Dandeker
1989   "Patronage: Relation and System." Pages 219-42 in *Patronage in*

Ancient Society. Edited by A. Wallace-Hadrill. Leicester-Nottingham Studies in Ancient Society 1. London and New York: Routledge.

Jolowicz, F., and B. Nicholas
1972   *Historical Introduction to the Study of Roman Law.* 3d ed. Cambridge: Cambridge University Press.

Jones, G. H.
1984   *1 and 2 Kings.* NCB. Grand Rapids: Eerdmans.

Kapelrud, A. S.
1963   "Temple Building, a Task for the Gods and Kings." *Or* 32: 56-62.

Kaser, M.
1973   "Die Beziehung von Lex und Ius und die XII Tafeln." Pages 523-46 in vol. 2 of *Studi in memoria di Guido Donatuti.* Edited by Università degli studi di Parma. Facoltà di giurisprudenza. 3 vols. Milan: Cisalpino-La golidardica.

Kelly, J. M.
1964   "The Meaning of the Lex Aquilia." *LQR* 80: 73-83.
1971   "Further Reflections on the 'Lex Aquilia.'" Pages 235-41 in vol. 1 of *Studi in Onore di Edoardo Volterra.* 6 vols. Università di Roma Facoltà di giurisprudenza 45. Rome and Milan: Giuffrè.
1974   "A Note on 'Threefold Mancipation.'" Pages 183-86 in *Daube Noster: Essays in Legal History for David Daube.* Edited by A. Watson. Edinburgh: Scottish Academic Press.

Kemp, B. J.
1989   *Ancient Egypt: Anatomy of a Civilization.* London and New York: Routledge.

Kienast, B.
1978   *Die altbabylonischen Briefe und Urkunden aus Kisurra.* 2 vols. Wiesbaden: Steiner.

King, L.
1912   *Babylonian Boundary-Stones and Memorial Tablets in the British Museum.* London: British Museum.

Kirk, G. S.
1975   *The Cambridge Ancient History.* Vol. 2/2: *History of the Middle East and the Aegean Region, c. 1380-1000 B.C.* 3d ed. Cambridge: Cambridge University Press.

Klengel, H.
1980   "Mord und Busseleistung in spätbronzezeitlichen Syrien." Pages 189-97 in *Death in Mesopotamia: Papers Read at the XXVIe Rencontre Assyriologique International.* Edited by B. Alster. CRRAI 26; Mesopotamia 8. Copenhagen: Akademisk Forlag.

Klíma, J.
1972 "La perspective historique des lois hammourabiennes." *Comptes-rendus des séances de l'Académie des inscriptions et belles-lettres* 1972: 297-317.

Klíma, J., H. P. H. Petschow, G. Cardascia, and V. Korošec
1971 "Gesetze." Pages 234-97 in vol. 3 of *Reallexikon der Assyriologie.* Edited by E. Ebeling et al. 16 vols. Berlin: de Gruyter, 1928-.

Knudtzon, J. A., ed.
1907-15 *Die El-Amarna-Tafeln.* 2 vols. Vorderasiastische Bibliothek. Leipzig: Hinrichs. Reprinted Aalen: Zeller, 1964.

Kohler, J., and A. Ungnad
1913 *Assyrische Rechtsurkunden, in Umschrift und Übersetzung nebst einem Index der Personen-Namen und Rechtserläuterungen.* Leipzig: Pfeiffer.

Kornfeld, W.
1950 "L'adultère dans l'orient antique." *RB* 57: 92-109.

Korošec, V.
1957 "La codification dans le domains du droit Hittite." *RIDA* 4: 93-105

Koschaker, P.
1917 *Rechtsvergleichende Studien zur Gesetzgebung Hammurapis Königs von Babylon.* Leipzig: Hinrichs und Veit.
1924 "Beiträge zum altbabylonischen Recht." *ZA* 35: 194-212.
1928 *Neue Keilschriftrechtliche Rechtsurkunden aus der El-Amarna-Zeit.* Leipzig: Hirzel.

Kramer, S. N.
1963 *The Sumerians: Their History, Culture, and Character.* Chicago: University of Chicago Press.
1983 The Ur-Nammu Code: Who Was Its Author? *Or* 52: 453-56.

Kraus, F. R.
1958 *Ein Edikt des Königs Ammi-ṣaduqa von Babylon.* SDIOAP 5. Leiden: Brill.
1959 "Briefschreibübungen im altbabylonischen Schulunterricht." *JEOL* 16: 16-39.
1960 "Ein zentrales Problem des altmesopotamiscchen Rechtes: Was ist der Codex Hammu-rabi?" *Geneva NS* 8: 283-96.
1964 *Briefe aus dem British Museum: CT 43 and 44.* AbB 1. Leiden, Brill.
1969 "Erbrechtliche Terminologie im alten Mesopotamien." Pages 18-57 in *Essays on Oriental Laws of Succession.* Edited by J. Brugman. SDIOAP 9. Leiden: Brill.

1973 *Vom mesopotamischen Menschen der altbabylonischen Zeit und seiner Welt. Eine Reihe Vorlesungen.* MKNAW 36/6. Amsterdam: North Holland.

1979 "Akkadische Wörter and Ausdrücke, XII." *RA* 73: 51-62.

1984 *Königliche Verfügungen in Altbabylonischer Zeit.* SDIOAP 11. Leiden: Brill.

Kruchten, J. M.

1981 *Le décret d'Horemheb: tradition, commentaire épigraphique, philologique et institutionnel.* Brussels: Éditions de l'Université de Bruxelles.

Kuemmerlin-McLean, J. K.

1992 "Magic (OT)." Pages 468-71 in vol. 4 of *The Anchor Bible Dictionary.* Edited by David Noel Freedman. 6 vols. New York: Doubleday.

Kuhl, C.

1934 "Neue Dokumente zum Verständis von Hosea 2, 4-15." *ZAW* 11: 102-9.

Kühne, C.

1973 *Die Chronologie der internationalen Korrespondenz von El-Amarna.* AOAT 17. Neukirchen-Vluyn: Neukirchener Verlag.

Kunkel, W.

1973 *An Introduction to Roman Legal and Constitutional History.* Translated by J. M. Kelly. Oxford: Clarendon.

Kwasman, T.

1988 *Neo-Assyrian Legal Documents in the Kouyunjik Collection of the British Museum.* Studia Pohl, Series Maior 14. Rome: Pontifical Biblical Institute.

Kwasman, T., and S. Parpola

1991 *Legal Transactions of the Royal Court of Nineveh, Part I: Tiglath-Pileser III through Esarhaddon.* SAA 6. Helsinki: Helsinki University Press.

Lacey, W.

1966 "Homeric *Hedna* and Penelope's *Kurios.*" *JHS* 86: 55-68.

Læssøe, J.

1950 "On the Fragments of the Hammurabi Code." *JCS* 4: 173-87.

Lafont, S.

see: Démare-Lafont, S.

Lambert, M.

1956 "Les 'reformes' d'Urukagina." *RA* 50:169-84.

1968 "Notes Brèves 5." *RA* 62: 96.

Lambert, W. G.

1960a *Babylonian Wisdom Literature.* Oxford: Clarendon.

1960b   "Gilgameš in Religious, Historical and Omen Texts and the Historicity of Gilgameš." Pages 39-56 in *Gilgameš et sa légende: Études recueillies*. Edited by P. Garelli. Cahiers du Groupe François Thureau-Dangin. Paris: Klincksieck.

1966   "The 'Tamitu' Texts." Pages 119-23 in *La Divination en Mésopotamie Ancienne et dans les régions voisines. XIVth Rencontre Assyriologique Internationale, Strasbourg, 2-6 juillet 1965*. CRRAI 14. Paris: Presses universitaires France.

Landsberger, B.

1937   *Materialien zum sumerischen Lexikon: Vokabulare und Formularbücher, unter Mitwirkung von Fachgenossen*. Vol. I: *Die Serie* ana ittišu. Rome: Pontifical Biblical Institute.

1939   "Die babylonischen Termini für Gesetz und Recht." Pages 219-34 in *Symbolae ad iura orientis antiqui pertinentes Paulo Koschaker dedicatae*. Edited by T. Folkers et al. SDIOAP 2. Leiden: Brill.

Latte, K.

1933   "Mord." Cols. 280-81 in vol. 16/1 of *Paulys Realenzyklopädie der klassischen Altertumswissenschaft*. New Edition: *Der neue Pauly: Enzyklopädie der Antike*. Edited by H. Cancik and H. Schneider. Stuttgart: Metzler, 1996.

Leaf, W.

1887   "The Trial Scene in Iliad 18." *JHS* 8: 122-32.

Leemans, W. F.

1946   "*Kidinnu:* Un symbole de droit divin babylonien." Pages 36-70 in *Symbolae ad jus et historiam antiquitatis pertinentes, Julio Christiano van Oven dedicatae*. Edited by M. David, B. A. van Groningen, and E. M. Meijers. Leiden: Brill.

1968   "King Hammurapi as Judge." Pages 107-29 in vol. 2 of *Symbolae iuridicae et historicae Martino David dedicatae*. Edited by J. Ankum, R. Feenstra, and W. F. Leemans. 2 vols. SDIOAP 2. Leiden: Brill.

1988   "Aperçu sur les textes juridiques d'Emar." *JESHO* 31: 207-42.

1991   "Quelques considérations à propos d'une étude récente du droit du Proche-Orient ancien." *BO* 48: 409-20.

Leichty, E.

1970   *The Omen Series* Šumma Izbu. TCS 4. Locust Valley, N. Y.: Augustin.

Leist, B. W.

1884   *Graeco-italische Rechtsgeschichte*. Jena: Fischer.

Lejeune, M.

1965   "Le ΔΑΜΟΣ dans la société mycénienne." *Revue des Études Grecques* 78: 3-16.

Lemche, N. P.
1995a   "Justice in Western Asia in Antiquity, or: Why No Laws Were Needed!" *Chicago-Kent Law Review* 70: 1695-1716.
1995b   "Kings and Clients: On Loyalty between the Ruler and the Ruled in Ancient 'Israel.'" *Semeia* 66: 119-32.
1996   "From Patronage Society to Patronage Society." Pages 106-20 in *The Origins of the Ancient Israelite States*. Edited by V. Fritz and P. R. Davies. JSOTSup 228. Sheffield: Sheffield Academic.

Lenclud, G.
1988   "Des idées et des hommes: patronage électoral et culture politique en corse." *Revue Française de Science Politique* 38: 770-82.

Lenel, O.
1922   Review of H. F. Jolowicz. *Original Scope of the Lex Aquilia and the Question of Damages. ZSSR (Rom. Abt.)* 43: 575.

Lenel, O., ed.
1901-03   *Edictum Perpetuum: An Essay of Reconstruction*. 2 vols. Paris: Larose.

Levine, B.
1968   "*mulugu/melug*: The Origins of a Talmudic Legal Institution." *JAOS* 88: 271-85.

Lévy-Bruhl, H.
1958   "Le deuxième chapitre de la loi Aquilia." *RIDA* 5: 507-17.

Lewy, J.
1937   "Old Assyrian Documents from Asia Minor." *Archives d'histoire du droit oriental* 1: 91-108.
1958   "The Biblical Institution of *deror* in the Light of Accadian Documents." *EI* 5: 21-31.

Lichtheim, M.
1976   *Ancient Egyptian Literature: A Book of Readings*. Vol. 2: *The New Kingdom*. Berkeley: University of California Press.

Linke, B.
1995   *Von der Verwandtschaft zum Staat: Die Entstehung politischer Organisationsformen in der frührömischen Geschichte*. Stuttgart: Steiner.

Lintott, A.
1972   "Provocatio." Pages 226-67 in *Aufstieg und Niedergang der römischen Welt: Geschichte und Kultur Roms im Spiegel der neueren Forschung*. Vol. 1/2. Edited by H. Temporini. Berlin and New York: de Gruyter.

Liverani, M.
1967   "Contrasti e confluenze di concezioni politiche nell'età di El-Amarna." *RA* 61: 1-18.

1983   "Political Lexicon and Political Ideologies in the Amarna Letters."
         Berytus 31: 41-56.
1990   *Prestige and Interest: International Relations in the Near East ca.
         1600-1100 B.C.* HANES 1. Padova: Sargon.
2000   "The 'Great Powers' Club." Pages 15-27 in *Amarna Diplomacy: The
         Beginnings of International Relations.* Edited by R. Cohen and R.
         Westbrook. Baltimore: Johns Hopkins University Press.
2001   *International Relations in the Ancient Near East 1600-1100 B.C.* New
         York: Palgrave.

Lloyd, G. E. R.
1970   *Early Greek Science: Thales to Aristotle.* New York: Norton.

Locher, C.
1986   *Die Ehre einer Frau in Israel: Exegetische und rechtsvergleichende
         Studien zu Deuteronomium 22,13-21.* OBO 70. Göttingen: Vanden-
         hoeck & Ruprecht; Freiburg: Universitätsverslag.

Loewenstamm, S.
1980a   "The Cumulative Oath of Witnesses and Parties in Mesopotamian
         Law." Pages 341-45 in *Comparative Studies in Biblical and Ancient
         Oriental Literatures.* AOAT 204. Neukirchen-Vluyn: Neukirchener
         Verlag.
1980b   "The Laws of Adultery and the Law of Murder in Biblical and Meso-
         potamian Law." Pages 146-53 in *Comparative Studies in Biblical and
         Ancient Oriental Literatures.* AOAT 204. Neukirchen-Vluyn: Neu-
         kirchener Verlag.

MacCormack, G.
1967   "Nexi, Iudicati and Addicti in Livy." *ZSSR (Rom. Abt.)* 84: 350-55.
1983   "The T'ang Code: Early Chinese Law." *Irish Jurist* 18: 132-50.

MacDowell, D. M.
1978   *The Law in Classical Athens.* London: Thames and Hudson; Ithaca:
         Cornell University Press.
1999   *Athenian Homicide Law in the Age of Orators.* 2d ed. Manchester:
         Manchester University Press.

Maekawa, K.
1973-74 "The Development of the É-MÍ in Lagash during Early Dynastic III."
         Mesopotamia 8-9: 77-144.

Magdalene, F. R.
2003   "On the Scales of Righteousness: Law and Story in the Book of Job."
         Ph.D. diss. Iliff School of Theology and University of Denver (Colo-
         rado Seminary), 2003.
2007   *On the Scales of Righteousness: Neo-Babylonian Trial Law and the*

Book of Job. Brown Judaic Studies Series 348. Providence, R.I.: Program in Judaic Studies, Brown University, 2007.

Maine, H.
1861   *Ancient Laws.* Reprint edition Tucson: University of Arizona Press, 1986.

Malul, M.
1985   "The *bukannum*-Clause—Relinquishment of Rights by Previous Right-Holder." *ZA* 75: 66-77.
1988   *Studies in Mesopotamian Legal Symbolism.* AOAT 221. Neukirchen-Vluyn: Neukirchener Verlag.
1990   *The Comparative Method in Ancient Near Eastern and Biblical Legal Studies.* AOAT 227. Kevelaer and Neukirchen-Vluyn: Butzon & Bercker and Neukirchener Verlag.

Marcks, E.
2000   "English Law in Early Hong Kong: Colonial Law as a Means for Control and Liberation." *Texas International Law Journal* 35: 265-88.

Matthews, V. H., and D. C. Benjamin
1993   *Social World of Ancient Israel 1250-587 BCE.* Peabody, Mass.: Hendrickson.

McKeating, H.
1979   "Sanctions against Adultery in Ancient Israelite Society, with Some Reflections on Methodology in the Study of Old Testament Ethics." *JSOT* 11: 57-72.

Meier, G.
1937   *Die assyrische Beschwörungssammlung Maqlû.* Berlin: Berger.

Méléze-Modrzejewski, J.
1993   "Aut nascuntur aut fiunt." Pages 1-25 in *Statut personnel et liens de famille dans les droits de l'antiquité.* Hampshire, Great Britain: Aldershot; Brookfield, Vt.: Variorum.

Mendelsohn, I.
1949   *Slavery in the Ancient Near East.* New York: Oxford University Press.

Mendenhall, G.
1954   "Ancient Oriental and Biblical Law." *BA* 17: 26-46.

Messerschmidt, L.
1911-22   *Keilschrifttexte aus Assur historischen Inhalts.* 2 vols. WVDOH 16, 37. Leipzig: Hinrichs. Reprinted Innsbruck: Zeller, 1972.

Meyers, C. L., and E. M. Meyers
1993   *Zechariah 9-14.* AB 25C. New York: Doubleday.

Mieroop, M. van de
1987   "The Archive of Balmunamhe." *AfO* 34: 1-29.

Moran, W. L.
1959   "The Scandal of the 'Great Sin' at Ugarit." *JNES* 12: 280-81.
1991   "Ashurbanipal's Message to the Babylonians (ABL 301), with an Ex-
         cursus on Figurative *biltu*." Pages 320-31 in *Ah, Assyria: Studies in
         Assyrian History and Ancient Near Eastern Historiography Presented
         to Hayim Tadmor*. Edited by M. Cogan and I. Eph'al. Scripta Hiero-
         solymitana 33. Jerusalem: Magnes.
1992   *The Amarna Letters*. Baltimore: The Johns Hopkins University Press.
Morgenstern, J.
1930   "The Book of the Covenant, Pt. 2." *HUCA* 7: 19-258.
Morris, I.
1986   "The Use and Abuse of Homer." *Classical Antiquity* 5: 81-138.
Moyer, J. C.
1983   "Hittite and Israelite Cult Practices." Pages 19-38 in *Scripture in Con-
         text 2*. Edited by W. W. Hallo, J. C. Moyer, and L. G. Perdue. Winona
         Lake, Ind.: Eisenbrauns.
Muellner, L. C.
1976   *The Meaning of Homeric EYXOMAI through its Formulas*. Innsbruker
         Beiträge zur Sprachwissenschaft 13. Innsbruck: Institut für Sprach-
         wissenschaft der Universität Innsbruck.
Muffs, Y.
1969   *Studies in Aramaic Legal Papyri from Elephantine*. SDIOAP 8.
         Leiden: Brill. Reprinted as *Studies in the Aramaic Legal Papyri from
         Elephantine*. HdO 66. Leiden: Brill, 2003.
Mühl, M.
1933   *Untersuchungen zur altorientalischen und althellenischen Gesetz-
         gebung*. Klio, Beihefte zur alten Geschichte 29. Leipzig: Dieterich.
Müller, D. H.
1903   *Die Gesetze Hammurabis und ihr Verhältnis zur mosaischen Gesetz-
         gebung sowie zu den 12 Tafeln*. Vienna: A. Hölder. Reprinted
         Amsterdam: Philo, 1975.
Na'aman, N.
2000   "The Egyptian-Canaanite Correspondence." Pages 125-38 in *Amarna
         Diplomacy: The Beginnings of International Relations*. Edited by R.
         Cohen and R. Westbrook. Baltimore: Johns Hopkins University Press.
Nagy, G.
1990   *Pindar's Homer*. Baltimore: Johns Hopkins University Press.
Naveh, J.
1982   *Early History of the Alphabet: An Introduction to West Semitic Epi-
         graphy and Palaeography*. Jerusalem: Magnes; Leiden: Brill.

Neher, A.
1954   "Le symbolisme conjugal: expression de l'histoire dans l'Ancien Test-
        ament." *RHPR* 34: 30-49.
Neugebauer, O.
1969   *The Exact Sciences in Antiquity.* 2d ed. New York: Dover.
Nobrega, V. L. de
1967   "L'*iniuria* dans la loi des XII Tables." *Romanitas* 8: 250-70.
Nörr, D.
1972   *Divisio et Partitio: Bemerkungen zur römischen Rechtsquellenlehre
        und zur antiken Wissenschaftstheorie.* Berlin: Schweitzer.
1976   "Pomponius." Pages 496-604 in *Aufstieg und Niedergang der röm-
        ischen Welt: Geschichte und Kultur Roms im Spiegel der neueren For-
        schung.* Vol. 2/15. Edited by H. Temporini. Berlin and New York: de
        Gruyter.
1986   "Texte zur Lex Aquilia." Pages 211-19 in *Iuris professio: Festgabe für
        Max Kaser zum 80. Geburtstag.* Edited by H.-P. Benöhr et al. Vienna:
        Böhlau.
Northern Securities Co v. United States. 193 *US* 197 (1904), Holmes dissent.
Noth, M.
1962   *Exodus.* Translated by J. S. Bowden. OTL. Philadelphia: Westminster.
Nothdurft, W.
1978   "Noch einmal Πέιραρ/Πείρατα bei Homer." *Glotta* 56: 25-40.
Nougayrol, J.
1951   [Title unavailable] *Comptes Rendus des séances de l'Académie des
        inscriptions et belles-lettres* 1951: 42-47.
1955   *Le palais royal d'Ugarit III: Textes accadiens et hourrites des
        archives est, ouest et centrales.* Mission de Ras Shamra 6. Paris:
        Imprimerie Nationale
1956   *Le Palais Royal d'Ugarit IV.* Mission Ras-Shamra 9. Paris: Imprime-
        rie Nationale
1957   "Les fragments en pierre du code Hammourabien I." *Journal Asiatique*
        245: 339-66.
1958   "Les fragments en pierre du code Hammourabien II." *Journal Asiatique*
        246: 143-55.
O'Callaghan, R. T.
1954   "A New Inheritance Contract from Nippur." *JCS* 8: 137-43.
Oliver, H.
1984   "The Effectiveness of the Old Babylonian *Mēšarum* Decree." *JNSL*
        12: 107-13.
Oppenheim, A. L.
1967   *Letters from Mesopotamia.* Chicago: University of Chicago Press.

Oppenheim, A. L., et al., eds.
1956-   *The Assyrian Dictionary of the Oriental Institute of Chicago.* Chicago:
           Oriental Institute of the University of Chicago.

Ostwald, M.
1969   *Nomos and the Beginnings of Athenian Democracy.* Oxford: Clarendon.

Otten, H.
1981   *Die Apologie Hattusilis III: Das Bild der Überliefergung.* StBoT 24.
           Wiesbaden: Harrassowitz.

Otto, E.
1988a   "Interdependenzen zwischen Geschichte und Rechtsgeschichte des
           antiken Israels." *Rechtshistorisches Journal* 7: 347-68. Reprinted at
           pages 75-93 in *Kontinuum und Proprium. Studien zur Sozial- und
           Rechtsgeschichte des Alten Orients und des Alten Testaments.* OBC 8.
           Wiesbaden: Harrassowitz, 1996.

1988b   "Die rechtsgeschichtliche Entwicklung des Depositenrechts in altori-
           entalischen und altisraelitischen Rechtskorpora." *ZSSR (Rom. Abt.)*
           105: 1-31. Reprinted at pages 139-63 in *Kontinuum und Proprium:
           Studien zur Sozial- und Rechtsgeschichte des Alten Orients und des
           Alten Testaments.* OBC 8. Wiesbaden: Harrassowitz, 1996.

1988c   *Wandel der Rechtsbegründungen in der Gesellschaftsgeschichte des
           antiken Israel: Eine Rechtsgeschichte des 'Bundesbuchs' Ex XX 22-
           XXIII 13.* StudBib 3. Leiden: Brill.

1994   "Aspects of Legal Reforms and Reformulations in Ancient Cuneiform
           and Israelite Law." Pages 160-96 in *Theory and Method in Biblical
           and Cuneiform Law: Revision, Interpolation and Development.* Edited
           by B. M. Levinson. JSOTSup 181. Sheffield: Sheffield Academic.

Page, D. L.
1959   *History and the Homeric Iliad.* Berkeley: University of California
           Press.

Parker, R.
1983   *Miasma: Pollution and Purification in Early Greek Religion.* Oxford:
           Clarendon.

Parpola, S.
1983   *Letters from Assyrian Scholars to the Kings Esarhaddon and Assur-
           banipal.* 2 vols. AOAT 5. Kevelaer: Butzon & Bercker.

1993   *Letters from Assyrian and Babylonian Scholars.* SAA 10. Helsinki:
           Helsinki University Press.

Parpola, S., and K. Watanabe
1988   *Neo-Assyrian Treaties and Loyalty Oaths.* SAA 2. Helsinki: Helsinki
           University Press.

Paul, S.
1970   *Studies in the Book of the Covenant in the Light of Cuneiform and Biblical Laws.* VTSup 18. Leiden: Brill.
Pernice, A.
1867   *Zur Lehre von den Sachbeschädigungen nach römischem Rechte.* Weimar: Böhlau.
Perysinakis, I.
1991   "Penelope's *EEDNA* Again." *CQ* 41: 297-302.
Peters, E. L.
1968   "The Tied and the Free." Pages 167-88 in *Contribution to Mediterranean Sociology.* Edited by I. G. Peristiany. Paris: Mouton.
Petschow, H. P. H.
1965   "Zur Systematik und Gesetzestechnik im Codex Hammurabi." *ZA* 57: 146-72.
1968   "Zur 'Systematik' in den Gesetzen von Eshnunna." Pages 131-43 in vol. 2 of *Symbolae iuridicae et historicae Martino David dedicatae.* Edited by J. Ankum, R. Feenstra, and W. F. Leemans. 2 vols. SDIOAP 2. Leiden: Brill.
1974   *Mittelbabylonische Rechts- und Wirtschaftsurkunden der Hilprecht-Sammlung Jena.* ASAW philologisch-historische Klasse 64/4. Berlin: Akademie-Verlag.
1984   "Die §§ 45 and 46 des Codex Ḫammurapi—Ein Beitrag zum altbabylonischen Bodenpachtrecht und zum Problem: Was ist der Codex Ḫammurapi." *ZA* 74: 181-212.
1986   "Beiträge zum Codex Hammurapi." *ZA* 76:17-75.
Pettinato, G.
1979   *Ebla: un impero inciso nell'argilla.* Milan: Mondadori.
Pfeiffer, R. H., ed.
1935   *State Letters of Assyria.* New Haven: American Oriental Society.
Pfeiffer R. H., and E. A. Speiser, eds.
1936   *One Hundred New Selected Nuzi Texts.* AAOS 16. New Haven: American Schools for Oriental Research.
Pflüger, H. H.
1942   "Die Gerichtsszene auf dem Schilde des Achilleus." *Hermes* 77: 146-48.
Phillips, A.
1970   *Ancient Israel's Criminal Law: A New Approach to the Decalogue.* Oxford: Blackwell; New York: Schocken.
1981   "Another Look at Adultery." *JSOT* 20: 3-25.

Pitt-Rivers, J. A.
1971   *The People of the Sierra.* 2d ed. Chicago: University of Chicago Press. 1st ed., 1954.

Porten, B., and A. Yardeni, eds.
1989   *Textbook of Aramaic Documents from Ancient Egypt.* 2 vols. Texts and Studies for Students. Jerusalem: Hebrew University, Department of the History of the Jewish People; Winona Lake, Ind.: Eisenbrauns.

Postgate, J. N.
1973   *The Governor's Palace Archive.* CTN 2. London: British School of Archaeology in Iraq.

1988   *The Archive of Urad-Šerūa and His Family. A Middle Assyrian Household in Government Service.* Pubblicazioni del progetto "Analisi electtronica del cuneiforme." Corpus Medio-Assiro. Rome: Denicola.

Preiser, W.
1969   "Zur rechtilchen Natur der altorientalischen Gesetze." Pages 17-36 in *Festschrift für Karl Englisch.* Frankfurt: Klostermann.

Primmer, A.
1970   "Homerische Gerichtsszenen." *Wiener Studien* 4: 5-13.

Pringsheim, F.
1959   "The Origin of the 'Lex Aquilia.'" Pages 233-44 in *Droits de l'antiquité sociologie juridique: Mélanges Henri Lévy-Bruhl.* Publications de l'Institut de droit romain de l'Université de Paris 17. Paris: Recueil Sirey.

Pritchard, J. B., ed.
1969   *Ancient Near Eastern Texts Relating to the Old Testament.* 3d ed. with supplement. Princeton: Princeton University Press.

Pugsley, D.
1969a   "Furtum in the XII Tables." *Irish Jurist* 4: 139-52.
1969b   "The Origins of the Lex Aquilia." *LQR* 85: 50-73.

Raaflaub, K.
1986   "From Protection and Defense to Offense and Participation: Stages in the Conflict of the Orders." Pages 198-243 in *Social Struggles in Archaic Rome: New Perspectives on the Conflict of Orders.* Edited by K. Raaflaub. Berkeley and Los Angeles: University of California Press.

Rabello, A. M.
1979   *Effetti personali della "Patria Potestas."* Milan: Giuffrè.

Rabinowitz, J. J.
1959   "The 'Great Sin' in Ancient Egyptian Marriage Contracts." *JNES* 18: 73.

Rebuffat, R.
1966   "Les Phéniciens à Rome." *MEFR* 78: 7-48.

Reiner, E.
1958   *Šurpu: A Collection of Sumerian and Akkadian Incantations.* AfO
         Beiheft 11. Graz: Weidner.
Renger, J.
1972   "Flucht als soziales Problem in der altbabylonischen Gesellschaft."
         Pages 167-82 in *Gesellschaftsklassen im Alten Zweistromland und in
         den angrenzenden Gebieten. 18. Rencontre Assyriologique Interna-
         tionale. München. 29. Juni bis 3. Juli 1970.* Edited by D. O. Edzard.
         CRRAI 18. ABAW philosophisch-historische Klasse n.f. 75. Munich:
         Bayerische Akademie der Wissenschaften, with Beck.
1973   "Who Are All Those People?" *Or (NS)* 42: 259-73.
1975   "Heilige Hochzeit. A. Philologisch." Pages 251-59 in vol. 4 of *Real-
         lexikon der Assyriologie.* Edited by E. Ebeling et al. 16 vols. Berlin: de
         Gruyter, 1928-
1976   "Hammurapis Stele 'König der Gerechtigkeit': Zur Frage von Recht
         und Gesetz in der altbabylonischen Zeit." *WO* 8: 228-35.
Reynolds, F.
2003   *The Babylonian Correspondence of Esarhaddon and Letters to Assur-
         banipal and Sin-Šarru-Iškun from Northern and Central Babylonia.*
         SAA 18. Helsinki: Helsinki University Press.
Riccobono, S., and J. Baviera, eds.
1968   *Fontes iuris Romani anteiustiniani.* 3 vols. Florence: Barbèra.
Rich, J.
1989   "Patronage and Interstate Relations in the Roman Republic." Pages
         117-35 in *Patronage in Ancient Society.* Edited by A. Wallace-Hadrill.
         Leicester-Nottingham Studies in Ancient Society 1. London and New
         York: Routledge.
Richard, J.
1986   "Patricians and Plebeians: The Origins of a Social Dichotomy." Page
         105-29 in *Social Struggles in Archaic Rome: New Perspectives on the
         Conflict of Orders.* Edited by K. Raaflaub. Berkeley and Los Angeles:
         University of California Press.
Ries, G.
1984   "Ein neubabylonischer Mitgiftprozess (559 v. Chr.): Gleichzeitig ein
         Beitrag zur Frage der Geltung keilschriftlicher Gesetze." Pages 345-63
         in *Gedächtnisschrift für Wolfgang Kunkel.* Edited by D. Nörr and D.
         Simon. Frankfurt: Klostermann.
Rofé, A.
1986   "Methodological Aspects of the Study of Biblical Law." Pages 1-16 in
         Jewish Law Association Studies 2: The Jerusalem Conference Volume.
         Edited by B. S. Jackson. Jewish Law Association Studies 2; Academic

Studies in the History of Judaism. Atlanta: Scholars Press. Reprinted Binghamton, N.Y.: Global Publications, 2000.

Roller, M.

2001   *Constructing Autocracy: Aristocrats and Emperors in Julio-Claudian Rome.* Princeton: Princeton University Press.

Roth, M.

1979   "Scholastic Tradition and Mesopotamian Law." Ph.D. diss. University of Pennsylvania.

1983   "The Slave and the Scoundrel: CBS 10467, a Sumerian Mortality Tale?" *JAOS* 103: 275-82.

1987   "Homicide in the Neo-Assyrian Period." Pages 351-66 in *Language, Literature and History: Philological and Historical Studies Presented to Erica Reiner.* Edited by F. Rochberg-Halton. AOS 67. New Haven: American Oriental Society.

1988   "'She Will Die by the Iron Dagger': Adultery and Neo-Babylonian Marriage." *JESHO* 31: 186-206.

1989   *Babylonian Marriage Agreements 7th-3rd Centuries B.C.* AOAT 222. Kevelaer: Butzon & Bercker; Neukirchen-Vluyn: Neukirchener Verlag.

1997   *Law Collections from Mesopotamia and Asia Minor.* 2d ed. SBLWAW 6. Atlanta: Scholars Press. 1st ed., 1995.

Russo, J., and R. Knox

1989   "Agamemnon's Test: Iliad 2.73-75." *Classical Antiquity* 8: 174-80.

Sachers, E.

1953   "Potestas patria." Col. 1087 in vol. 43 of *Paulys Realenzyklopädie der klassischen Altertumswissenschaft.* New Edition: *Der neue Pauly: Enzyklopädie der Antike.* Edited by H. Cancik and H. Schneider. Stuttgart: Metzler, 1996.

Saller, R. P.

1982   *Personal Patronage under the Early Empire.* Cambridge: Cambridge University Press.

San Nicolò, M.

1931   *Beiträge zur Rechtsgeschitchte im Bereiche der keilschriftrechtlichen Rechtsquellen.* Serie A: Forelesninger 13. Cambridge, Mass.: Harvard University Press; Oslo: Aschehoug.

1932   "Parerga Babylonica V: Ein Fall §§202-205 KḪ in einer Urkunde aus Emutbal." *ArOr* 4: 179-92.

San Nicolò, M., and H. P. H. Petschow

1960   *Babylonische Rechtsurkunden aus dem 6. Jahrhundert v. Chr.* ABAW philosophisch-historische Klasse n.F. 51. Munich: Bayerische Akademie der Wissenschaften.

Schiller, A. A.
1978   *Roman Law: Mechanisms of Development.* New York: Mouton.
Schloen, J. D.
2001   *The House of the Father as Fact and Symbol: Patrimonialism in Uga-rit and the Ancient Near East.* Studies in Archaeology and History of the Levant 2, Harvard Semitic Museum Publications. Winona Lake, Ind.: Eisenbrauns.
Schmitz, P.
1995   "The Phoenician Text from the Etruscan Sanctuary at Pyrgi." *JAOS* 115: 559-75.
Schoneveld, J.
1973   "Le sang du cambrioleur: Exode 22:1,2." Pages 335-40 in *Symbolae biblicae et mesopotamicae Francisco Mario Theodoro de Liagre Böhl dedicatae.* Edited by M. A. Beek, A. A. Kampman, C. Nijland and J. Ryckmans. Leiden: Brill.
Schorr, M.
1913   *Urkunden des altbabylonischen Zivil- und Prozessrechts.* Vorderasia-tische Bibliothek 5. Leipzig: Hinrich. Reprinted Leipzig: Zentral-Antiquariat, 1968.
Schuler, E. von
1957   *Hethitische Dienstanweisungen.* AfO Beiheft 10. Innsbruck: Biblio-Verlag. Reprinted 1967.
1959   "Hethitische Königerlässe als Quellen der Rechtsfindung und ihr Verhältnis zum kodifizierten Recht." Pages 435-72 in *Festschrift Johannes Friedrich zum 65. Geburtstag am 27. August 1958 gewidmet.* Edited by R. von Kienle. Heidelberg: Winter.
Schwienhorst-Schönberger, L.
1990   *Das Bundesbuch (Ex. 20,22-23,33): Studien zu seiner Entstehung und Theologie.* BZAW 188. Berlin: de Gruyter.
Scullard, H. H.
1967   *The Etruscan Cities and Rome.* London: Thames & Hudson; Ithaca: Cornell University Press.
1973   *Roman Politics, 220-150 B.C.* 2d ed. Oxford: Clarendon. Reprinted Westport, Conn.: Greenwood, 1981.
Sefati, Y., and J. Klein
2001   "The Role of Women in Mesopotamian Witchcraft." Pages 569-87 in vol. 2 of *Sex and Gender in the Ancient Near East: Proceedings of the XLVIIe Rencontre Assyriologique Internationale.* Edited by S. Parpola and R. M. Whiting. 2 vols. CRRAI 47. Helsinki: The Neo-Assyrian Text Corpus Project.

Segal, S. P.
1989   "Postbiblical Jewish Criminal Law and Theology." *JLA* 9: 107-18.
Segerstedt, T. T.
1942   "Customs and Codes." *Theoria* 8: 3-22, 126-53.
Seidl, E.
1951   *Einführung in die ägyptische Rechtsgeschichte bis zum Ende des Neuen Reiches*. 2d ed. ÄF 10. Glückstadt and New York: Augustin.
Sellin, E., and G. Fohrer
1965   *Einleitung in das Alte Testament*. 10th ed. Heidelberg: Quelle & Meyer.
Selms, A. van
1950   "The Goring Ox in Babylonian and Biblical Law." *ArOr* 18: 321-30.
Shinan, A., ed.
1977   *Proceedings of the 6th World Congress of Jewish Studies*. 2 vols. Jerusalem: World Union of Jewish Studies.
Sick, U.
1984   "Die Tötung eines Menschen und ihre Ahndung in den keilschriftlichen Rechtssammlungen unter Berücksichtigung rechtsvergleichender Aspeckte." 2 vols. Ph.D. diss. University of Tübingen. Self-published.
Siegel, B. J.
1947   "Slavery during the Third Dynasty of Ur." *American Anthropologist* N.S. 49 no. 1, part 2. Reprinted as *Slavery during the Third Dynasty of Ur*. Memoir Series of the American Anthropological Association 66. New York: Kraus Reprint Co., 1969.
Silverman, S.
1977   "Patronage as Myth." Pages 7-19 in *Patrons and Clients in Mediterranean Societies*. Edited by E. Gellner and J. Waterbury. London: Duckworth; Hanover, N. H.: Center for Mediterranean Studies of the American Universities Field Staff.
Simon, D. V.
1965   "Begriff und Tatbestand der Iniuria im altrömischen Recht." *ZSSR (Rom. Abt.)* 82: 132-87.
Simpson, W. K.
1973   *The Literature of Ancient Egypt: An Anthology of Stories, Instructions, and Poetry*. New Haven: Yale University Press.
Snaith, N. H.
1966   "The Daughters of Zelophehad." *VT* 16: 124-27.
Snodgrass, A.
1974   "An Historical Homeric Society?" *JHS* 94: 114-25.

Soden, W. von
1965-81 *Akkadisches Handwörterbuch.* 3 vols. Wiesbaden: Harrassowitz.
Speleers, L.
1925 *Recueil des inscriptions de l'Asie antérieure des Musées Royaux du Cinquantenaire à Bruxelles.* Brussels: Musées Royaux d'art et d'histoire Bruxelles.
Stackert, J.
2006 "Why Does Deuteronomy Legislate Cities of Refuge? Asylum in the Covenant Collection [Exodus 21:12–14] and Deuteronomy [19:1–13]." *JBL* 125: 23-49.
Steible, H.
1982 *Die altsumerischen Bau- und Weihinschriften.* FAOS 5. Wiesbaden: Steiner.
Stein, P.
1966 *Regulae Iuris: From Juristic Rules to Legal Maxims.* Edinburgh: Edinburgh University Press.
Steinkeller, P.
1989 Sale Documents of the Ur III Period. FAOS 17. Stuttgart and Wiesbaden: Steiner.
Steinwenter, A.
1925 *Die Streitbeendigung durch Urteil, Schiedsspruch und Vergleich nach griechischenm Rechte.* Munich: Beck.
1948 "Die Gerichtsszene auf dem Schild des Achilles." Pages 7-15 in *Studi in onore di Siro Solazzi nel cinquantesimo anniversario del suo insegnamento universitario.* Edited by V. Arangio-Ruiz. Naples: Jovene.
Stol, M.
1993 *Epilepsy in Babylonia.* CM 2. Groningen: Styx.
Strassmaier, J. N.
1889 *Inschriften von Nabonidus, König von Babylon (555-538 v. Chr.).* Leipzig: Pfeiffer.
1890a *Inschriften von Cambyses, König von Babylon (529-521 v. Chr.).* Leipzig: Pfeiffer.
1890b *Inschriften von Cyrus, König von Babylon (538-529 v. Chr.).* Leipzig: Pfeiffer.
1890c *Inschriften von Darius, König von Babylon (521-485 v. Chr.).* Leipzig: Pfeiffer.
Stroud, R. S.
1968 *Drakon's Law on Homicide.* University of California Publications, Classical Studies 3. Berkeley: University of California Press.

Szlechter, E.
1950   "Essai d'explication des clauses: *muttatam gullubu abbuttam šakānu et abbuttam gullubu*." *ArOr* 17: 391-418.
1954   *Les Lois d'Eshnunna*. Publications de l'institut de droit romain de l'université de Paris 12. Paris: Recueil Sirey.
1965   "La 'loi' dans la Mésopotamie ancienne." *RIDA* 12: 55-77.

Tadmor, H.
1977   "A Lexicographical Text from Hazor." *IEJ* 27: 98-102.

Thompson, T.
1995   "'House of David': An Eponymic Referent to Yahweh as Godfather." *Scandinavian Journal of the Old Testament* 9: 59-74.

Thomsen, M. L.
2001   "Witchcraft and Magic in Mesopotamia." Pages 1-96 in *Witchcraft and Magic in Europe: Biblical and Pagan Societies*. Edited by F. R. Cryer and M. L. Thomsen. Philadelphia: University of Pennsylvania Press.

Thureau-Dangin, F.
1924   "La correspondance de Hammurapi avec Šamaš-hasir." *RA* 21: 1-58.
1937   "Trois contrats de Ras-Shamra." *Syria* 18: 245-55.

Uchitel, A.
1988   "The Archives of Mycenaean Greece and the Ancient Near East." Pages 19-30 in *Society and Economy in the Eastern Mediterranean, c. 1500-1000 B.C.: Proceedings of the International Symposium Held at the University of Haifa from the 28th of April to the 2nd of May, 1985*. Edited M. Heltzer and E. Lipiński. OLA 23. Leuven: Peeters.

Vatin, C.
1982   "Poinē, Timē, Thoiē dans le droit homérique." *Ktèma* 7: 275-80.

Veenhof, K.
1982   "A Deed of Manumission and Adoption from the Later Old Assyrian Period." Pages 359-85 in *Zikir Šumim: Assyriological Studies Presented to F. R. Kraus on the Occasion of His Seventieth Birthday*. Edited by G. van Driel. Leiden: Brill.
1995   "'In Accordance with the Words of the Stele': Evidence for Old Assyrian Legislation." *Chicago-Kent Law Review* 70: 1717-44.

Verboven, K.
2002   *The Economy of Friends: Economic Aspects of Amicitia and Patronage in the Late Republic*. Collection Latomus 269. Brussels: Éditions Latomus.

Versnel, H. S.
1970   *Triumphus: An Inquiry into the Origin, Development and Meaning of the Roman Triumph*. Leiden: Brill.

Viberg, Å.
1992   *Symbols of Law: A Contextual Analysis of Legal Symbolic Acts in the Old Testament.* ConBOT 34. Stockholm: Almqvist & Wiksell.

Visscher, F. de
1931   *Études de droit Romain.* Paris: Recueil Sirey.

Volterra, E.
1937   *Diritto Romano e Diritti Orientali.* Bologna: Zanichelli.

Wagner-Hasel, B.
1988   "Geschlecht und Gabe: Zum Brautgütersystem bei Homer." *ZSSR (Rom. Abt.)* 105: 41-49.

Waldock, A. J. A.
1966   *Sophocles, the Dramatist.* Cambridge: Cambridge University Press.

Wallace, R., and R. Westbrook
1989   Review of M. Gagarin, *Early Greek Law. American Journal of Philology* 110: 362-67.

Wallace-Hadrill, A.
1989   "Patronage in Roman Society: From Republic to Empire." Pages 63-87 in *Patronage in Ancient Society.* Edited by A. Wallace-Hadrill. Leicester-Nottingham Studies in Ancient Society 1. London and New York: Routledge.

Walters, S. D.
1970   "The Sorceress and Her Apprentice: A Case Study of an Accusation." *JCS* 23: 27-38.

Waterbury, J.
1977   "An Attempt to Put Patrons and Clients in Their Place." Pages 329-42 in *Patrons and Clients in Mediterranean Societies.* Edited by E. Gellner and J. Waterbury. London: Duckworth; Hanover, N. H.: Center for Mediterranean Studies of the American Universities Field Staff.

Waterman, L.
1916   *Business Documents of the Hammurapi Period.* Ancient Mesopotamian Tests and Studies. London: Ams Press (= *AJSL* 29-30 [1912-1914])

Waterman, L., ed.
1930-36   *Royal Correspondence of the Assyrian Empire.* University of Michigan Studies, Humanistic Series 17-20. Ann Arbor, Mich.: University of Michigan Press.

Watson, A.
1975a   "Personal Injuries in the XII Tables." *TvR* 43: 213-22.

1975b   *Rome of the XII Tables: Persons and Property.* Princeton: Princeton University Press.

1975c   "Si Adorat Furto." *Labeo* 21: 193-96.

1991   *Studies in Roman Private Law.* London and Rio Grande, Ohio: Hambledon.

Weidner, E. F.

1937   "Das Alter der mittelassyrischen Gesetztexte." *AfO* 12: 46-54.

1952-53   "Keilschrifttexte nach Kopien von T.G. Pinches." *AfO* 16: 35-46.

1954-56a   "Die astrologische Serie Enûma Anu Enlil (Fortsetzung)." *AfO* 17: 71-89.

1954-56b   "Hochverrat gegen Nebukadnezar II." *AfO* 17: 1-9.

1954-56c   "Hof- und Harems-Erlässe assyrischer Könige aus dem 2. Jahrtausend v.Chr." *AfO* 17: 257-93.

Weinfeld, M.

1972   *Deuteronomy and the Deuteronomic School.* Oxford: Clarendon.

1977   "Judge and Officer in Ancient Israel and the Ancient Near East." *IOS* 7: 65-88.

1983   "Social and Cultic Institutions in the Priestly Source against Their Ancient Near Eastern Background." Pages 95-129 in *Proceedings of the Eighth World Congress of Jewish Studies Held at the Hebrew University of Jerusalem, August 16-21, 1981: Panel Sessions, Biblical Studies, and Hebrew Language.* Publication of the World Union of Jewish Studies. Jerusalem: Magnes.

1985   *Justice and Righteousness in Israel and the Nations. Equality and Freedom in Ancient Israel in Light of Social Justice in the Ancient Near East.* Jerusalem: Magnes (in Hebrew).

1995   *Social Justice in Ancient Israel and in the Ancient Near East.* Jerusalem: Magnes; Minneapolis: Fortress.

Weingreen, J.

1966   "The Case of the Daughters of Zelophahad." *VT* 16: 518-22.

Wender, D.

1978   *The Last Scenes of the Odyssey.* Mnemosyne, biblio classica Batava, Supplementum 52. Leiden: Brill.

Werner, R.

1967   *Hethitische Gerichtsprotokolle.* StBoT 4. Wiesbaden: Harrassowitz.

Westbrook, R.

1971a   "Jubilee Laws." *Israel Law Review* 6: 209-26. Reprinted at pages 36-57 in *Property and the Family in Biblical Law.* JSOTSup 113. Sheffield: Sheffield Academic.

1971b   "Purchase of the Cave of Machpelah." *Israel Law Review* 6: 29-38. Reprinted at pages 24-35 in *Property and the Family in Biblical Law.* JSOTSup 113. Sheffield: Sheffield Academic.

1971c	"Redemption of Land." *Israel Law Review* 6: 367-75. Reprinted at pages 58-68 in *Property and the Family in Biblical Law*. JSOTSup 113. Sheffield: Sheffield Academic.
1982a	"Old Babylonian Marriage Law." 2 vols. Ph.D. diss. Yale University.
1982b	"Sabbatical Year" (in Hebrew). Columns 112-19 in vol. 8 of *Encyclopedia Biblica*. Edited by B. Mazar. 10 vols. Jerusalem: Bialik Institute, 1950-.
1984	"The Enforcement of Morals in Mesopotamian Law." *JAOS* 104: 753-56.
1985a	"Biblical and Cuneiform Law Codes." *RB* 92: 247-65. Reprinted at pages 495-511 in vol. 1 of *Folk Law*. Edited by A. D. Renteln and A. Dundes. 2 vols. New York and London: Garland Publishing, 1994.
1985b	"The Price Factor in the Redemption of Land." *RIDA* 32: 97-127.
1986a	"Lex Talionis and Exodus 21, 22-25." *RB* 93: 52-69.
1986b	"The Prohibition on Restoration of Marriage in Deuteronomy 24:1-4." Pages 387-405 in *Studies in Bible*. Edited by S. Japhet. Scripta Hierosolymitana 31. Jerusalem: Magnes.
1986c	Review of M. Weinfeld, *Justice and Righteousness in Israel and Among the Nations*. RB 93: 602-5.
1988a	"The Nature and Origins of the Twelve Tables." *ZSSR (Rom. Abt.)* 105: 74-121.
1988b	*Old Babylonian Marriage Law*. AfO Beiheft 23. Horn: Berger.
1988c	Review of D. Patrick, *Old Testament Law*. *Biblical Archaeologist* 51: 59-60.
1988d	*Studies in Biblical and Cuneiform Law*. Cahiers de la Revue Biblique 26. Paris: Gabalda.
1989a	"Cuneiform Law Codes and the Origins of Legislation." *ZA* 79: 201-22.
1989b	"Restrictions on Alienation of Property in Early Roman Law." Pages 207-13 in *New Perspectives in the Roman Law of Property*. Edited by P. Birks. Oxford: Oxford University Press.
1990a	"1 Samuel 1:8." *JBL* 109: 114-15.
1990b	"Adultery in Ancient Near Eastern Law." *RB* 97: 542-80.
1991a	"The Phrase 'His Heart is Satisfied' in Ancient Near Eastern Legal Sources." *JAOS* 111: 219-24.
1991b	*Property and the Family in Biblical Law*. JSOTSup 113. Sheffield: Sheffield Academic.
1992a	"Crimes and Punishments." Pages 546-56 in vol. 5 of *Anchor Bible Dictionary*. Edited by D. N. Freedman. 6 vols. New York: Doubleday.

1992b   "The Trial Scene in the Iliad." *HSCP* 94: 53-76.

1994a   "The Deposit Law of Exodus 22,6-12." *ZAW* 106: 390-403.

1994b   "Mitgift." Pages 273-83 in vol. 8 of *Reallexikon der Assyriologie*. Edited by E. Ebeling et al. 16 vols. Berlin: de Gruyter, 1928-.

1994c   "The Old Babylonian Term *napṭaru*." *JCS* 46: 41-46.

1994d   Review of C. Carmichael, ed., *Collected Works of David Daube*, Vol. 1: *Talmudic Law. ZSSR* (*Rom. Abt.*) 111: 702-3.

1994e   "What Is the Covenant Code?" Pages 13-34 in *Theory and Method in Biblical and Cuneiform Law: Revision, Interpolation and Development*. Edited by B. M. Levinson. JSOTSup 181. Sheffield: Sheffield Academic. Reprinted 2006.

1995a   "The Coherence of the Lex Aquilia." *RIDA* 42: 437-71.

1995b   "A Death in the Family: Codex Eshnunna 17-18 Revisited." *Studies in Honour of Reuven Yaron*. Edited by M. Rabello. *Israel Law Review* 29: 32-42.

1995c   "Muntehe." Pages 425-26 in vol. 8 of *Reallexikon der Assyriologie*. Edited by E. Ebeling et al. 16 vols. Berlin: de Gruyter, 1928-.

1995d   "Riddles in Deuteronomic Law." Pages 159-74 in *Bundesdokument und Gesetz: Studien zum Deuteronomium*. Edited by G. Braulik. Herders Biblische Studien 4. Freiburg: Herder.

1995e   "Slave and Master in Ancient Near Eastern Law." *Chicago-Kent Law Review* 70: 631- 76.

1995f   "Social Justice in the Ancient Near East." Pages 149-63 in *Social Justice in the Ancient World*. Edited by K. Irani and M. Silver. Westport, Conn.: Greenwood Press.

1996a   "Biblical Law." Pages 1-17 in *An Introduction to the History and Sources of Jewish Law*. Edited by N. S. Hecht et al. Oxford: Oxford University Press.

1996b   "zíz.da/*kiššātum*." *WZKM* 86: 449-59.

1997   "A Matter of Life and Death." *JANES* 25: 61-70.

1999a   "Codex Hammurabi and the Ends of the Earth." Pages 101-3 in vol. 3 of *Landscapes: Territories, Frontiers and Horizons in the Ancient Near East*. Edited by L. Milano et al. HANEM 3. Padova: Sargon.

1999b   "International Law in the Amarna Age." Pages 28-41 in *Amarna Diplomacy: The Beginning of International Relations*. Edited by R. Cohen and R. Westbrook. Baltimore: Johns Hopkins University Press.

1999c   "Legalistic Glosses in Biblical Narratives." *Israel Law Review* 33: 787-97.

1999d   "Lois Sumériennes." Columns 204-15 in *Supplément au Dictionnaire de la Bible*. Edited by J. Briend and M. Quesnel. Paris: Letouzey et Ané.

1999e   Review of E. Dombradi, *Die Darstellung des Rechtsaustrags in den altbabylonischen Prozessurkunden. Or (NS)* 68: 122-27.

1999f   "Vitae Necisque Potestas." *Historia* 48: 203-23.

2000a   "Babylonian Diplomacy in the Amarna Letters." *JAOS* 120: 377-82.

2000b   "Codification and Canonization." Pages 33-47 in *La codification des lois dans l'antiquité: Actes du Colloque de Strasbourg 27-29 Novembre 1997*. Edited by E. Lévy. Travaux du Centre de Recherche sur le Proche-Orient et la Grèce antiques 16. Paris: de Boccard.

2003a   "The Case of the Elusive Debtors: CT 4 6a and CT 6 34b." *ZA* 93: 199-207.

2003b   "Emar and Vicinity." Pages 657-91 in *A History of Ancient Near Eastern Law*. Edited by R. Westbrook. Leiden: Brill.

2003c   "Evidentiary Procedure in the Middle Assyrian Laws." *JCS* 55: 75-85.

2003d   "Introduction: The Character of Ancient Near Eastern Law." Pages 1-90 in vol. 1 of *A History of Ancient Near Eastern Law*. Edited by R. Westbrook. 2 vols. HdO 72. Leiden and New York: Brill.

2003e   "Old Babylonian Period." Pages 360-430 in *A History of Ancient Near Eastern Law*. Edited by R. Westbrook. Leiden: Brill.

2003f   "A Sumerian Freedman." Pages in 333-39 *Literatur, Politik und Recht in Mesopotamien. Festschrift für Claus Wilcke*. Edited by W. Sallaberger et al. OBC 14. Wiesbaden: Harrassowitz.

2005a   "Elisha's True Prophecy in 2 Kings 3." *JBL* 124: 530-32.

2005b   "Judges in the Cuneiform Sources." *Maarav* 12: 27-39.

2005c   "Patronage in the Ancient Near East." *JESHO* 48: 210-33.

2005d   "Penelope's Dowry and Odysseus' Kingship." Pages 3-23 in *Symposion 2001: Vorträge zur griechischen und hellenistischen Rechtsgeschichte*. Edited by R. W. Wallace and M. Gagarin. Akten der Gesellschaft für griechische und hellenistische Rechtsgeschichte 16. Vienna: Österreichische Akademie der Wissenschaften.

2005e   "Polygamie." Pages 600-2 in vol. 10 of *Reallexikon der Assyriologie*. Edited by E. Ebeling et al. 16 vols. Berlin: de Gruyter, 1928-.

Westbrook, R., ed.

2003   *A History of Ancient Near Eastern Law*. 2 vols. HdO 72. Leiden: Brill.

Westbrook, R., and C. Wilcke

1974-77   "The Liability of an Innocent Purchaser of Stolen Goods in Early Mesopotamian Law." *AfO* 25: 111-15.

Westbrook, R., and R. Woodard

1990   "The Edict of Tudhaliya IV." *JAOS*: 110: 641-59.

Westrup, C. W.

1950   *Introduction to Early Roman Law*. Vol. 4/1. Oxford: Oxford University Press.

Wieacker, F.
1956   "Zwölftafelprobleme." *RIDA* 3: 459-91.
1967   "Die XII Tafeln in ihrem Jahrhundert." Pages 291-362 in *Les origines de la république romaine*. Entretiens sur l'antiquité classique. Vandoeuvres: Fondation Hardt pour l'études de l'antiquité classique.

Wilcke, C.
1969   "ku-li." *ZA* 59: 65-99.
1985   "Familiengründung im alten Babylonien." Pages 213-317 in *Geschlechtsreife und Legitimation zur Zeugung*. Veröffentlichungen des Instituts für Historische Anthropologie 1. Edited by E. W. Müller. Freiburg and Munich: Alber.

Willetts, R. F., ed.
1967   *The Law Code of Gortyn*. KadmosSup 1. Berlin: de Gruyter.

Williams, J.
1964   "Concerning One of the Apodictic Formulas." *VT* 14: 484-89.

Wiseman, D. J.
1953   *The Alalakh Tablets*. British School of Archaeology in Ankara, Occasional Publications 2. London: British School of Archaeology in Ankara.
1962   "The Laws of Hammurabi Again." *JSS* 7: 161-72.

Wolf, J. G.
1970   "Lanx und Licium: Das Ritual der Haussuchung im altrömischen Recht." Pages 59-79 in *Sympotica Franz Wieacker: Sexagenario Sasbachwaldeni a suis libata*. Göttingen: Vandenhoeck & Ruprecht.

Wolff, H. J.
1946   "The Origin of Judicial Litigation among the Greeks." *Traditio* 4: 31-87. Reprinted at pages 1-90 in Wolff, H. J. *Beiträge zur Rechtsgeschichte Altgriechenlands und des hellenisch-römischen Ägyptens*. Weimar: Böhlaus Nachfolger, 1961 (in German).

Wright, D. P.
2003   "The Laws of Hammurabi as a Source for the Covenant Collection (Exodus 20:23-23:19)." *Maarav* 10: 11-87.
2006   "The Laws of Hammurabi and the Covenant Code: A Response to Bruce Wells." *Maarav* 10: 209-58.

Yaron, R.
1959   "Redemption of Persons in the Ancient Near East." *RIDA* 6: 155-76.
1960   "Minutiae on Roman Divorce." *TvR* 28:1-12.
1962a   "Forms in the Laws of Eshnunna." *RIDA* 9: 137-53.
1962b   "Vitae Necisque Potestas." *TvR* 30: 243-51.
1965   "Varia on Adoption." *JJP* 15: 171-83.

1966   "The Goring Ox in Near Eastern Laws." *Israel Law Review* 1: 396-406.
1967   "Si adorat furto." *TvR* 34: 510-24.
1968   "Si pater filium ter venum buit." *TvR* 36: 52-72.
1969   *The Laws of Eshnunna.* Jerusalem: Magnes.
1974   "Semitic Elements in Early Rome." Pages 343-57 in *Daube Noster: Essays in Legal History for David Daube.* Edited by A. Watson. Edinburgh: Scottish Academic.
1988a   "The Evolution of Biblical Law." Pages 77-108 in *La Formazione del diritto nel vicino oriente antico.* Edited by A. Theodorides et al. Pubblicazioni dell'Istituto di diritto romano e del diritti dell'Oriente mediterraneo 65. Rome: Edizioni Scientifiche Italiane.
1988b   *The Laws of Eshnunna.* 2d ed. Jerusalem: Magnes; Leiden: Brill.
1993a   "*kurrum ṣibtam uṣṣab* 'das kor wird Zins hinzufügen': Weiteres zu §18A der Gesetze von Ešnunna." *ZA* 83: 206-18.
1993b   "Stylistic Conceits: The Negated Antonym." *JANES* 22: 141-48.
Yildiz, F.
1981   "A Tablet of Codex Ur-Nammu from Sippar." *Or* 5: 87-97.
Yoffee, N.
1977   *The Economic Role of the Crown in the Old Babylonian Period.* BiMes 5. Malibu: Undena.
Zaccagnini, C.
2000   "The Interdependence of the Great Powers." Pages 141-53 in *Amarna Diplomacy: The Beginnings of International Relations.* Edited by R. Cohen and R. Westbrook. Baltimore: Johns Hopkins University Press.
Zuckerman, A.
1977   "Clientelist Politics in Italy." Pages 63-79 in *Patrons and Clients in Mediterranean Societies.* Edited by E. Gellner and J. Waterbury. London: Duckworth; Hanover, N. H.: Center for Mediterranean Studies of the American Universities Field Staff.
Zulueta, F. de
1946-53   *The Institutes of Gaius.* 2 vols. Oxford: Clarendon.

Index of Authors

12
124 - oval oath it
210 - King's oath it again
I ever do it again
may I be killed
213 - Thievish

Index of Subjects

Abraham, 28, 171, 210, 247, 272-73
Absalom, 320
academic method, ancient, xiii, 8,
    12, 19, 35-36, 40, 73-74, 76-
    77, 106, 108, 112, 125, 164,
    248, 311, 368, 377-78; *see also*
    scientific treatise
acceptilatio, 363-64
accusations, 136, 256, 261, 280,
    282, 291, 294, 296, 352-53,
    362, 366, 393
Achilles, 303, 320-22, 335, 342,
    344-47
  shield of, 303, 319
acquisitions, 66, 172-73, 189, 341,
    385
actio furti concepti, 57-58, 67-68
adjudication, xviii
administration, 89, 146, 224, 235,
    306
administration of justice, 94, 306,
    317, 343
administrative documents, 92, 106,
    111, 174
adoption, 12-13, 95, 180, 184-85,
    377, 392, 396
adrogatio, 392, 396, 409, 411
adstipulatio, 364
adstipulator, 355, 363-64, 374

adultery, 43, 103, 129, 155, 245-46,
    245-87, 293, 295, 297, 299,
    307, 393, 395, 403-4, 408-11
aestimatio, 361
Agamemnon, 315-16, 321, 335, 342,
    344-45
ager publicus, 372
agriculture, 70, 80, 84, 86, 110, 151,
    153-54, 158, 168, 209, 222,
    243, 286, 309, 319, 365, 371
Ajax, 320-21
Akkadian, 29-32, 34, 42, 55, 103,
    113, 120, 144, 151-53, 162-63,
    165, 171, 198, 204, 221, 261,
    263, 271, 275-76, 330, 332,
    339, 341, 364, 386, 408
Alalakh, xi, 103, 164, 187, 212-13,
    330
Alexander the Great, 29, 162
alphabet, 315
Amalekites, 17
Amarna, xi, 223, 233, 341
ana ittišu, 3, 254
Anatolia, xi, 29-30, 143, 161-63,
    306, 330, 341, 407
Antinous, 322, 340, 342, 347, 349,
    353
ao. furti oblati, 57
apodictic style, 97-100, 110-14, 116

Index of Ancient Sources

The sources listed below are arranged in the following order: Cuneiform, Biblical, Greek and Roman, Egyptian, Phoenician, Aramaic, and Rabbinic.

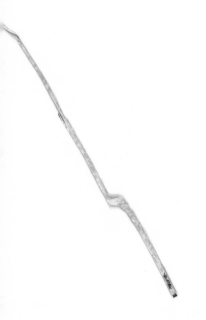